Philosophy of Religion: An Anthology

Philosophy of Religion: An Anthology

LOUIS P. POJMAN

The University of Mississippi

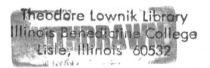
Wadsworth Publishing Company

Belmont, California / A Division of Wadsworth, Inc.

Philosophy Editor: *Kenneth King*
Editorial Assistants: *Debbie Fox, Linda Cazanov*
Production: *Mary Forkner, Publication Alternatives*
Print Buyer: *Ruth Cole*
Designers: *Lois Stanfield, Al Burkhardt*
Copy Editor: *Kathleen Engelberg*
Cover: *Al Burkhardt*
Cover Photograph: *© Frank Siteman/Jeroboam, Inc.*
Signing Representative: *Melinda Horan*

Printed in the United States of America

1 2 3 4 5 6 7 8 9 10—91 90 89 88 87

ISBN 0-534-06672-0

Library of Congress Cataloging-in-Publication Data

Philosophy of religion.

  Includes bibliographies and index.
  1. Religion — Philosophy.   I. Pojman, Louis P.
BL51.P532 1986   200'.1   86-11162
ISBN 0-534-06672-0

Dedicated to the memory of my father and mother, Louis A. and Helen Pojman

Contents

---

* An asterisk indicates a more challenging article.

PART II   The Argument from Religious Experience   91

PART III   The Problem of Evil   151

PART IV   The Attributes of God   197

PART **VIII**   **Religion and Ethics**   493

Preface

Questions concerning the existence of God may be the most important that we can ask and try to answer. If God, an omnibenevolent, supremely powerful being who interacts with the world, exists, then it is of the utmost importance that we come to know that fact and learn as much as possible about God and his plan. The implications of such a fact affect our understanding of the world and ourselves. If God exists, the world is not accidental, a product of mere chance and necessity, but a home designed for rational and sentient beings. The universe is his handiwork, a place of personal purposefulness. We are not alone in the world struggling for justice but are working together with one whose plan is to redeem the world from evil. Most importantly, there is someone to whom we are responsible and to whom we owe absolute devotion and worship. Other implications follow for our self-understanding, the way we ought to live our lives, and prospects for continued life after death.

Of course, it may be false that a supreme being exists, and many people have lived well without believing in God. Laplace, when asked about his faith, is reported to have replied, "I have no need of that hypothesis." But the testimony of humankind is against him. Millions have needed and been inspired by this notion. So much inspiration issues from the idea of God that we could say that if God doesn't exist, the idea is the greatest invention of the human mind. What are all the world's works of literature, art, music, drama, architecture, science, and philosophy compared to this simple concept? Anthony Kenny put it as follows:

If there is no God, then God is incalculably the greatest single creation of the human imagination. No other creation of the imagination has been so fertile of ideas, so great an inspiration to philosophy, to literature, to painting, sculpture, architecture, and drama. Set beside the idea of God, the most original inventions of mathematicians and the most unforgetable characters in drama are minor products of the imagination: Hamlet and the square root of minus one pale into insignificance by comparison.*

The field of philosophy of religion documents the history of humanity's quest for a supreme being. Even if God does not exist, the arguments centering on this quest are interesting in their own right for their ingenuity and subtlety, apart from their possible soundness. It may be argued that the Judeo-Christian tradition has informed our self-understanding to such a degree that every person who wishes to be well informed must come to grips with the arguments and counterarguments surrounding its claims. Hence, even if one rejects the assertions of religion, it is important to understand what is being rejected and why.

Whether religious beliefs are true or justified is the overarching concern of the readings included in this volume. The central issues of religion are examined and subjected to rigorous philosophical analysis so that well-informed conclusions may be drawn. I have endeavored to put together a balanced work, consisting of the best articles both pro and con on the rele-

---

* *Faith and Reason* (New York, Columbia University Press, 1983), 59.

xi

vant issues. The criteria of inclusion were cogency, clarity, and accessibility to college undergraduates. I have given a wider range of views and levels of difficulty than is generally the case with textbook anthologies in the hope that introductory as well as advanced classes may use this work. I have tried both in the introductions and the selections to give a fair hearing to both sides on the issues, suppressing my own inclinations in many cases. The order of the articles in some instances reflects the development of the argument, but in other instances (especially in the case of the arguments for the existence of God) it reflects pedagogical purposes. Of course, a teacher may have students read these articles in any order he or she desires.

It is impossible to include all of the areas of religion in which philosophical analysis is relevant. I have concentrated on arguments concerning the decisive features of theistic religion. Selectivity has demanded that some areas that divide theists be omitted, such as the particular beliefs of the various theistic religions, Judaism, Christianity, and Islam; and I have not been able to deal with Eastern religions.

This leaves several important problems open to investigation. The eight parts of this book take up the major issues in classical and contemporary philosophy of religion: the existence of God, the argument from religious experience, the attributes of God, the problem of evil, miracles, the question of survival after death, the relation of faith to reason, and the relation of ethics to religion. I have given extended coverage to the faith-reason debate since religious epistemology is at the heart of philosophy of religion and is recognized as such in contemporary discussion.

This anthology consists of both classical and contemporary work in philosophy of religion. It brings together in one volume some of the most important work in the field, including the recent work of J. L. Mackie, Alvin Plantinga, Richard Swinburne, Philip Quinn, Robert Merrihew Adams, and William Alston. Articles by William Rowe, Gary Gutting, and Stephen T. Davis appear in print here for the first time. I have made a fresh, accessible translation and selection of Kierkegaard's work on subjectivity and truth from the *Concluding Unscientific Postscript*, which will benefit those interested in understanding his thought. Part 7, section D, "Rationality and Justified Religious Belief," contains some of the most recent material in religious epistemology, centered on Alvin Plantinga's arguments that belief in God may be properly basic.

For the reader's benefit I have included brief introductions to each part and section of the book as well as brief summary statements at the beginning of each article. I have also included an annotated bibliography at the end of each part of this work. As already mentioned, although this work is meant primarily for introductory courses, I have included a few more difficult readings for advanced students or those in introductory classes who wish to pursue a topic further. (These articles are marked with an asterisk in the table of contents.) The more difficult articles are intended for those students who enjoy the challenge of pursuing an argument further than might be necessary for an introductory course. Some sections contain more of these articles than others. This is partly due to my judgment of where the cutting edge of the general subject lies.

This book has been structured in such a way as to be used with William Rowe's *An Introduction: Philosophy of Religion*, which has chapters corresponding to all but two of the sections included in this book. Rowe's work may usefully be consulted as a commentary to these readings. Because I expect the reader either to have the help of Rowe's book or the benefit of a teacher's guidance, I have kept the introductions short.

I would like to express my thanks to all the reviewers who offered me their excellent suggestions along the way, suggestions that have helped to shape this work. These include William Rowe, Purdue University; H. Michael Awalt, Belmont College; John Donnelly, University of San Diego; Frederick Ferre, University of Georgia; Ted Klein, Texas Christian University; George I. Mavrodes, University of Michigan; Richard Purtill, Western Washington University; W. Jay Wood, Wheaton College; Keith E. Yandell, University of Wisconsin, Madison. Ken King, the sponsoring editor, who is responsible for getting this work under way and published, was extremely helpful at every stage of development. His assistant, Debbie Fox, expertly facilitated matters. I am very grateful to Mary Forkner of Publication Alternatives and her copy editor, Kathleen Engelberg, for their care in the editing and production of the final manuscript.

This work is dedicated to the memory of my mother and father, who taught me to wrestle with these issues at a very early age. I hope this anthology helps others to make progress in understanding both the questions and the possible answers.

Louis P. Pojman

TRADITIONAL ARGUMENTS FOR THE EXISTENCE OF GOD

Can the existence of God be demonstrated or made probable by argument? The debate between those who believe that reason can demonstrate that God exists and those who do not has an ancient lineage, going back to Protagoras (ca. 450 BC) and Plato (427–347 BC). The Roman Catholic church has traditionally held that the existence of God is demonstrable by human reason. The strong statement of the First Vatican Council (1870) indicates that human reason is adequate to arrive at a state of knowledge:

> If anyone says that the one and true God, our creator and Lord, cannot be known with certainty with the natural light of human reason by means of the things that have been made: let him be anathema.

Many others, including theists of various denominations, among them Catholics, have denied that human reason is adequate to arrive at knowledge or demonstrate the existence of God.

Arguments for the existence of God divide into two main groups: a priori and a posteriori arguments. An *a posteriori argument* is based on premises that can be known only by means of experience of the world (e.g., that there is a world, events have causes, and so forth). An *a priori argument*, on the other hand, rests on premises that can be known to be true independently of experience of the world. One need only clearly conceive of the proposition in order to see that it is true.

In this work we consider two types of a posteriori arguments for the existence of God and one a priori argument. The a posteriori arguments are the cosmological argument and the teleological argument. The a priori argument is the ontological argument; we offer two forms of that argument type. We have also included a section on the relevance of these arguments, sometimes called "the proofs."

The question before us in this part of our work is, What do the arguments for the existence of God establish? Do any of them demonstrate beyond reasonable doubt the existence of a supreme being or deity? Do any of them make it probable (given the evidence at hand) that such a being exists?

1

I.A The Cosmological Argument for the Existence of God

All the versions of the cosmological argument begin with the a posteriori assumptions that the universe exists and that something outside the universe is required to explain its existence. That is, the universe is *contingent,* depending on something outside of itself for its existence. That "something else" is logically prior to the universe. It constitutes the reason for the existence of the universe. Such a being is God.

One version of the cosmological argument is called the "First Cause argument." The first two arguments given by St. Thomas Aquinas in our readings serve as examples of it. The general outline goes something like this:

1. Everything (every event or state of affairs or object) has a cause. That is, for everything that exists (E), there is some other thing (C) that existed before E existed; and C produced E—that is, without C, E would not have existed. But C itself was caused by a prior cause C_1, and C_1 by still another cause before it, and so on.
2. An infinite regress is impossible. The series of causes and effects cannot go on indefinitely but must have a beginning.
3. So there must be a First Cause capable of producing everything besides itself (which is not produced but is a necessary being).
4. Such a being must be an infinite, necessary being, that is, God.
5. Therefore, God exists.

This sort of argument can be challenged at every point, and you will find many of these challenges in Bertrand Russell's comments (in his dialogue with Father Copleston) and in Paul Edward's article, "A Critique of the Cosmological Argument." You will decide whether the challenges are successful. We may first ask, Must everything have a cause? A significant number of physicists would deny that the principle of causality applies to some behavior of subatomic particles. These particles seem to behave randomly, and their behavior can be predicted only statistically. This noncausal thesis has been confirmed by certain experiments, though the issue is controversial. Some physicists offer other explanations. In any case, the question should be raised, How do we know that everything must have a cause?

The second premise may be challenged with the question, How do we know that an infinite regress of causes is impossible? We have infinite series in mathematics. Why not in physics too? Do we understand enough about the world to rule out such a series? If we can imagine an infinite series into the future, why not allow its possibility into the past?

Regarding the third and fourth premises, in using the notion of an infinite being to explain the world have we really solved anything? For don't we still have to explain what an infinite being is? Isn't this simply a case of explaining the obscure with the even more obscure? And do we help our argument any by calling this unknown being God? Does the notion of a necessary being make any sense? We usually apply the notion of "necessity" to logically necessary propositions (such as that a contradiction is necessarily false or that two plus two equals four is necessarily true). What sense does it make to say that a being must necessarily exist?

There are responses to these challenges, some of which are found in Richard Taylor's article, "The Cosmological Argument: A Defense." However, Taylor's argument is a version of Aquinas's third way. It is based on the notion of the principle of sufficient reason (PSR): Everything must have an explanation to account for it. To paraphrase Leibniz, who first introduced the principle, there is a sufficient reason why everything that is, is the way it is and not otherwise. A mere fact in isolation is not intelligible. Taylor makes use of this principle, which he takes as intuitively certain, to argue that the existence of the universe demands some explanation, some sufficient reason why it is the way it is and not some other way or not at all. Taylor contends that it is only the mind-dulling familiarity of the world that prevents us from asking this question. We need to think afresh about what we have before us. To illustrate this, he asks us to imagine that while walking in the woods we come upon a six-foot-high translucent ball and are mystified by it. We would want to know how it came to be where it is and as it is. We would want a reason for its existence. Our need of an explanation for the universe is no less pressing.

Now, some truths depend on something else and are called *contingent*. Others depend only on themselves and are called *necessary*. Taylor illustrates the difference this way. It is a contingent truth that there is a warm stone by my window. The stone doesn't have to be by my window. I might never have brought it home from the beach in the first place, and it wouldn't be warm if the blinds were not up so that the sun could shine on it. So it is only contingently true that there is a warm stone by my window. On the other hand, it is not merely accidentally true that all the points of a circle are equidistant from the center. This truth depends on nothing but itself. It is a necessary truth. Similarly it is a necessary truth that if the stone by my window has a body, it has extension.

Put very briefly, Taylor argues that the world is like unto the six-foot-high translucent ball, a contingent object requiring an explanation. As a dependent or contingent being, it must ultimately be explained through reference to a necessary being that has its reason for its own existence in itself. And this, argues Taylor, is what we call God.

You will want to decide whether Taylor's version of the argument meets the objections leveled against it by Russell and Edwards.

I.A.1   The Five Ways

THOMAS AQUINAS

The Benedictine monk Thomas Aquinas (1225–1274) is considered by many to be the greatest theologian in Western religion. The five ways of showing the existence of God given in this selection are versions of the cosmological argument; put simply, their strategies are as follows: The first way concerns the fact that there is change (or motion) and argues that there must be an Unmoved Mover that originates all change but itself is not moved. The second way is from the idea of causation and argues that there must be a first cause to explain the existence of cause. The third way is from the idea of contingency. It argued that since there are dependent beings (e.g., humans), there must be an independent or necessary being on whom the dependent beings rely for their subsistence. The fourth way is from excellence, and it argues that since there are degrees of excellence, there must be a perfect being from whence cometh all excellences. The final way is from the harmony of things. There is a harmony of nature, which calls for an explanation. The only sufficient explanation is that there is a divine designer who planned this harmony.

The First Way: The Argument from Change

The existence of God can be shown in five ways. The first and clearest is taken from the idea of motion. (1) Now it is certain, and our senses cor-

Reprinted from *Summa Theologica*, trans. Laurence Shapcote (London: O. P. Benziger Brothers, 1911).

roborate it, that some things in this world are in motion. (2) But everything which is in motion is moved by something else. (3) For nothing is in motion except in so far as it is in potentiality in relation to that towards which it is in motion. (4) Now a thing causes movement in so far as it is in actuality. For to cause movement is nothing else than to bring something from potentiality to actuality; but a thing cannot be brought from potentiality to actuality except by something which exists in actuality, as, for example, that which is hot in actuality, like fire, makes wood, which is only hot in potentiality, to be hot in actuality, and thereby causes movement in it and alters it. (5) But it is not possible that the same thing should be at the same time in actuality and in potentiality in relation to the same thing, but only in relation to different things; for what is hot in actuality cannot at the same time be hot in potentiality, though it is at the same time cold in potentiality. (6) It is impossible, therefore, that in relation to the same thing and in the same way anything should both cause movement and be caused, or that it should cause itself to move. (7) Everything therefore that is in motion must be moved by something else. If therefore the thing which causes it to move be in motion, this too must be moved by something else, and so on. (8) But we cannot proceed to infinity in this way, because in that case there would be no first mover, and in consequence, neither would there by any other mover; for secondary movers do not cause movement except they be moved by a first mover, as, for example, a stick cannot cause movement unless it is moved by the hand. Therefore it is necessary to stop at some first mover which is moved by nothing else. And this is what we all understand God to be.

The Second Way: The Argument from Causation

The Second Way is taken from the idea of the Efficient Cause. (1) For we find that there is among material things a regular order of efficient causes. (2) But we do not find, nor indeed is it possible, that anything is the efficient cause of itself, for in

that case it would be prior to itself, which is impossible. (3) Now it is not possible to proceed to infinity in efficient causes. (4) For if we arrange in order all efficient causes, the first is the cause of the intermediate, and the intermediate the cause of the last, whether the intermediate be many or only one. (5) But if we remove a cause the effect is removed; therefore, if there is no *first* among efficient causes, neither will there be a last or an intermediate. (6) But if we proceed to infinity in efficient causes there will be no first efficient cause, and thus there will be no ultimate effect, nor any intermediate efficient causes, which is clearly false. Therefore it is necessary to suppose the existence of some first efficient cause, and this men call God.

The Third Way: The Argument from Contingency

The Third Way rests on the idea of the "contingent" and the "necessary" and is as follows: (1) Now we find that there are certain things in the Universe which are capable of existing and of not existing, for we find that some things are brought into existence and then destroyed, and consequently are capable of being or not being. (2) But it is impossible for all things which exist to be of this kind, because anything which is capable of not existing, at some time or other does not exist. (3) If therefore *all* things are capable of not existing, there was a time when nothing existed in the Universe. (4) But if this is true there would also be nothing in existence now; because anything that does not exist cannot begin to exist except by the agency of something which has existence. If therefore there was once nothing which existed, it would have been impossible for anything to begin to exist, and so nothing would exist now. (5) This is clearly false. Therefore all things are not contingent, and there must be something which is necessary in the Universe. (6) But everything which is necessary either has or has not the cause of its necessity from an outside source. Now it is not possible to proceed to infinity in necessary things which have a cause of their necessity, as has been proved in the case of efficient causes. Therefore it is necessary to suppose the existence of something which is necessary in itself, not having the cause of its necessity from any outside source, but which is the cause of necessity in others. And this "something" we call God.

The Fourth Way: The Argument from Degrees of Excellence

The Fourth Way is taken from the degrees which are found in things. (1) For among different things we find that one is more or less good or true or noble; and likewise in the case of other things of this kind. (2) But the words "more" or "less" are used of different things in proportion as they approximate in their different ways to something which has the particular quality in the highest degree—e.g., we call a thing hotter when it approximates more nearly to that which is hot in the highest degree. There is therefore something which is true in the highest degree, good in the highest degree and noble in the highest degree; (3) and consequently there must be also something which has being in the highest degree. For things which are true in the highest degree also have being in the highest degree (see Aristotle, *Metaphysics*, 2). (4) But anything which has a certain quality of any

kind in the highest degree is also the cause of all the things of that kind, as, for example, fire which is hot in the highest degree is the cause of all hot things (as is said in the same book). (5) Therefore there exists something which is the cause of being, and goodness, and of every perfection in all existing things; and this we call God.

The Fifth Way: The Argument from Harmony

The Fifth Way is taken from the way in which nature is governed. (1) For we observe that certain things which lack knowledge, such as natural bodies, work for an End. This is obvious, because they always, or at any rate very frequently, operate in the same way so as to attain the best possible result. (2) Hence it is clear that they do not arrive at their goal by chance, but by purpose. (3) But those things which have no knowledge do not move towards a goal unless they are guided by someone or something which does possess knowledge and intelligence—e.g., an arrow by an archer. Therefore, there does exist something which possesses intelligence by which all natural things are directed to their goal; and this we call God.

I.A.2   A Debate on the Argument from Contingency

FATHER F. C. COPLESTON AND BERTRAND RUSSELL

Father F. C. Copleston (1907–1980) was professor of philosophy at Heythrop College in England and at the Gregorian University in Rome. He is famous for his multivolume History of Philosophy. *Bertrand Russell (1872–1970), one of the most important philosophers of this century, was an ag-*

nostic who argued against Christian belief. In this famous BBC radio debate of 1948 Copleston defends the argument from contingency, which Russell attacks.

This debate was broadcast in 1948 on the Third Program of the British Broadcasting Corporation. It was published in *Humanitas* (Manchester) and reprinted in *Why I Am Not a Christian,* by Bertrand Russell (London: George Allen & Unwin, 1957). Copyright © 1957 by Allen and Unwin, Ltd. Reprinted by permission of Simon & Schuster, Inc.

Copleston: As we are going to discuss the existence of God, it might perhaps be as well to come to some provisional agreement as to what we understand by the term "God." I presume that we mean a supreme personal being—distinct from the world and creator of the world. Would you agree—provisionally at least—to accept this statement as the meaning of the term "God"?

Russell: Yes, I accept this definition.

Copleston: Well, my position is the affirmative position that such a being actually exists, and that His existence can be proved philosophically. Perhaps you would tell me if your position is that of agnosticism or of atheism. I mean, would you say that the non-existence of God can be proved?

Russell: No, I should not say that: my position is agnostic.

Copleston: Would you agree with me that the problem of God is a problem of great importance? For example, would you agree that if God does not exist, human beings and human history can have no other purpose than the purpose they choose to give themselves, which—in practice—is likely to mean the purpose which those impose who have the power to impose it?

Russell: Roughly speaking, yes, though I should have to place some limitation on your last clause.

Copleston: Would you agree that if there is no God—no absolute Being—there can be no absolute values? I mean, would you agree that if there is no absolute good that the relativity of values results?

Russell: No, I think these questions are logically distinct. Take, for instance, G. E. Moore's *Principia Ethica,* where he maintains that there is a distinction of good and evil, that both of these are definite concepts. But he does not bring in the idea of God to support that contention.

Copleston: Well, suppose we leave the question of good till later, till we come to the moral argument, and I give first a metaphysical argument. I'd like to put the main weight on the metaphysical argument based on Leibniz's argument from "Contingency" and then later we might discuss the moral argument. Suppose I give a brief statement on the metaphysical argument and that then we go on to discuss it?

Russell: That seems to me to be a very good plan.

The Argument from Contingency

Copleston: Well, for clarity's sake, I'll divide the argument into distinct stages. First of all, I should say, we know that there are at least some beings in the world which do not contain in themselves the reason for their existence. For example, I depend on my parents, and now on the air, and on food, and so on. Now, secondly, the world is simply the real or imagined totality or aggregate of individual objects, none of which contain in themselves alone the reason for their existence. There isn't any world distinct from the objects which form it, any more than the human race is something apart from the members. Therefore, I should say, since objects or events exist, and since no object of experience contains within itself the reason of its existence, this reason, the totality of objects, must have a reason external to itself. That reason must be an existent being. Well, this being is either itself the reason for its own existence, or it is not. If it is, well and good. If it is not, then we must proceed farther. But if we proceed to infinity in that sense, then there's no explanation of existence at all. So, I should say, in order to explain existence, we must come to a being which contains within itself the reason for its own existence, that is to say, which cannot not exist.

Russell: This raises a great many points and it is not altogether easy to know where to begin, but I think that, perhaps, in answering your argument, the best point at which to begin is the question of necessary being. The word "necessary," I should maintain, can only be applied significantly to propositions. And, in fact, only to such as are analytic—that is to say—such as it is self-contradictory to deny. I could only admit a necessary being if there were a being whose existence it is self-contradictory to deny. I should like to know whether you would accept Leibniz's division of propositions into truths of reason and truths of fact. The former—the truths of reason—being necessary.

Copleston: Well, I certainly should not subscribe to what seems to be Leibniz's idea of truths of reason and truths of fact, since it would appear that, for him, there are in the long run only analytic propositions. It would seem that for Leibniz truths of fact are ultimately reducible to truths of reason. That is to say, to analytic propositions, at least for an omniscient mind. Well, I couldn't agree with that. For one thing it would fail to meet the requirements of the experience of freedom. I don't want to uphold the whole philosophy of Leibniz. I have made use of his argument from contingent to necessary being, basing the argument on the principle of sufficient reason, simply because it seems to me a brief and clear formulation of what is, in my opinion, the fundamental metaphysical argument for God's existence.

Russell: But, to my mind, "a necessary proposition" has got to be analytic. I don't see what else it can mean. And analytic propositions are always complex and logically somewhat late. "Irrational animals are animals" is an analytic proposition; but a proposition such as "This is an animal" can never be analytic. In fact, all the propositions that can be analytic are somewhat late in the build-up of propositions.

Copleston: Take the proposition "If there is a contingent being then there is a necessary being." I consider that that proposition hypothetically expressed is a necessary proposition. If you are going to call every necessary proposition an analytic proposition, then—in order to avoid a dispute in terminology—I would agree to call it analytic, though I don't consider it a tautological proposition. But the proposition is a necessary proposition only on the supposition that there is a contingent being. That there is a contingent being actually existing has to be discovered by experience, and the proposition that there is a contingent being is certainly not an analytic proposition, though once you know, I should maintain, that there is a contingent being, it follows of necessity that there is a necessary being.

Russell: The difficulty of this argument is that I don't admit the idea of a necessary being and I don't admit that there is any particular meaning in

calling other beings "contingent." These phrases don't for me have a significance except within a logic that I reject.

Copleston: Do you mean that you reject these terms because they won't fit in with what is called "modern logic"?

Russell: Well, I can't find anything that they could mean. The word "necessary," it seems to me, is a useless word, except as applied to analytic propositions, not to things.

Copleston: In the first place, what do you mean by "modern logic?" As far as I know, there are somewhat differing systems. In the second place, not all modern logicians surely would admit the meaninglessness of metaphysics. We both know, at any rate, one very eminent modern thinker whose knowledge of modern logic was profound, but who certainly did not think that metaphysics are meaningless or, in particular, that the problem of God is meaningless. Again, even if all modern logicians held that metaphysical terms are meaningless, it would not follow that they were right. The proposition that metaphysical terms are meaningless seems to me to be a proposition based on an assumed philosophy. The dogmatic position behind it seems to be this: What will not go into my machine is non-existent, or it is meaningless; it is the expression of emotion. I am simply trying to point out that anybody who says that a particular system of modern logic is the sole criterion of meaning is saying something that is over-dogmatic; he is dogmatically insisting that a part of philosophy is the whole of philosophy. After all, a "contingent" being is a being which has not in itself the complete reason for its existence, that's what I mean by a contingent being. You know, as well as I do, that the existence of neither of us can be explained without reference to something or somebody outside us, our parents, for example. A "necessary" being, on the other hand, means a being that must and cannot not exist. You may say that there is no such being, but you will find it hard to convince me that you do not understand the terms I am using. If you do not understand them, then how can you be entitled to say that such a being does not exist, if that is what you do say?

Russell: Well, there are points here that I don't propose to go into at length. I don't maintain the meaninglessness of metaphysics in general at all. I maintain the meaninglessness of certain particular terms—not on any general ground, but simply because I've not been able to see an interpretation of those particular terms. It's not a general dogma—it's a particular thing. But those points I will leave out for the moment. And I will say that what you have been saying brings us back, it seems to me, to the ontological argument that there is a being whose essence involves existence, so that his existence is analytic. That seems to me to be impossible, and it raises, of course, the question what one means by existence, and as to this, I think a subject named can never be significantly said to exist but only a subject described. And that existence, in fact, quite definitely is not a predicate.

Copleston: Well, you say, I believe, that it is bad grammar, or rather bad syntax to say for example ''T. S. Eliot exists''; one ought to say, for example, ''He, the author of *Murder in the Cathedral,* exists.'' Are you going to say that the proposition, ''The cause of the world exists,'' is without meaning? You may say that the world has no cause; but I fail to see how you can say that the proposition that ''the cause of the world exists'' is meaningless. Put it in the form of a question: ''Has the world a cause?'' or ''Does a cause of the world exist?'' Most people surely would understand the question, even if they don't agree about the answer.

Russell: Well, certainly the question ''Does the cause of the world exist?'' is a question that has meaning. But if you say ''Yes, God is the cause of the world'' you're using God as a proper name; then ''God exists'' will not be a statement that has meaning; that is the position that I'm maintaining. Because, therefore, it will follow that it cannot be an analytic proposition ever to say that this or that exists. For example, suppose you take as your subject ''the existent round-square,'' it would look

like an analytic proposition that ''the existent round-square exists,'' but it doesn't exist.

Copleston: No, it doesn't, then surely you can't say it doesn't exist unless you have a conception of what existence is. As to the phrase ''existent round-square,'' I should say that it has no meaning at all.

Russell: I quite agree. Then I should say the same thing in another context in reference to a ''necessary being.''

Copleston: Well, we seem to have arrived at an impasse. To say that a necessary being is a being that must exist and cannot not exist has for me a definite meaning. For you it has no meaning.

Russell: Well, we can press the point a little, I think. A being that must exist and cannot not exist, would surely, according to you, be a being whose essence involves existence.

Copleston: Yes, a being the essence of which is to exist. But I should not be willing to argue the existence of God simply from the idea of His essence because I don't think we have any clear intuition of God's essence as yet. I think we have to argue from the world of experience to God.

Russell: Yes, I quite see the distinction. But, at the same time, for a being with sufficient knowledge, it would be true to say ''Here is this being whose essence involves existence!''

Copleston: Yes, certainly if anybody saw God, he would see that God must exist.

Russell: So that I mean there is a being whose essence involves existence although we don't know that essence. We only know there is such a being.

Copleston: Yes, I should add we don't know the essence a *priori*. It is only a *posteriori* through our experience of the world that we come to a knowledge of the existence of that being. And then one argues, the essence and existence must be identical. Because if God's essence and God's existence was not identical, then some sufficient reason for this existence would have to be found beyond God.

Russell: So it all turns on this question of sufficient reason, and I must say you haven't defined "sufficient reason" in a way that I can understand—what do you mean by sufficient reason? You don't mean cause?

Copleston: Not necessarily. Cause is a kind of sufficient reason. Only contingent being can have a cause. God is His own sufficient reason; and He is not cause of Himself. By sufficient reason in the full sense I mean an explanation adequate for the existence of some particular being.

Russell: But when is an explanation adequate? Suppose I am about to make a flame with a match. You may say that the adequate explanation of that is that I rub it on the box.

Copleston: Well, for practical purposes—but theoretically, that is only a partial explanation. An adequate explanation must ultimately be a total explanation, to which nothing further can be added.

Russell: Then I can only say that you're looking for something which can't be got, and which one ought not to expect to get.

Copleston: To say that one has not found it is one thing; to say that one should not look for it seems to me rather dogmatic.

Russell: Well, I don't know. I mean, the explanation of one thing is another thing which makes the other thing dependent on yet another, and you have to grasp this sorry scheme of things entire to do what you want, and that we can't do.

Copleston: But are you going to say that we can't, or we shouldn't even raise the question of the existence of the whole of this sorry scheme of things—of the whole universe?

Russell: Yes, I don't think there's any meaning in it at all. I think the word "universe" is a handy word in some connections, but I don't think it stands for anything that has a meaning.

Copleston: If the word is meaningless, it can't be so very handy. In any case, I don't say that the universe is something different from the objects which compose it (I indicated that in my brief summary of the proof), what I'm doing is to look for the reason, in this case the cause of the objects—the real or imagined totality of which constitute what we call the universe. You say, I think

that the universe—or my existence if you prefer, or any other existence—is unintelligible?

Russell: First may I take up the point that if a word is meaningless it can't be handy. That sounds well but isn't in fact correct. Take, say, such a word as "the" or "than." You can't point to any object that those words mean, but they are very useful words; I should say the same of "universe." But leaving that point, you ask whether I consider that the universe is unintelligible. I shouldn't say unintelligible—I think it is without explanation. Intelligible, to my mind, is a different thing. Intelligible has to do with the thing itself intrinsically and not with its relations.

Copleston: Well, my point is that what we call the world is intrinsically unintelligible, apart from the existence of God. You see, I don't believe that the infinity of the series of events—I mean a horizontal series, so to speak—if such an infinity could be proved, would be in the slightest degree relevant to the situation. If you add up chocolates you get chocolates after all and not a sheep. If you add up chocolates to infinity, you presumably get an infinite number of chocolates. So if you add up contingent beings to infinity, you still get contingent beings, not a necessary being. An infinite series of contingent beings will be, to my way of thinking, as unable to cause itself as one contingent being. However, you say, I think, that it is illegitimate to raise the question of what will explain the existence of any particular object?

Russell: It's quite all right if you mean by explaining it, simply finding a cause for it.

Copleston: Well, why stop at one particular object? Why shouldn't one raise the question of the cause of the existence of all particular objects?

Russell: Because I see no reason to think there is any. The whole concept of cause is one we derive from our observation of particular things; I see no reason whatsoever to suppose that the total has any cause whatsoever.

Copleston: Well, to say that there isn't any cause is not the same thing as saying that we shouldn't look for a cause. The statement that there isn't any cause should come, if it comes at all, at the end of the inquiry, not the beginning. In any case, if the total has no cause, then to my way of thinking it must be its own cause, which seems to me impossible. Moreover, the statement that the world is simply there if in answer to a question, presupposes that the question has meaning.

Russell: No, it doesn't need to be its own cause, what I'm saying is that the concept of cause is not applicable to the total.

Copleston: Then you would agree with Sartre that the universe is what he calls "gratuitous"?

Russell: Well, the word "gratuitous" suggests that it might be something else; I should say that the universe is just there, and that's all.

Copleston: Well, I can't see how you can rule out the legitimacy of asking the question how the total, or anything at all comes to be there. Why something rather than nothing, that is the question? The fact that we gain our knowledge of causality empirically, from particular causes, does not rule out the possibility of asking what the cause of the series is. If the word "cause" were meaningless or if it could be shown that Kant's view of the matter were correct, the question would be illegitimate I agree; but you don't seem to hold that the word "cause" is meaningless, and I do not suppose you are a Kantian.

Russell: I can illustrate what seems to me your fallacy. Every man who exists has a mother, and it seems to me your argument is that therefore the human race must have a mother, but obviously the human race hasn't a mother—that's a different logical sphere.

Copleston: Well, I can't really see any parity. If I were saying "every object has a phenomenal cause, therefore, the whole series has a phenomenal cause," there would be a parity; but I'm not saying that; I'm saying, every object has a phenomenal cause if you insist on the infinity of the series—but the series of phenomenal causes is an insufficient explanation of the series. Therefore, the series has not a phenomenal cause but a transcendent cause.

Russell: That's always assuming that not only every particular thing in the world, but the world as a whole must have a cause. For that assumption

I see no ground whatever. If you'll give me a ground I'll listen to it.

Copleston: Well, the series of events is either caused or it's not caused. If it is caused, there must obviously be a cause outside the series. If it's not caused then it's sufficient to itself, and if it's sufficient to itself it is what I call necessary. But it can't be necessary since each member is contingent, and we've agreed that the total has no reality apart from its members, therefore, it can't be necessary. Therefore, it can't be (caused)—uncaused—therefore it must have a cause. And I should like to observe in passing that the statement "the world is simply there and is inexplicable" can't be got out of logical analysis.

Russell: I don't want to seem arrogant, but it does seem to me that I can conceive things that you say the human mind can't conceive. As for things not having a cause, the physicists assure us that individual quantum transitions in atoms have no cause.

Copleston: Well, I wonder now whether that isn't simply a temporary inference.

Russell: It may be, but it does show that physicists' minds can conceive it.

Copleston: Yes, I agree, some scientists—physicists—are willing to allow for indetermination within a restricted field. But very many scientists are not so willing. I think that Professor Dingle, of London University, maintains that the Heisenberg uncertainty principle tells us something about the success (or the lack of it) of the present atomic theory in correlating observations, but not about nature in itself, and many physicists would accept this view. In any case, I don't see how physicists can fail to accept the theory in practice, even if they don't do so in theory. I cannot see how science could be conducted on any other assumption than that of order and intelligibility in nature. The physicist presupposes, at least tacitly, that there is some sense in investigating nature and looking for the causes of events, just as the detective presupposes that there is some sense in looking for the cause of a murder. The metaphysician assumes that there is sense in looking for the reason or cause of phenomena, and, not being a

Kantian, I consider that the metaphysician is as justified in his assumption as the physicist. When Sartre, for example, says that the world is gratuitous, I think that he has not sufficiently considered what is implied by "gratuitous."

Russell: I think—there seems to me a certain unwarrantable extension here; a physicist looks for causes; that does not necessarily imply that there are causes everywhere. A man may look for gold without assuming that there is gold everywhere; if he finds gold, well and good, if he doesn't he's had bad luck. The same is true when the physicists look for causes. As for Sartre, I don't profess to know what he means, and I shouldn't like to be thought to interpret him, but for my part, I do think the notion of the world having an explanation is a mistake. I don't see why one should expect it to have, and I think you say about what the scientist assumes is an over-statement.

Copleston: Well, it seems to me that the scientist does make some such assumption. When he experiments to find out some particular truth, behind that experiment lies the assumption that the universe is not simply discontinuous. There is the possibility of finding out a truth by experiment. The experiment may be a bad one, it may lead to no result, or not to the result that he wants, but that at any rate there is the possibility, through experiment, of finding out the truth that he assumes. And that seems to me to assume an ordered and intelligible universe.

Russell: I think you're generalizing more than is necessary. Undoubtedly the scientist assumes that this sort of thing is likely to be found and will often be found. He does not assume that it will be found, and that's a very important matter in modern physics.

Copleston: Well, I think he does assume or is bound to assume it tacitly in practice. It may be that, to quote Professor Haldane, "when I light the gas under the kettle, some of the water molecules will fly off as vapor, and there is no way of finding out which will do so," but it doesn't follow necessarily that the idea of chance must be introduced except in relation to our knowledge.

Russell: No it doesn't—at least if I may believe what he says. He's finding out quite a lot of things—the scientist is finding out quite a lot of things that are happening in the world, which are, at first, beginnings of causal chains—first causes which haven't in themselves got causes. He does not assume that everything has a cause.

Copleston: Surely that's a first cause within a certain selected field. It's a relatively first cause.

Russell: I don't think he'd say so. If there's a world in which most events, but not all, have causes, he will then be able to depict the probabilities and uncertainties by assuming that this particular event you're interested in probably has a cause. And since in any case you won't get more than probability that's good enough.

Copleston: It may be that the scientist doesn't hope to obtain more than probability, but in raising the question he assumes that the question of explanation has a meaning. But your general point then, Lord Russell, is that it's illegitimate even to ask the question of the cause of the world?

Russell: Yes, that's my position.

Copleston: If it's a question that for you has no meaning, it's of course very difficult to discuss it, isn't it?

Russell: Yes, it is very difficult. What do you say—shall we pass on to some other issue?

I.A.3   A Critique of the Cosmological Argument

P A U L   E D W A R D S

Paul Edwards is professor of philosophy at Brooklyn College, City University of New York. In this article he follows Russell, attacking the cosmological argument and arguing that it fails at several different points.

I

The so-called "cosmological proof" is one of the oldest and most popular arguments for the existence of God. It was forcibly criticized by Hume, Kant, and Mill, but it would be inaccurate to consider the argument dead or even moribund. Catholic philosophers, with hardly any exception, appear to believe that it is as solid and conclusive as ever. Thus Father F. C. Copleston confidently championed it in his Third Programme debate with Bertrand Russell, and in America, where Catholic writers are more sanguine, we are told by a Jesuit professor of physics that "the existence of an intelligent being as the First Cause of the universe can be established by *rational scientific inference.*"[1]

I am absolutely convinced [the same writer continues] that any one who would give the same consideration to that proof (the cosmological argument), as outlined for example in William Brosnan's *God and Reason,* as he would give to a line of argumentation found in the *Physical Review* or the *Proceedings of the Royal Society* would be forced to admit that the cogency of this argument for the existence of God far outstrips that which is found in the reasoning which Chadwick uses to prove the existence of the neutron, which today is accepted as certain as any conclusion in the physical sciences.

Mild theists like the late Professor Dawes Hicks and Dr. [A. C.] Ewing, who concede many of Hume's and Kant's criticisms, nevertheless contend that the argument possesses a certain core of truth. In popular discussions it also crops up again and again—for example, when believers address atheists with such questions as "You tell me where the universe came from!" Even philosophers who reject the cosmological proof sometimes embody certain of its confusions in the formulation of their own position. In the light of all this, it may be worth while to undertake a fresh examination of the argument with special attention to the fallacies that were not emphasized by the older critics.

II

The cosmological proof has taken a number of forms, the most important of which are known as the "causal argument" and "the argument from contingency," respectively. In some writers, in Samuel Clarke for example, they are combined, but it is best to keep them apart as far as possible. The causal argument is the second of the "five ways" of Aquinas and roughly proceeds as follows: we find that the things around us come into being as the result of the activity of other things. These causes are themselves the result of the activity of other things. But such a causal series cannot "go back to infinity." Hence there must be a first member, a member which is not itself caused by any preceding member—an uncaused or "first" cause.

It has frequently been pointed out that even if this argument were sound it would not establish the existence of *God.* It would not show that the first cause is all-powerful or all-good or that it is in any sense personal. Somebody believing in the eternity of atoms, or of matter generally, could quite consistently accept the conclusion. Defenders of the causal argument usually concede this and insist that the argument is not in itself

Reprinted from *The Rationalist Annual,* 1959, edited by Hector Hawton. Reprinted by permission of Paul Edwards. Footnotes edited.

meant to prove the existence of God. Supplementary arguments are required to show that the first cause must have the attributes assigned to the deity. They claim, however, that the argument, if valid, would at least be an important step towards a complete proof of the existence of God.

Does the argument succeed in proving so much as a first cause? This will depend mainly on the soundness of the premise that an infinite series of causes is impossible. Aquinas supports this premise by maintaining that the opposite belief involves a plain absurdity. To suppose that there is an infinite series of causes logically implies that nothing exists now; but we know that plenty of things do exist now; and hence any theory which implies that nothing exists now must be wrong. Let us take some causal series and refer to its members by the letters of the alphabet:

$$A \rightarrow B \ . \ . \ . \ W \rightarrow X \rightarrow Y \rightarrow Z$$

Z stands here for something presently existing, e.g. Margaret Truman. Y represents the cause or part of the cause of Z, say Harry Truman. X designates the cause or part of the cause of Y, say Harry Truman's father, etc. Now, Aquinas reasons, whenever we take away the cause, we also take away the effect: if Harry Truman had never lived, Margaret Truman would never have been born. If Harry Truman's father had never lived, Harry Truman and Margaret Truman would never have been born. If A had never existed, none of the subsequent members of the series would have come into existence. But it is precisely A that the believer in the infinite series is "taking away." For in maintaining that the series is infinite he is denying that it has a first member; he is denying that there is such a thing as a first cause; he is in other words denying the existence of A. Since without A, Z could not have existed, his position implies that Z does not exist now; and that is plainly false.

This argument fails to do justice to the supporter of the infinite series of causes. Aquinas has failed to distinguish between the two statements:

(1) A did not exist, and
(2) A is not uncaused.

To say that the series is infinite implies (2), but it does not imply (1). The following parallel may be

helpful here: Suppose Captain Spaulding had said, "I am the greatest explorer who ever lived," and somebody replied, "No, you are not." This answer would be denying that the Captain possessed the exalted attribute he had claimed for himself, but it would not be denying his existence. It would not be "taking him away." Similarly, the believer in the infinite series is not "taking A away." He is taking away the privileged status of A; he is taking away its "first causiness." He does not deny the *existence* of A or of any particular member of the series. He denies that A or anything else *is the first member* of the series. Since he is not taking A away, he is not taking B away, and thus he is also not taking X, Y, or Z away. His view, then, does not commit him to the absurdity that nothing exists now, or more specifically, that Margaret Truman does not exist now. It may be noted in this connection that a believer in the infinite series is not necessarily denying the existence of supernatural beings. He is merely committed to denying that such a being, if it exists, is uncaused. He is committed to holding that whatever other impressive attributes a supernatural being might possess, the attribute of being a first cause is not among them.

The causal argument is open to several other objections. Thus, even if otherwise valid, the argument, would not prove a *single* first cause. For there does not seem to be any good ground for supposing that the various causal series in the universe ultimately merge. Hence even if it is granted that no series of causes can be infinite the possibility of a plurality of first members has not been ruled out. Nor does the argument establish the *present* existence of the first cause. It does not prove this, since experience clearly shows that an effect may exist long after its cause has been destroyed.

III

Many defenders of the causal argument would contend that at least some of these criticisms rest on a misunderstanding. They would probably go further and contend that the argument was not quite fairly stated in the first place—or at any rate that if it was fair to some of its adherents it was not fair to others. They would in this connection distinguish between two types of causes—what they call "causes *in fieri*" and what they call "causes *in esse*." A cause *in fieri* is a factor which brought or helped to bring an effect into existence. A cause *in esse* is a factor which "sustains" or helps to sustain the effect "in being." The parents of a human being would be an example of a cause *in fieri*. If somebody puts a book in my hand and I keep holding it up, his putting it there would be the cause *in fieri,* and my holding it would be the cause *in esse* of the book's position. To quote Father [G. H.] Joyce:

> If a smith forges a horse-shoe, he is only a cause *in fieri* of the shape given to the iron. That shape persists after his action has ceased. So, too, a builder is a cause *in fieri* of the house which he builds. In both cases the substances employed act as causes *in esse* as regards the continued existence of the effect produced. Iron, in virtue of its natural rigidity, retains in being the shape which it has once received; and, similarly, the materials employed in building retain in being the order and arrangement which constitute them into a house.[2]

Using this distinction, the defender of the argument now reasons in the following way. To say that there is an infinite series of causes *in fieri* does not lead to any absurd conclusions. But Aquinas is concerned only with causes *in esse* and an infinite series of *such* causes is impossible. In the words of the contemporary American Thomist, R. P. Phillips:

> Each member of the series of causes possesses being solely by virtue of the actual present operation of a superior cause. . . . Life is dependent, *inter alia,* on a certain atmospheric pressure, this again on the continual operation of physical forces, whose being and operation depends on the position of the earth in the solar system, which itself must endure relatively unchanged, a state of being which can only be continuously produced by a definite—if unknown— constitution of the material universe. This constitution, however, cannot be its own cause. That a thing should cause itself is impossible: for in order that it may cause it is necessary for it to exist, which it cannot do, on the hypothesis, until it has been caused. So it must *be* in order to cause itself. Thus, not being

uncaused nor yet its own cause, it must be caused by another, which produces and preserves it. It is plain, then, that as no member of this series possesses being except in virtue of the actual present operation of a superior cause, if there be no first cause actually operating none of the dependent causes could operate either. We are thus irresistibly led to posit a first efficient cause which, while itself uncaused, shall impart causality to a whole series. . . .

> The series of cause which we are considering is not one which stretches back into the past; so that we are not demanding a beginning of the world at some definite moment reckoning back from the present, but an actual cause now operating, to account for the present being of things.[3]

Professor Phillips offers the following parallel to bring out his point:

> In a goods train each truck is moved and moves by the action of the one immediately in front of it. If then we suppose the train to be infinite, i.e. that there is no end to it, and so no engine which starts the motion, it is plain that no truck will move. To lengthen it out to infinity will not give it what no member of it possesses of itself, viz. the power of drawing the truck behind it. If then we see any truck in motion we know there must be an end to the series of trucks which gives causality to the whole.[4]

Father Joyce introduces an illustration from Aquinas to explain how the present existence of things may be compatible with an infinite series of causes *in fieri* but not with an infinite series of causes *in esse.*

> When a carpenter is at work, the series of efficient causes on which his work depends is necessarily limited. The final effect, e.g. the fastening of a nail is caused by a hammer: the hammer is moved by the arm: and the motion of his arm is determined by the motor-impulses communicated from the nerve centres of the brain. Unless the subordinate causes were limited in number, and were connected with a starting-point of motion, the hammer must remain inert; and the nail will never be driven in. If the series be supposed infinite, no work will ever take place. But if there is question of causes on which the work is not essentially dependent, we cannot draw the same conclusion. We may suppose the carpenter to have broken an infinite number of hammers, and as often to have replaced the broken tool by a fresh one. There is nothing in such a supposition which excludes the driving home of the nail.

The supporter of the infinite series of causes, Joyce also remarks, is

. . . asking us to believe that although each link in a suspended chain is prevented from falling simply because it is attached to the one above it, yet if only the chain be long enough, it will, taken as a whole, need no support, but will hang loose in the air suspended from nothing.

This formulation of the causal argument unquestionably circumvents one of the objections mentioned previously. If Y is the cause *in esse* of an effect, Z, then it must exist as long as Z exists. If the argument were valid in this form it would therefore prove the present and not merely the past existence of a first cause. In this form the argument is, however, less convincing in another respect. To maintain that all "natural" or "phenomenal" objects—things like tables and mountains and human beings—require a cause *in fieri* is not implausible, though even here Mill and others have argued that strictly speaking only *changes* require a causal explanation. It is far from plausible, on the other hand, to claim that all natural objects require a cause *in esse*. It may be granted that the air around us is a cause *in esse* of human life and further that certain gravitational forces are among the causes *in esse* of the air being where it is. But when we come to gravitational forces or, at any rate, to material particles like atoms or electrons it is difficult to see what cause *in esse* they require. To those not already convinced of the need for a supernatural First Cause some of the remarks by Professor Phillips in this connection appear merely dogmatic and question-begging. Most people would grant that such particles as atoms did not cause themselves, since, as Professor Phillips observes, they would in that event have had to exist before they began existing. It is not at all evident, however, that these particles cannot be uncaused. Professor Phillips and all other supporters of the causal argument immediately proceed to claim that there is something else which needs no cause *in esse*. They themselves admit thus, that there is nothing self-evident about the proposition that everything must have a cause *in esse*. Their entire procedure here lends substance

to Schopenhauer's gibe that supporters of the cosmological argument treat the law of universal causation like "a hired cab which we dismiss when we have reached our destination."

But waiving this and all similar objections, the restatement of the argument in terms of causes *in esse* in no way avoids the main difficulty which was previously mentioned. A believer in the infinite series would insist that his position was just as much misrepresented now as before. He is no more removing the member of the series which is supposed to be the first cause *in esse* than he was removing the member which had been declared to be the first cause *in fieri*. He is again merely denying a privileged status to it. He is not denying the reality of the cause *in esse* labelled "A." He is not even necessarily denying that it possesses supernatural attributes. He is again merely taking away its "first causiness."

The advocates of the causal argument in either form seem to confuse an infinite series with one which is long but finite. If a book, Z, is to remain in its position, say 100 miles up in the air, there must be another object, say another book, Y, underneath it to serve as its support. If Y is to remain where it is, it will need another support, X, beneath it. Suppose that this series of supports, one below the other, continues for a long time, but eventually, say after 100,000 members, comes to a first book which is not resting on any other book or indeed on any other support. In that event the whole collection would come crashing down. What we seem to need is a first member of the series, a first support (such as the earth) which does not need another member as *its* support, which in other words is "self-supporting."

This is evidently the sort of picture that supporters of the First Cause argument have before their minds when they rule out the possibility of an infinite series. But such a picture is not a fair representation of the theory of the infinite series. A *finite* series of books would indeed come crashing down, since the first or lowest member would not have a predecessor on which it could be supported. If the series, however, were infinite this would not be the case. In that event every member *would* have a predecessor to support itself on and there would be no crash. That is to say: a crash can be avoided either by a finite series with a first self-supporting member or by an infinite series. Similarly, the present existence of motion is equally compatible with the theory of a first unmoved mover and with the theory of an infinite series of moving objects; and the present existence of causal activity is compatible with the theory of a first cause *in esse* as much as with the theory of an infinite series of such causes.

The illustrations given by Joyce and Phillips are hardly to the point. It is true that a carpenter would not, *in a finite time-span,* succeed in driving in a nail if he had to carry out an infinite number of movements. For that matter, he would not accomplish this goal in a finite time if he broke an infinite number of hammers. However, to make the illustrations relevant we must suppose that he has infinite time at his disposal. In that case he would succeed in driving in the nail even if he required an infinite number of movements for this purpose. As for the goods train, it may be granted that the trucks do not move unless the train has an engine. But this illustration is totally irrelevant as it stands. A relevant illustration would be that of engines, each moved by the one in front of it. Such a train would move if it were infinite. For every member of this series there would be one in front capable of drawing it along. The advocate of the infinite series of causes does not, as the original illustration suggests, believe in a series whose members are not really causally connected with one another. In the series he believes in every member is genuinely the cause of the one that follows it.

IV

No staunch defender of the cosmological argument would give up at this stage. Even if there were an infinite series of causes *in fieri* or *in esse,* he would contend, this still would not do away with the need for an ultimate, a first cause. As Father Copleston put it in his debate with Bertrand Russell:

Every object has a phenomenal cause, if you insist on the infinity of the series. But the series of phenomenal causes is an insufficient explanation of the series. Therefore, the series has not a phenomenal cause, but a transcendent cause. . . .

An infinite series of contingent beings will be, to my way of thinking, as unable to cause itself as one contingent being.

The demand to find the cause of the series as a whole rests on the erroneous assumption that the series is something over and above the members of which it is composed. It is tempting to suppose this, at least by implication, because the word "series" is a noun like "dog" or "man." Like the expression "this dog" or "this man" the phrase "this series" is easily taken to designate an individual object. But reflection shows this to be an error. If we have explained the individual members there is nothing additional left to be explained. Supposing I see a group of five Eskimos standing on the corner of Sixth Avenue and 50th Street and I wish to explain why the group came to New York. Investigation reveals the following stories:

- Eskimo No. 1 did not enjoy the extreme cold in the polar region and decided to move to a warmer climate.
- No. 2 is the husband of Eskimo No. 1. He loves her dearly and did not wish to live without her.
- No. 3 is the son of Eskimos 1 and 2. He is too small and too weak to oppose his parents.
- No. 4 saw an advertisement in the *New York Times* for an Eskimo to appear on television.
- No. 5 is a private detective engaged by the Pinkerton Agency to keep an eye on Eskimo No. 4.

Let us assume that we have now explained in the case of each of the five Eskimos why he or she is in New York. Somebody then asks: "All right, but what about the group as a whole; why is *it* in New York?" This would plainly be an absurd question. There is no group over and above the five members, and if we have explained why each of the five members is in New York we have *ipso facto* explained why the group is there. It is just as absurd to ask for the cause of the series as a whole as distinct from asking for the causes of individual members.

V

It is most unlikely that a determined defender of the cosmological line of reasoning would surrender even here. He would probably admit that the series is not a thing over and above its members and that it does not make sense to ask for the cause of the series if the cause of each member has already been found. He would insist, however, that when he asked for the explanation of the entire series, he was not asking for its *cause*. He was really saying that a series, finite or infinite, is not "intelligible" or "explained" if it consists of nothing but "contingent" members. To quote Father Copleston once more:

What we call the world is intrinsically unintelligible apart from the existence of God. The infinity of the series of events, if such an infinity could be proved, would not be in the slightest degree relevant to the situation. If you add up chocolates, you get chocolates after all, and not a sheep. If you add up chocolates to infinity, you presumably get an infinite number of chocolates. So, if you add up contingent beings to infinity, you still get contingent beings, not a necessary being.

This last quotation is really a summary of the "contingency argument," the other main form of the cosmological proof and the third of the five ways of Aquinas. It may be stated more fully in these words: All around us we perceive contingent beings. This includes all physical objects and also all human minds. In calling them "contingent" we mean that they might not have existed. We mean that the universe can be *conceived* without this or that physical object, without this or that human being, however certain their actual existence may be. These contingent beings we can trace back to other contingent beings—e.g. a human being to his parents. However, since these other beings are also contingent, they do not provide a real or full explanation. The contingent beings we originally wanted explained have not yet become intelligi-

ble, since the beings to which they have been traced back are no more necessary than they were. It is just as true of our parents, for example, as it is of ourselves, that they might not have existed. We can then properly explain the contingent beings around us only by tracing them back ultimately to some necessary being, to something which exists necessarily, which has "the reason for its existence within itself." The existence of contingent beings, in other words, implies the existence of a necessary being.

This form of cosmological argument is even more beset with difficulties than the causal variety. In the first place, there is the objection, stated with great force by Kant, that it really commits the same error as the ontological argument in tacitly regarding existence as an attribute or characteristic. To say that there is a necessary being is to say that it would be a self-contradiction to deny its existence. This would mean that at least one existential statement is a necessary truth; and this in turn presupposes that in at least one case existence is contained in a concept. But only a characteristic can be contained in a concept and it has seemed plain to most philosophers since Kant that existence is not a characteristic, that it can hence never be contained in a concept, and that hence no existential statement can ever be a necessary truth. To talk about anything "existing necessarily" is in their view about as sensible as to talk about round squares, and they have concluded that the contingency-argument is quite absurd.

It would lead too far to discuss here the reasons for denying that existence is a characteristic. I will assume that this difficulty can somehow be surmounted and that the expression "necessary being," as it is intended by the champions of the contingency-argument, might conceivably apply to something. There remain other objections which are of great weight. I shall try to state these by first quoting again from the debate between Bertrand Russell and Father Copleston:

Russell: . . .It all turns on this question of sufficient reason, and I must say you haven't defined "sufficient reason" in a way that I can understand—what do you mean by sufficient reason? You don't mean cause?

Copleston: Not necessarily. Cause is a kind of sufficient reason. Only contingent being can have a cause. God is his own sufficient reason; and he is not cause of himself. By sufficient reason in the full sense I mean an explanation adequate for the existence of some particular being.

Russell: But when is an explanation adequate? Suppose I am about to make a flame with a match. You may say that the adequate explanation of that is that I rub it on the box.

Copleston: Well for practical purposes—but theoretically, that is only a partial explanation. An adequate explanation must ultimately be a total explanation, to which nothing further can be added.

Russell: Then I can only say that you're looking for something which can't be got, and which one ought not to expect to get.

Copleston: To say that one has not found it is one thing; to say that one should not look for it seems to me rather dogmatic.

Russell: Well, I don't know. I mean, the explanation of one thing is another thing which makes the other thing dependent on yet another, and you have to grasp this sorry scheme of things entire to do what you want, and that we can't do.

Russell's main point here may be expanded in the following way. The contingency-argument rests on a misconception of what an explanation is and does, and similarly on what it is that makes phenomena "intelligible." Or else it involves an obscure and arbitrary redefinition of "explanation," "intelligible," and related terms. Normally, we are satisfied that we have explained a phenomenon if we have found its cause or if we have exhibited some other uniform or near-uniform connection between it and something else. Confining ourselves to the former case, which is probably the most common, we might say that a phenomenon, Z, has been explained if it has been traced back to a group of factors, a, b, c, d, etc., which are its cause. These factors are the full and real explanation of Z, quite regardless of whether they are pleasing or displeasing, admirable or con-

temptible, necessary or contingent. The explanation would not be adequate only if the factors listed are not really the cause of Z. If they are the cause of Z, the explanation would be adequate, even though each of the factors is merely a "contingent" being.

Let us suppose that we have been asked to explain why General Eisenhower won the elections of 1952. "He was an extremely popular general," we might answer, "while Stevenson was relatively little known; moreover there was a great deal of resentment over the scandals in the Truman Administration." If somebody complained that this was only a partial explanation we might mention additional antecedents, such as the widespread belief that the Democrats had allowed communist agents to infiltrate the State Department, that Eisenhower was a man with a winning smile, and that unlike Stevenson he had shown the good sense to say one thing on race relations in the North and quite another in the South. Theoretically, we might go further and list the motives of all American voters during the weeks or months preceding the elections. If we could do this we would have explained Eisenhower's victory. We would have made it intelligible. We would "understand" why he won and why Stevenson lost. Perhaps there is a sense in which we might make Eisenhower's victory even more intelligible if we went further back and discussed such matters as the origin of American views on Communism or of racial attitudes in the North and South. However, to explain the outcome of the election in any ordinary sense, loose or strict, it would not be necessary to go back to prehistoric days or to the amoeba or to a first cause, if such a first cause exists. Nor would our explanation be considered in any way defective because each of the factors mentioned was a "contingent" and not a necessary being. The only thing that matters is whether the factors were really the cause of Eisenhower's election. If they were, then it has been explained although they are contingent beings. If they were not the cause of Eisenhower's victory, we would have failed to explain it even if each of the factors were a necessary being.

If it is granted that, in order to explain a phenomenon or to make it intelligible, we need not bring in a necessary being, then the contingency-argument breaks down. For a series, as was already pointed out, is not something over and above its members; and every contingent member of it could in that case be explained by reference to other contingent beings. But I should wish to go further than this and it is evident from Russell's remarks that he would do so also. Even if it were granted, both that the phrase "necessary being" is meaningful and that all explanations are defective unless the phenomena to be explained are traced back to a necessary being, the conclusion would still not have been established. The conclusion follows from this premise together with the additional premise that *there are* explanations of phenomena in the special sense just mentioned. It is this further premise which Russell (and many other philosophers) would question. They do not merely question, as Copleston implies, whether human beings can ever obtain explanations in this sense, but whether they *exist*. To assume without further ado that phenomena have explanations or an explanation in this sense is to beg the very point at issue. The use of the same word "explanation" in two crucially different ways lends the additional premise a plausibility it does not really possess. It may indeed be highly plausible to assert that phenomena have explanations, whether we have found them or not, in the ordinary sense in which this usually means that they have causes. It is then tempting to suppose, because of the use of the same word, that they also have explanations in a sense in which this implies dependence on a necessary being. But this is a gross *non sequitur*.

VI

It is necessary to add a few words about the proper way of formulating the position of those who reject the main premise of the cosmological argument, in either of the forms we have considered. It is sometimes maintained in this connection that in order to reach a "self-existing" entity it is not necessary to go beyond the universe: the universe itself (or "Nature") is "self-existing." And this in turn is sometimes expanded into the statement that while all individual things "within" the universe are caused, the universe itself is uncaused. Statements of this kind are found in Büchner, Bradlaugh, Haeckel, and other free-thinkers of the nineteenth and early twentieth century. Sometimes the assertion that the universe is "self-existing" is elaborated to mean that *it* is the "necessary being." Some eighteenth-century unbelievers, apparently accepting the view that there is a necessary being, asked why Nature or the material universe could not fill the bill as well or better than God.

"Why," asks one of the characters in Hume's *Dialogues*, "may not the material universe be the necessarily existent Being? . . . We dare not affirm that we know all the qualities of matter; and for aught we can determine, it may contain some qualities, which, were they known, would make its non-existence appear as great a contradiction as that twice two is five."

Similar remarks can be found in Holbach and several of the Encyclopedists.

The former of these formulations immediately invites the question why the universe, alone of all "things," is exempted from the universal sway of causation. "The strong point of the cosmological argument," writes Dr. Ewing, "is that after all it does remain incredible that the physical universe should just have happened . . . It calls out for some further explanation of some kind." The latter formulation is exposed to the criticism that there is nothing any more "necessary" about the existence of the universe or Nature as a whole than about any particular thing within the universe.

I hope some of the earlier discussions in this article have made it clear that in rejecting the cosmological argument one is not comitted to either of these propositions. If I reject the view that there is a supernatural first cause, I am not thereby committed to the proposition that there is a *natural* first cause, and even less to the proposition that a mysterious "thing" called "the universe" qualifies for this title. I may hold that there is no "universe" over and above individual things of various sorts; and, accepting the causal principle, I may proceed to assert that all these things are caused by other things, and these other things by yet other things, and so on, *ad infinitum*. In this way no arbitrary exception is made to the principle of causation. Similarly, if I reject the assertion that God is a "necessary being," I am not committed to the view that the universe is such an entity. I may hold that it does not make sense to speak of anything as a "necessary being" and that even if there were such a thing as the universe it could not be properly considered a necessary being.

However, in saying that nothing is uncaused or that there is no necessary being, one is not committed to the view that everything, or for that matter anything, is merely a "brute fact." Dr. Ewing laments that "the usual modern philosophical views opposed to theism do not try to give any rational explanation of the world at all, but just take it as a brute fact not to be explained." They thus fail to "rationalize" the universe. Theism, he concedes, cannot completely rationalize things either since it does not show "how God can be his own cause or how it is that he does not need a cause." Now, if one means by "brute fact" something for which there *exists* no explanation (as distinct from something for which no explanation is in our possession), then the theists have at least one brute fact on their hands, namely God. Those who adopt Büchner's formulation also have one brute fact on their hands, namely "the universe." Only the position I have been supporting dispenses with brute facts altogether. I don't know if this is any special virtue, but the defenders of the cosmological argument seem to think so.

Notes

1. J. S. O'Connor, "A Scientific Approach to Religion," *The Scientific Monthly* (1940), p. 369; my italics.
2. *The Principles of Natural Theology*, p. 58.
3. *Modern Thomistic Philosophy*, Vol. II, pp. 284–85.
4. Ibid., p. 278.

I.A.4   The Cosmological Argument: A Defense

RICHARD TAYLOR

Richard Taylor is professor of philosophy at the University of Rochester. In this article he argues that the existence of the world demands an explanation and that the notion of a deity who is a necessary being satisfies that demand.

Suppose you were strolling in the woods and, in addition to the sticks, stones, and other accustomed litter of the forest floor, you one day came upon some quite unaccustomed object, something not quite like what you had ever seen before and would never expect to find in such a place. Suppose, for example, that it is a large ball, about

From Richard Taylor, *Metaphysics*, 3rd ed., copyright © 1983, pp. 91–99. Reprinted by permission of Prentice-Hall, Inc., Englewood Cliffs, N.J.

your own height, perfectly smooth and translucent. You would deem this puzzling and mysterious, certainly, but if one considers the matter, it is no more inherently mysterious that such a thing should exist than that anything else should exist. If you were quite accustomed to finding such objects of various sizes around you most of the time, but had never seen an ordinary rock, then upon finding a large rock in the woods one day you would be just as puzzled and mystified. This illustrates the fact that something that is mysterious ceases to seem so simply by its accustomed presence. It is strange indeed, for example, that a world such as ours should exist; yet few men are very often struck by this strangeness, but simply take it for granted.

Suppose, then, that you have found this translucent ball and are mystified by it. Now whatever else you might wonder about it, there is one thing you would hardly question; namely, that it did not appear there all by itself, that it owes its existence to something. You might not have the remotest idea whence and how it came to be there, but you would hardly doubt that there was an explanation. The idea that it might have come from nothing at all, that it might exist without there being any explanation of its existence, is one that few people would consider worthy of entertaining.

This illustrates a metaphysical belief that seems to be almost a part of reason itself, even though few men ever think upon it; the belief, namely, that there is some explanation for the existence of anything whatever, some reason why it should exist rather than not. The sheer nonexistence of anything, which is not to be confused with the passing out of existence of something, never requires a reason; but existence does. That there should never have been any such ball in the forest does not require any explanation or reason, but that there should ever be such a ball does. If one were to look upon a barren plain and ask why there is not and never has been any large translucent ball there, the natural response would be to ask why there should be; but if one finds such a ball, and wonders why it is there, it is not quite so natural to ask why it should *not* be, as though existence should simply be taken for granted. That anything should not exist, then, and that, for instance, no such ball should exist in the forest, or that there should be no forest for it to occupy, or no continent containing a forest, or no earth, nor any world at all, do not seem to be things for which there needs to be any explanation or reason; but that such things should be, does seem to require a reason.

The principle involved here has been called the principle of sufficient reason. Actually, it is a very general principle, and is best expressed by saying that, in the case of any positive truth, there is some sufficient reason for it, something which, in this sense, makes it true—in short, that there is some sort of explanation, known or unknown, for everything.

Now some truths depend on something else, and are accordingly called *contingent,* while others depend only upon themselves, that is, are true by their very natures and are accordingly called *necessary.* There is, for example, a reason why the stone on my window sill is warm; namely, that the sun is shining upon it. This happens to be true, but not by its very nature. Hence, it is contingent, and depends upon something other than itself. It is also true that all the points of a circle are equidistant from the center, but this truth depends upon nothing but itself. No matter what happens, nothing can make it false. Similarly, it is a truth, and a necessary one, that if the stone on my window sill is a body, as it is, then it has a form, because this fact depends upon nothing but itself for its confirmation. Untruths are also, of course, either contingent or necessary, it being contingently false, for example, that the stone on my window sill is cold, and necessarily false that it is both a body and formless, because this is by its very nature impossible.

The principle of sufficient reason can be illustrated in various ways, as we have done, and if one thinks about it, he is apt to find that he presupposes it in his thinking about reality, but it cannot be proved. It does not appear to be itself a necessary truth, and at the same time it would be most odd to say it is contingent. If one were to try proving it, he would sooner or later have to appeal to considerations that are less plausible than the principle itself. Indeed, it is hard to see how one could even make an argument for it, without already assuming it. For this reason it might properly be called a presupposition of reason itself. One can deny that it is true, without embarrassment or fear of refutation, but one is then apt to find that what he is denying is not really what the principle asserts. We shall, then, treat it here as a datum—not something that is provably true, but as something which all men, whether they ever reflect upon it or not, seem more or less to presuppose.

The Existence of a World

It happens to be true that something exists, that there is, for example, a world, and although no one ever seriously supposes that this might not be so, that there might exist nothing at all, there still seems to be nothing the least necessary in this, considering it just by itself. That no world should ever exist at all is perfectly comprehensible and seems to express not the slightest absurdity. Considering any particular item in the world it seems not at all necessary in itself that it should ever have existed, nor does it appear any more necessary that the totality of these things, or any totality of things, should ever exist.

From the principle of sufficient reason it follows, of course, that there must be a reason, not only for the existence of everything in the world but for the world itself, meaning by "the world" simply everything that ever does exist, except God, in case there is a god. This principle does not imply that there must be some purpose or goal for everything, or for the totality of all things; for explanations need not, and in fact seldom are, teleological or purposeful. All the principle requires is that there be some sort of reason for everything. And it would certainly be odd to maintain that everything in the world owes its existence to something, that nothing in the world is either purely accidental, or such that it just bestows its own being upon itself, and then to deny this of the world itself. One can indeed *say* that the world is in some sense a pure accident, that there simply is no reason at all why this or any world should exist, and one can equally say that the world exists by its very nature, or is an inherently necessary being. But it is at least very odd and arbitrary to deny of this existing world the need for any sufficient reason, whether independent of itself or not, while presupposing that there is a reason for every other thing that ever exists.

Consider again the strange ball that we imagine has been found in the forest. Now we can hardly doubt that there must be an explanation for the existence of such a thing, though we may have no notion what that explanation is. It is not, moreover, the fact of its having been found in the forest rather than elsewhere that renders an explanation necessary. It matters not in the least where it happens to be, for our question is not how it happens to be *there* but how it happens to exist at all. If we in our imagination annihilate the forest, leaving

only this ball in an open field, our conviction that it is a contingent thing and owes its existence to something other than itself is not reduced in the least. If we now imagine the field to be annihilated, and in fact everything else as well to vanish into nothingness, leaving only this ball to constitute the entire physical universe, then we cannot for a moment suppose that its existence has thereby been explained, or the need of any explanation eliminated, or that its existence is suddenly rendered self-explanatory. If we now carry this thought one step further and suppose that no other reality ever has existed or ever will exist, that this ball forever constitutes the entire physical universe, then we must still insist on there being some reason independent of itself why it should exist rather than not. If there must be a reason for the existence of any particular thing, then the necessity of such a reason is not eliminated by the mere supposition that certain other things do *not* exist. And again, it matters not at all what the thing in question is, whether it be large and complex, such as the world we actually find ourselves in, or whether it be something small, simple and insignificant, such as a ball, a bacterium, or the merest grain of sand. We do not avoid the necessity of a reason for the existence of something merely by describing it in this way or that. And it would, in any event, seem quite plainly absurd to say that if the world were comprised entirely of a single ball about six feet in diameter, or of a single grain of sand, then it would be contingent and there would have to be some explanation other than itself why such a thing exists, but that, since the actual world is vastly more complex than this, there is no need for an explanation of its existence, independent of itself.

Beginningless Existence

It should now be noted that it is no answer to the question, why a thing exists, to state *how long* it has existed. A geologist does not suppose that he has explained why there should be rivers and mountains merely by pointing out that they are old. Similarly, if one were to ask, concerning the ball of which we have spoken, for some sufficient reason for its being, he would not receive any answer upon being told that it had been there since yesterday. Nor would it be any better answer to say that it had existed since before anyone could remember, or even that it had existed; for the question was not one concerning its age but its existence. If, to be sure, one were to ask where a given thing came from, or how it came into being, then upon learning that it had always existed he would learn that it never really *came* into being at all; but he could still reasonably wonder why it should exist at all. If, accordingly, the world—that is, the totality of all things excepting God, in case there is a god—had really no beginning at all, but has always existed in some form or other, then there is clearly no answer to the question, where it came from and when; it did not, on this supposition, *come* from anything at all, at any time. But still, it can be asked why there is a world, why indeed there is a beginningless world, why there should have perhaps always been something rather than nothing. And, if the principle of sufficient reason is a good principle, there must be an answer to that question, an answer that is by no means supplied by giving the world an age, or even an infinite age.

Creation

This brings out an important point with respect to the concept of creation that is often misunderstood, particularly by those whose thinking has been influenced by Christian ideas. People tend to think that creation—for example, the creation of the world by God—*means* creation *in time,* from which it of course logically follows that if the world had no beginning in time, then it cannot be the creation of God. This, however, is erroneous, for creation means essentially *dependence,* even in Christian theology. If one thing is the creation of another, then it depends for its existence on that other, and this is perfectly consistent with saying that both are eternal, that neither ever came into being, and hence, that neither was ever created at any point of time. Perhaps an analogy will help

convey this point. Consider, then, a flame that is casting beams of light. Now there seems to be a clear sense in which the beams of light are dependent for their existence upon the flame, which is their source, while the flame, on the other hand, is not similarly dependent for its existence upon them. The beams of light arise from the flame, but the flame does not arise from them. In this sense, they are the creation of the flame; they derive their existence from it. And none of this has any reference to time; the relationship of dependence in such a case would not be altered in the slightest if we supposed that the flame, and with it the beams of light, had always existed, that neither had ever *come* into being.

Now if the world is the creation of God, its relationship to God should be thought of in this fashion; namely, that the world depends for its existence upon God, and could not exist independently of God. If God is eternal, as those who believe in God generally assume, then the world may (though it need not) be eternal too, without that altering in the least its dependence upon God for its existence, and hence without altering its being the creation of God. The supposition of God's eternality, on the other hand, does not by itself imply that the world is eternal too; for there is not the least reason why something of finite duration might not depend for its existence upon something of infinite duration—though the reverse is, of course, impossible.

God

If we think of God as "the creator of heaven and earth," and if we consider heaven and earth to include everything that exists except God, then we appear to have, in the foregoing considerations, fairly strong reasons for asserting that God, as so conceived, exists. Now of course most people have much more in mind than this when they think of God, for religions have ascribed to God ever so many attributes that are not at all implied by describing him merely as the creator of the world; but that is not relevant here. Most religious persons do, in any case, think of God as being at least the creator, as that being upon which every-thing ultimately depends, no matter what else they may say about him in addition. It is, in fact, the first item in the creeds of Christianity that God is the "creator of heaven and earth." And, it seems, there are good metaphysical reasons, as distinguished from the persuasions of faith, for thinking that such a creative being exists.

If, as seems clearly implied by the principle of sufficient reason, there must be a reason for the existence of heaven and earth—i.e., for the world—then that reason must be found either in the world itself, or outside it, in something that is literally supranatural, or outside heaven and earth. Now if we suppose that the world—i.e., the totality of all things except God—contains within itself the reason for its existence, we are supposing that it exists by its very nature, that is, that it is a necessary being. In that case there would, of course, be no reason for saying that it must depend upon God or anything else for its existence; for if it exists by its very nature, then it depends upon nothing but itself, much as the sun depends upon nothing but itself for its heat. This, however, is implausible, for we find nothing about the world or anything in it to suggest that it exists by its own nature, and we do find, on the contrary, ever so many things to suggest that it does not. For in the first place, anything that exists by its very nature must necessarily be eternal and indestructible. It would be a self-contradiction to say of anything that it exists by its own nature, or is a necessarily existing thing, and at the same time to say that it comes into being or passes away, or that it ever could come into being or pass away. Nothing about the world seems at all like this, for concerning anything in the world, we can perfectly easily think of it as being annihilated, or as never having existed in the first place, without there being the slightest hint of any absurdity in such a supposition. Some of the things in the universe are, to be sure, very old; the moon, for example, or the stars and the planets. It is even possible to imagine that they have always existed. Yet it seems quite impossible to suppose that they owe their existence to nothing but themselves, that they bestow existence upon themselves by their very natures, or that they are in themselves

things of such nature that it would be impossible for them not to exist. Even if we suppose that something, such as the sun, for instance, has existed forever, and will never cease, still we cannot conclude just from this that it exists by its own nature. If, as is of course very doubtful, the sun has existed forever and will never cease, then it is possible that its heat and light have also existed forever and will never cease; but that would not show that the heat and light of the sun exist by their own natures. They are obviously contingent and depend on the sun for their existence, whether they are beginningless and everlasting or not.

There seems to be nothing in the world, then, concerning which it is at all plausible to suppose that it exists by its own nature, or contains within itself the reason for its existence. In fact, everything in the world appears to be quite plainly the opposite, namely, something that not only need not exist, but at some time or other, past or future or both, does not in fact exist. Everything in the world seems to have a finite duration, whether long or short. Most things, such as ourselves, exist only for a short while; they come into being, then soon cease. Other things, like the heavenly bodies, last longer, but they are still corruptible, and from all that we can gather about them, they too seem destined eventually to perish. We arrive at the conclusion, then, that although the world may contain some things that have always existed and are destined never to perish, it is nevertheless doubtful that it contains any such thing and, in any case, everything in the world is capable of perishing, and nothing in it, however long it may already have existed and however long it may yet remain, exists by its own nature, but depends instead upon something else.

Although this might be true of everything in the world, is it necessarily true of the world itself? That is, if we grant, as we seem forced to, that nothing in the world exists by its own nature, that everything in the world is contingent and perishable, must we also say that the world itself, or the totality of all these perishable things, is also contingent and perishable? Logically, we are not forced to, for it is logically possible that the totality of all perishable things might itself be imperishable, and hence, that the world might exist by its own nature, even though it is comprised exclusively of things that are contingent. It is not logically necessary that a totality should share the defects of its members. For example, even though every man is mortal, it does not follow from this that the human race, or the totality of all men, is also mortal; for it is possible that there will always be human beings, even though there are no human beings who will always exist. Similarly, it is possible that the world is in itself a necessary thing, even though it is comprised entirely of things that are contingent.

This is logically possible, but it is not plausible. For we find nothing whatever about the world, any more than in its parts, to suggest that it exists by its own nature. Concerning anything in the world, we have not the slightest difficulty in supposing that it should perish, or even that it should never have existed in the first place. We have almost as little difficulty in supposing this of the world itself. It might be somewhat hard to think of everything as utterly perishing and leaving no trace whatever of its ever having been, but there seems to be not the slightest difficulty in imagining that the world should never have existed in the first place. We can, for instance, perfectly easily suppose that nothing in the world had every existed except, let us suppose, a single grain of sand, and we can thus suppose that this grain of sand has forever constituted the whole universe. Now if we consider just this grain of sand, it is quite impossible for us to suppose that it exists by its very nature, and could never have failed to exist. It clearly depends for its existence upon something other than itself, if it depends on anything at all. The same will be true if we consider the world to consist, not of one grain of sand, but of two, or of a million, or, as we in fact find, of a vast number of stars and planets and all their minuter parts.

It would seem, then, that the world, in case it happens to exist at all—and this is quite beyond doubt—is contingent and thus dependent upon something other than itself for its existence, if it depends upon anything at all. And it must depend upon something, for otherwise there could be no reason why it exists in the first place. Now that upon which the world depends must be something that either exists by its own nature or does not. If it does not exist by its own nature, then it, in turn, depends for its existence upon something else, and so on. Now then, we can say either of two things: namely, (1) that the world depends for its existence upon something else, which in turn depends on still another thing, this depending upon still another, *ad infinitum;* or (2) that the world derives its existence from something that exists by its own nature and that is accordingly eternal and imperishable, and is the creator of heaven and earth. The first of these alternatives, however, is impossible, for it does not render a sufficient reason why anything should exist in the first place. Instead of supplying a reason why any world should exist, it repeatedly begs off giving a reason. It explains what is dependent and perishable in terms of what is itself dependent and perishable, leaving us still without a reason why perishable things should exist at all, which is what we are seeking. Ultimately, then, it would seem that the world, or the totality of contingent or perishable things, in case it exists at all, must depend upon something that is necessary and imperishable, and that accordingly exists, not in dependence upon something else, but by its own nature.

"Self-Caused"

What has been said thus far gives some intimation of what meaning should be attached to the concept of a self-caused being, a concept that is quite generally misunderstood, sometimes even by scholars. To say that something—God, for example—is self-caused, or is the cause of its own existence, does not mean that this being brings itself into existence, which is a perfectly absurd idea. Nothing can *bring* itself into existence. To say that something is self-caused (*causa sui*) means only that it exists, not contingently or in dependence upon something else, but by its own nature, which is only to say that it is a being which is such that it can neither come into being nor perish. Now whether such a being in fact exists or not, there is in any case no absurdity in the idea. We have found, in fact, that the principle of sufficient reason seems to point to the existence of such a being, as that upon which the world, with everything in it, must ultimately depend for its existence.

"Necessary Being"

A being that depends for its existence upon nothing but itself, and is in this sense self-caused, can equally be described as a necessary being; that is to say, a being that is not contingent, and hence not perishable. For in the case of anything that exists by its own nature and is dependent upon nothing else, it is impossible that it should not exist, which is equivalent to saying that it is necessary. Many persons have professed to find the gravest difficulties in this concept, too, but that is partly because it has been confused with other notions. If it makes sense to speak of anything as an *impossible* being, or something that by its very nature does not exist, then it is hard to see why the idea of a necessary being, or something that in its very nature exists, should not be just as comprehensible. And of course, we have not the slightest difficulty in speaking of something, such as a square circle or a formless body, as an impossible being. And if it makes sense to speak of something as being perishable, contingent, and dependent upon something other than itself for its existence, as it surely does, then there seems to be no difficulty in thinking of something as imperishable and dependent upon nothing other than itself for its existence.

"First Cause"

From these considerations we can see also what is properly meant by a first cause, an appellative that has often been applied to God by theologians, and

that many persons have deemed an absurdity. It is a common criticism of this notion to say that there need not be any first cause, because the series of causes and effects that constitute the history of the universe might be infinite or beginningless and must, in fact, be infinite in case the universe itself had no beginning in time. This criticism, however, reflects a total misconception of what is meant by a first cause. *First* here does not mean first in time, and when God is spoken of as a first cause, he is not being described as a being which, at some time in the remote past, *started* everything. To describe God as a first cause is only to say that he is literally a *primary* rather than a secondary cause, an *ultimate* rather than a derived cause, or a being upon which all other things, heaven and earth, ultimately depend for their existence. It is, in short, only to say that God is the creator, in the sense of creation explained above. Now this, of course, is perfectly consistent with saying that the world is eternal or beginningless. As we have seen, one gives no reason for the existence of a world merely by giving it an age, even if it is supposed to have an infinite age. To use a helpful analogy, we can say that the sun is the first cause of daylight and, for that matter, of the moonlight of the night as well, which means only that daylight and moonlight ultimately depend upon the sun for their existence. The moon, on the other hand, is only a secondary or derivative cause of its light. This light would be no less dependent upon the sun if we affirmed that it had no beginning, for an ageless and beginningless light requires a source no less than an ephemeral one. If we supposed that the sun has always existed, and with it its light, then we would have to say that the sun has always been the first—i.e., the primary or ultimate—cause of its light. Such is precisely the manner in which God should be thought of, and is by theologians often thought of, as the first cause of heaven and earth.

I.B   The Teleological Argument for the Existence of God

The teleological argument for the existence of God begins with the premise that the world exhibits intelligent purpose or order, and it proceeds to the conclusion that there must be or probably is a divine intelligence, a supreme designer, to account for the observed or perceived intelligent purpose or order. Although the argument has been cited in Plato, in the Bible (Romans, chapter 1), and in Cicero, the clearest sustained treatment of it is found in William Paley's *Natural Theology* (1802). In his opening chapter, included here as our first selection, he offers his famous "watch" argument, which begins as follows:

> In crossing a heath, suppose I pitched my foot against a stone, and were asked how the stone came to be there, I might possibly answer, that, for anything I knew to the contrary, it had lain there for ever; nor would it, perhaps, be very easy to show the absurdity of this answer. But suppose I found a watch upon the ground, and it should be inquired how the watch happened to be in that place, I should hardly think of the answer which I had before given—that, for anything I knew, the watch might have always been there. Yet why should not this answer serve for the watch as well as for the stone? Why is it not as admissible in the second case, as in the first?

Paley argues that just as we infer an intelligent designer to account for the purpose-revealing watch, we must analogously infer an intelligent grand designer to account for the purpose-revealing world. "Every indication of contrivance, every manifestation of design, which existed in the watch, exists in the works of nature; with the difference, on the side of nature, of being greater and more, and that in a degree which exceeds all computation." The skeleton of the argument looks like this:

1. Human artifacts are products of intelligent design (purpose).
2. The universe resembles these human artifacts.
3. Therefore, the universe is (probably) a product of intelligent design (purpose).
4. But the universe is vastly more complex and gigantic than a human artifact.
5. Therefore, there probably is a powerful and vastly intelligent designer who designed the universe.

Ironically, Paley's argument was attacked even before Paley had set it down, for David Hume (1711–1776) had long before written his famous *Dialogues Concerning Natural Religion* (published posthumously in 1779), the classic critique of the teleological argument. Paley seems to have been unaware of it. A selection from the *Dialogue* is included as our second reading. In it, the natural theologian, Cleanthes, debates the orthodox believer, Demea, and the skeptic or critic, Philo, who does most of the serious arguing.

Hume, through Philo, attacks the argument from several different angles. He argues first of all that the universe is not sufficiently like the productions of human design to support the argument. Philo puts it as follows:

> But can you think, Cleanthes, that your usual phlegm and philosophy have been preserved in so wide a step as you have taken, when you compare to the universe, houses, ships, furniture, machines; and from their similarity in some circumstances infer a similarity in their causes? . . . But can a conclusion, with any propriety, be transferred from the parts to the whole? Does not the great disproportion bar all comparison and inferences? From observing the growth of a hair, can we learn anything concerning the generation of a man?

We cannot argue from the parts to the whole. You, the reader, will want to test this judgment with some possible counterexamples.

Philo's second objection is that the analogy from artifact to divine designer fails because we have no other universe with which to compare this one. We would need to make such a comparison in order to decide if it were the kind of universe that was designed or simply the kind that developed on its own. As C. S. Peirce put it, "Universes are not as plentiful as blackberries." Since there is only one of them, we have no standard of comparison by which to judge it. Paley's answer to this would be that if we could find one clear instance of purposiveness in nature (e.g., the eye), it would be sufficient to enable us to conclude that there is probably an intelligent designer. Hume makes several other points against the design argument, which you will want to examine on your own.

A modern objection to the argument, one that was anticipated by Hume, is that based on Darwinian evolution, which has cast doubt upon the notion of teleological explanation altogether. In his *Origin of Species* (1859) Darwin claimed that the process of development from simpler organisms to more complex ones took place gradually over millions of years through an apparently nonpurposive process of trial and error, of natural selection and survival of the fittest. As Julian Huxley put it, the evolutionary process

> results immediately and automatically from the basic property of living matter—that of self-copying, but with occasional errors. Self-copying leads to multiplication and competition; the errors in self-copying are what we call mutations, and mutations will inevitably confer different degrees of biological advantage or disadvantage on their possessors. The consequence will be differential reproduction down the generations—in other words, natural selection.*

As important as Darwin's contribution is in offering us an alternative model of biological development, it doesn't altogether destroy the argument from design. The theist can still argue that the process of natural selection is the *way* an ultimate designer is working out his purpose for the world. The argument from design could still be used as an argument to the best explanation.

---

*Evolution As Process (New York: Harper & Row, 1953), 4.

Such an argument is set forth in the third and final reading in this section, "The Argument from Design," excerpted from Richard Swinburne's *The Existence of God* (1979). Swinburne, a modern Cleanthes, rejects all deductive forms of arguments for the existence of God, but in their place he sets a series of inductive arguments: versions of the cosmological argument, the teleological argument, the argument from religious experience, and others. Although none of these alone proves the existence of God or shows it to be more probable than not, each adds to the probability of God's existence. Together they constitute a cumulative case for theism. There is something crying for an explanation: Why does this grand universe exist? Together the arguments for God's existence provide a plausible explanation of the existence of the universe, of why we are here, of why there is anything at all and not just nothing.

Swinburne's arguments are set in terms of confirmation theory. He distinguishes arguments that are "P-inductive" (in which the premises make the conclusion probable) from those that are "C-inductive" (in which the premises confirm the probability of the conclusion or make it more probable than it otherwise would be—although without showing the conclusion to be more probable than not). The cosmological and teleological arguments are, according to Swinburne, good C-inductive arguments. Since there is no counterargument to theism (note that Swinburne believes he can successfully meet the argument from evil; see Part 3 below), and since religious experience offers "considerable evidential force" in favor of theism, the cumulative effect is "sufficient to make theism all over probable."

The chapter on teleological arguments in Swinburne's book contains the essential structure of the confirmation argument used in the rest of his arguments. From it you should be able to figure out the kind of case he makes for those other arguments. A few notes are crucial to an understanding of Swinburne's essay. First of all, Swinburne believes that scientific, purely deterministic accounts—what he calls the Hempel account—are not the only type of explanatory theory. We can also explain things in terms of rational intentions or agency. Indeed, a full explanation often demands such an account. Theism makes use of such a personal explanatory account.

Secondly, Swinburne puts a great deal of weight on the notion of simplicity. All things being equal, if theory *A* is simpler than theory *B*, theory *A* is to be accepted as the better explanatory account. This is a version of Occam's razor, which counsels us not to multiply entities unnecessarily. You will want to think through this principle and decide whether or to what degree it applies to the teleological argument. Does Swinburne's account get more mileage from such a principle than is warranted?

Finally, Swinburne uses Bayes's theorem to sustain his argument: Let h = a theory or hypothesis; let e = the evidential phenomena; and let k = our background knowledge. Then $P(h/k)$ represents the prior probability of h, and $P(e/h,k)$ represents the probability of the phenomena occurring given our hypothesis and our background knowledge. $P(h/e,k)$ represents the probability of h being true given the available evidence and our background knowledge. You do not need to understand the intricacies of Bayes's theorem in order to follow Swinburne's reasoning, but you should beware of his use of k, the background knowledge. What does it come to? What is our background knowledge (minus the evidence in question) with regard to the hypothesis that God exists?

We turn now to the readings.

I.B.1 The Watch and the Watchmaker

WILLIAM PALEY

William Paley (1743–1805), Archdeacon of Carlisle, was a leading evangelical apologist. His most important work is Natural Theology, or Evidences of the Existence and Attributes of the Deity Collected from the Appearances of Nature *(1802), the first chapter of which is reprinted here. Paley argues that just as we infer an intelligent designer to account for the purpose-revealing watch, so likewise we must infer an intelligent Grand Designer to account for the purpose-revealing world.*

Statement of the Argument

In crossing a heath, suppose I pitched my foot against a *stone*, and were asked how the stone came to be there, I might possibly answer, that, for anything I knew to the contrary, it had lain there

for ever; nor would it, perhaps, be very easy to show the absurdity of this answer. But suppose I found a *watch* upon the ground, and it should be inquired how the watch happened to be in that place, I should hardly think of the answer which I had given—that, for anything I knew, the watch might have always been there. Yet why should not this answer serve for the watch as well as for the stone? why is it not as admissible in the second case as in the first? For this reason, and for no other; viz., that, when we come to inspect the watch, we perceive (what we could not discover in the stone) that its several parts are framed and put together for a purpose, e.g. that they are so formed and adjusted as to produce motion, and that motion so regulated as to point out the hour of the day; that, if the different parts had been differently shaped from what they are, if a different size from what they are, or placed after any other manner, or in any other order than that in which they are placed, either no motion at all would have been carried on in the machine, or none which

From William Paley, *Natural Theology, or Evidences of the Existence and Attributes of the Deity Collected from the Appearances of Nature* (1802).

would have answered the use that is now served by it. To reckon up a few of the plainest of these parts, and of their offices, all tending to one result:—We see a cylindrical box containing a coiled elastic spring, which, by its endeavor to relax itself, turns round the box. We next observe a flexible chain (artificially wrought for the sake of flexure) communicating the action of the spring from the box to the fusee. We then find a series of wheels, the teeth of which catch in, and apply to, each other, conducting the motion from the fusee to the balance, and from the balance to the pointer, and, at the same time, by the size and shape of those wheels, so regulating that motion as to terminate in causing an index, by an equable and measured progression, to pass over a given space in a given time. We take notice that the wheels are made of brass, in order to keep them from rust; the springs of steel, no other metal being so elastic; that over the face of the watch there is placed a glass, a material employed in no other part of the work, but in the room of which, if there had been any other than a transparent substance, the hour could not be seen without opening the case. This mechanism being observed, (it requires indeed an examination of the instrument, and perhaps some previous knowledge of the subject, to perceive and understand it; but being once, as we have said, observed and understood,) the inference, we think, is inevitable, that the watch must have had a maker; that there must have existed, at some time, and at some place or other, an artificer or artificers who formed it for the purpose which we find it actually to answer; who comprehended its construction, and designed its use.

I. Nor would it, I apprehend, weaken the conclusion, that we had never seen a watch made; that we had never known an artist capable of making one; that we were altogether incapable of executing such a piece of workmanship ourselves, or of understanding in what manner it was performed; all this being no more than what is true of some exquisite remains of ancient art, of some lost arts, and, to the generality of mankind, of the more curious productions of modern manufacture. Does one man in a million know how oval frames are turned? Ignorance of this kind exalts our opinion of the unseen and unknown artist's skill, if he be unseen and unknown, but raises no doubt in our minds of the existence and agency of such an artist, at some former time, and in some place or other. Nor can I perceive that it varies at all the inference, whether the question arise concerning a human agent, or concerning an agent of a different species, or an agent possessing, in some respect, a different nature.

II. Neither, secondly, would it invalidate our conclusion, that the watch sometimes went wrong, or that it seldom went exactly right. The purpose of the machinery, the design, and the designer, might be evident, and, in the case supposed, would be evident, in whatever way we accounted for the irregularity of the movement, or whether we could account for it or not. It is not necessary that a machine be perfect, in order to show with what design it was made; still less necessary, where the only question is, whether it were made with any design at all.

III. Nor, thirdly, would it bring any uncertainty into the argument, if there were a few parts of the watch, concerning which we could not discover, or had not yet discovered, in what manner they conduced to the general effect; or even some parts, concerning which we could not ascertain whether they conduced to that effect in any manner whatever. For, as to the first branch of the case, if by the loss, or disorder, or decay of the parts in question, the movement of the watch were found in fact to be stopped, or disturbed, or retarded, no doubt would remain in our minds as to the utility or intention of these parts, although we should be unable to investigate the manner according to which, or the connection by which, the ultimate effect depended upon their action or assistance; and the more complex is the machine, the more likely is this obscurity to arise. Then, as to the second thing supposed, namely, that there were parts which might be spared without prejudice to the movement of the watch, and that he had proved this by experiment, these superfluous parts, even if we were completely assured that they were such, would not vacate the reasoning which we had instituted concerning other parts. The indication of contrivance remained, with respect to them, nearly as it was before.

IV. Nor, fourthly, would any man in his senses think the existence of the watch, with its various machinery, accounted for, by being told that it was one out of possible combinations of material forms; that whatever he had found in the place where he found the watch, must have contained some internal configuration or other; and that this configuration might be the structure now exhibited, viz., of the works of a watch, as well as a different structure.

V. Nor, fifthly, would it yield his inquiry more satisfaction, to be answered, that there existed in things a principle of order, which had disposed the parts of the watch into their present form and situation. He never knew a watch made by the principle of order; nor can he even form to himself an idea of what is meant by a principle of order, distinct from the intelligence of the watchmaker.

VI. Sixthly, he would be surprised to hear that the mechanism of the watch was no proof of contrivance, only a motive to induce the mind to think so:

VII. And not less surprised to be informed, that the watch in his hand was nothing more than the result of the laws of *metallic* nature. It is a perversion of language to assign any law as the efficient, operative cause of anything. A law presupposes an agent; for it is only the mode according to which an agent proceeds; it implies a power; for it is the order according to which that power acts. Without this agent, without this power, which are both distinct from itself, the *law* does nothing, is nothing. The expression, "the law of metallic nature," may sound strange and harsh to a philosophic ear; but it seems quite as justifiable as some others which are more familiar to him such as "the law of vegetable nature," "the law of animal nature," or, indeed, as "the law of nature" in general, when assigned as the cause of phenomena in exclusion of agency and power, or when it is substituted into the place of these.

VIII. Neither, lastly, would our observer be driven out of his conclusion, or from his confidence in its truth, by being told that he knew nothing at all about the matter. He knows enough for his argument: he knows the utility of the end: he knows the subserviency and adaptation of the means to the end. These points being known, his ignorance of other points, his doubts concerning other points, affect not the certainty of his reasoning. The consciousness of knowing little need not beget a distrust of that which he does know. . . .

Application of the Argument

Every indication of contrivance, every manifestation of design, which existed in the watch, exists in the works of nature; with the difference, on the side of nature, of being greater and more, and that in a degree which exceeds all computation. I mean that the contrivances of nature surpass the contrivances of art, in the complexity, subtilty, and curiosity of the mechanism; and still more, if possible, do they go beyond them in number and variety; yet in a multitude of cases, are not less evidently mechanical, not less evidently contrivances, not less evidently accommodated to their end, or suited to their office, than are the most perfect productions of human ingenuity. . . .

I.B.2   A Critique of the Design Argument

DAVID HUME

The Scottish empiricist and skeptic David Hume (1711–1776) is one of the most important philosophers who ever lived. The Dialogues Concerning Natural Religion *(published posthumously in 1779) contains the classic critique of the argument from design. Our reading is from Parts 2 and 5 of this dialogue. Cleanthes, who opens our selection, is a natural theologian, the Paley of his time, who opposes both the orthodox believer, Demea, and the skeptic, Philo. It is Philo who puts forth the major criticisms against the argument from design.*

Cleanthes: Look round the world: Contemplate the whole and every part of it: You will find it to be nothing but one great machine, subdivided into an infinite number of lesser machines, which again admit of subdivisions to a degree beyond what human senses and faculties can trace and explain. All these various machines, and even their most minute parts, are adjusted to each other with an accuracy which ravishes into admiration all men who have ever contemplated them. The curious adapting of means to ends, throughout all nature, resembles exactly, though it much exceeds, the productions of human contrivance; of human design, thought, wisdom, and intelligence. Since therefore the effects resemble each other, we are led to infer, by all the rules of analogy, that the causes also resemble, and that the Author of Nature is somewhat similar to the mind of man, though possessed of much larger faculties, proportioned to the grandeur of the work which he has executed. By this argument a *posteriori*, and by this argument alone, do we prove at once the existence of a Deity and his similarity to human mind and intelligence.

From David Hume, *Dialogues Concerning Natural Religion* (1779).

Demea: I shall be so free, *Cleanthes*, said *Demea*, as to tell you that from the beginning I could not approve of your conclusion concerning the similarity of the Deity to men; still less can I approve of the mediums by which you endeavor to establish it. What! No demonstration of the Being of God! No abstract arguments! No proofs a *priori*! Are these which have hitherto been so much insisted on by philosophers all fallacy, all sophism? Can we reach no farther in this subject than experience and probability? I will say not that this is betraying the cause of a Deity; but surely, by this affected candor, you give advantages to atheists which they never could obtain by the mere dint of argument and reasoning.

Philo: What I chiefly scruple in this subject, said *Philo*, is not so much that all religious arguments are by *Cleanthes* reduced to experience, as that they appear not be even the most certain and irrefragable of that inferior kind. That a stone will fall, that fire will burn, that the earth has solidity, we have observed a thousand and a thousand times; and when any new instance of this nature is presented, we draw without hesitation the accustomed inference. The exact similarity of the cases gives us a perfect assurance of a similar event, and a stronger evidence is never desired nor sought after. But wherever you depart, in the least, from the similarity of the cases, you diminish proportionably the evidence; and may at last bring it to a very weak *analogy*, which is confessedly liable to error and uncertainty. After having experienced the circulation of the blood in human creatures, we make no doubt that it takes place in *Titius* and *Maevius*; but from its circulation in frogs and fishes it is only a presumption, though a strong one, from analogy that it takes place in men and other animals. The analogical reasoning is much weaker when we infer the circulation of the sap in vegetables from our experience that the blood circulates in animals; and those who hastily followed that imperfect analogy are found, by more accurate experiments, to have been mistaken.

If we see a house, *Cleanthes,* we conclude, with the greatest certainty, that it had an architect or builder because this is precisely that species of effect which we have experienced to proceed from that species of cause. But surely you will not affirm that the universe bears such a resemblance to a house that we can with the same certainty infer a similar cause, or that the analogy is here entire and perfect. The dissimilitude is so striking that the utmost you can here pretend to is a guess, a conjecture, a presumption concerning a similar cause; and how that pretension will be received in the world, I leave you to consider.

Cleanthes: It would surely be very ill received, replied *Cleanthes;* and I should be deservedly blamed and detested did I allow that the proofs of a Deity amounted to no more than a guess or conjecture. But is the whole adjustment of means to ends in a house and in the universe so slight a resemblance? The economy of final causes? The order, proportion, and arrangement of every part? Steps of a stair are plainly contrived that human legs may use them in mounting; and this inference is certain and infallible. Human legs are also contrived for walking and mounting; and this inference, I allow, is not altogether so certain because of the dissimilarity which you remark; but does it, therefore, deserve the name only of presumption or conjecture?

Demea: Good God! cried *Demea,* interrupting him, where are we? Zealous defenders of religion allow that the proofs of a Deity fall short of perfect evidence! And you, *Philo,* on whose assistance I depended in proving the adorable mysteriousness of the Divine Nature, do you assent to all these extravagant opinions of *Cleanthes?* For what other name can I give them? or, why spare my censure when such principles are advanced, supported by such an authority, before so young a man as *Pamphilus?*

Philo: You seem not to apprehend, replied *Philo,* that I argue with *Cleanthes* in his own way, and, by showing him the dangerous consequences of his tenets, hope at last to reduce him to our opinion. But what sticks most with you, I observe, is the representation which *Cleanthes* has made of the argument a *posteriori;* and, finding that that argument is likely to escape your hold and vanish into air, you think it so disguised that you can scarcely believe it to be set in its true light. Now, however much I may dissent, in other respects, from the dangerous principle of *Cleanthes,* I must allow that he has fairly represented that argument, and I shall endeavor so to state the matter to you that you will entertain no further scruples with regard to it.

Were a man to abstract from everything which he knows or has seen, he would be altogether incapable, merely from his own ideas, to determine what kind of scene the universe must be, or to give the preference to one state or situation of things above another. For as nothing which he clearly conceives could be esteemed impossible or implying a contradiction, every chimera of his fancy would be upon an equal footing; nor could he assign any just reason why he adheres to one idea or system, and rejects the others which are equally possible.

Again, after he opens his eyes and contemplates the world as it really is, it would be impossible for him at first to assign the cause of any one event, much less of the whole of things, or of the universe. He might set his fancy a rambling, and she might bring him in an infinite variety of reports and representations. These would all be possible; but, being all equally possible, he would never of himself give a satisfactory account for his preferring one of them to the rest. Experience alone can point out to him the true cause of any phenomenon.

Now, according to this method of reasoning, *Demea,* it follows (and is, indeed, tacitly allowed by *Cleanthes* himself) that order, arrangement, or the adjustment of final causes, is not of itself any proof of design, but only so far as it has been experienced to proceed from that principle. For aught we can know a *priori,* matter may contain the source or spring of order originally within itself, as well as mind does; and there is no more difficulty in conceiving that the several elements, from an internal unknown cause, may fall into the most exquisite arrangement, than to conceive that their ideas, in the great universal mind, from a like internal unknown cause, fall into that arrangement. The equal possibility of both these suppositions is allowed. But, by experience, we find, according to *Cleanthes,* that there is a difference between them. Throw several pieces of steel together, without shape or form; they will never arrange themselves so as to compose a watch. Stone and mortar and wood, without an architect, never erect a house. But the ideas in a human mind, we see, by an unknown, inexplicable economy, arrange themselves so as to form the plan of a watch or house. Experience, therefore, proves that there is an original principle of order in mind, not in matter. From similar effects we infer similar causes. The adjustment of means to ends is alike in the universe, as in a machine of human contrivance. The causes, therefore, must be resembling.

I was from the beginning scandalized, I must own, with this resemblance which is asserted between the Deity and human creatures, and must conceive it to imply such a degradation of the Supreme Being as no sound theist could endure. With your assistance, therefore, *Demea,* I shall endeavor to defend what you justly call the adorable mysteriousness of the Divine Nature, and shall refute this reasoning of *Cleanthes,* provided he allows that I have made a fair representation of it.

When *Cleanthes* had assented, *Philo,* after a short pause, proceeded in the following manner.

That all inferences, *Cleanthes,* concerning fact are founded on experience, and that all experimental reasonings are founded on the supposition that similar causes prove similar effects, and similar effects similar causes, I shall not at present much dispute with you. But observe, I entreat you, with what extreme caution all just reasoners proceed in the transferring of experiments to similar cases. Unless the cases be exactly similar, they repose no perfect confidence in applying their past observation to any particular phenomenon. Every alteration of circumstances occasions a doubt concerning the event; and it requires new experiments to prove certainly that the new circumstances are of no moment or importance. A change in bulk, situation, arrangement, age, dis-

position of the air, or surrounding bodies; any of these particulars may be attended with the most unexpected consequences. And unless the objects be quite familiar to us, it is the highest temerity to expect with assurance, after any of these changes, an event similar to that which before fell under our observation. The slow and deliberate steps of philosophers here, if anywhere, are distinguished from the precipitate march of the vulgar, who, hurried on by the smallest similitude, are incapable of all discernment or consideration.

But can you think, *Cleanthes,* that your usual phlegm and philosophy have been preserved in so wide a step as you have taken when you compared to the universe houses, ships, furniture, machines; and, from their similarity in some circumstances, inferred a similarity in their causes? Thought, design, intelligence, such as we discover in men and other animals, is no more than one of the springs and principles of the universe, as well as heat or cold, attraction or repulsion, and a hundred others which fall under daily observation. It is an active cause by which some particular parts of nature, we find, produce alterations on other parts. But can a conclusion, with any propriety, be transferred from parts to the whole? Does not the great disproportion bar all comparison and inference? From observing the growth of a hair, can we learn anything concerning the generation of a man? Would the manner of a leaf's blowing, even though perfectly known, afford us any instruction concerning the vegetation of a tree?

But allowing that we were to take the *operations* of one part of nature upon another for the foundation of our judgment concerning the *origin* of the whole (which never can be admitted), yet why select so minute, so weak, so bounded a principle as the reason and design of animals is found to be upon this planet? What peculiar privilege has this little agitation of the brain which we call "thought", that we must thus make it the model of the whole universe? Our partiality in our own favor does indeed present it on all occasions, but sound philosophy ought carefully to guard against so natural an illusion.

So far from admitting, continued *Philo,* that the operations of a part can afford us any just conclusion concerning the origin of the whole, I will not allow any one part to form a rule for another part if the latter be very remote from the former. Is there any reasonable ground to conclude that the inhabitants of other planets possess thought, intelligence, reason, or anything similar to these faculties in men? When nature has so extremely diversified her manner of operation in this small globe, can we imagine that she incessantly copies herself throughout so immense a universe? And if thought, as we may well suppose, be confined merely to this narrow corner, and has even there so limited a sphere of action, with what propriety can we assign it for the original cause of all things? The narrow views of a peasant who makes his domestic economy the rule for the government of kingdoms is in comparison a pardonable sophism.

But were we ever so much assured that a thought and reason resembling the human were to be found throughout the whole universe, and were its activity elsewhere vastly greater and more commanding than it appears in this globe; yet I cannot see why the operations of a world constituted, arranged, adjusted, can with any propriety be extended to a world which is in its embryostate, and is advancing towards that constitution and arrangement. By observation we know somewhat of the economy, action, and nourishment of a finished animal; but we must transfer with great caution that observation to the growth of a foetus in the womb, and still more to the formation of an animalcule in the loins of its male parent. Nature, we find, even from our limited experience, possesses an infinite number of springs and principles which incessantly discover themselves on every change of her position and situation. And what new and unknown principles would actuate her in so new and unknown a situation as that of the formation of a universe, we cannot, without the utmost temerity, pretend to determine.

A very small part of this great system, during a very short time, is very imperfectly discovered to us; and do we thence pronounce decisively concerning the origin of the whole?

Admirable conclusion! Stone, wood, brick, iron, brass, have not, at this time, in this minute globe of earth, an order or arrangement without human art and contrivance; therefore, the universe could not originally attain its order and arrangement without something similar to human art. But is a part of nature a rule for another part very wide of the former? Is it a rule for the whole? Is a very small part a rule for the universe? Is nature in one situation a certain rule for nature in another situation vastly different from the former?

And can you blame me, *Cleanthes,* if I here imitate the prudent reserve of *Simonides,* who, according to the noted story, being asked by *Hiero, What God was?* desired a day to think of it, and then two days more; and after than manner continually prolonged the term, without ever bringing in his definition or description? Could you even blame me if I had answered, at first, *that I did not know,* and was sensible that this subject lay vastly beyond the reach of my faculties? You might cry out skeptic and raillier, as much as you pleased; but, having found in so many other subjects much more familiar the imperfections and even contradictions of human reason, I never should expect any success from its feeble conjectures in a subject so sublime and so remote from the sphere of our observation. When two *species* of objects have always been observed to be conjoined together, I can *infer,* by custom, the existence of one wherever I *see* the existence of the other; and this I call an argument from experience. But how this argument can have place where the objects, as in the present case, are single, individual, without parallel or specific resemblance, may be difficult to explain. And will any man tell me with a serious countenance that an orderly universe must arise from some thought and art like the human because we have experience of it? To ascertain this reasoning it were requisite that we had experience of the origin of worlds; and it is not sufficient, surely, that we have seen ships and cities arise from human art and contrivance. . . .

Philo: But to show you still more inconveniences, continued *Philo,* in your anthropomorphism, please to take a new survey of your principles. *Like effects prove like causes.* This is the experimental argument; and this, you say too, is the sole theological argument. Now it is certain that the liker the effects are which are seen and the liker the causes which are inferred, the stronger is the argument. Every departure on either side diminishes the probability and renders the experiment less conclusive. You cannot doubt of the principle; neither ought you to reject its consequences.

All the new discoveries in astronomy which prove the immense grandeur and magnificence of the works of nature are so many additional arguments for a Deity, according to the true system of theism; but, according to your hypothesis of experimental theism, they become so many objections, by removing the effect still farther from all resemblance to the effects of human art and contrivance. For if *Lucretius,* even following the old system of the world, could exclaim:

> Who is strong enough to rule the sum, who to hold in hand and control the mighty bridle of the unfathomable deep? who to turn about all the heavens at one time, and warm the fruitful worlds with ethereal fires, or to be present in all places and at all times.[1]

If Tully[2] esteemed this reasoning so natural as to put it into the mouth of his Epicurean:

> What power of mental vision enabled your master Plato to descry the vast and elaborate architectural process which, as he makes out, the deity adopted in building the structure of the universe? What method of engineering was employed? What tools and levers and derricks? What agents carried out so vast an understanding? And how were air, fire, water, and earth enabled to obey and execute the will of the architect?

If this argument, I say, had any force in former ages, how much greater must it have at present when the bounds of nature are so infinitely enlarged and such a magnificent scene is opened to us? It is still more unreasonable to form our idea of so unlimited a cause from our experience of the narrow productions of human design and invention.

The discoveries by microscopes, as they open a new universe in miniature, are still objections, according to you; arguments, according to me. The farther we push our researches of this kind, we are still led to infer the universal cause of all to

be vastly different from mankind, or from any object of human experience and observation.

And what say you to the discoveries in anatomy, chemistry, botany? . . . *Cleanthes:* These surely are no objections, replied *Cleanthes;* they only discover new instances of art and contrivance. It is still the image of mind reflected on us from innumerable objects. *Philo:* Add a mind *like the human,* said *Philo. Cleanthes:* I know of no other, replied *Cleanthes. Philo:* And the liker, the better, insisted *Philo. Cleanthes:* To be sure, said *Cleanthes.*

Philo: Now, *Cleanthes,* said *Philo,* with an air of alacrity and triumph, mark the consequences. *First,* by this method of reasoning you renounce all claim to infinity in any of the attributes of the Deity. For, as the cause ought only to be proportioned to the effect, and the effect, so far as it falls under our cognizance, is not infinite: What pretensions have we, upon your suppositions, to ascribe that attribute to the Divine Being? You will still insist that, by removing him so much from all similarity to human creatures, we give in to the most arbitrary hypothesis, and at the same time weaken all proofs of his existence.

Secondly, you have no reason, on your theory, for ascribing perfection to the Deity, even in his finite capacity; or for supposing him free from every error, mistake, or incoherence, in his undertakings. There are many inexplicable difficulties in the works of Nature which, if we allow a perfect author to be proved *a priori,* are easily solved, and become only seeming difficulties from the narrow capacity of man, who cannot trace infinite relations. But according to your method of reasoning, these difficulties become all real; and, perhaps, will be insisted on as new instances of likeness to human art and contrivance. At least, you must acknowledge that it is impossible for us to tell, from our limited views, whether this system contains any great faults or deserves any considerable praise if compared to other possible and even real systems. Could a peasant, if the *Aeneid* were read to him, pronounce that poem to be absolutely faultless, or even assign to it its proper rank among the productions of human wit, he who had never seen any other production?

But were this world ever so perfect a production, it must still remain uncertain whether all the excellences of the work can justly be ascribed to the workman. If we survey a ship, what an exalted idea must we form of the ingenuity of the carpenter who framed so complicated, useful, and beautiful a machine? And what surprise must we feel when we find him a stupid mechanic who imitated others, and copied an art which, through a long succession of ages, after multiplied trials, mistakes, corrections, deliberations, and controversies, had been gradually improving? Many worlds might have been botched and bungled, throughout an eternity, ere this system was struck out; much labor lost; many fruitless trials made; and a slow but continued improvement carried on during infinite ages in the art of world-making. In such subjects, who can determine where the truth, nay, who can conjecture where the probability lies, amidst a great number of hypotheses which may be proposed, and a still greater which may be imagined?

And what shadow of an argument, continued Philo, can you produce from your hypothesis to prove the unity of the Deity? A great number of men join in building a house or ship, in rearing a city, in framing a commonwealth; why may not several deities combine in contriving and framing a world? This is only so much greater similarity to human affairs. By sharing the work among several, we may so much further limit the attributes of each, and get rid of that extensive power and knowledge which must be supposed in one deity, and which, according to you, can only serve to weaken the proof of his existence. And if such foolish, such vicious creatures as man can yet often unite in framing and executing one plan, how much more those deities or demons, whom we may suppose several degrees more perfect?

To multiply causes without necessity is indeed contrary to true philosophy, but this principle applies not to the present case. Were one deity antecedently proved by your theory who were possessed of every attribute requisite to the production of the universe, it would be needless, I own (though not absurd), to suppose any other deity existent. But while it is still a question

whether all these attributes are united in one subject or dispersed among several independent beings; by what phenomena in nature can we pretend to decide the controversy? Where we see a body raised in a scale, we are sure that there is in the opposite scale, however concealed from sight, some counterpoising weight equal to it; but it is still allowed to doubt whether that weight be an aggregate of several distinct bodies or one uniform united mass. And if the weight requisite very much exceeds anything which we have ever seen conjoined in any single body, the former supposition becomes still more probable and natural. And intelligent being of such vast power and capacity as is necessary to produce the universe, or, to speak in the language of ancient philosophy, so prodigious an animal, exceeds all analogy and even comprehension.

But further, *Cleanthes,* men are mortal, and renew their species by generation; and this is common to all living creatures. The two great sexes of male and female, says *Milton,* animate the world. Why must this circumstance, so universal, so essential, be excluded from those numerous and limited deities? Behold, then, the theogeny of ancient times brought back upon us.

And why not become a perfect anthropomorphite? Why not assert the deity or deities to be corporeal, and to have eyes, a nose, mouth, ears, etc.? *Epicurus* maintained that no man had ever seen reason but in a human figure; therefore, the gods must have a human figure. And this argument, which is deservedly so much ridiculed by *Cicero,* becomes, according to you, solid and philosophical.

In a word, *Cleanthes,* a man who follows your hypothesis is able, perhaps, to assert or conjecture that the universe sometime arose from something like design: But beyond that position he cannot ascertain one single circumstance, and is left afterwards to fix every point of his theology by the utmost license of fancy and hypothesis. This world, for aught he knows, is very faulty and imperfect, compared to a superior standard; and was only the first rude essay of some infant deity who afterwards abandoned it, ashamed of his lame performance: It is the work only of some dependent, inferior deity, and is the object of derision to his superiors: It is the production of old age and dotage in some superannuated deity; and ever since his death has run on at adventures, from the first impulse and active force which it received from him. . . . You justly give signs of horror, *Demea*, at these strange suppositions; but these, and a thousand more of the same kind, are *Cleanthes'* suppositions, not mine. From the moment the attributes of the Deity are supposed finite, all these have place. And I cannot, for my part, think that so wild and unsettled a system of theology is, in any respect, preferable to none at all.

Cleanthes: These suppositions I absolutely disown, cried *Cleanthes:* They strike me, however, with no horror, especially when proposed in that rambling way in which they drop from you. On the contrary, they give me pleasure when I see that, by the utmost indulgence of your imagination, you never get rid of the hypothesis of design in the universe, but are obliged at every turn to have recourse to it. To this concession I adhere steadily; and this I regard as a sufficient foundation for religion.

Notes

1. *On the Nature of Things,* II, 1096–1099 (trans. by W. D. Rouse).
2. Tully was a common name for the Roman lawyer and philosopher, Marcus Tullius Cicero, 106–43 BC. The excerpt is from *The Nature of the Gods,* I, viii, 19 (trans. by H. Rackham).

I.B.3   The Argument from Design

RICHARD SWINBURNE

Richard Swinburne is the Nolloth Professor of Philosophy of Religion at Oxford University. He has written several articles on the traditional arguments for the existence of God. The following selection is from The Existence of God *(1979), in which he rejects all deductive forms of arguments for the existence of God but, in their place, sets a series of inductive arguments. In this selection he presents an inductive version of the argument from design. His strategy is to show that several of the arguments, though only minimally suggestive when taken in isolation, together make a cumulative case for the truth of theism.*

I understand by an argument from design one which argues from some general pattern of order in the universe or provision for the needs of conscious beings to a God responsible for these phenomena. An argument from a general pattern of order I shall call a teleological argument. In the definition of 'teleological argument' I emphasize the words 'general pattern'; I shall not count an argument to the existence of God from some particular pattern of order manifested on a unique occasion as a teleological argument.

Two Forms of Teleological Argument

I begin with the distinction between spatial order and temporal order, between what I shall call regularities of co-presence and regularities of succession. An example of a regularity of co-presence would be a town with all its roads at right angles to each other, or a section of books in a library arranged in alphabetical order of authors. Regularities of succession are simple patterns of behaviour of objects, such as their behaviour in accordance with the laws of nature—for example, Newton's laws.

Many of the striking examples of order in the universe evince an order which is due both to a regularity of co-presence and to a regularity of succession. A working car consists of many parts so adjusted to each other that it follows the instructions of the driver delivered by his pulling and pushing a few levers and buttons and turning a wheel, to take passengers whither he wishes. Its order arises because its parts are so arranged at some instant (regularity of co-presence) that, the laws of nature being as they are (regularity of succession) it brings about the result neatly and efficiently. The order of living animals and plants likewise results from regularities of both types.

Men who marvel at the order of the universe may marvel at either or both of the regularities of co-presence and of succession. The thinkers of the eighteenth century to whom the argument from design appealed so strongly were struck almost exclusively by the regularities of co-presence. They marvelled at the order in animals and plants; but since they largely took for granted the regularities of succession, what struck them about the animals and plants, as to a lesser extent about machines made by men, was the subtle and coherent arrangement of their millions of parts. Paley's *Natural Theology* dwells mainly on details of comparative anatomy, on eyes and ears and muscles and bones arranged with minute precision so as to operate with high efficiency, and in the *Dialogues* Hume's Cleanthes produces the same kind of examples: 'Consider, anatomize the eye, survey its structure and contrivance, and tell me from your own feeling, if the idea of a contriver does not immediately flow in upon you with a force like that of sensation.'

The eighteenth-century argument from spatial order seems to go as follows. Animals and plants have the power to reproduce their kind, and so, given the past existence of animals and plants, their present existence is to be expected. But what is vastly surprising is the existence of animals and plants at all. By natural processes they can only come into being through generation. But we know that the world has not been going on for ever, and so the great puzzle is the existence of the first animals and plants in 4004 BC or whenever exactly it was that animals and plants began to exist. Since they could not have come about by natural scientific processes, and since they are very simi-

lar to the machines, which certain rational agents, viz. men, make, it is very probable that they were made by a rational agent—only clearly one much more powerful and knowledgeable than men.

In the *Dialogues*, through the mouth of Philo, Hume made some classical objections to the argument in this form, some of which have some force against all forms of the argument; I shall deal with most of these as we come to appropriate places in this chapter. Despite Hume's objections, the argument is, I think, a very plausible one—given its premises. But one of its premises was shown by Darwin and his successors to be clearly false. Complex animals and plants can be produced through generation by less complex animals and plants—species are not eternally distinct; and simple animals and plants can be produced by natural processes from inorganic matter. This discovery led to the virtual disappearance of the argument from design from popular apologetic—mistakenly, I think, since it can easily be reconstructed in a form which does not rely on the premises shown to be false by Darwin. This can be done even for the argument from spatial order.

We can reconstruct the argument from spatial order as follows. We see around us animals and plants, intricate examples of spatial order in the ways which Paley set out, similar to machines of the kind which men make. We know that these animals and plants have evolved by natural processes from inorganic matter. But clearly this evolution can only have taken place, given certain special natural laws. These are first, the chemical laws stating how under certain circumstances inorganic molecules combine to make organic ones, and organic ones combine to make organisms. And secondly, there are the biological laws of evolution stating how organisms have very many offspring, some of which vary in one or more characteristics from their parents, and how some of these characteristics are passed on to most offspring, from which it follows that, given shortage of food and other environmental needs, there will be competition for survival, in which the fittest will survive. Among organisms very well fitted for survival will be organisms of such complex and subtle construction as to allow easy adaptation to a changing environment. These organisms will evince great spatial order. So the laws of nature are such as, under certain circumstances, to give rise to striking examples of spatial order similar to the machines which men make. Nature, that is, is a machine-making machine. In the twentieth century men make not only machines, but machine-making machines. They may therefore naturally infer from nature which produces animals and plants, to a creator of nature similar to men who make machine-making machines.

This reconstructed argument is now immune to having some crucial premiss shown false by some biologist of the 1980s. The facts to which its premisses appeal are too evident for that—whatever the details, natural laws are clearly such as to produce complex organisms from inorganic matter under certain circumstances. But although this is so, I do not find the argument a very strong one, and this is because of the evident paucity of organisms throughout the universe. The circumstances under which nature behaves as a machine-making machine are rare. For that reason nature does not evince very strongly the character of a machine-making machine and hence the analogies between the products of natural processes on the one hand and machines on the other are not too strong. Perhaps they give a small degree of probability to the hypothesis that a rational agent was responsible for the laws of evolution in some ways similar to the rational agents who make machines, but the probability is no more than that.

I pass on to consider a form of teleological argument which seems to me a much stronger one—the teleological argument from the temporal order of the world. The temporal order of the universe is, to the man who bothers to give it a moment's thought, an overwhelmingly striking fact about it. Regularities of succession are all-pervasive. For simple laws govern almost all successions of events. In books of physics, chemistry, and biology we can learn how almost everything in the world behaves. The laws of their behaviour can be set out by relatively simple formulae which men can understand and by means of which they can successfully predict the future. The orderliness of the universe to which I draw attention here is its

conformity to formula, to simple, formulable, scientific laws. The orderliness of the universe in this respect is a very striking fact about it. The universe might so naturally have been chaotic, but it is not—it is very orderly.

That the world has this very peculiar characteristic may be challenged in various ways. It may be said of the order which we seem to see in the universe that we impose the order on the world, that it is not there independently of our imposition. Put another way, all that this temporal order amounts to, it might be said, is a coincidence between how things have been so far in the world and the patterns which men can recognize and describe, a coincidence which is itself susceptible of an explanation in terms of natural selection. In fact, however, the temporal order of the world is something deeper than that. The premiss of a good teleological argument is not that so far (within his life or within human history) things have conformed to a pattern which man can recognize and describe. The premiss is rather that things have and will continue to conform to such a pattern however initial conditions vary, however men interfere in the world. If induction is justified, we are justified in supposing that things will continue to behave as they have behaved in the kinds of respect which scientists and ordinary people recognize and describe. I assume that we are justified in believing that the laws of gravity and chemical cohesion will continue to hold tomorrow—that stones will fall, and desks hold together tomorrow as well as today—however initial conditions vary, however men interfere in the world. It may of course be doubted whether philosophers have given a very satisfactory account of what makes such beliefs justified (hence 'the problem of induction'); but I assume the common-sense view that they are justified. So the teleologist's premiss is not just that there has been in nature so far an order which men can recognize and describe; but there has been and will continue to be in nature an order, recognizable and describable by men certainly, but one which exists independently of men. If men are correct in their belief that the order which they see in the world is an order which will hold in the future as in the past, it is clearly not an imposed or invented order. It is there in nature. For man cannot make nature conform subsequently to an order which he has invented. Only if the order is there in nature is nature's future conformity to be expected.

An objector may now urge that although the order of the universe is an objective matter, nevertheless, unless the universe were an orderly place, men would not be around to comment on the fact. (If there were no natural laws, there would be no regularly functioning organisms, and so no men.) Hence there is nothing surprising in the fact that men find order—they could not possibly find anything else. This conclusion is clearly a little too strong. There would need to be quite a bit of order in and around our bodies if men are to exist and think, but there could be chaos outside the earth, so long as the earth was largely unaffected by that chaos. There is a great deal more order in the world than is necessary for the existence of humans. So men could still be around to comment on the fact even if the world were a much less orderly place than it is. But quite apart from this minor consideration, the argument still fails totally for a reason which can best be brought out by an analogy. Suppose that a madman kidnaps a victim and shuts him in a room with a card-shuffling machine. The machine shuffles ten packs of cards simultaneously and then draws a card from each pack and exhibits simultaneously the ten cards. The kidnapper tells the victim that he will shortly set the machine to work and it will exhibit its first draw, but that unless the draw consists of an ace of hearts from each pack, the machine will simultaneously set off an explosion which will kill the victim, in consequence of which he will not see which cards the machine drew. The machine is then set to work, and to the amazement and relief of the victim the machine exhibits an ace of hearts drawn from each pack. The victim thinks that this extraordinary fact needs an explanation in terms of the machine having been rigged in some way. But the kidnapper, who now reappears, casts doubt on this suggestion. 'It is hardly surprising', he says, 'that the machine draws only aces of hearts. You could not possibly see anything else. For you would not be here to see anything at all, if any

other cards had been drawn.' But of course the victim is right and the kidnapper is wrong. There is indeed something extraordinary in need of explanation in ten aces of hearts being drawn. The fact that this peculiar order is a necessary condition of the draw being perceived at all makes what is perceived no less extraordinary and in need of explanation. The teleologist's starting-point is not that we perceive order rather than disorder, but that order rather than disorder is there. Maybe only if order is there can we know what is there, but that makes what is there no less extraordinary and in need of explanation.

So the universe is characterized by vast, all-pervasive temporal order, the conformity of nature to formula, recorded in the scientific laws formulated by men. Now this phenomenon, like the very existence of the world, is clearly something 'too big' to be explained by science. If there is an explanation of the world's order it cannot be a scientific one, and this follows from the nature of scientific explanation. For, in scientific explanation we explain particular phenomena as brought about by prior phenomena in accord with scientific laws; or we explain the operation of scientific laws in terms of more general scientific laws (and perhaps also particular phenomena). Thus we explain the operation of Kepler's laws in terms of the operation of Newton's laws (given the masses, initial velocities, and distances apart of the sun and planets); and we explain the operation of Newton's laws in terms of the operation of Einstein's field equations for space relatively empty of matter. Science thus explains particular phenomena and low-level laws in terms partly of high-level laws. But from the very nature of science it cannot explain the highest-level laws of all; for they are that by which it explains all other phenomena.

At this point we need to rephrase our premises in terms of the *powers-and-liabilities account* of science, which we have seen reason for preferring to the Hempelian account. On this account what the all-pervasive temporal order amounts to is the fact that throughout space and time there are physical objects of various kinds, every such object having the powers and liabilities which are described in laws of nature—e.g. the power of attracting each other physical object in the universe with a force of $\gamma mm^1/r^2$ dynes (where γ is the gravitational constant) the liability always to exercise this power, and the liability to be attracted by each other body in the universe with a force of $\gamma mm^1/r^2$ dynes and so on. From the fact that it has such general powers it follows that an object will have certain more specific powers, given the kind of object that it is. For example, given that it has a mass of 1 gram, it will follow that it has the power of attracting each other body in the universe with a force of $\gamma m^1/r^2$ dynes. This picture allows us to draw attention to one feature of the orderliness of the universe which the other picture makes it easy to ignore. Unlike the feature to which I have drawn attention so far, it is not one of which men have always known; it is one which the atomic theory of chemistry strongly suggested, and the discovery of fundamental particles confirmed. It is this. The physical objects scattered throughout space and time are, or are composed of, particles of a few limited kinds, which we call fundamental particles. Whether the protons and electrons which we suppose to be the fundamental particles are in fact fundamental, or whether they are composed of yet more fundamental particles (e.g. quarks) which are capable of independent existence is not altogether clear—but what does seem clear is that if there are yet more fundamental particles, they too come in a few specific kinds. Nature only has building-blocks of a few kinds. Each particle of a given kind has a few defining properties which determine its behaviour and which are specific to that kind. Thus all electrons have a mass of $\frac{1}{2}MeV/c^2$, a charge of -1, a spin of $\frac{1}{2}$, etc. All positrons have other properties the same as electrons, but a charge of $+1$. All protons have a mass of $938\ MeV/c^2$, a charge of $+1$, and a spin of $\frac{1}{2}$. And so on. There are innumerably many particles which belong to each of a few kinds, and no particles with characteristics intermediate between those of two kinds. The properties of fundamental kinds, that is, which give specific form to the general powers which all objects have, belong to a small class; and the powers and liabilities of large-scale objects are determined by those of their fundamental components. Particles have

constant characteristics over time; they only change their characteristics, or are destroyed or converted into other particles by reason of their own liabilities (e.g. to decay) or the action of other particles acting in virtue of their powers.

Put in these terms then, the orderliness of nature is a matter of the vast uniformity in the powers and liabilities of bodies throughout endless time and space, and also in the paucity of kinds of components of bodies. Over centuries long, long ago and over distances distant in millions of light years from ourselves the same universal orderliness reigns. There are, as we have seen, explanations of only two kinds for phenomena—scientific explanation and personal explanation. Yet, although a scientific explanation can be provided of why the more specific powers and liabilities of bodies hold (e.g. why an electron exerts just the attractive force which it does) in terms of more general powers and liabilities possessed by all bodies (put in Hempelian terms—why a particular natural law holds in terms of more general natural laws), science cannot explain why all bodies do possess the same very general powers and liabilities. It is with this fact that scientific explanation stops. So either the orderliness of nature is where all explanation stops, or we must postulate an agent of great power and knowledge who brings about through his continuous action that bodies have the same very general powers and liabilities (that the most general natural laws operate); and, once again, the simplest such agent to postulate is one of infinite power, knowledge, and freedom, i.e. God. An additional consideration here is that it is clearly vastly simpler to suppose that the existence and the order of the world have the same cause, and the considerations which lead us to postulate a being of infinite power, knowledge, and freedom as the cause of the former reinforce the considerations which lead us to postulate such a cause for the latter.

In the *Dialogues* Hume made the objection— why should we not postulate many gods to give order to the universe, not merely one? 'A great number of men join in building a house or a ship, in rearing a city, in framing a commonwealth, why may not several deities combine in framing a world?' Hume again is aware of the obvious counter-objection to his suggestion. 'To multiply causes without necessity is . . . contrary to true philosophy.' He claims, however, that the counter-objection does not apply here, because (in my terminology) although the supposition that there is one god is a simpler supposition than the supposition that there are many, 'in postulating many persons to be responsible for the order of the universe we are postulating persons more like to men in power and knowledge—that is we are putting forward a hypothesis which fits in better with our background knowledge of what there is in the world. That may be. But Hume's hypothesis is very complicated—we want to ask about it such questions as why are there just 333 deities (or whatever the number is), why do they have powers of just the strength which they do have, and what moves them to cooperate as closely as obviously they do; questions of a kind which obtrude far less with the far simpler and so less arbitrary theistic hypothesis. Even if Hume were right in supposing that the prior probability of his hypothesis were as great as that of theism (because the fit with background knowledge of the former cancels out the simplicity of the latter) (and I do not myself think that he is right), the hypothesis of theism nevertheless has greater explanatory power than the Humean hypothesis and is for that reason more probable. For theism leads us to expect that we will find throughout nature one pattern of order. But if there were more than one deity responsible for the order of the universe, we would expect to see characteristic marks of the handiwork of different deities in different parts of the universe, just as we see different kinds of workmanship in the different houses of a city. We would expect to find an inverse square of law of gravitation obeyed in one part of the universe, and in another part a law which was just short of being an inverse square law—without the difference being explicable in terms of a more general law. It is enough to draw this absurd conclusion to see how wrong the Humean objection is.

So I shall take as the alternatives—the first, that the temporal order of the world is where explanation stops, and the second, that the temporal order of the world is due to the agency of God; and I shall ignore the less probable possibilities that the order is to be explained as due to the agency of an agent or agents of finite power. The proponent of the teleological argument claims that the order of nature shows an orderer—God.

The Force of the Second Form of Teleological Argument

The teleological argument, whether from temporal or spatial order, is, I believe, a codification by philosophers of a reaction to the world deeply embedded in the human consciousness. Men see the comprehensibility of the world as evidence of a comprehending creator. The prophet Jeremiah lived in an age in which the existence of a creator-god of some sort was taken for granted. What was at stake was the extent of his goodness, knowledge, and power. Jeremiah argued from the order of the world that he was a powerful and reliable god, that god was God. He argued to the power of the creator from the extent of the creation—'The host of heaven cannot be numbered, neither the sand of the sea measured'; and he argued that its regular behaviour showed the reliability of the creator, and he spoke of the 'covenant of the day and night' whereby they follow each other regularly, and 'the ordinances of heaven and earth',[1] and he used their existence as an argument for the trustworthiness of the God of Jacob. The argument from temporal order has been with us ever since.

You get the argument from temporal order also in Aquinas's fifth way, which runs as follows:

The fifth way is based on the guidedness of nature. An orderedness of actions to an end is observed in all bodies obeying natural laws, even when they lack awareness. For their behaviour hardly ever varies, and will practically always turn out well; which shows that they truly tend to a goal, and do not merely hit it by accident. Nothing however that lacks awareness tends to a goal, except under the direction of someone with awareness and with understanding; the arrow, for example requires an archer. Everything in nature, therefore is directed to its goal by someone with understanding and this we call 'God'.[2]

Aquinas argues that the regular behaviour of each inanimate thing shows that some animate being is directing it (making it move to achieve some purpose, attain some goal); and from that he comes—rather quickly—to the conclusion that one 'being with understanding' is responsible for the behaviour of all inanimate things.

It seems to me fairly clear that no argument from temporal order—whether Aquinas's fifth way or any other argument can be a good deductive argument. For although the premiss is undoubtedly correct—a vast pervasive order characterizes the world—the step from premiss to conclusion is not a valid deductive one. Although the existence of order may be good evidence of a designer, it is surely compatible with the non-existence of one—it is hardly a logically necessary truth that all order is brought about by a person. And although, as I have urged, the supposition that one person is responsible for the orderliness of the world is much simpler and so more probable than the supposition that many persons are, nevertheless, the latter supposition seems logically compatible with the data—so we must turn to the more substantial issue of whether the argument from the temporal order of the world to God is a good inductive argument. We had reached the conclusion that either the vast uniformity in the powers and liabilities of bodies was where explanation stopped, or that God brings this about by his continuous action, through an intention constant over time.

Let us represent by e this conformity of the world to order, and let h be the hypothesis of theism. It is not possible to treat a teleological argument in complete isolation from the cosmological argument. We cannot ask how probable the premiss of the teleological argument makes theism, independently of the premiss of the cosmological argument, for the premiss of the teleological argument entails in part the premiss of the cosmological argument. That there is order of the kind described entails at least that there is a physical universe. So let k be now, not mere tautological evidence, but the existence of a complex physical universe (the premiss of the version of the cosmological argument to which I devoted most attention). Let us ask how much more probable does

the orderliness of such a universe make the existence of God than does the mere existence of the universe.

With these fillings, we ask whether $P(h/e.k) > P(h/k)$ and by how much. As we have seen $P(h/e.k)$ will exceed $P(h/k)$ if and only if $P(e/h.k) > P(e/\sim h.k)$. Put in words with our current fillings for h, e, and k, the existence of order in the world confirms the existence of God if and only if the existence of this order in the world is more probable if there is a God than if there is not. We saw in Chapter 6 that where h is the hypothesis that there is a God $P(e/h.k)$ may exceed $P(e/\sim h.k)$, either because e cannot be explained in any other way and is very unlikely to occur uncaused or because God has a character such that he is more likely to bring about e than alternative states. With respect to the cosmological argument, I suggested that its case rested solely on the first consideration. Here I shall suggest that again the first consideration is dominant, but that the second has considerable significance also.

Let us start with the first consideration. e is the vast uniformity in the powers and liabilities possessed by material objects—$P(e/\sim h.k)$ is the probability that there should be that amount of uniformity in a God-less world, that this uniform distribution of the powers of things should be where explanation terminates, that they be further inexplicable. That there should be material bodies is strange enough; but that they should all have such similar powers which they inevitably exercise, seems passing strange. It is strange enough that physical objects should have powers at all—why should they not just be, without being able to make a difference to the world? But that they should all, throughout infinite time and space, have some general powers identical to those of all other objects (and they all be made of components of very few fundamental kinds, each component of a given kind being identical in all characteristics with each other such component) and yet there be no cause of this at all seems incredible. The universe is complex as we urged, in the last chapter, in that there are so many bodies of different shapes, etc., and now we find an underlying orderliness in the identity of powers and paucity of kinds of components of bodies. Yet this orderliness, if there is no explanation of it in terms of the action of God, is the orderliness of coincidence—the fact that one body has certain powers does not explain the fact that a second body has—not the simplicity of a common underlying explanation. The basic complexity remains in the vast number of different bodies in which the orderliness of identical powers and components is embodied. It is a complexity too striking to occur unexplained. It cries out for explanation in terms of some single common source with the power to produce it. Just as we would seek to explain all the coins' of the realm having an identical pattern in terms of their origin from a common mould, or all of many pictures' having a common style in terms of their being painted by the same painter, so too should we seek to explain all physical objects' having the same powers in terms of their deriving them from a common source. On these grounds alone $P(e/h.k) \geqslant P(e/k)$, and so $P(h/e.k) \geqslant P(h/k).$[3]

I think, however, that we can go further by bringing in considerations from God's character—we saw in Chapter 6 that God will bring about a state of affairs if it is over all a good thing that he should, he will not bring about a state of affairs if it is over all a bad thing that he should, and that he will only bring about a state of affairs if it is in some way a good thing that he should. Put in terms of reasons—he will always act on overriding reasons and cannot act except for a reason. Now there are two reasons why human beings produce order. One is aesthetic—beauty comes in the patterns of things, such as dances and songs. Some sort of order is a necessary condition of phenomena having beauty; complete chaos is just ugly—although of course not any order is beautiful. The second reason why a human being produces order is that when there is order he or other rational agents can perceive that order and utilize it to achieve ends. If we see that there is a certain pattern of order in phenomena we can then justifiably predict that that order will continue, and that enables us to make predictions about the future on which we can rely. A librarian puts books in an alphabetical order of authors in order that he and users of the library who come to know that the

order is there may subsequently be able to find any book in the library very quickly (because, given knowledge of the order, we can predict whereabouts in the library any given book will be).

God has similar reasons for producing an orderly, as opposed to a chaotic universe. In so far as some sort of order is a necessary condition of beauty, and it is a good thing—as it surely is—that the world be beautiful rather than ugly, God has reason for creating an orderly universe. Secondly, I shall argue in Chapter 10 that it is good that God should make finite creatures with the opportunity to grow in knowledge and power. Now if creatures are going consciously to extend their control of the world, they will need to know how to do so. There will need to be some procedures which they can find out, such that if they follow those procedures, certain events will occur. This entails the existence of temporal order. There can only be such procedures if the world is orderly, and, I should add, there can only be such procedures ascertainable by men if the order of the world is such as to be discernible by men. To take a simple example, if hitting things leads to them breaking or penetrating other things, and heating things leads to them melting, men can discover these regularities and utilize them to make artefacts such as houses, tables, and chairs. They can heat iron ore to melt it to make nails, hammers, and axes, and use the latter to break wood into the right shapes to hammer together with nails to make the artefacts. Or, if light and other electro-magnetic radiation behave in predictable ways comprehensible by men, men can discover those ways and build telescopes and radio and television receivers and transmitters. A world must evince the temporal order exhibited by laws of nature if men are to be able to extrapolate from how things have behaved in the past, to how they will behave in the future, which extrapolation is necessary if men are to have the knowledge of how things will behave in the future, which they must have in order to be able to extend their control over the world. (There would not need to be complete determinism—agents themselves could be exempt from the full rigours of determinism, and there might be violations of natural laws from time to time. But basically the world has to be governed by laws of nature if agents are consciously to extend their control of the world.) If I am right in supposing that God has reason to create finite creatures with the opportunity to grow in knowledge and power, then he has reason to create temporal order. So I suggest that God has at least these two reasons for producing an orderly world. Maybe God has reasons for not making creatures with the opportunity to grow in knowledge and power, and so the second reason for his creating an orderly universe does not apply. But with one possible, and, I shall show, irrelevant qualification, the first surely does. God may choose whether or not to make a physical universe, but if he does, he has reason for making a beautiful and so an orderly one. God has reason, if he does make a physical universe, not to make a chaotic or botched-up one. The only reason of which I can think why God should make the universe in some respects ugly would be to give to creatures the opportunity to discover the aesthetic merits of different states of affairs and through cooperative effort to make the world beautiful for themselves. But then the other argument shows that if they are to be able to exercise such an opportunity the world will need to be orderly in some respects. (There will have to be predictable regularities which creatures may utilize in order to produce beautiful states of affairs.) So, either way, the world will need to be orderly. It rather looks as if God has overriding reason to make an orderly universe if he makes a universe at all. However, as I emphasized, human inquiry into divine reasons is a highly speculative matter. But it is nevertheless one in which men are justified in reaching tentative conclusions. For God is postulated to be an agent like ourselves in having knowledge, power, and freedom, although to an infinitely greater degree than we have. The existence of the analogy legitimizes us in reaching conclusions about his purposes, conclusions which must allow for the quantitative difference, as I have tried to do.

So I suggest that the order of the world is evidence of the existence of God both because its occurrence would be very improbable *a priori* and also because, in virtue of his postulated character, he has very good, apparently overriding, reason for making an orderly universe, if he makes a universe at all. It looks as if $P(e/h.k)$ equals 1. For both reasons $P(e/h.k) \gg P(e/ \sim h.k)$ and so $P(h/e.k) \gg P(h/k)$. I conclude that the teleological argument from temporal order is a good C-inductive argument to the existence of God.†

Let us look at the argument from a slightly different angle. It is basically an argument by analogy, an analogy between the order in the natural world (the temporal order codified in laws of nature) and the patterns of order which men often produce (the ordered books on library shelves, or the temporal order in the movements of a dancer or the notes of a song). It argues from similarity between phenomena of two kinds B and B^* to similarity between their causes A and A^*. In view of the similarities between the two kinds of order B and B^*, the theist postulates a cause (A^*) in some respects similar to A (men); yet in view of the dissimilarities the theist must postulate a cause in other respects different. All arguments by analogy do and must proceed in this way. They cannot postulate a cause in all respects similar. They postulate a cause who is such that one would expect him to produce phenomena similar to B in the respects in which B^* are similar to B and different from B in the respects in which B^* are different from B.

All argument from analogy works like this. Thus various properties of light and sound were known in the nineteenth century, among them that both light and sound are reflected, refracted, diffracted, and show interference phenomena. In the case of sound these were known to be due to disturbance of the medium, air, in which it is transmitted. What could one conclude by analogy about the cause of the relection, etc., of light? One could conclude that the propagation of light was, like the propagation of sound, the propagation of a

---

† Earlier in the book Swinburne distinguishes a P-inductive argument from a C-inductive argument. A P-inductive argument is one in which the premises make the conclusion probable. A C-inductive argument is one in which the premises *add* to the probability of the conclusion (i.e., make it more probable than it would otherwise be).

wave-like disturbance in a medium. But one could not conclude that it was the propagation of a disturbance in the same medium—air, since light passed through space empty of air. Scientists had to postulate a separate medium—aether, the disturbance of which was responsible for the reflection, etc., of light. And not merely does all argument by analogy proceed like this, but all inductive inference can be represented as argument by analogy. For all inductive inference depends on the assumption that in certain respects things continue the same and in other respects they differ. Thus that crude inference from a number of observed swans all having been white to the next swan's being white is an argument by analogy. For it claims that the next swan will be like the observed swans in one respect—colour, while being unlike them in other respects.

In our case the similarities between the temporal order which men produce and the temporal order in nature codified in scientific laws mean postulating as cause of the latter a person who acts intentionally. The dissimilarities between the kinds of order include the world-wide extent of the order in nature in comparison with the very narrow range of order which men produce. This means postulating as cause of the former a person of enormous power and knowledge. Now, as we saw in Chapter 2, a person has a body if there is a region of the world under his direct control and if he controls other regions of the world only by controlling the former and by its movements having predictable effects on the outside world. Likewise he learns about the world only by the world having effects on this region. If these conditions are satisfied, the person has a body, and the stated region is that body. But if a person brings about directly the connections between things, including the predictable connections between the bodies of other persons and the world, there is no region of the world, goings-on in which bring about those connections. The person must bring about those connections as a basic action. His control of the world must be immediate, not mediated by a body. So the dissimilarities between the two kinds of order necessarily lead to the postulation of a non-embodied person (rather than an

embodied person) as cause of the temporal order in nature.

These considerations should suffice to rebut that persistent criticism of the argument from design which we have heard ever since Hume that, taken seriously, the argument ought to be postulating an embodied god, a giant of a man. 'Why not', wrote Hume, 'become a perfect anthropomorphite? Why not assert the deity or deities to be corporeal, and, to have eyes, a nose, mouth, ears, etc.?' The answer is the simple one that dissimilarities between effects lead the rational man to postulate dissimilarities between causes, and that this procedure is basic to inductive inference.

It is true that the greater the dissimilarities between effects, the weaker is the argument to the existence of a similar cause; and it has been a traditional criticism of the argument from design represented as an argument by analogy that the analogy is weak. The dissimilarities between the natural world and the effects which men produce are indeed striking; but the similarities between these are also, I have been suggesting, striking—in both there is the conformity of phenomena to a simple pattern of order detectable by men. But although the dissimilarities are perhaps sufficiently great to make the argument not a good P-inductive argument, this chapter suggests that it remains a good C-inductive argument. The existence of order in the universe increases significantly the probability that there is a God, even if it does not by itself render it probable.

The Argument from Beauty

We saw that God has reason, apparently overriding reason, for making, not merely any orderly world (which we have been considering so far) but a beautiful world—at any rate to the extent to which it lies outside the control of creatures. (And he has reason too, I would suggest, even in whatever respects the world does lie within the control of creatures, to give them experience of beauty to develop, and perhaps also some ugliness to annihilate.) So God has reason to make a basically beautiful world, although also reason to leave some of the beauty or ugliness of the world within the power of creatures to determine; but he would seem to have overriding reason not to make a basically ugly world beyond the powers of creatures to improve. Hence, if there is a God there is more reason to expect a basically beautiful world than a basically ugly one—by the principles of Chapter 6. *A priori,* however, there is no particular reason for expecting a basically beautiful rather than a basically ugly world. In consequence, if the world is beautiful, that fact would be evidence for God's existence. For, in this case, if we let k be 'there is an orderly physical universe', e be 'there is a beautiful universe', and h be 'there is a God', $P(e/h.k)$ will be greater than $P(e/k)$; and so by our previous principles the argument from e to h will be another good C-inductive argument.

Few, however, would deny that our universe (apart from its animal and human inhabitants, and aspects subject to their immediate control) has that beauty. Poets and painters and ordinary men down the centuries have long admired the beauty of the orderly procession of the heavenly bodies, the scattering of the galaxies through the heavens (in some ways random, in some ways orderly), and the rocks, sea, and wind interacting on earth, 'The spacious firmament on high, and all the blue aethereal sky', the water lapping against 'the old eternal rocks', and the plants of the jungle and of temperate climates, contrasting with the desert and the Arctic wastes. Who in his senses would deny that here is beauty in abundance? If we confine ourselves to the argument from the beauty of the inanimate and plant worlds, the argument surely works.

Notes

1. Jer. 33: 20f. and 25f.
2. St. Thomas Aquinas, *Summa Theologiae,* la, 2.3, trans. T. McDermott, OP (London, 1964).
3. '$\gg$' means 'is much greater than'. '$\ll$' means 'is much less than'.

I.C The Ontological Argument for the Existence of God

The ontological argument for the existence of God is the most intriguing of all the arguments for theism. It is one of the most remarkable arguments ever set forth. First devised by Anselm (1033–1109), Archbishop of Canterbury in the eleventh century, the argument has continued to puzzle and fascinate philosophers ever since. Let the testimony of the agnostic philosopher Bertrand Russell serve as a typical example here:

> I remember the precise moment, one day in 1894, as I was walking along Trinity Lane [at Cambridge University where Russell was a student], when I saw in a flash (or thought I saw) that the ontological argument is valid. I had gone out to buy a tin of tobacco; on my way back, I suddenly threw it up in the air, and exclaimed as I caught it: "Great Scott, the ontological argument is sound!"*

The argument is important not only because it claims to be an a priori proof for the existence of God but also because it is the primary locus of such philosophical problems as whether existence is a property and whether the notion of necessary existence is intelligible. Furthermore, it has special religious significance because it is the only one of the traditional arguments that clearly concludes to the necessary properties of God, that is, his omnipotence, omniscience, omnibenevolence, and other great-making properties.

Although there are many versions of the ontological argument and many interpretations of some of these, most philosophers agree on the essential form of Anselm's version in the second chapter of his *Proslogium*. Anselm believes that God's existence is so absolutely certain that only a fool would doubt or deny it. Yet he desires understanding to fulfill his faith. "And so, Lord, do thou, who dost give understanding to faith, give me, so far as thou knowest it to be profitable, to understand that thou art as we believe; and that thou art that which we believe. And indeed, we believe that thou art a being than which nothing greater can be conceived. Or is there no such nature, since the fool hath said in his heart, there is no God?"

The argument that follows may be treated as a reductio ad absurdum argument. That is, it begins with a supposition (*S:* suppose that the greatest conceivable being exists in the mind alone) that is contradictory to what one desires to prove. One then goes about showing that (*S*) together with other certain or self-evident assumptions (A_1 and A_2) yields a contradiction, which in turn demonstrates that the contradictory of (*S*) must be true: A greatest possible being must exist in reality. You, the reader, can work out the details of the argument.

A monk named Gaunilo, a contemporary of Anselm's, sets forth the first objection to Anselm's argument. Accusing Anselm of pulling rabbits out of hats, he tells the story of a delectable lost island, one that is more excellent than all lands. Since it is better that such a perfect island exist in reality than simply in the mind alone, this Isle of the Blest must necessarily exist. Anselm's reply is that the analogy fails, for unlike the greatest possible being, the greatest possible island can be conceived as not existing. Recently, Alvin Plantinga has clarified Anselm's point. There simply are some properties that have intrinsic maximums and some properties that do not. No matter how wonderful we make the Isle of the Blest, we can conceive of a more wonderful island. The greatness of islands is like the greatness of numbers in this respect. There is no greatest natural number, for no matter how large the number we choose, we can always conceive of one twice as large. On the other hand, the properties of God have intrinsic maximums. For example, perfect

---

* *Autobiography of Bertrand Russell* (New York: Little, Brown & Co., 1967).

knowledge has an intrinsic maximum: For any proposition, an omniscient being knows whether it is true or false.

Our next reading is the critique by Immanuel Kant (1724–1804), who accused the proponent of the argument of defining God into existence. Kant claims that Anselm makes the mistake of treating 'existence' or 'being' as a first-order predicate like 'blue' or 'great'. When we say that the castle is blue, we are adding a property (viz., blueness) to the idea of a castle, but when we say that the castle *exists*, we are not adding anything to the concept of a castle. We are saying only that the concept is exemplified or instantiated. In Anselm's argument 'existence' is treated as a first-order predicate, which adds something to the concept of an entity and makes it *greater*. This, according to Kant, is the fatal flaw in the argument.

In our third reading, "The Ontological Argument," Alvin Plantinga analyzes Anselm's argument, defends it against Kant's criticism, and then constructs a modal version of the argument. That is, the argument is set forth in terms of the modes of possibility and necessity or in terms of possible and necessary existence. The key premise, number (29) in this essay, is this: "There is a possible world in which maximal greatness is instantiated." Plantinga explicates and defends this premise, which rests on the premise that a being has maximal excellence in every possible world and which therefore entails the existence of God. Plantinga believes that this version of the ontological argument is sound, but he doesn't claim that it proves that God exists (for the argument works only if (29) is true, and it may not be). But there is nothing irrational about believing (29). His argument "establishes not the truth of theism, but its rational acceptability."

Following Plantinga's article is William Rowe's explication of how modal versions of the ontological argument work. Specifically, Rowe analyzes and critiques Plantinga's version. Appreciating the subtlety and validity of the argument itself, he argues that Plantinga's

assessment of what his modal version of the argument does is inaccurate. Plantinga claims that the argument shows that one can rationally accept theism, but Rowe thinks that all he has shown is that one may not be foolish to accept it.

Our final reading is a short article by David and Marjorie Haight entitled "An Ontological Argument for the Devil." The Haights turn the ontological argument on its head and claim that one can use it to prove that the devil exists as the supreme being. The argument goes like this:

1. I have a concept of something than which nothing *worse* can be conceived.
2. If that "something" did not actually, or in fact, exist, it would not be "that than which nothing worse could be conceived," because something could always be conceived to be much worse, namely, something that actually exists.
3. This "greatest something" we shall call the devil.
4. Therefore, the devil exists.

The argument thus parallels the ontological argument for the existence of God. The Haights claim that, *mutatis mutandis*, the same considerations that support the version that argues to the existence of God support the version that leads to the existence of the devil as the supreme being. But since there can be only one supreme being, it is a toss-up between the two versions and one decides between them only by faith. So the ontological argument, if valid, brings us back to a point of faith, not of theoretical reason.

There are many other considerations involved in the ontological argument that are not dealt with in our readings. For a clear discussion of the wider issues involved in this argument, see William Rowe's introductory work, *Philosophy of Religion* (chapter 3, "The Ontological Argument"). However, the readings before you will most likely provide more than enough to whet your appetite.

I.C.1   The Ontological Argument

S T . A N S E L M

St. Anselm (1033–1109), Abbot of Bec and later Archbishop of Canterbury, is the originator of one of the most intriguing arguments ever devised by the human mind, the ontological argument for the existence of a supremely perfect being. After the short selection from Anselm's Proslogium, *there follows a brief selection from Gaunilo's reply,* In Behalf of the Fool, *and a counterresponse by Anselm.*

St. Anselm's Presentation

Truly there is a God, although the fool hath said in his heart, There is no God.

And so, Lord, do thou, who dost give understanding to faith, give me, so far as thou knowest it to be profitable, to understand that thou art as we believe; and that thou art that which we believe. And, indeed, we believe that thou art a being than which nothing greater can be conceived. Or is there no such nature, since the fool hath said in his heart, there is no God? (Psalms xiii, 1). But, at any rate, this very fool, when he hears of this being of which I speak—a being than which nothing greater can be conceived—understands what he hears, and what he understands is in his understanding; although he does not understand it to exist.

For, it is one thing for an object to be in the understanding, and another to understand that the object exists. When a painter first conceives of what he will afterwards perform, he has it in his understanding, but he does not yet understand it to be, because he has not yet performed it. But

Reprinted from *Anselm's Basic Writings*, translated by S. W. Deane, 2d ed. (La Salle, Ill.: Open Court Publishing Company, 1962), by permission of the publisher.

after he has made the painting, he both has it in his understanding, and he understands that it exists, because he has made it.

Hence, even the fool is convinced that something exists in the understanding, at least, than which nothing greater can be conceived. For, when he hears of this, he understands it. And whatever is understood, exists in the understanding. And assuredly that, than which nothing greater can be conceived, cannot exist in the understanding alone. For, suppose it exists in the understanding alone: then it can be conceived to exist in reality; which is greater.

Therefore, if that, than which nothing greater can be conceived, exists in the understanding alone, the very being, than which nothing greater can be conceived, is one, than which a greater can be conceived. But obviously this is impossible. Hence, there is no doubt that there exists a being, than which nothing greater can be conceived, and it exists both in the understanding and in reality.

God cannot be conceived not to exist.—God is that, than which nothing greater can be conceived.—That which can be conceived not to exist is not God.

And it assuredly exists so truly, that it cannot be conceived not to exist. For, it is possible to conceive of a being which cannot be conceived not to exist; and this is greater than one which can be conceived not to exist. Hence, if that, than which nothing greater can be conceived, can be conceived not to exist, it is not that, than which nothing greater can be conceived. But this is an irreconcilable contradiction. There is, then, so truly a being than which nothing greater can be conceived to exist, that it cannot even be conceived not to exist; and this being thou art, O Lord, our God.

So truly, therefore, dost thou exist, O Lord, my God, that thou canst not be conceived not to exist; and rightly. For, if a mind could conceive of a being better than thee, the creature would rise above the Creator; and this is most absurd. And, indeed, whatever else there is, except thee alone, can be conceived not to exist. To thee alone, therefore, it belongs to exist more truly than all other beings, and hence in a higher degree than all others. For, whatever else exists does not exist so truly, and hence in a less degree it belongs to it to exist. Why, then, has the fool said in his heart, there is no God (Psalms xiii, 1), since it is so evident, to a rational mind, that thou dost exist in the highest degree of all? Why, except that he is dull and a fool?

How the fool has said in his heart what cannot be conceived.—A thing may be conceived in two ways: (1) when the word signifying it is conceived: (2) when the thing itself is understood. As far as the word goes, God can be conceived not to exist; in reality he cannot.

But how has the fool said in his heart what he could not conceive; or how is it that he could not conceive what he said in his heart? since it is the same to say in the heart, and to conceive.

But, if really, nay, since really, he both conceived, because he said in his heart; and did not say in his heart, because he could not conceive; there is more than one way in which a thing is said in the heart or conceived. For, in one sense, an object is conceived, when the word signifying it is conceived; and in another, when the very entity, which the object is, is understood.

In the former sense, then, God can be conceived not to exist; but in the latter, not at all. For no one who understands what fire and water are can conceive fire to be water, in accordance with the nature of the facts themselves, although this is possible according to the words. So, then, no one who understands what God is can conceive that God does not exist; although he says these words in his heart, either without any or with some foreign, signification. For, God is that than which a greater cannot be conceived. And he who thoroughly understands this, assuredly understands that this being so truly exists, that not even in concept can it be non-existent. Therefore, he who understands that God so exists, cannot conceive that he does not exist.

I thank thee, gracious Lord, I thank thee; because what I formerly believed by thy bounty, I now so understand by thine illumination, that if I were unwilling to believe that thou dost exist, I should not be able not to understand this to be true.

Gaunilo's Criticism

For example: it is said that somewhere in the ocean is an island, which, because of the difficulty, or rather the impossibility, of discovering what does not exist, is called the lost island. And they say that this island has an inestimable wealth of all manner of riches and delicacies in greater abundance than is told of the Islands of the Blest; and that having no owner or inhabitant, it is more excellent than all other countries, which are inhabited by mankind, in the abundance with which it is stored.

Now if some one should tell me that there is such an island, I should easily understand his words, in which there is no difficulty. But suppose that he went on to say, as if by a logical inference: "You can no longer doubt that this island which is more excellent than all lands exists somewhere, since you have no doubt that it is in your understanding. And since it is more excellent not to be in the understanding alone, but to exist both in the understanding and in reality, for this reason it must exist. For if it does not exist, any land which really exists will be more excellent than it; and so the island already understood by you to be more excellent will not be more excellent."

If a man should try to prove to me by such reasoning that this island truly exists, and that its existence should no longer be doubted, either I should believe that he was jesting, or I know not which I ought to regard as the greater fool: myself,

---

Gaunilo, a monk, was a contemporary of St. Anselm's.

supposing that I should allow this proof; or him, if he should suppose that he had established with any certainty the existence of this island. For he ought to show first that the hypothetical excellence of this island exists as a real and indubitable fact, and in no wise as any unreal object, or one whose existence is uncertain, in my understanding.

St. Anselm's Rejoinder

A criticism of Gaunilo's example, in which he tries to show that in this way the real existence of a lost island might be inferred from the fact of its being conceived.

But, you say, it is as if one should suppose an island in the ocean, which surpasses all lands in its fertility, and which, because of the difficulty, or rather the impossibility, of discovering what does not exist, is called a lost island; and should say that there can be no doubt that this island truly exists in reality, for this reason, that one who hears it described easily understands what he hears.

Now I promise confidently that if any man shall devise anything existing either in reality or in concept alone (except that than which a greater cannot be conceived) to which he can adapt the sequence of my reasoning, I will discover that thing, and will give him his lost island, not to be lost again.

But it now appears that this being than which a greater is inconceivable cannot be conceived not to be, because it exists on so assured a ground of truth; for otherwise it would not exist at all.

Hence, if any one says that he conceives this being not to exist, I say that at the time when he conceives of this either he conceives of a being than which a greater is inconceivable, or he does not conceive at all. If he does not conceive, he does not conceive of the non-existence of that of which he does not conceive. But if he does conceive, he certainly conceives of a being which cannot be even conceived not to exist. For if it could be conceived not to exist, it could be conceived to have a beginning and an end. But this is impossible.

He, then, who conceives of this being conceives of a being which cannot be even conceived not to exist; but he who conceives of this being does not conceive that it does not exist; else he conceives what is inconceivable. The non-existence, then, of that than which a greater cannot be conceived is inconceivable.

I.C.2   A Critique of the Ontological Argument

IMMANUEL KANT

The German philosopher Immanuel Kant (1724–1804) in his remarkable work Critique of Pure Reason *(1781), from which our selection is taken, set forth a highly influential critique of the ontological argument. Essentially, the objection is that "existence is not a predicate," whereas the opposite is assumed to be true in the various forms of*

the ontological argument. That is, when you say that Mary is my mother, you are noting some property that describes or adds to who Mary is. But when you say, "Mary, my mother, exists," you are not telling us anything new about Mary; you are simply affirming that the concepts in question are exemplified. 'Existence' is a second-order predicate or property, not to be treated as other first-order, normal predicates or properties are.

From *Kant's Critique of Pure Reason*, translated by Norman Kemp Smith. Copyright © 1967 by St. Martin's Press, Inc., and used with permission of the publisher.

The Impossibility of an Ontological Proof of the Existence of God

It is evident, from what has been said, that the concept of an absolutely necessary being is a concept of pure reason, that is, a mere idea the objective reality of which is very far from being proved by the fact that reason requires it. For the idea instructs us only in regard to a certain unattainable completeness, and so serves rather to limit the understanding than to extend it to new objects. But we are here faced by what is indeed strange and perplexing, namely, that while the inference from a given existence in general to some absolutely necessary being seems to be both imperative and legitimate, all those conditions under which alone the understanding can form a concept of such a necessity are so many obstacles in the way of our doing so.

In all ages men have spoken of an *absolutely necessary* being, and in so doing have endeavored, not so much to understand whether and how a thing of this kind allows even of being thought, but rather to prove its existence. There is, of course, no difficulty in giving a verbal definition of the concept, namely, that it is something the non-existence of which is impossible. But this yields no insight into the conditions which make it necessary to regard the non-existence of a thing as absolutely unthinkable. It is precisely these conditions that we desire to know, in order that we may determine whether or not, in resorting to this concept, we are thinking anything at all. The expedient of removing all those conditions which the understanding indispensably requires in order to regard something as necessary, simply through the introduction of the word *unconditioned,* is very far from sufficing to show whether I am still thinking anything in the concept of the unconditionally necessary, or perhaps rather nothing at all.

Nay more, this concept, at first ventured upon blindly, and now become so completely familiar, has been supposed to have its meaning exhibited in a number of examples; and on this account all further enquiry into its intelligibility has seemed to be quite needless. Thus the fact that every geomet-rical proposition, as, for instance, that a triangle has three angles, is absolutely necessary, has been taken as justifying us in speaking of an object which lies entirely outside the sphere of our understanding as if we understood perfectly what it is that we intend to convey by the concept of that object.

All the alleged examples are, without exception, taken from *judgments,* not from *things* and their existence. But the unconditioned necessity of judgments is not the same as an absolute necessity of things. The absolute necessity of the judgment is only a conditioned necessity of the thing, or of the predicate in the judgment. The above proposition does not declare that three angles are absolutely necessary, but that, under the condition that there is a triangle (that is, that a triangle is given), three angles will necessarily be found in it. So great, indeed, is the deluding influence exercised by this logical necessity that, by the simple device of forming an a priori concept of a thing in such a manner as to include existence within the scope of its meaning, we have supposed ourselves to have justified the conclusion that because existence necessarily belongs to the object of this concept— always under the condition that we posit the thing as given (as existing)—we are also of necessity, in accordance with the law of identity, required to posit the existence of its object, and that this being is therefore itself absolutely necessary—and this, to repeat, for the reason that the existence of this being has already been thought in a concept which is assumed arbitrarily and on condition that we posit its object.

If, in an identical proposition, I reject the predicate while retaining the subject, contradiction results; and I therefore say that the former belongs necessarily to the latter. But if we reject subject and predicate alike, there is no contradiction; for nothing is then left that can be contradicted. To posit a triangle, and yet to reject its three angles, is self-contradictory; but there is no contradiction in rejecting the triangle together with its three angles. The same holds true of the concept of an absolutely necessary being. If its existence is rejected, we reject the thing itself with all its predicates; and no question of contradiction can then arise. There is nothing outside it that would then be contradicted, since the necessity of the thing is not supposed to be derived from anything external; nor is there anything internal that would be contradicted, since in rejecting the thing itself we have at the same time rejected all its internal properties. "God is omnipotent" is a necessary judgment. The omnipotence cannot be rejected if we posit a Deity, that is, an infinite being; for the two concepts are identical. But if we say, "There is no God," neither the omnipotence nor any other of its predicates is given; they are one and all rejected together with the subject, and there is therefore not the least contradiction in such a judgment.

We have thus seen that if the predicate of a judgment is rejected together with the subject, no internal contradiction can result, and that this holds no matter what the predicate may be. The only way of evading this conclusion is to argue that there are subjects which cannot be removed, and must always remain. That, however, would only be another way of saying that there are absolutely necessary subjects; and that is the very assumption which I have called in question, and the possibility of which the above argument professes to establish. For I cannot form the least concept of a thing which, should it be rejected with all its predicates, leaves behind a contradiction; and in the absence of contradiction I have, through pure *a priori* concepts alone, no criterion of impossibility.

Notwithstanding all these general considerations, in which every one must concur, we may be challenged with a case which is brought forward as proof that in actual fact the contrary holds, namely, that there is one concept, and indeed only one, in reference to which the not-being or rejection of its object is in itself contradictory, namely, the concept of the *ens realissimum*. It is declared that it possesses all reality, and that we are justified in assuming that such a being is possible (the fact that a concept does not contradict itself by no means proves the possibility of its object: but the contrary assertion I am for the moment willing to allow). Now [the argument proceeds] "all reality" includes existence; existence

is therefore contained in the concept of a thing that is possible. If, then, this thing is rejected, the internal possibility of the thing is rejected—which is self-contradictory.

My answer is as follows. There is already a contradiction in introducing the concept of existence—no matter under what title it may be disguised—into the concept of a thing which we profess to be thinking solely in reference to its possibility. If that be allowed as legitimate, a seeming victory has been won; but in actual fact nothing at all is said; the assertion is a mere tautology. We must ask: Is the proposition that *this or that thing* (which, whatever it may be, is allowed as possible) *exists,* an analytic or a synthetic proposition? If it is analytic, the assertion of the existence of the thing adds nothing to the thought of the thing; but in that case either the thought, which is in us, is the thing itself, or we have presupposed an existence as belonging to the realm of the possible, and have then, on that pretext, inferred its existence from its internal possibility—which is nothing but a miserable tautology. The word "reality," which in the concept of the thing sounds other than the word "existence" in the concept of the predicate, is of no avail in meeting this objection. For if all positing (no matter what it may be that is posited) is entitled reality, the thing with all its predicates is already posited in the concept of the subject, and is assumed as actual; and in the predicate this is merely repeated. But if, on the other hand, we admit, as every reasonable person must, that all existential propositions are synthetic, how can we profess to maintain that the predicate of existence cannot be rejected without contradiction? This is a feature which is found only in analytic propositions, and is indeed precisely what constitutes their analytic character.

I should have hoped to put an end to these idle and fruitless disputations in a direct manner, by an accurate determination of the concept of existence, had I not found that the illusion which is caused by the confusion of a logical with a real predicate (that is, with a predicate which determines a thing) is almost beyond correction. Anything we please can be made to serve as a logical predicate; the subject can even be predicated of itself; for logic abstracts from all content. But a *determining* predicate is a predicate which is added to the concept of the subject and enlarges it. Consequently, it must not be already contained in the concept.

"*Being*" is obviously not a real predicate; that is, it is not a concept of something which could be added to the concept of a thing. It is merely the positing of a thing, or of certain determinations, as existing in themselves. Logically, it is merely the copula of a judgment. The proposition, "God is omnipotent," contains two concepts, each of which has its object—God and omnipotence. The small word "is" adds no new predicate, but only serves to posit the predicate *in its relation* to the subject. If, now, we take the subject (God) with all its predicates (among which is omnipotence), and say "God is," or "There is a God," we attach no new predicate to the concept of God, but only posit the subject in itself with all its predicates, and indeed posit it as being an *object* that stands in relation to my *concept*. The content of both must be one and the same; nothing can have been added to the concept, which expresses merely what is possible, by my thinking its object (through the expression "it is") as given absolutely. Otherwise stated, the real contains no more than the merely possible. A hundred real thalers do not contain the least coin more than a hundred possible thalers. For as the latter signify the concept, and the former the object and the positing of the object, should the former contain more than the latter, my concept would not, in that case, express the whole object, and would not therefore be an adequate concept of it. My financial position is, however, affected very differently by a hundred real thalers than it is by the mere concept of them (that is, of their possibility). For the object, as it actually exists, is not analytically contained in my concept, but is added to my concept (which is a determination of my state) synthetically; and yet the conceived hundred thalers are not themselves in the least increased through thus acquiring existence outside my concept.

By whatever and by however many predicates we may think a thing—even if we completely determine it—we do not make the least

addition to the thing which we further declare that this thing *is*. Otherwise, it would not be exactly the same thing that exists, but something more than we had thought in the concept; and we could not, therefore, say that the exact object of my concept exists. If we think in a thing every feature of reality except one, the missing reality is not added by my saying that this defective thing exists. On the contrary, it exists with the same defect with which I have thought it, since otherwise what exists would be something different from what I thought. When, therefore, I think a being as the supreme reality, without any defect, the question still remains whether it exists or not. For though, in my concept, nothing may be lacking of the possible real content of a thing in general, something is still lacking in its relation to my whole state of thought, namely, [in so far as I am unable to assert] that knowledge of this object is also possible *a posteriori*. And here we find the source of our present difficulty. Were we dealing with an object of the senses, we could not confound the existence of the thing with the mere concept of it. For through the concept the object is thought only as conforming to the *universal conditions* of possible empirical knowledge in general, whereas through its existence it is thought as belonging to the context of experience as a whole. In being thus connected with the *content* of experience as a whole, the concept of the object is not, however, in the least enlarged; all that has happened is that our thought has thereby obtained an additional possible perception. It is not, therefore, surprising that, if we attempt to think existence through the pure category alone, we cannot specify a single mark distinguishing it from mere possibility.

Whatever, therefore, and however much, our concept of an object may contain, we must go outside it, if we are to ascribe existence to the object. In the case of objects of the senses, this takes place through their connection with some one of our perceptions, in accordance with empirical laws. But in dealing with objects of pure thought, we have no means whatsoever of knowing their existence, since it would have to be known in a completely *a priori* manner. Our consciousness of all existence (whether immediately

through perception, or mediately through inferences which connect something with perception) belongs exclusively to the unity of experience; and [alleged] existence outside this field,
while not indeed such as we can declare to
be absolutely impossible, is of the nature of an assumption which we can never be in a position to
justify.

The concept of a supreme being is in many
respects a very useful idea; but just because it is a
mere idea, it is altogether incapable, by itself
alone, of enlarging our knowledge in regard to
what exists. It is not even competent to enlighten
us as to the *possibility* of any existence beyond
that which is known in and through experience.
The analytic criterion of possibility, as consisting
in the principle that bare positives (realities) give
rise to no contradiction, cannot be denied to it.
But since the realities are not given to us in their

specific characters; since even if they were, we
should still not be in a position to pass judgment;
since the criterion of the possibility of synthetic
knowledge is never to be looked for save in experience, to which the object of an idea cannot belong, the connection of all real properties in a
thing is a synthesis, the possibility of which we are
unable to determine *a priori*. And thus the celebrated Leibniz is far from having succeeded in
what he plumed himself on achieving—the comprehension *a priori* of the possibility of this sublime ideal being.

The attempt to establish the existence of a supreme being by means of the famous ontological
argument of Descartes is therefore merely so much
labor and effort lost; we can no more extend our
stock [theoretical] insight by mere ideas, than a
merchant can better his position by adding a few
noughts to his cash account.

I.C.3   The Ontological Argument

ALVIN PLANTINGA

*Alvin Plantinga is a professor of philosophy at the
University of Notre Dame and one of the leading
philosophers of religion today. In this reading,
Plantinga analyzes Anselm's argument, defends it
against Kant's criticism, and then constructs a modal version of the argument. That is, the argument
is set forth in terms of the modes of possibility and
necessity or in terms of possible and necessary
existence. The key premise becomes "There is a
possible world in which maximal greatness is instantiated." Plantinga explicates and defends this
premise, which rests on the premise that a being
has maximal excellence in every possible world
and which therefore entails the existence of God.
Plantinga believes that this version of the ontological argument is sound, but he doesn't claim that it*

*proves that God exists (for the argument works
only if (29) is true, and it may not be). But there is
nothing irrational about believing (29). His argument "establishes not the truth of theism, but its
rational acceptability."*

The third theistic argument I wish to discuss is the
famous "ontological argument" first formulated
by Anselm of Canterbury in the eleventh century.
This argument for the existence of God has fascinated philosophers ever since Anselm first stated
it. Few people, I should think, have been brought
to belief in God by means of this argument; nor
has it played much of a role in strengthening and
confirming religious faith. At first sight Anselm's
argument is remarkably unconvincing if not
downright irritating; it looks too much like a parlor
puzzle or word magic. And yet nearly every major

Reprinted from Alvin Plantinga, *God, Freedom and Evil* (New
York: Harper & Row, 1974) by permission of the author.

philosopher from the time of Anselm to the present has had something to say about it; this argument has a long and illustrious line of defenders extending to the present. Indeed, the last few years have seen a remarkable flurry of interest in it among philosophers. What accounts for its fascination? Not, I think, its religious significance, although that can be underrated. Perhaps there are two reasons for it. First, many of the most knotty and difficult problems in philosophy meet in this argument. Is existence a property? Are existential propositions—propositions of the form *x exists*—ever necessarily true? Are existential propositions about what they seem to be about? Are there, in any respectable sense of "are," some objects that do not exist? If so, do they have any properties? Can they be compared with things that do exist? These issues and a hundred others arise in connection with Anselm's argument. And second, although the argument certainly looks at first sight as if it ought to be unsound, it is profoundly difficult to say what, exactly, is wrong with it. Indeed, I do not believe that any philosopher has ever given a cogent and conclusive refutation of the ontological argument in its various forms. . . .

At first sight, [Anselm's] argument smacks of trumpery and deceit; but suppose we look at it a bit more closely. Its essentials are contained in these words:

> And assuredly that, than which nothing greater can be conceived, cannot exist in the understanding alone. For suppose it exists in the understanding alone; then it can be conceived to exist in reality; which is greater.
> Therefore, if that, than which nothing greater can be conceived, exists in the understanding alone, the very being, than which nothing greater can be conceived, is one, than which a greater can be conceived. But obviously this is impossible. Hence there is no doubt that there exists a being, than which nothing greater can be conceived, and it exists both in the understanding and in reality.

How can we outline this argument? It is best construed, I think, as a *reductio ad absurdum* argument. In a *reductio* you prove a given proposition *p* by showing that its denial, *not-p*, leads to (or more strictly, entails) a contradiction or some other kind of absurdity. Anselm's argument can be

seen as an attempt to deduce an absurdity from the proposition that there is no God. If we use the term "God" as an abbreviation for Anselm's phrase "the being than which nothing greater can be conceived," then the argument seems to go approximately as follows: Suppose

(1) God exists in the understanding but not in reality.
(2) Existence in reality is greater than existence in the understanding alone. (premise)
(3) God's existence in reality is conceivable. (premise)
(4) If God did exist in reality, then He would be greater than He is. [from (1) and (2)]
(5) It is conceivable that there is a being greater than God is. [(3) and (4)]
(6) It is conceivable that there be a being greater than the being than which nothing greater can be conceived. [(5) by the definition of "God"]

But surely (6) is absurd and self-contradictory; how could we conceive of a being greater than the being than which none greater can be conceived? So we may conclude that

(7) It is false that God exists in the understanding but not in reality

It follows that if God exists in the understanding, He also exists in reality; but clearly enough He *does* exist in the understanding, as even the fool will testify; therefore, He exists in reality as well.

Now when Anselm says that a being *exists in the understanding*, we may take him, I think, as saying that someone has *thought of* or thought about that being. When he says that something *exists in reality*, on the other hand, he means to say simply that the thing in question really does exist. And when he says that a certain state of affairs is *conceivable*, he means to say, I believe, that this state of affairs is possible in our broadly logical sense, there is a possible world in which it obtains. This means that step (3) above may be put more perspicuously as

(3') It is possible that God exists

and step (6) as

(6') It is possible that there be a being greater than the being than which it is not possible that there be a greater.

An interesting feature of this argument is that all of its premises are *necessarily* true if true at all. (1) is the assumption from which Anselm means to deduce a contradiction. (2) is a premise, and presumably necessarily true in Anselm's view; and (3) is the only remaining premise (the other items are consequences of preceding steps); it says of some *other* proposition (*God exists*) that it is possible. Propositions which thus ascribe a modality—possibility, necessity, contingency—to another proposition are themselves either necessarily true or necessarily false. So all the premises of the argument are, if true at all, necessarily true. And hence if the premises of this argument are true, then [provided that (6) is really inconsistent] a contradiction can be deduced from (1) together with necessary propositions; this means that (1) entails a contradiction and is, therefore, necessarily false. . . .

1. Kant's Objection

The most famous and important objection to the ontological argument is contained in Immanuel Kant's *Critique of Pure Reason*. Kant begins his criticism as follows:

If, in an identical proposition, I reject the predicate while retaining the subject, contradiction results; and I therefore say that the former belongs necessarily to the latter. But if we reject the subject and predicate alike, there is no contradiction; for nothing is then left that can be contradicted. To posit a triangle, and yet to reject its three angles, is self-contradictory; but there is no contradiction in rejecting the triangle together with its three angles. The same holds true of the concept of an absolutely necessary being. If its existence is rejected, we reject the thing itself with all its predicates; and no question of contradiction can then arise. There is nothing outside it that would then be contradicted, since the necessity of the thing is not supposed to be derived from anything external; nor is there anything internal that would be contradicted, since in rejecting the thing itself we have at the same time rejected all its internal properties. "God is omnipotent" is a necessary judgment. The omnipotence cannot be rejected if we posit a Deity, that is, an

infinite being; for the two concepts are identical. But if we say "There is no God," neither the omnipotence nor any other of its predicates is given; they are one and all rejected together with the subject, and there is therefore not the least contradiction in such a judgment. . . .

For I cannot form the least concept of a thing which, should it be rejected with all its predicates, leaves behind a contradiction.

One characteristic feature of Anselm's argument, as we have seen, is that if successful, it establishes that *God exists* is a *necessary* proposition. Here Kant is apparently arguing that no *existential* proposition—one that asserts the existence of something or other—is necessarily true; the reason, he says, is that no *contra-existential* (the denial of an existential) is contradictory or inconsistent. But in which of our several senses of inconsistent? What he means to say, I believe, is that no existential proposition is necessary in the broadly logical sense. And this claim has been popular with philosophers ever since. But why, exactly, does Kant think it's true? What is the argument? When we take a careful look at the purported reasoning, it looks pretty unimpressive; it's hard to make out an argument at all. The conclusion would apparently be this: if we deny the existence of something or other, we can't be contradicting ourselves; no existential proposition is necessary and no contra-existential is impossible. Why not? Well, if we say, for example, that God does not exist, then says Kant, "There is nothing outside it (i.e., God) that would then be contradicted, since the necessity of the thing is not supposed to be derived from anything external; nor is there anything internal that would be contradicted, since in rejecting the thing itself we have at the same time rejected all its internal properties."

But how is this even *relevant*? The claim is that *God does not exist* can't be necessarily false. What could be meant, in this context, by saying that there's nothing "outside of" God that would be contradicted if we denied His existence? What would contradict a proposition like *God does not exist* is some other proposition—*God does exist,* for example. Kant seems to think that if the proposition in question *were* necessarily false, it would have to contradict, not a proposition, but some *object* external to God—or else contradict some internal part or aspect or property of God. But this certainly looks like confusion; it is *propositions* that contradict each other; they aren't contradicted by objects or parts, aspects or properties of objects. Does he mean instead to be speaking of *propositions* about things external to God, or about his aspects or parts or properties? But clearly many such propositions do contradict *God does not exist;* an example would be *the world was created by God.* Does he mean to say that no *true* proposition contradicts *God does not exist?* No, for that would be to affirm the *nonexistence* of God, an affirmation Kant is by no means prepared to make.

So this passage is an enigma. Either Kant was confused or else he expressed himself very badly indeed. And either way we don't have any argument for the claim that contra-existential propositions can't be inconsistent. This passage seems to be no more than an elaborate and confused way of *asserting* this claim.

The heart of Kant's objection to the ontological argument, however, is contained in the following passage:

"Being" is obviously not a real predicate; that is, it is not a concept of something which could be added to the concept of a thing. It is merely the positing of a thing, or of certain determinations, as existing in themselves. Logically, it is merely the copula of a judgment. The proposition "God is omnipotent" contains two concepts, each of which has its object—God and omnipotence. The small word "is" adds no new predicate, but only serves to posit the predicate in its relation to the subject. If, now, we take the subject (God) with all its predicates (among which is omnipotence), and say "God is," or "There is a God," we attach no new predicate to the concept of God, but only posit it as an object that stands in relation to my concept. The content of both must be one and the same; nothing can have been added to the concept, which expresses merely what is possible, by my thinkings its object (through the expression "it is") as given absolutely. Otherwise stated, the real contains no more than the merely possible. A hundred real thalers not contain the least coin more than a hundred possible thalers. For as the latter signify the concept and the former the object and the positing of the concept, should the former contain more than the latter, my concept would not, in that case, express the

whole object, and would not therefore be an adequate concept of it. My financial position, however, is affected very differently by a hundred real thalers than it is by the mere concept of them (that is, of the possibility). For the object, as it actually exists, is not analytically contained in my concept, but is added to my concept (which is a determination of my state) synthetically; and yet the conceived hundred thalers are not themselves in the least increased through thus acquiring existence outside my concept.

By whatever and by however many predicates we may think a thing—even if we completely determine it—we do not make the least addition to the thing when we further declare that this thing is. Otherwise it would not be exactly the same thing that exists, but something more than we had thought in the concept: and we could not, therefore, say that the object of my concept exists. If we think in a thing every feature of reality except one, the missing reality is not added by my saying that this defective thing exists.

Now how, exactly is all this relevant to Anselm's argument? Perhaps Kant means to make a point that we could put by saying that it's not possible to *define things into existence.* (People sometimes suggest that the ontological argument is just such an attempt to define *God* into existence.) And this claim is somehow connected with Kant's famous but perplexing *dictum* that *being* (or existence) is not a real predicate or property. But how shall we understand Kant here? What does it mean to say that existence isn't (or is) a real property?

Apparently Kant thinks this is equivalent to or follows from what he puts variously as "the real *contains* no more than the merely possible"; "the *content* of both (i.e., concept and object) must be one and the same"; "being is not the concept of something that could be *added to* the concept of a thing," and so on. But what does all this mean? And how does it bear on the ontological argument? Perhaps Kant is thinking along the following lines. In defining a concept—*bachelor*, let's say, or *prime number*—one lists a number of properties that are *severally necessary* and *jointly sufficient* for the concept's applying to something. That is, the concept applies to a given thing only if that thing has each of the listed properties, and if a thing does have them all, then the concept in question applies to it. So, for example, to define the concept *bachelor* we list such properties as *being unmarried, being male, being over the age of twenty-five,* and the like. Take any one of these properties: a thing is a bachelor only if it has it, and if a thing has all of them, then it follows that it is a bachelor.

Now suppose you have a concept C that has application *contingently* if at all. That is to say, it is not necessarily true that there are things to which this concept applies. The concept *bachelor* would be an example; the proposition *there are bachelors,* while *true,* is obviously not necessarily true. And suppose P_1, P_2 . . . , P_n are the properties jointly sufficient and severally necessary for something's falling under C. Then C can be defined as follows:

- A thing x is an instance of C (i.e., C applies to x) if and only if x has P_1, P_2 . . . , P_n.

Perhaps Kant's point is this. There is a certain kind of mistake here we may be tempted to make. Suppose P_1, . . . , P_n are the defining properties for the concept *bachelor.* We might try to define a new concept *superbachelor* by adding *existence* to P_1, . . . , P_n. That is, we might say

- x is a superbachelor if and only if x has P_1, P_2, . . . , P_n, and x exists.

Then (as we might mistakenly suppose) just as it is a necessary truth that bachelors are unmarried, so it is a necessary truth that superbachelors exist. And in this way it looks as if we've defined superbachelors into existence.

But of course this is a mistake, and perhaps that is Kant's point. For while indeed it is a necessary truth that bachelors are unmarried, what this means is that the proposition

(8) Everything that is a bachelor is unmarried

is necessarily true. Similarly, then,

(9) Everything that is a superbachelor exists

will be necessarily true. But obviously it doesn't follow that there *are* any superbachelors. All that follows is that

(10) All the superbachelors there are *exist*

which is not really very startling. If it is a contingent truth, furthermore, that there are bachelors, it will be equally contingent that there are superbachelors. We can see this by noting that the defining properties of the concept *bachelor* are included among those of *superbachelor;* it is a necessary truth, therefore, that every superbachelor is a bachelor. This means that

(11) There are some superbachelors

entails

(12) There are some bachelors.

But then if (12) is contingent, so is (11). Indeed, the concepts *bachelor* and *superbachelor* are equivalent in the following sense: it is impossible that there exists an object to which one but not the other of these two concepts applies. We've just seen that every superbachelor must be a bachelor. Conversely, however, every bachelor is a superbachelor: for every bachelor exists and every existent bachelor is a superbachelor. Now perhaps we can put Kant's point more exactly. Suppose we say that a property or predicate P is *real* only if there is some list of properties P_1 to P_n such that the result of adding P to the list does not define a concept equivalent (in the above sense) to that defined by the list. It then follows, of course, that existence is not a real property or predicate. Kant's point, then, is that one cannot *define things into existence* because *existence* is not a real property or predicate in the explained sense.

2. The Irrelevance of Kant's Objection

If this is what he means, he's certainly right. But is it relevant to the ontological argument? Couldn't Anselm thank Kant for this interesting point and proceed merrily on his way? Where did he try to define God into being by adding existence to a list of properties that defined some concept? According to the great German philosopher and pessimist Arthur Schopenhauer, the ontological argument arises when "someone excogitates a conception, composed out of all sorts of predicates, among which, however, he takes care to include the predicate actuality or existence, either openly or wrapped up for decency's sake in some other predicate, such as perfection, immensity, or something of the kind." If this were Anselm's procedure—if he had simply added existence to a concept that has application contingently if at all—then indeed his argument would be subject to the Kantian criticism. But he didn't, and it isn't.

The usual criticisms of Anselm's argument, then, leave much to be desired. Of course, this doesn't mean that the argument is successful, but it does mean that we shall have to take an independent look at it. What about Anselm's argument? Is it a good one? The first thing to recognize is that the ontological argument comes in an enormous variety of versions, some of which may be much more promising than others. Instead of speaking of *the* ontological argument, we must recognize that what we have here is a whole family of related arguments. (Having said this I shall violate my own directive and continue to speak of *the* ontological argument.)

3. The Argument Restated

Let's look once again at our initial schematization of the argument. I think perhaps it is step (2)

(2) Existence in reality is greater than existence in the understanding alone

that is most puzzling here. Earlier we spoke of the properties in virtue of which one being is greater, just as a being, than another. Suppose we call them *great-making properties*. Apparently Anselm means to suggest that *existence* is a great-making property. He seems to suggest that a nonexistent being would be greater than in fact it is, if it did exist. But how can we make sense of that? How could there be a nonexistent being anyway? Does that so much as make sense?

Perhaps we can put this perspicuously in terms of possible worlds. You recall that an object may exist in some possible worlds and not others. There are possible worlds in which you and I do

not exist; these worlds are impoverished, no doubt, but are not on that account impossible. Furthermore, you recall that an object can have different properties in different worlds. In the actual world Paul J. Zwier is not a good tennis player; but surely there are worlds in which he wins the Wimbledon Open. Now if a person can have different properties in different worlds, then he can have different degrees of greatness in different worlds. In the actual world Raquel Welch has impressive assets; but there is a world RW_f in which she is fifty pounds overweight and mousy. Indeed, there are worlds in which she does not so much as exist. What Anselm means to be suggesting, I think, is that Raquel Welch enjoys very little greatness in those worlds in which she does not exist. But of course this condition is not restricted to Miss Welch. What Anselm means to say, more generally, is that for any being x and worlds W and W', if x exists in W but not in W', then x's greatness in W exceeds x's greatness in W'. Or, more modestly, perhaps he means to say that if a being x does not exist in a world W (and there is a world in which x does exist), then *there is at least one world* in which the greatness of x exceeds the greatness of x in W. Suppose Raquel Welch does not exist in some world W. Anselm means to say that there is at least one possible world in which she has a degree of greatness that exceeds the degree of greatness she has in that world W. (It is plausible, indeed, to go much further and hold that she has *no greatness at all* in worlds in which she does not exist.)

But now perhaps we can restate the whole argument in a way that gives us more insight into its real structure. Once more, use the term "God" to abbreviate the phrase "the being than which it is not possible that there be a greater." Now suppose

(13) God does not exist in the actual world

Add the new version of premise (2):

(14) For any being x and world W, if x does not exist in W, then there is a world W' such that the greatness of x in W' exceeds the greatness of x in W.

Restate premise (3) in terms of possible worlds:

(15) There is a possible world in which God exists.

And continue on:

(16) If God does not exist in the actual world, then there is a world *W'* such that the greatness of God in *W'* exceeds the greatness of God in the actual world. [from (14)]

(17) So there is a world *W'* such that the greatness of God in *W'* exceeds the greatness of God in the actual world. [(13) and (16)]

(18) So there is a possible being *x* and a world *W'* such that the greatness of *x* in *W'* exceeds the greatness of God in actuality. [(17)]

(19) Hence it's possible that there be a being greater than God is. [(18)]

(20) So it's possible that there be a being greater than the being than which it's not possible that there be a greater. (19), replacing "God" by what it abbreviates

But surely

(21) It's not possible that there be a being greater than the being than which it's not possible that there be a greater.

So (13) [with the help of premises (14) and (15)] appears to imply (20), which, according to (21), is necessarily false. Accordingly, (13) is false. So the actual world contains a being than which it's not possible that there be a greater—that is, God exists.

Now where, if anywhere, can we fault this argument? Step (13) is the hypothesis for *reductio,* the assumption to be reduced to absurdity, and is thus entirely above reproach. Steps (16) through (20) certainly look as if they follow from the items they are said to follow from. So that leaves only (14), (15), and (20). Step (14) says only that it is possible that God exists. Step (15) also certainly seems plausible: if a being doesn't even *exist* in a given world, it can't have much by way of greatness in that world. At the very least it can't have its *maximum* degree of greatness—a degree of greatness that it does not excel in any other world—in a world where it doesn't exist. And consider (20): surely it has the ring of truth. How could there be a

being greater than the being than which it's not possible that there be a greater? Initially, the argument seems pretty formidable.

4. Its Fatal Flaw

But there is something puzzling about it. We can see this if we ask what sorts of things (14) is supposed to be *about*. It starts off boldly: "For any being *x* and world *W*, . . ." So (14) is talking about worlds and beings. It says something about each world-being pair. And (16) follows from it, because (16) asserts of *God* and *the actual world* something that according to (14) holds of every being and world. But then if (16) follows from (14), God must be a *being*. That is, (16) follows from (14) only with the help of the additional premise that God is a being. And doesn't this statement—that God is a being—imply that *there is* or *exists* a being than which it's not possible that there be a greater? But if so, the argument flagrantly begs the question; for then we can accept the inference from (14) to (16) only if we already know that the conclusion is true.

We can approach this same matter by a slightly different route. I asked earlier what sorts of things (14) was *about;* the answer was: beings and worlds. We can ask the same or nearly the same question by asking about the *range* of the *quantifiers*—"for any being," "for any world"—in (14). What do these quantifiers range over? If we reply that they range over possible worlds and beings—*actually existing* beings—then the inference to (16) requires the additional premise that God is an actually existing being, that there *really is* a being than which it is not possible that there be a greater. Since this is supposed to be our conclusion, we can't very gracefully add it as a *premise.* So perhaps the quantifiers don't range just over actually existing beings. But what else is there? Step (18) speaks of a *possible being*—a thing that may not in fact exist, but *could* exist. Or we could put it like this. A possible being is a thing that exists in some possible world or other; a thing *x* for which there is a world *W*, such that if *W* had been actual, *x* would have existed. So (18) is really about worlds and *possible beings*. And what it says is this: take any possible being x and any possible world W. If x does not exist in W, then there is a possible world W ' where x has a degree of greatness that surpasses the greatness that it has in W. And hence to make the argument complete perhaps we should add the affirmation that God is a *possible being*.

But *are* there any possible beings—that is, *merely* possible beings, beings that don't in fact exist? If so, what sorts of things are they? Do they have properties? How are we to think of them? What is their status? And what reasons are there for supposing that there are any such peculiar items at all?

These are knotty problems: Must we settle them in order even to consider this argument? No. For instead of speaking of *possible beings* and the worlds in which they do or don't exist, we can speak of *properties* and the worlds in which they do or don't *have instances,* are or are not *instantiated* or *exemplified.* Instead of speaking of a possible being named by the phrase, "the being than which it's not possible that there be a greater," we may speak of the property *having an unsurpassable degree of greatness*—that is, *having a degree of greatness such that it's not possible that there exist a being having more.* And then we can ask whether this property is instantiated in this or other possible worlds. Later on I shall show how to restate the argument this way. For the moment please take my word for the fact that we can speak as freely as we wish about possible objects; for we can always translate ostensible talk about such things into talk about properties and the worlds in which they are or are not instantiated.

The argument speaks, therefore, of an unsurpassably great being—of a being whose greatness is not excelled by any being in any world. This being has a degree of greatness so impressive that no other being in any world has more. But here we hit the question crucial for this version of the argument. *Where* does this being have that degree of greatness? I said above that the same being may have different degrees of greatness in different worlds; in which world does the possible being in question have the degree of greatness in question?

All we are really told, in being told that God is a possible being, is this: among the possible beings there is one that in some world or other has a degree of greatness that is nowhere excelled.

And this fact is fatal to this version of the argument. I said earlier that (21) has the ring of truth; a closer look (listen?) reveals that it's more of a dull thud. For it is ambiguous as between

(21') It's not possible that there be a being whose greatness surpasses that enjoyed by the unsurpassably great being *in the worlds where its greatness is at a maximum*

and

(21") It's not possible that there be a being whose greatness surpasses that enjoyed by the unsurpassably great being *in the actual world.*

There is an important difference between these two. The greatest possible being may have different degrees of greatness in different worlds. Step (21') points to the worlds in which this being has its maximal greatness; and it says, quite properly, that the degree of greatness this being has in those worlds is nowhere excelled. Clearly this is so. The greatest possible being is a possible being who in some world or other has unsurpassable greatness. Unfortunately for the argument, however, (21') does not contradict (20). Or to put it another way, what follows from (13) [together with (14) and (15)] is not the denial of (21'). If that *did* follow, then the *reductio* would be complete and the argument successful. But what (20) says is not that there is a possible being whose greatness exceeds that enjoyed by the greatest possible being *in a world where the latter's greatness is at a maximum;* it says only that there is a possible being whose greatness exceeds that enjoyed by the greatest possible being *in the actual world*—where, for all we know, its greatness is *not* at a maximum. So if we read (21) as (21'), the *reductio* argument falls apart.

Suppose instead we read it as (21"). Then what it says is that there couldn't be a being whose greatness surpasses that enjoyed by the greatest possible being in Kronos, the actual world. So read, (21) does contradict (20). Unfortunately, however, we have no reason, so far, for thinking that (21″) is true at all, let alone necessarily true. If, among the possible beings, there is one whose greatness *in some world or other* is absolutely maximal—such that no being in any world has a degree of greatness surpassing it—then indeed there couldn't be a being that was greater than *that*. But it doesn't follow that this being has that degree of greatness in the *actual* world. It has it *in some world or other* but not necessarily in Kronos, the actual world. And so the argument fails. If we take (21) as (21′), then it follows from the assertion that God is a possible being; but it is of no use to the argument. If we take it as (21″), on the other hand, then indeed it is useful in the argument, but we have no reason whatever to think it true. So this version of the argument fails.

5. A Modal Version of the Argument

But of course there are many other versions; one of the argument's chief features is its many-sided diversity. The fact that *this* version is unsatisfactory does not show that *every* version is or must be. Professors Charles Hartshorne and Norman Malcolm claim to detect two quite different versions of the argument in Anselm's work. In the first of these versions *existence* is held to be a perfection or a great-making property; in the second it is *necessary existence*. But what could *that* amount to? Perhaps something like this. Consider a pair of beings *A* and *B* that both do in fact exist. And suppose that *A* exists in every other possible world as well—that is, if any other possible world has been actual, *A* would have existed. On the other hand, *B* exists in only some possible worlds; there are worlds *W* such that had any of *them* been actual, *B* would not have existed. Now according to the doctrine under consideration, *A* is so far greater than *B*. Of course, *on balance* it may be that *A* is not greater than *B*; I believe that the number seven, unlike Spiro Agnew, exists in every possible world; yet I should be hesitant to affirm on that account that the number seven is greater than Agnew. Necessary existence is just one of several great-making properties, and no doubt

Agnew has more of some of these others than does the number seven. Still, all this is compatible with saying that necessary existence is a great-making property. And given this notion, we can restate the argument as follows:

(22) It is possible that there is a greatest possible being.

(23) Therefore, there is a possible being that in some world *W′* or other has a maximum degree of greatness—a degree of greatness that is nowhere exceeded.

(24) A being *B* has the maximum degree of greatness in a given possible world *W* only if *B* *exists in every possible world.*

(22) and (24) are the premises of this argument; and what follows is that if *W′* had been actual, *B* would have existed in every possible world. That is, if *W′* had been actual, *B*'s nonexistence would have been impossible. But logical possibilities and impossibilities do not vary from world to world. That is to say, if a given proposition or state of affairs is impossible in at least one possible world, then it is impossible in every possible world. There are no propositions that in fact are possible but could have been impossible; there are none that are in fact impossible but could have been possible. Accordingly, *B*'s nonexistence is impossible in every possible world; hence it is impossible in *this* world; hence *B* exists and exists necessarily.

6. A Flaw in the Ointment

This is an interesting argument, but it suffers from at least one annoying defect. What it shows is that if it is possible that there be a greatest possible being (if the idea of a greatest possible being is coherent) and if that idea includes necessary existence, then in fact there is a being that exists in every world and in *some* world has a degree of greatness that is nowhere excelled. Unfortunately it doesn't follow that the being in question has the degree of greatness in question in Kronos, the actual world. For all the argument shows, this being might *exist* in the actual world but be pretty insignificant here. In some world or other it has maximal greatness; how does this show that it has such greatness in Kronos?

But perhaps we can repair the argument. J. N. Findlay once offered what can only be called an ontological *disproof* of the existence of God. Findlay begins by pointing out that God, if He exists, is an "adequate object of religious worship." But such a being, he says, would have to be a *necessary* being; and, he adds, this idea is incredible "for all who share a contemporary outlook." "Those who believe in necessary truths which aren't merely tautological think that such truths merely connect the *possible* instances of various characteristics with each other; they don't expect such truths to tell them whether there *will* be instances of any characteristics. This is the outcome of the whole medieval and Kantian criticism of the ontological proof." I've argued above that "the whole medieval and Kantian criticism" of Anselm's argument may be taken with a grain or two of salt. And certainly most philosophers who believe that there are necessary truths, believe that *some* of them *do* tell us whether there will be instances of certain characteristics; the proposition *there are no married bachelors* is necessarily true, and it tells us that there will be no instances whatever of the characteristic *married bachelor.* Be that as it may what is presently relevant in Findlay's piece is this passage:

Not only is it contrary to the demands and claims inherent in religious attitudes that their object should *exist* "accidentally"; it is also contrary to these demands that it should *possess its various excellences* in some merely adventitious manner. It would be quite unsatisfactory from the religious stand point, if an object merely *happened* to be wise, good, powerful, and so forth, even to a superlative degree. . . . And so we are led on irresistibly, by the demands inherent in religious reverence, to hold that an adequate object of our worship must possess its various excellences *in some necessary manner.*

I think there is truth in these remarks. We could put the point as follows. In determining the greatness of a being *B* in a world *W,* what counts is not merely the qualities and properties possessed by *B in W;* what *B* is like in *other* worlds is also relevant. Most of us who believe in God think of

Him as a being than whom it's not possible that there be a greater. But we don't think of Him as a being who, had things been different, would have been powerless or uninformed or of dubious moral character. God doesn't *just happen* to be a greatest possible being; He couldn't have been otherwise.

Perhaps we should make a distinction here between *greatness* and *excellence.* A being's excellence in a given world *W,* let us say, depends only upon the properties it has in *W;* its *greatness* in *W* depends upon these properties but also upon what it is like in other worlds. Those who are fond of the calculus might put it by saying that there is a function assigning to each being in each world a degree of excellence; and a being's *greatness* is to be computed (by someone unusually well informed) by integrating its excellence over all possible worlds. Then it is plausible to suppose that the maximal degree of greatness entails *maximal excellence in every world.* A being, then, has the maximal degree of *greatness* in a given world *W* only if it has *maximal excellence in every possible world.* But *maximal excellence* entails *omniscience, omnipotence,* and *moral perfection.* That is to say, a being *B* has maximal excellence in a world *W* only if *B* has omniscience, omnipotence, and moral perfection in *W*—only if *B* would have been omniscient, omnipotent, and morally perfect if *W* had been actual.

7. The Argument Restated

Given these ideas, we can restate the present version of the argument in the following more explicit way.

(25) It is possible that there be a being that has maximal greatness.

(26) So there is a possible being that in some world *W* has maximal greatness.

(27) A Being has maximal greatness in a given world only if it has maximal excellence in every world.

(28) A being has maximal excellence in a given

world only if it has omniscience, omnipotence, and moral perfection in that world.

And now we no longer need the supposition that necessary existence is a perfection; for obviously a being can't be omnipotent (or for that matter omniscient or morally perfect) in a given world unless it *exists* in that world. From (25), (27), and (28) it follows that there actually exists a being that is omnipotent, omniscient, and morally perfect; this being, furthermore, exists and has these qualities in every other world as well. For (26), which follows from (25), tells us that there is a possible world *W'*, let's say, in which there exists a being with maximal greatness. That is, had *W'* been actual, there would have been a being with maximal greatness. But then according to (27) this being has maximal excellence in every world. What this means, according to (28), is that in *W'* this being has omniscience, omnipotence, and moral perfection *in every world*. That is to say, if *W'* had been actual, there would have existed a being who was omniscient and omnipotent and morally perfect and who would have had these properties in every possible world. So if *W'* had been actual, it would have been *impossible* that there be no omnipotent, omniscient, and morally perfect being. But while *contingent* truths vary from world to world, what is logically impossible does not. Therefore, in every possible world *W* it is impossible that there be no such being; each possible world *W* is such that if it had been actual, it would have been impossible that there be no such being. And hence it is impossible in the *actual* world (which is one of the possible worlds) that there be no omniscient, omnipotent, and morally perfect being. Hence there really does exist a being who is omniscient, omnipotent, and morally perfect and who exists and has these properties in every possible world. Accordingly these premises, (25), (27), and (28), entail that God, so thought of, exists. Indeed, if we regard (27) and (28) as consequences of a *definition*—a definition of maximal greatness—then the only premise of the argument is (25).

But now for a last objection suggested earlier. What about (25)? It says that there is a *possible being* having such and such characteristics. But

what *are* possible beings? We know what *actual* beings are—the Taj Mahal, Socrates, you and I, the Grand Teton—these are among the more impressive examples of actually existing beings. But what is a *possible* being? Is there a possible mountain just like Mt. Rainier two miles directly south of the Grand Teton? If so, it is located at the same place as the Middle Teton. Does that matter? Is there another such possible mountain three miles east of the Grand Teton, where Jenny Lake is? Are there possible mountains like this all over the world? Are there also possible oceans at all the places where there are possible mountains? For any place you mention, of course, it is *possible* that there be a mountain there; does it follow that in fact *there is* a possible mountain there?

These are some questions that arise when we ask ourselves whether there are merely possible beings that don't in fact exist. And the version of the ontological argument we've been considering seems to make sense only on the assumption that there are such things. The earlier versions also depended on that assumption; consider for example, this step of the first version we considered:

(18) So there is a possible being *x* and a world *W'* such that the greatness of *x* in *W'* exceeds the greatness of God in actuality.

This possible being, you recall, was God Himself, supposed not to exist in the actual world. We can make sense of (18), therefore, only if we are prepared to grant that there are possible beings who don't in fact exist. Such beings exist in other worlds, of course; had things been appropriately different, they would have existed. But in fact they don't exist, although nonetheless there *are* such things.

I am inclined to think the supposition that there are such things—things that are possible but don't in fact exist—is either unintelligible or necessarily false. But this doesn't mean that the present version of the ontological argument must be rejected. For we can restate the argument in a way that does not commit us to this questionable idea. Instead of speaking of *possible beings* that do or do not exist in various possible worlds, we may speak of *properties* and the worlds in which they are or are not *instantiated*. Instead of speaking of the possible fat man in the corner, noting that he doesn't exist, we may speak of the property *being a fat man in the corner,* noting that it isn't instantiated (although it could have been). Of course, the *property* in question, like the property *being a unicorn,* exists. It is a perfectly good property which exists with as much equanimity as the property of equininity, the property of being a horse. But it doesn't happen to apply to anything. That is, in *this* world it doesn't apply to anything; in other possible worlds it does.

8. The Argument Triumphant

Using this idea we can restate this last version of the ontological argument in such a way that it no longer matters whether there are any merely possible beings that do not exist. Instead of speaking of the possible being that has, in some world or other, a maximal degree of greatness, we may speak of *the property of being maximally great* or *maximal greatness.* The premise corresponding to (25) then says simply that maximal greatness is possibly instantiated, i.e., that

(29) There is a possible world in which maximal greatness is instantiated.

And the analogues of (27) and (28) spell out what is involved in maximal greatness:

(30) Necessarily, a being is maximally great only if it has maximal excellence in every world

and

(31) Necessarily, a being has maximal excellence in every world only if it has omniscience, omnipotence, and moral perfection in every world.

Notice that (30) and (31) do not imply that there are possible but nonexistent beings—any more than does, for example,

(32) Necessarily, a thing is a unicorn only if it has one horn.

But if (29) is true, then there is a possible world *W* such that if it had been actual, then there would have existed a being that was omnipotent, omniscient, and morally perfect; this being, furthermore, would have had these qualities in every possible world. So it follows that if *W* had been actual, it would have been *impossible* that there be no such being. That is, if *W* had been actual,

(33) There is no omnipotent, omniscient, and morally perfect being

would have been an impossible proposition. But if a proposition is impossible in at least one possible world, then it is impossible in every possible world; what is impossible does not vary from world to world. Accordingly (33) is impossible in the *actual* world, i.e., impossible *simpliciter*. But if it is impossible that there be no such being, then there actually exists a being that is omnipotent, omniscient, and morally perfect; this being, furthermore, has these qualities essentially and exists in every possible world.

What shall we say of this argument? It is certainly valid; given its premise, the conclusion follows. The only question of interest, it seems to me, is whether its main premise—that maximal greatness *is* possibly instantiated—is *true*. I think it *is* true; hence I think this version of the ontological argument is sound.

But here we must be careful; we must ask whether this argument is a successful piece of natural theology, whether it *proves* the existence of God. And the answer must be, I think, that it does not. An argument for God's existence may be *sound*, after all, without in any useful sense proving God's existence. Since I believe in God, I think the following argument is sound:

- Either God exists or $7 + 5 = 14$
- It is false that $7 + 5 = 14$
- Therefore God exists.

But obviously this isn't a *proof*; no one who didn't already accept the conclusion, would accept the first premise. The ontological argument we've been examining isn't just like this one, of course, but it must be conceded that not everyone who understands and reflects on its central premise—

that the existence of a maximally great being is *possible*—will accept it. Still, it is evident, I think, that there is nothing *contrary to reason* or *irrational* in accepting this premise. What I claim for this

argument, therefore, is that it establishes, not the *truth* of theism, but its rational acceptability. And hence it accomplishes at least one of the aims of the tradition of natural theology.

I.C.4 Modal Versions of the Ontological Argument

WILLIAM ROWE

William Rowe is professor of philosophy at Purdue University. In this essay he critically analyzes Plantinga's version of the ontological argument, appreciating its brilliance but leveling some objections at what it claims to have accomplished.

It has sometimes been thought that two distinct ontological arguments can be found in chapters 2 and 3 of Anselm's *Proslogium*. It is clear that in chapter 2 Anselm intended to set forth an argument for God's existence. He there introduces his concept of God as a being than which none greater is possible, and he advances the principle that existence in reality contributes to the greatness of a being. He then argues that God, as conceived by him, exists in reality—for otherwise a being greater than the greatest possible being would be possible.[1] Having satisfied himself that God's existence has been established, in chapter 3 Anselm turns to consider the mode or way in which God exists. Some things, like cabbages and kings, exist only *contingently*. It is possible that they should not have existed at all. Put in the language of possible worlds, we might say that the possible world that happens to be actual contains cabbages and kings.[2] Other possible worlds, however, do no contain them; and had one of those worlds been the actual world, cabbages and kings would not have existed.

Does God exist only contingently? Anselm thought not, for a being would be greater if it ex-

isted in such a way that it logically could not fail to exist. Put in the language of possible worlds, a being would be greater if it is contained in *every* possible world rather than in just some possible worlds. So if God exists contingently, it would be possible for God to be greater than he is. Since it is not possible for God to be greater than he is, God must exist *necessarily*.

As I have interpreted Anselm, he did not intend in chapter 3 to be offering a further argument for God's existence. Instead, he wanted to determine whether God, whose existence he had already established in chapter 2 exists contingently or necessarily. But whatever his intentions may have been, it is not difficult to see in chapter 3 the makings of a distinct argument for God's existence. For chapter 3 presents us with the principle that *necessary existence,* no less than the *existence in reality* of chapter 2, contributes to the greatness of a being. If it is possible for Anselm's God to possess necessary existence, then that is the sort of existence he does possess—otherwise it would be possible for God to be greater.

Reflection on chapter 3 of Anselm's *Proslogium* has led philosophers to create various modal versions of the ontological argument. Among the most interesting versions is one set forth by Alvin Plantinga. Plantinga's version has the merit of extraordinary simplicity. By defining the concept of maximal greatness in a certain manner, Plantinga is able to boil down his version of the argument to the assertion of a single premise: that there is a possible world in which the property of maximal greatness is instantiated. Another merit of Plantinga's version is that it makes use of the idea of possible worlds, thus reducing the logic of the mo-

This article was written specifically for this volume and appears here for the first time.

dal argument to its most intuitive level. Before we consider his version, however, let's prepare ourselves for some of the questions we need to raise by examining two quite simple ontological arguments that are suggested by the reasoning in chapters 2 and 3 of Anselm's *Proslogium*.

Consider two distinct concepts of God that I will call G_1 and G_2. We shall define G_1 as follows:

> G_1 = the concept of an omnipotent, omniscient, wholly good being who is such that he exists with these perfections in the actual world.

G_2 is defined as follows:

> G_2 = the concept of an omnipotent, omniscient, wholly good being who is such that he exists with these perfections in every possible world.

Let us say that a *normal* concept C of a being or kind of being is *satisfied* in a given possible world just in case, were that world actual, that being or a being of that kind would exist. Thus the concept *elephant* is satisfied in our world, but the concept *unicorn* is not. For our world is actual and elephants do exist, but unicorns do not. In some other possible world, however, just the reverse is true—the concept *unicorn* is satisfied, but the concept *elephant* is not. For if that world were actual, at least one unicorn would exist, but no elephants would exist. Armed with this idea of what it is for a normal concept of a being (or kind of being) to be *satisfied* in a possible world, let's consider our two concepts of God introduced above.

With a little reflection, I think we can see that our first concept, G_1, may not be a *normal* concept. To ask whether the normal concept *unicorn* is satisfied in w is simply to ask whether a unicorn would exist if w were actual. Where w is some possible world other than the possible world that is in fact actual, the question of whether the concept *unicorn* is satisfied in w has nothing to do with whether unicorns, elephants, cabbages, or kings exist in the actual world. But this is not so with G_1. Whether G_1 is satisfied in w depends in part on what sorts of beings *actually exist*, what

sorts of beings exist in the actual world. It is not enough that w contains an omnipotent, omniscient, wholly good being. For unless *that being* exists in the actual world with just those perfections, G_1 is not satisfied in w. The important point to grasp here is that the satisfaction of G_1 in any possible world depends on the *actual existence* of an omnipotent, omniscient, wholly good being.[3]

The following argument is suggested by the reasoning of *Proslogium 2:*

(1) There is a possible world in which G_1 is satisfied.

Therefore,

(2) There exists an omnipotent, omniscient, wholly good being.

This argument is logically valid. Is its premise true? Well, that depends, as we've seen, on what beings are contained in the actual world. If every existing being has some moral defect, then there is no possible world in which G_1 is *in fact* satisfied.

For an argument to be a *proof* of its conclusion we must know its premise(s) to be true without basing that knowledge on a prior knowledge of its conclusion. Is it logically possible for some human being to know (1) to be true without basing that knowledge on knowing (2) to be true? It would be rash to answer no to this question. For it is difficult to draw *logical* limits to the ways in which human beings might come to know that a certain proposition is true. But perhaps we can say this much. It is exceedingly difficult to see how some human being would in fact come to a knowledge of (1) independently of knowing (2). So it is more than likely true that this argument is not a proof of its conclusion for any human being.

G_2 is a more far-reaching concept than is G_1. For G_1's being satisfied in a possible world w requires that the actual world contain an omnipotent, omniscient, wholly good being but allows that many other possible worlds lack such a being. G_2, however, is satisfied in a possible world w only if *every* possible world (including the actual world) contains an omnipotent, omniscient, wholly good being. In the spirit of *Proslogium 3,* if not the letter, we can construct the following argument.

(3) There is a possible world in which G_2 is satisfied.

Therefore,

(4) There necessarily exists an omnipotent, omniscient, wholly good being.

Once we realize that the satisfaction of G_2 in *any* possible world requires the existence of an omnipotent, omniscient, wholly good being in *every* possible world, we can appreciate the extraordinary difficulty of viewing this argument as a *proof* of its conclusion. Perhaps if we know that the actual world contains an omnipotent, omniscient, wholly good being, we might begin to ponder whether this being holds forth in all or just some possible worlds. But it is difficult to see how merely reflecting on the concept G_2 can enable us to know that it is satisfied in some possible world. For, as we've noted, its satisfaction in *any* possible world depends on what is contained in *every* possible world. But again, it would be unwise to declare that it is logically impossible for someone to come to know (3) independently of knowing (4), or even (2). But few, I believe, would be inclined to view this argument as a *proof* of its conclusion.

For reasons we need not consider here, Plantinga prefers to state his modal version of the ontological argument in terms of whether a certain property—the property of being maximally great—is instantiated in any possible world. For a property to be instantiated in a world *w* is for it to be true that if *w* were actual some thing would exist having that property. Thus the property of being an elephant is instantiated in our possible world, but the property of being a unicorn is not. Plantinga's property of being maximally great, however, is vastly different from such pedestrian properties as being an elephant or being a unicorn. The question of whether these two properties are instantiated in some possible but nonactual world *w* doesn't at all depend on whether the actual world contains elephants or unicorns. But Plantinga's property of being maximally great can be instantiated in some possible world *w* only if the actual world contains a being that is omnipotent, omniscient, and morally perfect. And even

this is not enough. Not only must the actual world contain an omnipotent, omniscient, and morally perfect being, but *every* possible world must contain a being having these marvelous attributes, and it must be the *same* being who has these attributes in all these different worlds. Once we understand all this, we can see what an extraordinary property it is to which Plantinga has drawn our attention. If any possible world whatever happens to lack an omnipotent, omniscient, and morally perfect being, then Plantinga's extraordinary property is an impossible property and is instantiated in no possible world.

Analogous to our argument concerning concept G_2, the following argument is valid:

(5) There is a possible world in which maximal greatness is instantiated.

Therefore,

(6) There necessarily exists an omnipotent, omniscient, and morally perfect being.

And, for reasons given in connection with our two earlier arguments, it is extremely unlikely that this argument is a *proof* of its conclusion.

Consider the property of being in less than perfect company, where it is understood that a person has that property in a world *w* just in case every person in *w* (human and nonhuman) has some degree of imperfection, however slight. It may be that we enjoy (or are burdened with) this property in the actual world. But even if we are not, surely, one would think, it is *possible* that this property be instantiated. Surely there is some possible world in which every person has some imperfection, however slight. But if so, then Plantinga's extraordinary property is impossible; there is no possible world in which it is instantiated. If either of these properties is instantiated in some world *w*, then the other is uninstantiated in *w* and in every other possible world. Since only one can be instantiated, which, if either, might it be? The instantiation of Plantinga's extraordinary property in a possible world *w* is *dependent* on what every other possible world contains—every possible world must contain an omnipotent, omniscient, and morally perfect being. The instantiation in *w* of the property of being in less than perfect company requires only that each person *in w* have some flaw, however slight. If you know nothing else relevant to your decision and had to bet on which property is possibly instantiated, knowing that both cannot be, which would you bet on?

Although Plantinga accepts the version of the ontological argument that he sets forth, he acknowledges that it is not a *proof* of its conclusion. It does not, he notes, establish the truth of theism. What then does the argument do? It establishes, Plantinga claims, the *rational acceptability* of theism. It does this, Plantinga argues, because the premise of the argument, proposition (5), is something that can be believed without violating any rule of reason concerning what we may or may not believe. Since we do no wrong in accepting (5), and since we acknowledge that (5) entails the truth of theism, we do no wrong in accepting the truth of theism. If it is not wrong for me to believe a proposition, then that proposition is rationally acceptable for me.

Perhaps the first point to note about Plantinga's claim is that in his view the premise of an argument may be rationally acceptable and may thus establish the rational acceptability of the argument's conclusion, even though one doesn't know the premise to be true, and even though the truth of the premise is a matter of significant controversy. After all, some who reflect on the amount of tragic evil in our world are committed to the view that the property of being in less than perfect company is instantiated in our world. Others, including a number who believe that there exists an omnipotent, omniscient, and morally perfect being, would insist that there is some possible world in which the property of being in less than perfect company is instantiated. Both groups, therefore, are committed to the denial of Plantinga's premise that there is some possible world in which maximal greatness is instantiated. Still others may hold that there is simply no way of telling whether maximal greatness is possibly instantiated. So the premise of Plantinga's argument is denied by many and held in question by others. Moreover, Plantinga offers no argument for his premise and acknowledges that reflecting on it

does not enable us to somehow *see* that it must be true; he does not claim that after sufficient reflection the inquiring mind somehow comes to find his premise *self-evident*.

What, then, does Plantinga claim for his premise? He claims, as we've seen, that it is not *irrational* to accept it, that in accepting it one does not violate any rules concerning what we may or may not believe. Of course, if it were a rule that one must not accept a premise unless one can prove it or has some good evidence for it, Plantinga would be unjustified in accepting his premise. But the "rule" just mentioned is difficult to defend. Perhaps what Plantinga holds is this: There are circumstances in which it is *permissible* to believe a proposition even though you cannot prove it and don't have good evidence for it. What are these circumstances? Well, one circumstance, surely, is that you have no good reason to think the proposition false. (Some think that the idea of a maximally great being is like the idea of a largest integer—an impossible object. But this may well be wrong. It might be that we have no good reason to think Plantinga's premise false.) The other circumstances that must obtain are difficult to specify. But if we agree with Plantinga about this, then I think we can say that it *may* be permissible for someone to believe Plantinga's premise. Plantinga says something much stronger. He says it is "evident" that believing his premise is permissible. This claim, I believe, is excessive. We need to be much clearer about the circumstances that must obtain for Plantinga's premise to be acceptable before we declare its acceptability with the unabashed assurance Plantinga here expresses.

Some philosophers declare that the ontological argument in all its versions commits some gross fallacy or contains some obviously false premise. Plantinga's careful work on the argument helps us to see that we can confidently reject such criticisms. But when the argument is set forth with care and rigor, we can see, I believe, how very difficult it is to know or establish the truth of its premise(s). (Indeed, in some versions one has great difficulty in even imagining how one might know the premise(s) without basing such knowledge on a prior knowledge of the conclusion.) I think Plantinga sees this as well. Anselm's high hope of discovering an argument that would conclusively establish God's existence remains unfulfilled, even in Plantinga's skillful hands. As a consolation prize, Plantinga proposes a weak sense of rational acceptability that he claims is satisfied by the premise of his modal version of the argument. Anselm thought that if we really understood the argument it would be obvious that it is a sound demonstration of the existence of God. To reject the argument, therefore, is to be foolish. Plantinga makes no such claim. He holds only that it is clear that one is not foolish to accept it. If I am right, all that has been shown is that it may not be foolish to accept it. To *establish* that it is not foolish requires that we become clear that its premise satisfies all the circumstances (whatever they are) that are required for it to be permissible to believe a proposition even though we cannot prove it and don't have good evidence for it.

Notes

1. This argument has fascinated philosophers and theologians for centuries. For an exposition of the argument and the major objections to it, see my essay, "The Ontological Argument," in my *Philosophy of Religion* (Belmont, Calif.: Wadsworth, 1978).

2. The idea of *possible worlds* is explained briefly and clearly in Alvin Plantinga's *God, Freedom and Evil* (New York: Harper & Row, 1974), 34–39.

3. G_1 is an *abnormal* concept if there is a possible world in which no perfect being exists. For in that case, G_1's being satisfied in w depends in part upon *which* possible world is actual. Suppose possible world w^* contains an omnipotent, omniscient, wholly good being, but possible world w^{**} does not. If w^* is the actual world, then depending on what w contains, G_1 may be satisfied in w. But if w^{**} is the actual world, then no matter what w contains, G_1 is not satisfied in w. G_2, although a more far-reaching concept than G_1, is, however, a *normal* concept. Although its being satisfied in w depends upon what is contained in every other possible world, its being satisfied in w does not depend on *which* possible world is actual.

I.C.5 An Ontological Argument for the Devil

DAVID AND MARJORIE HAIGHT

David and Marjorie Haight, who teach philosophy at Iowa State University, argue that the ontological argument for God's existence can be turned on its head and used to prove that the devil exists as the supreme being in place of a benevolent God.

After so many centuries of debate, much of it even quite recent, as to the credibility of Anselm's and others' ontological arguments for the existence of God, it seems only fair to the opposition that some such argument be proposed for Satan's existence. It must be noted, however, that in advocating the Devil's existence, we may be no more than playing the Devil's advocate.

Reprinted from *The Monist,* vol. 54 (1970), pp. 218–20, by permission of The Hegeler Institute, La Salle, Ill.

We intend to argue that *if* Anselm's first ontological argument successfully proves that God indeed exists, then, by parity of reasoning, Satan, or the devil, exists as well. Or, to put in conversely, we shall claim that if Satan does not exist, then neither can God, at least in terms of what the Anselmian argument asserts. Finally, we shall claim that if Satan does not exist, it will *not* be because of the possible fact that the ontological argument establishes God's existence, but rather it will be because of something that the Anselmian argument *presupposes,* which may not be provable in any argument.

Anselm's first argument, roughly, is as follows:

(1) I have a concept of something "than which nothing greater can be conceived."

(2) If that "something" did not actually, or in fact,

exist, it would not be "that than which nothing greater can be conceived," for something could always be conceived to be greater, viz., something that actually exists.

(3) This "greatest something" is, by logical equivalence, or definition, "God."

(∴) God exists.

An ontological argument for the devil, by analogue of reason, goes as follows:

(1) I have a concept of something than which nothing *worse* can be conceived.

(2) If that "something" did not actually, or in fact, exist, it would not be "that than which nothing worse could be conceived," because something could always be conceived to be much worse, viz., something that actually exists.

(3) This "greatest something" we shall call the Devil.

(∴) The Devil exists.

This second ontological argument, by parity of reasoning with the first, seems sound, if indeed, the first is. Is it not conceivable that not only do we have an idea of something that is the worst possible thing, but that it would *have* to exist if it truly *were* the worst possible thing? Hence, the very possibility of the Devil implies his actuality, just as the very possibility of God implies his existence. The logic is the same, in both cases: a devil would not be the Devil unless he existed and was therefore the most awful thing, just as a god would not be God unless he existed and was therefore the greatest thing.

This ontological argument for Satan seems shocking enough, at least at first reading, but something even more startling might be suggested: the two arguments are not only analogous—they are identical. Might it not be suggested that they both establish the existence of the *one* thing—call it God or Satan—namely, a supreme Being who is the "greatest" and the "worst" possible being. This suggestion, however, can be made good *only if* it can be plausibly argued that the word 'greater' in the first argument does *not* imply the word 'better'. For it is surely the case that if Anselm means "better" when he uses the word 'greater', there would be an overt contradiction between the two ontological arguments, viz., the conflict between a "best being" and a "worst being." But does Anselm, in fact, mean "better" by 'greater'? It has definitely been claimed, subsequent to Anselm, that his argument assumes "existence to be a perfection," or that it is *better* to be than not to be, and, with this supplementation, it certainly seems to be the case that Anselm equated the two terms or at least implied the one by the other.

But is this really explicit in Anselm's argument? Is he saying that existence is a perfection? If he is, then his argument seems question-begging, because the argument seems to assume what it purports to prove, viz., that it is better for God to exist than not to exist. Presumably, too, if existence is good, God must be good, but one may not be able to assume that existence is good without, first, proving that God exists and is good. Hence, one cannot, or must not, reverse the order of argument such as Anselm seems to do—one must not assume that existence is good or a perfection unless one has *already* proved God's existence. But, actually, the plausibility of Anselm's proof, at least as it has been here paraphrased, is partly contingent upon the word 'greater'. The "greatest" possible being must be God. Or, it might be the Devil, for it does not follow from Anselm's argument that God is good, only that he exists. And if the word 'greater' does not involve "perfection," then both ontological arguments establish the existence of one and only one being. It is then a matter of faith as to whether one calls it God or Satan, a benign *daemon* or a malicious demon. And this faith may, after all, be simply cause of itself.

I.D   The Relevance to Religion of the "Proofs"

What bearing do the traditional arguments for the existence of God have on religious life? Are the so-called proofs merely intellectual games that philosophers play, of no relevance for the believer or the unbeliever? In the nineteenth century the Christian existentialist Søren Kierkegaard (1813–1855) attacked the practice of trying to prove the existence of God. The arguments are useless, he claimed, for the believer doesn't need them and the unbeliever won't heed them. "Whoever therefore attempts to demonstrate the existence of God . . . is an excellent subject for a comedy of the higher lunacy."* What's more, continues Kierkegaard, rational endeavor with regard to the existence of God is a bad thing, for it distracts one from worship and service (see the article by Kierkegaard in Part 7 of this work).

We have included two articles with different responses to the question of the relevance of the proofs to religion. First, Steven M. Cahn, in his article "The Irrelevance to Religion of Philosophic Proofs for the Existence of God," continues the Kierkegaardian critique. Unbelievers won't heed the proofs, and believers don't need them, for they have something better—a self-validating experience of God, which for them is infallible. Furthermore, even if the proofs are successful, they are irrelevant for the practical moral life. For even if we know that God always wills what is morally good, simply knowing that God exists doesn't help us know what is morally good. Knowing that it is good to do God's will turns out to be an empty notion. This is another instance of the is/ought problem pointed out by David Hume.

So there remains only one possible way to know God's will. "One must undergo a personal experience in which one senses the presence of God and apprehends which of the putative holy books is the genuine one," Cahn writes. "One must undergo a self-validating experience, one which carries its own infallibility." In this case one doesn't need any further evidence or proof, and even if the "proof" turns out to be invalid, it doesn't matter to the believer. Religion will not be affected in the least by the outcome of the philosophic proofs.

In our second article, "What Good are Theistic Proofs?" by Stephen T. Davis, we have a more conciliatory view of the matter. Davis agrees with Cahn that the proofs do not succeed in convincing unbelievers and that believers aren't terribly affected by their fate. Nevertheless he does not believe that discussing the theistic proofs is a waste of time. They can be both philosophically and religiously valuable.

First Davis discusses in detail what a successful theistic proof would be. He rejects several formulations and concludes that such a proof would have to *demonstrate the rationality of belief in the existence of God.* That is, it would have to substantiate the theist's belief in God, showing it to be credible, and it would be an endeavor to prove this rationality to all rational persons. Davis believes that some versions of the ontological argument may meet this criterion; at least they have not been refuted.

Davis responds to the objection that the proofs don't convince skeptics and unbelievers by saying that this may be because none of the existing proofs are successful, or because the defenders have done a bad job defending them, or simply because it is difficult to persuade others in such a complicated matter.

Responding to Cahn's central point that it is foolish to try to prove something that you already know, Davis argues that sometimes believers are just what that term signifies: *believers.* They do not know or claim to know whether what they believe is really true. They are not absolutely certain about their beliefs,

---

* *Philosophical Fragments,* translated by David F. Swenson (Princeton: Princeton University Press, 1936), 34.

and so reasoning may give them added confidence.

In sum there are two benefits to be derived from a successful theistic proof (i.e., a proof demonstrating that it is rational to believe in the existence of God). First, it would allow theists to make full use of their rational faculties in arriving at or continuing in belief in God's existence. Second, it would show that belief is rationally justified. Davis's point about both of these benefits is that the religious and rational aspects of belief are not two separate domains. The religious includes the domain of rational justification and is not altogether separate from it. In the end, however, Davis concedes that the proofs are optional for theists. One believes not because of the proofs but because of religious experience.

You will want to ask yourself, Who is closer to the truth, Cahn or Davis? Or is the matter of rationality even more serious than either of these philosophers suggest? Why could not a strong argument (or a cumulative case) for the existence (or nonexistence) of God convince people and cause them to change their minds? I have known people to lose their faith because they concluded that the proofs didn't work, and I have known others to come to faith because they thought that the proofs were sufficiently convincing. How would Cahn account for these phenomena? What place do (or should) these arguments for God's existence have in your world view?

Although there are only two readings on this issue, the issue itself is discussed further under other topics in this book: in Part 2 on religious experience and in Part 7 on the relation of faith to reason. I hope these two articles stimulate your thinking on this matter and help you to work out your own positions as you continue through the succeeding parts of this volume.

I.D.1 The Irrelevance to Religion of Philosophic Proofs for the Existence of God

STEVEN M. CAHN

Steven M. Cahn is Acting Director for the Humanities for the Rockefeller Foundation. In this article he argues that the proofs are useless, since the believer doesn't need them and the unbeliever isn't convinced by them. Even if the nonbeliever were intellectually convinced by them, he or she would not necessarily have a religious experience, which is at the heart of religion.

Philosophic proofs for the existence of God have a long and distinguished history. Almost every major Western philosopher has been seriously concerned with defending or refuting such proofs.

Reprinted from the *American Philosophical Quarterly*, 6 (1969), by permission of the *American Philosophical Quarterly*. Footnotes deleted.

Furthermore, many contemporary philosophers have exhibited keen interest in such proofs. A survey of the philosophical literature of the past decade reveals quite a concentration of work in this area.

One might expect that religious believers would be vitally interested in discussions of this subject. One might suppose that when a proof of God's existence is presented and eloquently defended, believers would be most enthusiastic, and that when a proof is attacked and persuasively refuted, believers would be seriously disappointed. But this is not at all the case. Religious believers seem remarkably uninterested in philosophic proofs for the existence of God. They seem to consider discussion of such proofs as a sort of intellectual game which has no relevance to religious belief or activity. And this view is shared by proponents of both supernaturalist and naturalist varieties of religion. For example, Søren Kierkegaard, a foremost proponent of supernaturalist religion, remarked: "Whoever therefore attempts to demonstrate the existence of God . . . [is] an excellent subject for a comedy of the higher lunacy!" The same essential point is made in a somewhat less flamboyant manner by Mordecai M. Kaplan, a foremost proponent of naturalist religion, who remarks that the "immense amount of mental effort to prove the existence of God . . . was in vain, since unbelievers seldom become believers as a result of logical arguments."

In what follows, I wish to explain just why religious believers have so little interest in philosophic proofs for the existence of God. I wish to show that their lack of interest is entirely reasonable, and that whatever the philosophic relevance of such proofs, they have little or no relevance to religion.

The three classic proofs for the existence of God are the ontological, the cosmological, and the teleological. Each of these proofs is intended to prove something different. The ontological argument is intended to prove the existence (or necessary existence) of the most perfect conceivable Being. The cosmological argument is intended to prove the existence of a necessary Being who is the Prime Mover or First Cause of the universe. The teleological argument is intended to prove the existence of an all-good designer and creator of the universe.

Suppose we assume, contrary to what most philosophers, I among them, believe, that all of these proofs are valid. Let us grant the necessary existence (whatever than might mean) of the most perfect conceivable Being, a Being who is all-good and is the designer and creator of the universe. What implications can be drawn from this fact which would be of relevance to human life? In other words, what difference would it make in men's lives if God existed?

Perhaps some men would feel more secure in the knowledge that the universe had been planned by an all-good Being. Others, perhaps, would feel insecure, realizing the extent to which their very existence depended upon the will of this Being. In any case, most men, either out of fear or respect, would wish to act in accordance with the moral code advocated by this Being.

Note, however, that the proofs for the existence of God provide us with no hint whatever as to which actions God wishes us to perform, or what we ought to do so as to please or obey Him. We may affirm that God is all-good and yet have no way of knowing what the highest moral standards are. All we may be sure of is that whatever these standards may be, God always acts in accordance with them. One might assume that God would have implanted the correct moral standards in men's minds, but this seems doubtful in view of the wide variance in men's moral standards. Which of these numerous standards, if any, is the correct one is not known, and no appeal to a proof for the existence of God will cast the least light upon the matter.

For example, assuming that it can be proven that God exists, is murder immoral? One might argue that since God created man, it is immoral to murder, since it is immoral to destroy what God in His infinite wisdom and goodness has created. This argument, however, fails on several grounds. First, if God created man, He also created germs, viruses, disease-carrying rats, and man-eating sharks. Does it follow from the fact that God created these things that they ought not to be eliminated? Secondly, if God arranged for men to live, He also arranged for men to die. Does it follow from this that by committing murder we are assisting the work of God? Thirdly, if God created man, He provided him with the mental and physical capacity to commit murder. Does it follow from this that God wishes men to commit murder? Clearly, the attempt to deduce moral precepts from the fact of God's existence is but another case of trying to do what Hume long ago pointed out to be logically impossible, viz., the deduction of normative judgments from factual premises. No such deduction is valid, and, thus, any moral principle is consistent with the existence of God.

The fact that the proofs of God's existence afford no means of distinguishing good from evil has the consequence that no man can be sure of how to obey God and do what is best in His eyes. One may hope that his actions are in accord with God's standards, but no test is available to check on this. Some seemingly good men suffer great ills, and some seemingly evil men achieve great happiness. Perhaps in a future life these things are rectified, but we have no way of ascertaining which men are ultimately rewarded and which are ultimately punished.

One can imagine that if a group of men believed in God's existence, there would be most anxious to learn His will, and consequently, they would tend to rely upon those individuals who claimed to know the will of God. Diviners, seers, and priests would be in a position of great influence. No doubt competition between them would be severe, for no man could be sure which of these oracles to believe. Assuming that God made no effort to reveal His will by granting one of these oracles truly superhuman powers (though, naturally, each oracle would claim that he possessed such powers), no man could distinguish the genuine prophet from the fraud.

It is clear that the situation I have described is paralleled by a stage in the actual development of religion. What men wanted at this stage was some way to find out the will of God. Individual prophets might gain a substantial following, but prophets died and their vital powers died with them. What was needed on practical grounds was a permanent record of God's will as revealed to His special prophet. And this need was eventually met by the writing of holy books, books in which God's will was revealed in a permanent fashion.

But there was more than one such book. Indeed, there were many such books. Which was to be believed? Which moral code was to be followed? Which prayers were to be recited? Which rituals were to be performed? Proofs for the existence of God are silent upon these crucial matters.

There is only one possible avenue to God's will. One must undergo a personal experience in which one senses the presence of God and apprehends which of the putative holy books is the genuine one. But it is most important not to be deceived in this experience. One must be absolutely certain that it is God whose presence one is experiencing and whose will one is apprehending. In other words, one must undergo a self-validating experience, one which carries its own guarantee of infallibility.

If one undergoes what he believes to be such an experience, he then is certain which holy book is the genuine one, and consequently he knows which actions, prayers, and rituals God wishes him to engage in. But notice that if he knows this, he has necessarily validated the existence of God, for unless he is absolutely certain that he has experienced God's presence, he cannot be sure that the message he has received is true. Thus, he has no further need for a proof of God's existence.

For one who does not undergo what he believes to be such a self-validating experience, several possibilities remain open. He may accept the validity of another person's self-validating experience. He thereby accepts the holy book which has been revealed as genuine, and he thereby also accepts the existence of God, since unless he believed that this other person had experienced the presence of God, he would not accept this person's opinion as to which is the genuine book.

It is possible, however, that one does not accept the validity of another person's supposedly self-validating experience. This may be due either to philosophical doubts concerning the logical possibility of such an experience or simply to practical doubts that anyone has, in fact, ever undergone such an experience. In either case, adherence to a particular supernatural religion is unreasonable.

But having no adherence to a supernatural religion does not imply that one does not still face the serious moral dilemmas which are inherent in life. How are these dilemmas to be solved? To believe that God exists is of no avail, for one cannot learn His will. Therefore, one must use one's own judgment. But this need not be solely an individual effort. One may join others in a communal effort to propound and promulgate a moral code. Such a group may have its own distinctive prayers and rituals which emphasize various aspects of the group's beliefs. Such a naturalistic religious organization does not depend upon its members' belief in the existence of God, for such a belief is irrelevant to the religious aims and activities of the group.

Is it surprising then that proponents of both supernaturalist and naturalist religion are uninterested in philosophic proofs for the existence of God? Not at all. A supernaturalist believes in God because of a personal self-validating experience which has shown him (or someone he trusts) not only that God exists, but also what His will is. A philosophic proof of the existence of God is thus of no use to the supernaturalist. If the proof is shown to be valid, it merely confirms what he already knows on the much stronger evidence of personal experience. If the proof is shown to be invalid, it casts no doubt on a self-validating experience.

On the other hand, the naturalist believes either that no one has learned or that no one can learn the will of God. If, therefore, a proof for the existence of God is shown to be valid, this has no implications for the naturalist, for such a proof does not provide him with any information which he can utilize in his religious practice. If, on the contrary, a proof for the existence of God is shown to be invalid, this casts no doubt on the naturalist's religious views, since these views have been formulated independently of a belief in the existence of God.

Who, then, is concerned with philosophic proofs for the existence of God? First, there are those who believe that if such proofs are invalid, religion is thereby undermined. This is, as I have shown, a wholly erroneous view. Neither supernaturalist nor naturalist religion depends at all upon philosophic proofs for the existence of God. To attack religion on the grounds that it cannot provide a philosophic proof for the existence of God is an instance of *ignoratio elenchi*.

Secondly, there are those who believe that if the philosophic proofs for the existence of God are invalid, our moral commitments are necessarily undermined. This is also, as I have shown, a wholly erroneous view. It is, however, a common view, and one which underlies the so-called moral argument for the existence of God. According to this argument, it is only if one believes in the existence of God that one can reasonably commit oneself to respect the importance of moral values. This argument is invalid, however, for, as I have shown, belief in the existence of God is compatible with any and all positions on moral issues. It is only if one can learn the will of God that one can derive any moral implications from His existence.

Thirdly, there are philosophers who discuss proofs for the existence of God because of the important philosophical issues which are brought to light and clarified in such discussions. So long as philosophers are aware of the purpose which their discussions serve, all is well and good. It is when philosophers and others use discussions of this sort as arguments for and against religion that they overstep their bounds. Religion may be rationally attacked or defended, but to refute philosophic proofs for the existence of God is not to attack religion, and to support philosophic proofs for the existence of God is not to defend religion.

I.D.2   What Good Are Theistic Proofs?

STEPHEN T. DAVIS

Stephen T. Davis is professor of philosophy at Claremont McKenna College. In this essay he disagrees with Cahn on the value of the proofs. Davis first clarifies what a successful proof of the existence of God would be, and then he argues that, although believers do not need to define proofs to support their faith, nevertheless there are aspects of the exercise that are valuable for them.

One of the most interesting facts about the enterprise of trying to prove the existence of God is its longevity. In Book X of Plato's *Laws* (written in the fourth century BC) we find a version of what we now call the cosmological argument.[1] Ever since then, philosophers have spent a great deal of time and effort debating various attempts to prove that God exists. The arguments that we call the ontological, cosmological, teleological, and moral proofs have been enormously fascinating to philosophers of every stripe, even to many who have no other particular interest in religion or the philosophy of religion. This interest continues in the twentieth century—scores of books and hundreds of articles have been written on the theistic proofs in the past eighty years or so. One could almost say that debate about the existence of God is a consuming passion of twentieth-century philosophers of religion.

It is odd that this should be the case. For several reasons, theistic proofs are widely criticized and even denigrated—by believers and unbelievers in God alike. First, most (but not quite all) of the participants in the debate concede that none of the theistic proofs succeeds in demonstrating the existence of God. Second, and perhaps for the above reason, it is often pointed out that the theis-

tic proofs are unpersuasive; they just do not succeed in convincing unbelievers. For myself, I do not think I have every met anyone who was converted to belief in God because of one of the proofs. Third, theologians, religious people, and some philosophers play down or even scoff at the proofs as totally irrelevant to religious faith and practice. Believers don't need the proofs—why try to demonstrate something you already know? And the proofs, it is said, are cold, formal, and philosophical; they do not call for faith or commitment, nor do they meet our spiritual needs. Fourth, the "God" of the theistic proofs, it is said, is a mere philosophical abstraction (a "necessary being," the "Greatest Conceivable Being," the "Prime Mover," etc.) rather than the living God of the Bible. Finally, one recent theologian, Paul Tillich, rejects the proofs because (he says) they end up denying divine transcendence. To say that "God exists," Tillich claims, is to place God on the same level as the creatures. God becomes a "being" like all the other existing "beings" rather than "the ground of being."[2]

What good are the theistic proofs, then? Why bother trying to prove that God exists? Or why bother discussing seriously the attempts of others to do so? Is this not so much wasted effort? In this paper I will attempt to answer these questions. I do not believe that discussing theistic proofs need be a waste of time. That is, I believe the theistic proofs can be religiously and philosophically valuable. That is what I will try to show.

I

It will be helpful to begin by defining some terms. First, let us say that "God" is the God of theism, that is, a unique, eternal, all-powerful, all-knowing, and loving spirit who created the heavens and earth and works for the salvation of human beings.

This article was written specifically for this volume and appears in print here for the first time. The author would like to thank Professors Linda Zagzebski and Bill Alston for helpful comments on an earlier draft of this paper.

Second, let us say that a "theistic proof" is an argument whose conclusion is identical to or equivalent with the statement "God exists." It tries to prove that God is real or actual, that God exists independently of our minds. Third, let us say that an "argument" is a set of words arranged in a series of sentences in which one sentence consists of the conclusion and the other sentence or sentences consist of the premise or premises, and in which the premise or premises are designed to provide intellectual support for or proof of the conclusion. Fourth, let us say that a "valid" argument is one that makes no error in logic; accordingly, if the premises are true, the conclusion logically must be true. Finally, let us say that a "sound" argument is a valid argument all of whose premises are true.

The next question we need to ask is, What would constitute a *good* or *successful* theistic proof?[3] Let us see if we can answer this question by considering various theistic proofs. Suppose we begin with the following:

(1) All the people in Claremont are people;
(2) Some people believe in God;
(3) Therefore, God exists.

Now this is obviously a feeble attempt to prove the existence of God. Probably the most noticeable problem with it is that it is invalid—the conclusion does not follow from the premises. Let us then try to remedy this difficulty by coming up with a theistic proof that is formally valid:

(4) If God exists then God exists;
(5) God exists;
(6) Therefore, God exists.

But this argument too is feeble—doubtless few atheists or agnostics will come to believe in the existence of God because of it. It is true that the argument is *formally valid:* if (4) and (5) are true (6) must be true. That is, it is impossible for (4) and (5) to be true and (6) false. But the argument assumes in premise (5) exactly what it is trying to prove; accordingly, no sensible person who doubts the conclusion will grant premise (5). Classically, then, this is an argument that commits the infor-

mal fallacy of "begging the question." The argument, then, is *informally invalid*.

Consider also the following two arguments:

(7) Everything the Bible says is true;
(8) The Bible says that God exists;
(9) Therefore, God exists;

and

(10) Either God exists or 7 + 5 = 13;
(11) 7 + 5 does not = 13;
(12) Therefore, God exists.[4]

These arguments too seem to beg the question. As far as the first is concerned, it does so because no one who denies or doubts (9) will grant that both (7) and (8) are true. Premise (8) is perhaps beyond reproach, but (7) will be singularly unappealing to atheists or agnostics. The second argument is a bit more complicated; it is surely formally valid, and those who believe in God, as I do, will hold that it is also sound. Nearly everyone will grant (11), and I for one am happy to grant 10. But the problem again is that no sensible person who denies or doubts the conclusion will grant (10); there is no reason to grant (10) apart from a prior commitment to the existence of God. Thus this argument too begs the question.

Another major informal fallacy is that of "equivocation"—that is, using the same word in two different senses—as for example in the following argument: "The audience gave her a hand; therefore, the audience gave her something; therefore, the audience gave her something with five fingers." A theistic proof that commits the fallacy of equivocation might be stated as follows:

(13) I believe in God;
(14) Therefore, God exists;
(15) Therefore, God exists.

Here the word *exists* is used in two different ways. If premise (13) all by itself is to entail premise (14), then the word *exists* in (14) must mean something like "exists in my mind" (or as Anselm would have said, exists *in intellectu*). But if the above argument is to count as a theistic proof, then the word *exists* in (15) must mean something quite different. It must mean something like "exists independently of my mind" (exists *in re,* as Anselm would have it). Thus this argument too is quite worthless as an attempt to prove the existence of God.

We appear then so far to have arrived at two criteria that a theistic proof must satisfy in order to count as successful: it must be formally valid and it must be informally valid. That is, it must be the case that the truth of the premises logically requires the truth of the conclusion, and it must be the case that the argument avoids question begging, equivocation, and all other informal fallacies. But clearly these criteria are insufficient. Notice the following argument:

(16) Anything everyone believes is true;
(17) Everyone believes in the existence of God;
(18) Therefore, God exists.

This argument seems to me to satisfy both of the above criteria—it is valid both formally and informally—but it is clearly a poor attempt at a theistic proof. It fails, I think, because (16) and (17) are both false—the argument is unsound. (An argument is unsound if *any* of its premises is false, let alone if both or all of them are.) Thus it seems we must add some third criterion that has something to do with the truth of the premises. But here too we find complications; how exactly shall we specify this third criterion?

Which of the following shall we say that the premises of a successful theistic proof must be?

(a) possibly true;
(b) known to be possibly true;
(c) more reasonable or plausible than their denials;
(d) known to be more reasonable or plausible than their denials;
(e) reasonable or plausible;
(f) known to be reasonable or plausible;
(g) true;
(h) known to be true;
(i) necessarily true; or
(j) known to be necessarily true?

Some of these candidates can surely be ruled out—(a) and (b) are doubtless too weak; if they were acceptable the (16)–(18) argument might well count as a successful theistic proof, for both

(16) and (17) are possibly true and known to be so. Both (c) and (d) are also probably too weak. A premise might be just slightly more plausible than its denial; if so, we will want to deny that any theistic proof in which it appears is successful. And (i) and (j) are doubtless too strong. But where do we go from here? Which of the remaining candidates—(e), (f), (g), or (h)—shall we opt for? What we have concluded so far is that a successful theistic proof is formally and informally valid and satisfies one of the four remaining candidates for the third criterion. Which candidate we pick, it seems to me, will depend on our view as to the *purpose* of a theistic proof. Let us then ask, What is or ought to be the aim, goal, or purpose of a theistic proof?

II

Here too we find difficulties. There are several ways of envisioning the goal or purpose of a theistic proof. There is perhaps a common assumption behind most discussions of theistic proofs, an assumption made by both defenders and critics of these arguments, namely, that theism is in better epistemic shape, so to speak, if a theistic proof succeeds than it is if none succeeds. But beyond that point of general (but not quite universal) agreement, there are at least three ways in which we might try to define success for a theistic proof.

One possibility is to say that a successful theistic proof is one that *convinces people that God exists.* But which people? (a) Perhaps a successful proof convinces *everyone who hears and follows it* that God exists. But of course it is extremely doubtful that any proof will ever do that. (b) Perhaps then a successful proof is one that convinces every *rational* person who hears and follows it that God exists. This notion is a bit more promising than the first, but the difficulty here is that we will never be able to tell whether a proof is successful because we have no precise criteria for determining which people are rational. (c) Perhaps we ought to say that a successful proof is one that convinces all rational people *who believe its premises* that God exists. (I am assuming both here and elsewhere that it makes sense to speak of both believers and unbelievers in a proposition *p* as "being convinced" that *p* is true; in the second case but not the first a change of mind is involved.) But this is surely too liberal a notion of success. On the basis of this notion, the (7)–(9) and the (10)–(12) arguments above are probably successful theistic proofs, and that is something we do not want to grant. (d) Perhaps we ought to say that a successful theistic proof is one that convinces at least *some* of the people who hear and follow it that God exists. But this notion is also too liberal— probably lots of feeble theistic proofs (possibly including some of the ones mentioned above) will convince somebody somewhere that God exists.

Suppose we consider another possibility. A successful theistic proof, we might say, is one that *demonstrates the rationality of belief in God.* That is, it is one that substantiates or provides good grounds for belief in the existence of God. It creates a situation in which rational people who hear and follow the proof may rationally believe in the existence of God. But here too we face the question, To whom is a theistic proof addressed? Does a successful proof demonstrate to everyone the rationality of belief in God? Or just to all rational persons? Or just to all rational persons who believe the premises? Or just to some of the persons who hear and follow the proof?

A third possibility is to define a successful theistic proof as one that *strengthens the faith of theists,* that is, strengthens the conviction of those who already believe in God. But although some theistic proofs probably do achieve this end, and in some cases this might be an end well worth achieving, it is doubtful that we ought to understand success for a theistic proof in this way. For one thing, possibly something like the (7)–(9) argument above would strengthen the faith of some theists, but we will not want to call that argument a successful proof. Furthermore, in the case of the actual theistic proofs discussed by philosophers,—for example, the ontological, cosmological, teleological, and moral arguments—stronger aims than this one are clearly had in mind by the people who propose them.

It seems to me that the second of the above

possibilities is by far the most promising. Without claiming that this was precisely what was had in mind by such defenders of theistic proofs as Plato, Anselm, Aquinas, Paley, Kant, and so on, I will hold that the purpose, aim, or goal of a theistic proof is to *demonstrate the rationality of belief in the existence of God.* That is, what a theistic proof aims to do is substantiate the theist's belief in God, give a good reason for it, show that it is credible. And theistic proofs, I suggest, try to demonstrate the rationality of theistic belief to *all rational persons* (whoever exactly they are).

This causes me to say that the third criterion (besides formal validity and informal validity) of a good or successful theistic proof is either (e) or (f) above. That is, the premises of a good or successful theistic proof must be either *reasonable or plausible* or else *known to be reasonable or plausible.* Of course a theistic proof would be even more able to demonstrate the rationality of theism if it satisfied the stronger criterion that its premises must be *known to be true.* But I opt for the slightly weaker criterion because there are premises that have not been proved and that may not be known to be true but that, being recognized as at least plausible or rational, can appear as premises in a successful theistic proof.

I think for example of that statement that appears in many versions of the ontological argument, namely, "The Greatest Conceivable Being is a possible being." I would claim to know this statement, but surely many others would dispute such a claim. And I see no way of proving the statement apart from showing that the Greatest Conceivable Being is actual (all actual beings are possible beings). Nevertheless, if this being *seems* to me to be a possible being, and if I have apparently answered successfully all the known arguments to the contrary, then I know to be plausible the statement, "The Greatest Conceivable Being is a possible being." Accordingly, I can rationally believe the statement, and I can use it as a premise in a successful theistic proof.

Between candidates (e) and (f) for the third criterion of a successful theistic proof, (f) is to be preferred. It is crucial that the premises of a successful theistic proof be not just *plausible* but *known to be plausible.* But known to whom? They must be known by the people to whom the rationality of belief in the existence of God is to be demonstrated (including presumably, the person who offers the proof). If the premises of a theistic proof are plausible but the relevant people do not know them or recognize that they are plausible, the rationality of theism will not be demonstrated to them. Neither believers nor unbelievers in the existence of God will receive the intended benefit, namely, recognition of the rationality of belief in the existence of God.

Of course there may be premises that some people know to be plausible and others don't. (Notoriously, this situation seems frequently to occur in discussions of theistic proofs, e.g., with statements like "Every existing thing has a reason for its existence," or "The universe is like a watch.") If these premises appear in an otherwise successful theistic proof, then the rationality of belief in the existence of God will have been demonstrated to those who know that the premises in question are plausible (if there are any such people) but not to those who do not.

In summary, then, a good or successful theistic proof satisfies the following criteria:

1. It is formally valid;
2. It is informally valid;
3. Its premises are known to be plausible.

A theistic proof that satisfies these criteria (if any such argument ever does) demonstrates the rationality of belief in the existence of God. It shows that rational people can rationally believe in the existence of God.

III

What then would be the result if some logician or philosopher of religion were able to produce a successful, or at least apparently successful, theistic proof? Suppose it were an argument of the form we call *modus ponens* and went something like this:

(19) If *p* is true, then God exists;

(20) *p* is true;
(21) Therefore, God exists.

Or perhaps the argument might run as follows:

(22) If *q* is true, it is probable that God exists;
(23) *q* is true;
(24) Therefore, it is probable that God exists.

Now arguments of this form would surely be formally valid. Suppose that they were also informally valid and that the premises were known to be plausible. What would or should our reaction be?

Our first thought might be to return to the various criticisms mentioned at the outset of this paper that have been raised against theistic proofs. We might wonder what ought to be said about them in the light of the existence of an apparently successful theistic proof. So let us now take a second look at those criticisms. The first point was not so much a criticism as a recognition of the odd fact that debate about theistic proofs thrives despite general but not universal agreement that no actual theistic proof succeeds. But even if all this is true, it constitutes no good argument against the continued thriving of the industry. Perhaps the majority is wrong; perhaps some existing theistic proof succeeds despite the failure of the majority to recognize its success. (I myself hold that there are versions of the ontological argument that have not been refuted.) Or even if the majority is right and no theistic proof succeeds, perhaps engaging in the enterprise of discussing theistic proofs is valuable anyway, that is, for some other reason.

The second point was that theistic proofs don't convince religious skeptics and unbelievers to believe in the existence of God. That is surely true, but perhaps it is merely because no successful theistic proof yet exists; or perhaps it is because defenders of successful theistic proofs have thus far done a poor job of defending them; or perhaps it is because atheists and agnostics are too stubborn. Few arguments possess irresistible force; few coerce people on pain of irrationality, so to speak, into accepting their conclusions. So even if a successful theistic proof existed we should expect (as Norman Malcolm once suggested)[5] few conversions. It is always possible to find some reason to reject an argument whose conclusion one finds repugnant.

The third point was that theistic proofs are irrelevant to religious faith and practice. And it does seem odd to try to prove something that you already know—for example, that San Francisco is north of Los Angeles, or that Napoleon Bonaparte is dead. But perhaps it is not so odd to try to prove something you believe but do not know (which is how many theists would describe their cognitive state vis-à-vis the existence of God). And it is surely not at all odd to try to prove something you believe or even know, when the proof is aimed at someone else who neither knows nor believes it. It is also true that the theistic proofs do not do a good job of meeting human spiritual needs—the cosmological argument, for example, calls few people to religious commitment. The teleological argument does not tell us how to worship or pray. The moral argument does not teach us any lessons about forgiving each other. But why is that a problem? Naturally, there are many crucial tasks theistic proofs do not succeed in doing—for example, feeding hungry people. There are even crucial intellectual tasks theistic proofs do not succeed in doing—for example, solving the problem of evil. Is the fact that they fail to do these things a reason for us all to opt out of the debate over theistic proofs? Of course not. Perhaps there are other crucial tasks the theistic proofs *can* perform. (What they might be I will discuss below.)

The fourth point was that the "God" spoken of in the theistic proofs is a philosophical abstraction rather than the living God of the Bible. And one can appreciate what is being said here. As is well known, Aquinas finishes each of his "five ways" of demonstrating the existence of God with some such statement as, "and this everyone understands to be God." It has been frequently and correctly pointed out that what he claims here is not necessarily true. Despite Aquinas's attempts to argue otherwise, it is logically possible for a first mover, a first cause, and a necessary being that owes its necessity to no other being to exist without possessing such characteristic properties of God as omnipotence, omniscience, compassion, and so

on. The beings whose existence Aquinas tries to prove, in short, do not have to be God. Furthermore, the beings spoken of in typical theistic proofs do seem more like metaphysical principles than living beings. But the criticism of theistic proofs we are considering here would be immeasurably stronger, in my view, if it could be shown that such beings as "the Greatest Conceivable Being," "the Designer of the Universe," "the Prime Mover," and so on, *cannot* be God, that is, if some of their properties are inconsistent with some of the properties of the living God of the Bible. But that has not been shown and (I think) is not true.[6]

The fifth point was Tillich's insistence that God is not a "being" and that to try to prove "the existence of God" is illicitly to place God on the same level as finite beings. But I confess I have never been able to grasp how it lessens or destroys God's transcendence over the creatures to say that God is a being. Why can't we state that God "is a being" and "exists" without denying that God's existence is of a radically different sort than ours? And whether or not we choose to regard God as sharing some of our properties—for example, the property of being a being, the property of knowing the sum of six and five, the property of desiring peace on earth—we will still want to be free to ask whether or not God is real, whether the atheists are right or wrong. And I see no significant danger in using the word *exist* to ask the relevant questions or make the relevant affirmations. As long as we recognize the limitations of all human talk about God, and as long as we recognize that God "exists" in a different sense than we do, the enterprise of proposing, criticizing, and defending theistic proofs can continue.

IV

What good, then, do theistic proofs do? Why spend time arguing about them? I would prefer to approach the question by asking, What good would a *successful* theistic proof do (if one existed)? Naturally, the question and its answer might be quite different if I were instead to ask,

What good is done by the existing theistic proofs discussed by philosophers, that is, the ontological argument, the moral argument, and so on? I choose to proceed in the way I do because the main point behind discussions of these arguments seems to me to be in any case to see whether or not they are successful. Those who defend them think they are or might be (although their notions of "success" sometimes appear to differ from mine); those who criticize them think they are not.

In my view, there are two great benefits that would be derived from a successful theistic proof.[7] The two are closely related; and the first benefit (but not the second) is also derived from discussions of the actual theistic proofs, whether or not any one of them is successful. The first then is this: Theistic proofs show that theists do or at least can make full and thoroughgoing use of their rational faculties in arriving at or continuing in belief in the existence of God. I say this because it is frequently charged (oddly, by some who look sympathetically on religious faith as well as by some who do not) that faith in God is essentially irrational or at least arational, that is, is based on an "existential choice" that is not supported by evidence, arguments, or reasons.

The second and most important benefit that would derive from a successful theistic proof is that belief in the existence of God will have been shown to be rational or intellectually justified. (I do not claim, of course, that this is the *only* way such a belief can be shown to be rational.) The standard criticism of belief in the existence of God, namely, that it is naive or credulous or irrational to believe in the existence of something you can't see or measure or test or prove, will have been answered. I consider that this result will constitute a very great benefit indeed for theism.

If such a proof existed, the temptation for theists would be to use it as an evangelistic device. That is, they might try to use the proof to convince nonbelievers in the existence of God to become believers. And I suppose it is *possible* there might be some converts—a successful theistic proof might at least lead some folk to consider God more seriously than they had been doing, or it might for some folk remove intellectual obstacles

to belief in the existence of God. But that, I think, is about all it should be expected to do. As noted above, few arguments are intellectually coercive; I suspect there never will exist a discursive, deductive theistic proof that convinces all the rational people who attend to it.

One reason this is true is that in the face of even a successful theistic proof a stubborn atheist always has the option of denying one of its premises. And in some cases this might be a rational thing for the atheist to do. Similarly, if someone were clever enough to construct from premises I believed a proof of the nonexistence of God, I am quite sure that the first thing I would do would be to consider which of those premises to deny. The strength of my commitment to theism would outweigh my commitment to at least one of those premises. And, I claim, this might well be the rational thing for me to do.

But just when might it be rational for a person to deny a previously accepted premise in order rationally to reject a conclusion it entails or helps to entail? This is a complicated matter; I will suggest some criteria, but they should be taken as tentative suggestions only. Let us imagine an atheist, Jones, who is faced with the theistic proof with which we began:

(1) All the people in Claremont are people;
(2) Some people believe in God;
(3) Therefore, God exists.

Let us further suppose something that is obviously not in fact true, namely, that this is a *valid* argument. And if it is valid, then it is also *sound,* since surely premises (1) and (2) are true. Now since these premises seem to be not only true but *known to be plausible,* this argument—so we are supposing—meets our requirements of a successful theistic proof. Finally, let us suppose that Jones knows that these premises are plausible. What, then, can or should Jones do in the light of this imagined successful theistic proof?

It seems that Jones has three options. First, Jones might agree that our theistic proof is successful but still deny its conclusion. Second, Jones might agree that our theistic proof is successful and accepts its conclusion, that is, become a theist. Third, Jones might deny that our theistic proof is successful by denying the plausibility of premises (1), (2), or both. (Let us imagine it is the contingently true premise (2) that Jones would decide to dispute.) Now the first option is obviously unacceptable and must be rejected as irrational. The second option, however, is clearly acceptable; in the light of our successful theistic proof, we would want to say, Jones rationally *should* accept the truth of (3).

Whether the third option is acceptable seems to depend on various considerations. First, is Jones willing to pay the price of rationally rejecting (3)? That is, is Jones willing to deny the apparently plausible premise (2)? Second, how important in Jones's world view is the denial of (3)? Is it central or important enough to outweigh the cost of denying premise (2)? Third, how probable is the denial of (3) (i.e., atheism) versus the probability of (2)? I would argue, then, that if Jones is willing to deny (2), and if the denial of (3) is crucial to Jones's world view, and if Jones's best judgment is that the denial of (3) is more probable than the truth of premise (2), then Jones is rational in denying (2), despite its initial plausibility, in order rationally to deny (3).

In short, if you think a statement *p* is plausible or even true; and if you are utterly convinced that another statement *q* is false; and if you discover that *p* entails *q;* then you can rationally change your mind about *p* and deny it if you are willing to pay the price of doing so, if the denial of *q* is crucial to your world view, and if the denial of *q* seems far more probable to you that the truth or plausibility of *p.*

V

I have been arguing that rational discussion of theistic proofs is worthwhile. But in the end I do want to say that theistic proofs are very much *optional* for theists. The fact of the matter is this: I enjoy discussing theistic proofs; I consider the enterprise valuable, and I even consider that there do exist successful theistic proofs; nevertheless, the reason I am a theist has almost nothing to do with theistic proofs. It has a great deal to do with experiences I have had that I interpret in terms of the presence of God—experiences I find myself interpreting in terms of divine forgiveness, divine protection, divine guidance. That is why I claim to know that God exists. That is why I would be extremely suspicious of any apparently successful atheistic proof.

Let us return to the move Aquinas makes at the conclusion of each of the five ways—"and this everyone understands to be God." As noted, Aquinas errs in that he has not shown that the Prime Mover, and so on, can be none other than the Judeo-Christian God. Yet we can understand what he is doing here—he is, of course, connecting his philosophy and his theology. His method is first to prove the existence of a first mover, a first cause, and a necessary being who owes its necessity to no other being; he then does an inventory, so to speak, of all the beings he believes on other grounds to exist; finally, he asks, Which of them could be the same being as the being or beings proven in the five ways? The answer he finds, naturally enough, is that only *God* can be a first mover, a first cause, and a necessary being who owes its necessity to no other being. Thus he says, "and this everyone understands to be God."

My own view is that this "connecting" strategy of Aquinas (connecting his philosophical proofs with his theological convictions) is entirely acceptable. And this is surely the (usually implicit) strategy of many of those who offer theistic proofs. If you successfully prove that a given being exists, and if on other grounds there is good reason for you to think this being is God, then you have good reason to hold that you have successfully proved the existence of God. Or at least your proof will have achieved the aim mentioned earlier, namely, the aim of confirming your faith in God.

Notes

1. *The Collected Dialogues of Plato,* ed. Edith Hamilton and Huntington Cairns (New York: Pantheon, 1961), 1455–1479 (894A–899C).

2. See *Systematic Theology,* I (Chicago: Univ. of Chicago Press, 1951), 235–38.

3. Helpful work on this question has been done by George Mavrodes in his *Belief in God* (New York: Random House, 1970), 17–48, and by James F. Ross in his *Philosophical Theology* (Indianapolis: Bobbs-Merrill, 1969), 3–34.

4. This argument is discussed by Alvin Plantinga in *The Nature of Necessity* (Oxford: Clarendon Press, 1974), 217–18.

5. See "Anselm's Ontological Arguments," in *The Existence of God,* ed. John Hick (New York: Macmillan, 1964), 68.

6. See my *Logic and the Nature of God* (London: Macmillan, 1983), 145–53.

7. Another possible benefit of theistic proofs, which I am not able to discuss here, is their use in a cumulative, nondeductive argument for the broad truth of the theistic world view. Some contemporary philosophers have been engaged in making such a case; see, e.g., Basil Mitchell, *The Justification of Religious Belief* (New York: Oxford University Press, 1981), and Richard Swinburne, *The Existence of God* (Oxford: Clarendon Press, 1979).

Bibliography for Part I

General

Davies, Brian. *An Introduction to the Philosophy of Religion.* Oxford: Oxford Univ. Press, 1982. Readable and reliable, written from a distinctive theistic framework.

Mackie, J. L. *The Miracle of Theism.* Oxford: Oxford Univ. Press, 1982. A lively but uneven discussion of the proofs by one of the ablest atheist philosophers of our time.

Matson, Wallace. *The Existence of God.* Ithaca: Cornell Univ. Press, 1965. A cogent attack on the traditional arguments.

Ross, James. *Philosophical Theology.* Indianapolis: Hackett, 1969. Highly recommended for a discussion of the medieval sources and contemporary relevance.

Rowe, William. *Philosophy of Religion: An Introduction.* Belmont, Calif.: Wadsworth, 1978. A very readable and reliable introduction for beginners.

Swinburne, Richard. *The Existence of God.* Oxford: Clarendon Press, 1979. Perhaps the most sustained, if not the overall best, defense of the traditional arguments since the Middle Ages.

Yandell, Keith. *Christianity and Philosophy.* Grand Rapids, Mich.: Eerdmans, 1984. A rigorously analytic approach, full of outlines of arguments but lacking the thorough discussion that one might like.

The Cosmological Argument

Craig, William. *The Cosmological Argument from Plato to Leibniz.* New York: Barnes & Noble, 1980. A good survey of the history of the argument.

Rowe, William. *The Cosmological Argument.* Princeton: Princeton Univ. Press, 1975. A very thorough and penetrating study of the classic formulations (especially Aquinas, Scotus, and Clark).

The Teleological Argument

McPherson, Thomas. *The Argument from Design.* London: Macmillan, 1972. A good introduction to the various forms of the argument.

Salmon, Wesley. "Religion and Science: A New Look at Hume's Dialogue." *Philosophical Studies* 33 (1978):145.

Swinburne, Richard. "The Argument from Design." *Philosophy* 43 (1968):199–212. A detailed response to Hume.

———. "The Argument from Design—A Defence." *Religious Studies* 8 (1972):193–205.

Tennant, R. R. *Philosophical Theology.* Cambridge: Cambridge Univ. Press, 1928–30. A classic post-Humean version of the teleological argument.

The Ontological Argument

Barnes, Jonathan. *The Ontological Argument.* London: Macmillan, 1972. A good general discussion of the argument.

Plantinga, Alvin, ed. *The Ontological Argument from St. Anselm to Contemporary Philosophers.* Garden City, N.Y.: Doubleday, 1965.

PART II

THE ARGUMENT FROM RELIGIOUS EXPERIENCE

Why is religious experience problematical? If I say that I hear a sweet tune and you listen and say, "Yes, I hear it now too," we have no problem. But if you listen carefully and don't hear it, you might well wonder whether I am really hearing sounds or only imagine that I am. Perhaps we could bring in others to check the matter out. If they agree with me, well and good, but if they agree with you and don't hear the sounds, then we have a problem. Perhaps we could bring in an audiometer to measure the decibels in the room. If the meter confirms my report, then it is simply a case of my having better hearing than you and the rest of the witnesses. But if the meter doesn't register at all, then, assuming that it is in working order, we would have good evidence that I am only imagining that I am hearing sounds. There is little doubt but that I am not hearing the sounds except in my own mind. Perhaps I need to change my original claim and say, "Well, I *seem* to be hearing a sweet tune."

The problem we find in religious experience, as in this example, is that the experience is private. You have the sense of God forgiving you or an angel speaking to you, but I, who am in the same room with you, hear nothing and feel nothing unusual. You are praying and suddenly feel transported by grace and sense the unity of all reality. I, who am sitting next to you, wonder at the strange expression on your face and ask you if something is wrong. Perhaps you are having an epileptic seizure?

Yet religious experiences have been reported in great variety by many people, from dairy maids like Joan of Arc to mystics like Theresa of Avila and St. John of the Cross. They cannot simply be dismissed without serious analysis.

There are actually two levels of problem here. First, to what degree, if any, is the person having a religious experience justified in inferring from the psychological experience (the subjective aspect) to the existential or ontological reality of the content of the experience (the objective aspect)? Second, to what degree, if any, does the cumulative witness of those undergoing religious experience justify the claim that there is a God or a transcendent reality?

Traditionally, the argument from religious experience has not been one of the "proofs" for God's existence. At best, it has confirmed or branded on the soul what the proofs conveyed with icy logic. Many—among them, William James—believe that even without the proofs' being valid, religious experiences are self-authenticating for those who have them. Others, such as Wallace Matson (see the third reading) deny this and argue that a subjective experience alone never warrants an existential claim (that is, the claim that an object exists outside oneself). They believe it is a fallacy to go from the psychological experience of *X* to the reality of *X*. Philosophers like Gary Gutting and William Alston have recently disputed this claim. Some philosophers have argued that a sort of *consensus mysticum* is itself evidence for the reality of a divine being. In our readings, Gutting argues that the tremendous similarity of religious experiences is evidence of their validity and leads to the natural interpretation that they come from a benevolent and powerful being. Since Gutting's work is very recent, it hasn't been seriously challenged. Hence, I have offered a brief exploratory critique of my own.

Now, there are many psychological explanations of religious experience that cast doubt on its validity. One of the most famous is the Freudian interpretation. Freud claimed that religious experience was the result of the projection of the father image within oneself. The progression goes like this: When you were a child, you saw your father as a powerful hero who could do everything, meet all your needs, and overcome the normal obstacles that stood in your way at every step. When you grew older, you sadly realized that your father was fallible and very finite indeed. But you still had the need of the benevolent, all-powerful father. Subconsciously you projected your need for that long-lost parent onto the empty heavens and invented a god for yourself. Since this is a common phenomenon, all of us who have successfully projected daddy onto the big sky go to church or synagogue or the mosque or whatever and worship the illusion on our favorite holy day. But it is a myth. The sky is empty, and the sooner we realize it the better it will be for everyone.

This is one explanation of religious experience and religion in general. It is not a disproof of God's existence, simply a hypothesis. Even if it is true psychologically that we tend to think of God as a powerful and loving parent, it could still be the case that the parental relationship is God's way of teaching us about himself, by analogy.

Another explanation of religious experience is naturalism. According to this theory, all reality can be explained by reference to physical processes, so there is no need to bring in mysterious spiritual entities. There is no soul or spiritual reality, although there are values and consciousnesses that are explained with reference to functions of physical states. Consciousness, or mind, is a function of brain states, nothing more or less. The brain processes spatio-temporal experiences communicated to it through the senses. All learning is produced in this way. The mechanisms of the brain modify and coordinate the experiences, but there is no good reason to believe that the brain has access to extraphysical reality. There are problems with naturalism, but it is a coherent explanatory theory that rivals theism. In our readings, Wallace Matson represents this point of view.

The first reading in this part is an excerpt from William James's classic study, *The Varieties of Religious Experience* (1902). In this selection James describes mystical experience, which he considers to be the deepest kind of religious experience. It is something that transcends our ordinary, sensory experience and that cannot be described in terms of our normal concepts and language. It is 'ineffable experience'. The subject realizes that the experience "defies expression, that no adequate report of its content can be given in words," James writes. "It follows from this that its quality must be directly experienced; it cannot be imparted or transferred to others." And yet it contains a 'noetic quality', a content. It purports to convey truth about the nature of reality, namely, that there is a unity of all things and that that unity is spiritual, not material. It is antinaturalistic, pantheistic, and optimistic. Further, mystical states are *transient*—that is, they cannot be sustained for long—and they are *passive*—that is, the mystic is acted upon by divine deliverance. We may prepare ourselves for the experience, but it is not something that we do; it is something that happens to us.

James is cautious about what can be deduced from mystical experience. Although mystic states are and ought to be absolutely authoritative for the individuals to whom they come, "no authority emanates from them which should make it a duty for those who stand outside of them to accept their revelations uncritically." But their value for us, James argues, is that they show us a valid alternative to the "non-mystical rationalistic consciousness, based on understanding and the senses alone. They open up the possibility of other orders of truth, in which, so far as anything in us vitally responds to them, we may freely continue to have faith."

Our second selection is C. D. Broad's important article, "The Argument from Religious Experience" (1953), in which he considers the extent to which we can infer from religious experience to the existence of God. Broad likens the religious sense to an ear for music. There are a few people on the negative end who are spiritually tone deaf and a few on the positive end who are the founders of religions, the Bachs and Beethovens. In between are the ordinary followers of religion, who are like the average musical listeners, and above them are the saints, who are likened to those with a very fine ear for music.

The chief difference is that religion, unlike music, says something about the nature of reality. Is what it says true? And does religious experience lend any support to the truth claims of religion? Is religious experience *veridical?* Are the claims about "the nature of reality which are an integral part of the experience true or probable?" Broad considers the argument from mystical agreement, which goes as follows:

(1) There is an enormous unanimity among the mystics concerning the spiritual nature of reality.

(2) When there is such unanimity among observers as to what they believe themselves to be experiencing, it is reasonable to conclude that their experiences are veridical (unless we have good reason to believe that they are deluded).

(3) There are no positive reasons for thinking that mystical experiences are delusory.

(4) Therefore it is reasonable to believe that mystical experiences are veridical.

The weak premise is (3), for there is evidence that mystics are neuropathic or sexually repressed. In considering these charges, Broad admits some plausibility in them but suggests that they are not conclusive. Regarding the charge of neuropathology, he urges that "one might need to be slightly 'cracked' in order to have some peep-holes into the super-sensible world." With regard to sexual abnormality, it could simply be the case that no one who was "incapable of strong sexual desires and emotions could have anything worth calling religious experience."

His own guarded judgment is that, given what we know about the origins of religious belief and emotions, there is no reason to think that religious experience is "specially likely to be delusive or misdirected." On the other hand, the evidence suggests that the concepts and beliefs of even the best religions are "extremely inadequate to the facts which they express; that they are highly confused and are mixed up with a great deal of positive error and sheer nonsense; and that, if the human race goes on and continues to have religious experiences and to reflect on them, they will be altered and improved almost out of recognition."

Our third reading on religious experience is a section from Wallace Matson's book *The Existence of God* (1965). Matson first presents a brief analysis of perception. He then applies it to the notion of certifying the experience of a god. He notes that there are several conditions that must be fulfilled in normal perceptual reports, such as corroboration and publicity, that are not fulfilled in religious experiences. By itself, therefore, the testimony of the subject cannot be used to persuade others of its veridicality (unless we have independent evidence for the existence of a god, in which case we should expect such experiences).

Matson grants even less authority to experiences that are *unlike* ordinary perceptions. Even if the mystics are sane, their experiences have no authority for us. Their seeming authority comes from analogy with other esoteric knowledge. For example, physicists tell us that pi-mesons exist and that with an appropriate amount of study of mathematics and physics (i.e., by becoming physicists), most of us (but not all of us) could eventually come to learn how to confirm this belief. Similarly, mystics tell us that through prayer and meditation we could become mystics and have the chance of experiencing what they report. Of course, there is no guarantee that the process will succeed, any more than there is that we will master the material necessary to verify the existence of pi-mesons. Matson contends that this argument fails because of several disanalogies: (1) Physicists can still talk with one another without difficulty, but the mystic has no way of discussing the ineffable even with other mystics. (2) There is an agreed curriculum of study for the physicist but not for the mystic. (3) There is no need for faith in the process of physics as there is in mystical experience.

Matson compares the mystic to a seer among the blind who describes the sun's influence in bringing warmth. He argues that just as it would be unreasonable for the blind to believe such seers unless they could check out their reports in some way, so likewise it is reasonable for the "non-mystic to believe the mystic only if the mystic makes some checkable statements that show him to have a power of directly experiencing what the non-mystic knows about only indirectly."

Our fourth reading is an essay by Gary Gutting from his recent book, *Religious Belief and Religious Skepticism.* The significance of Gutting's work lies in its skepticism about the traditional arguments for the existence of God and its assertion that theistic belief can be based on religious experience alone. Gutting believes that his argument successfully "establishes the existence of a good and powerful being concerned about us, and [this] justifies a central core of religious belief." On this basis he argues that the essential validity of religion is vindicated. However, in a manner reminiscent of C. D. Broad (above), he finds that this sort of justified belief "falls far short of the claims of traditional religions and that detailed religious accounts are nearly as suspect as nonreligious accounts. The heart of true religious belief is a realization that we have *access* to God but only minimal reliable *accounts* of his nature and relation to us." Gutting develops three criteria that veridical religious experience must meet: They must be repeatable; they must be experienced by many in diverse places and cultures; and they must issue forth in morally better lives.

In the fifth essay in this part I offer a critique of Gutting's argument. I distinguish between a strong and a weak justification for religious belief. A strong justification would make it rationally obligatory for everyone to believe in the conclusion of an argument. A weak justification would only provide rational support for those who had had an "of-God" experience (or already accepted the world view that made such experiences likely). Gutting believes that he has given a strong justification for religious belief, but I argue that the argument from religious experience offers only weak justification. At the end of my essay I raise the question of why religious experience does not yield ways of checking the accuracy of its content or predictions that would confirm it.

In the last reading in this part, "Religious Experience and Religious Belief," William Alston argues that religious experience can provide grounds for religious belief. Comparing the epistemology of Christian religious experience with the epistemology of perceptual experience, Alston shows that although perceptual practices include more stringent requirements than religious practices, there are good reasons why the two should be different. Whereas the criteria for valid perceptual experiences include verifiability and predictability, God's being wholly other may preclude those criteria from applying to religious experience. One question that you may want to put to Alston's argument is that even though God's nature may preclude our being able to find regularities in his behavior, might not God, if he exists, be able to give us confirming data, signs to encourage and convince the seeker after truth?

II.1 Mysticism

W I L L I A M   J A M E S

William James (1842–1910), American philoso-
pher and psychologist, was one of the most influ-
ential thinkers of his time. He taught at Harvard
University and is considered, along with C. S.
Peirce, one of the fathers of pragmatism. The Vari-
eties of Religious Experience (1902) is his classic
study of religious experience. In this selection
James describes mystical experience which he
considers to be the deepest kind of religious expe-
rience. It is something that transcends our ordi-
nary, sensory experience and that cannot be de-
scribed in terms of our normal concepts and
language.

Over and over again in these lectures I have raised
points and left them open and unfinished until we
should have come to the subject of Mysticism.
Some of you, I fear, may have smiled as you noted
my reiterated postponements. But now the hour
has come when mysticism must be faced in good
earnest, and those broken threads wound up together. One may say truly, I think, that personal
religious experience has its root and centre in mystical states of consciousness; so for us, who in
these lectures are treating personal experience as
the exclusive subject of our study, such states of
consciousness ought to form the vital chapter from
which the other chapters get their light. Whether
my treatment of mystical states will shed more
light or darkness, I do not know, for my own constitution shuts me out from their enjoyment almost
entirely, and I can speak of them only at second
hand. But though forced to look upon the subject
so externally, I will be as objective and receptive
as I can; and I think I shall at least succeed in
convincing you of the reality of the states in ques-

tion, and of the paramount importance of their
function.

First of all, then, I ask, What does the expression "mystical states of consciousness" mean?
How do we part off mystical states from other
states?

The words "mysticism" and "mystical" are often used as terms of mere reproach, to throw at
any opinion which we regard as vague and vast
and sentimental, and without a base in either facts
or logic. For some writers a "mystic" is any person
who believes in thought-transference, or spirit-
return. Employed in this way the word has little
value: there are too many less ambiguous syno-
nyms. So, to keep it useful by restricting it, I will
do what I did in the case of the word "religion,"
and simply propose to you four marks which,
when an experience has them, may justify us in
calling it mystical for the purpose of the present
lectures. In this way we shall save verbal disputa-
tion, and the recriminations that generally go
therewith.

1. *Ineffability.*—The handiest of the marks by
which I classify a state of mind as mystical is negative. The subject of it immediately says that it defies expression, that no adequate report of its contents can be given in words. It follows from this
that its quality must be directly experienced; it
cannot be imparted or transferred to others. In this
peculiarity mystical states are more like states of
feeling than like states of intellect. No one can
make clear to another who has never had a certain
feeling, in what the quality or worth of it consists.
One must have musical ears to know the value of
a symphony; one must have been in love one's
self to understand a lover's state of mind. Lacking
the heart or ear, we cannot interpret the musician
or the lover justly, and are even likely to consider
him weak-minded or absurd. The mystic finds that
most of us accord to his experiences an equally
incompetent treatment.

From William James, *The Varieties of Religious Experience*
(New York: Longman, Green & Co., 1902).

2. *Noetic quality.*—Although so similar to states of feeling, mystical states seem to those who experience them to be also states of knowledge. They are states of insight into depths of truth unplumbed by the discursive intellect. They are illuminations, revelations, full of significance and importance, all inarticulate though they remain; and as a rule they carry with them a curious sense of authority for aftertime.

These two characters will entitle any state to be called mystical, in the sense in which I use the word. Two other qualities are less sharply marked, but are usually found. These are:—

3. *Transiency.*—Mystical states cannot be sustained for long. Except in rare instances, half an hour, or at most an hour or two, seems to be the limit beyond which they fade into the light of common day. Often, when faded, their quality can but imperfectly be reproduced in memory; but when they recur it is recognized; and from one recurrence to another it is susceptible of continuous development in what is felt as inner richness and importance.

4. *Passivity.*—Although the oncoming of mystical states may be facilitated by preliminary voluntary operations, as by fixing the attention, or going through certain bodily performances, or in other ways which manuals of mysticism prescribe; yet when the characteristic sort of consciousness once has set in, the mystic feels as if his own will were in abeyance, and indeed sometimes as if he were grasped and held by a superior power. This latter peculiarity connects mystical states with certain definite phenomena of secondary or alternative personality, such as prophetic speech, automatic writing, or the mediumistic trance. When these latter conditions are well pronounced, however, there may be no recollection whatever of the phenomenon, and it may have no significance for the subject's usual inner life, to which, as it were, it makes a mere interruption. Mystical states, strictly so-called, are never merely interruptive. Some memory of their content always remains, and a profound sense of their importance. They modify the inner life of the subject between the times of their recurrence. Sharp divisions in this

region are, however, difficult to make, and we find all sorts of gradations and mixtures.

These four characteristics are sufficient to mark out a group of states of consciousness peculiar enough to deserve a special name and to call for careful study. Let it then be called the mystical group.

Our next step should be to gain acquaintance with some typical examples. Professional mystics at the height of their development have often elaborately organized experiences and a philosophy based thereupon. But you remember what I said in my first lecture: phenomena are best understood when placed within their series, studied in their germ and in their over-ripe decay, and compared with their exaggerated and degenerated kindred. The range of mystical experience is very wide, much too wide for us to cover in the time at our disposal. Yet the method of serial study is so essential for interpretation that if we really wish to reach conclusions we must use it. I will begin, therefore, with phenomena which claim no special religious significance, and end with those of which the religious pretensions are extreme.

The simplest rudiment of mystical experience would seem to be that deepened sense of the significance of a maxim or formula which occasionally sweeps over one. "I've heard that said all my life," we exclaim, "but I never realized its full meaning until now." "When a fellow-monk," said Luther, "one day repeated the words of the Creed: 'I believe in the forgiveness of sins,' I saw the Scripture in an entirely new light; and straightway I felt as if I were born anew. It was as if I had found the door of paradise thrown wide open." This sense of deeper significance is not confined to rational propositions. Single words, and conjunctions of words, effects of light on land and sea, odors and musical sounds, all bring it when the mind is tuned aright. Most of us can remember the strangely moving power of passages in certain poems read when we were young, irrational doorways as they were through which the mystery of fact, the wildness and the pang of life, stole into our hearts and thrilled them. The words have now perhaps become mere polished surfaces for us; but lyric poetry and music are alive and significant only in proportion as they fetch these vague vistas of a life continuous with our own, beckoning and inviting, yet ever eluding our pursuit. We are alive or dead to the eternal inner message of the arts according as we have kept or lost this mystical susceptibility.

A more pronounced step forward on the mystical ladder is found in an extremely frequent phenomenon, that sudden feeling, namely, which sometimes sweeps over us, of having "been here before," as if at some indefinite past time, in just this place, with just these people, we were already saying just these things. As Tennyson writes:

Moreover, something is or seems
That touches me with mystic gleams,
Like glimpses of forgotten dreams—

Of something felt, like something here;
Of something done, I know not where;
Such as no language may declare.

Sir James Crichton-Browne has given the technical name of "dreamy states" to these sudden invasions of vaguely reminiscent consciousness. They bring a sense of mystery and of the metaphysical duality of things, and the feeling of an enlargement of perception which seems imminent but which never completes itself. In Dr. Crichton-Browne's opinion they connect themselves with the perplexed and scared disturbances of self-consciousness which occasionally precede epileptic attacks. I think that this learned alienist takes a rather absurdly alarmist view of an intrinsically insignificant phenomenon. He follows it along the downward ladder, to insanity; our path pursues the upward ladder chiefly. The divergence shows how important it is to neglect no part of a phenomenon's connections, for we make it appear admirable or dreadful according to the context by which we set it off.

Somewhat deeper plunges into mystical consciousness are met with in yet other dreamy states. Such feelings as these which Charles Kingsley describes are surely far from being uncommon, especially in youth:—

When I walk the fields, I am oppressed now and then with an innate feeling that everything I see has a meaning, if I could but understand it. And this feeling of being surrounded with truths which I cannot grasp amounts to indescribable awe sometimes. . . . Have you not felt that your real soul was imperceptible to your mental vision, except in a few hallowed moments?

. . . .

[An] incommunicableness of the transport is the keynote of all mysticism. Mystical truth exists for the individual who has the transport, but for no one else. In this, as I have said, it resembles the knowledge given to us in sensations more than that given by conceptual thought. Thought, with its remoteness and abstractness, has often enough in the history of philosophy been contrasted unfavorably with sensation. It is a commonplace of metaphysics that God's knowledge cannot be discursive but must be intuitive, that is, must be constructed more after the pattern of what in ourselves is called immediate feeling, that after that of proposition and judgment. But *our* immediate feelings have no content but what the five senses supply; and we have seen and shall see again that mystics may emphatically deny that the senses play any part in the very highest type of knowledge which their transports yield.

In the Christian church there have always been mystics. Although many of them have been viewed with suspicion, some have gained favor in the eyes of the authorities. The experiences of these have been treated as precedents, and a codified system of mystical theology has been based upon them, in which everything legitimate finds its place. The basis of the system is "orison" or meditation, the methodical elevation of the soul towards God. Through the practice of orison the higher levels of mystical experience may be attained. It is odd that Protestantism, especially evangelical Protestantism, should seemingly have abandoned everything methodical in this line. Apart from what prayer may lead to, Protestant mystical experience appears to have been almost exclusively sporadic. It has been left to our mind-curers to reintroduce methodical meditation into our religious life.

The first thing to be aimed at in orison is the mind's detachment from outer sensations for these interfere with its concentration upon ideal things. Such manuals as Saint Ignatius's Spiritual Exercises recommend the disciple to expel sensation by a graduated series of efforts to imagine holy scenes. The acme of this kind of discipline would be a semi-hallucinatory mono-ideism—an imaginary figure of Christ, for example, coming fully to occupy the mind. Sensorial images of this sort, whether literal or symbolic, play an enormous part in mysticism. But in certain cases imagery may fall away entirely, and in the very highest raptures it ends to do so. The state of consciousness becomes then insusceptible of any verbal description. Mystical teachers are unanimous as to this. Saint John of the Cross, for instance, one of the best of them, thus describes the condition called the "union of love," which, he says, is reached by "dark contemplation." In this the Deity compenetrates the soul, but in such a hidden way that the soul—

finds no terms, no means, no comparison whereby to render the sublimity of the wisdom and the delicacy of the spiritual feeling with which she is filled. . . . We receive this mystical knowledge of God clothed in none of the kinds of images, in none of the sensible representations, which our mind makes use of in other circumstances. Accordingly in this knowledge, since the senses and the imagination are not employed, we get neither form nor impression, nor can we give any account or furnish any likeness, although the mysterious and sweet-tasting wisdom comes home so clearly to the inmost parts of our soul. Fancy a man seeing a certain kind of thing for the first time in his life. He can understand it, use and enjoy it, but he cannot apply a name to it, nor communicate any idea of it, even though all the while it be a mere thing of sense. How much greater will be his powerlessness when it goes beyond the senses! This is the peculiarity of the divine language. The more infused, intimate, spiritual, and supersensible it is, the more does it exceed the senses, both inner and outer, and impose silence upon them. . . . The soul then feels as if placed in a vast and profound solitude, to which no created thing has access, in an immense and boundless desert, desert the more delicious the more solitary it is. There, in this abyss of wisdom, the soul grows by what it drinks in from the well-springs of the comprehension of love, . . . and recognizes, however sublime and learned may be the terms we employ, how utterly vile, insignificant, and improper they are, when we seek to discourse of divine things by their means.

I cannot pretend to detail to you the sundry stages of the Christian mystical life. Our time would not suffice, for one thing; and moreover, I confess that the subdivisions and names which we find in the Catholic books seem to me to represent nothing objectively distinct. So many men, so many minds; I imagine that these experiences can be as infinitely varied as are the idiosyncrasies of individuals.

The cognitive aspects of them, their value in the way of revelation, is what we are directly concerned with, and it is easy to show by citation how strong an impression they leave of being revelations of new depths of truth. Saint Teresa is the expert of experts in describing such conditions, so I will turn immediately to what she says of one of the highest of them, the "orison of union."

In the orison of union (says Saint Teresa) the soul is fully awake as regards God, but wholly asleep as regards things of this world and in respect of herself. During the short time the union lasts, she is as it were deprived of every feeling, and even if she would, she could not think of any single thing. Thus she needs to employ no artifice in order to arrest the use of her understanding: it remains so stricken with inactivity that she neither knows what she loves, nor in what manner she loves, nor what she wills. In short, she is utterly dead to the things of the world and lives solely in God. . . . I do not even know whether in this state she has enough life left to breathe. It seems to me she has not; or at least that if she does breathe, she is unaware of it. Her intellect would fain understand something of what is going on within her, but it has so little force now that it can act in no way whatsoever. So a person who falls into a deep faint appears as if dead. . . .

Thus does God, when he raises a soul to union with himself, suspend the natural action of all her faculties. She neither sees, hears, nor understands, so long as she is united with God. But this time is always short, and it seems even shorter than it is. God establishes himself in the interior of this soul in such a way, that when she returns to herself, it is wholly impossible for her to doubt that she has been in God, and God in her. This truth remains so strongly impressed on her that, even though many years should pass without the condition returning, she can neither forget the favor she received, nor doubt of its reality. If you, nevertheless, ask how it is possible that the soul can see and understand that she has been in , God, since during the union she has neither sight nor understanding, I reply that she does not see it then, but that she sees it clearly later, after she has returned to herself, not by any vision, but by a certitude which abides with her and which God alone can give her. I knew a person who was ignorant of the truth that God's mode of being in everything must be either by presence, by power, or by essence, but who, after having received the grace of which I am speaking, believed this truth in the most unshakable manner. So much so that, having consulted a half-learned man who was as ignorant on this point as she had been before she was enlightened, when he replied that God is in us only by ''grace,'' she disbelieved his reply, so sure she was of the true answer; and when she came to ask wiser doctors, they confirmed her in her belief, which much consoled her. . . .

But how, you will repeat, *can* one have such certainty in respect to what one does not see? This question, I am powerless to answer. These are secrets of God's omnipotence which it does not appertain to me to penetrate. All that I know is that I tell the truth; and I shall never believe that any soul who does not possess this certainty has ever been really united to God.

The kinds of truth communicable in mystical ways, whether these be sensible or supersensible, are various. Some of them relate to this world—visions of the future, the reading of hearts, the sudden understanding of texts, the knowledge of distant events, for example; but the most important revelations are theological or metaphysical.

Saint Ignatius confessed one day to Father Laynez that a single hour of meditation at Manresa had taught him more truths about heavenly things than all the teachings of all the doctors put together could have taught him. . . . One day in orison, on the steps of the choir of the Dominican church, he saw in a distinct manner the plan of divine wisdom in the creation of the world. On another occasion, during a procession, his spirit was ravished in God, and it was given him to contemplate, in a form and images fitted to the weak understanding of a dweller on the earth, the deep mystery of the holy Trinity. This last vision flooded his heart with such sweetness, that the mere memory of it in after times made him shed abundant tears.

Similarly with Saint Teresa.

One day, being in orison (she writes), it was granted me to perceive in one instant how all things are seen and contained in God. I did not perceive them in their proper form, and nevertheless the view I had of them was of a sovereign clearness, and has remained vividly impressed upon my soul. It is one of the most signal of all the graces which the Lord has granted me. . . . The view was so subtle and delicate that the understanding cannot grasp it.

She goes on to tell how it was as if the Deity were an enormous and sovereignly limpid diamond, in which all our actions were contained in such a way their full sinfulness appeared evident as never before. On another day, she relates, while she was reciting the Athanasian Creed—

Our Lord made me comprehend in what way it is that one God can be in three persons. He made me see it so clearly that I remained as extremely surprised as I was comforted, . . . and now, when I think of the holy Trinity, or hear It spoken of, I understand how the three adorable Persons form only one God and I experience an unspeakable happiness.

On still another occasion, it was given to Saint Teresa to see and understand in what wise the Mother of God had been assumed into her place in Heaven.

The deliciousness of some of these states seems to be beyond anything known in ordinary consciousness. It evidently involves organic sensibilities, for it is spoken of as something too extreme to be borne, and as verging on bodily pain. But it is too subtle and piercing a delight for ordinary words to denote. God's touches, the wounds of his spear, references to ebriety and to nuptial union have to figure in the phraseology by which it is shadowed forth. Intellect and senses both swoon away in these highest states of ecstasy. ''If our understanding comprehends,'' says Saint Teresa, ''it is in a mode which remains unknown to it, and it can understand nothing of what it comprehends. For my own part, I do not believe that it does comprehend, because, as I said, it does not understand itself to do so. I confess that it is all a mystery in which I am lost.'' In the condition called *raptus* or ravishment by theologians, breathing and circulation are so depressed that it is a question among the doctors whether the soul be or be not temporarily dissevered from the body. One must read Saint Teresa's descriptions and the very exact distinctions which she makes, to persuade one's self that one is dealing, not with imaginary experiences, but with phenomena which, however rare, follow perfectly definite psychological types.

To the medical mind these ecstasies signify nothing but suggested and imitated hypnoid states, on an intellectual basis of superstition, and a corporeal one of degeneration and hysteria. Undoubtedly these pathological conditions have existed in many and possibly in all the cases, but that fact tells us nothing about the value for knowledge of the consciousness which they induce. To pass a spiritual judgment upon these states, we must not content ourselves with superficial medical talk, but inquire into their fruits for life.

Their fruits appear to have been various. Stupefaction, for one thing, seems not to have been altogether absent as a result. You may remember the helplessness in the kitchen and schoolroom of poor Margaret Mary Alacoque. Many other ecstatics would have perished but for the care taken of them by admiring followers. The "other-worldliness" encouraged by the mystical consciousness makes this over-abstraction from practical life peculiarly liable to befall mystics in whom the character is naturally passive and the intellect feeble; but in natively strong minds and characters we find quite opposite results. The great Spanish mystics, who carried the habit of ecstasy as far as it has often been carried, appear for the most part to have shown indomitable spirit and energy, and all the more so for the trances in which they indulged.

Saint Ignatius was a mystic, but his mysticism made him assuredly one of the most powerfully practical human engines that ever lived. Saint John of the Cross, writing of the intuitions and "touches" by which God reaches the substance of the soul, tells us that—

They enrich it marvelously. A single one of them may be sufficient to abolish at a stroke certain imperfections of which the soul during its whole life had vainly tried to rid itself, and to leave it adorned with

virtues and loaded with supernatural gifts. A single one of these intoxicating consolations may reward it for all the labors undergone in its life—even were they numberless. Invested with an invincible courage, filled with an impassioned desire to suffer for its God, the soul then is seized with a strange torment—that of not being allowed to suffer enough.

Saint Teresa is as emphatic, and much more detailed. You may perhaps remember a passage I quoted from her in my first lecture. There are many similar pages in her autobiography. Where in literature is a more evidently veracious account of the formation of a new centre of spiritual energy, than is given in her description of the effects of certain ecstasies which in departing leave the soul upon a higher level of emotional excitement?

Often, infirm and wrought upon with dreadful pains before the ecstasy, the soul emerges from it full of health and admirably disposed for action . . . as if God had willed that the body itself, already obedient to the soul's desires, should share in the soul's happiness. . . . The soul after such a favor is animated with a degree of courage so great that if at that moment its body should be torn to pieces for the cause of God, it would feel nothing but the liveliest comfort. Then it is that promises and heroic resolutions spring up in profusion in us, soaring desires, horror of the world, and the clear perception of our proper nothingness. . . . What empire is comparable to that of a soul who, from this sublime summit to which God has raised her, sees all the things of earth beneath her feet, and is captivated by no one of them? How ashamed she is of her former attachments! How amazed at her blindness! What lively pity she feels for those whom she recognizes still shrouded in the darkness! . . . She groans at having ever been sensitive to points of honor, at the illusion that made her ever see as honor what the world calls by that name. Now she sees in this name nothing more than an immense lie of which the world remains a victim. She discovers, in the new light from above, that in genuine honor there is nothing spurious, that to be faithful to this honor is to give our respect to what deserves to be respected really, and to consider as nothing, or as less than nothing, whatsoever perishes and is not agreeable to God. . . . She laughs when she sees grave persons, persons of orison, caring for points of honor for which she now feels profoundest contempt. It is suitable to the dignity of their rank to act thus, they pretend, and it makes them more useful to others. But she knows that in despising the dignity of their rank for the pure love of God they would do more good in a single day than they would effect in ten years by preserving it. . . . She laughs at herself that there should ever have been a time in her life when she made any case of money, when she ever desired it. . . . Oh! if human beings might only agree together to regard it as so much useless mud, what harmony would then reign in the world! With what friendship we would all treat each other if our interest in honor and in money could but disappear from earth! For my own part, I feel as if it would be a remedy for all our ills.

Mystical conditions may, therefore, render the soul more energetic in the lines which their inspiration favors. But this could be reckoned an advantage only in case the inspiration were a true one. If the inspiration were erroneous, the energy would be all the more mistaken and misbegotten. So we stand once more before the problem of truth which confronted us at the end of the lectures on saintliness. You will remember that we turned to mysticism precisely to get some light on truth. Do mystical states establish the truth of those theological affections in which the saintly life has its root?

In spite of their repudiation of articulate self-description, mystical states in general assert a pretty distinct theoretic drift. It is possible to give the outcome of the majority of them in terms that point in definite philosophical directions. One of these directions is optimism, and the other is monism. We pass into mystical states from out of ordinary consciousness as from a less into a more, as from a smallness into a vastness, and at the same time as from an unrest to a rest. We feel them as reconciling, unifying states. They appeal to the yes-function more than to the no-function in us. In them the unlimited absorbs the limits and peacefully closes the account. Their very denial of every adjective you may propose as applicable to the ultimate truth—He, the Self, the Atman, is to be described by "No! no!" only, say the Upanishads—though it seems on the surface to be a no-function, is a denial made on behalf of a deeper yes. Whoso calls the Absolute anything in particular, or says that it is *this,* seems implicitly to shut it off from being *that*—it is as if he lessened it. So we deny the "this," negating the negation which it seems to us to imply, in the interests of the higher affirmative attitude by which we are possessed. The fountainhead of Christian mysti-

cism is Dionysius the Areopagite. He describes the absolute truth by negatives exclusively.

The cause of all things is neither soul nor intellect; nor has it imagination, opinion, or reason, or intelligence; nor is it reason or intelligence; nor is it spoken or thought. It is neither number, nor order, nor magnitude, nor littleness, nor equality, nor inequality, nor similarity, nor dissimilarity. It neither stands, nor moves, nor rests. . . . It is neither essence, nor eternity, nor time. Even intellectual contact does not belong to it. It is neither science nor truth. It is not even royalty or wisdom; not one; not unity; not divinity or goodness; nor even spirit as we know it (etc., *ad libitum*).

But these qualifications are denied by Dionysius, not because the truth falls short of them, but because it so infinitely excels them. It is above them. It is *super*-lucent, *super*-splendent, *super*-essential, *super*-sublime, *super* everything that can be named. Like Hegel in his logic, mystics journey towards the positive pole of truth only by the "Methode der Absoluten Negativität."

Thus comes the paradoxical expressions that so abound in mystical writings. As when Eckhart tells of the still desert of the Godhead, "where never was seen difference, neither Father, Son, nor Holy Ghost, where there is no one at home, yet where the spark of the soul is more at peace than in itself." As when Boehme writes of the Primal Love, that "it may fitly be compared to Nothing, for it is deeper than any Thing, and is as nothing with respect to all things, forasmuch as it is not comprehensible by any of them. And because it is nothing respectively, it is therefore free from all things, and is that only good, which a man cannot express or utter what it is, there being nothing to which it may be compared, to express it by." Or as when Angelus Silesius sings:—

> Gott ist ein lauter Nichts, ihn rührt kein Nun
>   noch Hier;
> Je mehr du nach ihm greiffst, je mehr
>   entwind er dir.

To this dialectical use, by the intellect, of negation as a mode of passage towards a higher kind of affirmation, there is correlated the subtlest of moral counterparts in the sphere of the personal will. Since denial of the finite self and its wants, since asceticism of some sort, is found in religious experience to be the only doorway to the larger and more blessed life, this moral mystery intertwines and combines with the intellectual mystery in all mystical writings.

Love (continues Behmen) [is Nothing, for] when thou art gone forth wholly from the Creature and from that which is visible, and art become Nothing to all that is Nature and Creature, then thou art in that eternal One, which is God himself, and then thou shalt feel within thee the highest virtue of Love. . . . The treasure of treasures for the soul is where she goeth out of the Somewhat into that Nothing out of which all things may be made. The soul here saith, *I have nothing,* for I am utterly stripped and naked; *I can do nothing,* for I have no manner of power, but am as water poured out; *I am nothing,* for all that I am is no more than an image of Being, and only God is to me I AM; and so, sitting down in my own Nothingness, I give glory to the eternal Being, and *will nothing* of myself, that so God may will all in me, being unto me my God and all things.

In Paul's language, I live, yet not I, but Christ liveth in me. Only when I become as nothing can God enter in and no difference between his life and mine remain outstanding.

This overcoming of all the usual barriers between the individual and the Absolute is the great mystic achievement. In mystic states we both become one with the Absolute and we become aware of our oneness. This is the everlasting and triumphant mystical tradition, hardly altered by differences of clime or creed. In Hinduism, in Neoplatonism, in Sufism, in Christian mysticism, in Whitmanism, we find the same recurring note, so that there is about mystical utterances an eternal unanimity which ought to make a critic stop and think, and which brings it about that the mystical classics have, as has been said, neither birthday nor native land. Perpetually telling of the unity of man with God, their speech antedates languages, and they do not grow old.

"That are Thou!" says the Upanishads, and the Vedantists add: "Not a part, nor a mode of That, but identically That, that absolute Spirit of the World." "As pure water poured into pure water remains the same, thus, O Gautama, is the Self of a thinker who knows. Water in water, fire in

fire, ether in ether, no one can distinguish them: likewise a man whose mind has entered into the self." 'Everyman,' says the Sufi Gulshan-Râz, whose heart is no longer shaken by any doubts, knows with certainty that there is no being save only One. . . . In his divine majesty the *me,* and *we,* the *thou,* are not found, for in the One there can be no distinction. Every being who is annulled and entirely separated from himself, hears resound outside of him this voice and this echo: *I am God:* he has an eternal way of existing, and is no longer subject to death.' " In the vision of God, says Plotinus, "what sees is not our reason, but something prior and superior to our reason. . . . He who thus sees does not properly see, does not distinguish or imagine two things. He changes, he ceases to be himself, preserves nothing of himself. Absorbed in God, he makes but one with him, like a centre of a circle coinciding with another centre." "Here," writes Suso, "the spirit dies, and yet is all alive in the marvels of the Godhead . . . and is lost in the stillness of the glorious dazzling obscurity and of the naked simple unity. It is in this modeless *where* that the highest bliss is to be found." "Ich bin so gross als Gott," sings Angelus Silesius again, "Er ist als ich so klein; Er kann nich über mich, ich unter ihm nicht sein."

In mystical literature such self-contradictory phrases as "dazzling obscurity," "whispering silence," "teeming desert," are continually met with. They prove that not conceptual speech, but music rather, is the element through which we are best spoken to by mystical truth. Many mystical scriptures are indeed little more than musical compositions.

He who would hear the voice of Nada, "the Soundless Sound," and comprehend it, he has to learn the nature of Dhâranâ. . . . When to himself his form appears unreal, as do on waking all the forms he sees in dreams; when he has ceased to hear the many, he may discern the ONE—the inner sound which kills the outer. . . . For then the soul will hear, and will remember. And then to the inner ear will speak THE VOICE OF THE SILENCE. . . . And now thy *Self* is lost in SELF, *thyself* unto THYSELF, merged in that SELF from which thou first didst radiate. . . . Behold! thou hast become the Light, thou hast become the Sound, thou art thy Master and thy God. Thou art

THYSELF the object of thy search: the VOICE unbroken, that resounds throughout eternities, exempt from change, from sin exempt, the seven sounds in one, the VOICE OF THE SILENCE. *Om tat Sat.*

These words, if they do not awaken laughter as you receive them, probably stir chords within you which music and language touch in common. Music gives us ontological messages which non-musical criticism is unable to contradict, though it may laugh at our foolishness in minding them. There is a verge of the mind which these things haunt; and whispers therefrom mingle with the operations of our understanding, even as the waters of the infinite ocean send their waves to break among the pebbles that lie upon our shores.

> Here begins the sea that ends not till the
>   world's end. Where we stand,
> Could we know the next high sea-mark set
>   beyond these waves that gleam,
> We should know what never man hath
>   known, nor eye of man hath scanned.
>   . . .
> Ah, but here man's heart leaps, yearning
>   towards the gloom with venturous glee,
> From the shore that hath no shore beyond it,
>   set in all the sea.

That doctrine, for example, that eternity is timeless, that our "immortality," if we live in the eternal, is not so much future as already now and here, which we find so often expressed to-day in certain philosophical circles, finds its support in a "hear, hear!" or an "amen," which floats up from that mysteriously deeper level. We recognize the passwords to the mystical region as we hear them, but we cannot use them ourselves; it alone has the keeping of "the password primeval."

I have now sketched with extreme brevity and insufficiency, but as fairly as I am able in the time allowed, the general traits of the mystic range of consciousness. *It is on the whole pantheistic and optimistic, or at least the opposite of pessimistic. It is anti-naturalistic, and harmonizes best with twice-bornness and so-called other-worldly states of mind.*

My next task is to inquire whether we can invoke it as authoritative. Does it furnish any *warrant for the truth* of the twice-bornness and supernaturality and pantheism which it favors? I must give my answer to this question as concisely as I can.

In brief my answer is this—and I will divide it into three parts:—

(1) Mystical states, when well developed, usually are, and have the right to be, absolutely authoritative over the individuals to whom they come.

(2) No authority emanates from them which should make it a duty for those who stand outside of them to accept their revelations uncritically.

(3) They break down the authority of the non-mystical or rationalistic consciousness, based upon the understanding and the senses alone. They show it to be only one kind of consciousness. They open out the possibility of other orders of truth, in which, so far as anything in us vitally responds to them, we may freely continue to have faith.

I will take up these points one by one.

1. As a matter of psychological fact, mystical states of a well-pronounced and emphatic sort *are* usually authoritative over those who have them. They have been "there," and know. It is vain for rationalism to grumble about this. If the mystical truth that comes to a man proves to be a force that he can live by, what mandate have we of the majority to order him to live in another way? We can throw him into a prison or a madhouse, but we cannot change his mind—we commonly attach it only the more stubbornly to its beliefs. It mocks our utmost efforts, as a matter of fact, and in point of logic it absolutely escapes our jurisdiction. Our own more "rational" beliefs are based on evidence exactly similar in nature to that which mystics quote for theirs. Our senses, namely, have assured us of certain states of fact; but mystical experiences are as direct perceptions of fact for those who have them as any sensations ever were for us. The records show that even though the five senses be in abeyance in them, they are absolutely sensational in their epistemological quality, if I may be pardoned the barbarous expression—that

is, they are face to face presentations of what seems immediately to exist.

The mystic is, in short, *invulnerable,* and must be left, whether we relish it or not, in undisturbed enjoyment of his creed. Faith, says Tolstoy, is that by which men live. And faith-state and mystic state are practically convertible terms.

2. But I now proceed to add that mystics have no right to claim that we ought to accept the deliverance of their peculiar experiences, if we are ourselves outsiders and feel no private call thereto. The utmost they can ever ask of us in this life is to admit that they establish a presumption. They form a consensus and have an unequivocal outcome; and it would be odd, mystics might say, if such a unanimous type of experience should prove to be altogether wrong. At bottom, however, this would only be an appeal to numbers, like the appeal of rationalism the other way; and the appeal to numbers has no logical force. If we acknowledge it, it is for "suggestive," not for logical reasons: we follow the majority because to do so suits our life.

But even this presumption from the unanimity of mystics is far from being strong. In characterizing mystic states as pantheistic, optimistic, etc., I am afraid I over-simplified the truth. I did so for expository reasons, and to keep the closer to the classic mystical tradition. The classic religious mysticism, it now must be confessed, is only a "privileged case." It is an *extract,* kept true to type by the selection of the fittest specimens and their preservation in "schools." It is carved out from a much larger mass; and if we take the larger mass as seriously as religious mysticism has historically taken itself, we find that the supposed unanimity largely disappears. To begin with, even religious mysticism itself, the kind that accumulates traditions and makes schools, is much less unanimous than I have allowed. It has been both ascetic and antinomianly self-indulgent within the Christian church. It is dualistic in Sankhya, and monistic in Vedanta philosophy. I called it pantheistic; but the great Spanish mystics are anything but pantheists. They are with few exceptions non-metaphysical minds, for whom "the category of personality" is absolute. The "union" of man with God is for

them much more like an occasional miracle than like an original identity. How different again, apart from the happiness common to all, is the mysticism of Walt Whitman, Edward Carpenter, Richard Jefferies, and other naturalistic pantheists, from the more distinctively Christian sort. The fact is that the mystical feeling of enlargement, union, and emancipation has no specific intellectual content whatever of its own. It is capable of forming matrimonial alliances with material furnished by the most diverse philosophies and theologies, provided only they can find a place in their framework for its peculiar emotional mood. We have no right, therefore, to invoke its prestige as distinctively in favor of any special belief, such as that in absolute idealism, or in the absolute monistic identity, or in the absolute goodness, of the world. It is only relatively in favor of all these things—it passes out of common human consciousness in the direction in which they lie.

So much for religious mysticism proper. But more remains to be told, for religious mysticism is only one half of mysticism. The other half has no accumulated traditions except those which the text-books on insanity supply. Open any one of these, and you will find abundant cases in which "mystical ideas" are cited as characteristic symptoms of enfeebled or deluded states of mind. In delusional insanity, paranoia, as they sometimes call it, we may have a *diabolical* mysticism, a sort of religious mysticism turned upside down. The same sense of ineffable importance in the smallest events, the same texts and words coming with new meanings, the same voices and visions and leadings and missions, the same controlling by extraneous powers; only this time the emotion is pessimistic: instead of consolations we have desolations; the meanings are dreadful; and the powers are enemies to life. It is evident from the point of view of their psychological mechanism, the classic mysticism and these lower mysticisms spring from the same mental level, from that great subliminal or transmarginal region of which science is beginning to admit the existence, but of which so little is really known. That region contains every kind of matter: "seraph and snake" abide there side by side. To come from thence is no infallible credential. What comes must be sifted and tested, and run the gauntlet of confrontation with the total context of experience, just like what comes from the outer world of sense. Its value must be ascertained by empirical methods, so long as we are not mystics ourselves.

Once more, then, I repeat that non-mystics are under no obligation to acknowledge in mystical states a superior authority conferred on them by their intrinsic nature.

3. Yet, I repeat once more, the existence of mystical states absolutely overthrows the pretension of non-mystical states to be the sole and ultimate dictators of what we may believe. As a rule, mystical states merely add a supersensuous meaning to the ordinary outward data of consciousness. They are excitements like the emotions of love or ambition, gifts to our spirit by means of which facts already objectively before us fall into a new expressiveness and make a new connection with our active life. They do not contradict these facts as such, or deny anything that our senses have immediately seized. It is the rationalistic critic rather who plays the part of denier in the controversy, and his denials have no strength, for there never can be a state of facts to which new meaning may not truthfully be added, provided the mind ascend to a more enveloping point of view. It must always remain an open question whether mystical states may not possibly be such superior points of view, windows through which the mind looks out upon a more extensive and inclusive world. The difference of the views seen from the different mystical windows need not prevent us from entertaining this supposition. The wider world would in that case prove to have a mixed constitution like that of this world, that is all. It would have its celestial and its infernal regions, its tempting and its saving moments, its valid experiences and its counterfeit ones, just as our world has them; but it would be a wider world all the same. We should have to use its experiences by selecting and subordinating and substituting just as is our custom in this ordinary naturalistic world; we should be liable to error just as we are now; yet the counting in of that wider world of meanings, and the serious dealing with it, might, in spite of all the perplexity, be indispensable stages in our approach to the final fullness of the truth.

In this shape, I think, we have to leave the subject. Mystical states indeed wield no authority due simply to their being mystical states. But the higher ones among them point in directions to which the religious sentiments even of non-mystical men incline. They tell of the supremacy of the ideal, of vastness, of union, of safety, and of rest. They offer us *hypotheses,* hypotheses which we may voluntarily ignore, but which as thinkers we cannot possibly upset. The supernaturalism and optimism to which they would persuade us may, interpreted in one way or another, be after all the truest of insights into the meaning of this life.

"Oh, the little more, and how much it is; and the little less, and what worlds away!" It may be that possibility and permission of this sort are all that our religious consciousness requires to live on. In my last lecture I shall have to try to persuade you that this is the case. Meanwhile, however, I am sure that for many of my readers this diet is too slender. If supernaturalism and inner union with the divine are true, you think, then not so much permission, as compulsion to believe, ought to be found. Philosophy has always professed to prove religious truth by coercive argument; and the construction of philosophies of this kind has always been one favorite function of the religious life, if we use this term in the large historic sense. But religious philosophy is an enormous subject, and in my next lecture I can only give that brief glance at it which my limits will allow.

II.2   The Argument from Religious Experience

C. D. BROAD

C. D. Broad (1887–1971) was a professor of philosophy at Cambridge University who wrote prolifically on philosophy of mind, philosophy of religion, and psychical research. In his article "The Argument from Religious Experience" (1953), he considers the extent to which we can infer from religious experience to the existence of God. Broad likens the religious sense to an ear for music. There are a few people on the negative end who are spiritually tone deaf and a few on the positive end who are the founders of religions, the Bachs and Beethovens. In between are the ordinary followers of religion, who are like the average musical listeners, and above them are the saints, who are likened to those with a very fine ear for music.

The chief difference is that religion, unlike music, says something about the nature of reality. Is what it says true? And does religious experience lend any support to the truth claims of religion? Is religious experience veridical? Are the claims about "the nature of reality which are an integral part of the experience true or probable?" Broad carefully considers these questions.

I shall confine myself in this article to specifically religious experience and the argument for the existence of God which has been based on it.

This argument differs in the following important respect from the other two empirical types of argument. The Argument from Design and the arguments from ethical premises start from facts which are common to every one. But some people seem to be almost wholly devoid of any specifically religious experience; and among those who have it the differences of kind and degree are enor-

Reprinted from C. D. Broad, *Religion, Philosophy and Psychical Research* (London: Routledge & Kegan Paul PLC, 1930), by permission of the publisher.

mous. Founders of religions and saints, e.g., often claim to have been in direct contact with God, to have seen and spoken with Him, and so on. An ordinary religious man would certainly not make any such claim, though he might say that he had had experiences which assured him of the existence and presence of God. So the first thing that we have to notice is that capacity for religious experience is in certain respects like an ear for music. There are a few people who are unable to recognize and distinguish the simplest tune. But they are in a minority, like the people who have absolutely no kind of religious experience. Most people have some light appreciation of music. But the differences of degree in this respect are enormous, and those who have not much gift for music have to take the statements of accomplished musicians very largely on trust. Let us, then, compare tone-deaf persons to those who have no recognizable religious experience at all; the ordinary followers of a religion to men who have some taste for music but can neither appreciate the more difficult kinds nor compose; highly religious men and saints to persons with an exceptionally fine ear for music who may yet be unable to compose it; and the founders of religions to great musical composers, such as Bach and Beethoven.

This analogy is, of course, incomplete in certain important respects. Religious experience raises three problems, which are different though closely interconnected. (i) What is the *psychological analysis* of religious experience? Does it contain factors which are present also in certain experiences which are not religious? Does it contain any factor which never occurs in any other kind of experience? If it contains no such factor, but is a blend of elements each of which can occur separately or in non-religious experiences, its psychological peculiarity must consist in the characteristic way in which these elements are blended in it. Can this peculiar structural feature of religious experience be indicated and described? (ii) What are the *genetic and causal conditions* of the existence of religious experience? Can we trace the origin and development of the disposition to have religious experiences (a) in the human race, and (b) in each individual? Granted that the disposition is present in nearly all individuals at the present time, can we discover and state the variable conditions which call it into activity on certain occasions and leave it in abeyance on others? (iii) Part of the content of religious experience is alleged knowledge or well-founded belief about the nature of reality, e.g., that we are dependent on a being who loves us and whom we ought to worship, that values are somehow conserved in spite of the chances and changes of the material world at the mercy of which they seem *prima facie* to be, and so on. Therefore there is a third problem. Granted that religious experience exists, that it has such-and-such a history and conditions, that it seems vitally important to those who have it, and that it produces all kinds of effects which would not otherwise happen, is it *veridical?* Are the claims to knowledge or well-founded belief about the nature of reality, which are an integral part of the experience, *true or probable?* Now, in the case of musical experience, there are analogies to the psychological problem and to the genetic or causal problem, but there is no analogy to the epistemological problem of validity. For, so far as I am aware, no part of the content of musical experience is alleged knowledge about the nature of reality; and therefore no question of its being veridical or delusive can arise.

Since both musical experience and religious experience certainly exist, any theory of the universe which was incompatible with their existence would be false, and any theory which failed to show the connexion between their existence and the other facts about reality would be inadequate. So far the two kinds of experience are in exactly the same position. But a theory which answers to the condition that it allows of the *existence* of religious experience and indicates the *connexion* between its existence and other facts about reality may leave the question as to its *validity* quite unanswered. Or, alternatively, it may throw grave

doubt on its cognitive claims, or else it may tend to support them. Suppose, e.g., that it could be shown that religious experience contains no elements which are not factors in other kinds of experience. Suppose further it could be shown that this particular combination of factors tends to originate and to be activated only under certain conditions which are known to be very commonly productive of false beliefs held with strong conviction. Then a satisfactory answer to the questions of psychological analysis and causal antecedents would have tended to answer the epistemological question of validity in the negative. On the other hand, it might be that the only theory which would satisfactorily account for the origin of the religious disposition and for the occurrence of actual religious experiences under certain conditions was a theory which allowed some of the cognitive claims made by religious experience to be true or probable. Thus the three problems, though entirely distinct from each other, may be very closely connected; and it is the existence of the third problem in connexion with religious experience which puts it, for the present purpose, in a different category from musical experience.

In spite of this essential difference the analogy is not to be despised, for it brings out at least one important point. If a man who had no ear for music were to give himself airs on that account, and were to talk *de haut en bas* about those who can appreciate music and think it highly important, we should regard him, not as an advanced thinker, but as a self-satisfied Philistine. And, then if he did not do this but only propounded theories about the nature and causation of musical experience, we might think it reasonable to feel very doubtful whether his theories would be adequate or correct. In the same way, when persons without religious experience regard themselves as being *on that ground* superior to those who have it, their attitude must be treated as merely silly and offensive. Similarly, any theories about religious experience constructed by persons who have little or none of their own should be regarded with grave suspicion. (For that reason it would be unwise to attach very much weight to anything that the present writer may say on this subject.)

On the other hand, we must remember that the possession of a great capacity for religious experience, like the possession of a great capacity for musical appreciation and composition, is no guarantee of high general intelligence. A man may be a saint or a magnificent musician and yet have very little common sense, very little power of accurate introspection or of seeing causal connexions, and scarcely any capacity for logical criticism. He may also be almost as ignorant about other aspects of reality as the non-musical or non-religious man is about musical or religious experience. If such a man starts to theorize about music or religion, his theories may be quite as absurd, though in a different way, as those made by persons who are devoid of musical or religious experience. Fortunately it happens that some religious mystics of a high order have been extremely good at introspecting and describing their own experiences. And some highly religious persons have had very great critical and philosophical abilities. St. Teresa is an example of the first, and St. Thomas Aquinas of the second.

Now I think it must be admitted that, if we compare and contrast the statements made by religious mystics of various times, races, and religions, we find a common nucleus combined with very great differences of detail. Of course the interpretations which they have put on their experiences are much more varied than the experiences themselves. It is obvious that the interpretations will depend in a large measure on the traditional religious beliefs in which various mystics have been brought up. I think that such traditions probably act in two different ways.

(i) The tradition no doubt affects the theoretical interpretation of experiences which would have taken place even if the mystic had been brought up in a different tradition. A feeling of unity with the rest of the universe will be interpreted very differently by a Christian who has been brought up to believe in a personal God and by a Hindu mystic who has been trained in a quite different metaphysical tradition.

(ii) The traditional beliefs, on the other hand, probably determine many of the details of the experience itself. A Roman Catholic mystic may have visions of the Virgin and the saints, whilst a Protestant mystic pretty certainly will not.

Thus the relations between the experiences and the traditional beliefs are highly complex. Presumably the outlines of the belief are determined by the experience. Then the details of the belief are fixed for a certain place and period by the special peculiarities of the experiences had by the founder of a certain religion. These beliefs then become traditional in that religion. Thenceforth they in part determine the details of the experiences had by subsequent mystics of that religion, and still more do they determine the interpretations which these mystics will put upon their experiences. Therefore, when a set of religious beliefs has once been established, it no doubt tends to produce experiences which can plausibly be taken as evidence for it. If it is a tradition in a certain religion that one can communicate with saints, mystics of that religion will seem to see and to talk with saints in their mystical visions; and this fact will be taken as further evidence for the belief that one can communicate with saints.

Much the same double process of causation takes place in sense-perception. On the one hand, the beliefs and expectations which we have at any moment largely determine what *interpretation* we shall put on a certain sensation which we should in any case have had then. On the other hand, our beliefs and expectations do to some extent determine and modify some of the sensible characteristics of the *sensa themselves*. When I am thinking only of diagrams a certain visual stimulus may produce a sensation of a sensibly flat sensum; but a precisely similar stimulus may produce a sensation of a sensibly solid sensum when I am thinking of solid objects.

Such explanations, however, plainly do not account for the first origin of religious beliefs, or for the features which are common to the religious experiences of persons of widely different times, races, and traditions.

Now, when we find that there are certain experiences which, though never very frequent in a high degree of intensity, have happened in a high degree among a few men at all times and places; and when we find that, in spite of differences in detail which we can explain, they involve certain fundamental conditions which are common and peculiar to them; two alternatives are open to us. (i) We may suppose that these men are in contact with an aspect of reality which is not revealed to ordinary persons in their everyday experience. And we may suppose that the characteristics which they agree in ascribing to reality on the basis of these experiences probably do belong to it. Or (ii) we may suppose that they are all subject to a delusion from which other men are free. In order to illustrate these alternatives it will be useful to consider three partly analogous cases, two of which are real and the third imaginary.

(a) Most of the detailed facts which biologists tells us about the minute structure and changes in cells can be perceived only by persons who have had a long training in the use of the microscope. In this case we believe that the agreement among trained microscopists really does correspond to facts which untrained persons cannot perceive. (b) Persons of all races who habitually drink alcohol to excess eventually have perceptual experiences in which they seem to themselves to see snakes or rats crawling about their rooms or beds. In this case we believe that this agreement among drunkards is merely a uniform hallucination. (c) Let us now imagine a race of beings who can walk about and touch things but cannot see. Suppose that eventually a few of them developed the power of sight. All that they might tell their still blind friends about colour would be wholly unintelligible to and unverifiable by the latter. But they would also be able to tell their blind friends a great deal about what the latter would feel if they were to walk in certain directions. These statements would be verified. This would not, of course, *prove* to the blind ones that the unintelligible statements about colour correspond to certain aspects of the world which they cannot perceive. But it would show that the seeing persons had a source of additional information about matters which the blind ones could understand and test for themselves. It would not be unreasonable then for the blind ones to believe that probably the seeing ones are also able to perceive other aspects of reality which they are describing correctly when they make their unintel-

ligible statements containing colour-names. The question then is whether it is reasonable to regard the agreement between the experiences of religious mystics as more like the agreement among trained microscopists about the minute structure of cells, or as more like the agreement among habitual drunkards about the infestation of their rooms by pink rats or snakes, or as more like the agreement about colours which the seeing men would express in their statements to the blind men.

Why do we commonly believe that habitual excess of alcohol is a cause of a uniform delusion and not a source of additional information? The main reason is as follows. The things which drunkards claim to perceive are not fundamentally different in kind from the things that other people perceive. We have all seen rats and snakes, though the rats have generally been grey or brown and not pink. Moreover the drunkard claims that the rats and snakes which he sees are literally present in his room and on his bed, in the same sense in which his bed is in his room and his quilt is on his bed. Now we may fairly argue as follows. Since these are the sort of things which we could see if they were there, the fact that we cannot seem them makes it highly probable that they are not there. Again, we know what kinds of perceptible effect would generally follow from the presence in a room of such things as rats or snakes. We should expect fox-terriers or mongooses to show traces of excitement, cheese to be nibbled, corn to disappear from bins, and so on. We find that no such effects are observed in the bedrooms of persons suffering from *delirium tremens*. It therefore seems reasonable to conclude that the agreement among drunkards is a sign, not of a revelation, but of a delusion.

Now the assertions in which religious mystics agree are not such that they conflict with what we can perceive with our senses. They are about the structure and organization of the world as a whole and about the relations of men to the rest of it. And they have so little in common with the facts of daily life that there is not much chance of direct collision. I think that there is only one important point on which there is conflict. Nearly all mystics seem to be agreed that time and change and unchanging duration are unreal or extremely superficial, whilst these seem to plain men to be the most fundamental features of the world. But we must admit, on the one hand, that these temporal characteristics present very great philosophical difficulties and puzzles when we reflect upon them. On the other hand, we may well suppose that the mystic finds it impossible to state clearly in ordinary language what it is that he experiences about the facts which underlie the appearance of time and change and duration. Therefore it is not difficult to allow that what we experience as the temporal aspect of reality corresponds in some sense to certain facts, and yet that these facts appear to us in so distorted a form in our ordinary experience that a person who sees them more accurately and directly might refuse to apply temporal names to them.

Let us next consider why we feel fairly certain that the agreement among trained microscopists about the minute structure of cells expresses an objective fact, although we cannot get similar experiences. One reason is that we have learned enough, from simpler cases of visual perception, about the laws of optics to know that the arrangement of lenses in a microscope is such that it will reveal minute structure, which is otherwise invisible, and will not simply create optical delusions. Another reason is that we know of other cases in which trained persons can detect things which untrained people will overlook, and that in many cases the existence of these things can be verified by indirect methods. Probably most of us have experienced such results of training in our own lives.

Now religious experience is not in nearly such a strong position as this. We do not know much about the laws which govern its occurrence and determine its variations. No doubt there are certain standard methods of training and meditation which tend to produce mystical experiences. These have been elaborated to some extent by certain Western mystics and to a very much greater extent by Eastern Yogis. But I do not think that we can see here, as we can in the case of microscopes and the training which is required to

make the best use of them, any conclusive reason why these methods should produce veridical rather than delusive experiences. Uniform methods of training and meditation would be likely to produce more or less similar experiences, whether these experiences were largely veridical or wholly delusive.

Is there any analogy between the facts about religious experience and the fable about the blind men some of whom gained the power of sight? It might be said that many ideals of conduct and ways of life, which we can all recognize now to be good and useful, have been introduced into human history by the founders of religions. These persons have made actual ethical discoveries which others can afterwards recognize to be true. It might be said that this is at least roughly analogous to the case of the seeing men telling the still blind men of facts which the latter could and did verify for themselves. And it might be said that this makes it reasonable for us to attach some weight to what founders of religions tell us about things which we cannot understand or verify for ourselves; just as it would have been reasonable for the blind men to attach some weight to the unintelligible statements which the seeing men made to them about colours.

I think that this argument deserves a certain amount of respect, though I should find it hard to estimate how much weight to attach to it. I should be inclined to sum up as follows. When there is a nucleus of agreement between the experiences of men in different places, times, and traditions, and when they all tend to put much the same kind of interpretation on the cognitive content of these experiences, it is reasonable to ascribe this agreement to their all being in contact with a certain objective aspect of reality *unless* there be some positive reason to think otherwise. The practical postulate which we go upon everywhere else is to treat cognitive claims as veridical unless there be some positive reason to think them delusive. This, after all, is our only guarantee for believing that ordinary sense-perception is veridical. We cannot *prove* that what people agree in perceiving really exists independently of them; but we do always assume that ordinary waking sense-perception is veridical unless we can produce some positive ground for thinking that it is delusive in any given case. I think it would be inconsistent to treat the experiences of religious mystics on different principles. So far as they agree they should be provisionally accepted as veridical unless there be some positive ground for thinking that they are not. So the next question is whether there is any positive ground for holding that they are delusive.

There are two circumstances which have been commonly held to cast doubt on the cognitive claims of religious and mystical experience. (i) It is alleged that founders of religions and saints have nearly always had certain neuropathic symptoms or certain bodily weaknesses, and that these would be likely to produce delusions. Even if we accept the premises, I do not think that this is a very strong argument. (a) It is equally true that many founders of religions and saints have exhibited great endurance and great power of organization and business capacity which would have made them extremely successful and competent in secular affairs. There are very few offices in the cabinet or in the highest branches of the civil service which St. Thomas Aquinas could not have held with conspicuous success. I do not, of course, regard this as a positive reason *for* accepting the metaphysical doctrines which saints and founders of religions have based on their experiences; but it is relevant as a *rebuttal* of the argument which we are considering. (b) Probably very few people of extreme genius in science or art are perfectly normal mentally or physically, and some of them are very crazy and eccentric indeed. Therefore it would be rather surprising if persons of religious genius were completely normal, whether their experiences be veridical or delusive. (c) Suppose, for the sake of argument, that there is an aspect of the world which remains altogether outside the ken of ordinary persons in their daily life. Then it seems very likely that some degree of mental and physical abnormality would be a necessary condition for getting sufficiently loosened from the objects of ordinary sense-perception to come into cognitive contact with this aspect of reality. Therefore the fact that those persons who claim to have this peculiar kind of cognition gen-

erally exhibit certain mental and physical abnormalities is rather what might be anticipated if their claims were true. One might need to be slightly 'cracked' in order to have some peep-holes into the super-sensible world. (d) If mystical experience were veridical, it seems quite likely that it would *produce* abnormalities of behaviour in those who had it strongly. Let us suppose, for the sake of argument, that those who have religious experience are in frequent contact with an aspect of reality of which most men get only rare and faint glimpses. Then such persons are, as it were, living in two worlds, while the ordinary man is living in only one of them. Or, again, they might be compared to a man who has to conduct his life with one ordinary eye and another of a telescopic kind. Their behaviour may be appropriate to the aspect of reality which they alone perceive and think all-important; but, for that very reason, it may be inappropriate to those other aspects of reality which are all that most men perceive or judge to be important and on which all our social institutions and conventions are built.

(ii) A second reason which is commonly alleged for doubt about the claims of religious experience is the following. It is said that such experience always originates from and remains mixed with certain other factors, e.g., sexual emotion, which are such that experiences and beliefs that arise from them are very likely to be delusive. I think that there are a good many confusions on this point, and it will be worth while to begin by indicating some of them.

When people say that B 'originated from' A, they are liable to confuse at least three different kinds of connexion between A and B. (i) It might be that A is a necessary but insufficient condition of the existence of B. (ii) It might be that A is a necessary and sufficient condition of the existence of B. Or (iii) it might be that B simply *is* A in a more complex and disguised form. Now, when there is in fact evidence only for the first kind of connexion, people are very liable to jump to the conclusion that there is the third kind of connexion. It may well be the case, e.g., that no one who was incapable of strong sexual desires and emotions could have anything worth calling religious experience. But it is plain that the possession of a strong capacity for sexual experience is not a *sufficient* condition of having a religious experience; for we know that the former quite often exists in persons who show hardly any trace of the latter. But, even if it could be shown that a strong capacity for sexual desire and emotion is *both* necessary and sufficient to produce religious experience, it would not follow that the latter is just the former in disguise. In the first place, it is not at all easy to discover the exact meaning of this metaphorical phrase when it is applied to psychological topics. And, if we make use of physical analogies, we are not much helped. A mixture of oxygen and hydrogen in presence of a spark is necessary and sufficient to produce water accompanied by an explosion. But water accompanied by an explosion is not a mixture of oxygen and hydrogen and a spark 'in a disguised form', whatever that may mean.

Now I think that the present rather vaguely formulated objection to the validity of the claims of religious experience might be stated somewhat as follows. 'In the individual, religious experience originates from, and always remains mixed with, sexual desires and emotions. The other generative factor of it is the religious tradition of the society in which he lives, the teachings of his parents, nurses, schoolmasters, etc. In the race religious experience originated from a mixture of false beliefs about nature and man, irrational fears, sexual and other impulses, and so on. Thus the religious tradition arose from beliefs which we now recognize to have been false and from emotions which we now recognize to have been irrelevant and misleading. It is now drilled into children by those who are in authority over them at a time of life when they are intellectually and emotionally at much the same stage as the primitive savages among whom it originated. It is, therefore, readily accepted, and it determines beliefs and emotional dispositions which persist long after the child has grown up and acquired more adequate knowledge of nature and of himself.'

Persons who use this argument might admit that it does not definitely *prove* that religious beliefs are false and groundless. False beliefs and irrational fears in our remote ancestors *might* con-

ceivably be the origin of true beliefs and of an appropriate feeling of awe and reverence in ourselves. And, if sexual desires and emotions be an essential condition and constituent of religious experience, the experience *may* nevertheless be veridical in important respects. We might merely have to rewrite one of the beatitudes and say 'Blessed are the *impure* in heart, for they shall see God'. But, although it is logically possible that such causes should produce such effects, it would be said that they are most unlikely to do so. They seem much more likely to produce false beliefs and misplaced emotions.

It is plain that this argument has considerable plausibility. But it is worth while to remember that modern science has almost as humble an ancestry as contemporary religion. If the primitive witch-smeller is the spiritual progenitor of the Archbishop of Canterbury, the primitive rain-maker is equally the spiritual progenitor of the Cavendish Professor of Physics. There has obviously been a gradual refinement and purification of religious beliefs and concepts in the course of history, just as there has been in the beliefs and concepts of science. Certain persons of religious genius, such as some of the Hebrew prophets and the founders of Christianity and of Buddhism, do seem to have introduced new ethico-religious concepts and beliefs which have won wide acceptance, just as certain men of scientific genius, such as Galileo, Newton, and Einstein, have done in the sphere of science. It seem somewhat arbitrary to count this process as a continual approximation to true knowledge of the material aspect of the world in the case of science, and to refuse to regard it as at all similar in the case of religion. Lastly, we must remember that all of us have accepted the current common-sense and scientific view of the material world on the authority of our parents, nurses, masters, and companions at a time when we had neither the power nor the inclination to criticize it. And most of us accept, without even understanding, the more recondite doctrines of contemporary physics simply on the authority of those whom we have been taught to regard as experts.

On the whole, then, I do not think that what we know of the conditions under which religious beliefs and emotions have arisen in the life of the individual and the race makes it reasonable to think that they are *specially* likely to be delusive or misdirected. At any rate any argument which starts from that basis and claims to reach such a conclusion will need to be very carefully handled if its destructive effects are to be confined within the range contemplated by its users. It is reasonable to think that the concepts and beliefs of even the most perfect religions known to us are extremely inadequate to the facts which they express; that they are highly confused and are mixed up with a great deal of positive error and sheer nonsense;

and that, if the human race goes on and continues to have religious experiences and to reflect on them, they will be altered and improved almost out of recognition. But all this could be said, *mutatis mutandis,* of scientific concepts and theories. The claim of any particular religion or sect to have complete or final truth on these subjects seems to me to be too ridiculous to be worth a moment's consideration. But the opposite extreme of holding that the whole religious experience of mankind is a gigantic system of pure delusion seems to me to be almost (though not quite) as far-fetched.

II.3   Skepticism on Religious Experience

WALLACE MATSON

Wallace Matson is professor of philosophy at the University of California at Berkeley. This selection is from his book The Existence of God *(1965). Matson first offers a brief analysis of perception. He then applies it to the notion of certifying the experience of a god. He notes that there are several conditions that must be fulfilled in normal perceptual reports, such as corroboration and publicity, that are not fulfilled in religious experiences. By itself, therefore, the testimony of the subject cannot be used to persuade others of its veridicality (unless we have independent evidence for the existence of a god, in which case we should expect such experiences).*

Experience

Now we can begin to consider reasons, offered as justifying belief in gods, that are at least on their face of the same sort as reasons granted by everyone to be good reasons in other contexts.

One kind of good reason for believing in the existence of X is that one has perceived X, one has had experience of X. To be sure, philosophers sometimes question, or write as if they were questioning, the cogency of such reasons. Some theorists of knowledge profess to find many difficulties in justifying belief in the existence of a tree "in reality," "out there," "independent of the perceiver" merely on the ground that normal persons truthfully report that they see, smell, kick, climb in, or cut down a tree. I shall, however, ignore all such skeptical cavils and take it for granted that seeing or smelling a tree is normally a good reason for believing that an "objective" tree exists ("normally" meaning: in the absence of special positive reasons for doubt, such as ingestion of drugs, paresis, crazy-house context, hypnotist in vicinity, etc.); that a certain recognizable and distinguishable taste—the "taste of gin"—is normally a good reason for believing there to be gin in the punch; that objects roughly similar to ourselves in appearance and behavior are also like us in possessing consciousnesses with roughly similar contents; in a word, I shall assume, naively if you like, that perception is in general valid ground for claiming knowledge, at the same time remaining aware, as everyone must, of the existence of illusions and delusions, and of the difficulty, in some cases, of distinguishing the veridical from the illusory.

Perception

We need to indicate, however, how it is that we distinguish between perceptions and other kinds of conscious or quasi-conscious experiences, such as feeling blue, having a toothache, and dreaming. Now some philosophers do not make a distinction here; they speak of "perceiving one's toothache," "perceiving a red patch" (tomato or afterimage alike), and "perceiving a pink elephant [or maybe elephantoid patch] chasing one in a dream." Although I believe that there are objections to this way of speaking which are more than merely verbal ones, this is not the place to argue the point.

The verb "perceive" is transitive, and takes as its grammatical object only a "that" clause or the name of a thing—usually physical, but we shall allow the possibility of its being mental, or if you prefer, spiritual—that is independent of the perceiver. Thus it is not correct to speak of perceiving pains, afterimages, and pink elephants. It is all right to say, "I *thought* I perceived a pink elephant (but of course I had delirium tremens at the time)," "I seemed to hear the doorbell (but I was mistaken; it was a ringing in the ear)," "the beamish boy perceived a jabberwock whiffling through the tulgey wood" (where the context indicates that the assertion is not to be taken as literally describing a fact).

One does not perceive qualities per se: "I saw something red" will do, but not "I saw red," except as a metaphor; nor the philosophical jargon "I saw a red patch," unless this is a description, say, of a feature of someone's shirt. ("Lemon juice is sour, though nothing is a sour taste."—Kotarbinski.) Whether it is possible to perceive ghoulies and ghosties and things that go bump in the night, turns on the factual question of whether such entities are or are not part of the furniture of the universe, with their own careers, independent of the anxieties of Scotsmen.

Seeing, hearing, tasting, smelling, and touching are kinds of perceiving, but there may be others. "Extrasensory perception" is not here assumed to be a contradiction in terms. In our usage it is a hypothesis, not a matter of definition, that every case of perception involves a process in a sense receptor.

Perception is analyzable into a conscious experience (CE) of a perceiver (P), the object (O) perceived, and a relation (R) between the object and the perception. The CE must reveal characters that the O really has. To defend this statement, or even to explain it fairly fully, would involve us in unnecessary complications. An example may help to convey the bearing of this requirement: a tomato really is red. Someone looks at a tomato in a darkroom (under a red light). If he follows our recommendations, he will not say, "I saw a white tomato," but rather, "I seemed to see a white tomato," or "The tomato looked white," i.e., "The experience I had was like what I would have had if, in normal illumination, I had seen a tomato that really was white."

R is a causal relation. O causes CE or is an indispensable part of the cause. If I have my eyes closed and experience a hallucination of a tomato in a dish, I am not perceiving a tomato, even if there happens to be a tomato in a dish in front of me.

To sum up these points, perception, as we shall use the word, requires a real object. This is the important distinction between it and two other kinds of conscious experiences: fellings and fantasies. "Feelings" are experiences which do not, in and of themselves, reveal any features of the outside world, and which are such that no one is tempted to suppose that they do: aches and pains, joy, anger are some examples. Of course it is not denied that one is often led to infer features of the outside world from feelings; and such inferences are often justified. From "seeing stars" we may infer a lump on the head; but "seeing stars" is not perceiving a lump on the head, any more than it is perceiving stars, or perceiving anything at all. "Fantasies" will here be employed as a general term for all conscious experiences that are similar (in form and content) to perceptions, and that it is natural to describe in the "It seemed as if I were perceiving . . ." locution, or in terms limited in their application to such experiences: "I dreamed that . . . ," "I pictured to myself the . . . ," "I imagined myself to be . . . ," etc. We subdivide fantasies into the subclasses of imaginings, those fantasies which the subject does not confuse with perception; and delusions, which the subject mistakes for perception.

Nothing is a perception that does not fulfill our conditions of revelation and causality. It is of course one of the major traditional problems of philosophy to develop criteria for knowing that these conditions are satisfied—for distinguishing, and knowing that one has distinguished, between perceptions and delusions. This is another morass that we shall skirt. Or at any rate we shall not wade in it more deeply than we have to.

Visions and Voices

We now return to our main problem, that of trying to determine what sort of experience might suffice to certify the existence of a god.

Experiences that might possibly accomplish this will either be like ordinary experiences or unlike them. Let us consider the former class first.

A god-certifying experience might be like a perception; indeed, it might even *be* a perception. Let us assume that someone is known to have perceived some person and the perceiver claims, on the basis of this experience, to have knowledge of the existence of a god.

The claim, if reasonable, must be based either on some reasons advanced by the allegedly divine personage perceived or on the character of the personage. We have already considered the latter case, and we have only to repeat our conclusion: very extraordinary behavior by the personage might confer some probability on the claim; but there is no convincing evidence of this ever having happened. The evidential value (if any) of such epiphanies is in confirming beliefs otherwise established, whether in the first instance rationally or not; but if the original belief was not based on rational considerations, the appearance cannot confer reasonableness on it.

But is not something more than superfluous corroboration to be expected from an appearance of a well-known personage of religion? For surely this would show that the personage in question was real, not merely mythical. Suppose that belief in god X is based on an ancient document, which among other assertions minutely describes Y, the immortal messenger of X. Suppose now that a being of precisely this description (there is not and could not be any mistake about it) appears out of nowhere and announces that he is Y, sent by X; after performing various miracles, he vanishes upward. Would this not confirm the claims of the document?

Of course it would. To say so, however, is not to concede any more than we have already admitted in discussing miracles. The tremendous, if not insuperable, difficulties of ruling out the possibility of hallucination would remain. The evidential value of an epiphany would be greatly increased if Y appeared to someone who had never heard of him or of the document in question. It is safe to say that there is no reason to suppose that any such Y (or X, for that matter) has ever appeared to anyone who had not previously heard of Y or X. There are famous instances of apparitions to *nonbelievers,* but this does not alter the case: the psychology of such phenomena is well enough understood. So far from anyone *knowing* that someone has perceived a supernatural personage, there is no reason to believe that it has ever occurred. For the ordinary tests for distinguishing perceptions from fantasies turn on the publicity of the phenomena. (It will be noted that no publicity requirement has been incorporated into our definition of perception.) If P reports that he sees or hears something of a size or loudness such that ordinary persons normally see and hear such things, and no one else in the vicinity sees it or hears it, the claim of perception is dismissed without further ado. A certain degree of corroboration by others, however, may be attained without validating the claim, because of the well-known phenomena of mass delusion. What is needed is that several persons, of normal eyesight, hearing, and intelligence, not predisposed to believe reports of the phenomenon, and so insulated from one another that the effects of suggestibility can be ruled out, should corroborate the apparition. There may be some reason to believe that such corroboration has been achieved for some "paranormal" manifestations investigated by psychical researchers. However, such evidence does not seem to be available to support any claim for the existence of a god, except at most a very inferior sort of deity (poltergeists and such). We can imagine what the evidence would be like that would support the sort of claim that we are interested in; but in fact such evidence does not exist. This is not to say that it may not be discovered in future; I am inclined to agree with C. D. Broad that theologians should be more interested in psychical research than they are.

To be sure, failure of publicity tests does not disprove the claim that an apparition of a god or his messenger is a perception. We have defined "perception" in such a way that if experience reveals certain characters of a being, and that being really exists and has those characters, and, furthermore, the being causes the subject to have the experience, then the experience is a perception. Publicity is only the most usual and reliable way in which we test whether the experience is of this nature. But as we have just pointed out, an experience may pass the test and still not be a perception; equally it might fail the test and still really be a perception. This possibility has to be seriously considered in the religious context, and perhaps in no other. For a god—a nature-controller, hence a perception-controller—might see fit to reveal himself selectively: just to the believer, or to the virtuous, or to the infidel in need of shock therapy; never to those whose hearts he had hardened or to those beyond some pale or other. Indeed, we can even imagine that such behavior might not be a matter of choice on the part of the god; it might be a law of nature or of supernature that a god of limited power could not "get through" except to those already somehow attuned to him. Such hypotheses would explain why A sees him and B does not, compatibly with A's really seeing him.

If that is the way some god chooses to behave, however, he does so at the price of depriving his epiphanies of evidential value. He really appears to A, we suppose; even so, A cannot know that he has been favored with a theophany, for in the absence of confirmation from fellow men, the hy-

pothesis that the appearance is delusory must have greater probability than that it is veridical. And even if A somehow did know (was rationally convinced of) the reality of the phenomenon, there still could be no reason for B to accept A's testimony concerning it.

The case is different if there is independent evidence for the existence of a god. In that case, there might be some probability, on that evidence, that the god would manifest himself, perhaps privately; and there could be ways of distinguishing genuine manifestations from spurious ones. To perceive the god, or his messengers, would then be to have confirmatory evidence for the existence of that god. But it seems equally clear that no such phenomena—no visions or voices—could ever of themselves establish, or confer the slightest degree of probability on, the existence of a god, either for the recipient of the visitation or for anyone else. (We have noted the one possible exception to this verdict: manifestation to someone utterly ignorant of the supposed existence of the god in question.) Unless the existence of the god is first established by some other means, there is not and cannot be any reason to believe that a private appearance of that god is not a delusion.

Mystical Experience

We must now see how the case stands with experiences unlike ordinary perceptions. At the outset it may seem clear that if epiphanies cannot establish the existence of gods, then experiences not involving personal appearances must be of even less evidential value. For an experience unlike a perception must either be a feeling—and we need not labor the point that a mere feeling or hunch, not confirmed or substantiated by something else, is without evidential value according to the ordinary canons of evidence—or else it must be something altogether unlike any ordinary experience. Now one trouble with apparitions is their privacy; but at least the nature of the experience can be communicated to others. One can say, "The being was such and such form and figure, and he spake thus and so." But if an experience is utterly unlike any that one's audience has undergone, then one cannot even describe it intelligibly. It is hard to imagine what evidential value an indescribable encounter might have to others.

To others. . . . But what about to the person who has it? We must consider these two cases separately.

Let us try to rid ourselves of prejudices. Let us try to determine in advance and in a vacuum, so to speak, what a direct experience of a god should be like; what would be the most "natural" (in some sense) form for such an encounter to take; and let us try to forget what we have heard already on this score.

Now God is totally unlike any object of our ordinary experience; and if it is allowable to speak of God as a sort of limiting case that finite deities might more or less approximate, then insofar as a deity approaches to the character of God just to that extent the deity moves farther and farther from the orbit of worldly doings. Just to that extent, also, the deity becomes interesting as a religious object, a fit object of worship. But likewise, just to the extent to which a deity is unlike an everyday object, so one should expect in advance that an encounter with him would be unlike an everyday encounter. Hence the presumption is that an immediate experience of God, or of any august deity, would be so very strange as to be partly or wholly indescribable.

Of course religious persons of a certain degree of sophistication realize this; that is why, if they put any credence at all in epiphanies, they take it for granted that the appearance is only of a messenger (*angellos*) of the god, not of the god himself. On the other hand, it is equally clear that the mere occurrence of an indescribable experience cannot be regarded, in advance, as evidence for the existence of a god or of anything else. And it is hard to see how one indescribable experience can be distinguished from another—at all events by one who only hears tell of such occurrences. It looks then as if an experience, to be evidence for the existence of a god, must be indescribable; but an indescribable experience cannot be evidence for anything; therefore no experience can be evidence for the existence of a god.

It is, however, only the spectator who is at this impasse. Possibly the man who has the experience is not thus embarrassed, and perhaps there is some way in which he can communicate something of evidential value to the spectator.

Experiences of a unique and indescribable sort, which are taken by their subjects to be revelatory of a god, are not very common; but they are common enough to have a name, "mystical experiences"; and they are reported in nearly all cultures. We shall use the term "mystic" to refer to the subject of such an experience. This usage should not be confused with the vaguer, usually derogatory, popular sense.

Although the content of the mystical experience is indescribable, this does not mean that the experience itself cannot be characterized. William James lists four properties:

1. *Ineffability.* . . . The subject of it immediately says that it defies expression, that no adequate report of its contents can be given in words. . . .
2. *Noetic quality.*—Although so similar to states of feeling, mystic states seem to those who experience them to be also of knowledge. They are states of insight into depths of truth unplumbed by the discursive intellect. They are illuminations, revelations, full of significance and importance, all inarticulate though they remain; and as a rule they carry with them a curious sense of authority for aftertime. . . .
3. *Transiency.*—Mystical states cannot be sustained for long. Except in rare instances, half an hour, or at most an hour or two, seems to be the limit beyond which they fade into the light of common day. . . .
4. *Passivity.*—Although the oncoming of mystical states may be facilitated by preliminary voluntary operations . . . when the characteristic sort of consciousness once has set in, the mystic feels as if his own will were in abeyance, and indeed sometimes as if he were grasped and held by a superior power.[1]

The ineffability of the mystical experience has not prevented the creation of a vast and fascinating mystical literature, in which mystics attempt to convey the feel of their experiences, and to state those insights into the nature of things that they say have been revealed to them.

First, mystics pretty generally agree that their experiences reveal the reality of an order of being distinct from, and in some sense higher than, the world perceived through the senses. Commonly the world of the senses is inferred to be mere confused appearance of this higher reality, or at any rate dependent on it.

Second, reality is revealed to be one; at all events, it is more accurately described as one than as many, though no description is quite right. In any case, reality is emphatically not the "one damned thing after another" that the average sensual man supposes it to be. Moreover, the unity of all things is a tighter unity than any mere regularity or fitting together of parts that science may discover. The unity revealed to the mystics (we are told) transcends the categories of subject and object altogether. The mystic, in his rapture, does not contemplate the unity of all things; he is absorbed into it.

Third, reality is perfect. All that is ultimately valuable is somehow embedded in it; all that is evil is somehow excluded, as "mere appearance" or what you will. Optimism seems to be universal among mystics—even among the Oriental mystics, whose view of the world of the senses is gloomy indeed. And that is just as one would expect: for whatever religion may be, certainly it is supposed to offer us some sort of deliverance from, compensation for, or means of coming to terms with the uneasinesses and horrors that permeate the ordinary condition of man in nature.

Finally, the human soul is identical with, or at least akin to, the supersensible reality. Whatever may be the status of the material world, the soul, or at least some part or aspect of it, is of the same stuff as ultimate reality. Hence it is capable of shuffling off its mortal coil, of escaping from its fleshly prison, and of experiencing the ultimate bliss of reabsorption into the Infinite. The mystical experience itself is usually interpreted as a temporary foretaste of the heavenly state.

These four insights seem to comprise the principal points of agreement found in mystics of dif-

ferent cultures. Within a particular culture or religious tradition, a more specific consensus may obtain, for instance, concerning the reality of the Holy Trinity; and such conclusions may be different from, even incompatible with, what mystics of other religious antecedents infer from their ecstasies. From this fact some critics are led to deny that there is any mystical unanimity, hence to explain away mystical experience as delusion, in effect the heroic degree of wishful thinking. Now certainly mystics do agree on some points and disagree on others; to a certain extent it is an arbitrary matter whether one emphasizes the agreements and explains away the disagreements or vice versa. But it is too much to expect that thousands of human beings, vastly separated in space and time, each with his own cultural and religious heritage, each being the subject of an experience of such a nature as not to be describable in any ordinary language, let alone translatable into all the others—it is too much to expect that all these men should agree on every plank of a metaphysical platform, that their separate interpretations of their separate experiences should be unmixed with circumambient ideas. Rather, any substantial agreement at all will take on an extraordinary and striking importance.

That many mystics, probably a majority, are in substantial agreement on the four points that we have sketched, seems to be a fact; at any rate we shall assume that it is. This is a fact, then, to be explained. The agreement goes very far toward canceling the suspicions otherwise aroused by the private and ineffable nature of the experience. One hypothesis to explain the agreement—a hypothesis that it would be sheer dogmatism to dismiss with no consideration—is that the mystics happen to be right.

Is it our business, however, to investigate the claims of mystics? For our study is of reasons for believing that there is a god; and mystics are not in agreement on the proposition. The existence of God, as an Infinite Personal Intelligence, is not part of the mystical consensus, which seems to point to a view that is more akin to pantheism than to the personal theism that we are scrutinizing. Mystical ecstasy is often described as union with a something—call it X; but more often than not this X is described as impersonal (or superpersonal, if that is different), as something identical with the whole of reality.

However, the relation of God to the world is a nice point in any theology; and it surely is not our business to dwell on the subtleties of that relation. Moreover, our study will be naive and trivial unless we emancipate ourselves from the crudities of anthropomorphism; yet one of the prices of the emancipation is the giving up of any comfortable, intuitive notion of personality, as the term is to be applied to God. All that clearly remains is some abstract notion of unity; and mysticism is surely not wanting in such a notion. In any case, many mystics (suspiciously, those reared in theistic cultures) agree that the experience reveals the existence of God, in a more or less orthodox sense of the proposition. We cannot therefore excuse ourselves from the task of looking into the bearing of their experience on our question.

It will simplify our study if we make certain assumptions. Let us assume that all the mystics we are to consider are unanimous in asserting that God-infinitely powerful, wise, and good Being, the source and support of all creation—exists. When asked for their reasons, they tell us that they know this with absolute certainty because the mystical experience has revealed it to them in such a manner that no doubt whatever is admissible. But when pressed further, they lapse into silence and only smile.

The nonmystic is put into an exasperating situation. Here he is being solicited to adopt an exotic metaphysic, on no better evidence than the say-so of certain persons who claim to have reasons, but who decline altogether to produce them, saying that language—which is adequate enough to describe quantum theory and relativity—is incapable of expressing those reasons. It is understandable if the nonmystic's reaction is to complain that the mystic is crazy. And evidence tending to support this conclusion is not difficult to find. The claim to possess a profound but inexpressible insight is characteristic of many psychotic states. The austerities and mortifications practiced by many mystics in order to "facilitate the oncoming

of mystical states" might be interpreted as systematic methods for driving oneself out of one's mind. The mystic ecstasy itself, as far as an outsider can judge, bears a sinister resemblance to intoxications that can be induced by drugs known to be deleterious to the higher nervous functions. It is well known that in many cultures drug-induced hallucinations are ritually cultivated; and it is not clear how, or even whether, these states are to be distinguished from true mystic ecstasy. It is somehow unseemly that the secret of the universe should be unveiled via eating mushrooms.

The mystic retorts that it is outrageous to suppose that men like Plato, St. Paul, Plotinus, and Pascal, and women like St. Theresa, were simply demented. In rebuttal the skeptic speaks of the proverbial thin line and points out that no one with even a superficial acquaintance with the great of the world, particularly the intellectually great, is under the illusion that they are as a class paradigms of mental health. The counterrebuttal is that the great mystics were great poets, philosophers, scientists, even administrators, because of their mysticism and not in spite of it. The beatific vision is a source of strength as well as of joy. Counter-counterrebuttal: various neuroses (if not psychoses) often have the effect of making their sufferers into most energetic and creative persons.

And so it goes. It might appear that the controversy could be resolved if more detailed clinical material were collected. There is, however, a more fundamental difficulty. Sanity must presumably be defined in terms of adjustment to reality; and the question here is, precisely, what *is* reality? If it is the everyday world, and only that, then pretty clearly the mystic is insane, temporarily or permanently. But to decide the issue this way would obviously beg the question.

We shall just leave the matter up in the air. Mysticism, for all we know, may be lunacy; and the ravings of lunatics, we may assume, are of no evidential value for any purpose except diagnosis. It is not unreasonable to suspect that mysticism is insanity. What is unreasonable is to conclude, in the present state of our knowledge, that it must be. In consequence, we are obliged to explore the hypothesis that mystics are sane.

In that case, their conviction must be taken seriously, as the firm belief of reasonable men arrived at on the basis of evidence available to them. And if they are being reasonable in believing, is it not reasonable for the nonmystics to share their belief on trust?

It may seem at this point that our answer must be negative, because the situation is identical with that of the absolute authority, which we have already rejected as a source of rational belief. But it is not, though the difference is subtle. The absolute authority urges us to believe him just because he is who he is, and for no other reason. The mystic, however, urges us to believe him because his belief is grounded in satisfactory evidence—though he cannot tell us what the evidence is. There is a real difference here, because if the existence of evidence is not even mentioned, then the question of possible access to it does not arise. But when the assertion is made that some kind of evidence exists, then it may after all prove possible to get access to it: the nonmystic may be given directions for becoming a mystic; or failing this, there may be some indirect method of establishing, by ordinary means, the existence and relevance of the evidence.

Physicists tell us that pi-mesons exist. This kind of assertion, and the evidence offered for it, may be taken as a paradigm case of objective existence ("out there"), public verifiability, inferences drawn from undoubted facts in accordance with impeccable canons of scientific procedure, and all the rest that the nonmystic charges the mystic with ignoring. For all that, the evidence for the existence of the pi-meson is in fact inaccessible to the author of this book and very likely to most of its readers. Indeed, the meaning of the sentence "There are pi-mesons" is not understood. The author takes it on faith that this sentence has a meaning to those who concern themselves with such matters and that evidence of its truth is available to them.

It is surely reasonable for me (and for you) to do this. It would be impertinent for us to say: "The alleged evidence for pi-mesons is the property of a small confraternity, who make no pretense of communicating it to anyone outside their clique. What imposture!" For the physicists' retort is unanswerable: "To be sure, the evidence for pi-mesons is in fact inaccessible to you—meaning that if it were before you in your present condition, you could not make anything of it. However, if you are of slightly higher than moderate intelligence, and are willing to devote a rather large amount of time and effort to the study of mathematics and physics, you can be put in a position to understand the evidence and judge for yourself. That is: you can become a physicist. To say that the evidence for the pi-meson is publicly verifiable does not mean that it is easy to comprehend, that it is available right now to the general public; it only means that someone who follows a stated procedure can arrive at comprehension."

The mystic's argument is parallel: "You refuse to believe anything not 'publicly verifiable,' as you put it? Very well. You say that physics is publicly verifiable, though admitting that to understand physics one must become a physicist. Surely then it cannot be unreasonable for us mystics to tell you that the way to understand mysticism is to become a mystic. Now here is the way you do it: fifteen minutes of contemplation the first day, increasing fifteen minutes a day for six weeks; the following breathing exercises . . . ; fasting . . . ; mortifications, etc., etc. After this, your chance of being illuminated will be a fair one. . . . Too difficult? Why should it be easier to penetrate the secret of the universe than to understand the pi-meson? You ask whether we guarantee success if the regimen is followed? Of course we don't! But then, what physicist ever guaranteed that everybody could become a physicist?"

The analogy is plausible. But there are disanalogies:

Item: Physicists, if they cannot talk to laymen, can still talk to one another without difficulty. But there is no technical vocabulary of mysticism enabling mystics to converse about their experiences in a precise manner even among themselves.

Item: There is an agreed curriculum for the study of physics. There is no agreed road to mystical illumination. The manuals vary in their prescriptions, and whole sects of mystics reject set procedures altogether.

Item: The discipline required of the would-be physicist is entirely intellectual. At no point in the proceedings is it made a condition of progress that he "have faith," reform his morals, or anything of that sort. It is otherwise with the mystic path.

Here we have a very serious objection. To lay it down that one must "believe in order to understand" is nothing less than to refuse to play the rational game. So-called evidence that counts as evidence only to believers is just not evidence at all in any recognizable sense of the word. It would be hardly less objectionable to claim that the evidence can be vouchsafed only to the "pure"— and practically it would amount to the same thing, since religions tend to make belief an indispensable condition of "purity." In plain language, what is being said is just this: "Unless you can manage somehow to believe without evidence, you cannot get any evidence." "Unless you really believe in fairies, you will never see any."

Only two considerations prevent this last objection from being fatal to the mystics' claim to rationality. The first is that we probably malign the mystics in complaining that they *always* make faith an antecedent condition of illumination. Perhaps there have been cases of unbelievers being converted all at once by an unsought-for and unexpected ecstasy: St. Paul on the road to Damascus (though that was a vision rather than a rapture). If not, even so the mystic might say that it *could* happen were it not for the lamentable fact that unbelievers, because of their unbelief, are unwilling to tread the rocky path. (Unbelievers in pi-mesons seldom bother to learn physics.) Second, it is after all conceivable that there should really be fairies, who are, however, too shy, or uninterested in proselytizing, to display themselves to vulgar cavilers; similarly, it is conceivable that the believer, and only the believer, is favored by evidence that would convert an unbeliever if it were presented to him—but there is a "law of supernature" that such pearls are not to be cast before swine. We may say if we like that such additional saving hypotheses become somewhat strained, besides being repugnant to our sense of what is fair in the rational game.

It seems fair to conclude, however, that while "But you can become a mystic" may have some force against the flat denial of evidential value to mystical experience, the question is not to be settled this way. For the rejoinder is not enough like "But you can become a physicist" and too much like "But you can become a telepathist." It behooves us all the more, therefore, to appraise the contention that mystical experience is not really different, in those respects that bear on its adequacy as evidence, from ordinary experience; and that, in consequence, people who do not have it ought to listen to people who do have it, for the same excellent reason that the blind should pay attention to the sighted.

Mystics often argue that the privacy and incommunicability of their experiences are characteristics shared by all experiences; the only reason they are noticed in the case of mysticism, but unnoticed about drunkenness, is that mysticism is rarer than drunkenness. But it is absurd to make mere rarity into an incurable evidential defect.

Some philosophers say that every experience is private and incommunicable. What is meant by this paradox is that the quality of the experience— "how it feels," roughly speaking—cannot be put into language. We can communicate its form— how long it takes, what brings it on, how it affects one's blood pressure, etc.; and we can say what it feels *like*. That is all.

When we describe what an experience is like, we do so via assumptions about antecedent experiences of our hearers and about their qualitative similarity to ours.

A: "What does the pudding taste like?" B: "It must have bananas in it." Such an interchange is as successful as any communication could be. If A has not been told all about the pudding, he knows something anyway; he can anticipate the taste of it, and when he tastes it he will not be surprised; he can use the information to decide whether he wants to order a portion for himself; and so on.

The communication is successful only because B can assume that A already knows how a banana tastes. Such an assumption is a reasonable one to make of an adult twentieth-century English-speaking person. Bananas are discriminable physical objects. I bite one; a certain taste-experience ensues. This experience I name "banana-taste." I see someone else bite a banana; I assume that some experience then occurs in him. By the rules of language this experience, whatever its quality, its feel, will be named "banana-taste" likewise. I assume furthermore that the quality of his experience is similar to mine.

A philosopher might challenge this assumption: "How do you know that his banana-taste isn't like your carrot-taste, or even quite unlike any experience you have ever had? All you know, and all you can know, is that he has taken a bite from the banana. What happens then is private to him; there is no conceivable way for you to find out what the quality of his experience is. You mustn't be deceived by the identity of name into supposing you know it in its innerness."

One could meet this challenge by pointing to the publicly observable similarity of his banana to my banana, the similarity of this physiology to mine, and the principle "same cause same effect." If the philosopher is not satisfied by this reasoning, the only thing to do is to say to him: "It doesn't matter. He has some sort of experience when he bites a banana. Whatever its quality, that quality is repeated, so he tells us, whenever he bites any banana. Now, when I tell him the pudding tastes as if it has banana mashed up in it, I succeed in conveying the only kind of information that could be called for in the circumstances: I give him a basis for expecting that repeatable quality (whatever its innerness may be) to be repeated yet once more if he tastes the pudding."

We have touched here on a point of some importance: success in communicating does not depend on knowledge shared by the communicators of the respective feels of their experiences. As far as language is concerned, the banana-taste simply is the experience one has when one bites a banana. To be sure, I believe, I think reasonably, that the quality or content of your banana-taste experience is like mine. But if this were not true—indeed, even if I knew that it was not true—I should go on talking about bananas in just the same way. We can sum this up by saying that language conveys the structure of experience but not its content.

Let us illustrate further. If someone reports that bananas taste just like oranges to him, then we know that his experience is *not* like ours; but what we know in this case is that the structures of our experiences differ: he fails to make a discrimination that we make. This is how we tell that some persons are color-blind. But as long as his discriminations correlate with the differences in the stimuli in the same way that ours do, there is no way we can tell whether the private experiential basis of his discriminations—the qualities, feels, contents of his experiences—are like ours or not.

Nor does language even attempt to describe contents as distinguished from structures, as is indicated by the clumsy and artificial vocabulary we have just had to employ in trying to talk about this distinction. If we suppose that it does, that is because we make a same-structure-same-contents assumption. (I am not questioning that assumption, only pointing it out.)

Another way of making this point is by analyzing what happens when one is asked to describe an experience to someone who has never had it. The same banana will do, if we suppose we lived a hundred years earlier, when bananas were uncommon in the northern hemisphere. You have never tasted a banana. I have. You ask me to describe its taste to you. All I can do is say that it tastes more like *this* than like *that* (where *this* and *that* are things you have tasted), though not *quite* the same as *this*. If I am clever enough, it may occur to me (as it did to one Victorian) to describe it as "a sort of pineapple-flavoured marrow."

The more disparate the experience I try to describe is from any my hearer has gone through, the greater the difficulties. "What does straight whisky taste like?" "Well, it is aromatic, and bitter-sweet—more sweet than bitter—and it burns on the way down." "Like very hot sweetened coffee, then?" "No, no, not that kind of bitter-sweet, and certainly not that kind of burn."

The climax is reached when one struggles to describe the experiences of one sense modality to a person deprived of that sense: "To describe colors to a blind man." One can say something meaningful and suggestive even here: somehow scarlet really is more like a trumpet blast than aquamarine is, and busy wallpaper is rather like walking over gravel; but this is not much help. If it is any help at all, that is because there is some remote similarity between seeing a tomato and hearing a trumpet. Even so, only the person with sight can know this; the blind man must take it on faith.

To return now to the mystic and his defense: the ineffability of mystic ecstasy is just this same ineffability of content that is met in every experience, no matter how commonplace. When the mystic speaks to the nonmystic haltingly, in puzzling metaphors, the same sort of thing is occurring as when a man with sight tries to describe vision to a blind man. The only difference is that mystic experience, not being sensory at all, lacks even that tenuous analogy to our other senses that sight has to hearing.

All that is very well, the nonmystic replies; but those who can see have a rich and precise vocabulary in which they can communicate with one another about their visual experiences; whereas, we must repeat, there is no analogous vocabulary shared by the mystics with which they can communicate among themselves. They talk to one another in the same puzzling metaphors that they address to the general public.

It is not too difficult for the mystic to counter this objection. The reason there is a rich vocabulary of visual terms is that visual experience is structurally complex: there are all sorts of different things to see, and all of them have names. The same is true, though in less degree, of other sense modalities. Mystic ecstasy, on the other hand, is absolutely simple structurally: there is just one object (if it is permissible to use this word) of the experience. Suppose there were just one visible object: say, the sun. Then men of vision would have very little to say to each other: "Have you seen *it* today?" would be about the extent of this talk. They would probably not even have such a word as "bright," since there would be nothing dim to contrast it with; only the total darkness of everything else, wholly other than the sun. Perhaps they would attempt to convey their experience to the blind by saying that the sun is "loud": it comes closer to the mark to describe the sun as

loud than as soft, though of course one should not suppose that it has the same kind of loudness that a thunderclap has. (The burn of whisky is not the same kind of burn as that of hot coffee.) But all these difficulties notwithstanding, they really would be seeing the sun, which really would be "out there"; moreover, they could explain why noonday is warmer than midnight, etc.

This analogy goes a long way toward vindicating mysticism against the ineffability objection. Let us see how far it can be stretched.

Our supposition must be that the sun is the only thing visible and that very few persons are able to see at all. Our question is: Would it be reasonable for the sightless majority to believe in the existence of the sun on the basis of what the few visionaries told them? Our supposition does not answer the question of itself; a belief can be true without being reasonable.

The question of reasonableness, here as always, turns on the question of what kind of evidence in support of the assertion could be produced by the sighted to the blind. We have already suggested that the sighted could explain why noonday is warmer than midnight. Let us follow this out.

The blind people are already aware of two warmth cycles, one of twenty-four hours, the other of 365 days. These cycles are for them brute facts; the visionaries explain them by the movements of the sun, the "source" of warmth. The blind people know that tomatoes will not grow inside wooden structures, but will grow outdoors or in glass houses. The men with sight explain that this is because wood obscures ("stops the sound of"?) the sun, whereas glass does not. The blind men, by endless fiddling with a convex lens, occasionally succeed in setting tinder on fire; the men with sight accomplish this every time straight off.

Now in such circumstances it would be reasonable for the blind men to believe the seers, precisely because the blind men would already have inferred the existence and properties of the sun! The seer would explain the daily cycle of warmth by saying: "There is a big fire up above that moves from east to west." But the blind men, familiar with the warming properties of terrestrial fire, would already have suspected the existence of a moving fiery object, and would have confirmed their hypothesis by various methods: the simplest to describe would perhaps be a convex lens, the position of which was governed by a heat-sensitive servomechanism. Blind men could learn for themselves, simply by feeling, the differential properties of wood and glass with respect to passage of the sun's rays. These men would therefore conclude, correctly, that the seers possessed the ability to perceive directly what "ordinary men" could know only indirectly, via apparatus and associated theory—as if someone were to arise among us who could "hear" radio waves, or "see" electrons making quantum jumps.

It is not to the point to object that our suppositious case is fantastic, that a race of blind men could not stay alive, much less contrive heat-sensitive servomechanisms. We have been talking about what is possible in principle; and it should be fairly easy to see that a blind man could know all of physics—not in the trivial sense of taking on credit what men with sight told him, but by having conducted the fundamental experiments and made the inferences from them. As far as knowing the structure of the physical world is concerned—and that is what physics is solely concerned with—sight is in principle a dispensable sense.

These assertions may be unconvincing, however, and justifying them would take us too far afield. Well then, let us suppose, if you prefer, a more plausible race of blind men—men incapable of building any sort of physicists' apparatus, quite unacquainted with technology. And suppose, now, that the seers appear. Then the brute fact of the warmth cycles is "explained" by the existence and travels of the sun. Really, however, this would be no explanation at all; one brute fact known to the blind would be correlated with another brute fact known to the seer. There would be no reason for the blind man to believe in the seer's fact, first, because there would be no way for him to check up on it; second, because there would be no way of connecting the two facts. Cf. someone who purported to "explain" baldness by a nonsensuous emanation from the bald man's pate.

We can now conclude this excursion into the land of the blind. If seers arose among the blind, the blind would have reason to believe what the seers told them only insofar as the seers' assertions were amenable to checking procedures that could be carried out by the blind men themselves, or at least were of the same general nature as checkable assertions. The qualification is necessary because, for example, it would be reasonable for the blind to believe seers' descriptions of sunspots, even if the blind had no independent means of verifying their existence—if the seers had first established their credibility by making a sufficient number of checkable statements. The main point is that it would not be reasonable for the blind to believe in the sun solely on the testimony of the seers. And we must not be misled by the fact that what the seers reported would be true.

If we now apply this analogy to the case of the mystic in relation to the nonmystic, it is easy to see what conclusion we must come to. At best, it is reasonable for the nonmystic to believe the mystic only if the mystic makes some checkable statements that show him to have a power of directly experiencing what the nonmystic knows about only indirectly—but nonetheless knows about independently of the mystic. In other words, the mystic, just like the seer of visions, could confirm and to some degree extend the nonmystic's knowledge of God—but his testimony could not be sufficient in itself to establish that knowledge in the first instance on a rational basis.

Mystics might object to the application of this analogy, on the ground that the blind-man-and-seer case refers only to what can be reasonably believed about facts in the realm of nature, whereas the mystic claims access to facts (if that is not a misleading word) about supernature. The mystic will tell us that he does not claim a "sixth sense" or anything like a sense; hence conclusions about the circumstances in which we should credit someone with having an extra sense are simply irrelevant.

Actually, however, we have given the mystic more than a run for his money. It must be harder to establish the possession of a faculty of intuition totally unlike a sense, for seeing into a realm totally unlike nature, than to present reasons for believing that one has some mode like the ordinary five senses of apprehending facts in some ways like those of ordinary experience.

Note

1. William James, *The Varieties of Religious Experience* (New York and London: Longmans, Green, 1902), Lect. XVI, pp. 380f.

II.4   A Modified Version of the Argument from Religious Experience

GARY GUTTING

Gary Gutting is professor of philosophy at the University of Notre Dame. Our fourth reading is a revised excerpt from his recent book, Religious Belief and Religious Skepticism. *The significance of Gutting's work lies in its skepticism about the traditional arguments for the existence of God and its assertion that theistic belief can be based on religious experience alone. Gutting believes that his argument successfully "establishes the existence of a good and powerful being concerned about us, and [this] justifies a central core of religious belief." On this basis he argues that the essential validity of religion is vindicated. However, in a manner reminiscent of C. D. Broad (above), he finds that this sort of justified belief "falls far short of the claims of traditional religions and that detailed religious accounts are nearly as suspect as nonreligious accounts. The heart of true religious belief is a realization that we have access to God but only minimal reliable accounts of his nature and relation to us." Gutting develops three criteria that veridical religious experience must meet: They must be repeatable; they must be experienced by many in diverse places and cultures; and they must issue forth in morally better lives.*

From Gary Gutting, *Religious Belief and Religious Skepticism* (Notre Dame: University of Notre Dame Press, 1982), with revisions made for this volume. Printed by permission of the publisher and author. Footnotes edited.

1. Experiences of God

At least since William James' classic work, it has been a commonplace that there are many varieties of religious experience. Oddly, however, philosophical analysts of religious experiences have often ignored this diversity and treated exceptional instances—mystical experiences and physical visions—as typical or even exhaustive of the type. By contrast, I propose to center my discussion on the particular type of religious experience that, though paid little explicit attention by philosophers, is one of the most common and most important in the lives of believers. This is the sort of experience that psychologists of religion call "direct awareness of the presence of God." James gives the following general characterization of such experiences:

> We may lay it down as certain that in the distinctively religious sphere of experience, many persons (how many we cannot tell) possess the objects of their belief, not in the form of mere conceptions which their intellect accepts as true, but rather in the form of quasi-sensible realities directly apprehended [*The Varieties of Religious Experience*, p. 65].

James cites a number of instances of this sort of experience:

> There was not a mere consciousness of something there, but fused in the central happiness of it, a startling awareness of some ineffable good. Not vague either, not like the emotional effect of some poem, or scene, or blossom, or music, but the sure knowledge of the close presence of a sort of mighty person, and after it went, the memory persisted as the one percep-

tion of reality. Everything else might be a dream, but not that [p. 63].

I remember the night, and almost the very spot on the hilltop, where my soul opened out, as it were, into the Infinite, and there was a rushing together of the two worlds, the inner and the outer. . . . I stood alone with Him who had made me, and all the beauty of the world, and love, and sorrow, and even temptation. I did not seek Him, but felt the perfect unison of my spirit with His. . . . The darkness held a presence that was all the more felt because it was not seen. I could not any more have doubted that *He* was there than that I was. I felt myself to be, if possible, the less real of the two [p. 67].

Of the following statement, James says, "Probably thousands of unpretending Christians would write an almost identical account":

God is more real to me than any thought or thing or person. I feel his presence positively, and the more as I live in closer harmony with his laws as written in my body and mind. I feel him in the sunshine or rain. . . . I talk to him as to a companion in prayer and praise, and our communion is delightful. He answers me again and again, often in words so clearly spoken that it seems my outer ear must have carried the tone, but generally in strong mental impressions [p. 70].

Finally, a few brief statements taken, James says, at random:

God surrounds me like the physical atmosphere. He is closer to me than my own breath. In him literally I live and move and have my being.

There are times when I seem to stand in his very presence, to talk with him. Answers to prayers have come, sometimes direct and overwhelming in their revelation of his presence and powers. . . .

I have the sense of a presence, strong, and at the same time soothing, which hovers over me. Sometimes it seems to enwrap me with sustaining arms [p. 71].

More systematic studies reveal the same phenomenon. A recent example is a survey of a random sample of a hundred British university students, two-thirds of whom said they have had religious experiences of some sort, with about one-fourth describing their experiences as "awareness of the presence of God."[1] The following are some representative comments by students reporting such experiences:

It was just about dark and I was looking out of the library window. . . . I was aware of everything going on around me, and I felt that everybody had rejected me—and I felt very alone. But at the same time I was aware of something that was giving me strength and keeping me going . . . protecting me ["Religious Experience Amongst a Group of Post-Graduate Students," p. 168].

It's something that is there all the time. One's awareness of it is limited by one's willingness to submit to it [p. 168].

When I pray . . . I am not praying in a vacuum; there is a response and I feel that at the time of praying, otherwise I think I'd eventually give it up [p. 170].

At university I began to feel the 'gay' life had nothing to offer, life seemed meaningless and all came to a climax about a month before 1st year exams. I was feeling pretty anxious. One night in my room, as I was going to bed, things were at a bursting point. I said, 'I give you my life, whoever you are.' I definitely felt somebody was there and something had been done. I felt relief but not much else, emotionally. It was like a re-direction and this was a gradual thing [pp. 172–173].

There is every reason to believe that at least a very large number of such reports are candid, that the experiences reported did in fact take place. The crucial question is whether any of the experiences are veridical, whether there is reason to think that there really is a powerful and benevolent nonhuman being experienced by people reporting religious experiences. But before discussing this issue, we need to become as clear as possible about the nature of the experiences in question. This is especially important because, as noted above, many philosophical critics of religious experience have simply ignored the existence of the sorts of experiences I have cited. Alasdair MacIntyre, for example, begins his discussion of religious experience by reducing all such experiences ("visions" in his terminology) to two classes:

. . . first, those visions which can properly be called such, that is, those where something is *seen;* and second, those where the experience is of a feeling-state or of a mental image, which are only called visions by an honorific extension of the term.

He then goes on to argue that religious experiences of the second type could never provide evidence for religious claims because "an experience of a distinctively 'mental' kind, a feeling-state or an image cannot of itself yield us any information about anything other than experience" ("Visions," p. 256). With regard to visions properly speaking, MacIntyre argues that they of course cannot be themselves literally of God, since he cannot be seen, and that we are never warranted in inferring from an *X* that we see to a *Y* that we do not see unless we have on other occasions experienced a correlation between *X* and *Y*. Whatever we may think of MacIntyre's arguments here (and the second seems particularly weak), it is clear that they do not apply to religious experiences of the sort we are concerned with, since these are neither reports of mere feeling-states or mental images nor claims to have literally seen saints, angels, or the like. Rather, they are experiences that are both *perceptual* (i.e., purporting to be of something other than the experiencer) and *nonsensory* (not of some object of the special senses). As such, they fall into neither of MacIntyre's two classes and so escape the objections he raises.

Similarly, Wallace Matson raises difficulties first for the veridicality of experiences of "voices and visions" and second for "mystical" experiences (i.e., extraordinary encounters that cannot be intelligibly described to those who have not had them). We have already noted that the experiences with which we are concerned are not of "visions or voices." But neither are they the mystic's ineffable raptures. Although they sometimes have aspects their subjects feel cannot be fully described, they can all be adequately if not completely expressed by saying that they are of a very powerful and very good nonhuman person who is concerned about us. Accordingly, Matson's objections to the veridicality of mystical experiences—which all derive from their apparently peculiar ineffability — are irrelevant to the experiences we are concerned with. These, to summarize, are not given as mere feelings or images, nor are they literal physical visions or ineffable mystical insights. Rather, they are perceptual but nonsensory experiences, purporting to be of a good and powerful being concerned with us.

But are these experiences actually of such a

being? A first crucial point is that no experience that purports to be of an external object, taken simply by itself, makes it reasonable to believe that there is such an object. There are no "phenomenological" features of an experience that will mark it off as of something real. (This is the valid core of Descartes' dream argument: there may be no intrinsic differences between a veridical and a nonveridical perceptual experience.) Given an experience that purports to be of *X*, we need to know more before we are entitled to believe that *X* exists. A useful way of putting this point is as follows: given an experience with *X* as its *intentional object,* we may still ask if it is reasonable to believe that *X* exists (that *X* is a real object). However, for this language not to be misleading, we need to note that saying "*E* has *X* as its intentional object" does not mean that *X* exists in some special nonreal way; rather it means that *E* has the internal character of being an "of-*X*" experience; i.e., it is the sort of experience that, if veridical, is of a really existing *X*. . . .

How, then, do of-*X* experiences support the claim that *X* exists? Richard Swinburne has recently suggested that such an experience provides *prima facie* evidence for the claim, evidence that will be decisive if there is not some overriding reason in our background knowledge for questioning the experience's veridicality. He formulates this suggestion in a "Principle of Credulity": "I suggest that it is a principle of rationality that (in the absence of special considerations) if it seems (epistemically) to a subject that *X* is present, then probably *X* is present; what one seems to perceive is probably so" (*The Existence of God*, p. 245). The "special considerations" that can impugn the veridicality of an of-*X* experience are of four sorts. There can be considerations that show: (1) "that the apparent perception was made under conditions or by a subject found in the past to be unreliable" (p. 260); (2) "that the perceptual claim was to have perceived an object of a certain kind in circumstances where similar perceptual claims have proved false" (p. 261); (3) "that on background evidence it is probable that *X* was not present" (p. 261); (4) "that whether or not *X* was there, *X* was probably not a cause of the experience of its seeming to me that *X* was there" (pp. 263–64). Swinburne argues that none of these conditions are conditions under which we have religious experiences (or receive reports of such experiences); so he concludes that the Principle of Credulity warrants the conclusion that God exists.

Swinburne is right in thinking that to understand properly the epistemic relation between of-*X* experiences and claims that *X* exists we need to recognize that the experience is *prima facie* evidence for the claim. But I think he misconstrues the sense in which the experience is *prima facie* evidence. He takes "*prima facie*" to mean that the evidence of the experience is by itself decisive unless there is some overriding consideration in our background knowledge. But this claim is too strong.

Suppose, for example, I walk into my study one afternoon and seem to see, clearly and distinctly, my recently deceased aunt sitting in my chair. We may assume that the conditions of this experience (my mental state, the lighting of the room, etc.) are not ones that we have reason to think produce unreliable perceptions. Thus, the first of Swinburne's defeating conditions does not hold. Nor, given normal circumstances, does the second condition hold. Most likely, I have no knowledge at all of circumstances in which experiences of the dead by apparently normal persons have turned out to be nonveridical. (We may even assume that I have never heard of anyone I regard as at all reliable reporting such an experience.) Further, knowing nothing at all about the habits or powers of the dead, I have no reason to think that my aunt could not now be in my study or, if present, could not be seen by me. So Swinburne's third and fourth conditions do not hold for this case. But, although none of the four defeating conditions Swinburne recognizes apply, it is obvious that I am not entitled, without further information, to believe that I have in fact seen my aunt. To be entitled to the belief I would need much more evidence—for example, numerous repetitions of the experience, other people having the same or similar experiences, a long visit in which the appearance behaved in ways characteristic of my aunt, information from the appearance that only

my aunt had access to, etc. The mere experience described above provides some slight support for the claim that my aunt is in my room, but, even in the absence of defeating conditions, not nearly enough to warrant believing it.

As this example suggests, an of-*X* experience in general provides *prima facie* evidence of *X*'s existence only in the sense of supplying some (but not sufficient) support for the claim that *X* exists. For belief in the claim to be warranted, the solitary of-*X* experience requires supplementation by additional corroborating experiences. It, along with the additional corroboration, provides an adequate cumulative case for the claim. In cases of kinds of objects of which we have frequently had veridical experiences, we can of course rightly believe that they exist, without further corroboration beyond our seeming to see them. But this is because we have good inductive reason to expect that the further corroborations will be forthcoming. With relatively unfamiliar objects—from elves to deceased aunts to divine beings—this sort of inductive reason is not available; and warranted assent must await further corroboration. . . .

C. B. Martin endorses the sort of view of experiential evidence I am suggesting.[2] He does not require a one-dimensional inference from a subjective experience to its veridicality, but he does insist on the relevance of further "checking procedures" if a subjective experience is claimed to yield an objective truth. For the case of ordinary sense perception (e.g., of a sheet of blue paper), we can, he says, make two sorts of claims. The first is just that the experience as a subjective episode is occurring: "There seems to be a sheet of blue paper." Here the experience is "self-authenticating"; that is, the mere fact of its occurrence is sufficient to establish the truth of the claim based on it. The second sort of claim is that the experience correctly represents an objective state of affairs: "There is a sheet of blue paper." Here, Martin notes, more than just the occurrence of the experience is relevant to the truth of the claim:

> The presence of a piece of blue paper is not to be read off from my experience of a piece of blue paper. Other things are relevant: What would a photograph reveal? Can I touch it? What do others see? It is only

when I admit the relevance of such checking procedures that I can lay claim to apprehending the paper, and, indeed, the admission of the relevance of such procedures is what gives meaning to the assertion that I am apprehending the paper. [p. 77].

Presumably, Martin does not mean that, when I have the experience of seeing a piece of paper, I am never entitled to believe that there actually is a piece of paper unless I have in fact carried out further checking procedures. As we have seen, the inductive background of ordinary experience usually obviates the need for such checking. But to claim that the paper is objectively present is to admit the relevance in principle of such checking procedures in the following sense: if such checking procedures should happen not to support the claim, then it becomes questionable; and, if for some reason, the claim is questioned, the procedure can and should be invoked to support it.

It seems to me that Martin, unlike Flew and Swinburne, is employing an essentially correct account of the role of experience in the establishment of objective-truth claims. The main elements of this account are: (1) an "of-X" experience is veridical only if, supposing it to be veridical, we should expect, in suitable circumstances, the occurrence of certain further experiences; (2) if these further experiences do not occur (given the suitable circumstances), we have no basis for accepting the experience as veridical; (3) if, in the relevant circumstances, the experiences occur, we do have a basis for accepting the experience as veridical; (4) if there is some reason for questioning the veridicality of the experience, then appeal to further expected experiences is needed before accepting the experience as veridical.

Since religious beliefs in general and the veridicality of religious experiences in particular are not rationally unquestionable, religious experiences need further corroboration. So here we must, contrary to Swinburne, insist on the need to support the veridicality claim by further checking procedures. Such checking procedures are not further premises in a one-dimensional proof of God's existence; rather, they contribute to a many-dimensional, cumulative experiential case for his reality.

Given this, Martin goes on to claim that in the case of religious experiences of God no further checking procedures are available: "There are no tests agreed upon to establish genuine experience of God and distinguish it decisively from the ungenuine" ("A Religious Way of Knowing," p. 79). Because this is so, he concludes, religious experiences cannot be rightly taken as establishing the objective reality of God; they show nothing besides the existence of certain human psychological states.

What is puzzling here is Martin's assumption that the need for further checking immediately excludes accepting the veridicality of religious experiences. For surely, at least for the class of experiences we are discussing, there are further experiences that would be expected, given their veridicality. Given the veridicality of the typical experience of a very good and very powerful being concerned about us, we would, for example, expect that: (1) those who have had such experiences once would be likely to have them again; (2) other individuals will be found to have had similar experiences; (3) those having such experiences will find themselves aided in their endeavors to lead morally better lives. All these expectations follow from the nature of the experienced being and its concern for us. If the being has soothed, inspired, or warned me once, it is reasonable to expect that it will do so again in appropriate circumstances. If it is concerned enough to contact *me*, it is reasonable to think that it will contact others in similar situations. Most important, if it is indeed an extraordinarily good, wise, and powerful being, there is reason to think that intimate contact with it will be of great help in our efforts to lead good lives (just as such contact with a human being of exemplary character and wisdom would be likely to have such a result). Further, for some religious experiences, all these expectations are fulfilled to a very high degree. (1) Many people have numerous "of-God" experiences and some even find themselves having a continual sense of the divine presence. (2) "Of-God" experiences are reported from almost every human culture, and the institutional traditions (e.g., churches) they sustain have been among the most enduring in human history. (3) In very many cases, those having "of-God" experiences undergo major moral transformations and find a purpose and strength of will they previously lacked.

It seems, then, that we can argue that religious experiences of God's presence do establish his existence. The experiences themselves give *prima facie* warrant to the claim that he exists, and the fulfillment of the expectations induced by the assumption that the experiences are veridical provides the further support needed for ultimate warrant. This form of an argument from religious experience could be impressively developed by employing detailed illustrations from the literature of religious experience. But here I want to proceed in a different direction, to examine the underpinnings of the argument by developing and discussing the major philosophical challenges to it. . . .

2. Explaining the Experiences Away

When we are presented with the claim that a given religious experience is truly a revelation of the divine, we are often inclined to point out that the occurrence of the experience can be as well or better explained without the assumption that it was in fact produced by an encounter with God. Thus, we make reference to Freudian projections and wish fulfillments, group-induced expectations, schizophrenic personalities, and even the biochemistry of puberty to account for various religious experiences. Do such explanations truly impugn the veridicality of the experiences they try to account for? An adequate answer requires some reflection on the logic of explanation.

A first crucial point is that no explanation is acceptable unless there is reason to think that the explanandum it yields is true. There are no acceptable explanations of why there are only seven planets. Here there are two importantly different cases. In the first, the above condition is readily satisfied because we have good independent grounds for thinking that the premises of the explanation (the explanans) are true and so can conclude by a sound argument from them to the truth of the explanandum. In the second case, we do not have adequate independent support for the

explanans, but rather hope that its successful explanation of the explanandum will help provide such support. In this case, we are justified in regarding the explanation as adequate only if we have good independent reason to think that the explanandum is true.

Let us now apply these comments to attempts to explain away the veridicality of an experience. To claim that an explanation of an experience shows that it is not veridical is to propose an explanans that yields an explanandum asserting the nonveridicality of the experience. The assertion will be justified only if there is reason to think the explanation is adequate, and this will be so only if there is reason to think the explanandum is true. In the first of the cases distinguished in the preceding paragraph, we can rightly regard the explanans itself as establishing the truth of the explanandum, and so the claim that the explanation has shown the nonveridicality of the experience is warranted. Thus, if we know on independent grounds that Jean-Paul has been taking mescaline and that taking mescaline usually causes him to have hallucinations of menacing crustaceans, then we have an explanation of his experience of menacing crustaceans that shows it to be nonveridical. But in the second case this conclusion may not be drawn. If we have no independent support for the claims of the explanans about Jean-Paul's drug use and its probable effects, then, in order to accept the explanation as adequate, we need to have independent support for the claim that Jean-Paul's experiences are nonveridical. In this case, then, the proposed explanation cannot be used to show that the experience it explains is nonveridical.

Our conclusion then must be that we can "explain away" a religious experience only by means of an explanans whose truth we can establish independently of its purported explanatory power. With this in mind, let us examine some standard attempts to explain away religious experiences.

It will be useful to distinguish two sorts of such attempts. The first are based on peculiarities of the individuals who have religious experiences; for example, it may be pointed out that a particular religious mystic shows signs of a psychosis that is typically associated with religious hallucinations.

The second are based on traits common to everyone (or at least everyone belonging to some very broad class); thus, a Freudian might note that we all have unconscious desires to believe in the divine reality allegedly revealed in religious experiences.

The first sort of attempt to explain away religious experiences faces the initial difficulty of severe limitation in scope of application. Even if the "of-God" experiences of some people can be discounted because of their psychological abnormalities, the large number of apparently normal people reporting such experiences makes it extremely unlikely that such an approach could explain away all or even most of these experiences. The approach would be successful only if we had independent reason for thinking that the experiences were nonveridical and could then use this fact to support the hypothesis that there are hidden abnormalities in those who have them. But then, of course, the psychological explanation would presuppose rather than establish the nonveridicality of the experiences it explained.

Furthermore, it is not even clear that the independent establishment of an individual's psychological or physiological abnormalities would ordinarily impugn the veridicality of his religious experiences. The presence of psychotic traits or a history of use of hallucinatory drugs will often impugn the reliability of an individual's sense experiences, because we know that such conditions cause sensory distortions. But it is not so obvious that factors suggesting the unreliability of a person's sense experiences suggest a similar unreliability of his nonsensory experiences. *A priori*, there is just as much reason to think that the abnormalities that inhibit perceptions of material objects might enhance perception of nonmaterial objects. Of course, we might discover correlations between certain psychological traits and the nonveridicality of the religious experiences of those who have them. But this would require some means, other than the appeal to psychological explanations, of determining the nonveridicality of religious experiences; and there is little likelihood that everyone reporting religious experiences would have the traits in question. So there is little

reason to think that this first approach to explaining away religious experiences will be successful.

What about explanations of religious experiences on the basis of traits common to all human beings? Freud, for example, claims that "religious ideas . . . are fulfillments of the oldest, strongest and most urgent wishes of mankind." For example:

> . . . the benevolent rule of a divine Providence allays our fear of the dangers of life; the establishment of a moral world-order ensures the fulfillment of the demands of justice . . . ; and the prolongation of earthly existence in a future life provides the local and temporal framework in which these wish-fulfillments shall take place.

Given that we so deeply desire the truth of religious claims, it is not surprising that many people have experiences that seem to support their truth. For, as common sense suggests and depth psychology shows, there are mechanisms whereby the mind is capable, in certain circumstances, of seeing or otherwise experiencing what it wants to. Hence, from a Freudian perspective, there is a relatively straightforward explanation of religious experiences. Moreover, the premises of this explanation (that we desire religious claims to be true, that the mind can produce experiences fulfilling its wishes) have strong support apart from their role in explaining religious experiences. So shouldn't we conclude that this sort of account does undermine the veridicality of religious experiences?

No. The difficulty is this: even if we do have independent knowledge of the existence and the nature of the mechanisms of wish fulfillment, the Freudian explanation of any specific religious experience requires not only that these mechanisms exist as *capacities* but that they be actually operative in the occurrences of the experiences being explained. But there is no way of seeing the actual operation of wish-fulfillment mechanisms; we can only postulate them as the best explanation of the occurrence of delusory experiences. Hence, to be entitled to assert the actual operation of wish-fulfillment mechanisms, we must first have good reason to think that the experiences they explain are nonveridical. So the Freudian attempt to explain away religious experience is inevitably question-begging.

The same sort of difficulty faces Marxist explanations, based, for example, on the ideas that religious beliefs support the power of the ruling class and that there are socioeconomic forces capable of causing individuals to have experiences supporting these beliefs. We would need to know that these forces were in fact operative in a given case and to know this independent of information about the nonveridicality of the experiences. Similar strictures apply to any other attempts at general explanations (via social, economic, psychological or other causes) of religious experiences and beliefs. It is not sufficient to show just that such causes *could* produce the experiences and beliefs. It must also be shown that they are in fact operative in given cases; and it is very hard to see how this can be done without assuming ahead of time that the experiences and beliefs are nonveridical.

It is sometimes suggested—by both Freudians and Marxists—that *all* experiences are psychologically or economically determined. If we knew this to be so, then we would be justified in appealing to economic or psychological causes to explain religious experiences. It is hard to see what evidence could be put forward for these claims of universal determinism. But, given any such claim, we must surely allow that experiences can be veridical (and known to be so) in spite of their being determined, or else fall into an extreme skepticism. But then the mere fact that a religious experience is psychologically or economically determined does not undermine its veridicality.

A final difficulty facing Freudian and Marxist critiques of religious experience—and critiques based on any other general views of human reality and its place in the world—is that their own basic beliefs and the "evidence" they are said to be based on seem at least as susceptible to being explained away as are religious beliefs and experiences. There are after all Freudian explanations of Marxism and Marxist explanations of Freudianism. (Not to mention the possibility of religious explanations of both.) The attempt to discredit general worldviews by proposing explanations

themselves based on rival worldviews is a two-edged sword that can easily be turned against those who wield it.

3. Religious Experiences and Religion

So far the objections we have considered have derived from epistemological considerations quite separate from, if not opposed to, the content of religious beliefs. In this section we turn to objections derived from religion itself. I will first examine the suggestion that the true God's transcendence and utter uniqueness make it impossible for him to be the object of a human experience (at least of the relatively straightforward perceptual experiences with which we are concerned).

More precisely, the difficulty can be formulated in this way: any object given in our experience must be properly characterizable in terms of our concepts. (On a Kantian view, the experience is possible only if the object is given under our concepts; on an empiricist view, we could abstract the concepts from the object as experienced.) But it is an essential feature of God that none of our concepts are properly applicable to him. For, if they were, he would be just another thing in our world, even if a preeminent one, and not the creator of this world. So, if a being is given as an object of our experience, one thing we can surely conclude is that it is not the God who created us and whom we worship. We may, on this view, allow for special "mystical experiences" that are not encounters with an external object but rapturous unions with God that, as the mystics insist, cannot be described in human language and concepts. But these are very different from the perceptions of God that are our focus here. Indeed, to the extent that mystical experiences are accepted as true manifestations of God, they show that our more mundane perceptions of a powerful and good person are not.

There are at least three important lines of response to this difficulty. First, it should be noted that the objection does not in fact question the veridicality of experiences of a good and powerful person concerned about us. At best, it shows that there is another religiously relevant being, not encountered in these experiences. If it is true that this unexperienceable being is the primary focus of religious belief, then our "of-God" experiences do not ground the central claim of religion. Nonetheless, the existence of the sort of being revealed in these experiences must be of very great importance for us. Second, even religious views that most emphasize the utter transcendence of God (e.g., some versions of Christianity and Hinduism) allow for the role of mediators (angels, lesser gods) between God and man. So even if our experiences are not strictly of God, they may still be important factors in our relation to him. Finally, there is the possibility—at the heart of Christianity in the doctrine of incarnation—that even a transcendent God might reveal himself to us by taking on a human form. Christians who hold that a man living among us was the transcendent God can hardly reject the possibility that this God could reveal himself to us in nonsensory experiences. This possibility is further supported by the fact that, even if none of our concepts are properly applicable to God, there must be some that are more adequate than others to his reality. Thus, it is surely less of a mistake to say that God is good and powerful than to say that he is neurotic and deciduous. But if this is so, there would seem to be room for an experience—although imperfect—of God in terms of the concepts most appropriate to him.

Another objection drawn from religion is based on the alleged wide diversity in the content of experiences of God and the apparent dependence of this content on the religious traditions of the experiencers. This diversity is undeniable if we take account of the entire range of religious experiences; but it is by far most prominent in the extreme cases of literal visions and the "private revelations" of the most advanced mystics. The Virgin Mary does not appear to Hindus; Moslems do not have mystical encounters with the Trinity. But at best this sort of diversity shows that religious experience does not establish the superiority of one religious tradition over others. The fact remains that in all traditions there are countless experiences of a superhuman loving power concerned about us; and even the otherwise divergent physical and mystical visions share this essential core of content.

There are, it is true, two crucial questions on which there are differences between and even within traditions: Is the divine reality truly other than that of the experiencer? And is the divine reality personal or impersonal? However, the difference between those who answer these questions affirmatively and those who answer them negatively is not so great as it might seem. Even those who emphasize the unity of God and self admit that God is other than the ordinary mundane self of our everyday life. So in spite of their insistence that there is an ultimate unity, they agree that the divine is other than the "finite" or "illusory" self that is transcended in rapturous union with the divine. Given this, they could surely also admit the possibility of an essentially veridical, although incomplete, encounter of the finite self with God. Similarly, those who encounter God as "impersonal" do not claim that he is more like a rock than a human being, but that even the category of 'person' is not adequate to his reality. Even so, there is no reason that an encounter with God as a person could not be partially revelatory of the divine nature or perhaps an experience of a mediator between us and God. So, despite the manifest diversity of religious experiences, there remains a content common to them all; and, apart from very uncommon instances of highly specific revelations via visions or mystical insights, it is possible to accept consistently the essential features of almost all religious experiences.

4. Religious Experiences and the Justification of Religious Belief

People candidly report that they have directly experienced the presence of a good and powerful nonhuman being concerned about us. The experiences are not isolated events in their lives but are followed by other and more intimate encounters with this being, sometimes even to the point of an abiding sense of its presence. These encounters are a source of moral strength and comfort, even more than we would expect from prolonged and intimate contact with the most admirable human. Further, similar experiences with similar effects are reported by great numbers of people from diverse times and places. There is no reason to think that these experiences do not have the perceptual character attributed to them, and there are no explanations of them (as a whole) as delusory that are not question-begging. Further, there are few if any other religious experiences that contradict their central content. Surely, we then have very good reason to believe that at least some of these experiences are veridical and hence that there is a good and powerful being, concerned about us, who has revealed himself to human beings. So much, I think, is established by our discussion so far.

To what extent does this conclusion justify religious belief? If we have in mind the beliefs of the great majority of religious people, the answer is: *very little.* Typically, religious belief includes substantive accounts of the nature of God (e.g., that he is omnipotent, omniscient, all-good, the creator of all things, triune, etc.), of his relations to man (e.g., that he became man to save us, that this salvation is carried out by sacramental acts within specific religious communities), of the moral ideals (self-sacrifice, love for all men) that should animate our lives, and of an afterlife dependent on the moral quality of our lives here on earth. Hardly anything of any such accounts is justified by knowing that there is a powerful and good being concerned about us. We can sum up the situation by saying that "of-God" experiences provide us much more with *access to* than with *accounts of* God. Of course, this access necessarily involves some minimal description of what is encountered, but this description falls far short of what is asserted by any major religion and of what is held by almost all believers.

However, these experiences still have very great significance. First and most importantly, they establish the crucial claim that religion as a pervasive phenomenon of human life is based on a genuine contact with a reality beyond ourselves. As C. D. Broad said after a characteristically judicious assessment of the veridicality of religious experiences:

> The claim of any particular religion or sect to have complete or final truth on these subjects seems to me to be too ridiculous to be worth a moment's consideration. But the opposite extreme of holding that the whole religious experience of mankind is a gigantic system of pure delusion seems to me to be almost (though not quite) as farfetched.

Further, the fact that the religious beliefs of mankind derive to at least some extent from an access to the divine warrants our taking seriously the major beliefs of the great world religions. These beliefs have been formed (in part at least) by the sustained and intimate contact of generations of people with a superhuman power; and so, even if they are not to be believed without question, they ought to be carefully and respectfully scrutinized as potential sources of truth. Finally, given the fact that the great world religions seem to be the main loci and sustainers of our access to God, there is good reason for anyone interested in attaining such access or in more deeply understanding what it reveals to take part in the life of some established religious community. (And to these considerations many can add the happiness and moral inspiration they find in the fellowship of a particular religious tradition.)

So it seems that accepting the veridicality of religious experiences can provide good reasons for associating ourselves with the great religious traditions of mankind. There is no a *priori* reason why this association must be with one particular tradition or even a specific church. But for many people there will be specific psychological and social factors that make their participation in just one tradition or church most valuable. Moreover, the richness and diversity of the religious life of any one major tradition suggests that most of us will lose little by so restricting our primary commitment. On the contrary, a refusal to participate fully in some specific "form of religious life" may lead to an abstract and superficial religiosity that will fall far short of profiting from what the religious experiences of humankind have to offer. So, for many people at least, there is good reason for a commitment to a particular religious community. . . .

Notes

1. D. Hay, "Religious Experience Amongst a Group of Post-Graduate Students—A Qualitative Study," *Journal for the Scientific Study of Religion* 18 (1979), pp. 164–82.
2. C. B. Martin, "A Religious Way of Knowing," in A. Flew and A. MacIntyre, eds., *New Essays in Philosophical Theology* (London: Macmillan, 1955). Page references will be given in the text.

II.5   A Critique of Gutting's Argument from Religious Experience

LOUIS POJMAN

In the fifth essay in this part I offer a critique of Gutting's argument. I distinguish between a strong and a weak justification for religious belief. A strong justification would make it rationally obligatory for everyone to believe in the conclusion of an argument. A weak justification would only provide rational support for those who had had an "of-God" experience (or already accepted the world-view that made such experiences likely). Gutting believes that he has given a strong justification for religious belief, but I argue that the argument from religious experience offers only weak justification.

This essay raises a few questions about the arguments from religious experience offered in the previous reading, Gary Gutting's "The Presence of God and the Justification of Religious Belief." To my knowledge, Gutting has written the most sustained modern defense of the argument, which he believes is sufficient to *establish* the existence of God. Gutting believes that the testimony of religious experience should convince any rational person that God exists. Let us say that, according

to Gutting, the argument from religious experience *strongly* justifies belief that God exists. If it were evidence for the believer him- or herself alone, it would only *weakly* justify belief in God. In this essay I challenge the strong thesis, not the weak one, making three criticisms of his argument:

(1) Religious experience is too amorphous and disparate to justify generalizing from it, as Gutting would have us do. That is, there are so many "varieties of religious experiences," often vague and mutually contradictory, that it is not clear whether they can provide us with the proper criteria for determining which "of-God" experiences we will consider veridical or worthy of privileged status.

(2) Justification of belief in the veridicality of religious experience is circular, so that such belief rests upon premises that are not self-evident to everyone. In effect, all assessment of the veridicality of religious experience depends on background beliefs.

(3) When taken seriously as a candidate for veridical experience, religious experience has the liability of not being confirmable in the same way that perceptual experience is. That is, although religious experience may sometimes be veridical, it cannot be checked as ordinary

This article was written specifically for this volume and appears in print here for the first time.

perceptual experience can be, nor can we make predictions from it. I will argue that this indicates that religious experience cannot be used as an argument for the existence of God in the way that Gutting uses it.

(1) Religious experience is amorphous and too varied to yield conclusive evidence for the existence of God. Consider the following various types of religious experiences, most of which can be documented in the literature:

1. A man senses himself absorbed into the One, wherein the subject-object distinction ceases to hold.
2. A woman senses the unity of all things and that she is nothing at all.
3. The Buddhist monk who is an atheist senses the presence of the living Buddha.
4. A person senses the presence of God, the Father of our Lord Jesus Christ.
5. The Virgin Mary appears to S (in a dream).
6. The Lord Jesus appears to Paul on the road one afternoon, though no one else realizes it.
7. A man senses the presence of Satan, which convinces him that Satan is the highest reality.
8. The goddess Athena appears to Achilles. He believes her to have sprung from Zeus's head. She promises that he will win the battle on the morrow.
9. Allah appears to S and tells him to purify the land by executing all infidels (e.g., Jews and Christians) whose false worship corrupts the land.
10. A guilt-ridden woman senses the presence of her long-deceased father, assuring her that he has forgiven her for her neglect of him while he was aging and dying.
11. A mother senses the presence of the spirit of the river. It tells her that her deformed infant belongs to the river and that she should throw it back.
12. A man senses the presence of the Trinity and understands how it could be that the three persons are one God, but he cannot tell others.
13. A person senses the presence of the demiurge who has created the universe but makes no pretense of being omnipotent or omni-benevolent.
14. An atheist senses a deep, infinite gratitude for the life of his son without believing in the least that a god exists (George Nakhnikian's personal example).
15. An atheist has a deep sense of nothingness in which she is absolutely convinced that the universe has manifested itself to her as a deep void.

The problem for those who would strongly justify belief in God from religious experience—that is, show that we are rationally obligated to believe the content of the experience—is to differentiate the valid interpretations from the invalid. Which of these experiences are valid? That is, which guarantee the truth of the propositions contained in the experience? An experience is valid for the believer or experient, but why should the nonexperient accept any of these reports? And why should the experient him- or herself continue to believe the content of the report after it is over, realizing that there are other possible interpretations of it or that others have had experiences that contradict it?

Note the disparity among the different types of "nonphysical" or religious experiences listed above; it would seem that they cancel each other out. There is not even any consensus that there is one supreme being who is benevolent. In fact experiences 1 through 3 do not involve a divine being at all. Contrary to what Gutting says about the virtual universality of god-experiences, in branches of Buddhism and Hinduism there are religious experiences, such as attaining nirvana, that do not involve a god. Furthermore, 7 supposes that the supreme being is evil, and 13 denies omnibenevolence. Experiences 14 and 15 have all the self-authenticating certainty of a religious experience but involve a conviction that no God exists. Do we understand how to distinguish genuine religious experiences from "spiritually" secular ones like 14? Why should we believe in the testimony of "of-God" experients but not in the testimony that is inconsistent with it (e.g., 1–3, 7–9, 11, 13, and 15)? The very *private* nature of religious experience should preclude our being hasty in inferring from the psychological state to the reality of the object of the experience.

Gutting recognizes the diversity of religious experiences but fails to realize how troublesome this is for his thesis. He tries to find a core in these experiences that suggests there is a "good and powerful nonhuman being who cares about us." Gutting admits that we can't derive very much from "of-God" experiences—only that there is a being who is more powerful than us, very powerful and very good. But even if his argument showed this to be true, is this a sufficient definition of 'God'? What would be the difference between this and Plato's finite demiurge (experience 13 in our list) or the guilt-ridden woman's sense of her father, (experience 10—he was Arthur Conan Doyle, a pugilist and a benevolent genius), who presumably was both mentally and physically more powerful than she? How would this show that there is a God, whom we should worship? How would this differ from ancestor worship or polytheism? Or a visitor from outer space? All of these could be "powerful, good, nonhuman, and caring for us." Why should we prefer the "of-God" experiences to the "of-a-supreme Devil" experiences? Gutting rejects the notion of self-authentication as the guarantee of the veridicality of these religious experiences. But if this is so, how does the experient tell the difference between the nonhuman being who cares for her and one who only pretends to care? And how does one reidentify the being who has appeared to one in a nonsensory form?

(2) Justification of belief in religious experience is circular, so that such belief rests upon premises that are not self-evident to everyone. If I am right about the difficulties in singling out "of-God" experiences from other deeply felt experiences, it would seem that we can only justify belief in the content of religious experience through circular reasoning, by setting forth hypothetical assumptions that we then take as constraints on the experience itself. For example, we suppose that God's

ways are mysterious and beyond understanding, and so we are ready to accept our fellow believer's testimony of a deep "of-God" experience. Or a polytheist believes that the hippopotomus-god appears in dreams to women with deformed children and asks for them back (the example of noted British anthropologist Mary Douglas), and so he credits his wife with a veridical experience when she reports having such an encounter in a dream.

It would seem, then, that whether our interpretations of religious experience are justified or not depends on our background beliefs. Our beliefs appear to form a network or web in which they are all variously linked and supported by other beliefs. Some beliefs (call them "core beliefs," e.g., my belief that two plus two equals four, or that there are other minds, or that I am not now dreaming) are more centrally located and have more interconnections than other beliefs, so that if they fall, one's entire noetic structure is greatly affected. Other beliefs are only loosely connected to our noetic structure (e.g., my belief that the Yankees will win the pennant this year, or that it is better to have an IBM pc computer than a TRS 80). Now, religious people and nonreligious people often have fundamentally different propositions at or near the center of their noetic structure. The religious person is already predisposed to have a theistic-type religious experience, and the nonreligious person is not usually so disposed (in the literature Christians have visions of Jesus, Hindus of Krishna, Buddhists of Buddha, ancient Greeks of Athena and Apollo, and so on). If you had been brought up in a Hindu culture, wouldn't you be more likely to have a Hindu religious experience than a Christian one? Would there be enough common elements in the two experiences to allow us to decide that both really converged to a common truth?

All experiencing takes place within the framework of a world view. Certain features of the world view may gradually or suddenly change in importance, thus producing a different total picture, but there is no such thing as neutral evaluation of the evidence. What we see depends to some degree on our background beliefs and our expectations. The farmer, the real estate agent, and the artist looking at the "same" field do not see the *same* field. Neither do the religious person and the atheist see the same thing when evaluating other people's religious experience.

It might be supposed that we could agree upon criteria of assessment in order to arrive at the best explanatory theory regarding religious experience, and there are, of course, competing explanations. There are Freudian, Marxian, and naturalist accounts which, suitably revised, seem to be as internally coherent as the sophisticated theist account. In order for one account to persuade us of its accuracy, it would have to win out over all the others, and we would first have to agree about the criteria to be met by explanatory accounts. But it could turn out that there are competing criteria, so that theory *A* would fulfill criteria 1 and 2 better than *B* and *C*; but *B* would fulfill criteria 3 and 4 better than the others; whereas *C* might have the best overall record without fulfilling any of the criteria best of all. It could be a close second for all of them. At this point it looks like the very formulation and preference of the criteria of assessment depend on which explanatory account one already embraces. The theist may single out *self-authentication* of the "of-God" experience, but that won't convince the atheist who suspects that criterion in the first place. It seems that there is no unambiguous, noncircular consensus about a hierarchy of criteria.

Gutting is confident of a core content that would be experienced (1) repeatedly, (2) by many, and (3) in such a way that those experiencing it would be led to live morally better lives. But why should this convince a naturalist who already has a coherent explanation of this phenomenon? Plato's "noble lie" presumably would have had the same effect, but it was still a lie. Even if we took a survey and discovered that the "of-God" experiences were common to all people, what would that in itself prove? We might still have grounds to doubt its veridicality. As Richard Gale notes, mere unanimity or agreement among observers is not a sufficient condition for the establishment of the truth of what is experienced.

Everybody who presses his finger on his eyeball will see double, everybody who stands at a certain spot in the desert will see a mirage, etc. The true criterion for objectivity is the Kantian one: An experience is objective if its contents can be placed in a spatio-temporal order with other experiences in accordance with scientific laws.*

Gale may go too far in limiting objectivity to that which is accessible to scientific laws, but his negative comments about unanimity are apposite.

Let me illustrate this point in another way. Suppose Timothy Leary devised a psychogenic pill that produced in everyone who took it a "deep religious experience" exactly like that described by the Western theistic mystics. Would this be good evidence for the existence of God? But suppose, further, that upon taking two of the same pills everyone had a religious experience exactly like one common only to a remote primitive tribe. In this experience, the experient had a deep sense of the presence of a pantheon of gods, one being a three-headed hippopotomus who created the lakes and rivers of the world but didn't care a bit about people. The fact that there was complete agreement about what was experienced in these states can hardly *by itself* constitute strong evidence for the truth of the existential claims of the experience. It would be likely that theists would take the experience to be veridical until they had a double dosage and the tribal people would believe in the double dosage but not the single dosage. Doesn't this indicate that it is our accepted background beliefs that predispose us to accept or reject what fits or doesn't fit into our world view?

(3) When taken seriously as a candidate for veridical experience, religious experience fails in not being confirmable in the same way that perceptual experience is. However, there is one criterion of assessment that stands out very impressively in the minds of all rational people—indeed, it is one of the criteria of rationality itself—but that is unduly ignored by proponents of the argument from religious experience like Gutting. It is the Achilles' heel (if anything is) of those who would place a great deal of weight on religious experi-

---

* "Mysticism and Philosophy," *Journal of Philosophy* 57 (1960): 479.

ence as *evidence* for the content of religion. This is the complex criterion of *checkability-predictability* (I link them purposefully). The chemist who says that Avogadro's hypothesis holds (i.e., equal volumes of gases measured at the same temperature and pressure contain an equal number of molecules) predicts exactly to what degree the inclusion of certain gases will increase the overall weight of a gaseous compound. Similarly, if, under normal circumstances, we heat water to 100 degrees Celsius, we can predict ahead of time that it will boil. If you doubt my observation, you can check it out yourself. After suitable experiment, we see these propositions confirmed in such a way as to leave little room for doubt in our minds about their truth. After taking a bit of chemistry, we see that they play a role in a wider network of beliefs that are mutually supportive. The perceptual beliefs force themself upon us.

This notion of predictability applies not only to physical hypotheses but to social hypotheses as well. For instance, an orthodox Marxist states that if Marxist theory is true, capitalism will begin to collapse in industrialized countries. If it doesn't, we begin to doubt the theory. Of course, the Marxist may begin to revise her theory and bring in ad hoc hypotheses to explain why the expected developments didn't occur, but the more she has to bring in, the weaker the hypothesis itself becomes. It is a fact of human experience that we come to believe many important propositions through experiment, either our own experiments or those of others (whom we take as authoritative—for the moment, at least). The presumption with regard to authority is that we could check out the propositions in question if we had the time or need to do so.

How do we confirm the truth of religious experience? Does it make any predictions that we could test in order to say, "Look and see, the fact that X occurs shows that the content of the religious experience is veridical"? How do we check on other people's religious experiences, especially if they purport to be nonsensory perceptions?

When Gutting rightly criticizes Swinburne's argument from religious experience, he states that in order to be justified in believing his dead aunt is in the room he "would need much more evi-

dence—for example, numerous repetitions of the experience, other people having the same or similar experiences, a long visit in which the appearance behaved in ways characteristic of my aunt, information from the appearance that only my aunt had access to." But why not apply this same set of criteria to "of-God" experiences and demand that it yield information about the future or even the past that we could check out?

The checkability factor is weak in Gutting's account. He claims that we have a duty to believe simply on the report of others, not on the basis of our own experience or of any special predictions that the experient can make. But, if the Bible is to be believed, this wasn't always the case, nor should it be today. We read in I Kings 18 that in order to convince the Israelites that Jahweh, and not Baal, was worthy of being worshipped. Elijah challenged the priests of Baal to a contest. He proposed that they prepare a bullock and call on Baal to set fire to it. Then he would do the same with Jahweh. The priests failed, but Elijah succeeded. Convincing evidence. Likewise, at the end of Mark we read of Jesus' telling his disciples that "signs shall follow them that believe; In my name they cast out devils; they shall speak with new tongues; They shall take up serpents; and if they drink any deadly thing, it shall not hurt them; they shall lay hands on the sick, and they shall recover" (Mark 16:17,18). Some believers doubt whether this text is authentic, and others seek to explain it away (e.g., "Jesus only meant his apostles and was referring to the apostolic age"), but if the contents of a religion were true, we might well expect some outward confirmation of it, such as we find in Elijah's actions at Mt. Carmel or in Jesus' miracles. The fact that religious experience isn't testable and doesn't yield any nontrivial predictions surely makes it less reliable than perceptual experience.

Not only does religious experience not usually generate predictions that are confirmed, but it sometimes yields false predictions. Witness an incident that happened to me as a student in an evangelical Christian college. A group of theists believes that the Bible is the inerrant word of God and cannot contain an untruth. Now the Gospel of Matthew records Jesus as saying that "if two of you shall agree on earth as touching anything that they shall ask, it shall be done for them of my Father which is in heaven" (18:19), and Matthew tells of faith being able to move mountains: "Nothing shall be impossible for you" (17:20). Verses in Mark confirm this, adding that God will answer our prayer if we pray in faith and do not doubt. So, one night a score or more of believers pray through the entire night for the healing of a student who is dying of cancer. They pray for her with childlike faith that God will heal her. As morning breaks, they feel the presence of God amongst them, telling them that their prayer has been answered. As they leave the room rejoicing, they get word that the woman has just died.

It is interesting to note that none of the participants lost faith in God because of this incident. Some merely dismissed it as one of the mysteries of God's ways, others concluded that the Bible wasn't to be taken literally, and still others concluded that they hadn't prayed hard enough or with enough faith. But as far as the argument for the veridicality of the content of religion is concerned, such an event has to be taken as part of the total data. How it weighs against the empirically successful prayers or the times when the content of the experience was confirmed, I have no idea, and I don't think Gutting has either. But unless we do have some idea, it is hard to see how the argument from religious experience can be used as strong evidence for the existence of God *to anyone else except those who had the experiences.* As William James concludes about mystical states (one form of religious experience), although those having the experience have a right to believe in their content, "no authority emanates from them which should make it a duty for those who stand outside of them to accept their revelations uncritically."

Finally, let me offer an illustration of what might be a publically verifiable experience of God, one that would be analogous to the kind of perceptual experience by which we check scientific hypotheses. What if tomorrow morning (8 A.M. central standard time) there was a loud trumpet call and all over North America people heard a

voice say, "I am the Lord, your God speaking. I have a message for you all. I am deeply saddened by the violence and lack of concern you have for each other. I am calling upon all nations to put aside your nuclear weapons. This same message is being delivered to all the other nations of the earth at different times today. I want you all to know that I shall take all means necessary to prevent a nuclear war and punish those nations who persist on the mad course on which they are now embarked. I love each one of you. A few signs will confirm this message. Later today, while speaking to Israel and the Arab states, I will cause an island to appear west of Lebanon in the Mediterranean that is intended as a homeland for the Palestinians. I will also cause the Sahara desert to become fruitful in order to provide food for the starving people in that area. But I will have you know that I shall not intervene often in your affairs. I'm making this exception simply because it is an emergency situation."

The same message was conveyed all over the world during the next twenty-four hours. The predictions were fulfilled. The question is, Would this be a religious experience or not? What is special about a religious experience? A feeling of divine presence (with all the self-authentication that you like)? Then we could imagine that many people had that sense while the voice spoke. Would you be helped by such an experience? If so, and if you believe in God, why do you suppose such an experience doesn't occur?

The standard objection, that this would be a case of God's *forcing* faith, just won't do. If this simply means that we would have more reason to believe than we do now, what is wrong with that? If beliefs are not voluntary actions but responses to experience, then all believing is, in a significant sense, forced on us. If believing is different from having faith (e.g., the devils believe that God exist but do not have faith in him), we can only say that such an experience would force belief but not faith. One would still have to choose whether to accept God or not. There would be more incentive to accept God, but wouldn't it be the right kind, that is, based on *good* evidence?

II.6   Religious Experience and Religious Belief

WILLIAM P. ALSTON

In the last reading in this part, "Religious Experience and Religious Belief," William Alston, professor of philosophy at Syracuse University and editor of Faith and Philosophy, *argues that religious experience can provide grounds for religious belief. Comparing the epistemology of Christian religious experience with the epistemology of perceptual experience, Alston shows that although perceptual practices include more stringent requirements than religious practices, there are good reasons why the two should be different. Whereas the criteria for valid perceptual experience include verifiability and predictability, God's being wholly other may preclude those criteria from applying to religious experience. Do not be intimidated by Alston's use of symbols; they are simply a convenient shorthand. For example, one of Alston's central theses is as follows: "CP will be J_{nw} for S provided S has no significant reason for regarding it as unreliable." Parsed out, this reads, "Christian practices are justified in the weak, normative sense for a person (S = subject) provided that the person has no significant reason for regarding that practice as unreliable."*

I

Can religious experience provide any ground or basis for religious belief? Can it serve to justify religious belief, or make it rational? This paper will differ from many others in the literature by virtue of looking at this question in the light of basic epistemological issues. Throughout we will be comparing the epistemology of religious experience with the epistemology of sense experience.

We must distinguish between experience directly, and indirectly, justifying a belief. It indirectly justifies belief B_1 when it justifies some other beliefs, which in turn justify B_1. Thus I have learned indirectly from experience that Beaujolais wine is fruity, because I have learned from experience that this, that, and the other bottle of Beaujolais is fruity, and these propositions support the generalization. Experience will directly justify a belief when the justification does not go through other beliefs in this way. Thus, if I am justified, just by virtue of having the visual experiences I am now having, in taking what I am experiencing to be a typewriter situated directly in front of me, then the belief that there is a typewriter directly in front of me is directly justified by that experience.

We find claims to both direct and indirect justification of religious beliefs by religious experience. Where someone believes that her new way of relating herself to the world after her conversion is to be explained by the Holy Spirit imparting supernatural graces to her, she supposes her belief *that the Holy Spirit imparts graces to her* to be directly justified by her experience. What she directly learns from experience is that she sees and reacts to things differently; this is then taken as a reason for supposing that the Holy Spirit is imparting graces to her. When, on the other hand, someone takes himself to be experiencing the presence of God, he thinks that his experience justifies him in supposing that God is *what* he is experiencing. Thus, he supposes himself to be directly justified by his experience in believing God to be present to him.

In this paper I will confine myself to the question of whether religious experience can provide direct justification for religious belief. This has implications for the class of experiences we shall be considering. In the widest sense 'religious experience' ranges over any experiences one has in connection with one's religious life, including any

Reprinted by permission of the author and of the editor of NOÛS, Vol. 16 (1982):3–12. Footnotes deleted.

joys, fears, or longings one has in a religious context. But here I am concerned with experiences that could be taken to *directly* justify religious beliefs, i.e. experiences that give rise to a religious belief and that the subject takes to involve a direct awareness of what the religious belief is about. To further focus the discussion, let's confine ourselves to beliefs to the effect that God, as conceived in theistic religions, is doing something that is directed to the subject of the experience—that God is speaking to him, strengthening him, enlightening him, giving him courage, guiding him, sustaining him in being, or just being present to him. Call these "*M*-beliefs" ('*M*' for manifestation').

Note that our question concerns what might be termed a general "epistemic practice", the accepting of *M*-beliefs on the basis of experience, rather than some particular belief of that sort. I hold that practices, or habits, of belief formation are the primary subject of justification and that particular beliefs are justified only by issuing from a practice (or the activation of a habit) that is justified. The following discussion of concepts of justification will provide grounds for that judgment.

Whether *M*-beliefs can be directly justified by experience depends, *inter alia,* on what it is to be justified in a belief. So let us take a look at that.

First, the justification about which we are asking is an "epistemic" rather than a "moral" or "prudential" justification. Suppose one should hold that the practice in question is justified because it makes us feel good. Even if this is true in a sense, it has no bearing on epistemic justification. But why not? What makes a justification *epistemic*? Epistemic justification, as the name implies, has something to do with knowledge, or, more broadly, with the aim at attaining truth and avoiding falsity. At a first approximation, I am justified in believing that *p* when, from the point of view of that aim, there is something O.K., all right, to be approved, about that fact that I believe that *p*. But when we come to spell this out further, we find that a fundamental distinction must be drawn between two different ways of being in an epistemically commendable position.

On the one hand there is what we may call a "normative" concept of epistemic justification (J_n), "normative" because it has to do with how we stand *vis-a-vis* norms that specify our intellectual obligations, obligations that attach to one *qua* cognitive subject, *qua* truth-seeker. Stated most generally, J_n consists in one's not having violated one's intellectual obligations. We have to say "not having violated" rather than "having fulfilled" because in all normative spheres, *being justified* is a negative status; it amounts to ones behavior not being in violation of the norms. If belief is under direct voluntary control, we may think of intellectual obligations as attaching directly to believing. Thus one might be obliged to refrain from believing in the absence of adequate evidence. But if, as it seems to me, belief is not, in general, under voluntary control, obligations cannot attach directly to believing. However, I do have voluntary control over moves that can influence a particular belief formation, e.g., looking for more evidence, and moves that can affect my general belief forming habits or tendencies e.g., training myself to be more critical of testimony. If we think of intellectual obligations as attaching to activities that are designed to influence belief formation, we may say that a certain epistemic practice is normatively justified provided it is not the case that the practitioner would not have engaged in it had he satisfied intellectual obligations to engage in activities designed to inhibit it. In other words, the practice is justified if and only if the practitioner did not fail to satisfy an obligation to inhibit it.

However epistemologists also frequently use the term 'justified' in such a way that it has to do not with how the subject stands *vis-a-vis* obligations, but rather with the strength of her epistemic position in believing that *p*, with how likely it is that a belief of that sort acquired or held in that way is true. To say that a practice is justified in this, as I shall say, "evaluative" sense, (J_e) is to say that beliefs acquired in accordance with that practice, in the sorts of circumstances in which human beings typically find themselves, are generally true. Thus we might say that a practice is J_e if and only if it is reliable.

One further complication in the notion of J_n remains to be canvassed. What is our highest reasonable aspiration for being J_n in accepting a belief on the basis of experience? Being J_n no matter what else is the case? A brief consideration of sense perception would suggest a negative answer. I may be justified in believing that there is a tree in front of me by virtue of the fact that I am currently having a certain kind of sense experience, but this will be true only in "favorable circumstances". If I am confronted with a complicated arrangement of mirrors, I may not be justified in believing that there is an oak tree in front of me, even though it looks for all the world as if there is. Again, it may look for all the world as if water is running uphill, but the general improbability of this greatly diminishes the justification the corresponding belief receives from that experience.

What this shows is that the justification provided by one's experience is only defeasibly so. It is inherently liable to be overriden, diminished, or cancelled by stronger considerations to the contrary. Thus the justification of beliefs about the physical environment that is provided by sense experience is a defeasible or, as we might say, *prima facie* justification. By virtue of having the experience, the subject is in a position such that she will be adequately justified in the belief *unless* there are strong enough reasons to the contrary.

It would seem that direct experiential justification for *M*-beliefs, is also, at most, *prima facie*. Beliefs about the nature and ways of God are often used to override *M*-beliefs, particularly beliefs concerning communications from God. If I report that God told me to kill all phenomenologists, fellow Christians will, no doubt, dismiss the report on the grounds that God would not give me any such injunction as that. I shall take it that both sensory experience and religious experience provide, at most, *prima facie* justification.

One implication of this stand is that a particular experiential epistemic practice will have to include some way of identifying defeaters. Different theistic religions, even different branches of the same religion, will differ in this regard, e.g., with respect to what sacred books, what traditions, what doctrines are taken to provide defeaters. We also find difference of this kind in perceptual prac-

tice. For example, with the progress of science new defeaters are added to the repertoire. Epistemic practices can, of course, be individuated with varying degrees of detail. To fix our thoughts with regard to the central problem of this paper let's think of a "Christian epistemic practice" (*CP*) that takes its defeaters from the Bible, the classic creeds, and certain elements of tradition. There will be differences between subsegments of the community of practitioners so defined, but there will be enough commonality to make it a useful construct. My foil to *CP*, the practice of forming beliefs about the physical environment on the basis of sense-experience, I shall call "perceptual practice" (*PP*).

Actually it will prove most convenient to think of each of our practices as involving not only the formation of beliefs on the basis of experience, but also the retention of these beliefs in memory, the formation of rationally self-evident beliefs, and various kinds of reasoning on the basis of all this. *CP* will be the richer complex, since it will include the formation of perceptual beliefs in the usual way, while *PP* will not be thought of as including the distinctive experiential practice of *CP*.

One final preliminary note. J_n is relative to a particular person's situation. If practice P_1 is quite unreliable, I may still be J_n in engaging in it either because I have no way of realizing its unreliability or because I am unable to disengage myself; while you, suffering from neither of these disabilities, are not J_n. When we ask whether a given practice is J_n, we shall be thinking about some normal, reasonably well informed contemporary member of our society.

II

Let's make use of all this in tackling the question as to whether one can be justified in *CP* and in *PP*. Beginning with J_n, we will first have to determine more precisely what one's intellectual obligations are *vis-a-vis* epistemic practices. Since our basic cognitive aim is to come into possession of as much truth as possible and to avoid false beliefs, it would seem that one's basic intellectual obligation *vis-a-vis* practices of belief formation would be to do what one can (or, at least, do as much as could reasonably be expected of one) to see to it that these practices are as *reliable* as possible. But this still leaves us with an option between a stronger and a weaker view as to this obligation. According to the stronger demand one is obliged to refrain (or try to refrain) from engaging in a practice unless one has adequate reasons for supposing it to be reliable. In the absence of sufficient reasons for considering the practice reliable, it is not justified. Practices are guilty until proved innocent. While on the more latitudinarian view one is justified in engaging in a practice provided one does not have sufficient reasons for regarding it to be unreliable. Practices are innocent until proved guilty. Let's take J_{ns} as an abbreviation for 'justified in the normative sense on the stronger requirement', and 'J_{nw}' as an abbreviation for 'justified in the normative sense on the weaker requirement'.

Now consider whether Mr. Everyman is J_{nw} in engaging in *PP*. It would seem so. Except for those who, like Parmenides and Bradley, have argued that there are ineradicable inconsistencies in the conceptual scheme involved in *PP*, philosophers have not supposed that we can show that sense perception is not a reliable guide to our immediate surroundings. Sceptics about *PP* have generally confined themselves to arguing that we can't show that perception is reliable; i.e., they have argued that *PP* is not J_{ns}. I shall assume without further ado that *PP* is J_{nw}.

J_{ns} and J_e can be considered together. Although a practice may actually be reliable without my having adequate reasons for supposing so, and *vice versa*, still in considering whether a given practice is reliable, we will be seeking to determine whether there *are* adequate reasons for supposing it reliable, that is whether Everyman *could* be possessed of such reasons. And if we hold, as we shall, that there are no such reasons, the question of whether they are possessed by one or another subject does not arise.

I believe that there are no adequate non-circular reasons for the reliability of *PP* but I will not be able to argue that point here. If I had a general argument I would unveil it, but, so far as I can see, this thesis is susceptible only of inductive support, by unmasking each pretender in turn. And since this issue has been in the forefront of the Western philosophical consciousness for several centuries, there have been many pretenders. I do not have time even for criticism of a few representative samples. Instead I will simply assume that *PP* is not J_{ns}, and then consider what bearing this widely shared view has on the epistemic status of *CP*.

If J_{nw} is the most we can have for perceptual practice, then if *CP* is also J_{nw} it will be in at least as strong an epistemic position as the former. (I shall assume without argument that *CP* can no more be noncircularly shown to be reliable than can *PP*.) And *CP* will be J_{nw} for *S*, provided *S* has no significant reasons for regarding it as unreliable. Are there any such reasons? What might they be? Well, for one thing, the practice might yield a system that is ineradicably internally inconsistent. (I am not speaking of isolated and remediable inconsistencies that continually pop up in every area of thought and experience.) For another, it might yield results that come into ineradicable conflict with the results of other practices to which we are more firmly committed. Perhaps some fundamentalist Christians are engaged in an epistemic practice that can be ruled out on such grounds as these. But I shall take it as obvious that one *can* objectify certain stretches of one's experience, or indeed the whole of one's experience, in Christian terms without running into such difficulties.

III

One may grant everything I have said up to this point and still feel reluctant to allow that *CP* is J_{nw}. *CP* does differ from *PP* in important ways, and it may be thought that some of these differences will affect their relative epistemic status. The following features of *PP*, which it does not share with *CP*, have been thought to have this kind of bearing.

1. Within *PP* there are standard ways of checking the accuracy of any particular perceptual belief.

2. By engaging in *PP* we can discover regularities in the behavior of the objects putatively observed, and on this basis we can, to a certain extent, effectively predict the course of events.
3. Capacity for *PP*, and practice of it, is found universally among normal adult human beings.
4. All normal adult human beings, whatever their culture, use basically the same conceptual scheme in objectifying their sense experience.

If *CP* includes *PP* as a proper part, as I ruled on above, how can it lack these features? What I mean is that there is no analogue of these features for that distinctive part of *CP* by virtue of which it goes beyond *PP*. The extra element of *CP* does not enable us to discover extra regularities, e.g., in the behavior of God, or increase our predictive powers. *M*-beliefs are not subject to interpersonal check in the same way as perceptual beliefs. The practice of forming *M*-beliefs on the basis of experience is not engaged in by all normal adults. And so on.

Before coming to grips with the alleged epistemic bearing of these differences, I want to make two preliminary points. (1) We have to engage in *PP* to determine that this practice has features 1.-4., and that *CP* lacks them. Apart from observation, we have no way of knowing that, e.g., while all cultures agree in their way of cognizing the physical environment they differ in their ways of cognizing the divine, or that *PP* puts us in a position to predict while *CP* doesn't. It might be thought that this is loading the dice in favor of my opponent. If we are to use *PP*, rather than some neutral source, to determine what features it has, shouldn't the same courtesy of self-assessment be accorded *CP*? Why should *it* be judged on the basis of what we learn about it from another practice, while that other practice is allowed to grade itself? To be sure, this is a serious issue only if answers to these questions *are* forthcoming from *CP* that differ from those we arrive at by engaging in *PP*. Fortunately, I can avoid getting involved in these issues by ruling that what I am interested in here is how *CP* looks from the standpoint of *PP*. The person I am primarily concerned to address is

one who, like all the rest of us, engages in *PP*, and who, like all of us except for a few outlandish philosophers, regards it as justified. My aim is to show this person that, on his own grounds, *CP* enjoys basically the same epistemic status as *PP*. Hence it is consonant with my purposes to allow *PP* to determine the facts of the matter with respect to both practices. (2) I could quibble over whether the contrast is as sharp as is alleged. Questions can be raised about both sides of the putative divide. On the *PP* side, is it really true that all cultures have objectified sense experience in the same way? Many anthropologists have thought not. And what about the idea that all *normal* adult human beings engage in the same perceptual practice? Aren't we loading the dice by taking participation in what we regard as standard perceptual practice as our basic criterion for normality? On the *CP* side, is it really the case that this practice reveals no regularities to us, or only that they are very different from regularities in the physical world? What about the point that God is faithful to His promises? Or that the pure in heart will see God? However, I believe that when all legitimate quibbles have been duly registered there will still be very significant differences between the two practices in these respects. So rather than contesting the factual allegations, I will concentrate on the *de jure* issue as to what bearing these differences have on epistemic status.

How could the lack of 1.-4. prevent *CP* from being J_{nw}? Only by providing an adequate ground for a judgment of unreliability. And why suppose that? Of course, the lack of these features implies that we lack certain reasons we might conceivably have had for regarding *CP* as reliable. If we could ascertain that *PP* has those features, without using *PP* to do so, that would provide us with strong reasons for judging *PP* to be reliable. And the parallel possibility is lacking for *CP*. This shows that we cannot have *certain* reasons for taking *CP* to be reliable, but it doesn't follow that we have reasons for unreliability. That would follow only if we could also premise that a practice is reliable *only if* (as well as *if*) it has 1.-4. And why suppose that?

My position is that it is a kind of parochialism that makes the lack of 1.-4. appear to betoken untrustworthiness. The reality *CP* claims to put us in touch with is conceived to be vastly different from the physical environment. Why should the sorts of procedures required to put us in effective cognitive touch with this reality not be equally different? Why suppose that the distinctive features of *PP* set an appropriate standard for the cognitive approach to God? I shall sketch out a possible state of affairs in which *CP* is quite trustworthy while lacking 1.-4., and then suggest that we have no reason to suppose that this state of affairs does not obtain.

Suppose, then, that

(A) God is too different from created beings, too "wholly other", for us to be able to grasp any regularities in His behavior.

Suppose further that

(B) for the same reason we can only attain the faintest, sketchiest, and most insecure grasp of what God is like.

Finally, suppose that

(C) God has decreed that a human being will be aware of His presence in any clear and unmistakable fashion only when certain special and difficult conditions are satisfied.

If all this is the case, then it is the reverse of surprising that *CP* should lack 1.-4. even if it does involve a genuine experience of God. It would lack 1.-2. because of (A). It is quite understandable that it should lack 4. because of (B). If our cognitive powers are not fitted to frame an adequate conception of God, it is not at all surprising that there should be wide variation in attempts to do so. This is what typically happens in science when investigators are grappling with a phenomenon no one really understands. A variety of models, analogues, metaphors, hypotheses, hunches are propounded, and it is impossible to secure universal agreement. 3. is missing because of (C). If very difficult conditions are set it is not surprising that few are chosen. Now it is compatible with (A)-(C) that

(D) religious experience should, in general, constitute a genuine awareness of the divine.

and that

(E) although any particular articulation of such an experience might be mistaken to a greater or lesser extent, indeed even though all such articulations might miss the mark to some extent, still such judgments will, for the most part, contain some measure of truth; they, or many of them, will constitute a useful approximation of the truth;

and that

(F) God's designs contain provision for correction and refinement, for increasing the accuracy of the beliefs derived from religious experience. Perhaps as one grows in the spiritual life ones spiritual sight becomes more accurate and more discriminating; perhaps some special revelation is vouchsafed under certain conditions; and there are many other conceivable possibilities.

If something like all this were the case then *CP* would be trustworthy even though it lacks features 1.-4. This is a conceivable way in which *CP* would constitute a road to the truth, while differing from *PP* in respects 1.-4. Therefore unless we have adequate reason for supposing that no such combination of circumstances obtains, we are not warranted in taking the lack of 1.-4. to be an adequate reason for a judgment of untrustworthiness.

Moreover it is not just that A.-C. constitute a bare possibility. In the practice of CP we seem to learn that this is the way things are. As for (A) and (B) it is the common teaching of all the higher religions that God is of a radically different order of being from finite substances and, therefore, that we cannot expect to attain the grasp of His nature and His doings that we have of worldly objects. As for (C), it is a basic theme in Christianity, and in other religions as well, that one finds God within one's experience, to any considerable degree, only as one progresses in the spiritual life. God is not available for *voyeurs*. Awareness of God, and understanding of His nature and His will for us, is not a purely cognitive achievement; it requires the involvement of the whole person; it takes a practical commitment and a practice of the life of the spirit, as well as the exercise of cognitive faculties.

Of course these results that we are using to defend *CP* are derived from that same practice. But in view of the fact that the favorable features of *PP*, 1.-4., are themselves ascertained by engaging in *PP*, our opponent is hardly in a position to fault us on this score. However I have not forgotten that I announced it as my aim to show that even one who engaged only in *PP* should recognize that *CP* is J_{nw}. For this purpose, I ignore what we learn in

CP and revert to the point that my opponent has no basis for ruling out the conjoint state of affairs A.-F., hence has no basis for taking the lack of 1.-4. to show *CP* to be untrustworthy, and hence has no reason for denying that *CP* is J_{nw}.

I conclude that *CP* has basically the same epistemic status as *PP* and that no one who subscribes to the former is in any position to cavil at the latter.

Bibliography for Part II

Freud, Sigmund. *The Future of an Illusion*. New York: Norton, 1961. Contains his famous theory that religion is the outgrowth of the projection of the father image.

Gale, Richard. "Mysticism and Philosophy." *Journal of Philosophy* 57 (1960). A clear analysis and cogent critique of some key concepts and arguments related to mystical experience. (Republished in *Contemporary Philosophy of Religion*, ed. Steven M. Cahn and David Shatz. Oxford: Oxford Univ. Press, 1982.)

Martin, C. B. "A Religious Way of Knowing." *Mind* 61 (1952). A watershed article. (Reprinted and expanded in his book *Religious Belief*. Chap. 5. Ithaca: Cornell Univ. Press, 1959.

Mavrodes, George. *Belief in God*. Chap. 3. New York: Random House, 1970. A good analysis.

Otto, Rudolf. *The Idea of the Holy*, translated by J. W. Harvey. Oxford: Oxford Univ. Press, 1923. A classic study of religious experience.

Rowe, William. *Philosophy of Religion*. Belmont, Calif.: Wadsworth, 1978. A valuable commentary on some of the major work in the field.

Stace, Walter T. *Time and Eternity*. Princeton: Princeton Univ. Press, 1952. An important study.

————, ed. *The Teaching of the Mystics*. New York: New American Library, 1960. Contains useful material, especially the article by Stace himself.

Swinburne, Richard. *The Existence of God*. Chap. 13. Oxford: Clarendon Press, 1979. Contains a cogently reasoned defense for the veridicality of religious experience.

Wainwright, William. "Mysticism and Sense Perception." *Religious Studies* 9 (1973). Perhaps the best modern analysis of mysticism.

PART III

THE PROBLEM OF EVIL

Is he willing to prevent evil, but not able? then he is impotent. Is he able, but not willing? then he is malevolent. Is he both able and willing? whence then is evil?

EPICURUS (341–270 BC)

We have been looking at arguments in favor of God's existence. The agnostic and atheist usually base their case on the *absence* of evidence for God's existence. But they have one arrow in their own quiver, an argument for disbelief. It is the problem of evil. From it the "atheologian" (one who argues against the existence of God) hopes either to neutralize any positive evidence for God's existence, based on whatever in the traditional arguments survives their criticism, or to demonstrate that it is unreasonable to believe in God.

The problem of evil arises from the paradox of an omnibenevolent, omnipotent deity's allowing the existence of evil. The Judeo-Christian tradition has affirmed these three propositions:

1. God is all-powerful (his powers include omniscience).
2. God is perfectly good.
3. Evil exists.

But if he is perfectly good, why does he allow evil to exist? Why didn't he create a better world, if not one without evil, at least one with substantially less evil than this world? Many have contended that this paradox, first articulated by Epicurus, is not just a paradox but an implicit contradiction, for it contains premises that are inconsistent with one another. They argue something like the following:

4. If God (an all-powerful, omniscient, omnibenevolent being) exists, there would be no (or no unnecessary) evil in the world.
5. There is evil (or unnecessary evil) in the world.
6. Therefore, God does not exist.

151

You will want to examine each of these premises carefully. A few words about them are in order. Generally, Western thought has distinguished between two types of evil: moral and natural. 'Moral evil' covers all those bad things for which humans are morally responsible. 'Natural evil' or 'surd evil' includes those terrible events that occur in nature of their own accord, such as hurricanes, tornadoes, earthquakes, volcano eruptions, natural diseases, and so on, that cause suffering to humans and animals. However, some defenses of theism affirm that all evil is essentially moral evil, with the devil brought in as the cause of natural evil.

The main defense of theism in the light of evil is the free will defense, going back as far as St. Augustine (354–430) and receiving modern treatment in the work of John Hick, Alvin Plantinga, and Richard Swinburne. The free will defense adds a fourth premise to Epicurus's paradox in order to show that premises 1–3 are consistent and not contradictory:

7. It is logically impossible for God to create free creatures and guarantee that they will never do evil.

Since it is a good thing to create free creatures who are morally responsible agents, there is no assurance that they will not also do evil.

This defense assumes a libertarian view of freedom of the will. That is, humans are free to choose between good and evil acts. They are not caused (though they may be influenced) to do one deed rather than the other; they are causally underdetermined. Given two identical situations with identical causal antecedents, an agent could do act *A* at one time and *B* at the other. This view is opposed to determinism as well as compatibilism (a view that tries to reconcile freedom of action with determinism). If you are committed to compatibilism or determinism, the free will defense will not be effective against the argument from evil. This matter is well treated in chapter 9 of J. L. Mackie's *The Miracle of Theism*.

Proponents of the free will defense claim that all moral evil derives from creatures' freedom of will. But how does the theist account for natural evil? There are two different ways. The first one, suggested by Alvin Plantinga (see Part 3 Bibliography), is to attribute natural evil, such as disease and tornadoes, to the work of the devil and his angels. The second way, favored by Swinburne, argues that natural evil is part and parcel of the nature of things, resulting from the combination of deterministic physical laws that are necessary for consistent action and the responsibility given to humans to exercise their freedom.

There is one further distinction necessary to work through this problem. Some theists attempt to answer the charge of inconsistency by simply showing that there is no formal contradiction in propositions 1–3; thus the nontheists haven't proved their point. But others want to go beyond this negative function and offer a plausible account of evil. These latter are called "theodicists," for they attempt to justify the ways of God before humankind. They endeavor to show that God allows the temporary evil in order to bring out greater good. Leibniz, Hick, and Swinburne, all included in our readings, are theodicists.

Let me outline the main points of the readings that follow. The six readings included here constitute three separate debates. The first two readings are classic formulations of opposite positions. In the first reading, "The Argument from Evil," David Hume argues through his persona Philo that not merely the fact of evil but the enormous amount of evil make it dubious that a deity exists. It is arguable that there is actually more evil than good in the world, so it is hard to see how one can harmonize the crucial propositions. In the second reading, "Theodicy: A Defense of Theism," Gottfried Leibniz (1646–1716) argues that the fact of evil in no way refutes theism, and he answers the kind of objections made by Hume. He contends that God permitted evil to exist in order to bring about greater good and that Adam's fall was a *felix culpa* ("happy sin") because it led to the incarnation of the Son of God, raising humanity to a higher destiny than would otherwise have been the case. He argues that although God can foresee the future, the future isn't determined since humans are still free.

We come to contemporary formulations. Our third reading, John Hick's "Evil and Soul-Making," is an example of a theodicy argument that is based on the free will defense. Theodicies can be of two different types depending on how they justify the ways of God in the face of evil. The Augustinian position is that God created humans without sin and set them in a sinless, paradisical world. However, humanity fell into sin through misuse of its free will. God's grace will save some of us, but others will perish everlastingly. In this division God's goodness is manifested, for his mercy redeems some and his justice is served on the rest. But there is another theory of theodicy, stemming from Irenaeus (120–202), in the tradition of the Greek Church. The Irenaean tradition views Adam not as a free agent rebelling against God but as a child. The fall is humanity's first faulty step in the direction of freedom. God is still working with humanity in order to bring it from undeveloped life (*bios*) to a state of self-realization in divine love, spiritual life (*zoe*). This life is viewed as the "vale of soul-making." Spiritual development requires obstacles and the opportunity to fail as well as to succeed. Hick declares that those who are opposed to the challenge that our freedom grants us are looking for a hedonistic paradise in which every desire is gratified and we are treated by God as pet animals rather than autonomous agents. On the other hand, those who accept the challenge of freedom consider themselves to be coworkers with God in bringing forth the kingdom of God.

In the fourth reading, "A Critique of Hick's Theodicy," Edward H. Madden and Peter H. Hare attack Hick's theory. They ask whether the amount of evil in the world is necessary for soul-making and accuse Hick of three fallacies, called "all or nothing," "it could be worse," and "slippery slope."

The *all or nothing* fallacy involves the idea that what we have is desirable because not having it at all would be far worse. "The erroneous assumption," write Madden and Hare, "is that we must have this thing either in its present form and amount or not at all. But it is often the case that only *some* amount of the thing in *some* form is necessary to the achievement of a desirable end." Hick concedes that there is an appalling amount of evil in the world but insists that the alternative is for humans to be mere puppets or pets. We may object to this set of extreme alternatives since we can easily imagine intermediate states where there is still great good but much less evil. Taking away Auschwitz or the Gulag Archepelago doesn't seem to leave the world any worse off.

It could be worse is the claim that "something is not really bad because it will be followed by all manner of desirable things." But this overlooks the fact that things could also be better. Hick seems to ignore the fact that although it is true that we can imagine the world's being a worse place than it is, we can also imagine it to be a far better place. The question is, Why hasn't God created this far better place?

The *slippery slope* fallacy states that if God once started eliminating evil from the world, he could not stop short of a perfect world. This notion overlooks the fact that humanity could be shown by God why a certain proportion of good to evil is ideal.

The third set of readings is taken from a symposium held in 1975 at the University of Lancaster in England under the auspices of the Royal Institute of Philosophy. Richard Swinburne defends a version of the theodicy argument against D. Z. Phillips, who contends that the very effort to explain the problem is a terrible mistake.

In "The Problem of Evil" Swinburne develops and refines the position of Leibniz and Hick, taking into account the kinds of objections that Madden and Hare have made. He distinguishes various forms of evil and shows how the theist can account for them, offering a plausible response to each objection.

Specifically, Swinburne distinguishes between active and passive evil, active evil being that directly caused by human (or rational) immoral action and passive evil being that caused by nonmoral actions or by nature itself. In order to meet the objection that God should not have allowed moral evil to occur, Swinburne appeals to the free will defense. It was logically impossible for God to make a world wherein humans are free but wherein they do not do evil. Regarding passive evil caused by humans, Swinburne argues that in order for humans to be fully responsible it was necessary for God to allow their effects on others to be significant. So there must be deterministic physical laws in nature that allow reliable expectations of how our behavior will affect others. This principle of uniformity of nature also explains the presence of passive evil not due to humans. The laws of nature are necessarily such that the good is interconnected with the bad. The same rain that causes one farmer's field to germinate ruinously floods another's. Although there are, no doubt, limits to the amount of evil God will allow, he cannot constantly intervene without eroding human responsibility or the laws of nature. Where those limits of evil are, no one of us finite humans can know. It is presumptuous to think otherwise.

In his critique of Swinburne's position, D. Z. Phillips attacks all such theodicies as futile and inappropriate. Likening Swinburne's approach to a journey, Phillips claims that it is one we ought not embark on. Swinburne, he feels, arrogantly rushes in where angels fear to tread. What theodicists try to explain is essentially a mystery; not only do their endeavors not solve anything, but they are an inappropriate response to the fact of evil. The existence of evil does not necessarily prevent one from being a theist. The point is rather that human suffering and pain must shake the morally sensitive person to the core and should not be treated as a logical puzzle to be solved at all cost "in an abstract and global way." Evil is an existential reality, one that destroys innocent humans and causes unspeakable suffering. The proper response before the hoary head of evil is moral action and a certain amount of commiseration with the afflicted. Swinburne fails to deal with the concreteness of evil, which we all experience and which overwhelms many of us.

Phillips' essay raises the point that even if theists can show that there is no apparent inconsistency in Epicurus's triad, they may have not done enough. There is psychological doubt that many good people, religious individuals among them, cannot help but experience in moments of intense suffering. The question is whether or not Phillips has committed an all or nothing fallacy. Can we not feel the agony and mystery of evil and at the same time attempt to provide explanations? Perhaps we need to make a distinction between two importantly different contexts, one being the context of normal human activity in which people engage in social interaction, the other being the context of philosophical analysis in which explanation and argument about anything at all is legitimate. Even so, one might well ask the theodicist whether the psychological dimension of the experience of evil should not be taken into account in setting the tone for the theory itself.

You will want to work out your own position on just how devastating the problem of evil is to the claims of theism. These readings are included to help you do just that.

III.1   The Argument from Evil

DAVID HUME

In his Dialogues Concerning Natural Religion, *David Hume (1711–1776) argues through his persona Philo that not merely the fact of evil but the enormous amount of evil make it dubious that a deity exists. It is arguable that there is actually more evil than good in the world, so it is hard to see how one can harmonize the crucial propositions.*

Part X

It is my opinion, I own, replied Demea, that each man feels, in a manner, the truth of religion within his own breast, and, from a consciousness of his imbecility and misery rather than from any reasoning, is led to seek protection from that Being on whom he and all nature is dependent. So anxious or so tedious are even the best scenes of life that futurity is still the object of all our hopes and fears. We incessantly look forward and endeavour, by prayers, adoration, and sacrifice, to appease those unknown powers whom we find, by experience, so able to afflict and oppress us. Wretched creatures that we are! What resource for us amidst the innumerable ills of life did not religion suggest some methods of atonement, and appease those terrors with which we are incessantly agitated and tormented?

I am indeed persuaded, said Philo, that the best and indeed the only method of bringing everyone to a due sense of religion is by just representations of the misery and wickedness of men. And for that purpose a talent of eloquence and strong imagery is more requisite than that of reasoning and argument. For is it necessary to prove what everyone feels within himself? It is only nec-

Reprinted from David Hume, *Dialogues Concerning Natural Religion* (1779; London: Longmans Green, 1878).

essary to make us feel it, if possible, more intimately and sensibly.

The people, indeed, replied Demea, are sufficiently convinced of this great and melancholy truth. The miseries of life, the unhappiness of man, the general corruptions of our nature, the unsatisfactory enjoyment of pleasures, riches, honours—these phrases have become almost proverbial in all languages. And who can doubt of what all men declare from their own immediate feeling and experience?

In this point, said Philo, the learned are perfectly agreed with the vulgar; and in all letters, *sacred* and *profane,* the topic of human misery has been insisted on with the most pathetic eloquence that sorrow and melancholy could inspire. The poets, who speak from sentiment, without a system, and whose testimony has therefore the more authority, abound in images of this nature. From Homer down to Dr. Young, the whole inspired tribe have ever been sensible that no other representation of things would suit the feeling and observation of each individual.

As to authorities, replied Demea, you need not seek them. Look round this library of Cleanthes. I shall venture to affirm that, except authors of particular sciences, such as chemistry or botany, who have no occasion to treat of human life, there is scarce one of those innumerable writers from whom the sense of human misery has not, in some passage or other, extorted a complaint and confession of it. At least, the chance is entirely on that side; and no one author has ever, so far as I can recollect, been so extravagant as to deny it.

There you must excuse me, said Philo: Leibniz has denied it, and is perhaps the first[1] who ventured upon so bold and paradoxical an opinion; at least, the first who made it essential to his philosophical system.

And by being the first, replied Demea, might

he not have been sensible of his error? For is this a subject in which philosophers can propose to make discoveries especially in so late an age? And can any man hope by a simple denial (for the subject scarcely admits of reasoning) to bear down the united testimony of mankind, founded on sense and consciousness?

And why should man, added he, pretend to an exemption from the lot of all other animals? The whole earth, believe me, Philo, is cursed and polluted. A perpetual war is kindled amongst all living creatures. Necessity, hunger, want stimulate the strong and courageous; fear, anxiety, terror agitate the weak and infirm. The first entrance into life gives anguish to the new-born infant and to its wretched parent; weakness, impotence, distress attend each stage of that life, and it is, at last, finished in agony and horror.

Observe, too, says Philo, the curious artifices of nature in order to embitter the life of every living being. The stronger prey upon the weaker and keep them in perpetual terror and anxiety. The weaker, too, in their turn, often prey upon the stronger, and vex and molest them without relaxation. Consider that innumerable race of insects, which either are bred on the body of each animal or, flying about, infix their stings in him. These insects have others still less than themselves which torment them. And thus on each hand, before and behind, above and below, every animal is surrounded with enemies which incessantly seek his misery and destruction.

Man alone, said Demea, seems to be, in part, an exception to this rule. For by combination in society he can easily master lions, tigers, and bears, whose greater strength and agility naturally enable them to prey upon him.

On the contrary, it is here chiefly, cried Philo, that the uniform and equal maxims of nature are most apparent. Man, it is true, can, by combination, surmount all his *real* enemies and become master of the whole animal creation; but does he not immediately raise up to himself *imaginary* enemies, the demons of his fancy, who haunt him with superstitious terrors and blast every enjoyment of life? His pleasure, as he imagines, be-

comes in their eyes a crime; his food and repose give them umbrage and offence; his very sleep and dreams furnish new materials to anxious fear; and even death, his refuge from every other ill, presents only the dread of endless and innumerable woes. Nor does the wolf molest more the timid flock than superstition does the anxious breast of wretched mortals.

Besides, consider, Demea: This very society by which we surmount those wild beasts, our natural enemies, what new enemies does it not raise to us? What woe and misery does it not occasion? Man is the greatest enemy of man. Oppression, injustice, contempt, contumely, violence, sedition, war, calumny, treachery, fraud—by these they mutually torment each other, and they would soon dissolve that society which they had formed were it not for the dread of still greater ills which must attend their separation.

But though these external insults, said Demea, from animals, from men, from all the elements, which assault us form a frightful catalogue of woes, they are nothing in comparison of those which arise within ourselves, from the distempered condition of our mind and body. How many lie under the lingering torment of diseases? Hear the pathetic enumeration of the great poet.

Intestine stone and ulcer, colic-pangs,
Demoniac frenzy, moping melancholy,
And moon-struck madness, pining atrophy,
Marasmus, and wide-wasting pestilence.
Dire was the tossing, deep the groans:
    Despair
Tended the sick, busiest from couch to
    couch.
And over them triumphant *Death* his dart
Shook: but delay'd to strike, though oft
    invok'd
With vows, as their chief good and final
    hope.[2]

The disorders of the mind, continued Demea, though more secret, are not perhaps less dismal and vexatious. Remorse, shame, anguish, rage, disappointment, anxiety, fear, dejection, despair—who has ever passed through life without cruel inroads from these tormentors? How many have scarcely ever felt any better sensations? Labour and poverty, so abhorred by everyone, are the certain lot of the far greater number; and those few privileged persons who enjoy ease and opulence never reach contentment or true felicity. All the goods of life united would not make a very happy man, but all the ills united would make a wretch indeed; and any one of them almost (and who can be free from every one?), nay, often the absence of one good (and who can possess all?) is sufficient to render life ineligible.

Were a stranger to drop on a sudden into this world, I would show him, as a specimen of its ills, an hospital full of diseases, a prison crowded with malefactors and debtors, a field of battle strewed with carcases, a fleet foundering in the ocean, a nation languishing under tyranny, famine, or pestilence. To turn the gay side of life to him and give him a notion of its pleasures—whether should I conduct him? To a ball, to an opera, to court? He might justly think that I was only showing him a diversity of distress and sorrow.

There is no evading such striking instances, said Philo, but by apologies which still further aggravate the charge. Why have all men, I ask, in all ages, complained incessantly of the miseries of life? . . . They have no just reason, says one: these complaints proceed only from their discontented, repining, anxious disposition. . . . And can there possibly, I reply, be a more certain foundation of misery than such a wretched temper?

But if they were really as unhappy as they pretend, says my antagonist, why do they remain in life? . . .

Not satisfied with life, afraid of death—

this is the secret chain, say I, that holds us. We are terrified, not bribed to the continuance of our existence.

It is only a false delicacy, he may insist, which a few refined spirits indulge, and which has spread these complaints among the whole race of mankind. . . . And what is this delicacy, I ask, which you blame? Is it anything but a greater sensibility to all the pleasures and pains of life? And if the man of a delicate, refined temper, by being so

much more alive than the rest of the world, is only so much more unhappy, what judgment must we form in general of human life?

Let men remain at rest, says our adversary, and they will be easy. They are willing artificers of their own misery. . . . No! reply I: an anxious languor follows their repose; disappointment, vexation, trouble, their activity and ambition.

I can observe something like what you mention in some others, replied Cleanthes, but I confess I feel little or nothing of it in myself, and hope that it is not so common as you represent it.

If you feel not human misery yourself, cried Demea, I congratulate you on so happy a singularity. Others, seemingly the most prosperous, have not been ashamed to vent their complaints in the most melancholy strains. Let us attend to the great, the fortunate emperor, Charles V, when, tired with human grandeur, he resigned all his extensive dominions into the hands of his son. In the last harangue which he made on that memorable occasion, he publicly avowed *that the greatest prosperities which he had ever enjoyed had been mixed with so many adversities that he might truly say he had never enjoyed any satisfaciton or contentment.* But did the retired life in which he sought for shelter afford him any greater happiness? If we may credit his son's account, his repentance commenced the very day of his resignation.

Cicero's fortune, from small beginnings, rose to the greatest lustre and renown; yet what pathetic complaints of the ills of life do his familiar letters, as well as philosophical discourses, contain? And suitably to his own experience, he introduces Cato, the great, the fortunate Cato protesting in his old age that had he a new life in his offer he would reject the present.

Ask yourself, ask any of your acquaintance, whether they would live over again the last ten or twenty years of their life. No! but the next twenty, they say, will be better:

And from the dregs of life, hope to receive
What the first sprightly running could not
    give.[3]

Thus, at last, they find (such is the greatness of human misery, it reconciles even contradictions) that they complain at once of the shortness of life and of its vanity and sorrow.

And is it possible, Cleanthes, said Philo, that after all these reflections, and infinitely more which might be suggested, you can still persevere in your anthropomorphism, and assert the moral attributes of the Deity, his justice, benevolence, mercy, and rectitude, to be of the same nature with these virtues in human creatures? His power, we allow, is infinite; whatever he wills is executed; but neither man nor any other animal is happy; therefore, he does not will their happiness. His wisdom is infinite; he is never mistaken in choosing the means to any end; but the course of nature tends not to human or animal felicity; therefore, it is not established for that purpose. Through the whole compass of human knowledge there are no inferences more certain and infallible than these. In what respect, then, do his benevolence and mercy resemble the benevolence and mercy of men?

Epicurus' old questions are yet unanswered.

Is he willing to prevent evil, but not able? then is he impotent. Is he able, but not willing? then is he malevolent. Is he both able and willing? whence then is evil?

You ascribe, Cleanthes, (and I believe justly) a purpose and intention to nature. But what, I beseech you, is the object of that curious artifice and machinery which she has displayed in all animals—the preservation alone of individuals, and propagation of the species? It seems enough for her purpose, if such a rank be barely upheld in the universe, without any care or concern for the happiness of the members that compose it. No resource for this purpose: no machinery in order merely to give pleasure or ease; no fund of pure joy and contentment; no indulgence without some want or necessity accompanying it. At least, the few phenomena of this nature are overbalanced by opposite phenomena of still greater importance.

Our sense of music, harmony, and indeed beauty of all kinds, gives satisfaction, without being absolutely necessary to the preservation and propagation of the species. But what racking pains, on the other hand, arise from gouts, grav-

els, megrims, toothaches, rheumatisms, where the injury to the animal machinery is either small or incurable? Mirth, laughter, play, frolic seem gratuitous satisfactions which have no further tendency; spleen, melancholy, discontent, superstition are pains of the same nature. How then does the Divine benevolence display itself, in the sense of you anthropomorphites? None but we mystics, as you were pleased to call us, can account for this strange mixture of phenomena, by deriving it from attributes infinitely perfect but incomprehensible.

And have you, at last, said Cleanthes smiling, betrayed your intentions, Philo? Your long agreement with Demea did indeed a little surprise me, but I find you were all the while erecting a concealed battery against me. And I must confess that you have now fallen upon a subject worthy of your noble spirit of opposition and controversy. If you can make out the present point, and prove mankind to be unhappy or corrupted, there is an end at once of all religion. For to what purpose establish the natural attributes of the Deity, while the moral are still doubtful and uncertain?

You take umbrage very easily, replied Demea, at opinions the most innocent and the most generally received, even amongst the religious and devout themselves; and nothing can be more surprising than to find a topic like this—concerning the wickedness and misery of man—charged with no less than atheism and profaneness. Have not all pious divines and preachers who have indulged their rhetoric on so fertile a subject, have they not easily, I say, given a solution of any difficulties which may attend it? This world is but a point in comparison of the universe; this life but a moment in comparison of eternity. The present evil phenomena, therefore, are rectified in other regions, and in some future period of existence. And the eyes of men, being then opened to larger views of things, see the whole connection of general laws, and trace, with adoration, the benevolence and rectitude of the Deity through all the mazes and intricacies of his providence.

No! replied Cleanthes, no! These arbitrary suppositions can never be admitted, contrary to matter of fact, visible and uncontroverted. Whence can any cause be known but from its known effects? Whence can any hypothesis be proved but from the apparent phenomena? To establish one hypothesis upon another is building entirely in the air; and the utmost we ever attain by these conjectures and fictions is to ascertain the bare possibility of our opinion, but never can we, upon such terms, establish its reality.

The only method of supporting Divine benevolence—and it is what I willingly embrace—is to deny absolutely the misery and wickedness of man. Your representations are exaggerated; your melancholy views mostly fictitious; your inferences contrary to fact and experience. Health is more common than sickness; pleasure than pain; happiness than misery. And for one vexation which we meet with, we attain, upon computation, a hundred enjoyments.

Admitting your position, replied Philo, which yet is extremely doubtful, you must at the same time allow that, if pain be less frequent than pleasure, it is infinitely more violent and durable. One hour of it is often able to outweigh a day, a week, a month of our common insipid enjoyments; and how many days, weeks, and months are passed by several in the most acute torments? Pleasure, scarcely in one instance, is ever able to reach ecstasy and rapture; and in no one instance can it continue for any time at its highest pitch and altitude. The spirits evaporate, the nerves relax, the fabric is disordered, and the enjoyment quickly degenerates into fatigue and uneasiness. But pain often, good God, how often! rises to torture and agony; and the longer it continues, it becomes still more genuine agony and torture. Patience is exhausted, courage languishes, melancholy seizes us, and nothing terminates our misery but the removal of its cause or another event which is the sole cure of all evil, but which, from our natural folly, we regard with still greater horror and consternation.

But not to insist upon these topics, continued Philo, though most obvious, certain, and important, I must use the freedom to admonish you, Cleanthes, that you have put the controversy upon a most dangerous issue, and are unawares introducing a total scepticism into the most essential articles of natural and revealed theology. What!

no method of fixing a just foundation for religion unless we allow the happiness of human life, and maintain a continued existence even in this world, with all our present pains, infirmities, vexations, and follies, to be eligible and desirable! But this is contrary to everyone's feeling and experience; it is contrary to an authority so established as nothing can subvert. No decisive proofs can ever be produced against this authority; nor is it possible for you to compute, estimate, and compare all the pains and all the pleasures in the lives of all men and of all animals; and thus, by your resting the whole system of religion on a point which, from its very nature, must forever be uncertain, you tacitly confess that that system is equally uncertain.

But allowing you what never will be believed, at least, what you never possibly can prove, that animal or, at least, human happiness in this life exceeds its misery, you have yet done nothing; for this is not, by any means, what we expect from infinite power, infinite wisdom, and infinite goodness. Why is there any misery at all in the world? Not by chance, surely. From some cause then. Is it from the intention of the Deity? But he is perfectly benevolent. Is it contrary to his intention? But he is almighty. Nothing can shake the solidity of this reasoning, so short, so clear, so decisive, except we assert that these subjects exceed all human capacity, and that our common measures of truth and falsehood are not applicable to them—a topic which I have all along insisted on, but which you have, from the beginning, rejected with scorn and indignation.

But I will be contented to retire still from this intrenchment, for I deny that you can ever force me in it. I will allow that pain or misery in man is *compatible* with infinite power and goodness in the Deity, even in your sense of these attributes: what are you advanced by all these concessions? A mere possible compatibility is not sufficient. You must *prove* these pure, unmixt, and uncontrollable attributes from the present mixed and confused phenomena, and from these alone. A hopeful undertaking! Were the phenomena ever so pure and unmixed, yet, being finite, they would be insufficient for that purpose. How much more, where they are also so jarring and discordant!

Here, Cleanthes, I find myself at ease in my argument. Here I triumph. Formerly, when we argued concerning the natural attributes of intelligence and design, I needed all my sceptical and metaphysical subtilty to elude your grasp. In many views of the universe and of its parts, particularly the latter, the beauty and fitness of final causes strike us with such irresistible force that all objections appear (what I believe they really are) mere cavils and sophisms; nor can we then imagine how it was ever possible for us to repose any weight on them. But there is no view of human life or of the condition of mankind from which, without the greatest violence, we can infer the moral attributes or learn that infinite benevolence, conjoined with infinite power and infinite wisdom, which we must discover by the eyes of faith alone. It is your turn now to tug the labouring oar, and to support your philosophical subtilties against the dictates of plain reason and experience.

Notes

1. That sentiment had been maintained by Dr. King and some few others before Leibniz, though by none of so great fame as that German philosopher.
2. Milton: *Paradise Lost,* Bk. XI.
3. John Dryden, *Aureng-Zebe,* Act IV, sc. 1.

III.2   Theodicy: A Defense of Theism

GOTTFRIED LEIBNIZ

Gottfried Wilhelm Leibniz (1646–1716) was a German idealist who tried to set forth a thoroughgoing theodicy, a justification of the ways of God. In this selection he argues that the fact of evil in no way refutes theism, and he answers the kind of objections made by Hume. He contends that God permitted evil to exist in order to bring about greater good and that Adam's fall was a felix culpa (a "happy sin") because it led to the incarnation of the Son of God, raising humanity to a higher destiny than would otherwise have been the case. He argues that although God can foresee the future, the future isn't determined since humans are still free.

Reprinted from Gottfried Leibniz, *The Theodicy: Abridgement of the Argument Reduced to Syllogistic Form* (1710).

Some intelligent persons have desired that this supplement be made [to the Theodicy], and I have the more readily yielded to their wishes as in this way I have an opportunity again to remove certain difficulties and to make some observations which were not sufficiently emphasized in the work itself.

I. *Objection.* Whoever does not choose the best is lacking in power, or in knowledge, or in goodness.

God did not choose the best in creating this world.

Therefore, God has been lacking in power, or in knowledge, or in goodness.

Answer. I deny the minor, that is, the second premise of this syllogism; and our opponent proves it by this.

Prosyllogism. Whoever makes things in which there is evil, which could have been made without any evil, or the making of which could have been omitted, does not choose the best.

God has made a world in which there is evil; a world, I say, which could have been made without any evil, or the making of which could have been omitted altogether.

Therefore, God has not chosen the best.

Answer. I grant the minor of this prosyllogism; for it must be confessed that there is evil in this world which God has made, and that it was possible to make a world without evil, or even not to create a world at all, for its creation has depended on the free will of God; but I deny the major, that is, the first of the two premises of the prosyllogism, and I might content myself with simply demanding its proof; but in order to make the matter clearer, I have wished to justify this denial by showing that the best plan is not always that which seeks to avoid evil, since it may happen that *the evil is accompanied by a greater good.* For example, a general of an army will prefer a great victory with a slight wound to a condition without wound and without victory. We have proved this more fully in the large work by making it clear, by instances taken from mathematics and elsewhere, that an imperfection in the part may be required for a greater perfection in the whole. In this I have followed the opinion of St. Augustine, who has said a hundred times, that God has permitted evil in order to bring about good, that is, a greater good; and that of Thomas Aquinas (in libr. II. sent. dist. 32, qu. I, art. 1), that the permitting of evil tends to the good of the universe. I have shown that the ancients called Adam's fall *felix cupla,* a happy sin, because it had been retrieved with immense advantage by the incarnation of the Son of God, who has given to the universe something nobler than anything that ever would have been among creatures except for it. For the sake of a clearer understanding, I have added, following many good authors, that it was in accordance with order and the general good that God allowed to certain creatures the opportunity of exercising their liberty, even when he foresaw that they would turn to evil, but which he could so well rectify; because it was not fitting that, in order to hinder sin, God should always act in an extraordinary manner. To overthrow this objection, therefore, it is sufficient to show that a world with evil might be better than a world without evil; but I have gone even farther, in the work, and have even proved that this universe must be in reality better than every other possible universe.

II. *Objection.* If there is more evil than good in intelligent creatures, then there is more evil than good in the whole work of God.

Now, there is more evil than good in intelligent creatures.

Therefore, there is more evil than good in the whole work of God.

Answer. I deny the major and the minor of this conditional syllogism. As to the major, I do not admit it at all, because this pretended deduction from a part to the whole, from intelligent creatures to all creatures, supposes tacitly and without proof that creatures destitute of reason cannot enter into comparison nor into account with those which possess it. But why may it not be that the surplus of good in the non-intelligent creatures which fill the world, compensates for, and even incomparably surpasses, the surplus of evil in the rational creatures? It is true that the value of the latter is greater; but, in compensation, the others are beyond comparison the more numerous, and it may be that the proportion of number and quantity surpasses that of value and of quality.

As to the minor, that is no more to be admitted; that is, it is not at all to be admitted that there is more evil than good in the intelligent creatures. There is no need even of granting that there is more evil than good in the human race, because it is possible, and in fact very probable, that the glory and the perfection of the blessed are incomparably greater than the misery and the imperfection of the damned, and that here the excellence of the total good in the smaller number exceeds the total evil in the greater number. The blessed approach the Divinity, by means of a Divine Mediator, as near as may suit these creatures, and make such progress in good as is impossible for the damned to make in evil, approach as nearly as they may to the nature of demons. God is infinite, and the devil is limited; the good may and does go to infinity, while evil has its bounds. It is therefore possible, and is credible, that in the comparison of the blessed and the damned, the contrary of that which I have said might happen in the comparison of intelligent and non-intelligent creatures, takes place; namely, it is possible that in the comparison of the happy and the unhappy, the proportion of degree exceeds that of number, and that in the comparison of intelligent and non-intelligent creatures, the proportion of number is greater than that of value. I have the right to suppose that a thing is possible so long as its impossibility is not proved;

and indeed that which I have here advanced is more than a supposition.

But in the second place, if I should admit that there is more evil than good in the human race, I have still good grounds for not admitting that there is more evil than good in all intelligent creatures. For there is an inconceivable number of genii, and perhaps of other rational creatures. And an opponent could not prove that in all the City of God, composed as well of genii as of rational animals without number and of an infinity of kinds, evil exceeds good. And although in order to answer an objection, there is no need of proving that a thing is, when its mere possibility suffices; yet, in this work, I have not omitted to show that it is a consequence of the supreme perfection of the Sovereign of the universe, that the kingdom of God is the most perfect of all possible states or governments, and that consequently the little evil there is,' is required for the consummation of the immense good which is found there.

III. *Objection.* If it is always impossible not to sin, it is always unjust to punish.

Now, it is always impossible not to sin; or, in other words, every sin is necessary.

Therefore, it is always unjust to punish.

The minor of this is proved thus:

1. *Prosyllogism.* All that is predetermined is necessary.

Every event is predetermined.

Therefore, every event (and consequently sin also) is necessary.

Again this second minor is proved thus:

2. *Prosyllogism.* That which is future, that which is foreseen, that which is involved in the causes, is predetermined.

Every event is such.

Therefore, every event is predetermined.

Answer. I admit in a certain sense the conclusion of the second prosyllogism, which is the minor of the first; but I shall deny the major of the first prosyllogism, namely, that every thing predetermined is necessary; understanding by the *necessity* of sinning, for example, or by the impossibility of not sinning, or of not performing any action, the necessity with which we are here concerned, that is, that which is essential and abso-

lute, and which destroys the morality of an action and the justice of punishments. For if anyone understood another necessity or impossibility, namely, a necessity which should be only moral, or which was only hypothetical (as will be explained shortly); it is clear that I should deny the major of the objection itself. I might content myself with this answer and demand the proof of the proposition denied; but I have again desired to explain my procedure in this work, in order to better elucidate the matter and to throw more light on the whole subject, by explaining the necessity which ought to be rejected and the determination which must take place. That *necessity* which is contrary to morality and which ought to be rejected, and which would render punishment unjust, is an insurmountable necessity which would make all opposition useless, even if we should wish with all our heart to avoid the necessary action, and should make all possible efforts to that end. Now, it is manifest that this is not applicable to voluntary actions, because we would not perform them if we did not choose to. Also their prevision and predetermination are not absolute, but presuppose the will: if it is certain that we shall perform them, it is not less certain that we shall choose to perform them. These voluntary actions and their consequences will not take place no matter what we do or whether we wish them or not; but, *through* that which we shall do and through that which we shall wish to do, which leads to them. And this is involved in prevision and in predetermination, and even constitutes their ground. And the necessity of such an event is called conditional or hypothetical, or the necessity of consequence, because it supposes the will, and the other *requisites;* whereas the necessity which destroys morality and renders punishment unjust and reward useless, exists in things which will be whatever we may do or whatever we may wish to do, and, in a word, is in that which is essential; and this is what is called an absolute necessity. Thus it is to no purpose, as regards what is absolutely necessary, to make prohibitions or commands, to propose penalties or prizes, to praise or to blame; it will be none the less. On the other hand, in voluntary actions and in that which depends upon them, precepts armed with power to punish and to recompense are very often of use and are included in the order of causes which make an action exist. And it is for this reason that not only cares and labors but also prayers are useful; God having had these prayers in view before he regulated things and having had that consideration for them which was proper. This is why the precept which says *ora et labora* (pray and work), holds altogether good; and not only those who (under the vain pretext of the necessity of events) pretend that the care which business demands may be neglected, but also those who reason against prayer, fall into what the ancients even then called the *lazy sophism*. Thus the predetermination of events by causes is just what contributes to morality instead of destroying it, and causes incline the will, without compelling it. This is why the *determination* in question is not a necessitation—it is certain (to him who knows all) that the effect will follow this inclination; but this effect does not follow by a necessary consequence, that is, one the contrary of which implies contradiction. It is also by an internal inclination such as this that the will is determined, without there being any necessity. Suppose that one has the greatest passion in the world (a great thirst, for example), you will admit to me that the soul can find some reason for resisting it, if it were only that of showing its power. Thus, although one may never be in a perfect indifference of equilibrium and there may be always a preponderance of inclination for the side taken, it, nevertheless, never renders the resolution taken absolutely necessary.

IV. *Objection.* Whoever can prevent the sin of another and does not do so, but rather contributes to it although he is well informed of it, is accessory to it.

God can prevent the sin of intelligent creatures; but he does not do so, and rather contributes to it by his concurrence and by the opportunities which he brings about, although he has a perfect knowledge of it.

Hence, etc.

Answer. I deny the major of this syllogism. For it is possible that one could prevent sin, but ought

not, because he could not do it without himself committing a sin, or (when God is in question) without performing an unreasonable action. Examples have been given and the application to God himself has been made. It is possible also that we contribute to evil and that sometimes we even open the road to it, in doing things which we are obliged to do; and, when we do our duty or (in speaking of God) when, after thorough consideration, we do that which reason demands, we are not responsible for the results, even when we foresee them. We do not desire these evils; but we are willing to permit them for the sake of a greater good which we cannot reasonably help preferring to other considerations. And this is a *consequent* will, which results from *antecedent* wills by which we will the good. I know that some persons, in speaking of the antecedent and consequent will of God, have understood by the *antecedent* that which wills that all men should be saved; and by the *consequent,* that which wills, in consequence of persistent sin, that some should be damned. But these are merely illustrations of a more general idea, and it may be said for the same reason that God, by his antecedent will, wills that men should not sin; and by his consequent or final and decreeing will (that which is always followed by its effect), he wills to permit them to sin, this permission being the result of superior reasons. And we have the right to say in general that the antecedent will of God tends to the production of good and the prevention of evil, each taken in itself and as if alone (*particulariter et secundum quid,* Thom. I, qu. 19, art. 6), according to the measure of the degree of each good and of each evil; but that the divine consequent or final or total will tends toward the production of as many goods as may be put together, the combination of which becomes in this way determined, and includes also the permission of some evils and the exclusion of some goods, as the best possible plan for the universe demands. Arminius, in his *Anti-perkinsus,* has very well explained that the will of God may be called consequent, not only in relation to the action of the creature considered beforehand in the divine understanding, but also in relation to other anterior divine acts of will. But this consideration of the passage cited from Thomas Aquinas, and that from Scotus (I. dist. 46, qu. XI), is enough to show that they make this distinction as I have done here. Nevertheless, if anyone objects to this use of terms let him substitute *deliberating* will, in place of antecedent, and *final* or decreeing will, in place of consequent. For I do not wish to dispute over words.

V. *Objection*. Whoever produces all that is real in a thing, is its cause.

God produces all that is real in sin.

Hence, God is the cause of sin.

Answer. I might content myself with denying the major or the minor, since the term *real* admits of interpretations which would render these propositions false. But in order to explain more clearly, I will make a distinction. *Real* signifies either that which is positive only, or, it includes also privative beings: in the first case, I deny the major and admit the minor; in the second case, I do the contrary. I might have limited myself to this, but I have chosen to proceed still farther and give the reason for this distinction. I have been very glad therefore to draw attention to the fact that every reality purely positive or absolute is a perfection; and that imperfection comes from limitation, that is, from the privative: for to limit is to refuse progress, or the greatest possible progress. Now God is the cause of all perfections and consequently of all realities considered as purely positive. But limitations or privations result from the original imperfection of creatures, which limits their receptivity. And it is with them as with a loaded vessel, which the river causes to move more or less slowly ac-

cording to the weight which it carries: thus its speed depends upon the river, but the retardation which limits this speed comes from the load. Thus in the *Theodicy*, we have shown how the creature, in causing sin, is a defective cause; how errors and evil inclinations are born of privation; and how privation is accidentally efficient; and I have justified the opinion of St. Augustine (lib. I. ad Simpl. qu. 2) who explains, for example, how God makes the soul obdurate, not by giving it something evil, but because the effect of his good impression is limited by the soul's resistance and by the circumstances which contribute to this resistance, so that he does not give it all the good which would overcome its evil. *Nec* (inquit) *ab illo erogatur aliquid quo homo fit deterior, sed tantum quo fit melior non erogatur*. But if God had wished to do more, he would have had to make either other natures for creatures or other miracles to change their natures, things which the best plan could not admit. It is as if the current of the river must be more rapid than its fall admitted or that the boats should be loaded more lightly, if it were necessary to make them move more quickly. And the original limitation or imperfection of creatures requires that even the best plan of the universe could not receive more good, and could not be exempt from certain evils, which, however, are to result in a greater good. There are certain disorders in the parts which marvelously enhance the beauty of the whole; just as certain dissonances, when properly used, render harmony more beautiful. But this depends on what has already been said in answer to the first objection. . . . .

III.3   Evil and Soul-Making

JOHN HICK

John Hick was for many years professor of theology at the University of Birmingham in England. He is now professor of philosophy at Claremont Graduate School. His book Evil and the God of Love *(1966), from which the following selection is taken, is considered one of the most thorough treatises on the problem of evil. "Evil and Soul-Making" is an example of a theodicy argument that is based on the free will defense. Theodicies can be of two differing types depending on how they justify the ways of God in the face of evil. The Augustinian position is that God created humans without sin and set them in a sinless, paradisical world. However, humanity fell into sin through misuse of its free will. God's grace will save some of us, but others will perish everlastingly. The second type of theodicy stems from the thinking of Irenaeus (120–202), of the Greek Church. The Irenaean tradition views Adam not as a free agent rebelling against God but as a child. The fall is humanity's first faulty step in the direction of freedom. God is still working with humanity in order to bring it from undeveloped life (bios) to a state of self-realization in divine love, spiritual life (zoe). This life is viewed as the "vale of soul-making." Hick favors this version and develops it in this reading.*

Fortunately there is another and better way. As well as the "majority report" of the Augustinian tradition, which has dominated Western Christendom, both Catholic and Protestant, since the time of Augustine himself, there is the "minority report" of the Irenaean tradition. This latter is both older and newer than the other, for it goes back to St. Irenaeus and others of the early Hellenistic Fathers of the Church in the two centuries prior to St.

Pp. 253–261 from *Evil and the God of Love*, revised edition, by John Hick. Copyright © 1966, 1977 by John Hick. Reprinted by permission of Harper & Row, Publishers, Inc. Footnotes edited.

Augustine, and it has flourished again in more developed forms during the last hundred years.

Instead of regarding man as having been created by God in a finished state, as a finitely perfect being fulfilling the divine intention for our human level of existence, and then falling disastrously away from this, the minority report sees man as still in process of creation. Irenaeus himself expressed the point in terms of the (exegetically dubious) distinction between the "image" and the "likeness" of God referred to in Genesis i.26: "Then God said, Let us make man in our image, after our likeness." His view was that man as a personal and moral being already exists in the image, but has not yet been formed into the finite likeness of God. By this "likeness" Irenaeus means something more than personal existence as such; he means a certain valuable quality of personal life which reflects finitely the divine life. This represents the perfecting of man, the fulfilment of God's purpose for humanity, the "bringing of many sons to glory," the creating of "children of God" who are "fellow heirs with Christ" of his glory.

And so man, created as a personal being in the image of God, is only the raw material for a further and more difficult stage of God's creative work. This is the leading of men as relatively free and autonomous persons, through their own dealings with life in the world in which He has placed them, towards that quality of personal existence that is the finite likeness of God. The features of this likeness are revealed in the person of Christ, and the process of man's creation into it is the work of the Holy Spirit. In St. Paul's words, "And we all, with unveiled faces, beholding the glory of the Lord, are being changed into his likeness (εἰκών) from one degree of glory to another; for this comes from the Lord who is the Spirit";[1] or again, "For God knew his own before ever they were, and also ordained that they should be shaped to the likeness (εἰκών) of his Son."[2] In Johannine terms, the movement from the image to the likeness is a transition from one level of existence, that of animal life (*Bios*), to another and higher level, that of eternal life (*Zoe*), which includes but transcends the first. And the fall of man was seen by Irenaeus as a failure within the second phase of this creative process, a failure that has multiplied the perils and complicated the route of the journey in which God is seeking to lead mankind.

In the light of modern anthropological knowledge some form of two-stage conception of the creation of man has become an almost unavoidable Christian tenet. At the very least we must acknowledge as two distinguishable stages the fashioning of *homo sapiens* as a product of the long evolutionary process, and his sudden or gradual spiritualization as a child of God. But we may well extend the first stage to include the development of man as a rational and responsible person capable of personal relationship with the personal Infinite who has created him. This first stage of the creative process was, to our anthropomorphic imaginations, easy for divine omnipotence. By an exercise of creative power God caused the physical universe to exist, and in the course of countless ages to bring forth within it organic life, and finally to produce out of organic life personal life; and when man had thus emerged out of the evolution of the forms of organic life, a creature had been made who has the possibility of existing in conscious fellowship with God. But the second stage of the creative process is of a different kind altogether. It cannot be performed by omnipotent power as such. For personal life is essentially free and self-directing. It cannot be perfected by divine fiat, but only through the uncompelled responses and willing co-operation of human individuals in their actions and reactions in the world in which God has placed them. Men may eventually become the perfected persons whom the New Testament calls "children of God," but they cannot be created ready-made as this.

The value-judgement that is implicitly being invoked here is that one who has attained to goodness by meeting and eventually mastering temptations, and thus by rightly making responsible choices in concrete situations, is good in a richer and more valuable sense than would be one created *ab initio* in a state either of innocence or of virtue. In the former case, which is that of the actual moral achievements of mankind, the individual's goodness has within it the strength of temptations overcome, a stability based upon an accumulation of right choices, and a positive and responsible character that comes from the investment of costly personal effort. I suggest, then, that it is an ethically reasonable judgement, even though in the nature of the case not one that is capable of demonstrative proof, that human goodness slowly built up through personal histories of moral effort has a value in the eyes of the Creator which justifies even the long travail of the soul-making process.

The picture with which we are working is thus developmental and teleological. Man is in process of becoming the perfected being whom God is seeking to create. However, this is not taking place—it is important to add—by a natural and inevitable evolution, but through a hazardous adventure in individual freedom. Because this is a pilgrimage within the life of each individual, rather than a racial evolution, the progressive fulfilment of God's purpose does not entail any corresponding progressive improvement in the moral state of the world. There is no doubt a development in man's ethical situation from generation to generation through the building of individual choices into public institutions, but this involves an accumulation of evil as well as of good. It is thus probable that human life was lived on much the same moral plane two thousand years ago or four thousand years ago as it is today. But nevertheless during this period uncounted millions of souls have been through the experience of earthly life, and God's purpose has gradually moved towards its fulfilment within each one of them, rather than within a human aggregate composed of different units in different generations.

If, then, God's aim in making the world is "the bringing of many sons to glory," that aim will naturally determine the kind of world that He has created. Antitheistic writers almost invariably assume a conception of the divine purpose which is contrary to the Christian conception. They assume that the purpose of a loving God must be to create a hedonistic paradise; and therefore to the extent that the world is other than this, it proves to them that God is either not loving enough or not powerful enough to create such a world. They think of God's relation to the earth on the model of a human being building a cage for a pet animal to dwell in. If he is humane he will naturally make his pet's quarters as pleasant and healthful as he can. Any respect in which the cage falls short of the veterinarian's ideal, and contains possibilities of accident or disease, is evidence of either limited benevolence or limited means, or both. Those who use the problem of evil as an argument against belief in God almost invariably think of the world in this kind of way. David Hume, for example, speaks of an architect who is trying to plan a house that is to be as comfortable and convenient as possible. If we find that "the windows, doors, fires, passages, stairs, and the whole economy of the building were the source of noise, confusion, fatigue, darkness, and the extremes of heat and cold" we should have no hesitation in blaming the architect. It would be in vain for him to prove that if this or that defect were corrected greater ills would result: "still you would assert in general, that, if the architect had had skill and good intentions, he might have formed such a plan of the whole, and might have adjusted the parts in such a manner, as would have remedied all or most of these inconveniences.³

But if we are right in supposing that God's purpose for man is to lead him from human *Bios*, or the biological life of man, to that quality of *Zoe*, or the personal life of eternal worth, which we seen in Christ, then the question that we have to ask is not, Is this the kind of world that an all-powerful and infinitely loving being would create as an environment for his human pets? or, Is the architecture of the world the most pleasant and convenient possible? The question that we have to ask is rather, Is this the kind of world that God might make as an environment in which moral beings may be fashioned, through their own free insights and responses, into "children of God"?

Such critics as Hume are confusing what heaven ought to be, as an environment for perfected finite beings, with what this world ought to be, as an environment for beings who are in process of becoming perfected. For if our general conception of God's purpose is correct the world is not intended to be a paradise, but rather the scene of a history in which human personality may be formed towards the pattern of Christ. Men are not to be thought of on the analogy of animal pets, whose life is to be made as agreeable as possible, but rather on the analogy of human children, who are to grow to adulthood in an environment whose primary and overriding purpose is not immediate pleasure but the realizing of the most valuable potentialities of human personality.

Needless to say, this characterization of God as the heavenly Father is not a merely random illustration but an analogy that lies at the heart of the Christian faith. Jesus treated the likeness between the attitude of God to man, and the attitude of human parents at their best towards their children, as providing the most adequate way for us to think about God. And so it is altogether relevant to a Christian understanding of this world to ask, How does the best parental love express itself in its influence upon the environment in which children are to grow up? I think it is clear that a parent who loves his children, and wants them to become the best human beings that they are capable of becoming, does not treat pleasure as the sole and supreme value. Certainly we seek pleasure for our children, and take great delight in obtaining it for them; but we do not desire for them unalloyed pleasure at the expense of their growth in such even greater values as moral integrity, unselfishness, compassion, courage, humour, reverence for the truth, and perhaps above all the capacity for love. We do not act on the premise that pleasure is the supreme end of life; and if the development of these other values sometimes clashes with the provision of pleasure, then we are willing to have our children miss a certain amount of this, rather than fail to come to possess and to be possessed by the finer and more precious qualities that are possible to the human personality. A child brought up on the principle that the only or the supreme value is pleasure would not be likely to become an ethically mature adult or an attractive or happy personality. And to most parents it seems more important to try to foster quality and strength of character in their children than to fill their lives at all times with the utmost possible degree of pleasure. If, then, there is any true analogy between God's purpose for his human creatures, and the purpose of loving and wise parents for their children, we have to recognize that the presence of pleasure and the absence of pain cannot be the supreme and overriding end for which the world exists. Rather, this world must be a place of soul-making. And its value is to be judged, not primarily by the quantity of pleasure and pain occurring in it at any particular moment, but by its fitness for its primary purpose, the purpose of soul-making.

In all this we have been speaking about the nature of the world considered simply as the God-given environment of man's life. For it is mainly in this connection that the world has been regarded in Irenaean and in Protestant thought. But such a way of thinking involves a danger of anthropocentrism from which the Augustinian and Catholic tradition has generally been protected by its sense of the relative insignificance of man within the totality of the created universe. Man was dwarfed within the medieval world-view by the innumerable hosts of angels and archangels above him— unfallen rational natures which rejoice in the immediate presence of God, reflecting His glory in the untarnished mirror of their worship. However, this higher creation has in our modern world lost its hold upon the imagination. Its place has been taken, as the minimizer of men, by the immensities of outer space and by the material universe's unlimited complexity transcending our present knowledge. As the spiritual environment envisaged by Western man has shrunk, his physical horizons have correspondingly expanded. Where the human creature was formerly seen as an insignificant appendage to the angelic world, he is now seen as an equally insignificant organic excrescence, enjoying a fleeting moment of consciousness on the surface of one of the planets of a minor star. Thus the truth that was symbolized for former ages by the existence of the angelic hosts is today impressed upon us by the vastness of the physical universe, countering the egoism of our species by making us feel that this immense prodigality of existence can hardly all exist for the sake of man— though, on the other hand, the very realization that it is not all for the sake of man may itself be salutary and beneficial to man!

However, instead of opposing man and nature as rival objects of God's interest, we should perhaps rather stress man's solidarity as an embodied being with the whole natural order in which he is embedded. For man is organic to the world; all his acts and thoughts and imaginations are conditioned by space and time; and in abstraction from nature he would cease to be human. We may, then, say that the beauties and sublimities and powers, the microscopic intricacies and macroscopic vastnesses, the wonders and the terrors of the natural world and of the life that pulses through it, are willed and valued by their Maker in a creative act that embraces man together with nature. By means of matter and living flesh God both builds a path and weaves a veil between Himself and the creature made in His image. Nature thus has permanent significance; for God has set man in a creaturely environment, and the final fulfilment of our nature in relation to God will accordingly take the form of an embodied life within "a new heaven and a new earth." And as in the present age man moves slowly towards that fulfilment through the pilgrimage of his earthly life, so also "the whole creation" is "groaning in travail," waiting for the time when it will be "set free from its bondage to decay."

And yet however fully we thus acknowledge the permanent significance and value of the natural order, we must still insist upon man's special character as a personal creature made in the image of God; and our theodicy must still centre upon the soul-making process that we believe to be taking place within human life.

This, then, is the starting-point from which we propose to try to relate the realities of sin and suffering to the perfect love of an omnipotent Creator. And as will become increasingly apparent, a theodicy that starts in this way must be eschatological in its ultimate bearings. That is to say, instead of looking to the past for its clue to the mystery of evil, it looks to the future, and indeed to that ultimate future to which only faith can look. Given the conception of a divine intention working in and through human time towards a fulfilment that lies in its completeness beyond human time, our theodicy must find the meaning of evil in the part that it is made to play in the eventual outworking of that purpose; and must find the justification of the whole process in the magnitude of the good to which it leads. The good that outshines all ill is not a paradise long since lost but a kingdom which is yet to come in its full glory and permanence.

Notes

1. II Corinthians iii. 18.
2. Romans viii. 29. Other New Testament passages expressing a view of man as undergoing a process of spiritual growth within God's purpose are: Ephesians ii. 21; iii. 16; Colossians ii. 19; I John iii. 2; II Corinthians iv. 16.
3. *Dialogues Concerning Natural Religion,* pt. xi. Kemp-Smith's ed. (Oxford: Clarendon Press, 1935), p. 251.

III.4   A Critique of Hick's Theodicy

E D W A R D H . M A D D E N and P E T E R H . H A R E

Edward H. Madden and Peter H. Hare teach philosophy at the State University of New York at Buffalo. In this selection they attack Hick's theory. They ask whether the amount of evil in the world is necessary for soul-making and accuse Hick of three fallacies, called "all or nothing," "it could be worse," and "slippery slope."

The intellectual honesty of John Hick is impressive. Unlike the majority of Christian apologists he does not try to find safety in the number of solutions but instead searchingly criticizes and disowns many of the favorite solutions. He concludes, nevertheless, the apologetics reduced to fighting trim is all the more effective. He believes that a sophisticated combination of the character-building and free-will solutions will serve. They show evil to serve God's purpose of "soul-making."

Reprinted from Edward H. Madden and Peter H. Hare, *Evil and the Concept of God* (1968), 83–90, 102–103. Courtesy of Charles C. Thomas, Publisher, Springfield, Illinois. Footnotes deleted.

Earlier we pointed out the difficulties involved in the usual formulations of the character-building and free-will solutions. We shall consider here how successful Hick is in avoiding these difficulties.

According to Hick,

man, created as a personal being in the image of God, is only the raw material for a further and more difficult stage of God's creative work. This is the leading of men as relatively free and autonomous persons through their own dealings with life in the world in which he has placed them, towards that quality of personal existence that is the finite likeness of God.

The basic trouble, he says, with antitheistic writers is that "they assume that the purpose of a loving God must be to create a hedonistic paradise." He concedes that evil is not serving any, even remote, hedonistic end, but insists that it is serving the end of the development of moral personalities in loving relation to God. It is logically impossible to do this either by forcing them to love him or by forcing them always to act rightly. A creature *forced* to love would not be genuinely loving and a creature *forced* to do the right would not be a moral personality. Only through freedom, suffering, and initial remoteness from God ("epistemic distance") can the sort of person God is looking for come about.

Before we discuss in detail the difficulties involved in Hick's position we will briefly describe three informal fallacies Hick adroitly uses in his solution. They are all fallacies which have been used in one form or another throughout the history of Christian apologetics, and we have had occasion to mention them in our discussion of other writers in the previous chapter. However, it will be convenient in discussing Hick's skillful and elaborate use of them to describe and label clearly these arguments: "All or nothing," "It could be worse," and "slippery slope."

All or nothing. This is the claim that something is desirable because its complete loss would be far worse than the evil its presence now causes. The erroneous assumption is that we must have this thing either in its present form and amount or not at all. But it is often the case that only *some* amount of the thing in *some* form is necessary to the achievement of a desirable end.

It could be worse. This is the claim that something is not really bad because it will be followed by all manner of desirable things. The erroneous assumption here is that showing that having these later desirable things is a great boon also shows that the original evil is a necessary and not gratuitous one. Actually it only shows that the situation would be still worse if the desirable things did not follow. To show that it could be worse does not show that it could not be better.

Slippery slope. This is the claim that if God once started eliminating evils of this world he would have no place to stop short of a "perfect" world in which only robots and not men were possible. The erroneous assumption is that God would have no criterion to indicate where on the slippery slope to stop and no ability to implement it effectively. The same argument is used in human affairs and the answer is equally clear. "Once we

venture, as we sometimes must, on a dangerous course which may lead to our salvation in a particular situation but which may also be the beginning of our path to perdition, the only answer we can give to the question 'Where will you stop?' is 'Wherever our intelligence tells us to stop!'"

Hick's use of the free-will solution is an example of the "all or nothing" fallacy. He concedes that there is an appalling amount of moral evil in the world but insists that it would be logically impossible for God to achieve his purpose of soul-making by creating puppets who always acted rightly. This is a position we have criticized elsewhere and we must show here how the same criticism applies to Hick.

Hick says that the difficulty with criticisms of the free-will solution has been that they suppose God would have done better to create man as a "pet animal" in a cage, "as pleasant and healthful" as possible. Undeniably critics of the free-will solution have often made this mistake, but it is a mistake easily avoided. We are prepared to grant that a better world would not have been created by making men as pet animals. However, the damaging question is whether God had only two alternatives: to create men with the unfortunate moral inclinations they have at present or to create men as pet animals. There are clearly other alternatives. There are, after all, many different ways for a parent to guide his child's moral growth while respecting his freedom.

Perhaps an analogy will be helpful. God, as Hick views him, might be described as headmaster to a vast progressive school where the absolute freedom of the students is sacred. He does not want to force any children to read textbooks because, he feels, that will only produce students who are more motivated by fear of punishment than by love of knowledge for its own sake. Every student must be left to educate himself as much as possible. However, it is quite unconvincing to argue that because rigid regulation has horrible consequences, almost no regulation is ideal—there are dangers in either extreme. And it is just as much of a mistake to argue that because the possibility of God's creation of men as pet animals is ghastly to contemplate, God's creation of men with the sort of freedom they have now is the best possible choice.

One of Hick's more unfortunate uses of the "all or nothing" argument appears in his justification of man's "initial epistemic distance" from God. He suggests that God has deliberately refrained from giving much knowledge of himself to men for fear that it would jeopardize the development of "authentic fiduciary attitudes" in men. God is fearful (in our analogy) that "spoon-feeding" his creatures will prevent them from developing genuine intellectual curiosity. Because he thinks that constant and thorough spoon-feeding will ruin their intellects, he advocates contact between schoolboy and teacher only once a year.

But we are being too kind in our analogy. God does not even think it wise to deliver a matriculation address to each student. Almost all students must be content with meager historical records of a matriculation address in the distant past and a hope of a commencement speech in the future. It is no wonder there have been student riots. The countless generations before Christ were especially destitute of faculty-student contact. And even now the vast amount of humanity in non-Christian parts of the world find it difficult to be admitted to the soul-making school at all.

Sometimes Hick feels the weakness of the "all or nothing" argument and accordingly shifts to the "it could be worse" strategy. "Christian theodicy must point forward to that final blessedness, and claim that this infinite future good will render worth while all the pain and travail and wickedness that has occurred on the way to it." To be sure, we should be grateful to God for not tormenting us for an eternity, but the question remains of why he is torturing us at all. However, this strategy is beside the point. Hick must still show us how all the suffering in this world is the most efficient way of achieving God's goal. Merely to assure the student who is threatening riot that in his old age he will somehow come to regard the indignities of his student days as rather unimportant is not to explain why those indignities must be visited upon him at all.

Although Hick does not himself feel confident

that in the Kingdom of God all men will completely forget their earthly sufferings, he suggests that, if such a loss of memory were to occur, it would help solve the problem of evil. However, we can concede complete heavenly amnesia and this concession does not move us any closer to a solution. If a man were to torture his wife, and afterwards somehow to remove completely the memory of the torture from her mind so that she returned to her earlier love of him, this would certainly be better than retaining the painful memory, but it still would not explain the necessity of torturing her in the first place.

Hick, however, candidly admits to a feeling that neither of the two strategies discussed above is completely effective in the last analysis and realizes that he must face "excessive or dysteleological suffering." Consequently he moves on to the "slippery slope" argument.

> Unless God eliminated all evils whatsoever there would always be relatively outstanding ones of which it would be said that He should have secretly prevented them. If, for example, divine providence had eliminated Hitler in his infancy, we might now point instead to Mussolini. . . . There would be nowhere to stop, short of divinely arranged paradise in which human freedom would be narrowly circumscribed.

He claims, in other words, that there would be no way of eliminating some evils without removing all of them with the effect of returning us to the "all or nothing" situation.

This argument fails because the erroneous assumption is made that in the process of removing evils God would not be able precisely to calculate the effect of each removal and stop at exactly the point at which soul making was most efficiently achieved. Presumably at that point men would still suffer and complain about their suffering, but it would be possible to offer them an explanation of the necessity of this amount of suffering as a means to the end of soul making. In the analogy we used earlier, no matter how much is done to increase faculty-student contact there will still be some student complaints, but presumably it is possible to reach a point at which such students can be shown how the present amount of faculty-student contact is precisely the right amount to maximize creative intellectual activity.

Hick even comes to admit that this third strategy is no more effective than the first two. He appears to be like a man flourishing toy weapons before an assailant, knowing that in the last analysis they cannot be effective, but hoping that the assailant will be scared off before he comes close enough to see that they are not genuine weapons. In the last analysis he must appeal to mystery. "I do not now have an alternative theory to offer that would explain in any rational or ethical way why men suffer as they do. The only appeal left is to mystery."

Hick's use of mystery is not the usual appeal to mystical experience or commitment so often made by theists. He suggests that mystery, too, contributes to soul-making. Here again he uses the "all or nothing" argument and asks us to imagine a world which contained no unjust, excessive, or apparently unnecessary misery, a world in which suffering could always be seen to be either punishment justly deserved or a part of moral training.

> In such a world human misery would not evoke deep personal sympathy or call forth organized relief and sacrificial help or service. For it is presupposed in these compassionate reactions both that the suffering is not deserved and that it is *bad* for the sufferer.

There are at least three ways of criticizing this strategy:

(a) It is quite possible to feel intense compassion for someone even though his suffering is understood to be an unavoidable means to an end, desirable both to the sufferer and to oneself. A husband may feel convinced that his wife's labor pains are a necessary means to a highly desirable end and at the same time feel great compassion. One can even feel compassion for the pain suffered by a criminal being punished in a way that one thinks is deserved.

(b) Even if some undeserved and unnecessary suffering is necessary to make possible compassion, it is obvious that a minute percentage of the present unnecessary suffering would do the job adequately.

(c) One must remember that while unjust suffering may increase compassion, it also creates massive resentment. This resentment often causes individuals indiscriminately to lash out at the world. The benefits of compassion are probably more than offset by the damage done by resentment.

However, Hick thinks that there is still one last justification for unjust suffering. He asks us to consider what would happen if all unjust suffering were eliminated. In such a world reward would be the predictable result of virtue and punishment the predictable outcome of wickedness. But in such a world doing right simply for its own sake—what Kant called the good will—would be impossible "for whilst the possibility of the good will by no means precludes that right action shall in fact eventually lead to happiness, and wrong action to misery, it does preclude this happening so certainly, instantly, and manifestly that virtue cannot be separate in experience and thought from its reward, or vice from its punishment."

This solution, itself a sign that the end is near at hand, can be rejected with confidence for the following reasons.

(a) This effort to solve the problem of evil does not do justice to the good sense God presumably would have were he to exist. God would certainly have sense enough to administer rewards and punishments in view of *motives* and not simply in view of what an agent *does*. It would already be an unjust response if God rewarded an agent for doing what is objectively right on prudential grounds alone.

(b) This effort misfires psychologically as well as theologically. If God usually rewarded men when they sincerely performed an act solely because it was right, this could only have a beneficial effect on human morality. If a parent regularly rewards the child who performs a good act only because he thinks it right more than he rewards a child performing the same act only to curry favor with the parent, this can only tend to reinforce the tendency to act virtuously.

(c) Even if completely regular rewarding of right-behavior would tend to undermine the good will, there is still every reason to believe that an enormous amount of the present unjust punishment could be eliminated without jeopardizing the possibility of acting from a sense of duty. The "all-or-nothing" fallacy is omnipresent in theistic arguments and its presence here at the end, after it had been supposedly rejected, comes as no surprise.

III.5   The Problem of Evil

RICHARD SWINBURNE

Richard Swinburne is Nolloth Professor of Philosophy of Religion at Oxford University. The following reading was presented at a symposium that took place in 1975 at the University of Lancaster in England under the auspices of the Royal Institute of Philosophy. Swinburne develops and refines the position of Leibniz and Hick, taking into account the kinds of objections that Madden and Hare have made. He distinguishes various forms of evil and shows how the theist can account for them, offering a plausible response to each objection.

Introduction

God is, by definition, omniscient, omnipotent, and perfectly good. By "omniscient" I understand "one who knows all true propositions." By "omnipotent" I understand "able to do anything logically possible." By "perfectly good" I understand "one who does no morally bad action," and I include among actions omissions to perform some action. The problem of evil is then often stated as the problem whether the existence of God is compatible with the existence of evil. Against the suggestion of compatibility, an atheist often suggests that the existence of evil entails the nonexistence of God. For, he argues, if God exists, then being omniscient, he knows under what circumstances evil will occur, if he does not act; and being omnipotent, he is able to prevent its occurrence. Hence, being perfectly good, he will prevent its occurrence and so evil will not exist. Hence the existence of God entails the nonexistence of evil. Theists have usually attacked this argument by denying the claim that necessarily a perfectly good being, foreseeing the occurrence of evil and able to prevent it, will prevent it. And indeed, if evil is understood in the very wide way in which it normally is understood in this context, to include physical pain of however slight a degree, the cited claim is somewhat implausible. For it implies that if through my neglecting frequent warnings to go to the dentist, I find myself one morning with a slight toothache, then necessarily, there does not exist a perfectly good being who foresaw the evil and was able to have prevented it. Yet it seems fairly obvious that such a being might well choose to allow me to suffer some mild consequences of my folly—as a lesson for the future which would do me real harm.

The threat to theism seems to come, not from the existence of evil as such, but rather from the existence of evil of certain kinds and degrees—severe undeserved physical pain or mental anguish, for example. I shall therefore list briefly the kinds of evil which are evident in our world, and ask whether their existence in the degrees in which we find them is compatible with the existence of God. I shall call the man who argues for compatibility the theodicist, and his opponent the antitheodicist. The theodicist will claim that it is not morally wrong for God to create or permit the various evils, normally on the grounds that doing so is providing the logically necessary conditions of greater goods. The antitheodicist denies these claims by putting forward moral principles which have as consequences that a good God would not under any circumstances create or permit the evils in question. I shall argue that these moral principles are not, when carefully examined, at all obvious, and indeed that there is a lot to be said for their negations. Hence I shall conclude that it is plausible to suppose that the existence of these evils is compatible with the existence of God.

Since I am discussing only the compatibility of various evils with the existence of God, I am perfectly entitled to make occasionally some (non–self-contradictory) assumption, and argue that if it was true, the compatibility would hold. For if *p* is compatible with *q*, given *r* (where *r* is not self-contradictory), then *p* is compatible with *q* simpliciter. It is irrelevant to the issue of compatibility whether these assumptions are true. If, however, the assumptions which I make are clearly false, and if also it looks as if the existence of God is compatible with the existence of evil *only* given those assumptions, the formal proof of compatibility will lose much of interest. To avoid this danger, I shall make only such assumptions as are not clearly false—and also in fact the ones which I shall make will be ones to which many theists are already committed for entirely different reasons.

The Problem of Evil: Types

What then is wrong with the world? First, there are painful sensations, felt both by men, and, to a lesser extent, by animals. Second, there are painful emotions, which do not involve pain in the literal sense of this word—for example, feelings of loss and failure and frustration. Such suffering exists mainly among men, but also, I suppose, to some small extent among animals too. Third, there are evil and undesirable states of affairs, mainly states of men's minds, which do not involve suffering. For example, there are the states of mind of hatred and envy; and such states of the world as rubbish tipped over a beauty spot. And

fourth, there are the evil actions of men, mainly actions having as foreseeable consequences evils of the first three types, but perhaps other actions as well—such as lying and promise breaking with no such foreseeable consequences. As before, I include among actions, omissions to perform some actions. If there are rational agents other than men and God (if he exists), such as angels or devils or strange beings on distant planets, who suffer and perform evil actions, then their evil feelings, states, and actions must be added to the list of evils.

I propose to call evil of the first type physical evil, evil of the second type mental evil, evil of the third type state evil, and evil of the fourth type moral evil. Since there is a clear contrast between evils of the first three types, which are evils that happen to men or animals or the world, and evils of the fourth type, which are evils that men do, there is an advantage in having one name for evils of any of the first three types—I shall call these passive evils. I distinguish evil from mere absence of good. Pain is not simply the absence of pleasure. A headache is a pain, whereas not having the sensation of drinking whiskey is, for many people, mere absence of pleasure. Likewise, the feeling of loss in bereavement is an evil involving suffering, to be contrasted with the mere absence of the pleasure of companionship. Some thinkers have, of course, claimed that a good God would create a "best of all (logically) possible worlds" (i.e., a world than which no better is logically possible), and for them the mere absence of good creates a problem since it looks as if a world would be a better world if it had that good. For most of us, however, the mere absence of good seems less of a threat to theism than the presence of evil, partly because it is not at all clear whether any sense can be given to the concept of a best of all possible worlds (and if it cannot then of logical necessity there will be a better world than any creatable world) and partly because even if sense can be given to this concept it is not at all obvious that God has an obligation to create such a world—to whom would he be doing an injustice if he did not? My concern is with the threat to theism posed by the existence of evil.

Objection 1: God Ought Not to Create Evildoers

Now much of the evil in the world consists of the evil actions of men and the passive evils brought about by those actions. (These include the evils brought about intentionally by men, and also the evils which result from long years of slackness by many generations of men. Many of the evils of 1975 are in the latter category, and among them many state evils. The hatred and jealousy which many men and groups feel today result from an upbringing consequent on generations of neglected opportunities for reconciliations.) The antitheodicist suggests as a moral principle (*P1*) that a creator able to do so ought to create only creatures such that necessarily they do not do evil actions. From this it follows that God would not have made men who do evil actions. Against this suggestion the theodicist naturally deploys the free-will defense, elegantly expounded in recent years by Alvin Plantinga. This runs roughly as follows: it is not logically possible for an agent to make another agent such that necessarily he freely does only good actions. Hence if a being G creates a free agent, he gives to the agent power of choice between alternative actions, and how he will exercise that power is something which G cannot control while the agent remains free. It is a good thing that there exist free agents, but a logically necessary consequence of their existence is that their power to choose to do evil actions may sometimes be realized. The price is worth paying, however, for the existence of agents performing free actions remains a good thing even if they sometimes do evil. Hence it is not logically possible that a creator create free creatures "such that necessarily they do not do evil actions." But it is not a morally bad thing that he create free creatures, even with the possibility of their doing evil. Hence the cited moral principle is implausible.

The free-will defense as stated needs a little filling out. For surely there could be free agents who did not have the power of moral choice, agents whose only opportunities for choice were between morally indifferent alternatives—between jam and marmalade for breakfast, between watching the news on BBC 1 or the news on ITV. They might lack this power either because they lacked the power of making moral judgments (i.e., lacked moral discrimination); or because all their actions which were morally assessable were caused by factors outside their control; or because they saw with complete clarity what was right and wrong and had no temptation to do anything except the right. The free-will defense must claim, however, that it is a good thing that there exist free agents with the power and opportunity of choosing between morally good and morally evil actions, agents with sufficient moral discrimination to have some idea of the difference and some (though not overwhelming) temptation to do other than the morally good. Let us call such agents humanly free agents. The defense must then go on to claim that it is not logically possible to create humanly free agents such that necessarily they do not do morally evil actions. Unfortunately, this latter claim is highly debatable, and I have no space to debate it. I propose therefore to circumvent this issue as follows. I shall add to the definition of humanly free agents, that they are agents whose choices do not have fully deterministic precedent causes. Clearly then it will not be logically possible to create humanly free agents whose choices go one way rather than another, and so not logically possible to create humanly free agents such that necessarily they do not do evil actions. Then the free-will defense claims that (*P1*) is not universally true; it is not morally wrong to create humanly free agents—despite the real possibility that they will do evil. Like many others who have discussed this issue, I find this a highly plausible suggestion. Surely as parents we regard it as a good thing that our children have power to do free actions of moral significance—even if the consequence is that they sometimes do evil actions. This conviction is likely to be stronger, not weaker, if we hold that the free actions with which we are concerned are ones which do not have fully deterministic precedent causes. In this way we show the existence of God to be compatible with the existence of moral evil—but only subject to a very big assumption—that men are humanly free agents. If they are not, the compatibility shown by the free-will defense is of little interest. For the agreed exception to (P1) would not then justify a creator making men who did evil actions; we should need a different exception to avoid incompatibility. The assumption seems to me not clearly false, and is also one which most theists affirm for quite other reasons. Needless to say, there is no space to discuss the assumption here.

Objection 2: Against Passive Evil

All that the free-will defense has shown so far, however (and all that Plantinga seems to show), is grounds for supposing that the existence of moral evil is compatible with the existence of God. It has not given grounds for supposing that the existence of evil consequences of moral evils is compatible with the existence of God. In an attempt to show an incompatibility, the antitheodicist may suggest instead of (P1), (P2)—that a creator able to do so ought always to ensure that any creature whom he creates does not cause passive evils, or at any rate passive evils which hurt creatures other than himself. For could not God have made a world where there are humanly free creatures, men with the power to do evil actions, but where those actions do not have evil consequences, or at any rate evil consequences which affect others—e.g., a world where men cannot cause pain and distress to other men? Men might well do actions which are evil either because they were actions which they believed would have evil consequences or because they were evil for some other reason (e.g., actions which involved promise breaking) without them in fact having any passive evils as consequences. Agents in such a world would be like men in a simulator training to be pilots. They can make mistakes, but no one suffers through those mistakes. Or men might do evil actions which did have the evil consequences which were foreseen but which damaged only themselves. . . .

I do not find (P2) a very plausible moral principle. A world in which no one except the agent was affected by his evil actions might be a world in which men had freedom but it would not be a

world in which men had responsibility. The theodicist claims that it would not be wrong for God to create interdependent humanly free agents, a society of such agents responsible for each other's well-being, able to make or mar each other.

Fair enough, the antitheodicist may again say. It is not wrong to create a world where creatures have responsibilities for each other. But might not those responsibilities simply be that creatures had the opportunity to benefit or to withhold benefit from each other, not a world in which they had also the opportunity to cause each other pain? One answer to this is that if creatures have only the power to benefit and not the power to hurt each other, they obviously lack any very strong responsibility for each other. To bring out the point by a caricature—a world in which I could choose whether or not to give you sweets, but not whether or not to break your leg or make you unpopular, is not a world in which I have a very strong influence on your destiny, and so not a world in which I have a very full responsibility for you. Further, however, there is a point which will depend on an argument which I will give further on. In the actual world very often a man's withholding benefits from another is correlated with the latter's suffering some passive evil, either physical or mental. Thus if I withhold from you certain vitamins, you will suffer disease. Or if I deprive you of your wife by persuading her to live with me instead, you will suffer grief at the loss. Now it seems to me that a world in which such correlations did not hold would not necessarily be a better world than the world in which they do. The appropriateness of pain to bodily disease or deprivation, and of mental evils to various losses or lacks of a more spiritual kind, is something for which I shall argue in detail a little later.

So then the theodicist objects to (P2) on the grounds that the price of possible passive evils for other creatures is a price worth paying for agents to have great responsibilities for each other. It is a price which (logically) must be paid if they are to have those responsibilities. Here again a reasonable antitheodicist may see the point. In bringing up our own children, in order to give them responsibility, we try not to interfere too quickly in their quarrels—even at the price, sometimes, of younger children getting hurt physically. We try not to interfere, first, in order to train our children for responsibility in later life and second because responsibility here and now is a good thing in itself. True, with respect to the first reason, whatever the effects on character produced by training, God could produce without training. But if he did so by imposing a full character on a humanly free creature, this would be giving him a character which he had not in any way chosen or adopted for himself. Yet it would seem a good thing that a creator should allow humanly free creatures to influence by their own choices the sort of creatures they are to be, the kind of character they are to have. That means that the creator must create them immature, and allow them gradually to make decisions which affect the sort of beings they will be. And one of the greatest privileges which a creator can give to a creature is to allow him to help in the process of education, in putting alternatives before his fellows.

Objection 3: The Quantity of Evil

Yet though the antitheodicist may see the point, in theory, he may well react to it rather like this. "Certainly some independence is a good thing. But surely a father ought to interfere if his younger son is really getting badly hurt. The ideal of making men free and responsible is a good one, but there are limits to the amount of responsibility which it is good that men should have, and in our world men have too much responsibility. A good God would certainly have intervened long ago to stop some of the things which happen in our world." Here, I believe, lies the crux—it is simply a matter of quantity. The theodicist says that a good God could allow men to do to each other the hurt they do, in order to allow them to be free and responsible. But against him the antitheodicist puts forward as a moral principle (*P3*) that a creator able to do so ought to ensure that any creature whom he creates does not cause passive evils as many and as evil as those in our world. He says

that in our world freedom and responsibility have gone too far—produced too much physical and mental hurt. God might well tolerate a boy hitting his younger brothers, but not Belsen.

The theodicist is in no way committed to saying that a good God will not stop things getting too bad. Indeed, if God made our world, he has clearly done so. There are limits to the amount and degree of evil which are possible in our world. Thus there are limits to the amount of pain which a person can suffer—persons live in our world only so many years and the amount which they can suffer at any given time (if mental goings-on are in any way correlated with bodily ones) is limited by their physiology. Further, theists often claim that from time to time God intervenes in the natural order which he has made to prevent evil which would otherwise occur. So the theodicist can certainly claim that a good God stops too much sufferings—it is just that he and his opponent draw the line in different places. The issue as regards the passive evils caused by men turns ultimately to the quantity of evil. To this crucial matter I shall return toward the end of the paper.

The Interconnectedness of Good and Evil

We shall have to turn next to the issue of passive evils not apparently caused by men. But, first, I must consider a further argument by the theodicist in support of the free-will·defense and also an argument of the antitheodicist against it. The first is the argument that various evils are logically necessary conditions for the occurrence of actions of certain especially good kinds. Thus for a man to bear his suffering cheerfully there has to be suffering for him to bear. There have to be acts which irritate for another to show tolerance of them. Likewise, it is often said, acts of forgiveness, courage, self-sacrifice, compassion, overcoming temptation, etc., can be performed only if there are evils of various kinds. Here, however, we must be careful. One might reasonably claim that all that is necessary for some of these good acts (or acts as good as these) to be performed is belief in the existence of certain evils, not their actual existence. You can show compassion toward someone who appears to be suffering, but is not really; you can forgive someone who only appeared to insult you, but did not really. But if the world is to be populated with imaginary evils of the kind needed to enable creatures to perform acts of the above specially good kinds, it would have to be a world in which creatures are generally and systematically deceived about the feelings of their fellows—in which the behavior of creatures generally and unavoidably belies their feelings and intentions. I suggest, in the tradition of Descartes (*Meditations* 4, 5 and 6), that it would be a morally wrong act of a creator to create such a deceptive world. In that case, given a creator, then, without an immoral act on his part, for acts of courage, compassion, etc., to be acts open to men to perform, there have to be various evils. Evils give men the opportunity to perform those acts which show men at their best. A world without evils would be a world in which men could show no forgiveness, no compassion, no self-sacrifice. And men without that opportunity are deprived of the opportunity to show themselves at their noblest. For this reason God might well allow some of his creatures to perform evil acts with passive evils as consequences, since these provide the opportunity for especially noble acts.

Against the suggestion of the developed free-will defense that it would be justifiable for God to permit a creature to hurt another for the good of his or the other's soul, there is one natural objection which will surely be made. This is that it is generally supposed to be the duty of men to stop other men hurting each other badly. So why is it not God's duty to stop men hurting each other badly? Now the theodicist does not have to maintain that it is never God's duty to stop men hurting each other; but he does have to maintain that it is not God's duty in circumstances where it clearly is our duty to stop such hurt if we can—e.g., when men are torturing each other in mind or body in some of the ways in which they do this in our world and when, if God exists, he does not step in.

Now different views might be taken about the extent of our duty to interfere in the quarrels of others. But the most which could reasonably be claimed is surely this—that we have a duty to interfere in three kinds of circumstances—(1) if an oppressed person asks us to interfere and it is probable that he will suffer considerably if we do not, (2) if the participants are children or not of sane mind and it is probable that one or other will suffer considerably if we do not interfere, or (3) if it is probable that considerable harm will be done to others if we do not interfere. It is not very plausible to suppose that we have any duty to interfere in the quarrels of grown sane men who do not wish us to do so, unless it is probable that the harm will spread. Now note that in the characterization of each of the circumstances in which we would have a duty to interfere there occurs the word "probable," and it is being used in the "epistemic" sense—as "made probable by the total available evidence." But then the "probability" of an occurrence varies crucially with which community or individual is assessing it, and the amount of evidence which they have at the time in question. What is probable relative to your knowledge at t_1 may not be at all probable relative to my knowledge at t_2. Hence a person's duty to interfere in quarrels will depend on their probable consequences relative to that person's knowledge. Hence it follows that one who knows much more about the probable consequences of a quarrel may have no duty to interfere where another with less knowledge does have such a duty—and conversely. Hence a God who sees far more clearly than we do the consequences of quarrels may have duties very different from ours with respect to particular such quarrels. He may know that the suffering that A will cause B is not nearly as great as B's screams might suggest to us and will provide (unknown to us) an opportunity to C to help B recover and will thus give C a deep responsibility which he would not otherwise have. God may very well have reason for allowing particular evils which it is our bounden duty to attempt to stop at all costs simply because he knows so much more about them than we do. And this is no ad hoc hypothesis—it follows directly from the characterization of the kind of circumstances in which persons have a duty to interfere in quarrels.

We may have a duty to interfere in quarrels when God does not for a very different kind of reason. God, being our creator, the source of our beginning and continuation of existence, has rights over us which we do not have over our fellow-men. To allow a man to suffer for the good of his or someone else's soul one has to stand in some kind of parental relationship toward him. I don't have the right to let some stranger Joe Bloggs suffer for the good of his soul or of the soul of Bill Snoggs, but I do have *some* right of this kind in respect of my own children. I may let the younger son suffer *somewhat* for the good of his and his brother's soul. I have this right because in small part I am responsible for his existence, its beginning and continuance. If this is correct, then a fortiori, God who is, ex hypothesi, so much more the author of our being than are our parents, has so many more rights in this respect. God has rights to allow others to suffer, while I do not have those rights and hence have a duty to interfere instead. In these two ways the theodicist can rebut the objection that if we have a duty to stop certain particular evils which men do to others, God must have this duty too.

Objection 4: Passive Evil Not Due to Human Action

In the free-will defense, as elaborated above, the theist seems to me to have an adequate answer to the suggestion that necessarily a good God would prevent the occurrence of the evil which men cause—if we ignore the question of the quantity of evil, to which I will return at the end of my paper. But what of the passive evil apparently not due to human action? What of the pain caused to men by disease or earthquake or cyclone, and what too of animal pain which existed before there were men? There are two additional assumptions, each of which has been put forward to allow the free-will defense to show the compatibility of the existence of God and the existence of such evil. The first is

that, despite appearances, men are ultimately responsible for disease, earthquake, cyclone, and much animal pain. There seem to be traces of this view in Genesis 3:16–20. One might claim that God ties the goodness of man to the well-being of the world and that a failure of one leads to a failure of the other. Lack of prayer, concern, and simple goodness lead to the evils in nature. This assumption, though it may do some service for the free-will defense, would seem unable to account for the animal pain which existed before there were men. The other assumption is that there exist humanly free creatures other than men, which we may call fallen angels, who have chosen to do evil, and have brought about the passive evils not brought about by men. These were given the care of much of the material world and have abused that care. For reasons already given, however, it is not God's moral duty to interfere to prevent the passive evils caused by such creatures. This defense has recently been used by, among others, Plantinga. This assumption, it seems to me, will do the job, and is not *clearly* false. It is also an assumption which was part of the Christian tradition long before the free-will defense was put forward in any logically rigorous form. I believe that this assumption may indeed be indispensable if the theist is to reconcile with the existence of God the existence of passive evils of certain kinds, e.g., certain animal pain. But I do not think that the theodicist need deploy it to deal with the central cases of passive evils not caused by men—mental evils and the human pain that is a sign of bodily malfunctioning. Note, however, that if he does not attribute such passive evils to the free choice of some other agent, the theodicist must attribute them to the direct action of God himself, or rather, what he must say is that God created a universe in which passive evils must necessarily occur in certain circumstances, the occurrence of which is necessary or at any rate not within the power of a humanly free agent to prevent. The antitheodicist then naturally claims, that although a creator might be justified in allowing free creatures to produce various evils, nevertheless (P4) a creator is never justified in creating a world in which evil results except by the action of a humanly free agent. Against this the theodicist tries to sketch reasons which a good creator might have for creating a world in which there is evil not brought about by humanly free agents. One reason which he produces is one which we have already considered earlier in the development of the free-will defense. This is the reason that various evils are logically necessary conditions for the occurrence of actions of certain especially noble kinds. This was adduced earlier as a reason why a creator might allow creatures to perform evil acts with passive evils as consequences. It can also be adduced as a reason why he might himself bring about passive evils—to give further opportunities for courage, patience, and tolerance. I shall consider here one further reason that, the theodicist may suggest, a good creator might have for creating a world in which various passive evils were implanted, which is another reason for rejecting (*P4*). It is, I think, a reason which is closely connected with some of the other reasons which we have been considering why a good creator might permit the existence of evil.

A creator who is going to create humanly free agents and place them in a universe has a choice of the kind of universe to create. First, he can create a finished universe in which nothing needs improving. Humanly free agents know what is right, and pursue it; and they achieve their purposes without hindrance. Second, he can create a basically evil universe, in which everything needs improving, and nothing can be improved. Or, third, he can create a basically good but half-finished universe—one in which many things need improving, humanly free agents do not altogether know what is right, and their purposes are often frustrated; but one in which agents can come to know what is right and can overcome the obstacles to the achievement of their purposes. In such a universe the bodies of creatures may work imperfectly and last only a short time; and creatures may be morally ill-educated, and set their affections on things and persons which are taken from them. The universe might be such that it requires long generations of cooperative effort between

creatures to make perfect. While not wishing to deny the goodness of a universe of the first kind, I suggest that to create a universe of the third kind would be no bad thing, for it gives to creatures the privilege of making their own universe. Genesis 1 in telling of a God who tells men to "subdue" the earth pictures the creator as creating a universe of this third kind; and fairly evidently—given that men are humanly free agents—our universe is of this kind.

Now a creator who creates a half-finished universe of this third kind has a further choice as to how he molds the humanly free agents which it contains. Clearly he will have to give them a nature of some kind, that is, certain narrow purposes which they have a natural inclination to pursue until they choose or are forced to pursue others—e.g., the immediate attainment of food, sleep, and sex. There could hardly be humanly free agents without some such initial purposes. But what is he to do about their knowledge of their duty to improve the world—e.g., to repair their bodies when they go wrong, so that they can realize long-term purposes, to help others who cannot get food to do so, etc.? He could just give them a formal hazy knowledge that they had such reasons for action without giving them any strong inclination to pursue them. Such a policy might well seem an excessively laissez-faire one. We tend to think that parents who give their children no help toward taking the right path are less than perfect parents. So a good creator might well help agents toward taking steps to improve the universe. We shall see that he can do this in one of two ways.

An action is something done for a reason. A good creator, we supposed, will give to agents some reasons for doing right actions—e.g., that they are right, that they will improve the universe. These reasons are ones of which men can be aware and then either act on or not act on. The creator could help agents toward doing right actions by making these reasons more effective causally; that is, he could make agents so that by nature they were inclined (though not perhaps compelled) to pursue what is good. But this would be to impose a moral character on agents, to give them wide general purposes which they naturally pursue, to make them naturally altruistic, tenacious of purpose, or strong-willed. But to impose a character on creatures might well seem to take away from creatures the privilege of developing their own characters and those of their fellows. We tend to think that parents who try too forcibly to impose a character, however good a character, on their children, are less than perfect parents.

The alternative way in which a creator could help creatures to perform right actions is by sometimes providing additional reasons for creatures to do what is right, reasons which by their very nature have a strong causal influence. Reasons such as improving the universe or doing one's duty do not necessarily have a strong causal influence, for as we have seen creatures may be little influenced by them. Giving a creature reasons which by their nature were strongly causally influential on a particular occasion on any creature whatever his character, would not impose a particular character on a creature. It would, however, incline him to do what is right on that occasion and maybe subsequently too. Now if a reason is by its nature to be strongly causally influential it must be something of which the agent is aware which causally inclines him (whatever his character) to perform some action, to bring about some kind of change. What kind of reason could this be except the existence of an unpleasant feeling, either a sensation such as a pain or an emotion such as a feeling of loss or deprivation? Such feelings are things of which agents are conscious, which cause them to do whatever action will get rid of those feelings, and which provide reason for performing such action. An itch causally inclines a man to do whatever will cause the itch to cease, e.g., scratch, and provides a reason for doing that action. Its causal influence is quite independent of the agent—saint or sinner, strong-willed or weak-willed, will all be strongly inclined to get rid of their pains (though some may learn to resist the inclination). Hence a creator who wished to give agents some inclination to improve the world without giving them a character, a wide set of general purposes which they naturally pursue, would tie some of the im-

perfections of the world to physical or mental evils.

To tie desirable states of affairs to pleasant feelings would not have the same effect. Only an existing feeling can be causally efficacious. An agent could be moved to action by a pleasant feeling only when he had it, and the only action to which he could be moved would be to keep the world as it is, not to improve it. For men to have reasons which move men of any character to actions of perfecting the world, a creator needs to tie its imperfections to unpleasant feelings, that is, physical and mental evils.

There is to some considerable extent such tie-up in our universe. Pain normally occurs when something goes wrong with the working of our body which is going to lead to further limitation on the purposes which we can achieve; and the pain ends when the body is repaired. The existence of the pain spurs the sufferer, and others through the sympathetic suffering which arises when they learn of the sufferer's pain, to do something about the bodily malfunctioning. Yet giving men such feelings which they are inclined to end involves the imposition of no character. A man who is inclined to end his toothache by a visit to the dentist may be saint or sinner, strong-willed or weak-willed, rational or irrational. Any other way of which I can conceive of giving men an inclination to correct what goes wrong, and generally to improve the universe, would seem to involve imposing a character. A creator could, for example, have operated exclusively by threats and promises, whispering in men's ears, "unless you go to the dentist, you are going to suffer terribly," or "if you go to the dentist, you are going to feel wonderful." And if the order of nature is God's creation, he does indeed often provide us with such threats and promises—not by whispering in our ears but by providing inductive evidence. There is plenty of inductive evidence that unattended cuts and sores will lead to pain; that eating and drinking will lead to pleasure. Still, men do not always respond to threats and promises or take the trouble to notice inductive evidence (e.g., statistics showing the correlation between smoking and cancer). A creator could have made men so that they naturally took more account of inductive evidence. But to do so would be to impose character. It would be to make men, apart from any choice of theirs, rational and strong-willed.

Many mental evils too are caused by things going wrong in a man's life or in the life of his fellows and often serve as a spur to a man to put things right, either to put right the cause of the particular mental evil or to put similar things right. A man's feeling of frustration at the failure of his plans spurs him either to fulfill those plans despite their initial failure or to curtail his ambitions. A man's sadness at the failure of the plans of his child will incline him to help the child more in the future. A man's grief at the absence of a loved one inclines him to do whatever will get the loved one back. As with physical pain, the spur inclines a man to do what is right but does so without imposing a character—without, say, making a man responsive to duty, or strong-willed.

Physical and mental evils may serve as spurs to long-term cooperative research leading to improvement of the universe. A feeling of sympathy for the actual and prospective suffering of many from tuberculosis or cancer leads to acquisition of knowledge and provision of cure for future sufferers. Cooperative and long-term research and cure is a very good thing, the kind of thing toward which men need a spur. A man's suffering is never in vain if it leads through sympathy to the work of others which eventually provides a long-term cure. True, there could be sympathy without a sufferer for whom the sympathy is felt. Yet in a world made by a creator, there cannot be sympathy on the large scale without a sufferer, for whom the sympathy is felt, unless the creator planned for creatures generally to be deceived about the feelings of their fellows; and that, we have claimed, would be morally wrong.

So generally many evils have a biological and psychological utility in producing spurs to right action without imposition of character, a goal which it is hard to conceive of being realized in any other way. This point provides a reason for the rejection of (P4). There are other kinds of reason which have been adduced reasons for rejecting

(P4)—e.g., that a creator could be justified in bringing about evil as a punishment—but I have no space to discuss these now. I will, however, in passing, mention briefly one reason why a creator might make a world in which certain mental evils were tied to things going wrong. Mental suffering and anguish are a man's proper tribute to losses and failures, and a world in which men were immunized from such reactions to things going wrong would be a worse world than ours. By showing proper feelings a man shows his respect for himself and others. Thus a man who feels no grief at the death of his child or the seduction of his wife is rightly branded by us as insensitive, for he has failed to pay the proper tribute of feeling to others, to show in his feeling how much he values them, and thereby failed to value them properly—for valuing them properly involves having proper reactions of feeling to their loss. Again, only a world in which men feel sympathy for losses experienced by their friends, is a world in which love has full meaning.

So, I have argued, there seem to be kinds of justification for the evils which exist in the world, available to the theodicist. Although a good creator might have very different kinds of justification for producing, or allowing others to produce, various different evils, there is a central thread running through the kind of theodicy which I have made my theodicist put forward. This is that it is a good thing that a creator should make a half-finished universe and create immature creatures, who are humanly free agents, to inhabit it; and that he should allow them to exercise some choice over what kind of creatures they are to become and what sort of universe is to be (while at the same time giving them a slight push in the direction of doing what is right); and that the creatures should have power to affect not only the development of the inanimate universe but the well-being and moral character of their fellows, and that there should be opportunities for creatures to develop noble characters and do especially noble actions. My theodicist has argued that if a creator is to make a universe of this kind, then evils of various kinds may inevitably—at any rate temporarily—belong to such a universe; and that it is not a morally bad thing to create such a universe despite the evils.

The Quantity of Evil

Now a morally sensitive antitheodicist might well in principle accept some of the above arguments. He may agree that in principle it is not wrong to create humanly free agents, despite the possible evils which might result, or to create pains as biological warnings. But where the crunch comes, it seems to me, is in the amount of evil which exists in our world. The antitheodicist says, all right, it would not be wrong to create men able to harm each other, but it would be wrong to create men able to put each other in Belsen. It would not be wrong to create backaches and headaches, even severe ones, as biological warnings, but not the long severe incurable pain of some diseases. In reply the theodicist must argue that a creator who allowed men to do little evil would be a creator who gave them little responsibility; and a creator who gave them only coughs and colds, and not cancer and cholera would be a creator who treated men as children instead of giving them real encouragement to subdue the world. The argument must go on with regard to particular cases. The antitheodicist must sketch in detail and show his adversary the horrors of particular wars and diseases. The theodicist in reply must sketch in detail and show his adversary the good which such disasters make possible. He must show to his opponent men working together for good, men helping each other to overcome disease and famine; the heroism of men who choose the good in spite of temptation, who help others not merely by giving them food but who teach them right and wrong, give them something to live for and something to die for. A world in which this is possible can only be a world in which there is much evil as well as great good. Interfere to stop the evil and you cut off the good.

Like all moral arguments this one can be settled only by each party pointing to the consequences of his opponent's moral position and trying to show that his opponent is committed to

implausible consequences. They must try, too, to show that each other's moral principles do or do not fit well with other moral principles which each accepts. The exhibition of consequences is a long process, and it takes time to convince an opponent even if he is prepared to be rational, more time than is available in this paper. All that I claim to have *shown* here is that there is no *easy proof* of incompatibility between the existence of evils of the kinds we find around us and the existence of God. Yet my sympathies for the outcome of any more detailed argument are probably apparent, and indeed I may have said enough to convince some readers as to what that outcome would be.

My sympathies lie, of course, with the theodicist. The theodicist's God is a god who thinks the higher goods so worthwhile that he is prepared to ask a lot of man in the way of enduring evil. Creatures determining in cooperation their own character and future, and that of the universe in which they live, coming in the process to show charity, forgiveness, faith, and self-sacrifice is such a worthwhile thing that a creator would not be unjustified in making or permitting a certain amount of evil in order that they should be realized. No doubt a good creator would put a limit on the amount of evil in the world and perhaps an end to the struggle with it after a number of years. But if he allowed creatures to struggle with evil, he would allow them a real struggle with a real enemy, not a parlor game. The antitheodicist's mistake lies in extrapolating too quickly from *our* duties when faced with evil to the duties of a creator, while ignoring the enormous differences in the circumstances of each. Each of us at one time can make the existing universe better or worse only in a few particulars. A creator can choose the kind of universe and the kind of creatures there are to be. It seldom becomes us in our ignorance and weakness to do anything more than remove the evident evils—war, disease, and famine. We seldom have the power or the knowledge or the right to use such evils to forward deeper and longer-term goods. To make an analogy, the duty of the weak and ignorant is to eliminate cowpox and not to spread it, while the doctor has a duty to spread it (under carefully controlled conditions). But a creator who made or permitted his creatures to suffer much evil and asked them to suffer more is a very demanding creator, one with high ideals who expects a lot. For myself I can say that I would not be too happy to worship a creator who expected too little of his creatures. Nevertheless such a God does ask a lot of creatures. A theodicist is in a better position to defend a theodicy such as I have outlined if he is prepared also to make the further additional claim—that God knowing the worthwhileness of the conquest of evil and the perfecting of the universe by men, shared with them this task by subjecting himself as man to the evil in the world. A creator is more justified in creating or permitting evils to be overcome by his creatures if he is prepared to share with them the burden of the suffering and effort.

III.6   The Problem of Evil: A Critique of Swinburne

D. Z. PHILLIPS

D. Z. Phillips is professor of philosophy at Swansea University in Wales. He is one of the leading proponents of what has become known as Wittgensteinian fideism (see Part 7, Section C). In this critique of Swinburne's position, he attacks all such theodicies as futile and inappropriate, arguing that theodicists arrogantly rush in where angels fear to thread. What theodicists try to explain is essentially a mystery; not only do their endeavors not solve anything, but they are an inappropriate response to the fact of evil. The existence of evil does not necessarily prevent one from being a theist. The point is rather that human suffering and pain must shake the morally sensitive person to the core and should not be treated as a logical puzzle to be solved at all cost. Evil is an existential reality, one that destroys innocent humans and causes unspeakable suffering. The proper response before the hoary head of evil is moral action and commiseration with the afflicted.

Reprinted from *Reason and Religion*, edited by Stuart C. Brown. Copyright © 1977 by the Royal Institute of Philosophy. Used by permission of the publisher, Cornell University Press. Subheads added; footnotes deleted.

Introduction: False Journeys

For practical purposes it would be considered unfortunate if two symposiasts agreed with each other on too many points. If disagreements are too extreme, however, there is a danger of them passing each other by. The first possibility in no way threatens the present symposium, but the second poses a real problem. Kierkegaard once depicted a source of confusion in philosophy as thoroughly investigating details of a road one should not have turned into in the first place. As far as I can see, Swinburne is far down such a road. Nevertheless, in my reply, I shall for the most part comment on features of the road on which he chooses to travel. My reason for doing so is that many of Swinburne's assumptions about the Great Architect must, on his own admission, pass the compatibility test with respect to what goes on in and what we know about the highways and byways of human life. If it can be shown that what Swinburne asks us to think about the roads he travels on and the people who live there distorts what we know or goes beyond the limits of what we are prepared to think, this in itself would be a reason against extrapolating possibilities of divine policy or reasoning from such dubious facts. I shall do no more than hint at some reasons why we should not turn into Swinburne's way in the first place. I fear that the extent of my disagreement makes it impossible to fulfill either task adequately, but at least I hope to indicate the various directions in which my misgivings lie.

Before we begin our travels, let us note Swinburne's terms of reference for the journey. Since various ills and misfortunes can be found in the streets where we live, religious believers are faced with difficulties which are often referred to as the problem of evil: how are evils compatible with the existence of an omnipotent, omniscient, all-good God? A theodicist is someone who seeks to answer this question by justifying God's ways to men, by showing us why things are as they are and, in particular, why that which appears to be evil to us has been sent or created by God for the general good of mankind: a little evil does no one any harm and even the greatest evil, on closer examination, turns out to be worth the price. With this context in mind, let us follow Swinburne on his travels.

The Free Will Defense

His first observation is that all men are guilty of some wrong actions. Could men have been naturally good? This is a logical and not a factual question. Does the supposition make sense? If not, it makes no sense either to blame God for not creating perfect human beings. Swinburne holds that it is "not logically possible to create humanly free agents such that necessarily they do not do morally evil actions." Let us first ask whether we could have a world in which men always make the right decisions and where no actual evil exists. If we are retaining, as this talk may be doing, a world such as ours, where deliberations and temptations are what we know them to be, these assumptions soon run into conceptual difficulties. Consider the following course of argument: Someone may say that acquiring moral conceptions entails the existence of actual evil in the world. For example, a child may be taught to condemn selfishness by being restrained from performing a selfish action. His arm may be pulled back as it reaches for a third cream bun. Moral condemnation, it may be

said, develops partly by commenting on what is actually taking place. To this it may be retorted that disdain of evil could be taught by means of hypothetical inference without actual evils taking place. For example, a child may be told that if human beings were killed as animals are killed that would be a bad thing. Putting this suggestion aside for the moment, how could evil thoughts be eliminated? Someone may think that the possibility of saints whose lives are characterized by spontaneous virtues constitutes an answer to this question. Their generosity of spirit may be such that they do not entertain such thoughts. This reply, however, does not work. The impressiveness of saints cannot be explained by an attempt to isolate their characteristics in this way. We are impressed by the generosity of spirit which saints may possess, precisely because they possess it in a world where it is all too easy to think otherwise of other human beings. These observations about the saints admit of wider reference. Generosity, kindness, loyalty, truth, etc., do get their identity in a world where meanness, cruelty, disloyalty and lies are also possible. We see the importance of virtues not in face of apparent or possible evils, but in face of actual evils. Swinburne himself rejects the possibility of a world where God has seen to it that people only seem to be harmed, since God would be guilty of deception if this were the case. The objection, however, is logical, not moral. When we think we ought to be generous is it in face of apparent need or real need? How would we know the difference? The point is that we cannot, according to the argument. But this "cannot" is unintelligible, for no distinction between what can and cannot be known exists to give it any import. God, on this argument, suffers the same fate as Descartes's malignant demon. If we now look again at the question, Could there be a world where men are naturally good? we can see, for reasons already given, that such a world could not contain people we would call good. Even so, would a world of such people, whatever we call them, be a better world than the world we know? I have no idea how to answer this question.

Swinburne doubts whether the notion of the best of all logically possible worlds makes sense, but even if it did, he cannot see how God could have any obligation to create it. He does, however, think it makes sense to compare a universe without actual evil, a finished universe, with our own, a half-finished universe. Swinburne says, "While not wishing to deny the goodness of a universe of the first kind, I suggest that to create a universe of the [other] kind would be no bad thing, for it gives to creatures the privilege of making their own universe." Putting aside the dubious character of this privilege for the moment, I take it that Swinburne would also say that God could have no obligation to create such a universe. If Swinburne's conception of God were allowed, and that, as we shall see, is to allow a great deal, what can be made of Swinburne's defense of him? Swinburne asks, ". . . . to whom would he be doing an injustice if he did not?" The suggestion seems to be that God has no obligation to create a world of any particular kind, since prior to his act of creation, there are no people to harm! But this is no defense. If God were asked why he created such a world for people to live in instead of creating a better one, should his reply be, "They wouldn't know the difference", an appropriate reply, even if it could not be uttered, would be, "No, but you did!"

Having raised some difficulties concerning the possibility of a world of naturally good men which contains no actual evil and Swinburne's claim that God could not have an obligation to create the best of all possible worlds if that notion made sense, we see that new difficulties arise in the light of Swinburne's further observations. His strategy is placed in the context of the free-will defense, a defense which "must claim that it is a good thing that there exist free agents with the power and opportunity of choosing between morally good and morally evil actions, agents with sufficient moral discrimination to have some idea of the difference and some (though not overwhelming) temptation to do other than the morally good." Objections have been made to this defense by some philosophers who ask why God has not ensured or seen to it that men as a result of their free deliberations always make the right decisions. Swinburne says that God has not done this be-

cause it would be an imposition of character on man and therefore morally wrong. My difficulty is that I have the prior problem of not knowing what it means to speak of God either ensuring or not ensuring, seeing to it or not seeing to it, where the development of human character is concerned. My difficulties can be discussed in two contexts: first, the difficulty of the metaphysical level at which the "ensuring" or "seeing to it" is supposed to take place, and second, the difficulty of knowing what it would be to see to or ensure the formation of human character.

First, then, the question of the metaphysical character of God ensuring that human beings have such-and-such characters. There is no difficulty in locating natural events or intentional acts which have influenced a person's character in specific ways. But here I can say that there may or may not have been such effects, or that some people were affected and others not or that different people were affected in different ways. Even if we say that such-and-such an event or action must have an effect of a specifiable kind, there is still a question of how such an effect is taken up into the rest of a person's life. If I want to speak of "ensuring" or "seeing to it" that a person exhibits a certain "character" then I'd think of something akin to posthypnotic suggestion. Here, although the person so influenced "obeys the command" and "gives reasons" for his conduct, we do not accept such behavior without reservation as an instance of what we would call obeying a command or giving reasons. There are features of his behavior which lead us to detect rationalization. Of course, on a given occasion, one may be taken in. A man may exhibit anger as the result of a suggestion made to him while under hypnosis in a situation where anger would have been a natural response in any case. The point to stress is not that the seeing to it or the ensuring is always detected, but that we know what it means to speak of detecting it. Add to this the possibility of our having independent knowledge of the hypnosis in the first place. Such direct knowledge is not given to us in God's case, and so we are trying to contemplate what God may or may not have done on the basis of what we already know. My difficulty is to find a discernible difference in human affairs which would confirm or refute these speculations. Those who think it makes sense to speak of God ensuring that men, after free deliberation, always make the right decisions, do not want to think of God as the divine hypnotist since (a) that is not the kind of behavior God is said to ensure and (b) God's ensuring is not something we can clearly discern as sometimes present and sometimes absent in human affairs, but as that which ensures that human affairs are what they are in the first place. My difficulty, I suppose, concerns the intelligibility of thinking of creation as an act of ensuring or seeing to things, similar in character to acts of ensuring or seeing to things that we know, different only in the resources available and the scale of operation.

Second, I find difficulty in knowing what it means to speak of someone ensuring or seeing to it that human characters are of such-and-such a kind. Swinburne does not find this difficult to imagine. He simply thinks it would be a bad thing for God to do, just as it would be a bad thing for parents to do:

> The creator could help agents toward doing right actions by making these reasons more effective causally; that is, he could make agents so that by nature they were inclined (though not perhaps compelled) to pursue what is good. But this would be to impose a moral character on agents, to give them wide general purposes which they naturally pursue, to make them naturally altruistic, tenacious of purpose, or strong-willed. But to impose a character on creatures might well seem to take away from creatures the privilege of developing their own characters and those of their fellows. We tend to think that parents who try too forcibly to impose a character, however good a character, on their children, are less than perfect parents.

Someone might well argue from the same facts to the opposite conclusion. A parent who wants to ensure or see to it that his child has one sort of character rather than another, it may be said, is not necessarily interfering with the freedom of the child. If we do not regard such measures as an interference with freedom, despite our ignorance and all the mistakes we make, why should a logical or moral limit be drawn on God, who is not ignorant nor liable to error, seeing to it that human beings freely develop in the right way? I do not want to enter the dispute over whether either program for parental attitudes is right or wrong, since my difficulties over the intelligibility of the program remain. I am not denying that measures taken by parents may influence the development of their children in the way hoped for by the parents. I deliberately speak in the subjunctive mood and speak of hope, since I think it important to distinguish between the retrospective judgment, "I influenced the development of my child's character" or "I did what I could" with the claim, "I ensured or saw to it that my child's character developed in a certain way". Measures taken in hope recognize that such measures are taken in contexts where a great deal is outside the control of the agent, and a wise parent may recognize that this does not simply happen to be true. He would not know what it would mean if someone wanted to talk of parental influence on development of character in any other way. Greater control would recall visions of posthypnotic behavior, something we wouldn't include in developments of character at all. Thus the wise parent may say, "I thank my lucky stars that I was able to help the development of my child's character" or "I thank God that I was able to help my child." These references to God or lucky stars, here, are not references to those agents who *did* ensure the outcome. On the contrary, these utterances are themselves reactions to the fact that what is contingent, in the hands of God, we might say, has gone in a certain way. It is ironic that the debate about whether God should or should not have seen to the development of human characters, uproots the language of things being in God's hands from one of its natural contexts, a context which gets much of its force from the fact that talk of ensuring or seeing to it that outcomes are of one sort or another has no place in it.

Pseudoresponsibility

Having spent a little time considering Swinburne's treatment of the question whether men could have been naturally good and whether God could have seen to it that men developed freely in this direction, I want now to consider his defense of God based on more specific evils which he has observed. This shift of attention corresponds to the first two moral principles of the antitheodicist which Swinburne wants to attack. So far he would claim to have disposed of the principle "that a creator able to do so ought to create only creatures such that necessarily they do not do evil actions." He intends next to consider the modified second principle, namely, "that a creator able to do so ought always to ensure that any creature whom he creates does not cause passive evils, or at any rate passive evils which hurt creatures other than himself." Swinburne's general theodicist strategy within which he attempts to show the implausibility of this principle is "that it is not morally wrong for God to create or permit the various evils, normally on the grounds that doing so is providing the logically necesary conditions of greater goods." What is the greater good which justifies the harm that we do to others? Swinburne replies,

A world in which no one except the agent was affected by his evil actions might be a world in which men had freedom but it would not be a world in which men had responsibility. . . . So then the theodicist objects . . . on the grounds that the price of possible passive evils for other creatures is a price worth paying for agents to have great responsibilities for each other. It is a price which (logically) must be paid if they are to have those responsibilities.

Swinburne's analysis is not an analysis of moral responsibility, but of pseudoresponsibility; it involves a vulgarization of the concept. From the truth that we could not feel responsible unless we were responsible to someone or for something, it does not follow that someone or something should be regarded as opportunities for us to feel responsible. If we remind someone of his responsibilities, we are directing his attention to concerns other than himself. Swinburne's analysis makes these concerns the servants of that self. Compare: "He recognizes the importance of his job" with "His job makes him feel important". Similarly, instead of sometimes feeling responsible for or a responsibility toward the afflictions of others, we would, in terms of Swinburne's analysis, look on those afflictions as opportunities for feeling responsible. It is

as if the Parable of the Good Samaritan were thought to show that unlike the priest and the levite, the Samaritan did not pass by an opportunity of feeling responsible.

Furthermore, even if the feeling of responsibility had not been vulgarized in Swinburne's analysis, it would not follow that a responsible reaction justifies the evil or suffering which occasions it. This has been well expressed by W. Somerset Maugham:

It may be that courage and sympathy are excellent and that they could not come into existence without danger and suffering. It is hard to see how the Victoria Cross that rewards the soldier who has risked his life to save a blinded man is going to solace *him* for the loss of his sight. To give alms shows charity, and charity is a virtue, but does *that* good compensate for the evil of the cripple whose poverty has called it forth?

The Problem of the Quantity of Evil

Let us go further down Swinburne's road. He has noticed already that men intentionally bring evil to others, but now he also notices that there is quite a lot of evil around. Therefore he feels that a third moral principle advanced by the antitheodicist needs answering, namely, "that a creator able to do so ought to ensure that any creature whom he creates does not cause passive evils as many and as evil as those in our world." God may have laid out a moral obstacle race for mankind, but are the obstacles too difficult? A defender of the third moral principle "says that in our world freedom and responsibility have gone too far—produced too much physical and mental hurt. God might well tolerate a boy hitting his younger brother, but not Belsen." Swinburne admits that this would be a telling criticism if true, but as he looks around him he does not believe it is true. On the contrary, Swinburne believes that God has created a world where the men are sorted out from the boys. It means "that the creator must create them immature, and allow them gradually to make decisions which affect the sort of beings they will be." This is why Swinburne calls our world "a half-finished universe". The words are well chosen, since the picture is of a finishing school with God as the benevolent headmaster setting the tests. But does Swinburne's God pass the test of benevolence? It is hard to see that he does when we hear Swinburne's argument to show that in allowing evil God has not gone too far:

> There are limits to the amount and degree of evil which is possible in our world. Thus there are limits to the amount of pain which a person can suffer— persons only live in our world so many years and the amount which they can suffer at any given time (if mental goings-on are in any way correlated with bodily ones) is limited by their physiology. . . . So the theodicist can certainly claim that a good God stops too much suffering—it is just that he and his opponent draw the line in different places.

Can the theodicist make such a claim on the basis of Swinburne's argument? I think not. There is an unwarrantable transition in the argument from talk of the world to talk about human beings, and, more important, from conceivable limits to actual limits. Of course, for any evils in the world we mention, more can be conceived of, but this is neither here nor there as far as the question of whether human beings are visited with greater afflictions than they can bear is concerned. Swinburne argues that since any human being can stand only so much suffering and we can conceive of more, it follows that God has not produced unlimited suffering and therefore has not gone too far. But, clearly, he has produced too much suffering for that human being and has gone too far for him. Such questions cannot be answered in an abstract or global way. What constitutes a limit or going too far for one person may not do so for another. In order to judge whether a human being has suffered more than he can bear, we need to refer to actual limits, not conceivable limits. By judging actual limits as if they were conceivable limits, Swinburne could deny that even a person's death could count as going too far in his case. "After all," he might say, "he could have died a worse death"! I find this whole defense rather perverse. God's finishing school is one where everyone is finished in one sense or another. Either they are well finished, educated to maturity by their experience in the moral obstacle race, or they are finished off completely by it. If the finishing off were done by someone who was solely the bringer of death, then, in certain circumstances, he could be described as the bringer of welcome release. But this is not true of Swinburne's God. Since the bringer of death is also the bringer of afflictions, he who devised the whole fiendish obstacle race, one cannot even attribute to him the compassion with which a dog may be put out of his misery. On the contrary, as each candidate fails to make the grade, it is surely more appropriate to say with Thomas Hardy that thus God has ended his play. Let us hurry from this scene.

As he goes further down his road, Swinburne thinks that the possibility of evil can be justified in terms of the opportunities for noble actions it provides:

> given a creator, then, without an immoral act on his part, for acts of courage, compassion, etc., to be acts open to men to perform, there have to be various evils. Evils give men the opportunity to perform those acts which show men at their best. A world without evils would be a world in which men could show no forgiveness, no compassion, no self-sacrifice. And men without that opportunity are deprived of the opportunity to show themselves at their noblest. For this reason God might well allow some of his creatures to perform evil acts with passive evils as consequences, since these provide the opportunity for especially noble acts.

This argument ignores a great deal, its main defect being its one-sided optimism. Why should evil beget good? One cannot feel remorse without having done wrong, but evil may give one an appetite for more. One cannot show forgiveness without something to forgive, but that something may destroy or prompt savage reactions. In a man's own life natural evils such as illness or social evils such as poverty may debase and destroy him. Swinburne says,

> Pain normally occurs when something goes wrong with the working of our body which is going to lead to further limitation on the purposes which we can achieve; and the pain ends when the body is repaired. The existence of the pain spurs the sufferer, and others through the sympathetic suffering which

arises when they learn of the sufferer's pain, to do something about the bodily malfunctioning. Yet giving men such feelings which they are inclined to end involves the imposition of no character.

Swinburne is faced with formidable contrary testimony often expressed in art or from recollection of experience. Here are some of Settembrini's comments to Hans Castorp in Thomas Mann's *The Magic Mountain:*

> You said that the sight of dullness and disease going hand in hand must be the most melancholy in life. I grant you, I grant you that. I too prefer an intelligent ailing person to a consumptive idiot. But I take issue where you regard the combination of disease with dullness as a sort of aesthetic inconsistency, an error in taste on the part of nature, a "dilemma for the human feelings", as you were pleased to express yourself. When you professed to regard disease as something so refined, so—what did you call it?— possessing a "certain dignity"—that it doesn't "go with" stupidity. That was the expression you used. Well, I say no! Disease has nothing refined about it, nothing dignified. Such a conception is in itself pathological, or at least tends in that direction. . . . Do not, for heaven's sake, speak to me of the ennobling effects of physical suffering! A soul without a body is as inhuman and horrible as a body without a soul— though the latter is the rule and the former the exception. It is the body, as a rule, which flourishes exceedingly, which draws everything to itself, which usurps the predominant place and lives repulsively emancipated from the soul. A human being who is first of all an invalid is *all* body; therein lies his inhumanity and his debasement. In most cases he is little better than a carcass.

Here too are W. Somerset Maugham's recollections of what he saw in hospital wards as he trained for the medical profession:

> At that time (a time to most people of sufficient ease, when peace seemed certain and prosperity secure) there was a school of writers who enlarged upon the moral value of suffering. They claimed that it was salutary. They claimed that it increased sympathy and enhanced the sensibilities. They claimed that it opened to the spirit new avenues of beauty and enables it to get into touch with the mystical kingdom of God. They claimed that it strengthened the character, purified it from its human grossness, and brought to him who did not avoid but sought it a more perfect happiness . . . I set down in my note-books, not

once or twice, but in a dozen places, the facts that I had seen. I knew that suffering did not ennoble; it degraded. It made men selfish, mean, petty, and suspicious. It absorbed them in small things. It did not make men more than men; it made them less than men; and I wrote ferociously that we learn resignation not by our own suffering, but by the suffering of others.

Not only need evil not occasion goodness, but goodness itself may occasion evils. Swinburne does not consider these possibilities. The depth of a man's love may lead him to kill his wife's lover or to be destroyed when the object of his love is lost to him. A man whose love was mediocre would not have done either of these things. Love has as much to do with the terrible as with the wonderful. The presence of goodness in some may be the cause of hatred in others. Budd's goodness is more than Claggart can bear and it is the very possibility that deep love may be a reality which Iago cannot admit into his dark soul.

On his travels Swinburne has seen how human beings intervene from time to time to help each other in their troubles. Sometimes, when fortunate, they can prevent those troubles occurring, and they often try to prevent things getting worse. He realizes then that he has to answer the question why his God does not intervene in circumstances where mere mortals would not hesitate. His answers are not encouraging. Roughly, they amount to saying that just as parents know more than their children and are often right not to act when their offspring beg them to do so, so God, the Father of us all, knowing more than we know, refrains from acting despite the cries of the afflicted. Here is a sample:

> Hence a God who sees far more clearly than we do the consequences of quarrels may have duties very different from ours with respect to particular such quarrels. He may know that the suffering that A will cause B is not nearly as great as B's screams may suggest to us and will provide (unknown to us) an opportunity to C to help B recover and will thus give C a deep responsibility which he would not otherwise have.

I have already commented on the character of such a sense of responsibility, and that is not my purpose now. It is true that sometimes considering a matter further is a sign of reasonableness and maturity. But this cannot be stated absolutely, since at other times readiness to be open-minded about matters is a sign of a corrupt mind. There are screams and screams, and to ask of what use are the screams of the innocent, as Swinburne's defense would have us do, is to embark on a speculation we should not even contemplate. We have our reasons, final human reasons, for putting a moral full stop at many places. If God has other reasons, they are his reasons, not ours, and they do not overrule them. That is why, should he ask us to consider them, we, along with Ivan Karamazov, respectfully, or not so respectfully, return him the ticket. So when Swinburne says, ''The argument must go on with regard to particular cases. . . . The exhibition of consequences is a long process, and it takes time to convince an opponent even if he is prepared to be rational, more time than is available in this paper,'' one must not be misled by apparent reasonableness. Being prepared to consider the consequences of doing something is not the hallmark of moral reasonableness. Often, when the invitation to consider consequences is made, the appropriate reply is ''Get thee behind me, Satan!'' And if there is a ''higher'' form of reasoning among God and his angels, where such matters are open for compromise and calculation, then so much the worse for God and his angels. If they reason in this way in the heavenly places, we can say with Wallace Stevens, ''Alas that they should wear our colors there''. . . .

The Moral Insensitivity of Theodicies

Having traveled with Swinburne to the end of the road he has chosen to go down, noting various ills and misfortunes to which human beings are subject, we are now in a position to summarize the answer to the problem of evil which he brings before us: There are doubts as to whether it makes sense to imagine men who are naturally good without actual evils in the world. It is equally

doubtful to say that God ought to have seen to it that men freely reach the right decisions. Even if the notion of the best of all logically possible worlds made sense, God would have no obligation to create such a world, for whom would he harm if he did not? There are good reasons for saying that the various evils in the world are compatible with the existence of an omnipotent, omniscient, all-good God. Such evils as we bring on others give us the opportunity of feeling responsible, and that is a good thing. After all, such evils are not unlimited, since there is a limit to what anyone can stand. Evils give us an opportunity to be seen at our best in reacting to them. God does not intervene to prevent evil when any decent human being would, because he has a wider knowledge of the situations in which evils occur. In order to prompt us in the right direction without imposing characters on us, God has seen to it that physical and mental evils are linked to things going wrong. Looking back at the details of his case, Swinburne says that ''a morally sensitive antitheodicist might well in principle accept some of the above arguments.'' This conclusion is a somewhat embarrassing one since it is evident from my comments that one of the strongest criticisms available to the antitheodicist would be the moral insensitivity of the theodicist's case. There is an example in Billie Holiday's autobiography which combines many of the circumstances to which Swinburne calls our attention but which also sums up the fragility of his optimistic analyses. She tells of a well-known jazz personality who was a drug addict:

> I can tell you about a big-name performer who had a habit and a bad one. There were times when he had it licked. And other times it licked him. It went around that way for years. He was well known, like me, which makes it worse. He had bookings to make, contracts to fulfil. In the middle of one engagement he was about to crack up and go crazy because he had run out of stuff. There was no way in God's world that he could kick cold turkey and make three shows a day. There wasn't a doctor in town who would be seen looking at him. His wife got so scared he'd kill himself that she tried to help him the only way she knew—by risking her own neck and trying to get him what he needed. She went out in the street like a pigeon, begging everyone she knew for help. Finally she found someone who sold her some stuff for an

arm and a leg. It was just her luck to be carrying it back to her old man when she was arrested.

She was as innocent and clean as the day she was born. But she knew that if she tried to tell that to the cops it would only make her a "pusher" under the law, liable for a good long time in jail. She thought if she told them she was a user, and took some of the stuff in her pocket to prove it, they might believe her, feel sorry for her, go easy on her. And she could protect her man. So that's what she did. She used junk for the first time to prove to the law she wasn't a pusher. And that's the way she got hooked. She's rotting in jail right now. Yes siree bob, life is just a bowl of cherries.

Later, Billie Holiday sums up her own attitude, "If you expect nothing but trouble, maybe a few happy days will turn up. If you expect happy days, look out."

In replying to Swinburne's arguments I have chosen in the main to comment on his reading of the fortunes and misfortunes of human life, a reading which is to serve in the construction of a theodicy. Theodicies, such as Swinburne's, are marked by their order, optimism and progress. If we want to appreciate why Swinburne should not have turned down the road on which he chooses to travel in the first place, this, above all, is what has to be put aside. Throughout Swinburne's paper, the main emphasis, with only an occasional hint of difficulties, is on the world as a God-given setting in which human beings can exercise rational choices which determine the kind of people they are to become. This is neither the world I know, nor the world in which Swinburne lives. Ours is a world where disasters of natural and moral kinds can strike without rhyme or reason. Where, if much can be done to influence character, much can also bring about such influence over which we have no control. Character has as much, and probably more, to do with reacting to the unavoidable, as with choosing between available alternatives. Commenting on a similar order, progress and optimism to Swinburne's in recent moral philosophy, I had reason to quote Hardy's comments on the limits which life placed on Tess's endeavors:

Nature does not often say "See!" to her poor creature at a time when seeing can lead to happy doing; or reply "Here!" to a body's cry of "Where?" till the hide-and-seek has become an irksome, outworn game. We may wonder whether at the acme and summit of the human progress these anachronisms will be corrected by a finer intuition, a closer interaction of the social machinery than that which now jolts us round and along; but such completeness is not to be prophesied, or even conceived as possible.

And yet, even such poor creatures are heard to talk of God. In the context of this reply I can only hint at the import of such talk, talk which I do not claim is all of a piece or capable of being fitted into a neat theological system. I have already suggested in discussing what might be meant by someone who said the outcome was in the hands of God, that the force of the belief depends on the absence of the kind of higher level planning so essential to Swinburne's theodicy. The same is true of talk of God's grace in face of life's evils. In order even to reach the threshold of understanding what might be meant here, the sheer pointlessness of those evils has to be admitted. One has to see, for example, that there is no reason why these natural disasters should have come our way. One has to be ready to answer in face of one's cry, "Why is this happening to me?", "Why shouldn't it?" This recognition of the pointlessness of suffering in this sense can lead in various directions. It has led some to speak of the absurd, but it has led others to speak of all things as God's gifts, and of things not being one's own by right or reason, but by the grace of God. It is not my purpose to advocate these uses of language, but simply to note their existence. Again, in other contexts, a person may wonder in relation to his own character what he can do something about and what has been given by God; that is, what cannot be changed, but which he must come to terms with. On wider issues there may be much agonizing over whether something, marriage, for example, is of God, something fixed and unalterable with which we must come to terms, or whether we are confusing a human institution with God's will and erecting a barrier with no more than a nominal reality which prevents us receiving God's gifts of happiness. Such contexts as these do not imply the dismissal of those considerations which have led people to talk of the problem of evil. On the contrary, without the human cry from the midst of afflictions no sense can be made of these religious responses, and there may be constant tensions of various kinds between the responses and the evils which surround them. The responses are not, however, recognitions of a higher order, but one way of understanding the lack of such an order. Even when the response is understood in this way, it may well be regarded by those who cannot share it as an evil response.

Hardy complains ironically in face of the limits and limitations Tess had to face or fail to face, that "why so often the coarse appropriates the finer . . . the wrong man the woman, the wrong woman the man, many thousand years of analytical philosophy have failed to explain to our sense of order." In the context already mentioned I commented that Hardy, of course, was not looking for explanations. Swinburne looks for explanations. Any sense of order with which one would have

been satisfied would be defective just for that reason. That must be my verdict on Swinburne's theodicy. Swinburne admits that his God does ask a lot of his creatures, but says,

A theodicist is in a better position to defend a theodicy such as I have outlined if he is prepared also to make the further additional claim—that God knowing the worthwhileness of the conquest of evil and the perfecting of the universe by men, shared with them this task by subjecting himself as man to the evil in the world. A creator is more justified in creating or permitting evils to be overcome by his creatures if he is prepared to share with them the burden of the suffering and effort.

Not so, for if the visit to our world were by a God such as Swinburne describes, those who said that there was no room at the inn would be right. We should not be at home to such callers. And if perchance we were asked to choose between this visitor and another, we should unhesitatingly demand, "Give us Prometheus!"

Bibliography for Part III

Lewis, C. S. *The Problem of Pain*. London: Geoffrey Bles, 1940. Clearly and cogently written.

Mackie, J. L. "Evil and Omnipotence." *Mind* 64 (1955):200–212. One of the earlier contemporary attacks on the existence of God from the argument from evil, used in many anthologies.

———. *The Miracle of Theism*. Chap. 9. Oxford: Oxford Univ. Press, 1982. An insightful and well-argued chapter from an atheist's point of view.

McCloskey, H. J. "God and Evil." *The Philosophical Quarterly* 10 (1960):97–114. A sharp attack on theism, arguing that given the problem of evil theism is indefensible.

Pike, Nelson. "Hume on Evil." *The Philosophical Review* 72 (1963):180–97. A trenchant criticism of Hume's position.

Plantinga, Alvin. *The Nature of Necessity*. Chap. 9. Oxford: Clarendon Press, 1974. An excellent article developing in detail a version of the free will defense. In this version all evil is reduced to moral evil, with the devil being held accountable for natural evil. (A more accessible version of this argument is found in Plantinga's work *God, Freedom and Evil*. New York: Harper & Row, 1974.)

Rowe, William. "The Problem of Evil and Some Varieties of Atheism." *American Philosophical Quarterly* 7 (1970):335–41.

Schlesinger, George N. "Suffering and Evil." In

Contemporary Philosophy of Religion, edited by Steven M. Cahn and David Shatz. Oxford: Oxford Univ. Press, 1982. Schlesinger argues that when a complaint applies to every situation, it applies to none. Hence, since one could always complain that God could have created a better world, one cannot complain that this one could be better.

Swinburne, Richard. *The Existence of God.* Chap. 11. Oxford: Oxford Univ. Press, 1978. This contains a fuller defense than is presented in the reading included in this volume.

———. "Natural Evil." *American Philosophical Quarterly* 15 (1978):295–301. A detailed response to the charge that natural evil undermines theism.

Wainwright, William J. "God and the Necessity of Physical Evils." *Sophia* 11 (1972):16–19.

PART IV

THE ATTRIBUTES OF GOD

In the Judeo-Christian tradition God is viewed as having attributes that set him apart from other beings as supreme. Traditionally, some of these attributes have been omnibenevolence (being perfectly good), timelessness (eternity), immutability (changelessness), omnipotence (being all-powerful), and omniscience (being all-knowing). From time to time each of these attributes has been challenged, and some philosophers and theologians have suggested that there are problems with all of them. The problem of evil casts doubt on benevolence and omnipotence. The notion of timeless eternity gives rise to problems in transitivity. The notion of immutability seems inconsistent with the biblical idea that God loves, forgives, and acts. The notion of omnipotence gives rise to such puzzles as whether God can create a stone heavier than he can lift and whether he can sin, and the notion of omniscience leads to the possibility of eliminating free will in humans.

In the last few decades the assault on these attributes has come from within the theistic community as well as from without. Process theologians have denied all but the first attribute, omnibenevolence, arguing that the other four are holdovers from ancient Greek philosophy and are not found in the Bible at all. For them God need not be all-powerful and all-knowing in order to be the Creator of the Universe and our loving savior; and since God, like other persons, grows in wisdom and insight, he must be able to change and, consequently, be in time rather than timeless. On the other hand, all of the above attributes have had their defenders. In this part of our work we examine the three most controversial of God's attributes—his eternity, his omniscience, and his omnipotence—and present arguments on both sides of these issues.

IV.A. Time and Eternity

Thy years do not come and go; while these years of ours do come and go, in order that they all may come. All Thy years stand together [and in one non-extended instant], for they stand still, nor are those going away cut off by those coming, for they do not pass away, but these years of ours shall all be when they are all no more. Thy years are but one day, and Thy day is not a daily recurrent, but today. Thy present day does not give place to tomorrow, nor, indeed, does it take the place of yesterday. Thy present day is eternity.*

All theists agree that God exists as an eternal being. The question is how to interpret this notion. Does God's eternality put him outside of time, or may he still be inside? That is, is his eternity *timeless* or does it have *temporal duration* (sometimes such words as *everlasting* or *temporally eternal* indicate the second position). The notion of the eternal as timelessness first appears in Parmenides' poem "The Way to Truth," in which he says of the One, "It neither was at any time nor will be since it is now all at once a single whole." He and his disciple, Zeno, denied the reality of time. The concept of the eternal was further developed by Plato in the *Timaeus*, in which it is glorified as infinitely superior to the temporal. The *Timaeus* deeply influenced the early Church, and through Augustine and Boetius the doctrine of eternity (as timelessness) made its way into Christian thought, becoming the dominant position in mainstream Christianity. In the Middle Ages and the Reformation period it was embraced by Anselm, Aquinas, Luther, Calvin, and the vast majority of theologians but challenged by Duns Scotus and William of Ockham. In recent times Anthony Kenny, Nelson Pike, and Nicholas

Wolterstorff, among others, have argued that the notion of timelessness is unbiblical and incoherent and should be replaced with the notion of everlastingness.

In our readings Brian Davies defends the traditional timeless notion of God's eternity, and Stephen T. Davis argues that the notion of *temporally eternal* should be substituted for the timeless notion. In the first reading, Davis sets forth the contrasting ideas of "timeless eternity" and "temporal eternity." The former posits a God who is outside time and lacks both temporal location and extension. All events are simultaneously present to God. Temporal eternity, on the other hand, posits a God who has both temporal location and extension. Davis offers three arguments in favor of temporal eternity: (1) The concept of God's creative activity makes far more sense if we accept the notion that he exists in time. For if God creates a given temporal thing, his act of creation itself must be temporal. (2) A timeless being cannot be the personal, caring, involved God of the Bible. (3) The notion of simultaneity of timeless eternity seems to result in absurd consequences with regard to time; for if events in 3021 BC are no earlier than the events of 1986 for God, then time must be illusory. But there is no good reason to deem time illusory. Hence the notion of timeless eternity seems incoherent. This point is stated with elegance by Anthony Kenny:

Indeed, the whole concept of a timeless eternity, the whole of which is simultaneous with every part of time, seems to be radically incoherent. For simultaneity as ordinarily understood is a transitive relation. If *A* happens at the same time as *B*, and *B* happens at the same time as *C*, then *A* happens at the same time as *C*. If the BBC programme and the ITV programme both start when Big Ben strikes ten, then they both start at the same time. But in St. Thomas' view, my typing of this paper is simultaneous with the whole of eternity. Again, on this view, the great fire of Rome is simultaneous

---

* St. Augustine, *Confessions*, bk. 11, chap. 13, translated by V. J. Bourke, in *The Fathers of the Church* (New York: Catholic University of America Press, 1953), 342f.

with the whole of eternity. Therefore, while I type these very words, Nero fiddles heartlessly on.*

Davis answers several objections to his view, concluding that the concept of temporal eternity is more coherent than the notion of timeless eternity.

In his contribution, "Timeless Eternity," Brian Davies argues just the opposite. He examines objections such as those Davis has raised and tries to answer them, beginning with Davis's first argument, that the concept of God's creative *activity* makes far more sense if we accept the notion that he exists in time (for if God creates a given temporal thing, his act of creation itself must be temporal). Davies claims that the very notion of a First Cause seems to demand that the cause of all else be outside the temporal order and that it be immutable. That is, a close reading of the cosmological argument seems to entail a God whose actions are of a different nature than ours.

With regard to the second objection, that a timeless being cannot be the personal, caring, involved God of the Bible, Davies seems to dismiss the personal language of the Bible as metaphorical. He contends that there is no guarantee that the sort of changeable God that the process theologians posit will not go out of existence. In response to the third objection, that the notion of simultaneity of timeless eternity seems to result in absurd consequences with regard to time, Davies argues that although things may be said to be brought about at some *time*, this does not entail that God must *exist at some time* in order to bring them about. Davies contends that it is coherent to talk about temporal differences from our point of view but not from God's. Hence the idea of timelessness is not incoherent but is rather the more plausible of the options, given the idea of a First Cause who causes all else, who must stand outside of the causal process as its wholly other initiator.

You, the reader, will decide which view is more plausible.

---

* "Divine Foreknowledge and Human Freedom," in *Aquinas: A Collection of Critical Essays,* edited by Anthony Kenny (New York: Doubleday, 1969), 264.

IV.A.1   Temporal Eternity

STEPHEN T. DAVIS

Stephen T. Davis is professor of philosophy at Claremont McKenna College. In his article he sets forth the contrasting ideas of "timeless eternity" and "temporal eternity." The former posits a God who is outside time and lacks both temporal location and extension, and the latter posits a God who has both temporal location and extension. Davis offers three arguments in favor of temporal eternity: (1) The concept of God's creative activity *makes far more sense if we accept the notion that he exists in time. For if God creates a given temporal thing, his act of creation itself must be temporal. (2) A timeless being cannot be the personal, caring, involved God of the Bible. (3) The notion of simultaneity of timeless eternity seems to result in absurd consequences with regard to time; for if events in 3021 BC are no earlier than the events of 1986 for God, then time must be illusory. But there is no good reason to deem time illusory. Hence the notion of timeless eternity seems incoherent.*

Reprinted from Stephen T. Davis, *Logic and the Nature of God* (Grand Rapids, Mich.: Eerdmans, 1983), by permission of the author. Copyright © Stephen T. Davis. Footnotes edited.

One divine property that we will deal with early in the book is God's eternality. It will be best if we discuss it here because one's opinion on this subject is likely to affect opinions one has about several other divine properties, especially omnipotence, omniscience and immutability. Thus we must now raise the thorny question of God's relation to time.

It is part of the Judeo-Christian tradition that God is eternal.

> Lord, thou has been our dwelling place in all
>   generations.
> Before the mountains were brought forth, or
>   ever thou hadst formed the earth and
>   the world, from everlasting to
>   everlasting thou art God.
> Thou turnest man back to the dust, and
>   sayeth, 'Turn back, O children of man!'
> For a thousand years in thy sight are but as
>   yesterday when it is past, or as a watch
>   in the night. (Ps. 90:1–4)

> Of old thou didst lay the foundation of the
>   earth, and the heavens are the work of
>   thy hands.
> They will perish, but thou dost endure; they
>   will all wear out like a garment.
> Thou changest them like raiment, and they
>   pass away; but thou art the same and
>   thy years have no end. (Ps. 102:25–7)

> I am the Alpha and the Omega, the first and
>   the last, the beginning and the end.
>   (Rev. 22:13)

But what does it mean to say that God is eternal? Jews and Christians agree that God's eternality entails that he has always existed and always will exist, that he has no beginning and no end. But from this central point there are two routes that might be taken. One is to say that God is *timelessly eternal* and the other is to say that he is *temporally eternal*.

Let us first consider the view that God is timelessly eternal or 'outside of time'. There are a variety of reasons a Christian might be tempted by this thesis. One might be to emphasize God's transcendence over his creation as much as possible.

Another might be to reconcile divine foreknowledge and human freedom. (Boethius and others have argued that human beings can be free despite God's knowledge of what they will do in their future because God's knowledge is timeless.) Another might be to retain consistency with other things one says about God, for example that he is immutable. (And it certainly does seem true that a timeless being—to be defined below—must be immutable.)

Whatever the reasons, a variety of Christian theologians and philosophers have claimed that God is timeless. For example, Anselm graphically depicts God's relation to time as follows:

> Thou wast not, then, yesterday, nor wilt thou be tomorrow; but yesterday and today and tomorrow thou art; or, rather, neither yesterday, nor today nor tomorrow thou art; but, simply, thou art, outside all time. For yesterday and today and tomorrow have no existence, except in time; but thou, although nothing exists without thee, nevertheless dost not exist in space or time, but all things exist in thee.[1]

That God is timeless was also claimed by Augustine and Boethius before Anselm, and was also held after him, notably by Aquinas and Schleiermacher. In a famous definition, Boethius called eternity 'the complete possession all at once of illimitable life'; it is a kind of 'now that stands still'. (Notice that Boethius is using 'eternal' as a synonym for 'timeless', which I am not.) Since God is eternal, he lives in what might be called an 'everlasting present'; he has an infinity of movable time—past, present and future—all at once everlastingly present to him. Boethius is perhaps most clear on this point when he speaks of divine foreknowledge:

> Wherefore since . . . God hath always an everlasting and present state, his knowledge also surpassing all motions of time, remaineth in the simplicity of his presence, and comprehending the infinite spaces of that which is past and to come, considereth all things in his simple knowledge, as though they were now in doing. So that, if thou wilt weigh his foreknowledge with which he discerneth all things, thou wilt more rightly esteem it to be the knowledge of a never fading instant than a foreknowledge as of a thing to come.[2]

Following Boethius, Aquinas stressed that for God there is no past, present and future, and no before and after, that all is 'simultaneously whole' for him.[3]

These statements are not easy to understand. What precisely is meant by the term 'timeless' or 'timeless being'? Following Nelson Pike, let us say that a given being is timeless if and only if it:

(1) lacks temporal location

and

(2) lacks temporal extension.[4]

A being lacks temporal location if it does not make sense to say of it, for example, that it existed before the French Revolution or that it will exist on Jimmy Carter's seventieth birthday. Thus, if God is timeless, statements like these cannot meaningfully be made about him. A being lacks temporal extension if it has no duration, i.e. if it makes no sense to say of it, for example, that it has lived for eighty years or that it was alive during the entire period of the Truman administration.

It is not easy to feel that one has fully grasped the notion of a timeless being. Perhaps this is in part because it is difficult to see precisely what criteria (1) and (2) imply. Very possibly they imply another characteristic of a timeless being, one which is also difficult to state and explicate precisely:

(3) Temporal terms have no significant application to him.

What is a 'temporal term'? Without wishing to suggest that my list is exhaustive, let me stipulate that a temporal term is one like those included in the following list: 'past', 'present', 'future', 'before', 'after', and other similar terms like 'simultaneous', 'always', 'later', 'next year', 'forever', 'at 6:00 p.m.', etc. Now there appears to be a sense in which temporal terms cannot meaningfully be predicated of a being that lacks temporal location and temporal extension. Neither the timeless being itself, nor its properties, actions or relations with other beings can be significantly modified by temporal terms. Thus if God is a timeless being,

the following sentences are either meaningless or necessarily false:

- God existed before Moses.
- God's power will soon triumph over evil.
- Last week God wrought a miracle.
- God will always be wiser than human beings.

Does this imply that time as we understand it is unreal, a kind of illusion? If the timeless being in question is God, the ultimate reality of the universe, the creator of the heavens and the earth, one might well push the argument in this way: if from God's point of view there is no past, present and future, and no before and after, then—it might well be argued—there is no ultimately real past, present and future, and no ultimately real relationship of before and after. Thus time as we experience it is unreal.

But the argument need not be pushed in this direction. Even if God is a timeless being, it can be argued that time is real and that our temporal distinctions are apt just because God created time (for us to live 'in'). Perhaps an analogy from space will help. Just because God is spaceless (he has no spatial location or extension) no one wants to say that space is unreal. It is just that God does not exist in space as we do. Similarly, he does not exist 'in' time, but time is still real, both for us and for God. Well then—one might want to ask at this point—if God is timeless is it or is it not meaningful to say that 'God existed before Moses' or that 'God will always be wiser than human beings'? The answer is that it depends on who you are: for us these statements are meaningful and true; for God they are meaningless or at least necessarily false.

Is the doctrine of divine timelessness coherent? I do not know. I suspect it is possible for a philosopher to lay out a concept of divine timelessness which I am unable to refute, i.e. prove incoherent. I will discuss one such attempt later in this chapter. However, throughout this book, for reasons I will presently explain, I do not propose to assume that God is timeless. In fact, I plan to make and argue for the assumption that God is 'temporally eternal'. In my view, this is a far simpler procedure, with far fewer theological dangers, as I will explain. For the fact is that every notion of divine timelessness with which I am familiar is subject to difficulties which, at the very least, seem serious.

I will argue against the doctrine of divine timelessness on two counts: first, that a timeless being cannot be the Christian God; and second, that the notion of a timeless being is probably incoherent. The first point has been convincingly argued by both Nelson Pike and Richard Swinburne.[5] I will not mention all of the traditional attributes of God they claim timelessness rules out; I will instead concentrate on just two: the claim that God is the creator of the universe, and the claim that God is a personal being who acts in human history, speaking, punishing, warning, forgiving, etc. Both notions are obviously crucial to Christianity; if timelessness really does rule them out this will constitute a very good reason for a Christian to reject the doctrine.

Notice the following argument:

(5) God creates x.
(6) x first exists at T.
(7) Therefore, God creates x at T.

If this argument is valid, it seems to rule out the possibility of a timeless God creating anything at all, the universe or anything in it, for 'x' here is a variable ranging over anything at all about which it is logically possible that it be created. The reason the argument rules out the doctrine that God is creator is that (7) cannot be true if God lacks temporal location. For we saw earlier that no temporal term like 'at T' can meaningfully be applied to a being or to the actions of a being that lacks temporal location and temporal extension. God is not the creator Christians have traditionally believed in if he is not the creator of things like me and the eucalyptus tree outside my office. But no timeless being can be the creator of such things since they came into existence at various points in time. Thus timelessness is inconsistent with the Christian view of God as creator.

But cannot God, so to speak, timelessly create something temporal? Aquinas, at least, argued that he can. God may create something at a certain point in time (say, create me in the year 1940), but

it does not follow from this, Aquinas would say, that God's act of creating occurred at that point in time (or indeed at any point in time); his creating may well be based on changeless and eternal aspects of his will. Thus Aquinas says:

> God's act of understanding and willing is, necessarily, His act of making. Now, an effect follows from the intellect and the will according to the determination of the intellect and the command of the will. Moreover, just as the intellect determines every other condition of the thing made, so does it prescribe the time of its making; for art determines not only that this thing is to be such and such, but that it is to be at this particular time, even as a physician determines that a dose of medicine is to be drunk at such a particular time. So that, if his act of will were of itself sufficient to produce the effect, the effect would follow anew from his previous decision, without any new action on his part. Nothing, therefore, prevents our saying that God's action existed from all eternity, whereas its effect was not present from eternity, but existed at that time when, from all eternity, He ordained it.[6]

Thus—so Aquinas would say—(5) and (6) in the above argument do not entail (7) after all.

Is Aquinas correct? It depends on what he means by 'eternity' in the above lines. If he means temporal eternity I believe he is correct. It may well be true that God can, so to speak, 'from all eternity create x at T'. I have no wish to deny this, at any rate. A temporally eternal being apparently can eternally (that is, at all points in time) will that a given temporal being come to exist at a certain point in time. Of course, this case is not precisely parallel to the case of Aquinas's physician at a given point in time willing that a dosage be taken at a later point in time. But nevertheless, as concerns temporal eternality, Aquinas appears to be correct: as it stands, the (5)–(7) argument is invalid.

But Aquinas's argument, which in my opinion successfully applies to temporally eternal things, does not apply to timeless things. (Notice that the physician in his example is not timeless.) Even if it is true that I was created in 1940 not because of a choice God made in 1940 (or at some other time) but because of a temporally eternal divine choice, this does not make the choice *timeless* in the sense of lacking temporal location and extension. Temporally eternal things certainly do have temporal extension. It would still make sense and quite possibly be true to say, 'God willed in 1940 that Davis exist' (although it would also be meaningful and perhaps equally true to make the same statement with 3469 B.C. or A.D. 2610 or any other date substituted for 1940). Equally, if all God's decisions and actions are temporally eternal they are *simultaneous* with each other; and statements like 'x's desire to create a and x's decision to do b are simultaneous' cannot, as we saw, meaningfully be made about a timeless being.[7] This too is to apply a temporal term—'simultaneous'—to it.

Of course, nothing prevents a defender of timelessness from simply insisting that an action (e.g. the causing of something to exist) can be timeless and the effect (e.g. its coming into existence) temporal. Such a person can ask why the temporality of the effect requires that the cause be temporal. But to anticipate a point I will make in more detail later, the answer to this is that we have on hand no acceptable concept of atemporal causation, i.e. of what it is for a timeless cause to produce a temporal effect. Surely, as Nelson Pike argues, in all the cases of causation with which we are familiar, a temporal relationship obtains between an action and its effect. We are in no position to deny that this need always be the case unless we are armed with a usable concept of atemporal causation, which we are not.

Let us return to the argument mentioned above:

(5) God creates x.
(6) x first exists at T.
(7) Therefore, God creates x at T.

What we need to notice is that (7) is ambiguous between (7a) and (7b):

(7a) God, at T, creates x.
(7b) God creates x, and x first exists at T.

Now (7a) clearly cannot be true of God if God is timeless—a being that performs some action at a certain point in time is temporal. So (7b) is the interpretation of (7) that will be preferred by the defender of divine timelessness. Notice that (7b) is simply the conjunction of (5) and (6), and accord-

ingly is indeed entailed by (5) and (6). But can (7b) be true of God if God is timeless? Only if we have available a usable concept of atemporal causation, which, as I say, we do not have. Therefore, we are within our rights in concluding that (5) and (6) entail that God is temporal, i.e. that a timeless being cannot be the creator of the universe.

Accordingly, it is not clear how a timelessly eternal being can be the creator of this temporal universe. If God creates a given temporal thing, then God's act of creation is itself temporal (though it may be temporally eternal). If God is timelessly eternal in the sense defined earlier, he cannot create temporal things.

Second, a timeless being cannot be the personal, caring, involved God we read about in the Bible. The God of the Bible is, above all, a God who cares deeply about what happens in history and who acts to bring about his will. He makes plans. He responds to what human beings, do, e.g. their evil deeds or their acts of repentance. He seems to have temporal location and extension. The Bible does not hesitate to speak of God's years and days (see Psalm 102:24, 27; Hebrews 1:12). And God seems to act in temporal sequences—first he rescues the children of Israel from Egypt and later he gives them the Law; first he sends his son to be born of a virgin and later he raises him from the dead. These are generalizations meant to be understood as covering the whole Bible rather than specific passages; nevertheless here are two texts where such points seem to be made:

> If you obey the commandments of the Lord your God . . . by loving the Lord your God, by walking in his ways, and by keeping his commandments and his statutes and his ordinances, then you shall live and multiply, and the Lord your God will bless you . . . But if your heart turns away, and you will not hear, but are drawn away to worship other gods and serve them, I declare to you this day, that you shall perish. (Deut. 30:16–18)

> In many and various ways God spoke of old to our fathers by the prophets; but in these last days he has spoken to us by a Son. (Heb. 1:1–2)

But the obvious problem here is to understand how a timeless being can plan or anticipate or remember or respond or punish or warn or forgive. All such acts seem undeniably temporal.[8] To make plans is to formulate intentions about the future. To anticipate is to look forward to what is future. To remember is to have beliefs or knowledge about what is past. To respond is to be affected by events that have occurred in the past. To punish is to cause someone to suffer because of something done in the past. To warn is to caution someone about dangers that might lie in the future. To forgive someone is to restore a past relationship that was damaged by an offense.

On both counts, then, it is difficult to see how a timeless being can be the God in which Christians have traditionally believed. It does not seem that there is any clear sense in which a timeless being can be the creator of the universe or a being who acts in time.

The other and perhaps more important argument against divine timelessness is that both the notion of a timeless being per se and the notion of a timeless being who is also omniscient are probably incoherent. The incoherence of the notion per se can be seen by considering carefully the Boethius-Anselm-Aquinas claim that for God all times are simultaneously present. Events occurring at 3021 B.C., at 1982, and at A.D. 7643, they want to say, are all 'simultaneously present' to God. If this just means that at any point in time God knows in full and complete detail what happens at any other point in time, I can (and do) accept it. But it clearly means something different and much stronger than this, and in this stronger sense (whatever precisely it comes to) the claim does not seem possibly true.[9]

That is, if the doctrine of timelessness requires us to say that the years 3021 B.C. and A.D. 7643 are simultaneous, then the doctrine is false, for the two are not simultaneous. They may of course be simultaneous in some sense if time is illusory. But since I see no good reason to affirm that time is illusory and every reason to deny that it is illusory, I am within my rights in insisting that the two indicated years are not simultaneous and that the doctrine of divine timelessness is accordingly probably false.

Suppose an event that occurred yesterday is the cause of an event that will occur tomorrow, e.g. suppose your having thrown a banana peel on the pavement yesterday will cause me to trip and break a bone tomorrow. How can the throwing of the banana peel and the breaking of the bone be simultaneous? Surely if the first caused the second the first must be temporally prior to the second; and if so, they are not simultaneous. (Perhaps some causes are simultaneous with their effects, but not causes of events of this sort.)

But the following objection might be raised: 'Any argument for the conclusion that timeless beings cannot exist must be mistaken for the simple reason that timeless beings do exist'. It has been seriously suggested, for example, that numbers are timeless beings. Thus William Kneale says:

> An assertion such as 'There is a prime number between five and ten' can never be countered sensibly by the remark 'You are out of date: things have altered recently.' And this is the reason why the entities discussed in mathematics can properly be said to have a timeless existence. To say only that they have a sempiternal or omnitemporal existence (i.e., an existence at all times) would be unsatisfactory because this way of talking might suggest that it is at least conceivable that they should at some time cease to exist, and that is an absurdity we want to exclude.[10]

Is the number seven, for example, timeless? I do not think so. (I agree that it is eternal and that it would be absurd to suggest that it might not exist; it is, in short, a sort of 'necessary being'.) But if the number seven is not just eternal but timeless, then on our earlier definition of 'timeless', the following statements cannot meaningfully be made:

- The number seven existed on 27 July 1883.
- The number seven was greater than the number six during the whole of the Punic wars.
- The number seven existed yesterday and will exist tomorrow.

But the number seven is not a timeless being; all three of these sentences, in my opinion, are not only meaningful but true. (The fact that the first might be taken by someone to suggest that the number seven might not exist at some time other than 27 July 1883 is only an interesting psychological fact about the person who misreads it in this way. The statement implies nothing of the sort.)

But defenders of divine timelessness can raise an objection to this argument that their notion is incoherent. They can say something like this:

Of course talk about 'eternal present', 'simultaneously whole', etc. seems incoherent to us. This is because such talk is at best a stumbling way of understanding a mystery—the mystery of God's transcendence over time—that we cannot really understand. Statements like 'my nineteenth birthday occurred before my twentieth' only seem indubitable to us because, unlike God, our minds are limited. If we had God's intellectual prowess, if we understood temporal reality as he does, we would see that this statement is false or inadequate or misleading. We would then see time correctly.

There may be some sense in which the claims being made here are true. I will not deny them, at any rate. . . . God's consciousness of time may indeed so far transcend ours that the best way we have of expressing it is by making apparently incoherent statements. But whether or not these claims are true, I am quite sure that we have no good reason to believe them. Like it or not, we are stuck with these limited minds of ours; if we want to be rational we have no choice but to reject what we judge to be incoherent. It may be true, in some sense, that some statements we presently consider true (like 'my nineteenth birthday occurred before my twentieth') are really false or inadequate or misleading when understood in some way which we cannot now understand. But it is irrational for us now to affirm that this is true. . . .

We have been discussing the notion of timelessness as an attempt to understand the Christian tradition that God is eternal. It can now be seen why I find the notion inadequate and why I much prefer the other alternative, which is to say that God is temporally eternal. Let us say that a temporally eternal being is (1) eternal in the sense that there never was or will be a moment when it does not exist, (2) temporal in the sense that it has both temporal location and temporal extension, and (3) temporal in the sense that the distinctions among past, present and future, and between before and after, can meaningfully be applied to it. If God is such a temporally eternal being, there are still several ways of understanding his relation to time.

Perhaps the simplest way is to say that time has always existed alongside God. This is difficult to state coherently—'Time has always existed' reduces to the tautology 'There is no moment of time in which time does not exist'. Perhaps it is better to state this view as the simple claim that time is not a contingent, created thing like the universe.

A second possibility is espoused by Augustine. He says that time was created by God, exists, and then will cease to exist. Before the creation of the universe and after the universe ceases to exist there exists not time but timeless eternity. Thus God has control over time—he created it and can presumably destroy it whenever he wants. While this view has some attractions—time or at least our consciousness of it does seem in some sense dependent on the existence of mutable things—a possible problem is that the notion of timeless eternity before the creation of the universe and after it ceases to exist may be just as difficult to understand as the doctrine of timeless eternity itself. This problem may well be solvable, however. In timeless eternity there will presumably be no appearance of temporal succession, i.e. of events occurring before or after each other, which is at least one of the fundamental problems connected with regarding God as timeless at the same time that we live in a world of apparent temporal succession.

A third possibility was suggested by the eighth-century church father John of Damascus. Time has always existed, John appears to say, yet is only measurable when things like the sun and moon exist. Thus before the creation there existed non-measurable time, and after the end of the heavens and the earth non-measurable time will again exist. Measurable time is what exists from the point of creation of the world to the point of its destruction.

Since it is probably the simplest, and since I see no danger in it for Christianity (as I will argue below), I will adopt the first alternative: time was not created; it necessarily exists (like numbers); it depends for its existence on nothing else. Time, perhaps, is an eternal aspect of God's nature rather than a reality independent of God. But the point is that God, on this view, is a temporal being. Past, present and future are real to him; he has simultaneity and succession in his states, acts and knowledge. He knows statements like 'Today is 24 April' and 'My nineteenth birthday occurred before my twentieth'. He has temporal location. It makes good sense to say: 'God exists today' and 'God was omniscient on Napoleon's birthday'. And he has temporal extension. It makes good sense to say 'God existed during the entire period of the Punic wars' and to ask, 'How long has God existed?' The answer to the latter is: forever.

The three main motives for the theory of timeless eternity, I suggested, were to reconcile human freedom and divine foreknowledge, to retain consistency with other things one says about God, and to exalt God's transcendence as much as possible. As to the first, I believe foreknowledge and freedom can be reconciled without appealing to any doctrine of timelessness. . . . As to the second, I do not believe that anything I say about God in this book (or indeed anything said about God in the Bible) logically requires that he be timeless. And as to the third, I feel no need to exalt God's transcendence in every possible way. What Christians must do, I believe, is emphasize God's transcendence over his creation in the ways that scripture does and in ways that seem essential to Christian theism. And I do not believe that the Bible teaches, implies or presupposes that God is timeless. Nor do I feel any theological or philosophical need to embrace timelessness.

Nor is there any reason to doubt that a temporal God who is 'in' time just as we are is everything the Judeo-Christian God is traditionally supposed to be. He can still be an eternal being, i.e. a being without beginning or end. He can still be the creator of the universe. He can still be immutable in the sense of remaining ever true to his promises and purposes and eternally retaining his essential nature. (But he cannot be immutable in other stronger senses.) He can still have complete knowledge of all past, present and future events. (If he 'transcends time', it is only in the sense that he has this power—a power no other being has.) He can still be the loving, omnipotent redeemer Christians worship.

Some might still wish to object to this as fol-

lows: 'Surely God must be free of all temporal limitations if he is truly God. But a temporal God is not so free. Thus God must be timeless'. The answer to this is that a temporally eternally God such as I have described is free of certain temporal limitations, e.g. he is free of our inability to remember things that happened hundreds of years ago. Furthermore, not even a timelessly eternal God is free of all temporal limitations, for he is actually unable to experience 'before' or 'after'. His nature limits him; he is unable to experience such things, for if he did experience them he would be temporal. There is temporal limitation whichever view we take. It appears that however we look at it, the doctrine of divine temporal eternity is greatly preferable to timeless eternity. So it is the former that I will embrace.

Notes

1. Anselm, *St Anselm: Basic Writings* (LaSalle, Illinois: Open Court Publishing Company, 1958) p. 25.

2. Boethius, *The Theological Treatises and the Consolation of Philosophy* (Loeb Classical Library, London: William Heinemann, 1918) pp. 403–5; cf. also pp. 21–3, 401–5.

3. *The Summa Theologica of St Thomas Aquinas* (London: Burns, Oates and Washbourne, 1920) Pt. I, Q. X, Arts. 2 and 4.

4. These points are taken from Nelson Pike's *God and Timelessness* (New York: Schocken Books, 1970) p. 7. Pike's work is an outstanding study of this subject and has influenced me at several points.

5. Ibid., pp. 97–118, 125–8; Richard Swinburne, *The Coherence of Theism* (Oxford University Press, 1977) pp. 221–2.

6. Thomas Aquinas, *Summa Contra Gentiles*, trans A.C. Pegis (Notre Dame, Indiana: University of Notre Dame Press, 1975) II, 35.

7. This has been argued by Nicholas Woltersdorff in his 'God Everlasting'. See *God and the Good*, ed. Clifton J. Orlebeke and Lewis B. Smedes (Grand Rapids, Michigan: William B. Eerdmans, 1975) pp. 181–203.

8. See Pike, *God and Timelessness*, pp. 128–9; Swinburne, *The Coherence of Theism* pp. 220–1.

9. See Swinburne, *The Coherence of Theism* pp. 220–1.

10. William Kneale, 'Time and Eternity in Theology', *Proceedings of the Aristotelian Society*, vol. 61 (1961) p. 98.

IV.A.2   Timeless Eternity

BRIAN DAVIES

Brian Davies is a Dominican friar and lecturer in philosophy at Blackfriars, Oxford, England. In this article he examines objections to the concept of timeless eternity such as those raised by Davis and tries to answer them by appealing to a difference between God's perspective and ours and to the implications of the argument from causality. The very notion of a First Cause seems to demand that the cause of all else be outside the temporal order and that it be immutable. That is, a close reading of the cosmological argument seems to entail a God whose actions are of a different nature than ours.

We have already seen that people who believe in the Judaeo-Christian concept of God have more to say about God than that there is one. They ascribe certain attributes to God. These have often been the subject of lengthy philosophical debate and it now seems appropriate to say something more about them than has so far been said in earlier chapters. It will not be possible to discuss all the attributes that have been ascribed to God within Judaeo-Christianity, but we can say something about some of the most important. The one I have chosen to talk about is eternity. The question that basically confronts us throughout is simply this: is it reasonable to suppose that there is a God with this attribute?

The Meaning of Divine Eternity

The notion of divine eternity is especially difficult to discuss since it has been understood in two distinct senses. For some people divine eternity

means timelessness; others, however, have urged that God is only eternal in the sense that he is without beginning or end.

Theologically speaking it is the notion of eternity as timelessness that has had the greatest influence. It can be found in writers like Anselm, Augustine of Hippo (354–430), Aquinas, John Calvin (1509–64), and Friedrich Schleiermacher (1768–1834). Perhaps its most famous exponent is Boethius (c.480–524), whose definition of eternity as timelessness has become classic. Eternity, says Boethius, 'is the complete, simultaneous and perfect possession of everlasting life' (*aeternitas est interminabilis vitae tota simul et perfecta possessio*).[1]

The claim that God is timeless involves two assertions. The first is that God has no temporal extension, i.e. that he has no duration. As Augustine puts it: 'Thy years do not come and go; while these years of ours do come and go, in order that they might come. . . . Thy present day does not give place to tomorrow, nor indeed, does it take the place of yesterday. Thy present day is eternity.'[2] Second, to say that God is timeless is to assert that God has no temporal location, i.e. that there is no 'before' and 'after' with him. As St. Anselm declares: 'So it is not that you existed yesterday, or will exist tomorrow, but that yesterday, today and tomorrow, you simply are. Or rather, you exist neither yesterday, today, nor tomorrow, but you exist directly right outside time.'[3]

This view of divine eternity is an exceedingly difficult one to grasp; but the second view is less demanding, at least at first glance. Here the idea is simply that God just goes on and on, that nothing brought him into existence and that there is no time in the future when he will cease to be. In his book *The Coherence of Theism* Swinburne adopts this understanding of divine eternity:

If a creator of the universe exists now, he must have existed at least as long as there have been other logically contingent existing things. . . . However, traditionally theists believe not merely that this spirit, God, exists now or has existed as long as created things, but that he is an eternal being. This seems to mean, firstly, that he has always existed—that there was no time at which he did not exist. . . . Let us put this point by saying that they believe that he is backwardly eternal. The supposition that a spirit of the above kind is backwardly eternal seems to be a coherent one. . . . The doctrine that God is eternal seems to involve, secondly, the doctrine that the above spirit will go on existing for ever. . . . I will put this point by saying that he is forwardly eternal. This too seems to be a coherent suggestion.[4]

Objections to a Timeless God

Since most of the controversy about God's eternity has begun with the notion of eternity as timelessness, perhaps we had better plunge into the deep end immediately and consider whether it is reasonable to talk in terms of a timeless God. A number of arguments have been advanced to the effect that it is not. At this stage I simply present them without comment.

One argument is concerned with the notions of coherence and conceivability. According to some people one cannot talk reasonably about a timeless God since the whole notion of timeless existence is incoherent or unintelligible. For one thing, we can have no idea of what such existence would be like. Secondly, if anything exists at all, it must exist at some time, for to exist at all is to exist at some time.

This argument is sometimes related to another. According to this one God cannot reasonably be said to be timeless since other things must be said of him, always assuming that he exists at all, and these other things are incompatible with his being timeless. In other words, the idea here is that the notion of a timeless God would render theism internally contradictory.

But what is it that critics find incompatible with God's timelessness? Three things mainly: God's personal perfection, God's ability to act, and God's knowledge.

The view that God's personal perfection rules

out his timelessness has been particularly popular in the twentieth century largely as a result of the work of a group of theologians called Process Theologians, of whom an eminent representative is Charles Hartshorne.[5] According to Hartshorne we regard people as fully personal if they are capable of love and if they are both passive, and thereby responsive to their environment, as well as active, and thereby able to take initiatives. In that case, however, God's personal perfection requires that he be able to love and that he be both passive and active. God must therefore sympathize with his creatures and be affected by what goes on in the world. Thus God undergoes joys and sorrows and his knowledge undergoes development. In short, God changes. But if God changes he cannot be timeless since a timeless being cannot really change in itself.

The point about God's ability to act is a conceptual one. The idea here is that if God acts then he must be in time since to act at all logically depends on acting at some time. Thus Swinburne says that 'If we say that P brings about X, we can always sensibly ask *when* does he bring it about? If we say that P punishes Q, we can always sensibly ask *when* does he punish Q. . . . If P at t brings about X, then necessarily X comes into existence (simultaneously with or) subsequently to P's action. . . . And so on.'[6]

Finally, the argument about God's knowledge is simply that if, as is commonly said, God is knowledgeable, if, indeed, he is omniscient, then he must know things now and he must have known them in the past. Furthermore, he must know them when they come about in the future. But all this must mean that he exists in time. Thus Anthony Kenny argues that if God is timeless then his knowledge is extremely restricted. 'It seems', he says, 'an extraordinary way of affirming God's omniscience if a person, when asked what God knows *now*, must say "Nothing", and when asked what he knew *yesterday*, must again say "Nothing", and must yet again say "Nothing" when asked what God will know *tomorrow*.'[7]

A final line of argument sometimes advanced against the reasonableness of belief in a timeless

God is one based on Scripture. The argument is simply that in Scripture the eternity of God is eternity in the sense of endless duration.

Are the Objections Conclusive?

In considering the merits of the above objections we can begin with the one about coherence and intelligibility. And perhaps the first thing to say is that it is obviously expressing an evident truth. We can put it by saying that if 'intelligible' means 'understandable', 'conceivable', 'imaginable', or something like that, then the reality referred to in talking of timeless existence is not intelligible. It seems very hard indeed to conjure up any picture of timeless existence. It might be said that we are already familiar with things that exist timelessly. What about numbers and logical truths? But whether and how these can be said to exist is a difficult philosophical problem. Nor does it seem particularly relevant to the question of God's timelessness. For whatever else may be true of numbers and logical truths, it surely cannot be that they exercise anything like the causality commonly ascribed to God. As far as theists are concerned, God is operative; and it is just here that the problem of intelligibility begins to bite. Whenever we think of things operating, whenever we think of things with causal power, we seem to be thinking of things existing in time. We are thinking of things like men pushing pens and acids burning through substances.

But it is one thing to say this and another to say that timeless existence is not intelligible in the strong sense that it is flatly impossible, or, as the first of our objections put it, incoherent. And a case can be made for denying this second and stronger contention.

It will help at this stage if the reader thinks back to some remarks made earlier. I have already pointed out that one way of deciding whether something could be so is to see whether there is any reason for thinking that it is so. Now someone who says that the notion of timeless existence is flatly impossible or incoherent means that there

could not be timeless existence. But there is reason for saying that there is.

Referring back to the argument of Chapter 5, it is, I suggest, reasonable to believe in a cause of all existing things; a cause, furthermore, which cannot be regarded as a particular thing over and against the many things that exist. If this is so, then there is timeless existence. Why? Because (a) the cause of all things cannot be said to change or even to be capable of changing, and (b) only what can be said to change or to be capable of changing can be in time. The defence of (a) is that if X can or does change, then X must be some particular thing, but the cause of all existing things cannot be such. The defence of (b) is that if X does not or cannot change, then no temporal predicates can intelligibly be ascribed to it. That is why we are tempted (if we are tempted) to say that numbers and logical truths are timeless. They are what they are in total independence of changes occurring in the universe. Nothing that happens is going to affect the number 9, and nothing that happens is going to alter the fact that nothing can be simultaneously perfectly square and perfectly round. The connection between time and change is also what leads writers like Hartshorne to deny that God is timeless. They want to ascribe change to God and this would seem to put him in time; he would *first* be like this and *then* be like that.

I suggest, then, that the notion of timeless existence is a coherent one and that sense can be given to it with reference to the cosmological argument, though it also seems that such existence is unimaginable. But what of the objections to the notion of a timeless God based on positions like those of Hartshorne, Swinburne, and Kenny?

Hartshorne's position has a number of advantages from the viewpoint of someone who wishes to believe in God. One of these lies in the fact that it understands God's eternity in terms of endless duration and can thereby be related to the dominant biblical way of talking about divine eternity. In other words, the last of the objections to a timeless God noted in the preceding section seems correct as a statement of fact. As John L. McKenzie shows, 'The philosophical concept of eternity is not clearly expressed in either the O.T. or N.T. The Hb. 'olam and the Gk. aiōn both signify primarily an indefinitely extended period of time beyond the lifetime of a single person.'[8] In his article on aiōn/aiōnios in Kittel's *Theological Dictionary of the New Testament*[9] Sasse sums up the New Testament position thus:

> The unending eternity of God and the time of the world, which is limited by its creation and conclusion, are contrasted with one another. Eternity is thought of as unending time—for how else can human thought picture it?—and the eternal being of God is represented as pre-existence and post-existence. . . . The NT took over the OT and Jewish view of divine eternity along with the ancient formulae. There was new development, however, to the extent that the statements concerning God's eternity were extended to Christ.

But whatever may be the biblical way of talking (and, as Sasse himself indicates, it need only be a way of talking), there are serious objections to Hartshorne's position. The major one should now be clear in the light of what I have already been arguing. For if it is said that God is the cause of the existence of all things then God cannot change and must be timeless.

Hartshorne, of course, may reply that if that is the case then he is not interested in God and prefers to stick with his timeful, personal deity. But if the argument of Chapters 5 and 6 is correct this move is open to an obvious objection. As Hartshorne sees it, God is involved in a social context just like men and women; in this sense his God is personal, and that is why he wants to speak of him experiencing joy and sorrow. According to Hartshorne, just as I can feel joy and sorrow at things, so can God. But if that is true then Hartshorne's God is just as much part of the world of existing and ordered things as men and women are, and it is therefore reasonable to hold that he is caused to exist by a source of existing things. In other words, the existence of Hartshorne's God raises the question of something beyond it. His God cannot be ultimate in the way that those who believe in God normally maintain that he is. Instead he is very much a being among beings. Nor, of course, is his future at all secure. Given that God is as Hart-

shorne describes him, it seems reasonable to regard his existence as dependent on a cause other than himself. But what guarantee does he have that this cause will not cease to bring it about that he exists? Here, at least, the notion of a timeless God has an advantage over that of a temporal one. Those who believe in God have regularly wanted to ascribe to him a kind of permanence or independence which will enable them to be confident that he will not cease to exist. But, clearly, if God is timeless then the idea of his ceasing to exist makes no sense. If X ceases to exist then it must be true that there was a time before this event when X existed, and X must therefore have existed at some time.

So much, then, for Hartshorne. But what of Swinburne's point about divine action? With reference to it one can again, I think, argue that we do not have good grounds for holding that talk about a timeless God is unreasonable.

At first glance what Swinburne says seems clearly true. That is to say, it is tempting to agree that:

1. If P brings about X we can ask 'When does he bring it about?'
2. If someone says that P punishes Y then it makes sense to ask when he does so.
3. If P at t brings about X then X comes into existence simultaneously with or subsequently to P's action.

But how do we know that 1–3 are always true? Swinburne, as far as I can see, just assumes that they must be, that they express logically necessary truths. And as long as we keep our mind fixed on their use of the variable letter P it is tempting to agree. But in a discussion of timelessness and God, P = God. And it is far from clear that 1–3 are logically true when God is their subject. For if there could be a God who is timeless then obviously they are not necessarily true. But, as we have seen, if God is taken to be the cause of existing things he must be timeless. Therefore they are not necessarily true. And the inference to make from this is that when, for example, God is said to bring things about then 'bring about' has a sense appropriate to its subject, God, a sense which does not allow us to be bound by the stipulations involved in arguments like the present one of Swinburne.

A possible reply to this line of thinking would be to say that if, for example, 'brings about' does not mean 'brings about at some time' then it means nothing at all. But I have already indicated why this need not be so. For, clearly, 'brings about' means 'causes', and if God can be both timeless and the cause of existing things then God can bring things about without being at some time in bringing them about. He cannot, of course, arrange that things in time brought about by him are brought about at no time. And this, perhaps, is partly what Swinburne is getting at. But the temporal reference here is wholly on the side of the things of which 'is brought about' is truly predicated. It is not necessarily on the side of what beings them about, and if what I have been arguing about God is correct, and if it is God who is said to bring these things about, then it could not be. In other words, if it is coherent to suppose that there is a timeless cause of existing things it is coherent to suppose (1) that things can be said to be brought about by God, (2) that these things can be brought about at some time, but (3) that God does not have to exist at some time to bring it about that 'brought about at some time' is true of whatever is brought about by God. To put it another way, we can certainly ask when something was brought about, but it is not logically necessary that what brings it about is itself something in time. This is because it is coherent to talk of a timeless cause of existing things.

It is also, I think, coherent to say that if X is timeless then X can still be knowledgeable. . . . It is relevant at this point to consider the suggestion that there is a contradiction in holding that X can be knowledgeable if X is timeless, i.e. that knowing is inevitably only open to something in time.

Why should one say that if X knows something then X knows it at some time? The obvious reply is that it is normally people, and sometimes animals, who are said to know things, and since people and animals exist in time (as far as we understand them) then that they know something is either true

at some time or not true at all. But just as it does not follow that if X brings Y about then X is in time, so it does not follow that if X knows something then X knows it at some time, though it may perhaps be that X can know timelessly something that is the case at some time. In seeing why this is so we must go back to the point about denying that some statement is logically possible because one has reason to think that what it asserts is actually true. And with reference to this point we also need to return to the conclusions arrived at in Chapter 6. As we saw, it seems reasonable to hold that there is an intelligent cause of the order in the universe, a cause which can also be said to be the cause of the existence of things. Now, while there seems no necessary connection between the notions 'being a cause' and 'being knowledgeable' (as I suggested in Chapter 5), there is such a connection between 'being intelligent' and 'being knowledgeable'; i.e. if X is intelligent then X is knowledgeable (except perhaps when X is the subject in statements like 'The most intelligent arrangement won the competition', which introduce a use of 'intelligent' not relevant to the present discussion—obviously a design is not knowledgeable, but nor is it intelligent in any other way than by showing that its designer is intelligent). Now, if this is so, it seems that if it is reasonable to say that there is an intelligent cause of the existence of things then it is reasonable to say that this cause is knowledgeable. Yet we have already seen that the cause of the existence of things can reasonably be regarded as timeless. The cause of the existence of things must therefore be both knowledgeable and timeless, in which case it is wrong to say that being knowledgeable and being timeless are logically incompatible. This in turn entails that a timeless God could yet be said to be knowledgeable.

At this stage, in the discussion, then, the position seems to be this: (1) It is coherent to suppose that there is timeless existence. (2) The notion of a changing, timeful God is open to objection. (3) It is coherent to suppose that things are brought about by what is timeless and knowledgeable. This means, I think, that the objections to a timeless God are answerable and that there is positive reason for saying that God is timeless. Thus there is positive reason for holding that God is eternal in the classical theistic sense of being timeless.

But it is, perhaps, worth adding one point. Suppose one opts for the view that God is eternal in the sense of existing for ever. And suppose an objector retorts that this is a nonsensical view since nothing can be conceived of as existing for ever. Would this mean that the endless-duration view of divine eternity entailed that there could not be a God? It has been strongly argued that it would not. Swinburne, for instance, suggests that if it is coherent to suppose that God exists at the present time then it is 'coherent to suppose that he exists at any other nameable time; and, if that is coherent, then surely it is coherent to suppose that there exists a being now such that however far back in time you count years you do not reach the beginning of its existence.'[10] He continues: 'We, perhaps, cease to exist at death. But we can surely conceive of a being now existent such that whatever future nameable time you choose, he has not by that time ceased to exist. . . . A being who is both backwardly and forwardly eternal we may term an eternal being.'[11] I am inclined to agree with Swinburne here, so perhaps the notion of eternity as continuous existence is not demonstrably meaningless. But whether it makes any sense to suppose that God could have eternity in this sense is another matter. So much depends on one's reaction to the view that God is timeless.

Notes

1. Boethius, *The Consolation of Philosophy*, book V, 6.
2. *Confessions*, book XI, 13.
3. *Proslogion*, chap. xix.
4. pp.210 f.
5. Cf. Charles Hartshorne, *The Logic of Perfection* (La Salle, Illinois, 1962).
6. *The Coherence of Theism*, p.221.
7. *Aquinas: A Collection of Critical Essays* (London and Melbourne, 1969), p.263.
8. John L. McKenzie, *Dictionary of the Bible* (London, 1975), pp.247 f.
9. Grand Rapids, Michigan, 1965, p.202.
10. *The Coherence of Theism*, p.211.
11. ibid.

IV.B God's Omniscience and Human Freedom

And before him no creature is hidden, but all are open and laid bare to the eyes of him with whom we have to do.

HEBREWS 4:13

The second attribute we consider here is God's omniscience, his power to know everything. Let us roughly define *knowledge* as true justified belief, in which the manner of justification is a proper one. As an illustration of this concept, let us say that if John knows some proposition *p* (e.g., the Kansas City Royals won the World Series in 1985), then (1) John believes that *p* is true; (2) *p* is true; (3) John has an adequate justification for his belief that *p* is true (e.g., he watched all seven games on television with an adequate knowledge of what was going on). We may define God's property of all-knowingness in the following way: For any proposition, God knows whether it is true or false. That is, all God's beliefs are justified and true. He holds no false beliefs at all. Certain questions immediately arise from the notion of omniscience. For example, much of our descriptive or propositional knowledge depends on knowledge by acquaintance, experiential knowledge. But experiential knowledge is particular to the individual experiencer. I cannot experience *your* taste of chocolate ice cream or feel *your* headache, so how can God be said to know our experiences if they are ours? Is his experience of our pain exactly similar to ours when he looks within us? Does he need to take on a body to experience the *kinds* of feelings that we experience?

I leave you to wrestle with these questions. For in this section I want to introduce you to the problem of omniscience in relation to human freedom. Let us define freedom of the will in this sense: An agent *S* freely does an act *A* if and only if *S* could have done otherwise in the situation. That is, although at time *t* in situation *x*, *S* does *A*, it could have been the case that *S* did some other act, for example, *B*. Given the identical antecedent conditions, *A* and *B* are both in *S*'s power as genuine alternatives. This is a different notion of freedom from that of the *compatibilist* (soft determinist), who views a free act as one that is causally determined but done voluntarily. The view that I have outlined is called the *libertarian* view of freedom of the will.

Now the problem arises when we combine the two propositions described above:

(1) God is omniscient.
(2) Humans act freely.

Let us examine how these two propositions produce a problem. If God knows that you will go to your early morning class tomorrow, are you free to stay in bed until noon? If God knows that you will do anything, are you free to do it or not to do it? For the compatibilist (one who tries to combine the notion of free action with the thesis that every action is causally determined), there is no contradiction between human freedom and God's omniscience because every action is determined whether or not God knows which actions we will perform. But for the libertarian there may be a problem in reconciling these two propositions.

Note first that reconciling freedom with knowledge isn't ordinarily a problem. I may predict during our philosophy class that you will get up at the end of class and walk out the door. Knowing a lot about you, I may have very good evidence that this is the kind of thing you are likely to do; I have a justification for my belief, which turns out to be true at the end of the hour when you fulfill my prediction. We would normally say that I knew that you would walk out the door. But this would in no way limit your freedom. You could have stayed in your seat if you had really wanted to do so. If we are really free, our free acts do not depend on whether anyone happens to know what we will do, for knowledge in itself does not cause actions. My knowing or not knowing that you will walk out the door has absolutely nothing to do with whether you will do it (unless, of course, I tell you, in which case it might affect your reasons for acting). So knowledge of action and freedom to act do not ordinarily seem to conflict at all. So why shouldn't we apply all this to God and say that God's foreknowledge of what we are going to do in no way causes us to do it? God simply knows ahead of time what we are going to do; that is,

(3) God's knowledge of human action is contingent upon what humans will actually do.

This is the classical position on freedom and omniscience. Boethius and, in our first reading, Augustine argued that God's knowledge is contingent on our choices.

However, other philosophers have objected to comparing our knowledge to God's. The above contingency applies to human, finite knowledge. At time t I believe that you will walk out the door at time $t + 1$. You can cause it to be the case that I have a false belief by staying in your seat through the next class or even fainting and thus having to be carried out the door. But God's knowledge, these philosophers contend, is not like human knowledge in that it is not contingent but necessary. That is, we cannot bring it about by our actions that God believes any falsehood. This is essentially the position of Nelson Pike in the second of our readings. If God, who by virtue of his omniscience believes at t that you will walk out of your class at $t + 1$, how can you be free to stay in your seat?

Pike states the classical position as follows:

(4) God exists at t and believes at t that you would walk out of the classroom at $t + 1$, and it is in your power to refrain from walking out of the classroom.

But if this is the case, then there seem to be only three possibilities:

(5) You could have brought it about at $t + 1$ that God held a false belief;

(6) It was in your power to bring it about that God really did not believe that you would walk out of the classroom at $t + 1$ even though he did hold this belief; or

(7) It was in your power to do something that would have brought it about that any person who believed that you would walk out of the room held a false belief and hence was not God; that is to say, God does not exist.

Since (5), (6), (7) seem to contradict (1) and (2) above, which explicitly states that God is omniscient and we are free, Pike concludes that an examination of the implications of God's essential omniscience shows that it is incompatible with human freedom. Either we must understand God's omniscience differently, or God is not omniscient, or humans are not free.

In our third reading Alvin Plantinga responds to Pike's position, arguing that there really is no incompatibility between divine omniscience and human freedom. Essentially, he argues that all the options—(5), (6), and (7)—can be suitably accommodated to the traditional view of God's omniscience and human freedom. For example, (5) can be read as follows:

(5a) It was in your power at $t + 1$ to do something such that if you had done it, then a belief that God *did hold* at t *would have been* false.

But (5a) is not at all paradoxical and does not imply that it was within your power to do something that would have caused God to hold a false belief. Plantinga carries out a similar strategy with regard to (6) and (7), which you will want to examine carefully. You might also want to read Pike's response to Plantinga in his article "Divine Foreknowledge, Human Freedom and Possible Worlds" (*The Philosophical Review*, April 1977), in which he contends that the problem does not disappear with Plantinga's strategy because divine omniscience entails God's essential knowledge holding in every possible world.

IV.B.1   Divine Foreknowledge and Human Free Will

ST. AUGUSTINE

St. Augustine (354–430), Bishop of Hippo in North Africa, one of the greatest thinkers in the history of the Christian Church, argues in this dialogue that God's foreknowledge of human actions does not necessitate those actions. Specifically, human sin was not committed because God knew that it would happen, but God knew that it would happen because he knows how humans will choose.

Evodius. Since this is so, I am deeply troubled by a certain question: how can it be that God has foreknowledge of all future events, and yet that we do not sin by necessity? Anyone who says that an event can happen otherwise than as God has foreknown it is making an insane and malicious attempt to destroy God's foreknowledge. If God, therefore, foreknew that a good man would sin (and you must grant this, if you admit with me that God foreknows all future events)—if this is the case, I do not say that God should not have made the man, for He made him good, and the sin of the man He made cannot hurt God at all (on the contrary, in making him, God showed His goodness, for He showed His justice in punishing the man and His mercy in forgiving him); I do not say that God should not have made the man, but I do say this: since He foreknew that the man would sin, the sin was committed of necessity, because God foreknew that it would happen. How can there be free will where there is such inevitable necessity?

. . . .

Augustine. Surely this is the question that troubles and perplexes you: how can the following two propositions, that [1] God has foreknowledge of all future events, and that [2] we do not sin by necessity but by free will, be made consis-

tent with each other? "If God foreknows that man will sin," you say, "it is necessary that man sin." If man must sin, his sin is not a result of the will's choice, but is instead a fixed and inevitable necessity. You fear now that this reasoning results either in the blasphemous denial of God's foreknowledge or, if we deny this, the admission that we sin by necessity, not by will. Or does some other point bother you?

E. No, nothing else right now.

A. You think that all things of which God has foreknowledge come about by necessity, and not by will?

E. Absolutely.

A. Now pay careful attention. Look at yourself a little and tell me this, if you can: how are you going to will tomorrow, to sin or to act rightly?

E. I do not know.

A. Do you think that God does not know either?

E. Of course I do not.

A. If God knows what you are going to will tomorrow and foresees how all men who exist now or will exist are going to will in the future, He foresees much more what He will do about just men and about wicked ones.

E. Yes. If God foreknows my deeds, I would say much more confidently that He foreknows His own deeds and foresees most certainly what He will do.

A. If everything of which God has foreknowledge happens, not by will, but by necessity, shouldn't you be careful lest you say that God does what He is going to do by necessity too, and not by will?

E. When I said that everything that God foreknows happens by necessity, I meant only those things which occur in His creation, not what occurs in Himself, since these latter are eternal.

A. By this reasoning, God is not involved in His own creation.

E. He has decided once and for all how the

order of the universe He created is to be carried out, and does not arrange anything by a new act of will.

A. Does He not make anyone happy?

E. Yes, He does.

A. Then He is responsible when someone becomes happy.

E. Yes.

A. If, then, for example, you are to be happy a year from now, He will make you happy a year from now.

E. Yes.

A. Therefore, God foreknows today what He will do in a year.

E. He has always foreknown this. I also agree that He also foreknows it now if it is going to be so.

A. Please tell me: it is not the case, is it, that you are not His creature? Won't your happiness occur in you?

E. Of course! I am His creature and my happiness will occur in me.

A. Therefore, your happiness will come about in you, not by will, but by the necessity of God's action.

E. God's will is my necessity.

A. So you will be happy against your will!

E. Had I the power to be happy, I would surely be happy now. I wish to be happy now, and am not, because it is God, not I, who makes me happy.

A. How clearly truth cries out from you! For you could not maintain that anything is in our power except actions that are subject to our own will. Therefore, nothing is so completely in our power as the will itself, for it is ready at hand to act immediately, as soon as we will. Thus we are right in saying that we grow old by necessity, not by will; or that we die by necessity, not by will, and so on. Who but a madman would say that we do not will with the will?

Therefore, though God foreknows what we shall will in the future, this does not prove that we do not will anything voluntarily. In regard to happiness, you said (as if I would deny it) that you do not make yourself happy. I say, however, that when you are to be happy, you shall not be happy against your will, but because you will to be happy. When, therefore, God foreknows that you will be happy, it cannot be otherwise, or else there would be no such thing as foreknowledge. Nevertheless, we are not forced to believe, as a consequence of this, that you are going to be happy when you do not want to be. This is absurd and far from the truth. Moreover, just as God's foreknowledge, which today is certain of tomorrow's happiness, does not take from you the will to be happy when you begin to be happy; in the same way, a will which deserves blame, if it is going to be blameworthy, will nonetheless remain a will, since God foreknew that it would be so.

See, please, how blindly a man says, "If God has foreknown my will, it is necessary that I will what God foreknows, since nothing can occur except as he has foreknown it. If, moreover, my act of will is subject to necessity, we must admit that I willed it not by will, but by necessity." Strange foolishness! How could it be that nothing happens otherwise than as God foreknew, if He foreknows that something is going to be willed when nothing is going to be willed? I pass over the equally astounding assertion that I just said this man makes: "It is necessary that I will in this way." By assuming necessity, he tries to exclude will. If it is necessary that he will, how can he will, if there is no will?

If he says, in another way, that since it is necessary that he will, this very will is not in his power, he is to be answered with what I just said when I asked whether you would be happy without willing it. You answered that you would be happy if it were in your power to be happy, and that you wanted to, but were not yet able. Then I interposed that the truth had cried out from you because we cannot deny that we have the power, unless we cannot obtain what we will through an act of will or unless the will is absent. When we will, if the will itself is lacking in us, we surely do not will. If it cannot happen that when we will we do not will, then the will is present in the one who wills. And nothing else is in our power except what is present to us when we will. Our will, therefore, is not a will unless it is in our power. And since it is indeed in our power, it is free in us.

What we do not, or cannot, have in our power is not free for us. So it follows that we do not deny that God has foreknowledge of all things to be, and yet that we will what we will. For when He has foreknowledge of our will, it is going to be the will that He has foreknown. Therefore, the will is going to be a will because God has foreknowledge of it. Nor can it be a will if it is not in our power. Therefore, God also has knowledge of our power over it. So the power is not taken from me by His foreknowledge; but because of His foreknowledge, the power to will will more certainly be present in me, since God, whose foreknowledge does not err, has foreknown that I shall have the power.

E. I no longer deny that whatever God foreknows must come to be, and that he foreknows our sins in such a way that our will still remains free in us and lies in our power.

IV.B.2   God's Foreknowledge and Human Free Will Are Incompatible

NELSON PIKE

Nelson Pike is professor of philosophy at the University of California at Irvine. In this article he argues that given commonly held theological assumptions about God's nature, no human action is free. If God exists at a given time and holds infallible beliefs concerning what agents will do in the future, those actions cannot be free, because they could, then, cause it to be the case that what God believed was false.

In Part V, Section III of his *Consolatio Philosophiae*, Boethius entertained (though he later rejected) the claim that if God is omniscient, no human action is voluntary. This claim seems intuitively false. Surely, given only a doctrine describing God's *knowledge*, nothing about the voluntary status of human actions will follow. Perhaps such a conclusion would follow from a doctrine of divine omnipotence or divine providence, but what connection could there be between the claim that God is *omniscient* and the claim that human actions are determined? Yet Boethius thought he saw a problem here. He thought that if one collected together just the right assumptions and principles regarding God's knowledge, one could derive the conclusion that if God exists, no human action is voluntary. Of course, Boethius did not think that all the assumptions and principles required to reach this conclusion are true (quite the contrary), but he thought it important to draw attention to them nonetheless. If a theologian is to construct a doctrine of God's knowledge which does not commit him to determinism, he must first understand that there is a way of thinking about God's knowledge which would so commit him.

In this paper, I shall argue that although his claim has a sharp counterintuitive ring, Boethius was right in thinking that there is a selection from among the various doctrines and principles clustering about the notions of knowledge, omniscience, and God which, when brought together, demand the conclusion that if God exists, no human action is voluntary. Boethius, I think, did not succeed in making explicit all of the ingredients in the problem. His suspicions were sound, but his discussion was incomplete. His argument needs to be developed. This is the task I shall undertake in the pages to follow. I should like to make clear at the outset that my purpose in rearguing this thesis is not to show that determinism is true, nor to show that God does not exist, nor to show that

Reprinted from Nelson Pike, "Divine Omniscience and Voluntary Action," *The Philosophical Review* 74 (January 1965) by permission of the author and the editor.

either determinism is true or God does not exist. Following Boethius, I shall not claim that the items needed to generate the problem are either philosophically or theologically adequate. I want to concentrate attention on the implications of a certain set of assumptions. Whether the assumptions are themselves acceptable is a question I shall not consider.

I

A. Many philosophers have held that if a statement of the form "A knows X" is true, then "A believes X" is true and "X" is true. As a first assumption, I shall take this partial analysis of "A knows X" to be correct. And I shall suppose that since this analysis holds for all knowledge claims, it will hold when speaking of God's knowledge. "God knows X" entails "God believes X" and "'X' is true."

Secondly, Boethius said that with respect to the matter of knowledge, God "cannot in anything be mistaken."[1] I shall understand this doctrine as follows. Omniscient beings hold no false beliefs. Part of what is meant when we say that a person is omniscient is that the person in question believes nothing that is false. But, further, it is part of the "essence" of God to be omniscient. This is to say that any person who is not omniscient could not be the person we usually mean to be referring to when using the name "God." To put this last point a little differently: if the person we usually mean to be referring to when using the name "God" were suddenly to lose the quality of omniscience (suppose, for example, He came to believe something false), the resulting person would no longer be God. Although we might call this second person "God" (I might call my cat "God"), the absence of the quality of omniscience would be sufficient to guarantee that the person referred to was not the same as the person formerly called by that name. From this last doctrine it follows that the statement "If a given person is God, that person is omniscient" is an a priori truth. From this we may conclude that the statement "If a given person is God, that person holds no false beliefs" is also an a priori truth. It would be conceptually impossible

for God to hold a false belief. "'X' is true" follows from "God believes X." These are all ways of expressing the same principle—the principle expressed by Boethius in the formula "God cannot in anything be mistaken."

A second principle usually associated with the notion of divine omniscience has to do with the scope or range of God's intellectual gaze. To say that a being is omniscient is to say that he knows everything. "Everything" in this statement is usually taken to cover future, as well as present and past, events and circumstances. In fact, God is usually said to have had foreknowledge of everything that has ever happened. With respect to anything that was, is, or will be the case, God knew, *from eternity,* that it would be the case.

The doctrine of God's knowing everything from eternity is very obscure. One particularly difficult question concerning this doctrine is whether it entails that with respect to everything that was, is, or will be the case, God knew *in advance* that it would be the case. In some traditional theological texts, we are told that God is *eternal* in the sense that He exists "outside of time," that is, in the sense that He bears no temporal relations to the events or circumstances of the natural world.[2] In a theology of this sort, God could not be said to have known that a given natural event was going to happen before it happened. If God knew that a given natural event was going to occur *before* it occurred, at least one of God's cognitions would then have occurred before some natural event. This, surely, would violate the idea that God bears no temporal relations to natural events.[3] On the other hand, in a considerable number of theological sources, we are told that God *has always* existed—that He existed long *before* the occurrence of any natural event. In a theology of this sort, to say that God is eternal is not to say that God exists "outside of time" (bears no temporal relations to natural events), it is to say, instead, God has existed (and will continue to exist) at each moment.[4] The doctrine of omniscience which goes with this second understanding of the notion of eternity is one in which it is affirmed that God *has always* known that what was going to happen in the natural world. John Calvin wrote as follows:

When we attribute foreknowledge to God, we mean that all things have ever been and perpetually remain before, his eyes, so that to his knowledge nothing is future or past, but all things are present; and present in such manner, that he does not merely conceive of them from ideas formed in his mind, as things remembered by us appear to our minds, but really he holds and sees them as if (*tanquam*) actually placed before him.[5]

All things are "present" to God in the sense that He "sees" them as if (*tanquam*) they were actually before Him. Further, with respect to any given natural event, not only is that event "present" to God in the sense indicated, it has *ever been and has perpetually remained* "present" to Him in that sense. This latter is the point of special interest. Whatever one thinks of the idea that God "sees" things as if "actually placed before him," Calvin would appear to be committed to the idea that God has *always known* what was going to happen in the natural world. Choose an event (*E*) and a time (*T₂*) at which *E* occurred. For any time (*T₁*) prior to T_2 (say, five thousand, six hundred, or eighty years prior to T_2), God knew at T_1 that *E* would occur at T_2. It will follow from this doctrine, of course, that with respect to any human action, God knew well in advance of its performance that the action would be performed. Calvin says, "when God created man, He foresaw what would happen concerning him." He adds, "little more than five thousand years have elapsed since the creation of the world."[6] Calvin seems to have thought that God foresaw the outcome of every human action well over five thousand years ago.

In the discussion to follow, I shall work only with this second interpretation of God's knowing everything *from eternity*. I shall assume that if a person is omniscient, that person has always known what was going to happen in the natural world—and, in particular, has always known what human actions were going to be performed. Thus, as above, assuming that the attribute of omniscience is part of the "essence" of God, the statement "For any natural event (including human actions), if a given person is God, that person would always have known that that event was going to occur at the time it occurred" must be treated as an a priori truth. This is just another way of stating a point admirably put by St. Augustine when he said: "For to confess that God exists and at the same time to deny that He has foreknowledge of future things is the most manifest folly. . . . One who is not prescient of all future things is not God."[7]

B. Last Saturday afternoon, Jones mowed his lawn. Assuming that God exists and is (essentially) omniscient in the sense outlined above, it follows that (let us say) eighty years prior to last Saturday afternoon, God knew (and thus believed) that Jones would mow his lawn at that time. But from this it follows, I think, that at the time of action (last Saturday afternoon) Jones was not *able*—that is, it was not *within Jones's power*—to refrain from mowing his lawn.[8] If at the time of action, Jones had been able to refrain from mowing his lawn, then (the most obvious conclusion would seem to be) at the time of action, Jones was able to do something which would have brought it about that God held a false belief eighty years earlier. But God cannot in anything be mistaken. It is not possible that some belief of His was false. Thus, last Saturday afternoon, Jones was not able to do something which would have brought it about that God held a false belief eighty years ago. To suppose that it was would be to suppose that, at the time of action, Jones was able to do something having a conceptually incoherent description, namely something that would have brought it about that one of God's beliefs was false. Hence, given that God believed eighty years ago that Jones would mow his lawn on Saturday, if we are to assign Jones the power on Saturday to refrain from mowing his lawn, this power must not be described as the power to do something that would have rendered one of God's beliefs false. How then should we describe it vis-à-vis God and His belief? So far as I can see, there are only two other alternatives. First, we might try describing it as the power to do something that would have brought it about that God believed otherwise than He did eighty years ago; or, secondly, we might try describing it as the power to do something that would have brought it about that God (Who, by hypothesis, existed eighty years earlier) did not exist eighty years earlier—that is, as the power to do something that would have brought it about that any person who believed eighty years ago that Jones would mow his lawn on Saturday (one of whom was, by hypothesis, God) held a false belief, and thus was not God. But again, neither of these latter can be accepted. Last Saturday afternoon, Jones was not able to do something that would have brought it about that God believed otherwise than He did eighty years ago. Even if we suppose (as was suggested by Calvin) that eighty years ago God knew Jones would mow his lawn on Saturday in the sense that He "saw" Jones mowing his lawn as if this action were occurring before Him, the fact remains that God knew (and thus believed) eighty years prior to Saturday that Jones would mow his lawn. And if God held such a belief eighty years prior to Saturday, Jones did not have the power on Saturday to do something that would have made it the case that God did not hold this belief eighty years earlier. No action performed at a given time can alter the fact that a given person held a certain belief at a time prior to the time in question. This last seems to be an a priori truth. For similar reasons, the last of the above alternatives must also be rejected. On the assumption that God existed eighty years prior to Saturday, Jones on Saturday was not able to do something that would have brought it about that God did not exist eighty years prior to that time. No action performed at a given time can alter the fact that a certain person existed at a time prior to the time in question. This, too, seems to me to be an a priori truth. But if these observations are correct, then, given that Jones mowed his lawn on Saturday, and given that God exists and is (essentially) omniscient, it seems to follow that at the time of action, Jones did not have the power to refrain from mowing his lawn. The upshot of these reflections would appear to be that Jones's mowing his lawn last Saturday cannot be counted as a voluntary action. Although I do not have an analysis of what it is for action to be *voluntary,* it seems to me that a situation in which it would be wrong to assign Jones the *ability* or *power* to do *other* than he did would be a situation in which it would also be wrong to speak of his action as voluntary.

As a general remark, if God exists and is (essentially) omniscient in the sense specified above, no human action is voluntary.[9]

As the argument just presented is somewhat complex, perhaps the following schematic representation of it will be of some use.

1. "God existed at T_1" entails "If Jones did X at T_2, God believed at T_1 that Jones would do X at T_2."
2. "God believes X" entails "'X' is true."
3. It is not within one's power at a given time to do something having a description that is logically contradictory.
4. It is not within one's power at a given time to do something that would bring it about that someone who held a certain belief at a time prior to the time in question did not hold that belief at the time prior to the time in question.
5. It is not within one's power at a given time to do something that would bring it about that a person who existed at an earlier time did not exist at that earlier time.
6. If God existed at T_1 and if God believed at T_1 that Jones would do X at T_2, then if it was within Jones's power at T_2 to refrain from doing X, then (1) it was within Jones's power at T_2 to do something that would have brought it about that God held a false belief at T_1, of (2) it was within Jones's power at T_2 to do something which would have brought it about that God did not hold the belief He held at T_1, or (3) it was within Jones's power at T_2 to do something that would have brought it about that any person who believed at T_1 that Jones would do X at T_2 (one of whom was, by hypothesis, God) held a false belief and thus was not God—that is, that God (who by hypothesis existed at T_1) did not exist at T_1.
7. Alternative 1 in the consequent of item 6 is false (from 2 and 3).
8. Alternative 2 in the consequent of item 6 is false (from 4).
9. Alternative 3 in the consequent of item 6 is false (from 5).
10. Therefore, if God existed at T_1 and if God believed at T_1 that Jones would do X at T_2,

then it was not within Jones's power at T_2 to refrain from doing X (from 6 through 9).

11. Therefore, if God existed at T_1, and if Jones did X at T_2, it was not within Jones's power at T_2 to refrain from doing X (from 1 and 10).

In this argument, items 1 and 2 make explicit the doctrine of God's (essential) omniscience with which I am working. Items 3, 4, and 5 express what I take to be part of the logic of the concept of ability or power as it applies to human beings. Item 6 is offered as an analytic truth. If one assigns Jones the power to refrain from doing X at T_2 (given that God believed at T_1 that he would do X at T_2), so far as I can see, one would have to describe this power in one of the three ways listed in the consequent of item 6. I do not know how to argue that these are the only alternatives, but I have been unable to find another. Item 11, when generalized for all agents and actions, and when taken together with what seems to me to be a minimal condition for the application of "voluntary action," yields the conclusion that if God exists (and is essentially omniscient in the way I have described) no human action is voluntary.

C. It is important to notice that the argument given in the preceding paragraphs avoids use of two concepts that are often prominent in discussions of determinism.

In the first place, the argument makes no mention of the *causes* of Jones's action. Say (for example, with St. Thomas)[10] that God's foreknowledge of Jones's action was, itself, the cause of the action (though I am really not sure what this means). Say, instead, that natural events or circumstances caused Jones to act. Even say that Jones's action had no cause at all. The argument outlined above remains unaffected. If eighty years prior to Saturday, God believed that Jones would mow his lawn at that time, it was not within Jones's power at the time of action to refrain from mowing his lawn. The reasoning that justifies this assertion makes no mention of a causal series preceding Jones's action.

Secondly, consider the following line of thinking. Suppose Jones mowed his lawn last Saturday. It was then *true* eighty years ago that Jones would

mow his lawn at that time. Hence, on Saturday, Jones was not able to refrain from mowing his lawn. To suppose that he was would be to suppose that he was able on Saturday to do something that would have made false a proposition that was *already true* eighty years earlier. This general kind of argument for determinism is usually associated with Leibniz, although it was anticipated in Chapter IX of Aristotle's *De Interpretatione*. It has been used since, with some modification, in Richard Taylor's article, "Fatalism."[11] This argument, like the one I have offered above, makes no use of the notion of causation. It turns, instead, on the notion of its being *true eighty years ago* that Jones would mow his lawn on Saturday.

I must confess that I share the misgivings of those contemporary philosophers who have wondered what (if any) sense can be attached to a statement of the form "It was true at T_1 that E would occur at T_2."[12] Does this statement mean that had someone believed, guessed, or asserted at T_1 that E would occur at T_2, he would have been right?[13] (I shall have something to say about this form of determinism later in this paper.) Perhaps it means that at T_1 there was sufficient evidence upon which to predict that E would occur at T_2.[14] Maybe it means neither of these. Maybe it means nothing at all.[15] The argument presented above presupposes that it makes straightforward sense to suppose that God (or just anyone) held a true belief eighty years prior to Saturday. But this is not to suppose that *what* God believed *was true eighty years prior to Saturday*. Whether (or in what sense) it was true eighty years ago that Jones would mow his lawn on Saturday is a question I shall not discuss. As far as I can see, the argument in which I am interested requires nothing in the way of a decision on this issue.

II

I now want to consider three comments on the problem of divine foreknowledge which seem to be instructively incorrect.

A. Leibniz analyzed the problem as follows:

They say that what is foreseen cannot fail to exist and they say so truly; but it follows not that what is foreseen is necessary. For necessary truth is that whereof the contrary is impossible or implies a contradiction. Now the truth which states that I shall write tomorrow is not of that nature, it is not necessary. Yet, supposing that God foresees it, it is necessary that it come to pass, that is, the consequence is necessary, namely that it exist, since it has been foreseen; for God is infallible. This is what is termed a *hypothetical necessity*. But our concern is not this necessity; it is an *absolute* necessity that is required, to be able to say that an action is necessary, that it is not contingent, that it is not the effect of free choice.[16]

The statement "God believed at T_1 that Jones would do X at T_2" (where the interval between T_1 and T_2 is, for example, eighty years) does not entail "'Jones did X at T_2' is necessary." Leibniz is surely right about this. All that will follow from the first of these statements concerning "Jones did X at T_2" is that the latter is *true,* not that it is *necessarily true.* But this observation has no real bearing on the issue at hand. The following passage from St. Augustine's formulation of the problem may help to make this point clear.

> Your trouble is this. You wonder how it can be that these two propositions are not contradictory and incompatible, namely that God has foreknowledge of all future events, and that we sin voluntarily and not by necessity. For if, you say, God foreknows that a man will sin, he must necessarily sin. But if there is necessity there is no voluntary choice of sinning, but rather fixed and unavoidable necessity.[17]

In this passage, the term "necessity" (or the phrase "by necessity") is not used to express a modal-logical concept. The term "necessity" is here used in contrast with the term "voluntary," not (as in Leibniz) in contrast with the term "contingent." If one's action is necessary (or by necessity), this is to say that one's action is not voluntary. Augustine says that if God has foreknowledge of human actions, the actions are necessary. But the form of this conditional is "*P* implies *Q*," not "*P* implies *N* (*Q*)." "*Q*" in the consequent of this conditional is the claim that human actions are not voluntary— that is, that one is not able, or does not have the power, to do other than he does.

Perhaps I can make this point clearer by reformulating the original problem in such a way as to make explicit the modal operators working within it. Let it be *contingently* true that Jones did X at T_2. Since God holds a belief about the outcome of each human action well in advance of its performance, it is then *contingently* true that God believed at T_1 that Jones would do X at T_2. But it follows from this that it is *contingently* true that at T_2 Jones was not able to refrain from doing X. Had he been (contingently) able to refrain from doing X at T_2, then either he was (contingently) able to do something at T_2 that would have brought it about that God held a false belief at T_1, or he was (contingently) able to do something at T_2 that would have brought it about that God believed otherwise than He did at T_1, or he was (contingently) able to do something at T_2 that would have brought it about that God did not exist at T_1. None of these latter is an acceptable alternative.

B. In *Concordia Liberi Arbitrii,* Luis de Molina wrote as follows:

> It was not that since He foreknew what would happen from those things which depend on the created will that it would happen; but, on the contrary, it was because such things would happen through the freedom of the will, that He foreknew it; and that He would foreknow the opposite if the opposite was to happen.[18]

Remarks similar to this one can be found in a great many traditional and contemporary theological texts. In fact, Molina assures us that the view expressed in this passage has always been "above controversy"—a matter of "common opinion" and "unanimous consent"—not only among the Church fathers, but also, as he says, "among all catholic men."

One claim made in the above passage seems to me to be truly "above controversy." With respect to any given action foreknown by God, God would have foreknown the opposite if the opposite was to happen. If we assume the notion of omniscience outlined in the first section of this paper, and if we agree that omniscience is part of the "essence" of God, this statement is a conceptual truth. I doubt if anyone would be inclined to dispute it. Also involved in this passage, however, is at least the suggestion of a doctrine that cannot be taken as an item of "common opinion" among *all* catholic men. Molina says it is not because God foreknows what He foreknows that men act as they do: it is because men act as they do that God foreknows what He foreknows. Some theologians have rejected this claim. It seems to entail that men's actions determine God's cognitions. And this latter, I think, has been taken by some theologians to be a violation of the notion of God as self-sufficient and incapable of being affected by events of the natural world.[19] But I shall not develop this point further. Where the view put forward in the above passage seems to me to go wrong in an interesting and important way is in Molina's claim that God can have foreknowledge of things that will happen "through the freedom of the will." It is this claim that I here want to examine with care.

What exactly are we saying when we say that God can know in advance what will happen *through the freedom of the will?* I think that what Molina has in mind is this. God can know in advance that a given man is going to *choose* to perform a certain action sometime in the future. With respect to the case of Jones mowing his lawn, God knew at T_1 that Jones would *freely decide* to mow his lawn at T_2. Not only did God know at T_1 that Jones would mow his lawn at T_2, He also knew at T_1 that this action would be performed *freely*. In the words of Emil Brunner, "God knows that which will take place in freedom in the future as something which happens in freedom."[20] What God knew at T_1 is that Jones would *freely* mow his lawn at T_2.

I think that this doctrine is incoherent. If God knew (and thus believed) at T_1 that Jones would *do* X at T_2,[21] I think it follows that Jones was not able to do other than X at T_2 (for reasons already given). Thus, if God knew (and thus believed) at T_1 that Jones would *do* X at T_2, it would follow that Jones did X at T_2, but *not freely*. It does not seem to be possible that God could have believed at T_1 that Jones would freely do X at T_2. If God believed at T_1 that Jones would do X at T_2, Jones's action at T_2 was not free; and if God *also* believed at T_1 that Jones would freely act at T_2, it follows that God held a false belief at T_1—which is absurd.

C. Frederich Schleiermacher commented on the problem of divine foreknowledge as follows:

> In the same way, we estimate the intimacy between two persons by the foreknowledge one has of the actions of the other, without supposing that in either case, the one or the other's freedom is thereby endangered. So even the divine foreknowledge cannot endanger freedom.[22]

St. Augustine made this same point in *De Libero Arbitrio*. He said:

> Unless I am mistaken, you would not directly compel the man to sin, though you knew beforehand that he was going to sin. Nor does your prescience in itself compel him to sin even though he was certainly going to sin, as we must assume if you have real prescience. So there is no contradiction here. Simply you know beforehand what another is going to do with his own will. Similarly God compels no man to sin, though he sees beforehand those who are going to sin by their own will.[23]

If we suppose (with Schleiermacher and Augustine) that the case of an intimate friend having foreknowledge of another's action has the same implications for determinism as the case of God's foreknowledge of human actions, I can imagine two positions which might then be taken. First, one might hold (with Schleiermacher and Augustine) that God's foreknowledge of human actions cannot entail determinism—since it is clear that an intimate friend can have foreknowledge of another's voluntary actions. Or, secondly, one might hold that an intimate friend cannot have foreknowledge of another's voluntary actions—since it is clear that God cannot have foreknowledge of such actions. This second position could take either of two forms. One might hold that since an intimate friend *can* have foreknowledge of another's actions, the actions in question cannot be voluntary. Or, alternatively, one might hold that since the other's actions *are* voluntary, the intimate friend cannot have foreknowledge of them.[24] But what I propose to argue in the remaining pages of this paper is that Schleiermacher and Augustine were mistaken in supposing that the case of an intimate friend having foreknowledge of other's actions has the same implications for determinism as the case of God's foreknowledge of human actions. What I want to suggest is that the argument I used above to show that God cannot have foreknowledge of voluntary actions cannot be used to show that an intimate friend cannot have foreknowledge of another's actions. Even if one holds that an intimate friend *can* have foreknowledge of another's voluntary actions, one ought not to think that the case is the same when dealing with the problem of divine foreknowledge.

Let Smith be an ordinary man and an intimate friend of Jones. Now, let us start by supposing that Smith believed at T_1 that Jones would do X at T_2. We make no assumption concerning the truth or falsity of Smith's belief, but assume only that Smith held it. Given only this much, there appears to be no difficulty in supposing that at T_2 Jones was able to do X and that at T_2 Jones was able to do not-X. So far as the above description of the case is concerned, it might well have been within Jones's power at T_2 to do something (namely, X) which would have brought it about that Smith held a true belief at T_1, and it might well have been within Jones's power at T_2 to do something (namely, not-X) which would have brought it about that Smith held a false belief at T_1. So much seems apparent.

Now let us suppose that Smith *knew* at T_1 that Jones would do X at T_2. This is to suppose that Smith correctly believed (with evidence) at T_1 that Jones would do X at T_2. It follows, to be sure, that Jones *did* X at T_2. But now let us inquire about what Jones was *able* to do at T_2. I submit that there is nothing in the description of this case that requires the conclusion that it was not within Jones's power at T_2 to refrain from doing X. By hypothesis, the belief held by Smith at T_1 was true. Thus, by hypothesis, Jones did X at T_2. But even if we assume that the belief held by Smith at T_1 was *in fact* true, we can add that the belief held by Smith at T_1 *might have* turned out to be false.[25] Thus, even if we say that Jones *in fact* did X at T_2, we can add that Jones *might not* have done X at T_2—meaning by this that it was within Jones's power at T_2 to refrain from doing X. Smith held a true belief which might have turned out to be false, and, correspondingly, Jones performed an action which he was able to refrain from performing. Given that Smith correctly believed at T_1 that Jones would do

X at T_2, we can still assign Jones the *power* at T_2 to refrain from doing X. All we need add is that the power in question is one which Jones *did not exercise*.

These last reflections have no application, however, when dealing with God's foreknowledge. Assume that God (being essentially omniscient) existed at T_1, and assume that He believed at T_1 that Jones would do X at T_2. It follows, again, that Jones did X at T_2. God's beliefs are true. But now, as above, let us inquire into what Jones was *able* to do at T_2. We cannot claim now, as in the Smith case, that the belief held by God at T_1 was *in fact* true but *might have* turned out to be false. No sense of "might have" has application here. It is a conceptual truth that God's beliefs are true. Thus, we cannot claim, as in the Smith case, that Jones *in fact* acted in accordance with God's beliefs but had the *ability* to refrain from so doing. The ability to refrain from acting in accordance with one of God's beliefs would be the ability to do something that would bring it about that one of God's beliefs was false. And no one could have an ability of this description. Thus, in the case of God's foreknowledge of Jones's action at T_2, if we are to assign Jones the ability at T_2 to refrain from doing X, we must understand this ability in some way other than the way we understood it when dealing with Smith's foreknowledge. In this case, either we must say that it was the ability at T_2 to bring it about that God believed otherwise than He did at T_1; or we must say that it was the ability at T_2 to bring it about that any person who believed at T_1 that Jones would do X at T_2 (one of whom was, by hypothesis, God) held a false belief and thus was not God. But, as pointed out earlier, neither of these last alternatives can be accepted.

The important thing to be learned from the study of Smith's foreknowledge of Jones's action is that the problem of divine foreknowledge has as one of its pillars the claim that truth is *analytically* connected with God's *beliefs*. No problem of determinism arises when dealing with human knowledge of future actions. This is because truth is not analytically connected with human belief even when (as in the case of human knowledge) truth is contingently conjoined to belief. If we suppose that Smith knows at T_1 that Jones will do X at T_2, what we are supposing is that Smith believes at T_1 that Jones will do X at T_2 and (as an additional, contingent, fact) that the belief in question is true. Thus having supposed that Smith knows at T_1 that Jones will do X at T_2, when we turn to a consideration of the situation of T_2 we can infer (1) that Jones *will* do X at T_2 (since Smith's belief is true), and (2) that Jones does not have the power at T_2 to do something that would bring it about that Jones did not *believe* as he did at T_1. But paradoxical though it may seem (and it seems paradoxical only at first sight), Jones can have the power at T_2 to do something that would bring it about that Smith did not have *knowledge* at T_1. This is simply to say that Jones can have the *power* at T_2 to do something that would bring it about that the belief held by Smith at T_1 (which was, in fact, true) was (instead) false. We are required only to add that since Smith's belief was in fact true (that is, was knowledge) Jones *did not* (in fact) *exercise* that power. But when we turn to a consideration of God's foreknowledge of Jones's action at T_2 the elbowroom between belief and truth disappears and, with it, the possibility of assigning Jones even the *power* of doing other than he does at T_2. We begin by supposing that God *knows* at T_1 that Jones will do X at T_2. As above, this is to suppose that God believes at T_1 that Jones will do X at T_2, and it is to suppose that this belief is true. But it is *not* an additional, contingent fact that the belief held by God is true. "God believes X" entails "X is true." Thus, having supposed that God knows (and thus believes) at T_1 that Jones will do X at T_2, we can infer (1) that Jones *will do X* at T_2 (since God's belief is true); (2) that Jones does not have the power at T_2 to do something that would bring it about that God did not hold the belief He held at T_1, and (3) that Jones does not have the power at T_2 to do something that would bring it about that the belief held by God at T_1 was false. This last is what we could *not* infer when truth and belief were only factually connected—as in the case of Smith's knowledge. To be sure, "Smith knows at T_1 that Jones will do X at T_2" and "God knows at T_1 that Jones will do X at T_2" both entail "Jones will do X at T_2" ("A knows X" entails "'X' is true"). But this similarity be-

tween "Smith knows X" and "God knows X" is not a point of any special interest in the present discussion. As Schleiermacher and Augustine rightly insisted (and as we discovered in our study of Smith's foreknowledge) the mere fact that someone knows in advance how another will act in the future is not enough to yield a problem of the sort we have been discussing. We begin to get a glimmer of the knot involved in the problem of divine foreknowledge when we shift attention away from the *similarities* between "Smith knows X" and "God knows X" (in particular, that they both entail "'X' is true") and concentrate instead on the logical *differences* which obtain between Smith's knowledge and God's knowledge. We get to the difference which makes the difference when, after analyzing the notion of knowledge as true belief (supported by evidence) we discover the radically dissimilar relations between truth and belief in the two cases. When truth is only factually connected with belief (as in Smith's knowledge) one can have the power (though, by hypothesis, one will not exercise it) to do something that would make the belief false. But when truth is analytically connected with belief (as in God's belief) no one can have the power to do something which would render the belief false.

To conclude: I have assumed that any statement of the form "A knows X" entails a statement of the form "A believes X" as well as a statement of the form "'X' is true." I have then supposed (as an analytic truth) that if a given person is omniscient, that person (1) holds no false beliefs, and (2) holds beliefs about the outcome of human actions in advance of their performance. In addition, I have assumed that the statement "If a given person is God that person is omniscient" is an a priori statement. (This last I have labeled the doctrine of God's essential omniscience.) Given these items (plus some premises concerning what is and what is not within one's power), I have argued that if God exists, it is not within one's power to do other than he does. I have inferred from this that if God exists, no human action is voluntary.

As emphasized earlier, I do not want to claim that the assumptions underpinning the argument are acceptable. In fact, it seems to me that a theologian interested in claiming both that God is omniscient and that men have free will could deny any one (or more) of them. For example, a theologian might deny that a statement of the form "*A* knows *X*" entails a statement of the form "*A* believes *X*" (some contemporary philosophers have denied this) or, alternatively, he might claim that this entailment holds in the case of human knowledge but fails in the case of God's knowledge. This latter would be to claim that when knowledge is attributed to God, the term "knowledge" bears a sense other than the one it has when knowledge is attributed to human beings. Then again, a theologian might object to the analysis of "omniscience" with which I have been working. Although I doubt if any Christian theologian would allow that an omniscient being could believe something false, he might claim that a given person could be omniscient although he did not hold beliefs about the outcome of human actions *in advance* of their performance. (This latter is the way Boethius escaped the problem.) Still again, a theologian might deny the doctrine of God's essential omniscience. He might admit that if a given person is God that person is omniscient, but he might deny that this statement formulates an a priori truth. This would be to say that although God is omniscient, He is not *essentially* omniscient. So far as I can see, within the conceptual framework of theology employing any one of these adjustments, the problem of divine foreknowledge outlined in this paper could not be formulated. There thus appears to be a rather wide range of alternatives open to the theologian at this point. It would be a mistake to think that commitment to determinism is an unavoidable implication of the Christian concept of divine omniscience.

But having arrived at this understanding, the importance of the preceding deliberations ought not to be overlooked. There is a pitfall in the doctrine of divine omniscience. That knowing involves believing (truly) is surely a tempting philosophical view (witness the many contemporary philosophers who have affirmed it). And the idea that God's attributes (including omniscience) are essentially connected to His nature, together with the idea that an omniscient being would hold no false beliefs and would hold beliefs about the outcome of human actions in advance of their performance, might be taken by some theologians as obvious candidates for inclusion in a finished Christian theology. Yet the theologian must approach these items critically. If they are embraced together, then if one affirms the existence of God, one is committed to the view that no human action is voluntary.

Notes

1. *Consolatio Philosophiae*, Bk. V, sec. 3, par. 6.
2. This position is particularly well formulated in St. Anselm's *Proslogium*, ch. xix and *Monologium*, chs. xxi–xxii; and in Frederich Schleiermacher's *The Christian Faith*, Pt. I, sec. 2, par. 51. It is also explicit in Boethius, op. cit., secs. 4–6, and in St. Thomas' *Summa Theologica*, Pt. I, Q. 10.
3. This point is explicit in Boethius, op. cit., secs. 4–6.
4. This position is particularly well expressed in William Paley's *Natural Theology*, ch. xxiv. It is also involved in John Calvin's discussion of predestination, *Institutes of the Christian Religion*, Bk. III, ch. xxi; and in some formulations of the first cause argument for existence of God, e.g., John Locke's *Essay Concerning Human Understanding*, Bk. IV, ch. x.
5. *Institutes of the Christian Religion*, Bk. III, ch. xxi; this passage trans. by John Allen (Philadelphia, 1813), II, 145.
6. Ibid., p. 144.
7. *City of God*, Bk. V, sec. 9.
8. The notion of someone being *able* to do something and the notion of something being *within one's power* are essentially the same. Traditional formulations of the problem of divine foreknowledge (e.g., those of Boethius and Augustine) made use of the notion of what is (and what is not) *within one's power*. But the problem is the same when framed in terms of what one is (and one is not) *able* to do. Thus, I shall treat the statements "Jones was able to do *X*," "Jones had the ability to do *X*," and "It was within Jones's power to do *X*" as equivalent. Richard Taylor, in "I Can," *Philosophical Review*, LXIX (1960), 78–89, has argued that the notion of ability or power involved in these last three statements is incapable of philosophical analysis. Be this as it may, I shall not here attempt such an analysis. In what follows I shall, however, be careful to affirm only those statements about what is (or is not) within one's power that would have to be preserved on any analysis of this notion having even the most distant claim to adequacy.
9. In Bk. II, ch. xxi, secs. 8–11 of the *Essay*, John

Locke says that an agent is not *free* with respect to a given action (i.e., that an action is done "under necessity") when it is not within the agent's power to do otherwise. Locke allows a special kind of case, however, in which an action may be *voluntary* though done under necessity. If a man chooses to do something without knowing that it is not within his power to do otherwise (e.g., if a man chooses to stay in a room without knowing that the room is locked), his action may be voluntary though he is not free to forbear it. If Locke is right in this (and I shall not argue the point one way or the other), replace "voluntary" with (let us say) "free" in the above paragraph and throughout the remainder of this paper.

10. *Summa Theologica*, Pt. I, Q. 14, a. 8.

11. *Philosophical Review*, LXXI (1962), 56–66. Taylor argues that if an event *E* fails to occur at T_2, then at T_1 it was true that *E* would fail to occur at T_2. Thus, at T_1, a necessary condition of anyone's performing an action sufficient for the occurrence of *E* at T_2 is missing. Thus at T_1, no one could have the power to perform an action that would be sufficient for the occurrence of *E* at T_2. Hence, no one has the power at T_1 to do something sufficient for the occurrence of an event at T_2 that is not going to happen. The parallel between this argument and the one recited above can be seen very clearly if one reformulates Taylor's argument, pushing back the time at which it was true that *E* would not occur at T_2.

12. For a helpful discussion of difficulties involved here, see Rogers Albritton's "Present Truth and Future Contingency," a reply to Richard Taylor's "The Problem of Future Contingency," both in the *Philosophical Review*, LXVI (1957), 1–28.

13. Gilbert Ryle interprets it this way. See "It Was To Be," *Dilemmas* (Cambridge, 1954).

14. Richard Gale suggests this interpretation in "Endorsing Predictions," *Philosophical Review*, LXX (1961), 378–385.

15. This view is held by John Turk Saunders in "Sea Fight Tomorrow?" *Philosophical Review*, LXVII (1958), 367–378.

16. *Théodicée*, Pt. I, sec. 37. This passage trans. by E. M. Huggard (New Haven, 1952), p. 144.

17. *De Libero Arbitrio*, Bk. III. This passage trans. by J. H. S. Burleigh, *Augustine's Earlier Writings* (Philadelphia, 1955).

18. This passage trans. by John Mourant, *Readings in the Philosophy of Religion* (New York, 1954), p. 426.

19. Cf. Boethius' *Consolatio*, Bk. V, sec. 3, par. 2.

20. *The Christian Doctrine of God*, trans. by Olive Wyon (Philadelphia, 1964), p. 262.

21. Note: no comment here about *freely* doing *X*.

22. *The Christian Faith*, Pt. I, sec. 2, par. 55. This passage trans. by W. R. Matthew (Edinburgh, 1928), p. 228.

23. Loc. cit.

24. This last seems to be the position defended by Richard Taylor in "Deliberation and Foreknowledge," *American Philosophical Quarterly*, I (1964).

25. The phrase "might have" as it occurs in this sentence does not express mere *logical* possibility. I am not sure how to analyze the notion of possibility involved here, but I think it is roughly the same notion as is involved when we say, "Jones might have been killed in the accident (had it not been for the fact that at the last minute he decided not to go)."

IV.B.3   God's Foreknowledge and Human Free Will Are Compatible

ALVIN PLANTINGA

Alvin Plantinga is professor of philosophy at the University of Notre Dame. In this article he appeals to the notion of possible worlds in order to show that Pike's logic misfires and that there really is no incompatibility between divine foreknowledge and human free will.

The last argument I wish to discuss is perhaps only mildly atheological. This is the claim that God's omniscience is incompatible with *human freedom*. Many people are inclined to think that if God is omniscient, then human beings are never free. Why? Because the idea that God is omniscient implies that at any given time God knows not only what *has* taken place and what *is* taking place, but also what *will* take place. He knows the future as well as the past. But now suppose He knows that Paul will perform some trivial action tomorrow—having an orange for lunch, let's say. If God knows in advance that Paul will have an orange for lunch tomorrow, then it must be the case that he'll have an orange tomorrow; and if it *must* be the case that Paul will have an orange tomorrow, then it isn't possible that Paul will *refrain* from so doing—in which case he won't be free to refrain, and hence won't be free with respect to the action of taking the orange. So if God knows in advance that a person will perform a certain action *A*, then that person isn't free with respect to that action. But if God is omniscient, then for any person and any action he performs, God knew in advance that he'd perform that action. So if God is omniscient, no one ever performs any free actions.

This argument may initially sound plausible,

but the fact is it is based upon confusion. The central portion can be stated as follows:

(49) If God knows in advance that *X* will do *A*, then it must be the case that *X* will do *A*

and

(50) If it must be the case that *X* will do *A*, then *X* is not free to refrain from *A*.

From (49) and (50) it follows that if God knows in advance that someone will take a certain action, then that person isn't free with respect to that action. But (49) bears further inspection. Why should we think it's *true*? Because, we shall be told, if God *knows* that *X* will do *A*, it *logically follows* that *X* will do *A*: it's necessary that if God knows that *p*, then *p* is true. But this defense of (49) suggests that the latter is *ambiguous*; it may mean either

(49a) Necessarily, if God knows in advance that *X* will do *A*, then indeed *X* will do *A*

or

(49b) If God knows in advance that *X* will do *A*, then it is necessary that *X* will do *A*.

The atheological argument requires the truth of (49b); but the above defense of (49) supports only (49a), not (49b). It is indeed necessarily true that if God (or anyone else) knows that a proposition *P* is true, then *P* is true; but it simply doesn't follow that if God knows *P*, then *P* is *necessarily* true. *If I know that Henry is a bachelor, then Henry is a bachelor* is a necessary truth; it does not follow that if I know that Henry is a bachelor, then it is necessarily true that he is. I know that Henry is a bachelor: what follows is only that *Henry is married* is false; it doesn't follow that it is necessarily false.

So the claim that divine omniscience is incompatible with human freedom seems to be based

Reprinted from Alvin Plantinga, *God, Freedom and Evil* (New York: Harper & Row, 1974), 66–72, by permission of the author.

upon confusion. Nelson Pike has suggested[1] an interesting revision of this old claim: he holds, not that human freedom is incompatible with God's being omniscient, but with God's being *essentially* omniscient. Recall (p. 50) that an object X has a property P *essentially* if X has P in every world in which X exists—if, that is, it is impossible that X should have existed but *lacked P*. Now many theologians and philosophers have held that at least some of God's important properties are essential to him in this sense. It is plausible to hold, for example, that God is essentially omnipotent. Things could have gone differently in various ways; but if there had been no omnipotent being, then God would not have existed. *He* couldn't have been powerless or limited in power. But the same may be said for God's *omniscience*. If God is omniscient, then He is unlimited in knowledge; He knows every true proposition and believes none that are false. If He is *essentially* omniscient, furthermore, then He not only *is not* limited in knowledge; He *couldn't* have been. There is no possible world in which He exists but fails to know some truth or believes some falsehood. And Pike's claim is that this belief—the belief that God is essentially omnipotent—is inconsistent with human freedom.

To argue his case Pike considers the case of Jones, who mowed his lawn at T_2—last Saturday, let's say. Now suppose that God is essentially omniscient. Then at any earlier time T_1—80 years ago, for example—God believed that Jones would mow his lawn at T_2. Since He is *essentially* omniscient, furthermore, it isn't possible that God falsely believes something; hence His having believed at T_1 that Jones would mow his lawn at T_2 entails that Jones does indeed mow his lawn at T_2. Pike's argument (in his own words) then goes as follows:

1. "God existed at T_1" entails "If Jones did X at T_2, God believed at T_1 that Jones would do X at T_2."
2. "God believes X" entails "X is true."
3. It is not within one's power at a given time to do something having a description that is logically contradictory.

4. It is not within one's power at a given time to do something that would bring it about that someone who held a certain belief at a time prior to the time in question did not hold that belief at the time prior to the time in question.
5. It is not within one's power at a given time to do something that would bring it about that a person who existed at an earlier time did not exist at that earlier time.
6. If God existed at T_1 and if God believed at T_1 that Jones would do X at T_2, then if it was within Jones' power at T_2 to refrain from doing X, then (1) it was within Jones' power at T_2 to do something that would have brought it about that God held a false belief at T_1, or (2) it was within Jones' power at T_2 to do something which would have brought it about that God did not hold the belief He held at T_1, or (3) it was within Jones' power at T_2 to do something that would have brought it about that any person who believed at T_1 that Jones would do X at T_2 (one of whom was, by hypothesis, God) held a false belief and thus was not God—that is, that God (who by hypothesis existed at T_1) did not exist at T_1.
7. Alternative 1 in the consequent of item 6 is false (from 2 and 3).
8. Alternative 2 in the consequent of item 6 is false (from 4).
9. Alternative 3 in the consequent of item 6 is false (from 5).
10. Therefore, if God existed at T_1 and if God believed at T_1 that Jones would do X at T_2, then it was not within Jones' power at T_2 to refrain from doing X (from 1 and 10).[2]

What about this argument? The first two premises simply make explicit part of what is involved in the idea that God is essentially omniscient; so there is no quarreling with them. Premises 3–5 also seem correct. But that complicated premise (6) warrants a closer look. What exactly does it say? I think we can understand Pike here as follows. Consider

(51) God existed at T_1, and God believed at T_1 that Jones would do *X* at T_2, and it was within Jones' power to refrain from doing *X* at T_2.

What Pike means to say, I believe, is that either (51) entails

(52) It was within Jones' power at T_2 to do something that would have brought it about that God held a false belief at T_1

or (51) entails

(53) It was within Jones' power at T_2 to do something that would have brought it about that God did not hold the belief He did hold at T_1

or it entails

(54) It was within Jones' power at T_2 to do something that would have brought it about that anyone who believed at T_1 that Jones would do X at T_2 (one of whom was by hypothesis God) held a false belief and thus was not God—that is, that God (who by hypothesis existed at T_1) did not exist at T_1.

[The remainder of Pike's reasoning consists in arguing that each of (52), (53), and (54) is necessarily false, if God is essentially omniscient; hence (51) is necessarily false, if God is essentially omniscient, which means that God's being essentially omniscient is incompatible with human freedom.] Now suppose we look at these one at a time. Does (51) entail (52)? No. (52) says that it was within Jones' power to do something—namely, refrain from doing X—such that if he had done that thing, then God *would have* held a false belief at T_1. But this does not follow from (51). If Jones had refrained from X, then a proposition that God *did in fact* believe would have been false; but if Jones had refrained from X at T_2, then God (since He is omniscient) *would not have believed at T_1 that Jones will do X at T_2*—indeed, He would have held the true belief that Jones will *refrain* from doing X at T_2. What follows from (51) is not (52) but only (52'):

(52') It was within Jones' power to do something such that if he had done it, then a belief that God *did hold* at T_1 *would have been* false.

But (52') is not at all paradoxical and in particular does not imply that it was within Jones' power to

do something that would have brought it about that God held a false belief.

Perhaps we can see this more clearly if we look at it from the vantage point of possible worlds. We are told by (51) both that in the actual world God believes that Jones does X at T_2 and also that it is within Jones' power to *refrain* from doing X at T_2. Now consider any world W in which Jones *does* refrain from doing X. In *that* world, a belief that God holds in the actual world—in Kronos—is false. That is, if W had been actual, then a belief that God does *in fact* hold would have been false. But it does not follow that in W God holds a false belief. For it doesn't follow that if W had been actual, God would have believed that Jones would do X at T_2. Indeed, if God is essentially omniscient (omniscient in every world in which He exists) what follows is that in W God did *not* believe at T_1 that Jones will do X at T_2; He believed instead that Jones will *refrain* from X. So (51) by no means implies that it was within Jones' power to bring it about that God held a false belief at T_1.

What about

(53) It was within Jones' power at T_2 to do something that would have brought it about that God did not hold the belief He did hold at T_1?

Here the first problem is one of understanding. How are we to take this proposition? One way is this. What (53) says is that it was within Jones' power, at T_2, to do something such that if he had done it, then at T_1 God would have held a certain belief and also *not* held that belief. That is, (53) so understood attributes to Jones the power to bring about a contradictory state of affairs [call this interpretation (53a)]. (53a) is obviously and resoundingly false; but there is no reason whatever to think that (51) entails it. What (51) entails is rather

(53b) It was within Jones' power at T_2 to do something such that if he had done it, then God would not have held a belief that in fact he did hold.

This follows from (51) but is perfectly innocent. For suppose again that (51) is true, and consider a world *W* in which Jones refrains from doing *X*. If God is essentially omniscient, then in this world *W* He is omniscient and hence does not believe at T_1 that Jones will do *X* at T_2. So what follows from (51) is the harmless assertion that it was within Jones' power to do something such that if he had done it, then God would not have held a belief that in fact (in the actual world) He did hold. But by no stretch of the imagination does it follow that if Jones had done it, then it would have been true that God *did* hold a belief He didn't hold. Taken one way (53) is obviously false but not a consequence of (51); taken the other it is a consequence of (51) but by no means obviously false.

(54) fares no better. What it says is that it was within Jones' power at T_2 to do something such that if he had done it, then God would not have been omniscient and thus would not have been God. But this simply doesn't follow from (51). The latter does, of course, entail

(54') It was within Jones' power to do something such that if he'd done it, then anyone who believed at T_1 that Jones would do *X* at T_2 would have held a false belief.

For suppose again that (51) is in fact true, and now consider one of those worlds *W* in which Jones refrains from doing *X*. In that world

(55) Anyone who believed at T_1 that Jones will do *X* at T_2 held a false belief

is true. That is, if *W* had been actual, (55) would have been true. But again in *W* God does not believe that Jones will do *X* at T_2; (55) is *true* in *W* but isn't relevant to God there. If Jones had refrained from *X*, then (55) would have been true. It

does not follow that God would not have been omniscient; for in those worlds in which Jones does not do *X* at T_2, God does not believe at T_1 that He does.

Perhaps the following is a possible source of confusion here. If God is *essentially* omniscient, then He is omniscient in every possible world in which He exists. Accordingly there is no possible world in which He holds a false belief. Now consider any belief that God does in fact hold. It might be tempting to suppose that if He is essentially omniscient, then He holds that belief in every world in which He exists. But of course this doesn't follow. It is not essential to Him to hold the beliefs He does hold; what is essential to Him is the quite different property of holding only true beliefs. So if a belief is true in Kronos but false in some world *W*, then in Kronos God holds that belief and in *W* He does not.

Much more should be said about Pike's piece, and there remain many fascinating details. I shall leave them to you, however. And by way of concluding our study of natural atheology: none of the arguments we've examined has prospects for success; all are unacceptable. There are arguments we haven't considered, of course; but so far the indicated conclusion is that natural atheology doesn't work.

Notes

1. Nelson Pike, "Divine Omniscience and Voluntary Action," *Philosophical Review* 74 (January 1965): 27.

2. Ibid., pp. 33–34.

IV.C   God's Omnipotence

Omnipotence has traditionally been seen as one of God's attributes, for if God is a being possessing all perfections, surely he must possess omnipotence as a significant perfection. But what exactly is omnipotence? Is it the ability to do just anything at all? Some philosophers, following Descartes, hold that it even includes violating logical truths. However, the implications of this view seem catastrophic for any intelligent talk of God (since all rational discussion presupposes the laws of logic). If we do not presuppose that the laws of logic apply to God, we might just as well say that God does and does not exist at the same time, for a contradiction fails to describe any state of affairs at all. Hence, the overwhelming majority of philosophers and theologians, at least since Aquinas, have not included the notion of doing the logically impossible as being part of the perfections of God. We may roughly define omnipotence as the ability to do whatever is not logically impossible. God can create a universe, but he cannot square a circle.

Still, there are problems with this definition. On the surface, at least, it does not seem contradictory to say that God could make a stone heavier than he could lift or that he could sin if he wanted to (though his being perfectly good keeps him from exercising this power). Consider the paradox of the stone argument, as formulated by Wade Savage*:

1. Either x can create a stone that x cannot lift, or x cannot create a stone that x cannot lift.
2. If x can create a stone that x cannot lift, then, necessarily, there is at least one task that x cannot perform (namely, lift the stone in question).
3. If x cannot create a stone that x cannot lift, then, necessarily, there is at least one act that x cannot perform (namely, create the stone in question).

4. Hence, there is at least one task that x cannot perform.
5. If x is an omnipotent being, then x can perform any task.
6. Therefore, x is not omnipotent.

Since x could be any being whatsoever, the paradox apparently proves that the notion of omnipotence is incoherent.

Note first that there are some things that traditional theism admits God cannot control. God cannot create free beings, capable of choosing right and wrong, without giving up his power to control them. Can God make a world that he cannot control? Can he limit his own omnipotence? Theologians are divided on this issue, some saying that God cannot give up his omnipotence, for he is *essentially* omnipotent and any such ability would be a weakness. Others disagree and say that a God who can voluntarily limit himself is more powerful than a God who cannot. For these theologians, God's omnipotence is *nonessential.*

Your response to the paradox of the stone may depend on which view of omnipotence you accept. In our readings, George Mavrodes embraces the first alternative, presupposing that God is *essentially* omnipotent and so *cannot* create a stone heavier than he can lift, because such an act turns out to be logically impossible. This solution has been criticized by Savage as a case of question begging, supposing as it does that the statement 'God is omnipotent' is necessarily true.

The second line of thought, which Alvin Plantinga and Richard Swinburne take, is that God's omnipotence would enable him to create such a stone but this fact does not lessen his ability *unless* he does indeed create such a stone. Swinburne is worth quoting at this point.

True, if an omnipotent being actually exercises (as opposed to merely possessing) his ability to

---

* The Philosophical Review 76 (1967), 75f.

bring about the existence of a stone too heavy for him subsequently to bring about its rising, then he will cease to be omnipotent. . . . But the omnipotence of a person at a certain time includes the ability to make himself no longer omnipotent, an ability which he may or may not choose to exercise. A person may remain omnipotent forever because he never exercises his power to create stones too heavy to lift, forces too strong to resist, or universes too wayward to control.*

Similar to the paradox of the stone but more crucial to our idea of God is the question of whether God's omnipotence gives him the power to sin! Again, Aquinas and many medieval theologians argue that such power would be pseudopower, in fact, impotence. Others, following William of Ockham, have argued that God necessarily cannot sin, because sin is defined as simply being that which is opposed to God's will and God cannot oppose his own will at one and the same time. (This view presupposes a divine command theory of goodness, which we examine in Part 8.) Still others, such as Richard Swinburne, argue that an omniscient and perfectly free being cannot sin because sin necessarily involves a failure in reason or free-

dom.† It is not clear that Swinburne's conditions for sin are the only possible ones. In our third reading Nelson Pike argues that omnipotence includes the ability to sin. It is logically possible for God to do evil, but it is highly unlikely that he ever will because he always happens to will to do good. God "cannot bring himself to do evil" because that would violate a "firm and stable feature of his nature."

Finally, Peter Geach argues that the whole notion of omnipotence is really a Greek extravagance and that the Scriptures know no such concept. The Bible offers us a notion of almightiness but not omnipotence. Geach's argument is similar to that of the process theologians, as represented by Charles Hartshorne. So long as God is powerful enough to create and sustain the heavens and the earth, including our lives, and so long as he knows a great deal more than we do, is able to forgive us our sins and raise the dead, and, most importantly, is perfectly good, God is eminently worthy of our worship. We do not need nor should we crave the logically neat but personally frigid omnipotent, immutable, and omniscient God of Greek philosophy; the personal God of the Bible is far more appropriate for our needs.

---

* *The Coherence of Theism* (Oxford: Oxford Univ. Press, 1977), 157f.

† Ibid., 202f.

IV.C.1 Is God's Power Limited?

ST. THOMAS AQUINAS

Thomas Aquinas (1225–1274), one of the greatest theologians in the Western tradition, argues that although it is difficult to explain what God's omnipotence is, it includes only those things that are logically possible. Since God contains all perfec-

tions and sinning is an imperfection, the ability to sin is not part of his omnipotence.

We proceed thus to the Third Article:

Objection 1. It seems that God is not omnipotent. For movement and passiveness belong to everything. But this is impossible for God, since He is immovable, as was said above. Therefore He is not omnipotent.

From *Summa Theologica*, part 1, in *The Basic Writings of St. Thomas Aquinas*, vol. 1, edited by Anton C. Pegis (New York: Random House, 1945), 262–64, by permission of the Anton Pegis Estate.

Obj. 2. Further, sin is an act of some kind. But God cannot sin, nor *deny Himself,* as it is said *2 Tim.* ii. 13. Therefore He is not omnipotent.

Obj. 3. Further, it is said of God that He manifests His omnipotence *especially by sparing and having mercy.* Therefore the greatest act possible to the divine power is to spare and have mercy. There are things much greater, however, than sparing and having mercy; for example, to create another world, and the like. Therefore God is not omnipotent.

Obj. 4. Further, upon the text, *God hath made foolish the wisdom of this world* (*I Cor.* i. 20), the *Gloss* says: *God hath made the wisdom of this world foolish* by showing those things to be possible which it judges to be impossible. Whence it seems that nothing is to be judged possible or impossible in reference to inferior causes, as the wisdom of this world judges them; but in reference to the divine power. If God, then were omnipotent, all things would be possible; nothing, therefore, impossible. But if we take away the impossible, then we destroy also the necessary; for what necessarily exists cannot possibly not exist. Therefore, there would be nothing at all that is necessary in things if God were omnipotent. But this is an impossibility. Therefore God is not omnipotent.

On the contrary, It is said: *No word shall be impossible with God* (*Luke* i. 37).

I answer that, All confess that God is omnipotent; but it seems difficult to explain in what His omnipotence precisely consists. For there may be a doubt as to the precise meaning of the word "all" when we say that God can do all things. If, however, we consider the matter aright, since power is said in reference to possible things, this phrase, *God can do all things,* is rightly understood to mean that God can do all things that are possible; and for this reason He is said to be omnipotent. Now according to the Philosopher a thing is said to be possible in two ways. First, in relation to some power; thus whatever is subject to human power is said to be possible to man. Now God cannot be said to be omnipotent through being able to do all things that are possible to created nature; for the divine power extends farther than that. If, however, we were to say that

God is omnipotent because He can do all things that are possible to His power, there would be a vicious circle in explaining the nature of His power. For this would be saying nothing else but that God is omnipotent because He can do all that He is able to do.

It remains, therefore, that God is called omnipotent because he can do all things that are possible absolutely; which is the second way of saying a thing is possible. For a thing is said to be possible or impossible absolutely, according to the relation in which the very terms stand to one another: possible, if the predicate is not incompatible with the subject, as that Socrates sits; and absolutely impossible when the predicate is altogether incompatible with the subject, as, for instance, that a man is an ass.

It must, however, be remembered that since every agent produces an effect like itself, to each active power there corresponds a thing possible as its proper object according to the nature of that act on which its active power is founded; for instance, the power of giving warmth is related, as to its proper object, to the being capable of being warmed. The divine being, however, upon which the nature of power in God is founded, is infinite; it is not limited to any class of being, but possesses within itself the perfection of all being. Whence, whatsoever has or can have the nature of being is numbered among the absolute possibles, in respect of which God is called omnipotent.

Now nothing is opposed to the notion of being except non-being. Therefore, that which at the same time implies being and non-being is repugnant to the notion of an absolute possible, which is subject to the divine omnipotence. For such cannot come under the divine omnipotence; not indeed because of any defect in the power of God, but because it has not the nature of a feasible or possible thing. Therefore, everything that does not imply a contradiction in terms is numbered among those possibles in respect of which God is called omnipotent; whereas whatever implies contradiction does not come within the scope of divine omnipotence, because it cannot have the aspect of possibility. Hence it is more appropriate to say that such things cannot be done, than that God cannot do them. Nor is this contrary to the word of the angel, saying: *No word shall be impossible with God* (*Luke* i. 37). For whatever implies a contradiction cannot be a word, because no intellect can possibly conceive such a thing.

Reply Obj. 1. God is said to be omnipotent in respect to active power, not to passive power, as was shown above. Whence the fact that He is immovable or impassible is not repugnant to His omnipotence.

Reply Obj. 2. To sin is to fall short of a perfect action; hence to be able to sin is to be able to fall short in action, which is repugnant to omnipotence. Therefore it is that God cannot sin, because of His omnipotence. Now it is true that the Philosopher says that *God can deliberately do what is evil.* But this must be understood either on a condition, the antecedent of which is impossible—as, for instance, if we were to say that God can do evil things if He will. For there is no reason why a conditional proposition should not be true, though both the antecedent and consequent are impossible: as if one were to say: *If man is an ass, he has four feet.* Or he may be understood to mean that God can do some things which now seem to be evil: which, however, if He did them, would then be good. Or he is, perhaps, speaking after the common manner of the pagans, who thought that men became gods, like Jupiter or Mercury.

Reply Obj. 3. God's omnipotence is particularly shown in sharing and having mercy, because in this it is made manifest that God has supreme power, namely, that He freely forgives sins. For it is not for one who is bound by laws of a superior to forgive sins of his own free choice. Or, it is thus shown because by sparing and having mercy upon men, He leads them to the participation of an infinite good; which is the ultimate effect of the divine power. Or it is thus shown because, as was said above, the effect of the divine mercy is the foundation of all the divine works. For nothing is due anyone, except because of something already given him gratuitously by God. In this way the divine omnipotence is particularly made manifest, because to it pertains the first foundation of all good things.

Reply Obj. 4. The absolute possible is not so called in reference either to higher causes, or to inferior causes, but in reference to itself. But that which is called possible in reference to some power is named possible in reference to its proximate cause. Hence those things which it belongs to God alone to do immediately—as, for example, to create, to justify, and the like—are said to be possible in reference to a higher cause. Those things, however, which are such as to be done by inferior causes, are said to be possible in reference to those inferior causes. For it is according to the condition of the proximate cause that the effect has contingency or necessity, as was shown above. Thus it is that the wisdom of the world is deemed foolish, because what is impossible to nature it judges to be impossible to God. So it is clear that the omnipotence of God does not take away from things their impossibility and necessity.

IV.C.2 Some Puzzles Concerning Omnipotence

GEORGE MAVRODES

George Mavrodes is professor of philosophy at the University of Michigan. In this reading he applies the Thomistic view of God's omnipotence to the paradox of the stone, arguing that since the para-dox entails doing something contradictory, it can be resolved.

Reprinted from *The Philosophical Review* 72 (1963), 221–23, by permission of the author and the editors.

The doctrine of God's omnipotence appears to claim that God can do anything. Consequently, there have been attempts to refute the doctrine by giving examples of things which God cannot do; for example, He cannot draw a square circle.

Responding to objections of this type, St. Thomas pointed out that "anything" should be here construed to refer only to objects, actions, or states of affairs whose descriptions are not self-contradictory.[1] For it is only such things whose nonexistence might plausibly be attributed to a lack of power in some agent. My failure to draw a circle on the exam may indicate my lack of geometrical skill, but my failure to draw a square circle does not indicate any such lack. Therefore, the fact that it is false (or perhaps meaningless) to say that God could draw one does no damage to the doctrine of His omnipotence.

A more involved problem, however, is posed by this type of question: can God create a stone too heavy for Him to lift? This appears to be stronger than the first problem, for it poses a dilemma. If we say that God can create a stone, then it seems that there might be such a stone. And if there might be a stone too heavy for Him to lift, then He is evidently not omnipotent. But if we deny that God can create such a stone, we seem to have given up His omnipotence already. Both answers lead us to the same conclusion.

Further, this problem does not seem obviously open to St. Thomas' solution. The form "x is able to draw a square circle" seems plainly to involve a contradiction, while "x is able to make a thing too heavy for x to lift" does not. For it may easily be true that I am able to make a boat too heavy for me to lift. So why should it not be possible for God to make a stone too heavy for Him to lift?

Despite this apparent difference, this second puzzle *is* open to essentially the same answer as the first. The dilemma fails because it consists of asking whether God can do a self-contradictory thing. And the reply that He cannot does no damage to the doctrine of omnipotence.

The specious nature of the problem may be seen in this way. God is either omnipotent or not.[2] Let us assume first that He is not. In that case the phrase "a stone too heavy for God to lift" may not be self-contradictory. And then, of course, if we assert either that God is able or that He is not able to create such a stone, we may conclude that He is

not omnipotent. But this is no more than the assumption with which we began, meeting us again after our roundabout journey. If this were all that the dilemma could establish it would be trivial. To be significant it must derive this same conclusion *from the assumption that God is omnipotent;* that is, it must show that the assumption of the omnipotence of God leads to a *reductio.* But does it?

On the assumption that God is omnipotent, the phrase "a stone too heavy for God to lift" becomes self-contradictory. For it becomes "a stone which cannot be lifted by Him whose power is sufficient for lifting anything." But the "thing" described by a self-contradictory phrase is absolutely impossible and hence has nothing to do with the doctrine of omnipotence. Not being an object of power at all, its failure to exist cannot be the result of some lack in the power of God. And, interestingly, it is the very omnipotence of God which makes the existence of such a stone absolutely impossible, while it is the fact that I am finite in power which makes it possible for me to make a boat too heavy for me to lift.

But suppose that some die-hard objector takes the bit in his teeth and denies that the phrase "a stone too heavy for God to lift" is self-contradictory, even on the assumption that God is omnipotent. In other words, he contends that the description "a stone too heavy for an omnipotent God to lift" is self-coherent and therefore describes an absolutely possible object. Must I then attempt to prove the contradiction which I assume above as intuitively obvious? Not necessarily. Let me reply simply that if the objector is right in this contention, then the answer to the original question is "Yes, God can create such a stone." It may seem that this reply will force us into the original dilemma. But it does not. For now the objector can draw no damaging conclusion from this answer. And the reason is that he has just now contended that such a stone is compatible with the omnipotence of God. Therefore, from the possibility of God's creating such a stone it cannot be concluded that God is not omnipotent. The objector cannot have it both ways. The conclusion which he himself wishes to draw from an affirmative answer to the original question is itself the required proof that the descriptive phrase which appears there is self-contradictory. And "it is more appropriate to say that such things cannot be done, than that God cannot do them."[3]

The specious nature of this problem may also be seen in a somewhat different way.[4] Suppose that some theologian is convinced by this dilemma that he must give up the doctrine of omnipotence. But he resolves to give up as little as possible, just enough to meet the argument. One way he can do so is by retaining the infinite power of God with regard to lifting, while placing a restriction on the sort of stone He is able to create. The only restriction required here, however, is that God must not be able to create a stone too heavy for Him to lift. Beyond that the dilemma has not even suggested any necessary restriction. Our theologian has, in effect, answered the original question in the negative, and he now regretfully supposes that this has required him to give up the full doctrine of omnipotence. He is now retaining what he supposes to be the more modest remnants which he has salvaged from that doctrine.

We must ask, however, what it is which he has in fact given up. Is it the unlimited power of God to create stones? No doubt. But what stone is it which God is now precluded from creating? The stone too heavy for Him to lift, of course. But we must remember that nothing in the argument required the theologian to admit any limit on God's power with regard to the lifting of stones. He still

holds that to be unlimited. And if God's power to lift is infinite, then His power to create may run to infinity also without outstripping that first power. The supposed limitation turns out to be no limitation at all, since it is specified only by reference to another power which is itself infinite. Our theologian need have no regrets, for he has given up nothing. The doctrine of the power of God remains just what it was before.

Nothing I have said above, of course, goes to prove that God is, in fact, omnipotent. All I have intended to show is that certain arguments intended to prove that He is not omnipotent fail. They fail because they propose, as tests of God's power, putative tasks whose descriptions are self-contradictory. Such pseudo-tasks, not falling within the realm of possibility, are not objects of power at all. Hence the fact that they cannot be performed implies no limit on the power of God, and hence no defect in the doctrine of omnipotence.

Notes

1. St. Thomas Aquinas, *Summa Theologiae*, Ia, q. 25, a. 3.
2. I assume, of course, the existence of God, since that is not being brought in question here.
3. St. Thomas, *loc. cit.*
4. But this method rests finally on the same logical relations as the preceding one.

IV.C.3 Omnipotence and God's Ability to Sin

NELSON PIKE

Nelson Pike is professor of philosophy at the University of California at Irvine. Starting with an important distinction between the use of God as a title and its use as a name, Pike argues that God's omnipotence is not an essential property and that the being who is called "God" could sin if he so desired. However, "the individual that is God cannot sin in that sinning would be contrary to a firm and stable feature of his nature."

Reprinted from the *American Philosophical Quarterly* 6 (1969), 208–16, by permission of the author and the editor.

In the first chapter of the *Epistle of James* (verse 13) it is said that "God cannot be tempted by evil." This idea recurs in the confessional literature of the Christian tradition,[1] and is stated in its fullest form in the theological doctrine of God's *impeccability*.[2] God is not only free from sin, He is incapable of moral deviation. God not only does not sin, He *cannot* sin. This is generally held to be part of what is communicated in the claim that God is perfectly good. On the surface, at least, this doctrine appears to be in conflict with the traditional Christian doctrine of divine omnipotence. An omnipotent being is one that can do all things possible. But, surely, it is possible to sin. Men do this sort of thing all the time. It would thus appear that if God is perfectly good (and thus impeccable), He cannot sin; and if God is omnipotent (and thus can do all things possible), He can sin.

This argument appears to be sophistical. We are tempted to dismiss it with a single comment, viz., it involves an equivocation on the model element in the statement "God can (cannot) sin." In the long run, I think (and shall try to show) that this single remark is correct. But that's in the long run; and in the interim there is a complicated and interesting terrain that has not yet been adequately explored. In this paper I shall discuss this matter in detail. After working through what I judge to be a number of conceptual tangles that have accumulated in this literature on this topic, I shall end by making a suggestion as to how the various senses of "God can (cannot) sin" ought to be sorted out.

I

I shall begin by identifying three assumptions that will work importantly in the discussion to follow.

First, I shall assume that within the discourse of the Christian religion, the term "God" is a descriptive expression having an identifiable meaning. It is not, e.g., a proper name. As part of this first assumption, I shall suppose, further, that "God" is a very special type of descriptive expression—what I shall call a *title*. A title is a term used to mark a certain position or value-status as does, e.g., "Caesar" in the sentence "Hadrian is Caesar." To say that Hadrian is Caesar is to say that Hadrian occupies a certain governmental position; more specifically, it is to say that Hadrian is Emperor of Rome. To affirm of some individual

that He is God is to affirm that that individual occupies some special position (e.g., that He is Ruler of the Universe) or that that individual has some special value-status (e.g., that He is a being a greater than which cannot be conceived).

Secondly, I shall assume that whatever the particular semantical import of the term "God" may be (i.e., whether it means, for instance, "Ruler of the Universe," "a being than which no greater can be conceived," etc.), the attribute-terms "perfectly good," "omnipotent," "omniscient," and the like, attach to it in such a way as to make the functions "If x is God, then x is perfectly good," "If x is God, then x is omnipotent," etc., necessary truths. It is a logically necessary condition of bearing the title "God," that an individual be perfectly good, omnipotent, omniscient, and so on for all of the standard attributes traditionally assigned to the Christian God. If we could assume that in order to be Emperor (as opposed to Empress) of Rome one had to be male (rather than female), then if "x is Caesar" means "x is Emperor of Rome," then "If x is Caesar, then x is male" would have the same logical status as I am assuming for "If x is God, then x is perfectly good," "If x is God, then x is omnipotent," etc.

If there is an individual (e.g., Yahweh) who occupies the position or has the value-status marked by the term "God," then that individual is perfectly good, omnipotent, omniscient, etc. If He were not, then He could not (logically) occupy the position or have the value-status in question. However, with respect to the predicate "perfectly good," I shall assume that any individual possessing the attribute named by this phrase might not (logically) have possessed that attribute. This assumption entails that any individual who occupies the position or who has the value-status indicated by the term "God" might not (logically) have held that position or had that status. It should be noticed that this third assumption covers only a *logical* possibility. I am not assuming that there is any real (e.i., material) possibility that Yahweh (if He exists) is not perfectly good. I am assuming only that the hypothetical function "If x is *Yahweh*, then x is perfectly good" differs from the hypothetical function "If x is *God*, then x is perfectly good" in that the former, unlike the latter, does not formulate a necessary truth. With Job, one might at least *entertain* the idea that Yahweh is not perfectly good. This is at least a *consistent* conjecture even though to assert such a thing would be to deny a well-established part of the Faith.[3]

I now want to make two further preliminary comments—one about the predicate "omnipotent" and one about the concept of moral responsibility.

Pre-analytically, to say that a given individual is omnipotent is to say that that individual has unlimited power. This is usually expressed in religious discourse with the phrase "infinite power." St. Thomas explicated the intuitive content of this idea as follows: "God is called omnipotent because He can do all things that are possible absolutely.[4] As traditionally understood, St. Thomas' formula must be given a relatively restricted interpretation. The permissive verb "do" in "do all things possible" is usually replaced with one of a range of more specific verbs such as "create," "bring about," "effect," "make-to-be," "produce," etc.[5] God's omnipotence is thus to be thought of as creative-power only. It is not to be understood as the ability to *do* anything at all, e.g., it is not to be interpreted as including the ability to swim the English Channel or ride a bicycle. God is omnipotent in that He can create, bring about, effect, make-to-be, produce, etc., anything possible absolutely. For St. Thomas, something is "possible absolutely" when its description is logically consistent. Thus, on the finished analysis, God is omnipotent insofar as He can bring about any consistently describable object or state of affairs. In his article on "omnipotence" in the *Catholic Encyclopedia*,[6] J. A. McHugh analyzes the notion in this way. It seems clear from the context of this piece that McHugh meant to be reformulating St. Thomas' view of the matter. I might add that I think this restricted interpretation of the preanalytical notion of infinite power is an accurate portrayal of the way this concept works in the ordinary as well as in most of the technical (theological) discourse of the Christian religion.

Now, let us suppose that an innocent child suffers a slow and torturous death by starvation. Let it be true that this event was avoidable and that no greater good was served by its occurrence. Let it also be true that neither the child (or its parents) committed an offense for which it (or its parents) could be righteously punished. This is a consistently describable state of affairs (whether or not it ever occurred). I think it is clear that an individual that knowingly brought this state of affairs about would be morally reprehensible.

We can now formulate the problem under discussion in this paper more rigorously than above. God is omnipotent. When read hypothetically, this statement formulates a necessary truth. On the analysis of "omnipotent" with which we are working, it follows that God (if He exists) can bring about any consistently describable state of affairs. However, God is perfectly good. Again, when read hypothetically, this statement formulates a necessary truth. Further, an individual would not qualify as perfectly good if he were to act in a morally reprehensible way. Thus, the statement "God acts in a morally reprehensible way" is logically incoherent. This is to say that "God sins" is a logical contradiction.[7] Hence, some consistently describable states of affairs are such that God (being perfectly good) could not bring them about.[8] The problem, then, is this: If God is both omnipotent and perfectly good, there are at least some consistently describable states of affairs that He both can and cannot bring about. There would thus appear to be a logical conflict in the claim that God is both omnipotent and perfectly good.

I think it is worth noting that the problem just exposed is not the same as the classical theological problem of evil. The problem of evil is generally formulated as follows: Evil exists. If God exists and is omnipotent, He could have prevented evil if He had wanted to. If God exists and is perfectly good, He would have wanted to. Since evil in fact exists, it follows that God does not exist. This argument is supposed to point up a conflict between the attribute of perfect goodness and the attribute of omnipotence. But the conflict is not of a rigorous sort. So far as this argument goes, it is logically possible for there to exist a being who is both perfectly good and omnipotent. The argument is supposed to show only that since it is contingently true that evil exists, it is contingently false that omnipotence and perfect goodness are possessed by a single individual. However, the problem we are now discussing has a sharper report than this. The argument generating this latter is supposed to show that there is a direct logical conflict between the attribute of perfect goodness and the attribute of omnipotence. No contingent premiss is employed (such as, e.g., that evil exists) and the conclusion drawn is that it is logically impossible (not just contingently false) that there exists an individual who is both omnipotent and perfectly good.

II

In reply to objection 2, article 3, question 25, Part I of the *Summa Theologica*, St. Thomas Aquinas writes as follows[9]

To sin is to fall short of a perfect action; hence to be able to sin is to be able to fall short in action, which is repugnant to omnipotence. Therefore, it is that God cannot sin, because of his omnipotence. Now, it is true that the philosopher says that *God can deliberately do what is evil*. But this must be understood either on condition, the antecedent of which is impossible—as, for instance, if we were to say that God can do evil things if He will. For there is no reason why a conditional proposition should not be true, though both the antecedent and the consequent are impossible; as if one were to say: *If a man is an ass, he has four feet*. Or, he may be understood to mean that God can do some things which now seem to be evil: which, however, if He did them, would then be good. Or he is, perhaps, speaking after the common manner of the pagans, who thought that men became gods, like Jupiter or Mercury.

In this passage St. Thomas offers three suggestions as to how the problem we are discussing might be solved. (I do not count the suggestion made in the last sentence of this passage because it is clear that St. Thomas is not here talking about *God* but about individuals such as Jupiter or Mercury who are mistakenly thought to be God by certain misguided pagans.) Let us look at these three suggestions:

(A) St. Thomas begins with the claim that "to sin is to fall short of a perfect action." He then says that an omnipotent being cannot fall short in action. The conclusion is that God cannot sin because He is omnipotent. Essentially this same reasoning is developed in slightly more detail in the seventh chapter of St. Anselm's *Proslogium*. Anselm says:[10]

But how art Thou omnipotent, if Thou are not capable of all things? or, if Thou canst not be corrupted and canst not lie . . . how are Thou capable of all things? Or else to be capable of these things is not power but impotence. For he who is capable of these things is capable of what is not for his good, and of what he ought not to do and the more capable of them he is, the more power have adversity and perversity against him; and the less has he himself against these.

Anselm concludes that since God is omnipotent, adversity and perversity have no power against Him and He is not capable of anything through impotence. Therefore, since God is omnipotent, He is not capable of performing morally reprehensible actions.

This argument is interesting. Both Thomas and Anselm agree that God is unable to sin. Their effort is to show that instead of being in conflict with the claim that God is omnipotent, the assignment of this inability is a direct consequence of this latter claim. However, I think that the reasoning fails. Let us agree that to the extent that an individual is such that "adversity and perversity" can prevail against him, to that extent is he weak—*morally* weak. He is then capable of "falling short in action," i.e., of doing "what he ought not to do." So far as I can see, an individual that is able to bring about any consistently describable state of affairs might well be morally weak. I can find no conceptual difficulty in the idea of a diabolical omnipotent being. Creative-power and moral strength are readily discernible concepts. If this is right, then it does not follow from the claim that God is omnipotent that He is unable to act in a morally reprehensible way. In fact, as was set out in the original statement of the problem, quite the opposite conclusion seems to be warranted. If a being is able to bring about *any* consistently describable state of affairs, it would seem that he should be able to bring about states of affairs the production of which would be morally reprehensible. St. Thomas' first suggestion thus seems to be ineffective as a solution to the problem we are confronting. (I shall have something more to say on this topic in the fourth section of this paper.)

(B) The Philosopher says that God can deliberately do what is evil. Looking for a way of understanding this remark whereby it can be squared with his own view on the matter, St. Thomas suggests that what Aristotle may have meant is that the individual that is God can do evil *if He wants to*. Thomas adds that this last statement might be true even if it is impossible that God should want to do evil and even if it is also impossible that He can do evil. The point seems to be that although the statements "The individual that is God wants to do evil" and "The individual that is God can do evil" are false (or impossible), the conditional statement containing the first of these statements as the antecedent and the second of these statements as the consequent, might nonetheless be true.

Consider the statement: "Jones has an ace in his hand if he wants to play it." This statement has the surface grammar of a conditional, but it is not a conditional. The item mentioned in the "if . . ." clause does not condition the item described in the rest of the statement. If Jones has an ace in his hand, he has an ace in his hand whether or not he wants to play it. What, then, does the "if . . ." clause do in this statement? I think that it serves as a way of recording a certain indeterminacy as to what will be done about (or, with respect to) the unconditional fact described in the rest of the statement. Whether or not this last remark is precisely right, the major point to be seen here is this: The statement "Jones has an ace in his hand if he wants to play it" is false if the statement "Jones has an ace in his hand" is false. We are here dealing with a use of "if . . ." that does not fit the analysis usually given conditional statements such as "I shall be nourished if I eat."

Now consider the statement: "Jones can wiggle his ear if he wants to." I think that this is another instance in which "if . . ." operates in a nonconditional capacity. If Jones has the ability to wiggle his ear, he has the ability whether or not he wants to wiggle his ear. The question of whether he wants to wiggle his ear is independent of whether he has the ability to do so. As in the case above, what the "if . . ." clause adds in this statement is not a condition on the claim that Jones has an ability. It serves as a way of recording the idea that there is some indeterminacy as to whether the ability that Jones has will be exercised. But again, I am less concerned with whether this last remark about the function of the "if . . ." clause is precisely right than I am with the relation between the truth values of "Jones can wiggle his ear if he wants to" and "Jones can wiggle his ear." In this case, as above, if Jones does not have the ability to wiggle his ear, then the statement "Jones can wiggle his ear if he wants to" is false. If the second of the above statements if false, then the first is false too.

St. Thomas says that the statement "God can sin if He wants to" is true. He adds that both the antecedent and the consequent of this conditional are "impossible." The trouble here, I think, is that "God can sin if He wants to" is not a conditional statement; and the most important point to be seen in this connection is that this statement is false if its component "God can sin" is false. But, St. Thomas clearly holds that "God can sin" is false (or impossible)—he says that God's inability to sin is a consequence of the fact that He is omnipotent. The conclusion must be that "God can sin if He wants to" is also false (or impossible). Thomas has not provided a way of understanding The Philosopher's claim that God can deliberately do what is evil. As long as St. Thomas insists that God does not have the ability to sin (which, he says, follows from the claim that God is omnipotent) he must deny that God can sin if He wants to. He must then reject The Philosopher's claim that God can deliberately do what is evil if this latter means that God can sin if He wants to.

(C) Still looking for a way of understanding the idea that God can deliberately do what is evil, St. Thomas' next suggestion is that God can do things which seem evil to us but which are such that if

God did them, they would not be evil. I think that there are at least two ways of understanding this comment.

First, Thomas may be suggesting that God has the ability to bring about states of affairs that are, in fact, good, but which seem evil to us due to our limited knowledge, sympathy, moral insight, etc. However, even if we were to agree that this is true, Thomas could draw no conclusion as regards the starving-child situation described earlier. We have specified this situation in such a way that it not only *seems* evil to us, but *is* evil in fact. We have included in our description of this case that the child suffers intensely; that this suffering is not deserved and that it might have been avoided. We have added that the suffering does not contribute to a greater good. Thus, this line of reasoning does not really help with the major problem we are discussing in this paper. We still have a range of consistently describable states of affairs that God (being perfectly good) cannot bring about. We thus still have reason to think that God (being perfectly good) is not omnipotent.

Secondly, St. Thomas may be suggesting that God has the ability to bring about *any* consistently describable states of affairs (including the starving-child situation), but that if *He* were to bring about such a situation, it would no longer count as evil. Let "evil" cover any situation which is such that if one were to (knowingly) bring it about (though it is avoidable), that individual would be morally reprehensible. The view we are now considering requires that we append a special theory about the meanings of the *other* value-terms involved in our discussion. In particular, it requires that when applied to God, the expressions "not morally reprehensible" and "perfectly good" be assigned meanings other than the ones they have when used to characterize individuals other than God. If a man were knowingly to bring about the starving-child situation, he would be morally reprehensible. He could no longer be described as perfectly good. But (so the argument goes) if God were to bring about the same situation, He might still count as perfectly good (not morally reprehensible) in the special senses of "not morally repre-

hensible" and "perfectly good" that apply *only* to God.

I have two comments to make about this second way of understanding St. Thomas' claim that God can do things that seem evil to us but which are such that if He did them, they would not be evil.

First, in my opinion the view we are now entertaining about the theological use of "perfectly good" and "not morally reprehensible" is one that was decisively criticized by Duns Scotus, Bishop Berkeley, and John Stuart Mill.[11] If God were to bring about circumstances such as the starving-child situation, He would be morally reprehensible and thus not perfectly good in the ordinary senses of these phrases. If we now contrive some special phrases (retaining the tabletures "not morally reprehensible" and "perfectly good") that might apply to God though He produces the situation in question, this will be of no special interest. Whatever *else* can be said of God, if He were to bring about the starving-child situation, He would not be an appropriate object of the *praise* we ordinarily convey with the phrase "perfectly good." He would be an appropriate object of the *blame* we ordinarily convey with the phrase "morally reprehensible." We might put this point as follows: If we deny that God is perfectly good in the ordinary sense of "perfectly good," and if we cover this move by introducing a technical, well-removed, sense of "perfectly good" that can apply to God though He brings about circumstances such as the starving-child situation, it may appear that we have solved the problem under discussion in this paper, but we haven't. We have eliminated conflict by agreeing that God lacks one of the "perfections," i.e., one of the qualities the possession of which makes an individual better (more praiseworthy) than he would otherwise be. Unless a being is perfectly good in the *ordinary* sense of "perfectly good," that being is not as praiseworthy as he might otherwise be. It was the sense of "perfectly good" that connects with the idea of being morally praiseworthy (in the ordinary sense) that gave rise to the problem in the first place. Surely, it is this sense of "perfectly good" that religious people have in mind when they characterize God as perfectly good.

The second remark I should like to make about this second interpretation of St. Thomas' third suggestion is that the view assigned to St. Thomas in this interpretation is one that he would most likely reject. I shall need a moment to develop this point.[12]

Consider the word "triangle" as it occurs in the discourse of geometry. Compare it with "triangle" as it is used in the discourse of carpentry or woodworking. Within the discourse of geometry, the criteria governing the use of this term are more strict than are the criteria governing its use in the discourse of carpentry. The geometrical figure is an exemplary (i.e., perfect) version of the shape embodied in the triangular block of wood. We reach an understanding of the geometrical shape by correcting imperfections (i.e., irregularities) in the shape of the triangular block. Now, let's ask whether "triangle" has the same meaning in the two cases. We might answer this question in either way. Once the relation between the criteria governing its use in the two cases is made clear, no one would be confused if we were to say that "triangle" has the same meaning in the two cases, and no one would be confused if we were to say that "triangle" has different meaning in the two cases. Regarding the relation between the criteria, the following point seems to me to be of considerable importance: If a block of wood is triangular, it has three angles that add up (roughly) to 180 degrees and its sides are (roughly) straight. *At least this much* is implied with respect to a geometrical figure when one characterizes it as a triangle. By this I mean that if one could find reasons sufficient for rejecting the claim that a given thing is a triangle as "triangle" is used in the discourse of carpentry (suppose that one of its sides is visibly curved or suppose it has four angles), these same reasons would be sufficient for rejecting the claim that the thing in question is a triangle as "triangle" is used in the discourse of geometry. In fact, more than this can be said. If one could find slight irregularities in the shape of a thing that would cause some hesitation or prompt some reservation about

whether it is a triangle as "triangle" is used in the discourse of carpentry, such irregularities would be sufficient to establish that the thing in question is not a triangle as "triangle" is used in the discourse of geometry.

According to St. Thomas, finite things are caused by God. They thus bear a "likeness" to God. God's attributes are exemplary-versions of the attributes possessed by finite things. We reach whatever understanding we have of God's attributes, by removing "imperfections" that attend these qualities when possessed by finite things.[13] With respect to the predicate "good," St. Thomas writes as follows in the *Summa Theologica* (Pt. I, Q. 6, A. 4):[14]

> Each being is called good because of the divine goodness, the first exemplar principle as well as the efficient and telic cause of all goodness. Yet it is nonetheless the case that each being is called good because of a likeness of the divine goodness by which it is denominated.

Again, in *questiones disputatae de veritate* (XXI, 4), St. Thomas says:

> Every agent is found to produce effects which resemble it. Hence, if the first goodness is the efficient cause of all things, it must imprint its likeness upon things which it produces. Thus each thing is called good because of an intrinsic goodness impressed upon it, and yet is further denominated good because of the first goodness which is the exemplar and efficient cause of all created goodness.

Shall we say that "good" has the same meaning when applied to God as it has when applied to things other than God (e.g. Socrates)? As above, it seems to me that the answer we give to this question is unimportant once we get this far into the discussion. We might say that "good" has the same meaning in the two cases, and we might say that it has different meanings in the two cases. We might even say (as St. Thomas sometimes says) that we are here dealing with a case in which "good" is "midway between" having the same meaning and having different meanings in the two cases. However, as above, the following point has importance regardless of how one answers the question about same or different meanings. When

St. Thomas affirms that God is good, I think he means to be saying *at least as much* about God as one would say about, e.g., Socrates, if one were to affirm that Socrates is good. A study of "good" in nontheological contexts reveals at least the minimum implications of the corresponding predication statements relating to God. If we could find reasons sufficient for rejecting the claim that a given thing is good as "good" is used in discourse about finite agents, these same reasons would be sufficient for rejecting the claim that the thing in question is good as "good" is used in discourse about the nature of God. In fact, if we could find moral irregularities sufficient to cause hesitations or prompt reservations about whether a thing is good as "good" is used in discourse about finite agents, these irregularities would be sufficient to establish that the agent under consideration is not good as "good" is used in the discourse of theology.

So far as I can see, St. Thomas would not endorse a technical, well-removed sense of the phrase "perfectly good" that could apply to God even if God were to bring about circumstances or states of affairs the production of which would be morally reprehensible (in the ordinary sense of "morally reprehensible"). When St. Thomas says that God is good, he means to be saying that God possesses the exemplary version of the quality assigned to Socrates in the sentence "Socrates is good." This is to say that while Socrates is good, God is *perfectly* good. But on this understanding of the matter, God could not be perfectly good were He to bring about the starving-child situation described earlier. If Socrates were to bring about such a situation, we would probably refuse to describe him as "good." At the very least, we would surely have hesitations or reservations concerning his moral goodness. But if such an action would be sufficient to cause hesitations concerning an application of "good" in discourse about finite agents, this same action would be sufficient to *defeat* an application of "good" in discourse about the nature of God. In this latter context, "good" means *"perfectly* good." The logic of this phrase will not tolerate even a minor moral irregularity.

III

I want now to discuss an approach to our problem that is very different from any of those suggested by St. Thomas. It is an approach taken by J. A. McHugh in the *Encyclopedia* article mentioned above. I think we can best get at the center of McHugh's thinking if we start with a review of that side of the problem generated by the concept of perfect goodness.

God is perfectly good. This is a necessary statement. If a being is perfectly good, that being does not bring about objects or states of affairs the production of which would be morally reprehensible. This, too, is a necessary truth. Thus, the statement "God brings about objects or states of affairs the production of which would be morally reprehensible" is logically contradictory. It follows that God cannot bring about such states of affairs. But, McHugh argues, this should not be taken as a reason for denying God's omnipotence. As St. Thomas has pointed out, a being may be omnipotent and yet not be able to do an act whose description is logically contradictory. (A being may be omnipotent though he is not able to make a round-square.) Since the claim that God acts in a morally reprehensible way is logically contradictory, God's inability to perform such acts does not constitute a limitation of power.

Consider the following argument: The term "Gid" is the title held by the most efficient of those who make only leather sandals. "Gid makes leather belts" is thus a logical contradiction. It follows that the individual that is Gid cannot make leather belts. But Gid may still be omnipotent. Though He does not have the ability to make leather belts, our analysis of "omnipotence" requires only that an omnipotent being be able to do an act whose description is logically consistent and "Gid makes leather belts" is logically inconsistent. Thus, Gid's inability to make leather belts does not constitute a limitation on his power.

I think it is plain that this last argument is deficient since its conclusion is absurd. I think, too, that in this case, two difficulties are forced pretty close to the surface.

First, the description of the kind of object that Gid is (allegedly) unable to make (viz., leather belts) is not logically contradictory. What is contradictory is the claim that *Gid makes them*. But our definition of "omnipotent" requires only that the *state of affairs* brought about be consistently describable (excluding, therefore, round squares). It does not require that a statement in which it is claimed that a given individual brings it about be consistent. Thus, if Gid does not have the ability to produce leather belts, he is not omnipotent on St. Thomas' definition of "omnipotent." If it follows from the definition of "Gid" that the individual who bears this title cannot make leather belts; and if this entails that the individual in question does not have the creative-ability to make belts, the conclusion must be that, by definition, the individual who bears this title is a limited being. I think the same kind of conclusion must be drawn in the case of God's ability to sin. If it follows from the definition of "God" that the individual bearing this title cannot bring about objects or states of affairs the production of which would be morally reprehensible; and if it follows from this that the individual bearing this title does not have the creative power necessary to bring about such states of affairs though they are consistently desirable; the conclusion is that the individual who is God is not omnipotent on the analysis of "omnipotent" that we are supposing. The fact (if it is a fact) that this creative limitation is built into the definition of "God" making "God sins" a logical contradiction does not disturb this conclusion. The upshot is, simply, that the term "God" has been so specified that an individual qualifying for this title could not be omnipotent. (Of course, this is awkward because it is also a condition of bearing this title that the individual in question be omnipotent.)

The second difficulty in the argument about Gid is this: The term "Gid" has been defined in such a way that "Gid makes leather belts" is logically contradictory. The conclusion drawn is that Gid *cannot* make belts. What this means is that if some individual makes leather belts, this is logically sufficient to assure that the individual in question does not bear the title "Gid." But it does not follow from this (as is supposed in the argu-

ment) that the individual who is Gid does not have the *ability* to make leather belts. All we can conclude is that if he does have this ability, it is one that he does not *exercise*. Thus, as is affirmed in the argument, the individual who is Gid might be omnipotent though he cannot make leather belts (and be Gid). If we suppose that he is omnipotent, we must conclude that he has the ability to make belts; but since, by hypothesis, the individual in question is Gid, we know (analytically) that he does not exercise this ability. Again, I think the same is true with respect to the argument about God's inability to sin. The term "God" has been so specified that the individual who is God *cannot* sin and be God. But it will not follow from this that the individual who is God does not have the *ability* to sin. He might have the creative power necessary to bring about states of affairs the production of which would be morally reprehensible. He is perfectly good (and thus God) insofar as He does not exercise this power.

IV

If we collect together a number of threads developed in the preceding discussions, I think we shall have enough to provide at least a tentative solution to the problem we have been discussing. I shall proceed by distinguishing three ways in which the statement "God cannot sin" might be understood.

"God cannot sin" might mean: "If a given individual sins, it follows logically that the individual does not bear the title 'God'." In this case, the "cannot" in "cannot sin" expresses logical impossibility. The sentence as a whole might be rewritten as follows: $N(x)$ (If x is God then x does not sin.) On the assumptions we are making in this paper, this statement is true. We have supposed that the meaning of the title term "God" is such that it is a logically necessary condition of bearing this title that one be perfectly good and thus that one not perform actions that are morally reprehensible.

Secondly, "God cannot sin" might mean that if a given individual is God, that individual does not have the ability to sin, i.e., He does not have the creative power necessary to bring about states of affairs the production of which would be morally reprehensible, such as, e.g., the starving-child situation described earlier. In this case, the "cannot" in "cannot sin" does not express logical impossibility. It expresses a material concept—that of a limitation of creative-power (as in, e.g., "I cannot make leather sandals"). On St. Thomas' analysis of "omnipotence" if the individual who is God (Yahweh) cannot sin in this sense, He is not omnipotent. Further, I think there is strong reason to suspect that if the individual that is God (Yahweh) cannot sin in this sense, He is not perfectly good either. Insofar as the phrase "perfectly good" applies to the individual that is God (Yahweh) as an expression of praise—warranted by the fact that this individual does not sin—God could not be perfectly good if He does not have the ability to sin. If an individual does not have the creative-power necessary to bring about evil states of affairs, he cannot be praised (morally) for failing to bring them about. Insofar as I do not have the physical strength necessary to crush my next door neighbor with my bare hands, it is not to my credit (morally) that I do not perform this heinous act.

Thirdly, "God cannot sin" might mean that although the individual that is God (Yahweh) has the ability (i.e., the creative power necessary) to bring about states of affairs the production of which would be morally reprehensible, His nature or character is such as to provide material assurance that He will not act in this way. This is the sense in which one might say that Jones, having been reared to regard animals as sensitive and precious friends, just *cannot* be cruel to animals. Here "cannot" is not to be analyzed in terms of the notion of logical impossibility and it does not mark a limitation on Jones's physical power he may be physically able to kick the kitten). It is used to express the idea that Jones is *strongly disposed* to be kind to animals or at least to avoid actions that would be cruel. We have a special locution in English that covers this idea. When we say that Jones cannot be cruel to animals, what we mean is that Jones cannot *bring himself* to be cruel to animals. On this third analysis of "God cannot sin,"

the claim conveyed in this form of words is that the individual that is God (Yahweh) is of such character that he cannot bring himself to act in a morally reprehensible way. God is strongly disposed to perform only morally acceptable actions.

Look back for a moment over the ground we have covered.

McHugh noticed that the statement "God sins" is logically incoherent. He thus (rightly) concluded that God cannot sin. He was here affirming that the semantical import of the title term "God" is such that an individual could not (logically) bear this title and be a sinner. McHugh's conclusion ("God cannot sin") was thus intended in the first sense just mentioned. But McHugh then went on to suppose that God cannot sin in a sense of this phrase that connects with the notion of omnipotence. This is the second sense mentioned above. This conclusion was not warranted. The individual who bears the title "God" (Yahweh) might have the creative power necessary to bring about objects or states of affairs the production of which would be morally reprehensible even though "God sins" is logically contradictory. The conclusion is, simply, that if an individual bears the title "God," He does not exercise this creative-power.

St. Thomas and St. Anselm said that God cannot sin in that "adversity and perversity cannot prevail against Him." This appears to be the claim put forward in the *Epistle of James* 1:13—the claim embodied in the theological doctrine of God's impeccability—viz., "God cannot be tempted by evil." The individual that is God has a very special kind of strength—moral strength, or strength of character. He is, as we say, "above temptation." Both Thomas and Anselm concluded that God's inability to sin has a direct connection with the notion of omnipotence. It is because God is omnipotent that He is unable to sin. This line of reasoning confuses the second and third senses of the statement "God cannot sin." If we say that the individual who is God cannot sin in this second sense (i.e., in the sense that connects with the idea of creative power and thus with the standard notion of omnipotence) this is not to assign that individual strength. It is to assign Him a very definite limitation. The strength-concept in this cluster of ideas is the notion of not being able to *bring one-self* to sin. God has a special strength of character. But this latter concept is expressed in the third sense of "God cannot sin." As I argued earlier, this third sense appears to have no logical connection with the idea of having or lacking the creative power to bring about consistently describable states of affairs. It thus appears to have no logical connection to the notion of omnipotence as this latter concept is explicated by St. Thomas.

The individual that is God cannot sin and bear the title "God." The individual that is God cannot sin in that sinning would be contrary to a firm and stable feature of His nature. These claims are compatible with the idea that the individual that is God has the ability (i.e., the creative power necessary) to bring about states of affairs the production of which would be morally reprehensible. All we need add is that there is complete assurance that He will not exercise this ability and that if He did exercise this ability (which is logically possible but materially excluded), He would not bear the title "God." Further, if God is to be omnipotent in St. Thomas' sense of "omnipotent," and if God is to be perfectly good in a sense of this phrase that expresses praise for the fact that He refrains from sinful actions, this appears to be the conclusion that *must* be drawn.

Notes

1. See, for example, the *Westminister Confession,* ch. V, sect IV and the *Longer Catechism of the Eastern Church,* sects. 156–57.

2. See the *Catholic Encyclopedia* (New York, Robert Appleton Co., 1967).

3. The truth of this assumption is argued at some length by C. B. Martin in the fourth chapter of his *Religious Belief* (Ithaca, Cornell Press, 1964).

4. *Summa Theologica,* Pt. I, Q. 25, a 3. This passage taken from *The Basic Writings of St. Thomas Aquinas,* ed. by Anton Pegis, p. 263.

5. These verbs are sometimes called "factitive verbs."

6. New York, Robert Appleton Co., 1911.

7. There is probably some distinction to be made between acting in a morally reprehensible way and sinning. However, for purposes of this discussion, I shall treat these concepts as one.

8. I am here assuming that if God brings about a given circumstance, He does so *knowingly*. God could not bring about a given circumstance by mistake. I think this follows from the idea that God is omniscient.

9. This passage is taken from *The Basic Writings of St. Thomas Aquinas, op. cit.,* p. 264.

10. This passage is taken from S. N. Deane, *St. Anselm* (LaSalle, Open Court, 1958), p. 14.

11. See Scotus' *Oxford Commentary on the Sentences of Peter Lombard,* Q.II ("Man's Natural Knowledge of God"), second statement, argument IV; Berkeley's *Alcephron,* Dialogue IV, sects. 16–22 (especially sect. 17); and J. S. Mill's *An Examination of Sir William Hamilton's Philosophy,* ch. 6. What follows in this paragraph is what I think constitutes the center of these three discussions.

12. The next two paragraphs are taken almost without change from the Introduction to my book *God and Timelessness* (London, Routledge and Kegan-Paul, 1969). What I say here about the relation between "triangle" as used in the discourse of geometry and "triangle" as used in the discourse of carpentry is very much like a thesis developed by John Stuart Mill in the text mentioned above.

13. In the *Summa Theologica* (Pt. I, Q. 14, a.1) St. Thomas says: "Because perfections flowing from God to creatures exist in a higher state in God Himself, whenever a name taken from any created perfection is attributed to God, there must be separated from its signification anything that belongs to the imperfect mode proper to creatures." (Quoted from *The Basic Writings of St. Thomas Aquinas, op. cit.,* p. 136.)

14. Both of the following passages were translated by George P. Klubertanz, S. J., *Thomas Aquinas on Analogy* (Chicago, Loyola Press, 1960), p. 55. For a good analysis of St. Thomas' views on the topic of theological predication, see the whole of Klubertanz' discussion in ch. III. For an enlightening discussion of how poorly St. Thomas has been understood on this topic (even by his most illustrious interpreters) see Klubertanz' remarks in ch. I and Berkeley's discussion of St. Thomas in *Alcephron,* IV, sects. 20–22. According to Berkeley, St. Thomas' doctrine of "analogy by proportionality" is to be regarded as an expression of the view we are now discussing.

IV.C.4   Omnipotence and Almightiness

PETER GEACH

Peter Geach is professor of philosophy at Leeds University in England. In this article he distinguishes the notion of omnipotence (the ability to do anything) from the notion of almightiness (God's power over all things) and argues that the latter is a Biblical concept but the former is not. He examines four versions of omnipotence and shows how each of them is defective.

It is fortunate for my purposes that English has the two words "almighty" and "omnipotent," and that apart from any stipulation by me the words have rather different associations and suggestions. "Almighty" is the familiar word that comes in the creeds of the Church; "omnipotent" is at home rather in formal theological discussions and controversies, e.g. about miracles and about the problem of evil. "Almighty" derives by way of Latin "omnipotens" from the Greek word "*pantokratōr*"; and both this Greek word, like the more classical "*pankratēs*," and "almighty" itself suggest God's having power *over* all things. On the other hand the English word "omnipotent" would ordinarily be taken to imply ability to *do* everything; the Latin word "omnipotens" also predominantly has this meaning in Scholastic writers, even though in origin it is a Latinization of "*pantocratōr*." So there already is a tendency to distinguish the two words; and in this paper I shall make the distinction a strict one. I shall use the world "almighty" to express God's power over all things, and I shall take "omnipotence" to mean ability to do everything.

I think we can in a measure understand what God's almightiness implies, and I shall argue that almightiness so understood must be ascribed to God if we are to retain anything like traditional

Reprinted from *Philosophy* 48 (1973) by permission of Cambridge University Press. Copyright © The Royal Institute of Philosophy 1973.

Christian belief in God. The position as regards omnipotence, or as regards the statement "God can do everything," seems to me to be very different. Of course even "God can do everything" may be understood simply as a way of magnifying God by contrast with the impotence of man. McTaggart described it as "a piece of theological etiquette" to call God omnipotent: Thomas Hobbes, out of reverence for his Maker, would rather say that "omnipotent" is an attribute of honour. But McTaggart and Hobbes would agree that "God is omnipotent" or "God can do everything" is not to be treated as a proposition that can figure as premise or conclusion in a serious theological argument. And I too wish to say this. I have no objection to such ways of speaking if they merely express a desire to give the best honour we can to God our Maker, whose Name only is excellent and whose praise is above heaven and earth. But theologians have tried *to prove* that God can do everything, or to derive conclusions from this thesis as a premise. I think such attempts have been wholly unsuccessful. When people have tried to read into "God can do everything" a signification not of Pious Intention but of Philosophical Truth, they have only landed themselves in intractable problems and hopeless confusions; no graspable sense has ever been given to this sentence that did not lead to self-contradiction or at least to conclusions manifestly untenable from a Christian point of view.

I shall return to this; but I must first develop what I have to say about God's almightiness, or power over all things. God is not just more powerful than any creature; no creature can compete with God in power, even unsuccessfully. For God is also the source of all power; any power a creature has comes from God and is maintained only for such time as God wills. Nebuchadnezzar submitted to praise and adore the God of heaven because he was forced by experience to realize that only by God's favour did his wits hold together from one end of a blasphemous sentence to the other end. Nobody can deceive God or circumvent him or frustrate him; and there is no question of God's trying to do anything and failing. In Heaven and on Earth, God does whatever he will. We shall see that some propositions of the form "God cannot do so-and-so" have to be accepted as true; but what God cannot be said to be able to do he likewise cannot will to do; we cannot drive a logical wedge between his power and his will, which are, as the Scholastics said, really identical, and there is no application to God of the concept of trying but failing.

I shall not spend time on citations of Scripture and tradition to show that this doctrine of God's almightiness is authentically Christian; nor shall I here develop rational grounds for believing it is a true doctrine. But it is quite easy to show that this doctrine is indispensable for Christianity, not a bit of old metaphysical luggage that can be abandoned with relief. For Christianity requires an absolute faith in the promises of God: specifically, faith in the promise that some day the whole human race will be delivered and blessed by the establishment of the Kingdom of God. If God were not almighty, he might will and not do; sincerely promise, but find fulfilment beyond his power. Men might prove untamable and incorrigible, and might kill themselves through war or pollution before God's salvific plan for them could come into force. It is uselsss to say that after the end of this earthly life men would live again; for as I have argued elsewhere, only the promise of God can give us any confidence that there will be an afterlife for men; and if God were not almighty, this promise too might fail. If God is true and just and unchangeable and almighty, we can have absolute confidence in his promises: otherwise we cannot—and there would be an end of Christianity.

A Christian must therefore believe that God is almighty; but he need not believe that God can do everything. Indeed, the very argument I have just used shows that a Christian must not believe that God can do everything: for he may not believe that God could possibly break his own word. Nor can a Christian even believe that God can do

everything that is logically possible; for breaking one's word is certainly a logically possible feat.

It seems to me, therefore, that the tangles in which people have enmeshed themselves when trying to give the expression "God can do everything" an intelligible and acceptable content are tangles that a Christian believer has no need to enmesh himself in; the spectacle of others enmeshed may sadden him, but need not cause him to stumble in the way of faith. The denial that God is omnipotent, or able to do everything, may seem dishonouring to God; but when we see where the contrary affirmation, in its various forms, has led, we may well cry out with Hobbes: "Can any man think God is served with such absurdities? . . . As if it were an acknowledgment of the Divine Power, to say, that which is, is not; or that which has been, has not been."

I shall consider four main theories of omnipotence. The first holds that God can do everything absolutely; everything that can be expressed in a string of words that makes sense; even if that sense can be shown to be self-contradictory, God is not bound in action, as we are in thought, by the laws of logic. I shall speak of this as the doctrine that God is *absolutely* omnipotent.

The second doctrine is that a proposition "God can do so-and-so" is true when and only when "so-and-so" represents a logically consistent description.

The third doctrine is that "God *can* do so-and-so" is true just if "God does so-and-so" is logically consistent. This is a weaker doctrine than the second; for "God is doing so-and-so" is logically consistent only when "so-and-so" represents a logically consistent description, but on the other hand there may be consistently describable feats which it would involve contradiction to suppose done *by God*.

The last and weakest view is that the realm of what can be done or brought about includes all future possibilities, and that whenever "God *will* bring so-and-so about" is logically possible, "God *can* bring so-and-so about" is true.

The first sense of "omnipotent" in which people have believed God to be omnipotent implies precisely: ability to do absolutely everything,

everything describable. You mention it, and God can do it. McTaggart insisted on using "omnipotent" in this sense only; from an historical point of view we may of course say that he imposed on the word a sense which it, and the corresponding Latin word, have not always borne. But Broad seems to me clearly unjust to McTaggart when he implies that in demolishing this doctrine of omnipotence McTaggart was just knocking down a man of straw. As Broad must surely have known, at least one great philosopher, Descartes, deliberately adopted and defended this doctrine of omnipotence: what I shall call the doctrine of absolute omnipotence.

As Descartes himself remarked, nothing is too absurd for some philosopher to have said it some time; I once read an article about an Indian school of philosophers who were alleged to maintain that it is only a delusion, which the wise can overcome, that anything exists at all—so perhaps it would not matter all that much that a philosopher is found to defend absolute omnipotence. Perhaps it would not matter all that much that the philosopher in question was a very great one; for very great philosophers have maintained the most preposterous theses. What does make the denial of absolute omnipotence important is not that we are thereby denying what a philosopher, a very great philosopher, thought he must assert, but that this doctrine has a live influence on people's religious thought—I should of course say, a pernicious influence. Some naive Christians would explicitly assert the doctrine; and moreover, I think McTaggart was right in believing that in popular religious thought a covert appeal to the doctrine is sometimes made even by people who would deny it if it were explicitly stated to them and its manifest consequences pointed out.

McTaggart may well have come into contact with naive Protestant defenders of absolute omnipotence when he was defending his atheist faith at his public school. The opinion is certainly not dead, as I can testify from personal experience. For many years I used to teach the philosophy of Descartes in a special course for undergraduates reading French; year by year, there were always two or three of them who embraced Descartes'

defence of absolute omnipotence *con amore* and protested indignantly when I described the doctrine as incoherent. It would of course have been no good to say I was following Doctors of the Church in rejecting the doctrine; I did in the end find a way of producing silence, though not, I fear, conviction, and going on to other topics of discussion; I cited the passages of the Epistle to the Hebrews which say explicitly that God cannot swear by anything greater than himself (vi.13) or break his word (vi.18). Fortunately none of them ever thought of resorting to the ultimate weapon which, as I believe George Mavrodes remarked, is available to the defender of absolute omnipotence; namely, he can always say: "Well, you've stated a difficulty, but of course being omnipotent God can overcome that difficulty, though I don't see how." But what I may call, borrowing from C. S. Lewis's story, victory by the Deplorable Word is a barren one; as barren as a victory by an incessant demand that your adversary should prove his premises or define his terms.

Let us leave these naive defenders in their entrenched position and return for a moment to Descartes. Descartes held that the truths of logic and arithmetic are freely made to be true by God's will. To be sure we clearly and distinctly see that these truths are necessary; they are necessary in our world, and in giving us our mental endowments God gave us the right sort of clear and distinct ideas to see the necessity. But though they are necessary, they are not necessarily necessary; God could have freely chosen to make a different sort of world, in which other things would have been necessary truths. The possibility of such another world is something we cannot *comprehend*, but only dimly *apprehend*; Descartes uses the simile that we may girdle a tree-trunk with our arms but not a mountain—but we can *touch* the mountain. Proper understanding of the possibility would be possessed by God, or, no doubt, by creatures in the alternative world, who would be endowed by God with clear and distinct ideas corresponding to the necessities of their world.

In recent years, unsound philosophies have been defended by what I may call shyster logicians: some of the more dubious recent developments of modal logic could certainly be used to defend Descartes. A system in which "possibly p" were a theorem—in which everything is possible—has indeed never been taken seriously; but modal logicians have taken seriously systems in which "possibly possibly p," or again "it is not necessary that necessarily p," would be a theorem for arbitrary interpretation of "p." What is more, some modern modal logicians notoriously take possible worlds very seriously indeed; some of them even go to the length of saying that what you and I vulgarly call the actual world is simply the world we happen to live in. People who take *both* things seriously—the axiom "possibly possibly p" and the ontology of possible worlds—would say: You mention any impossibility, and there's a possible world in which that isn't impossible but possible. And this is even further away out than Descartes would wish to go; for he would certainly not wish to say that "It is possible that God should not exist" is even *possibly* true. So *a fortiori* a shyster logician could fadge up a case for Descartes. But to my mind all that this shows is that modal logic is currently a rather disreputable discipline: not that I think modal notions are inadmissible—on the contrary, I think they are indispensable—but that current professional standards in the discipline are low, and technical ingenuity is mistaken for rigour. On that showing, astrology would be rigorous.

Descartes' motive for believing in absolute omnipotence was not contemptible: it seemed to him that otherwise God would be *subject to* the inexorable laws of logic as Jove was to the decrees of the Fates. The nature of logical truth is a very difficult problem, which I cannot discuss here. The easy conventionalist line, that it is our arbitrary way of using words that makes logical truth, seems to me untenable, for reasons that Quine among others has clearly spelled out. If I could follow Quine further in regarding logical laws as natural laws of very great generality—revisable in principle, though most unlikely to be revised, in a major theoretical reconstruction—then perhaps after all some rehabilitation of Descartes on this topic might be possible. But in the end I have to say that as we cannot say how a non-logical world

would look, we cannot say how a supra-logical God would act or how he could communicate anything to us by way of revelation. So I end as I began: a Christian need not and cannot believe in absolute omnipotence.

It is important that Christians should clearly realize this, because otherwise a half-belief in absolute omnipotence may work in their minds subterraneously. As I said, I think McTaggart was absolutely right in drawing attention to this danger. One and the same man may deny the doctrine of absolute omnipotence when the doctrine is clearly put to him, and yet reassure himself that God can certainly do so-and-so by using *merely* the premise of God's omnipotence. And McTaggart is saying this is indefensible. At the very least this "so-and-so" must represent a logically consistent description of a feat; and proofs of logical consistency are notoriously not always easy. Nor, as we shall see, are our troubles at an end if we assume that God *can* do anything whose description is logically consistent.

Logical consistency in the description of the feat is certainly a *necessary* condition for the truth of "God can do so-and-so": if "so-and-so" represents an inconsistent description of a feat, then "God can do so-and-so" is certainly a false and impossible proposition, since it entails "It could be the case that so-and-so came about"; so, by contraposition, if "God can do so-and-so" is to be true, or even logically possible, then "so-and-so" must represent a logically consistent description of a feat. And whereas only a minority of Christians have explicitly believed in absolute omnipotence, many have believed that a proposition of the form "God can do so-and-so" is true whenever "so-and-so" represents a description of a logically possible feat. This is our second doctrine of omnipotence. One classic statement of this comes in the *Summa Theologica* Ia q. xxv art. 3. Aquinas rightly says that we cannot explain "God can do everything" in terms of what is within the power of some agent; for "God can do everything any created agent can do," though true, is not a comprehensive enough account of God's power, which exceeds that of any created agent; and "God can do everything God can do" runs uselessly in a circle. So he puts forward the view that if the description "so-and-so" is in itself possible through the relation of the terms involved—if it does not involve contradictories' being true together—then "God can do so-and-so" is true. Many Christian writers have followed Aquinas in saying this; but it is not a position consistently maintainable. As we shall see, Aquinas did not manage to stick to the position himself.

Before I raise the difficulties against this thesis, I wish to expose a common confusion that often leads people to accept it: the confusion between self-contradiction and gibberish. C. S. Lewis in *The Problem of Pain* says that meaningless combinations of words do not suddenly acquire meaning simply because we prefix to them the two other words "God can," and Antony Flew has quoted this with just approval. But if we take Lewis's words strictly, his point is utterly trivial, and nothing to our purpose. For gibberish, syntactically incoherent combination of words, is quite different from self-contradictory sentences or descriptions; the latter certainly have an intelligible place in our language.

It is a common move in logic to argue that a set of premises A, B, C together yield a contradiction, and that therefore A and B as premises yield as conclusion the contradictory of C; some logicians have puritanical objections to this manoeuvre, but I cannot stop to consider them; I am confident, too, that neither Aquinas nor Lewis would share these objections to *reductio ad absurdum*. If, however, a contradictory formula were gibberish, *reductio ad absurdum* certainly would be an illegitimate procedure—indeed it would be a nonsensical one. So we have to say that when "so-and-so" represents a self-contradictory description of a feat, "God can do so-and-so" is likewise self-contradictory, but that being self-contradictory it is *not* gibberish, but merely false.

I am afraid the view of omnipotence presently under consideration owes part of its attractiveness to the idea that then "God can do so-and-so" would never turn out *false,* so that there would be no genuine counterexamples to "God can do everything." Aquinas says, in the passage I just now cited: "What implies contradiction cannot be

a word, for no understanding can conceive it." Aquinas, writing seven centuries ago, is excusable for not being clear about the difference between self-contradiction and gibberish; we are not excusable if we are not. It is not gibberish to say "a God can bring it about that in Alcalá there lives a barber who shaves all those and only those living in Alcalá who do not shave themselves"; this is a perfectly well-formed sentence, and not on the face of it self-contradictory; all the same, the supposed feat notoriously is self-contradictory, so this statement of what God can do is not nonsense but false.

One instance of a description of a feat that is really but not overtly self-contradictory has some slight importance in the history of conceptions of omnipotence. It appeared obvious to Spinoza that *God can bring about everything that God can bring about,* and that to deny this would be flatly incompatible with God's omnipotence (*Ethics* I.17, scholium). Well, the italicized sentence is syntactically ambiguous. "Everything that God can bring about God can bring about" is one possible reading of the sentence, and this is an obvious, indeed trivial predication about God, which must be true if there is a God at all. But the other way of taking the sentence relates to a supposed feat of *bringing about everything that God can bring about*—all of these bringable-about things *together*—and it says that God is capable of *this* feat. This is clearly the way Spinoza wishes us to take the sentence. But taken this way, it is not obvious at all; quite the contrary, it's obviously false. For among the things that are severally possible for God to bring about, there are going to be some pairs that are not *compossible*, pairs which it is logically impossible should both come about; and then it is beyond God's power to bring about such a pair together—let alone, to bring about all the things together which he can bring about severally.

This does not give us a description of a *logically possible* feat which God cannot accomplish. However, there is nothing easier than to mention feats which are logically possible but which God cannot do, if Christianity is true. Lying and promise-breaking are logically possible feats: but

Christian faith, as I have said, collapses unless we are assured that God cannot lie and cannot break his promises.

This argument is an *ad hominem* argument addressed to Christians; but there are well-known logical arguments to show that on any view there must be some logically possible feats that are beyond God's power. One good example suffices: making a thing which its maker cannot afterwards destroy. This is certainly a possible feat, a feat that some human beings have performed. Can God perform the feat or not? If he cannot there is already some logically possible feat which God cannot perform. If God can perform the feat, then let us suppose that he does: *ponatur in esse,* as medieval logicians say. Then we are supposing God to have brought about a situation in which he *has* made something he cannot destroy; and in that situation destroying this thing is a *logically* possible feat that God cannot accomplish, for we surely cannot admit the idea of a creature whose destruction is logically *impossible*.

There have been various attempts to meet this argument. The most interesting one is that the proposition "God cannot make a thing that he cannot destroy" can be turned round to "Anything that God can make he can destroy"—which does not even look like an objection to God's being able to do everything logically possible. But this reply involves the very same bracketing fallacy that I exposed a moment ago in Spinoza. There, you will remember, we had to distinguish two ways of taking "God can bring about everything that God can bring about":

A. Everything that God can bring about, God can bring about.
B. God can bring about the following feat: to bring about everything that God can bring about.

And we saw that A is trivially true, given that there *is* a God, and B certainly false. Here, similarly, we have to distinguish two senses of "God cannot make a thing that its maker cannot destroy":

A. Anything that its maker cannot destroy, God cannot make.

B. God cannot bring about the following feat: to make something that its maker cannot destroy.

And here A does contrapose, as the objectors would have it, to "Anything that God can make, its maker can destroy," which on the face of it says nothing against God's power to do anything logically possible. But just as in the Spinoza example, the B reading purports to describe a single feat, *bringing about everything that God can bring about* (this feat, I argued, is impossible for God, because logically impossible): so in our present case, the B reading purports to describe a single feat, *making something that its maker cannot destroy*. This, as I said, is a logically possible feat, a feat that men sometimes do perform; so we may press the question whether this is a feat God can accomplish or not; and either way there will be some *logically possible* feat God cannot accomplish. So this notion of omnipotence, like the Cartesian idea of absolute omnipotence, turns out to be obviously incompatible with Christian faith, and moreover logically untenable.

Let us see, then, if we fare any better with the third theory: the theory that the only condition for the truth of "God can do so-and-so" is that "God does so-and-so" or "God is doing so-and-so" must be logically possible. As I said, this imposes a more restrictive condition than the second theory: for there are many feats that we can consistently suppose to be performed but cannot consistently suppose to be performed by God. This theory might thus get us out of the logical trouble that arose with the second theory about the feat: *making a thing that its maker cannot destroy*. For though this is a logically possible feat, a feat some creatures do perform, it might well be argued that "*God* has made a thing that its maker cannot destroy" is a proposition with a buried inconsistency in it; and if so, then on the present account of omnipotence we need not say "God *can* make a thing that its maker cannot destroy."

This suggestion also, however, can easily be refuted by an example of great philosophical importance that I borrow from Aquinas. "It comes about that Miss X never loses her virginity" is plainly a logically possible proposition: and so also is "God brings it about that Miss X never loses her virginity." All the same, if it so happens that Miss X already has lost her virginity, "God *can* bring it about that Miss X never loses her virginity" is false (Ia q. xxv art. 4 ad 3 um). Before Miss X had lost her virginity, it would have been true to say this very thing; so what we can truly say about what God can do will be different at different times. This appears to imply a change in God, but Aquinas would certainly say, and I think rightly, that it doesn't really do so. It is just like the case of Socrates coming to be shorter than Theaetetus because Theaetetus grows up; here, the change is on the side of Theaetetus not of Socrates. So in our case, the change is really in Miss X not in God; something about her passes from the realm of possibility to the realm of *fait accompli,* and thus *no longer* comes under the concept of the accomplishable—*deficit a ratione possibilium* (Aquinas, loc. cit., ad 2 um). I think Aquinas's position here is strongly defensible; but if he does defend it, he has abandoned the position that God can do everything that it is not a priori impossible *for God to do,* let alone the position that God can bring about everything describable in a logically consistent way.

Is it a priori impossible for God to do something wicked? And if not, *could* God do something wicked? There have been expressed serious doubts about this: I came across them in that favourite of modern moral philosophers, Richard Price. We must distinguish, he argues, between God's natural and his moral attributes: if God is a free moral being, even as we are, it must not be absolutely impossible for God to do something wicked. There must be just a chance that God should do something wicked: no doubt it will be a really infinitesimal chance—after all, God has persevered in ways of virtue on a vast scale for inconceivably long—but the chance must be there, or God isn't free and isn't therefore laudable for his goodness. The way this reverend gentleman commends his Maker's morals is so startling that you may suspect me of misrepresentation; I can only ask any sceptic to check in Daiches

Raphael's edition of Price's work! Further comment on my part is I hope needless.

A much more restrained version of the same sort of thing is to be found in the Scholastic distinction between God's *potentia absoluta* and *potentia ordinata.* The former is God's power considered in abstraction from his wisdom and goodness, the latter is God's power considered as controlled in its exercise by his wisdom and goodness. Well, as regards a man it makes good sense to say: "He has the bodily and mental power to do so-and-so, but he certainly will not, it would be pointlessly silly and wicked." But does anything remotely like this make sense to say about Almighty God? If not, the Scholastic distinction I have cited is wholly frivolous.

Let us then consider our fourth try. Could it be said that the "everything" in "God can do everything" refers precisely to things that are not in the realm of *fait accompli* but of futurity? This will not do either. If God can promulgate promises to men, then as regards any promises that are not yet fulfilled we know that they certainly will be fulfilled: and in that case God clearly has not a *potentia ad utrumque*—a two-way power of either actualizing the event that will fulfil the promise or not actualizing it. God can then only do what will fulfil his promise. And if we try to evade this by denying that God can make promises known to men, then we have once more denied something essential to Christian faith, and we are still left with something that God cannot do.

I must here remove the appearance of a fallacy. God cannot but fulfil his promises, I argued; so he has not a two-way power, *potentia ad utrumque,* as regards these particular future events. This argument may have seemed to involve the fallacy made notorious in medieval logical treatises, of confusing the necessity by which something follows—*necessitas consequentiae*—with the necessity of that very thing which follows—*necessitas consequentis.* If it is impossible for God to promise and not perform, then if we know God has promised something we may infer with certainty that he will perform it. Surely, it may be urged, this is enough for Christian faith and hope; we need not go on to say that God *cannot not* bring about the future event in question. If we do that, are we not precisely committing the hoary modal fallacy I have just described?

I answer that there are various senses of "necessary." The future occurrence of such-and-such, when God has promised that such-and-such shall be, is of course not logically necessary; but it may be necessary in the sense of being, as Arthur Prior puts it, now unpreventable. If God *has* promised that Israel shall be saved, then there is nothing that anybody, even God, can do about that; this past state of affairs is now unpreventable. But it is also necessary in the same way that if God has promised then he will perform; God cannot do anything about that either—cannot make himself liable to break his word. So we have as premises "Necessarily p" and "Necessarily if p then q," in the same sense of "necessarily"; and from these premises it not merely necessarily follows that q— the conclusion in the necessitated form, "Necessarily q" with the same sense of "necessarily," follows from the premises. So if God has promised that Israel shall be saved, the future salvation of Israel is not only certain but inevitable; God must save Israel, because he cannot not save Israel without breaking his word given in the past and he can neither alter the past nor break his word.

Again, in regard to this and other arguments, some people may have felt discomfort at my not drawing in relation to God the sort of distinction between various applications of "can" that are made in human affairs: the "can" of knowing how to, the "can" of physical power to, the "can" of opportunity, the "can" of what fits in with one's plans. But of course the way we make these distinct applications of "he can" to a human agent will not be open if we are talking about God. There is no question of God's knowing how but lacking the strength, or being physically able to but not knowing how; moreover (to make a distinction that comes in a logical example of Aristotle's) though there is a right time when God may bring something about, it is inept to speak of his then having the opportunity to do it. (To develop this distinction: if "x" stands for a finite agent and

"so-and-so" for an act directly in x's power, there is little difference between "At time t it is suitable for x to bring so-and-so about" and "It is suitable for x to bring so-and-so about at time t"; but if "x" means God, the temporal qualification "at time t" can attach only to what is brought about; God does not live through successive times and find one more suitable than another.)

These distinct applications of "can" are distinct only for finite and changeable agents, not for a God whose action is universal and whose mind and character and design are unchangeable. There is thus no ground for fear that in talking about God we may illicitly slip from one sort of "can" to another. What we say God can do is always in respect of his changeless supreme power.

All the same, we have to assert different propositions at different times in order to say truly what God can do. What is past, as I said, ceases to be alterable even by God; and thus the truth-value of a proposition like "God can bring it about that Miss X never loses her virginity" alters once she has lost it. Similarly, God's promise makes a difference to what we can thereafter truly say God can do; it is less obvious in this case that the real change involved is a change in creatures, not in God, than it was as regards Miss X's virginity, but a little thought should show that the promulgation or making known of God's intention, which is involved in a promise, is precisely a change in the creatures to whom the promise is made.

Thus all the four theories of omnipotence that I have considered break down. Only the first overtly flouts logic; but the other three all involve logical contradictions, or so it seems; and moreover, all these theories have consequences fatal to the truth of Christian faith. The last point really ought not to surprise us; for the absolute confidence a Christian must have in God's revelation and promises involves, as I said at the outset, both a belief that God is almighty, in the sense I explained, and a belief that there are certain describable things that God cannot do and therefore will not do.

If I were to end the discussion at this point, I

should leave an impression of Aquinas's thought that would be seriously unfair to him; for although in the passage I cited Aquinas appears verbally committed to our second theory of omnipotence, it seems clear that this does not adequately represent his mind. Indeed, it was from Aquinas himself and from the *Summa Theologica* that I borrowed an example which refutes even the weaker third theory, let alone the second one. Moreover, in the other Summa (Book II, c. xxv) there is an instructive list of things that *Deus omnipotens* is rightly said not to be able to do. But the mere occurrence of this list makes me doubt whether Aquinas can be said to believe, in any reasonable interpretation, the thesis that God can do everything. That God is almighty in my sense Aquinas obviously did believe; I am suggesting that here his "omnipotens" means "almighty" rather than "omnipotent." Aquinas does not say or even imply that he has given an *exhaustive* list of kinds of case in which "God can do so-and-so" or "God can make so-and-so" turns out false; so what he says here does not commit him to "God can do everything" even in the highly unnatural sense "God can do everything that is not excluded under one or other of the following heads."

I shall not explore Aquinas's list item by item, because I have made open or tacit use of his considerations at several points in the foregoing and do not wish to repeat myself. But one batch of items raises a specially serious problem. My attention was drawn to the problem by a contribution that the late Mr. Michael Foster made orally during a discussion at the Socratic Club in Oxford. Aquinas tells us that if "doing so-and-so" implies what he calls passive potentiality, then "God can do so-and-so" is false. On this ground he excluded all of the following:

- God can be a body or something of the sort.
- God can be tired or oblivious.
- God can be angry or sorrowful.
- God can suffer violence or be overcome.
- God can undergo corruption.

Foster pointed out that as a Christian Aquinas was committed to asserting the contradictory of all these theses. *Contra factum non valet ratio;* it's no

good arguing that God cannot do what God has done, and in the Incarnation God did do all these things Aquinas said God cannot do. The Word that was God *was* made flesh (and the literal meaning of the Polish for this is: The Word became a body!); God the Son *was* tired and did sink into the oblivion of sleep; he *was* angry and sorrowful; he was bound like a thief, beaten, and crucified; and though we believe his Body did not decay, it suffered corruption in the sense of becoming a corpse instead of a living body—Christ in the Apocalypse uses of himself the startling words "I became a corpse," *"egenomēn nekros,"* and the Church has always held that the dead Body of Christ during the *triduum mortis* was adorable with Divine worship for its union to the Divine Nature.

Foster's objection to Aquinas is the opposite kind of objection to the ones I have been raising against the various theories of omnipotence I have discussed. I have been saying that these theories say by implication that God *can* do certain things which Christian belief requires one to say God *cannot* do; Foster is objecting that Aquinas's account says God *cannot* do some things which according to Christian faith God *can* do and has in fact done.

It would take me too far to consider how Aquinas might have answered this objection. It would not of course be outside his intellectual milieu; it is the very sort of objection that a Jew or Moor might have used, accepting Aquinas's account of what God cannot do, in order to argue against the Incarnation. I shall simply mention one feature that Aquinas's reply would have had: it would have to make essential use of the particle "as," or in Latin *"secundum quod."* God did become man, so God can become man and have a human body; but God *as* God cannot be man or have a body.

The logic of these propositions with "as" in them, reduplicative propositions as they are traditionally called, is a still unsolved problem, although as a matter of history it was a problem raised by Aristotle in the *Prior Analytics.* We must not forget that such propositions occur frequently in ordinary discourse; we use them there with an ill-founded confidence that we know our way around. Jones, we say, is Director of the Gnome Works and Mayor of Middletown; he gets a salary *as* Director and an expense allowance *as* Mayor; he signs one letter *as* Director, another *as* Mayor. We say all this, but how far do we understand the logical relations of what we say? Very little, I fear. One might have expected some light and leading from medieval logicians; the theological importance of reduplicative propositions did in fact lead to their figuring as a topic in medieval logical treatises. But I have not found much that is helpful in such treatments as I have read.

I hope to return to this topic later. Meanwhile, even though it has nothing directly to do with almightiness or omnipotence, I shall mention one important logical point that is already to be found in Aristotle. A superficial grammatical illusion may make us think that "A as P is Q" attaches the predicate "Q" to a complex subject "A as P." But Aristotle insists, to my mind rightly, on the analysis: "A" subject, "is as P, Q" predicate—so that we have not a complex subject-term, but a complex predicate-term; clearly, this predicate entails the simple conjunctive predicate "is both P and Q" but not conversely. This niggling point of logic has in fact some theological importance. When theologians are talking about Christ as God and Christ as Man, they may take the two phrases to be two logical subjects of predication, if they have failed to see the Aristotelian point; and then they are likely to think or half think that Christ as God is one entity or *Gegenstand* and Christ as Man is another. I am sure some theologians have yielded to this temptation, which puts them on a straight road to the Nestorian heresy.

What Aquinas would have done, I repeat, to meet Foster's objection in the mouth of a Jew or Moor is to distinguish between what we say God can do, *simpliciter,* and what we say God *as God*

can do, using the reduplicative form of proposition. Now if we do make such a distinction, we are faced with considerable logical complications, particularly if we accept the Aristotelian point about the reduplicative construction. Let us go back to our friend Jones: there is a logical difference between:

1. Jones as Mayor can attend this committee meeting.
2. Jones can as Mayor attend this committee meeting.

as we may see if we spell the two out a little:

1. Jones as Mayor has the opportunity of attending the committee meeting.
2. Jones has the opportunity of (attending this committee meeting as Mayor).

We can easily see now that 1 and 2 are logically distinct: for one thing, if Jones is not yet Mayor but has an opportunity of becoming Mayor and *then* attending the committee meeting, 2 would be true and 1 false. And if we want to talk about what Jones as Mayor *cannot* do, the complexities pile up; for then we have to consider how the negation can be inserted at one or other position in a proposition of one of these forms, and how all the results are logically related.

All this is logical work to be done if we are to be clear about the implications of saying that God can or cannot do so-and-so, or again that God *as God* can or cannot do so-and-so. It is obvious, without my developing the matter further, that the logic of all this will not be simple. It's a far cry from the simple method of bringing our question "Can God do so-and-so?" under a reassuring principle "God can do *everything*." But I hope I have made it clear that any reassurance we get that way is entirely spurious.

Bibliography for Part IV

Davis, Stephen T. *Logic and The Nature of God.* Grand Rapids, Mich.: Eerdmans, 1983. A very perceptive and lucid analysis of the attributes of God.

Geach, Peter. *Providence and Evil.* Cambridge: Cambridge Univ. Press, 1977. An important work on the attributes of God.

Hartshorne, Charles. *The Divine Reality.* New Haven, Conn.: Yale Univ. Press, 1948. A very good exposition of the process theological view of God and his attributes.

Kenny, Anthony, ed. *Aquinas: A Collection of Critical Essays.* New York: Doubleday, 1969. In this good collection Kenny's own essay on divine foreknowledge and human freedom stands out.

Kretzmann, Norman. "Omniscience and Immutability." *Journal of Philosophy* 63 (1966): 409–21. A cogent article on the incoherence of the notion of immutability.

Pike, Nelson. *God and Time.* Ithaca, N.Y.: Cornell Univ. Press, 1970. A seminal work that has rightly played a central role in the debate on God's eternity.

Stump, Eleonore, and Norman Kretzmann. "Eternity." *Journal of Philosophy* 78 (August 1981): 429–58. Perhaps the most sophisticated defense of the traditional view of God's timeless eternity ever written.

Swinburne, Richard. *The Coherence of Theism.* Oxford: Oxford Univ. Press, 1977. A highly original work on the attributes of God, cogently argued.

Urban, Linwood, and Douglas Walton, eds. *The Power of God.* Oxford: Oxford Univ. Press, 1978. The best available collection of articles on divine omnipotence.

Wolterstorff, Nicholas. "God Everlasting." In *God and the Good,* edited by C. Orlebeke and L. Smedes. Grand Rapids, Mich.: Eerdmans, 1975. Possibly the best defense of the thesis that God's eternity is temporal rather than timeless.

PART V

MIRACLES AND REVELATION

What are miracles, and are they possible? Should miracles necessarily be defined as violations of the laws of nature? This notion has been disputed on the basis of the contention that in the Bible, which is the witness to the most significant alleged miracles in the Judeo-Christian tradition, there is no concept of nature as a closed system of law. For the Biblical writers, miracles signify simply an "extraordinary coincidence of a beneficial nature."[*]

This view is proposed by R. F. Holland in his article "The Miraculous," in which the following story is illustrative:

> A child riding his toy motor-car strays on to an unguarded railway crossing near his house and a wheel of his car gets stuck down the side of one of the rails. An express train is due to pass with the signals in its favour and a curve in the track makes it impossible for the driver to stop his train in time to avoid any obstruction he might encounter on the crossing. The mother coming out of the house to look for her child sees him on the crossing and hears the train approaching. She runs forward shouting and waving. The little boy remains seated in his car looking downward engrossed in the task of pedalling it free. The brakes of the train are applied and it comes to rest a few feet from the child. The mother thanks God for the miracle; which she never ceases to think of as such, although, as she in due course learns, there was nothing supernatural about the manner in which the brakes of the train came to be applied. The driver had fainted, for a reason that had nothing to do with the presence of the child on the line, and the brakes were applied automatically as his hand ceased to exert pressure on the control lever. He fainted on this particular afternoon because his blood pressure had risen after an exceptionally heavy lunch during which he had quarrelled with a colleague, and the change in blood pressure caused a clot of blood to be dislodged and circulate. He fainted at the time when he did on the afternoon in question because this was the time at which the coagulation in his blood stream reached the brain.[†]

Was this a miracle, or was it not? It is if we define miracles in Fuller's biblical sense. It is not if we define them in an interventionist sense. We can certainly understand the woman's feeling on the matter, and perhaps in some mysterious way God had 'allowed' nature to run its course so that the little boy would be saved. Perhaps we need not be overly exclusionary but say

---

[*] R. H. Fuller, *Interpreting the Miracle* (London, 1968), 8.

[†] *American Philosophical Quarterly*, 2 (1965).

that if there is a God, each sense is valid: the *weaker* sense of an extraordinary coincidence and the *stronger* sense of a violation of the laws of nature. Nonetheless, what is philosophically interesting as well as controversial with regard to miracles is the stronger sense, that of a violation of the laws of nature by a divine force. It is this sense of miracles that we consider in this part of our work.

The most celebrated article ever written on miracles is by David Hume. In section 10 of *An Enquiry Concerning Human Understanding* he set forth an argument against belief in miracles that provoked a lively response in his day and has continued to be the subject of vigorous dispute up to the present day. The three articles that follow Hume's in our readings all deal with Hume's argument, so it is important that you read it carefully. Let us analyze it briefly. Hume begins his attack on miracles by appealing to the biases of his Scottish Presbyterian readers. He tells of a marvelous proof that Dr. Tillotson has devised against the Roman Catholic doctrine of transubstantiation, the doctrine that the body and blood of Christ are present in Holy Communion. Tillotson argues that since the evidence of the senses is of the highest rank and since it is evident that it must diminish in passing through the original witnesses to their disciples, the doctrine of transubstantiation is always contrary to the rules of reasoning and opposed to our sense experience.

1. Our evidence for the truth of transubstantiation is less than the evidence of our senses. (Even for the apostles this was the case, and their testimony must diminish in authority in passing from them to their disciples).
2. A weaker evidence can never destroy a stronger. (That is, we are not justified in believing the weaker evidence over the stronger.)
3. Therefore, we are not warranted in believing in transubstantiation. (Even if the doctrine of transubstantiation were clearly revealed in the Scriptures, it would be against the rule of reason to give our assent to it).

No doubt Hume's Protestant readers were delighted with such a sound refutation of the doctrine of transubstantiation. But the mischievous Hume now turns the knife on his readers. A wise person always proportions one's belief to the evidence, he goes on. One has an enormous amount of evidence for the laws of nature, so that any testimony to the contrary is to be seriously doubted. Although miracles, as violations of the laws of nature, are not logically impossible, we are never justified in believing in one. The skeleton of the argument contained in the reading goes something like this:

1. One ought to proportion one's belief to the evidence.
2. Sense perception is generally better evidence than testimony (if for no other reason than that valid testimony is based on another's sense experience).
3. Therefore, when there is a conflict between sense experience and testimony, one ought to believe according to sense perception.

4. Sense perception does not reveal any miracles to us (but rather the presumption of natural law prevails).
5. Therefore, we are never justified in believing in miracles, but we are justified in believing in the naturalness of all events.

Since we have enormous evidence in favor of the uniformity of nature, every testimony of a miracle must be weighed against that preponderance and be found wanting. But what if we believe that we personally have beheld a miracle? Aren't we justified in believing one in that case? No, for given the principle of induction (that every time we pursue an event *far enough*, we discover it to have a natural cause), we are still not justified in believing the event to be a miracle. Rather we ought to look further (*far enough*) until we discover the natural cause. The only exception to this rule (or "proof" against miracles) is if it would be even more miraculous for a miracle not to have occurred: "That no testimony is sufficient to establish a miracle, unless the testimony be of such a kind, that its falsehood would be more marvelous, than the fact, which it endeavors to establish; and even in that case there is a mutual destruction of argument, and the superior only gives us an assurance suitable to that degree of force, which remains, after deducting the inferior." The best we can hope for is an agnostic standoff in the matter.

But the criteria that would have to be fulfilled would be that (1) A sufficient number of witnesses of (2) good sense and education and (3) integrity and reputation would have to testify to a (4) public performance of the incident. Hume offers several putative examples of such cases and argues that they are really not fulfilled in any of them.

One of the most vigorous critics of Hume has been Richard Swinburne, who in our second reading takes issue with him. Swinburne first inquires whether there could be evidence that a law of nature had been violated and, second, whether there could be evidence that the violation was due to a god. To satisfy the first inquiry, we would have to have good reason to believe that an event has occurred contrary to the predictions of a law that we had good reason to believe to be a law of nature; and furthermore we would have to have good reason to believe that events similar to the event would not occur in circumstances similar to those of the original occurrence. For if the event were repeatable, we would have to account for both events through the formulation of a law.

Swinburne gives as an illustration of a successful occurrence that of someone levitating (i.e., rising into the air and remaining there). If the event were sufficiently nonrepeatable and defied every attempt to work it into a lawlike framework, we would have good reason to believe that the event was a violation of the laws of nature. Here Hume seems to put the standards of justified belief too high, for given a high quality of witness, there is no reason for not believing that a violation of nature's laws had taken place.

But to be a miracle the violation of a natural law would have to be the work of a god, who is not a material object. What kind of evidence would we have to have to believe that a divine being had intervened in our world?

Here Swinburne distinguishes between situations in which we do and in which we do not have sufficient circumstantial evidence to warrant our attributing the anomolous event to the work of an invisible deity. The circumstantial evidence must be strong before we are justified in believing that an event is a genuine miracle—for example, the case of Elijah's calling on Yahweh to send fire and consume his offering on Mt. Carmel (1 Kings 18). Such an event would be sufficiently analogous to normal human agency to justify our believing that a divine being caused it. But all this supposes that we do have some independent evidence for the existence of a divine being in the first place, which justifies our seeing anomolous events as genuine miracles.

Our third reading is "Miracles and Testimony" by the late J. L. Mackie of Oxford University, a man who loved Hume and exemplified his thought. In this revised Humean account of miracles, Mackie argues that the evidence for miracles will never in practice be very great. The argument is epistemological, not ontological. That is, while miracles may be logically possible (and may indeed have occurred), we are never justified in believing in one. The concept of a miracle is a coherent one, but, Mackie argues, the *double* burden of showing both that the event took place *and* that it violated the laws of nature will be extremely hard to lift, for "whatever tends to show that it would have been a violation of natural law tends for that very reason to make it most unlikely that it actually happened." Correspondingly, the deniers of miracles have two strategies of defense. They may argue that the event took place but wasn't a violation of a law of nature (the event simply followed an unknown law of nature); or they can admit that if the event had happened, it would indeed have been a violation of a law of nature, but for that reason "there is a very strong presumption against its having happened, which it is most unlikely that any testimony will be able to outweigh."

Our fourth reading, Richard L. Purtill's "Miracles: What If They Happen?", continues the critique of Hume begun by Swinburne. Purtill argues that a two-stage case for the occurrence of miracles can be made: first, an argument for the general possibilities of miracles, and second, an argument for the actuality of miracles. Comparing the laws of nature to the laws of a nation, Purtill argues that a miracle is analogous to an exception to the law of the land—for example, President Ford's pardoning of Richard Nixon after Watergate.

Regarding the question of whether we have evidence that a miracle ever took place, Purtill looks at various reports of miracles and sets up limiting criteria—for example, they must not be utterly fantastic, as fairy tales are; they must be interwoven into the larger fabric of the religion; there must be independent evidence for the truth of the religion. Purtill then examines the miracles of Christ in the light of those criteria and concludes that it is very likely that those miracles are genuine. If we already have reason to believe in a God who is active in human affairs, we should expect miracles; but if we do not have such independent reason to believe in God, we will be far less likely to believe in divine interventions.

In our final reading in this section, "Miracles and Revelation," Richard Swinburne takes up the matter of miracles where he left off in his previous article. There he argued, contra Hume, that miracles were possible. Here he argues that given the proviso that the existence of God is a plausible hypothesis or assumption, it is reasonable to expect that he would reveal himself in human history and that he would confirm the revelation by miracles (including predictive prophecy). Swinburne here sets forth the criteria that would have to be met were a religion to claim that it is based on that revelation.

V.1   Against Miracles

DAVID HUME

The reading by David Hume that follows is the most celebrated article ever written on miracles. In it Hume sets forth an argument against belief in miracles that provoked a lively response in his day and has continued to be the subject of vigorous dispute up to the present day. Hume begins his attack on miracles by appealing to the biases of his Scottish Presbyterian readers. He tells of a marvelous proof that Dr. Tillotson has devised against the Roman Catholic doctrine of transubstantiation, the doctrine that the body and blood of Christ are present in Holy Communion. Tillotson argues that since the evidence of the senses is of the highest rank and since it is evident that it must diminish in passing through the original witnesses to their disciples, the doctrine of transubstantiation is always contrary to the rules of reasoning and opposed to our sense experience.

No doubt Hume's Protestant readers were delighted with such a sound refutation of the doctrine of transubstantiation. But the mischievous Hume now turns the knife on his readers. A wise person always proportions one's belief to the evidence, he goes on. One has an enormous amount of evidence for the laws of nature, so that any testimony to the contrary is to be seriously doubted. Although miracles, as violations of the laws of nature, are not logically impossible, we are never justified in believing in one. Since we have enormous evidence in favor of the uniformity of nature, every testimony of a miracle must be weighed against that preponderance and be found wanting.

Reprinted from David Hume, *An Enquiry Concerning Human Understanding* (Oxford: Oxford Univ. Press, 1748). Footnotes edited.

Part I.

There is, in Dr. Tillotson's writings, an argument against the *real presence,* which is as concise, and elegant, and strong as any argument can possibly be supposed against a doctrine, so little worthy of a serious refutation. It is acknowledged on all hands, says that learned prelate, that the authority, either of the scripture or of tradition, is founded merely in the testimony of the apostles, who were eye-witnesses to those miracles of our Saviour, by which he proved his divine mission. Our evidence, then, for the truth of the *Christian* religion is less than the evidence for the truth of our senses; because, even in the first authors of our religion, it was no greater; and it is evident it must diminish in passing from them to their disciples; nor can any one rest such confidence in their testimony, as in the immediate object of his senses. But a weaker evidence can never destroy a stronger; and therefore, were the doctrine of the real presence ever so clearly revealed in scripture, it were directly contrary to the rules of just reasoning to give our assent to it. It contradicts sense, though both the scripture and tradition, on which it is supposed to be built, carry not such evidence with them as sense; when they are considered merely as external evidences, and are not brought home to every one's breast, by the immediate operation of the Holy Spirit.

Nothing is so convenient as a decisive argument of this kind, which must at least *silence* the most arrogant bigotry and superstition, and free us from their impertinent solicitations. I flatter myself, that I have discovered an argument of a like nature, which, if just, will, with the wise and learned, be an everlasting check to all kinds of superstitious delusion, and consequently, will be useful as long as the world endures. For so long, I presume, will the accounts of miracles and prodigies be found in all history, sacred and profane.

Though experience be our only guide in reasoning concerning matters of fact; it must be acknowledged, that this guide is not altogether infallible, but in some cases is apt to lead us into errors. One, who in our climate, should expect better weather in any week of June than in one of December, would reason justly, and conformably to experience; but it is certain, that he may happen, in the event, to find himself mistaken. However, we may observe, that, in such a case, he would have no cause to complain of experience; because it commonly informs us beforehand of the uncertainty, by that contrariety of events, which we may learn from a diligent observation. All effects follow not with like certainty from their supposed causes. Some events are found, in all countries and all ages, to have been constantly conjoined together: Others are found to have been more variable, and sometimes to disappoint our expectations; so that, in our reasonings concerning matter of fact, there are all imaginable degrees of assurance, from the highest certainty to the lowest species of moral evidence.

A wise man, therefore, proportions his belief to the evidence. In such conclusions as are founded on an infallible experience, he expects the event with the last degree of assurance, and regards his past experience as a full *proof* of the future existence of that event. In other cases, he proceeds with more caution: He weighs the opposite experiments: He considers which side is supported by the greater number of experiments: to that side he inclines, with doubt and hesitation; and when at last he fixes his judgement, the evidence exceeds not what we properly call *probability*. All probability, then, supposes an opposition of experiments and observations, where the one side is found to overbalance the other, and to produce a degree of evidence, proportioned to the superiority. A hundred instances or experiments on one side, and fifty on another, afford a doubtful expectation of any event; though a hundred uniform experiments, with only one that is contradictory, reasonably beget a pretty strong degree of assurance. In all cases, we must balance the opposite experiments, where they are opposite, and deduct the smaller number from the greater, in order to know the exact force of the superior evidence.

To apply these principles to a particular instance; we may observe, that there is no species of reasoning more common, more useful, and even necessary to human life, than that which is derived from the testimony of men, and the reports of eye-witnesses and spectators. This species of reasoning, perhaps, one may deny to be founded on the relation of cause and effect. I shall not dispute about a word. It will be sufficient to observe that our assurance in any argument of this kind is derived from no other principle than our observation of the veracity of human testimony, and of the usual conformity of facts to the reports of witnesses. It being a general maxim, that no objects have any discoverable connexion together, and that all the inferences, which we can draw from one to another, are founded merely on our experience of their constant and regular conjunction; it is evident, that we ought not to make an exception to this maxim in favour of human testimony, whose connexion with any event seems, in itself, as little necessary as any other. Were not the memory tenacious to a certain degree; had not men commonly an inclination to truth and a principle of probity; were they not sensible to shame, when detected in a falsehood: Were not these, I say, discovered by *experience* to be qualities, inherent in human nature, we should never repose the least confidence in human testimony. A man delirious, or noted for falsehood and villany, has no manner of authority with us.

And as the evidence, derived from witnesses and human testimony, is founded on past experience, so it varies with the experience, and is regarded either as a *proof* or a *probability*, according at the conjunction between any particular kind of report and any kind of object has been found to be constant or variable. There are a number of circumstances to be taken into consideration in all judgements of this kind; and the ultimate standard, by which we determine all disputes, that may arise concerning them, is always derived from experience and observation. Where this experience is not entirely uniform on any side, it is attended with an unavoidable contrariety in our judgements, and with the same opposition and mutual destruction of argument as in every other kind of evidence. We frequently hesitate concerning the reports of others. We balance the opposite circumstances, which cause any doubt or uncertainty; and when we discover a superiority on any side, we incline to it; but still with a diminution of assurance, in proportion to the force of its antagonist.

This contrariety of evidence, in the present case, may be derived from several different causes; from the opposition of contrary testimony; from the character or number of the witnesses; from the manner of their delivering their testimony; or from the union of all these circumstances. We entertain a suspicion concerning any matter of fact, when the witnesses contradict each other; when they are but few, or of a doubtful character; when they have an interest in what they affirm; when they deliver their testimony with hesitation, or on the contrary, with too violent asseverations. There are many other particulars of the same kind, which may diminish or destroy the force of any argument, derived from human testimony.

Suppose, for instance, that the fact, which the testimony endeavors to establish, partakes of the extraordinary and the marvellous; in that case, the evidence, resulting from the testimony, admits of a diminution, greater or less, in proportion as the fact is more or less unusual. The reason why we place any credit in witnesses and historians, is not derived from any *connexion,* which we perceive *a priori,* between testimony and reality, but because we are accustomed to find a conformity between them. But when the fact attested is such a one as has seldom fallen under our observation, here is a contest of two opposite experiences; of which the one destroys the other, as far as its force goes, and the superior can only operate on the mind by the force, which remains. The very same principle of experience, which gives us a certain degree of assurance in the testimony of witnesses, gives us also, in this case, another degree of assurance against the fact, which they endeavour to establish; from which contradition there necessarily

arises a counterpoize, and mutual destruction of belief and authority.

I should not believe such a story were it told me by Cato, was a proverbial saying in Rome, even during the lifetime of that philosophical patriot. The incredibility of a fact, it was allowed, might invalidate so great an authority.

The Indian prince, who refused to believe the first relations concerning the effects of frost, reasoned justly; and it naturally required very strong testimony to engage his assent to facts, that arose from a state of nature, with which he was unacquainted, and which bore so little analogy to those events, of which he had had constant and uniform experience. Though they were not contrary to his experience, they were not conformable to it.

But in order to encrease the probability against the testimony of witnesses, let us suppose, that the fact, which they affirm, instead of being only marvellous, is really miraculous; and suppose also, that the testimony considered apart and in itself, amounts to an entire proof; in that case, there is proof against proof, of which the strongest must prevail, but still with a diminution of its force, in proportion to that of its antagonist.

A miracle is a violation of the laws of nature; and as a firm and unalterable experience has established these laws, the proof against a miracle, from the very nature of the fact, is as entire as any argument from experience can possibly be imagined. Why is it more than probable, that all men must die; that lead cannot, of itself, remain suspended in the air; that fire consumes wood, and is extinguished by water; unless it be, that these events are found agreeable to the laws of nature, and there is required a violation of these laws, or in other words, a miracle to prevent them? Nothing is esteemed a miracle, if it ever happen in the common course of nature. It is no miracle that a man, seemingly in good health, should die on a sudden: because such a kind of death, though more unusual than any other, has yet been frequently observed to happen. But it is a miracle, that a dead man should come to life; because that has never been observed in any age or country. There must, therefore, be a uniform experience against every miraculous event, otherwise the event would not merit that appellation. And as a uniform experience amounts to a proof, there is here a direct and full *proof*, from the nature of the fact, against the existence of any miracle; nor can such a proof be destroyed, or the miracle rendered credible, but by an opposite proof, which is superior.[1]

The plain consequence is (and it is a general maxim worthy of our attention), 'That no testimony is sufficient to establish a miracle, unless the testimony be of such a kind, that its falsehood would be more miraculous, than the fact, which it endeavours to establish; and even in that case there is a mutual destruction of arguments, and the superior only gives us an assurance suitable to that degree of force, which remains, after deducting the inferior.' When anyone tells me, that he saw a dead man restored to life, I immediately consider with myself, whether it be more probable, that this person should either deceive or be deceived, or that the fact, which he relates, should really have happened. I weigh the one miracle against the other; and according to the superiority, which I discover, I pronounce my decision, and always reject the greater miracle. If the falsehood of his testimony would be more miraculous, than the event which he relates; then, and not till then, can he pretend to command my belief or opinion.

Part II.

In the foregoing reasoning we have supposed, that the testimony, upon which a miracle is founded, may possibly amount to an entire proof, and that the falsehood of that testimony would be a real prodigy: But it is easy to shew, that we have been a great deal too liberal in our concession, and that there never was a miraculous event established on so full an evidence.

For *first*, there is not to be found, in all history, any miracle attested by a sufficient number of men, of such unquestioned good-sense, education, and learning, as to secure us against all delusion in themselves; of such undoubted integrity, as to place them beyond all suspicion of any design to deceive others; of such credit and reputation in the eyes of mankind, as to have a great deal to lose in case of their being detected in any falsehood; and at the same time, attesting facts performed in such a public manner and in so celebrated a part of the world, as to render the detection unavoidable: All which circumstances are requisite to give us a full assurance in the testimony of men.

Secondly. We may observe in human nature a principle which, if strictly examined, will be found to diminish extremely the assurance, which we might, from human testimony, have, in any kind of prodigy. The maxim, by which we commonly conduct ourselves in our reasonings, is, that the objects, of which we have no experience, resembles those, of which we have; that what we have found to be most usual is always most probable; and that where there is an opposition of arguments, we ought to give the preference to such as are founded on the greatest number of past observations. But though, in proceeding by this rule, we readily reject any fact which is unusual and incredible in an ordinary degree; yet in advancing farther, the mind observes not always the same rule; but when anything is affirmed utterly absurd and miraculous, it rather the more readily admits of such a fact, upon account of that very circumstance, which ought to destroy all its authority. The passion of *surprise* and *wonder,* arising from miracles, being an agreeable emotion, gives a sensible tendency towards the belief of those events, from which it is derived. And this goes so far, that even those who cannot enjoy this pleasure immediately, nor can believe those miraculous events, of which they are informed, yet love to partake of the satisfaction at second-hand or by rebound, and place a pride and delight in exciting the admiration of others.

With what greediness are the miraculous accounts of travellers received, their descriptions of sea and land monsters, their relations of wonderful adventures, strange men, and uncouth manners? But if the spirit of religion join itself to the love of wonder, there is an end of common sense; and human testimony, in these circumstances, loses all pretensions to authority. A religionist may be an enthusiast, and imagine he sees what has no reality: he may know his narrative to be false, and yet persevere in it, with the best intentions in the world, for the sake of promoting so holy a cause: or even where this delusion has not place, vanity, excited by so strong a temptation, operates on him more powerfully than on the rest of mankind in any other circumstances; and self-interest with equal force. His auditors may not have, and commonly have not, sufficient judgement to canvass his evidence: what judgement they have, they renounce by principle, in these sublime and mysterious subjects: or if they were ever so willing to employ it, passion and a heated imagination disturb the regularity of its operations. Their credulity increases his impudence: and his impudence overpowers their credulity.

Eloquence, when at its highest pitch, leaves little room for reason or reflection; but addressing itself entirely to the fancy or the affections, captivates the willing hearers, and subdues their understanding. Happily, this pitch it seldom attains. But what a Tully or a Demosthenes could scarcely effect over a Roman or Athenian audience, every *Capuchin,* every itinerant or stationary teacher can perform over the generality of mankind, and in a higher degree, by touching such gross and vulgar passions.

The many instances of forged miracles, and prophecies, and supernatural events, which, in all ages, have either been detected by contrary evidence, or which detect themselves by their absurdity, prove sufficiently the strong propensity of mankind to the extraordinary and the marvellous, and ought reasonably to beget a suspicion against all relations of this kind. This is our natural way of thinking, even with regard to the most common and most credible events. For instance: There is no kind of report which rises so easily, and spreads so quickly, especially in country places and provincial towns, as those concerning marriages; insomuch that two young persons of equal condition never see each other twice, but the whole neighborhood immediately join them together. The pleasure of telling a piece of news so interesting, of propagating it, and of being the first reporters of it, spreads the intelligence. And this is so well known, that no man of sense gives attention to these reports, till he find them confirmed by some greater evidence. Do not the same passions, and others still stronger, incline the generality of mankind to believe and report, with the greatest vehemence and assurance, all religious miracles?

Thirdly. It forms a strong presumption against all supernatural and miraculous relations, that they are observed chiefly to abound among ignorant and barbarous nations; or if a civilized people has ever given admission to any of them, that people will be found to have received them from ignorant and barbarous ancestors, who transmitted them with that inviolable sanction and authority, which always attend received opinions. When we peruse the first histories of all nations, we are apt to imagine ourselves transported into some new world; where the whole frame of nature is disjointed, and every element performs its operations in a different manner, from what it does at present. Battles, revolutions, pestilence, famine and death, are never the effect of those natural causes, which we experience. Prodigies, omens, oracles, judgements, quite obscure the few natural events, that are intermingled with them. But as the former grow thinner every page, in proportion as we advance nearer the enlightened ages, we soon learn, that there is nothing mysterious or supernatural in the case, but that all proceeds from the usual propensity of mankind towards the marvellous, and that, though this inclination may at intervals receive a check from sense and learning, it can never be thoroughly extirpated from human nature.

It is strange, a judicious reader is apt to say, upon the perusal of these wonderful historians, *that such prodigious events never happen in our days.* But it is nothing strange, I hope, that men should lie in all ages. You must surely have seen instances enough of that frailty. You have yourself heard many such marvellous relations started, which, being treated with scorn by all the wise and judicious, have at last been abandoned even by the vulgar. Be assured, that those renowned lies, which have spread and flourished to such a monstrous height, arose from like beginnings; but being sown in a more proper soil, shot up at last into prodigies almost equal to those which they relate. . . .

I may add as a *fourth* reason, which diminishes the authority of prodigies, that there is no testimony for any, even those which have not been expressly detected, that is not opposed by an infinite number of witnesses; so that not only the miracle destroys the credit of testimony, but the testimony destroys itself. To make this the better understood, let us consider, that, in matters of religion, whatever is different is contrary; and that it is impossible the religions of ancient Rome, of Turkey, of Siam, and of China should, all of them, be established on any solid foundation. Every miracle, therefore, pretended to have been wrought in any of these religions (and all of them abound in miracles), as its direct scope is to establish the particular system to which it is attributed; so has it the same force, though more indirectly, to overthrow every other system. In destroying a rival system, it likewise destroys the credit of those miracles, on which that system was established; so that all the prodigies of different religions are to be ragarded as contrary facts, and the evidences of these prodigies, whether weak or strong, as opposite to each other. According to this method of reasoning, when we believe any miracle of Mahomet or his successors, we have for our warrant the testimony of a few barbarous Arabians: And on the other hand, we are to regard the authority of Titus Livius, Plutarch, Tacitus, and, in short, of all the authors and witnesses, Grecian, Chinese, and Roman Catholic, who have related any miracle in their particular religion; I say, we are to regard their testimony in the same light as if they had mentioned that Mahometan miracle, and had in express terms contradicted it, with the same certainty as they have for the miracle they relate. This argument may appear over subtile and refined; but is not in reality different from the reasoning of a judge, who supposes, that the credit of two witnesses, maintaining a crime against any one, is destroyed by the testimony of two others, who affirm him to have been two hundred leagues distant, at the same instant when the crime is said to have been committed. . . . .

There is also a memorable story related by Cardinal de Retz, which may well deserve our consideration. When that intriguing politician fled into Spain, to avoid the persecution of his enemies, he passed through Saragossa, the capital of Arragon, where he was shewn, in the cathedral, a man, who had served seven years as a doorkeeper, and was well known to every body in town, that had ever paid his devotions at that church. He had been seen, for so long a time, wanting a leg; but recovered that limb by the rubbing of holy oil upon the stump; and the cardinal assures us that he saw him with two legs. This miracle was vouched by all the canons of the church; and the whole company in town were appealed to for a confirmation of the fact; whom the cardinal found, by their zealous devotion, to be thorough believers of the miracle. Here the relater was also cotemporary to the supposed prodigy, of an incredulous and libertine character, as well as of great genius; the miracle of so *singular* a nature as could scarcely admit of a counterfeit, and the witnesses very numerous, and all of them, in a manner, spectators of the fact, to which they gave their testimony. And what adds mightily to the force of the evidence, and may double our surprise on this occasion, is, that the cardinal himself, who relates the story, seems not to give any credit to it, and consequently cannot be suspected of any concurrence in the holy fraud. He considered justly, that it was not requisite, in order to reject a fact of this nature, to be able accurately to disprove the testimony, and to trace its falsehood, through all the circumstances of knavery and credulity which produced it. He knew, that, as this was commonly altogether impossible at any small distance of time and place; so was it extremely difficult, even where one was immediately present, by reason of the bigotry, ignorance, cunning, and roguery of a great part of mankind. He therefore concluded, like a just reasoner, that such an evidence carried falsehood upon the very face of it, and that a miracle, supported by any human testimony, was more properly a subject of derision than of argument.

There surely never was a greater number of miracles ascribed to one person, than those, which were lately said to have been wrought in France upon the tomb of Abbé Paris, the famous Jansenist, with whose sanctity the people were so long deluded. The curing of the sick, giving hearing to the deaf, and sight to the blind, were every where talked of as the usual effects of that holy sepulchre. But what is more extraordinary; many of the miracles were immediately proved upon the spot, before judges of unquestioned integrity, attested by witnesses of credit and distinction, in a learned age, and on the most eminent theatre that is now in the world. Nor is this all: a relation of them was published and dispersed every where; nor were the *Jesuits,* though a learned body, supported by the civil magistrate, and determined enemies to those opinions, in whose favour the miracles were said to have been wrought, ever able distinctly to refute or detect them. Where shall we find such a number of circumstances, agreeing to the corroboration of one fact? And what have we to oppose to such a cloud of witnesses, but the absolute impossibility or miraculous nature of the events, which they relate? And this surely, in the eyes of all reasonable people, will alone be regarded as a sufficient refutation.

Is the consequence just, because some human testimony has the utmost force and authority in some cases, when it relates the battle of Philippi or Pharsalia for instance; that therefore all kinds of testimony must, in all cases, have equal force and authority? Suppose that the Caesarean and Pompeian factions had, each of them, claimed the victory in these battles, and that the historians of each party had uniformly ascribed the advantage to their own side; how could mankind, at this distance, have been able to determine between them? The contrariety is equally strong between the miracles related by Herodotus or Plutarch, and those delivered by Mariana, Bede, or any monkish historian.

The wise lend a very academic faith to every report which favours the passion of the reporter; whether it magnifies his country, his family, or himself, or in any other way strikes in with his natural inclinations and propensities. But what greater temptation than to appear a missionary, a prophet, an ambassador from heaven? Who would not encounter many dangers and difficulties, in order to attain so sublime a character? Or if, by the help of vanity and a heated imagination,

a man has first made a convert of himself, and entered seriously into the delusion; who ever scruples to make use of pious frauds, in support of so holy and meritorious a cause?

The smallest spark may here kindle into the greatest flame; because the materials are always prepared for it. The *avidum genus auricularum,* the gazing populace, receive greedily, without examination, whatever sooths superstition, and promotes wonder.

How many stories of this nature have, in all ages, been detected and exploded in their infancy? How many more have been celebrated for a time, and have afterwards sunk into neglect and oblivion? Where such reports, therefore, fly about, the solution of the phenomenon is obvious; and we judge in conformity to regular experience and observation, when we account for it by the known and natural principles of credulity and delusion. And shall we, rather than have a recourse to so natural a solution, allow of a miraculous violation of the most established laws of nature?

I need not mention the difficulty of detecting a falsehood in any private or even public history, at the place, where it is said to happen; much more when the scene is removed to ever so small a distance. Even a court of judicature, with all the authority, accuracy, and judgement, which they can employ, find themselves often at a loss to distinguish between truth and falsehood in the most recent actions. But the matter never comes to any issue, if trusted to the common method of altercations and debate and flying rumours; especially when men's passions have taken part on either side.

In the infancy of new religions, the wise and learned commonly esteem the matter too inconsiderable to deserve their attention or regard. And when afterwards they would willingly detect the cheat, in order to undeceive the deluded multitude, the season is now past, and the records and witnesses, which might clear up the matter, have perished beyond recovery.

No means of detection remain, but those which must be drawn from the very testimony itself of the reporters: and these, though always sufficient with the judicious and knowing, are commonly too fine to fall under the comprehension of the vulgar.

Upon the whole, then, it appears, that no testimony for any kind of miracle has ever amounted to a probability, much less to a proof; and that, even supposing it amounted to a proof, it would be opposed by another proof; derived from the very nature of the fact, which it would endeavour to establish. It is experience only, which gives authority to human testimony; and it is the same experience, which assures us of the laws of nature. When, therefore, these two kinds of experience are contrary, we have nothing to do but substract the one from the other, and embrace an opinion, either on one side or the other, with that assurance which arises from the remainder. But according to the principle here explained, this substraction, with regard to all popular religions, amounts to an entire annihilation; and therefore we may establish it as a maxim, that no human testimony can have such force as to prove a miracle, and make it a just foundation for any such system of religion.

I beg the limitations here made may be remarked, when I say, that a miracle can never be proved, so as to be the foundation of a system of religion. For I own, that otherwise, there may possibly be miracles, or violations of the usual course of nature, of such a kind as to admit of proof from human testimony; though, perhaps, it will be impossible to find any such in all the records of history. Thus, suppose, all authors, in all languages, agree, that, from the first of January 1600, there was a total darkness over the whole earth for eight days: suppose that the tradition of this extraordinary event is still strong and lively among the people: that all travellers, who return from foreign countries, bring us accounts of the same tradition, without the least variation or contradiction: it is evident, that our present philosophers, instead of doubting the fact, ought to receive it as certain, and ought to search for the causes whence it might be derived. The decay, corruption, and dissolution of nature, is an event rendered probable by so many analogies, that any phenomenon, which seems to have a tendency towards that catastrophe, comes within the reach of human testimony, if that testimony be very extensive and uniform.

But suppose, that all the historians who treat of England, should agree, that, on the first of January 1600, Queen Elizabeth died; that both before and after her death she was seen by her physicians and the whole court, as is usual with persons of her rank; that here successor was acknowledged and proclaimed by the parliament; and that, after being interred a month, she again appeared, resumed the throne, and governed England for three years: I must confess that I should be surprised at the concurrence of so many odd circumstances, but should not have the least inclination to believe so miraculous an event. I should not doubt of her pretended death, and of those other public circumstances that followed it: I should only assert it to have been pretended, and that it neither was, nor possibly could be real. You would in vain object to me the difficulty, and almost impossibility of deceiving the world in an affair of such consequence; the wisdom and solid judgement of that renowned queen; with the little or no advantage which she could reap from so poor an artifice: All this might astonish me; but I would still reply, that the knavery and folly of men are such common phenomena, that I should rather believe the most extraordinary events to arise from their concurrence, than admit of so signal a violation of the laws of nature.

But should this miracle be ascribed to any new system of religion; men, in all ages, have been so much imposed on by ridiculous stories of that kind, that this very circumstance would be a full proof of a cheat, and sufficient, with all men of sense, not only to make them reject the fact, but even reject it without farther examination. Though the Being to whom the miracle is ascribed, be, in this case, Almighty, it does not, upon that account, become a whit more probable; since it is impossible for us to know the attributes or actions of such a Being, otherwise than from the experience which we have of his productions, in the usual course of nature. This still reduces us to past observation, and obliges us to compare the instances of the violation of truth in the testimony of men, with those of the violation of the laws of nature by miracles, in order to judge which of them is most likely and probable. As the violations of truth are more common in the testimony concerning religious miracles, than in that concerning any other matter of fact; this must diminish very much the authority of the former testimony, and make us form a general resolution, never to lend any attention to it, with whatever specious pretence it may be covered.

Lord Bacon seems to have embraced the same principles of reasoning. 'We ought,' says he, 'to make a collection or particular history of all monsters and prodigious births or productions, and in a word of every thing new, rare, and extraordinary in nature. But this must be done with the most severe scrutiny, lest we depart from truth. Above all, every relation must be considered as suspicious, which depends in any degree upon religion, as the prodigies of Livy: And no less so, every thing that is to be found in the writers of natural magic or alchimy, or such authors, who seem, all of them, to have an unconquerable appetite for falsehood and fable.

I am the better pleased with the method of reasoning here delivered, as I think it may serve to confound those dangerous friends or disguised enemies to the *Christian Religion,* who have undertaken to defend it by the principles of human reason. Our most holy religion is founded on *Faith,* not on reason; and it is a sure method of exposing it to put it to such a trial as it is, by no means, fitted to endure. To make this more evident, let us examine those miracles, related in scripture; and not to lose ourselves in too wide a field, let us confine ourselves to such as we find in the *Pentateuch,* which we shall examine, according to the principles of those pretended Christians, not as the word or testimony of God himself, but as the production of a mere human writer and historian. Here then we are first to consider a book, presented to us by a barbarous and ignorant people, written in an age when they were still more barbarous, and in all probability long after the facts which it relates, corroborated by no concurring testimony, and resembling those fabulous accounts, which every nation gives of its origin. Upon reading this book, we find it full of prodigies and miracles. It gives an account of a state of the world and of human nature entirely different from the present: Of our fall from that state: Of the age of man, extended to near a thousand years: Of the destruction of the world by a deluge: Of the arbitrary choice of one people, as the favourites of heaven; and that people the countrymen of the author: Of their deliverance from bondage by prodigies the most astonishing imaginable: I desire any one to lay his hand upon his heart, and after a serious consideration declare, whether he thinks that the falsehood of such a book, supported by such a testimony, would be more extraordinary and miraculous than all the miracles it relates; which is, however, necessary to make it be received, according to the measures of probability above established.

What we have said of miracles may be applied, without any variation, to prophecies; and indeed, all prophecies are real miracles, and as such only, can be admitted as proofs of any revelation. If it did not exceed the capacity of human nature to foretell future events, it would be absurd to employ any prophecy as an argument for a divine mission or authority from heaven. So that, upon the whole, we may conclude, that the *Christian Religion* not only was at first attended with miracles, but even at this day cannot be believed by any reasonable person without one. Mere reason is insufficient to convince us of its veracity: And whoever is moved by *Faith* to assent to it, is conscious of a continued miracle in his own person, which subverts all the principles of his understanding, and gives him a determination to believe what is most contrary to custom and experience.

Note

1. Sometimes an event may not, *in itself, seem* to be contrary to the laws of nature, and yet, if it were real, it might, by reason of some circumstances, be denominated a miracle; because, in *fact,* it is contrary to these laws. Thus if a person, claiming a divine authority, should command a sick person to be well, a healthful man to fall down dead, the clouds to pour rain, the winds to blow, in short, should order many natural events, which immediately follow upon his command; these might justly be esteemed miracles, because they are really, in this case, contrary to the laws of nature.

For if any suspicion remain, that the event and command concurred by accident, there is no miracle and no transgression of the laws of nature. If this suspicion be removed, there is evidently a miracle, and a transgression of these laws; because nothing can be more contrary to nature than that the voice or command of a man should have such an influence. A miracle may be accurately defined, *a transgression of a law of nature by a particular volition of the Deity, or by the interposition of some invisible agent.* A miracle may either be discoverable by men or not. This alters not its nature and essence. The raising of a house or ship into the air is a visible miracle. The raising of a feather, when the wind wants ever so little of a force requisite for that purpose, is as real a miracle, though not so sensible with regard to us.

V.2   For the Possibility of Miracles

RICHARD SWINBURNE

One of the most vigorous critics of Hume has been Richard Swinburne, professor of philosophy of religion at Oxford University, who in our second reading takes issue with him. Swinburne first inquires whether there could be evidence that a law of nature had been violated and, second, whether there could be evidence that the violation was due to a god. To satisfy the first inquiry, we would have to have good reason to believe that an event has occurred contrary to the predictions of a law that we had good reason to believe to be a law of nature; and furthermore we would have to have good reason to believe that events similar to the event would not occur in circumstances similar to those of the original occurrence. For if the event were repeatable, we would have to account for both events through the formulation of a law. Swinburne's example is levitation, a person's rising into the air and remaining there.

But to be a miracle the violation of a natural law would have to be the work of a god, who is not a material object. What kind of evidence would we have to have to believe that a divine being had intervened in our world? Here Swinburne distinguishes between situations in which we do and in which we do not have sufficient circumstantial evidence to warrant our attributing the anomolous event to the work of an invisible

deity. The circumstantial evidence must be strong before we are justified in believing that the event is a genuine miracle. An answer to a prayer, for example, fulfills the necessary conditions.

In this article I wish to investigate whether there could be strong historical evidence for the occurrence of miracles, and contrary to much writing which has derived from Hume's celebrated chapter "Of Miracles," I shall argue that there could be. I understand by a miracle a violation of a law of Nature by a god, that is, a very powerful rational being who is not a material object (viz., is invisible and intangible). My definition of a miracle is thus approximately the same as Hume's: "a transgression of a law of nature by a particular volition of the Deity or by the interposition of some invisible agent."[1] It has been questioned by many biblical scholars whether this is what the biblical writers understood by the terms translated into English 'miracle'. I do not propose to enter into this controversy. Suffice it to say that many subsequent Christian theologians have understood by 'miracle' roughly what I understand by the term and that much medieval and modern apologetic which appeals to purported miracles as evidence of the truth of the Christian revelation has had a similar understanding of miracle to mine.

I shall take the question in two parts. I shall enquire first whether there could be evidence that a law of nature has been violated, and secondly, if

Reprinted from Richard Swinburne, "Miracles," *Philosophical Quarterly* 18 (1968), by permission of the publisher, Basil Blackwell.

there can be such evidence, whether there could be evidence that the violation was due to a god.

First, then, can there be evidence that a law of nature has been violated? It seems natural to understand, as Ninian Smart[2] does, by a violation of a law of nature, an occurrence of a non-repeatable counter-instance to a law of nature. Clearly, as Hume admitted, events contrary to predictions of formulae which we had good reason to believe to be laws of nature often occur. But if we have good reason to believe that they have occurred and good reason to believe that similar events would occur in similar circumstances, then we have good reason to believe that the formulae which we previously believed to be the laws of nature were not in fact such laws. Repeatable counter-instances do not violate laws of nature, they just show propositions purporting to state laws of nature to be false. But if we have good reason to believe that an event E has occurred contrary to predictions of a formula L which we have good reason to believe to be a law of nature, and we have good reason to believe that events similar to E would not occur in circumstances as similar as we like in any respect to those of the original occurrence, then we do not have reason to believe that L is not a law of nature. For any modified formula which allowed us to predict E would allow us to predict similar events in similar circumstances and hence, we have good reason to believe, would give false predictions. Whereas if we leave the formula L unmodified, it will, we have good reason to believe, give correct predictions in all other conceivable circumstances. Hence if we are to say that any law of nature is operative in the field in question we must say that it is L. This seems a natural thing to say rather than to say that no law of nature operates in the field. Yet E is contrary to the predictions of L. Hence, for want of a better expression, we say that E has violated the law of nature L. If the use of the word 'violated' suggests too close an analogy between laws of nature and civil or moral laws, that is unfortunate. Once we have explained, as above, what is meant by a violation of a law of nature, no subsequent confusion need arise.

The crucial question, not adequately dis-

cussed by Smart, however, is what would be good reason for believing that an event E, if it occurred, was a non-repeatable as opposed to a repeatable counter-instance to a formula L which we have on all other evidence good reason to believe to be a law of nature. The evidence that E is a repeatable counter-instance would be that a new formula L^1 fairly well confirmed by the data as a law of nature can be set up. A formula is confirmed by data, if the data obtained so far are predicted by the formula, if new predictions are successful and if the formula is a simple and coherent one relative to the collection of data.

Compatible with any finite set of data, there will always be an infinite number of possible formulae from which the data can be predicted. We can rule out many by further tests, but however many tests we make we shall still have only a finite number of data and hence an infinite number of formulae compatible with them.

But some of these formulae will be highly complex relative to the data, so that no scientist would consider that the data were evidence that those formulae were true laws of nature. Others are very simple formulae such that the data can be said to provide evidence that they are true laws of nature. Thus suppose the scientist's task is to find a formula accounting for marks on a graph, observed at $(1, 1)$, $(2, 2)$, $(3, 3)$, and $(4, 4)$, the first number of each pair being the x co-ordinate and the second the y co-ordinate. One formula which would predict these marks is $x = y$. Another one is $(x - 1)(x - 2)(x - 3)(x - 4) + x = y$. But clearly we would not regard the data as supporting the second formula. It is too clumsy a formula to explain four observations. Among simple formulae supported by the data, the simplest is the best supported and regarded, provisionally, as correct. If the formula survives further tests, that increases the evidence in its favour as a true law.

Now if for E and for all other relevant data we can construct a formula L^1 from which the data can be derived and which either makes successful predictions in other circumstances where L makes bad predictions, or is a fairly simple formula, so that from the fact that it can predict E, and L cannot, we have reason to believe that its predictions, if tested, would be better than those of *L* in other circumstances, then we have good reason to believe that *L¹* is the true law in the field. The formula will indicate under what circumstances divergencies from *L* similar to *E* will occur. The evidence thus indicates that they will occur under these circumstances and hence that *E* is a repeatable counter-instance to the original formula *L*.

Suppose, however, that for *E* and all the other data of the field we can construct no new formula *L¹* which yields more successful predictions than *L* in other examined circumstances, nor one which is fairly simple relative to the data; but for all the other data except *E* the simple formula *L* does yield good predictions. And suppose that as the data continue to accumulate, *L* remains a completely successful predictor and there remains no reason to suppose that a simple formula *L¹* from which all the other data and *E* can be derived can be constructed. The evidence then indicates that the divergence from *L* will not be repeated and hence that *E* is a non-repeatable counter-instance to a law of nature *L*.

Here is an example. Suppose *E* to be the levitation (viz., rising into the air and remaining floating on it) of a certain holy person. *E* is a counter-instance to otherwise well substantiated laws of mechanics *L*. We could show *E* to be a repeatable counter-instance if we could construct a formula *L¹* which predicted *E* and also successfully predicted other divergences from *L,* as well as all other tested predictions of *L*; or if we could construct *L¹* which was comparatively simple relative to the data and predicted *E* and all the other tested predictions of *L,* but predicted divergences from *L* which had not yet been tested. *L¹* might differ from *L* in that, according to it, under certain circumstances bodies exercise a gravitational repulsion on each other, and the circumstance in which *E* occurred was one of those circumstances. If *L¹* satisfied either of the above two conditions, we would adopt it, and we would then say that under certain circumstances people do levitate and so *E* was not a counter-instance to a law of nature. However, it might be that any modification which we made to the laws of mechanics to allow them to predict *E* might not yield any more successful

predictions than *L* and they be so clumsy that there was no reason to believe that their predictions not yet tested would be successful. Under these circumstances we would have good reasons to believe that the levitation of the holy person violated the laws of nature.

If the laws of nature are statistical and not deterministic, it is not in all cases so clear what counts as a counter-instance to them. How improbable does an event have to be to constitute a counter-instance to a statistical law? But this problem is a general one in the philosophy of science and does not raise any issues peculiar to the topic of miracles.

It is clear that all claims about what does or does not violate the laws of nature are corrigible. New scientific knowledge may force us to revise any such claims. But all claims to knowledge about matters of fact are corrigible, and we must reach provisional conclusions about them on the evidence available to us. We have to some extent good evidence about what are the laws of nature, and some of them are so well established and account for so many data that any modifications to them which we could suggest to account for the odd counter-instance would be so clumsy and *ad hoc* as to upset the whole structure of science. In such cases the evidence is strong that if the purported counter-instance occurred it was a violation of the laws of nature. There is good reason to believe that the following events, if they occurred, would be violations of the laws of nature: levitation; resurrection from the dead in full health of a man whose heart has not been beating for twenty-four hours and who was, by other criteria also, dead; water turning into wine without the assistance of chemical apparatus or catalysts; a man getting better from polio in a minute.

So then we could have the evidence that an event *E* if it occurred was a non-repeatable counter-instance to a true law of nature *L*. But Hume's argument here runs as follows. The evidence, which *ex hypothesi* is good evidence, that *L* is a true law of nature is evidence that *E* did not occur. We have certain other evidence that *E* did occur. In such circumstances, writes Hume, the wise man "weighs the opposite experiments. He considers which side is supported by the greater number of experiments."[3] Since he supposes that the evidence that E occurred would be that of testimony, Hume concludes "that no testimony is sufficient to establish a miracle, unless the testimony be of such a kind, that its falsehood would be more miraculous, than the fact which it endeavours to establish."[4] He considers that this condition is not in fact satisfied by any purported miracle, though he seems at times to allow that it is logically possible that it might be.

One wonders here at Hume's scale of evidence. Suppose two hundred witnesses claiming to have observed some event E, an event which, if it occurred, would be a non-repeatable counter-instance to a law of nature. Suppose these to be witnesses able and anxious to show that E did not occur if there were grounds for doing so. Would not their combined evidence give us good reason to believe that E occurred? Hume's answer which we can see from his discussion of two apparently equally well authenticated miracles is—No. But then, one is inclined to say, is not Hume just being bigoted, refusing to face facts? It would be virtually impossible to draw up a table showing how many witnesses and of what kind we need to establish the occurrence of an event which, if it occurred, would be a non-repeatable counter-instance to a law of nature. Each purported instance has to be considered on its merits. But certainly one feels that Hume's standards of evidence are too high. What, one wonders, would Hume himself say if he saw such an event?

But behind Hume's excessively stringent demands on evidence there may be a philosophical point which he has not fully brought out. This is a point made by Flew in justification of Hume's standards of evidence: "The justification for giving the 'scientific' this ultimate precedence here over the 'historical' lies in the nature of the propositions concerned and in the evidence which can be displayed to sustain them . . . the candidate historical proposition will be particular, often singular, and in the past tense. . . . But just by reason of this very pastness and particularity it is no longer possible for anyone to examine the subject directly for himself . . . the law of nature will, un-

like the candidate historical proposition, be a general nomological. It can thus in theory, though obviously not always in practice, be tested at any time by any person."[5]

Flew's contrast is, however, mistaken. Particular experiments on particular occasions only give a certain and far from conclusive support to claims that a purported scientific law is true. Any person can test for the truth of a purported scientific law, but a positive result to one test will only give limited support to the claim. Exactly the same holds for purported historical truths. Anyone can examine the evidence, but a particular piece of evidence only gives limited support to the claim that the historical proposition is true. But in the historical as in the scientific case, there is no limit to the amount of evidence. We can go on and on testing for the truth of historical as well as scientific propositions. We can look for more and more data which can only be explained as effects of some specified past event, and data incompatible with its occurrence, just as we can look for more and more data for or against the truth of some physical law. Hence the truth of the historical proposition can also "be tested at any time by any person."

What Hume seems to suppose is that the only evidence about whether an event E happened is the written or verbal testimony of those who would have been in a position to witness it, had it occurred. And as there will be only a finite number of such pieces of testimony, the evidence about whether or not E happened would be finite. But this is not the only testimony which is relevant—we need testimony about the character and competence of the original witnesses. Nor is testimony the only type of evidence. All effects of what happened at the time of the alleged occurrence of E are also relevant. Far more than in Hume's day we are today often in a position to assess what occurred by studying the physical traces of the event. Hume had never met Sherlock Holmes with his ability to assess what happened in the room from the way in which the furniture lay, or where the witness was yesterday from the mud on his boot. As the effects of what happened at the time of the occurrence of E are always with us in some form, we can always go on examining them yet more carefully. Further, we need to investigate whether E, if it did occur, would in fact have brought about the present effects, and whether any other cause could have brought about just these effects. To investigate these issues involves investigating which scientific laws operate (other than the law L of which it is claimed that E was a violation), and this involves doing experiments *ad lib*. Hence there is no end to the amount of new evidence which can be had. The evidence that the event E occurred can go on mounting up in the way that evidence that L is a law of nature can do. The wise man in these circumstances will surely say that he has good reason to believe that E occurred, but also that L is a true law of nature and so that E was a violation of it.

So we could have good reason to believe that a law of nature has been violated. But for a violation of a law of nature to be a miracle, it has to be caused by a god, that is, a very powerful rational being who is not a material object. What could be evidence that it was?

To explain an event as brought about by a rational agent with intentions and purposes is to give an entirely different kind of explanation of its occurrence from an explanation by scientific laws acting on precedent causes. Our normal grounds for attributing an event to the agency of an embodied rational agent A is that we or others perceived A bringing it about *or* that it is the sort of event that A typically brings about and that A, and no one else of whom we have knowledge, was in a position to bring it about. The second kind of ground is only applicable when we have prior knowledge of the existence of A. In considering evidence for a violation E of a law of nature being due to the agency of a god, I will distinguish two cases, one where we have good reason on grounds other than the occurrence of violations of laws of nature to believe that there exists at least one god, and one where we do not.

Let us take the second case first. Suppose we have no other good reason for believing that a god exists, but an event E then occurs which, our evidence indicates, is a non-repeatable counter-instance to a true law of nature. Now we cannot attribute E to the agency of a god by seeing the

god's body bring E about, for gods do not have bodies. But suppose that E occurs in ways and circumstances C strongly analogous to those in which occur events brought about by human agents, and that other violations occur in such circumstances. We would then be justified in claiming that E and other such violations are, like effects of human actions, brought about by agents, but ones unlike men in not being material objects. This inference would be justified because, if an analogy between effects is strong enough, we are always justified in postulating slight difference in causes to account for slight difference in effects. Thus if because of its other observable behaviour we say that light is a disturbance in a medium, then the fact that the medium, if it exists, does not, like other media, slow down material bodies passing through it, is not by itself (viz., if there are no other disanalogies) a reason for saying that the light is not a disturbance in a medium, but only for saying that the medium in which light is a disturbance has the peculiar property of not resisting the passage of material bodies. So if, because of very strong similarity between the ways and circumstances of the occurrence of E and other violations of laws of nature to the ways and circumstances in which effects are produced by human agents, we postulate a similar cause—a rational agent, the fact that there are certain disanalogies (viz., we cannot point to the agent, say where his body is) does not mean that our explanation is wrong. It only means that the agent is unlike humans in not having a body. But this move is only justified if the similarities are otherwise strong. Nineteenth-century scientists eventually concluded that for light the similarities were not strong enough to outweigh the dissimilarities and justify postulating the medium with the peculiar property.

Now what similarities in the ways and circumstances C of their occurrence could there be between E (and other violations of laws of nature) and the effects of human actions to justify the postulation of similar causes? Suppose that E occurred in answer to a request. Thus E might be an explosion in my room, totally inexplicable by the laws of nature, when at the time of its occurrence there were in a room on the other side of the corridor men in turbans chanting "O God of the Sikhs, may there be an explosion in Swinburne's room." Suppose, too, that when E occurs a voice, but not the voice of an embodied agent, is heard giving reasonable reasons for granting the request. When the explosion occurs in my room, a voice emanating from no man or animal or man-made machine is heard saying "Your request is granted. He deserves a lesson." Would not all this be good reason for postulating a rational agent other than a material object who brought about E and the other violations, an agent powerful enough to change instantaneously by intervention the properties of things, viz., a god? Clearly if the analogy were strong enough between the ways and circumstances in which violations of laws of nature and effects of human action occur, it would be. If furthermore the prayers which were answered by miracles were prayers for certain kinds of events (e.g., relief of suffering, punishment of ill-doers) and those which were not answered by miracles were for events of different kinds, then this would show something about the character of the god. Normally, of course, the evidence adduced by theists for the occurrence of miracles is not as strong as I have indicated that very strong evidence would be. Violations are often reported as occurring subsequent to prayer for them to occur, and seldom otherwise; but voices giving reason for answering such a request are rare indeed. Whether in cases where voices are not heard but the occurrence of a violation E and of prayer for its occurrence were both well confirmed, we would be justified in concluding that the existence of a god who brought E about is a matter of whether the analogy is strong enough as it stands. The question of exactly when an analogy is strong enough to justify an inference based on it is a difficult one. But my only point here is that if the analogy were strong enough, the inference would be justified.

Suppose now that we have other evidence for the existence of a god. Then if E occurs in the circumstances C, previously described, that E is due to the activity of a god is more adequately substantiated, and the occurrence of E gives further support to the evidence for the existence of a god. But if we already have reason to believe in the existence of a god, the occurrence of E not under circumstances as similar as C to those under which human agents often bring about results, could nevertheless sometimes be justifiably attributed to his activity. Thus, if the occurrence of E is the sort of thing that the only god of whose existence we have evidence would wish to bring about if he has the character suggested by the other evidence for his existence, we can reasonably hold him responsible for the occurrence of E which would otherwise be unexplained. The healing of a faithful blind Christian contrary to the laws of nature could reasonably be attributed to the God of the Christians, if there were other evidence for his existence, whether or not the blind man or other Christians had ever prayed for that result.

For these reasons I conclude that we can have good reason to believe that a violation of a law of nature was caused by a god, and so was a miracle.

I would like to make two final points, one to tidy up the argument and the other to meet a further argument put forward by Hume which I have not previously discussed.

Entia non sunt multiplicanda praeter necessitatem.—Unless we have good reason to do so we ought not to postulate the existence of more than one god, but to suppose that the same being answers all prayers. But there could be good reason to postulate the existence of more than one god, and evidence to this effect could be provided by miracles. One way in which this could happen is that prayers for a certain kind of result, for example, shipwreck, which began "O, Neptune" were often answered, and also prayers for a different kind of result, for example, success in love, which began "O, Venus" were also often answered, but prayers for a result of the first kind beginning "O, Venus," and for a result of the second kind beginning "O, Neptune" were never answered. Evidence for the existence of one god would in general support, not oppose, evidence for the existence of a second one since, by suggesting that there is one rational being other than those whom we can see, it makes more reasonable the postulation of another one.

The second point is that there is no reason at

all to suppose that Hume is in general right to claim that "every miracle . . . pretended to have been wrought in any . . . (religion) . . . as its direct scope is to establish the particular system to which it is attributed; so has it the same force, though more indirectly, to overthrow every other system. In destroying a rival system it likewise destroys the credit of those miracles on which that system was established."[6] If Hume were right to claim that evidence for the miracles of one religion was evidence against the miracles of any other, then indeed evidence for miracles in each would be poor. But in fact evidence for a miracle "wrought in one religion" is only evidence against the occurrence of a miracle "wrought in another religion" if the two miracles, if they occurred, would be evidence for propositions of the two religious systems incompatible with each other. It is hard to think of pairs of alleged miracles of this type. If there were evidence for a Roman Catholic miracle which was evidence for the doctrine of transubstantiation and evidence for a Protestant miracle which was evidence against it, here we would have a case of the conflict of evidence which, Hume claims, occurs generally with alleged miracles. But it is enough to give this example to see that most alleged miracles do not give rise to conflicts of this kind. Most alleged miracles, if they occurred, would only show the power of god or gods and their concern for the needs of men, and little else.

My main conclusion, to repeat it, is that there are no logical difficulties in supposing that there could be strong historical evidence for the occurrence of miracles. Whether there is such evidence is, of course, another matter.

Notes

1. David Hume, *An Enquiry Concerning Human Understanding*, ed. L. A. Selby-Bigge (Oxford, 2nd ed., 1902), p. 115, footnote.
2. Ninian Smart, *Philosophers and Religious Truth* (London, 1964), Ch. II.
3. Op. cit., p. 111.
4. Op. cit., p. 116.
5. Antony Flew, *Hume's Philosophy of Belief* (London, 1961), pp. 207 ff.
6. Op. cit., pp. 121ff.

V.3   Miracles and Testimony

J. L. MACKIE

Our third reading is "Miracles and Testimony" by the late J. L. Mackie of Oxford University. In this revised Humean account of miracles, Mackie argues that the evidence for miracles will never in practice be very great. The argument is epistemological, not ontological. That is, while miracles may be logically possible (and may indeed have occurred), we are never justified in believing in one. The concept of a miracle is a coherent one, but, Mackie argues, the double burden of showing both that the event took place and that it violated the laws of nature will be extremely hard to lift, for "whatever tends to show that it would have been a violation of natural law tends for that very reason to make it most unlikely that it actually happened." Correspondingly, the deniers of miracles have two strategies of defense. They may argue that the event took place but wasn't a violation of a law of nature (the event simply followed an unknown law of nature); or they can admit that if the event had happened, it would indeed have been a violation of a law of nature, but for that reason "there is a very strong presumption against its having happened, which it is most unlikely that any testimony will be able to outweigh."

(a) Introduction

Traditional theism, as defined in the Introduction, does not explicitly include any contrast between the natural and the supernatural. Yet there is a familiar, if vague and undeveloped, notion of the natural world in contrast with which the theistic doctrines stand out as asserting a supernatural reality. The question whether and how there can be evidence for what, if real, would be supernatural is therefore one of central significance. Besides, explicit assertions about supernatural occurrences, about miracles or divine interventions which have disrupted the natural course of events, are common in nearly all religions: alleged miracles are often cited to validate religious claims. Christianity, for example, has its share of these. In the life of Christ we have the virgin birth, the turning of water into wine, Christ's walking on the water, his healing of the sick, his raising of Lazarus from the dead, and, of course, the resurrection. The Roman Catholic church will not recognize anyone as a saint unless it is convinced that at least two miracles have been performed by the supposed saint, either in his or her life or after death.

The usual purpose of stories about miracles is to establish the authority of the particular figures who perform them or are associated with them, but of course these stories, with their intended interpretation, presuppose such more general religious doctrines as that of the existence of a god. We can, therefore, recognize, as one of the supports of traditional theism, an argument from miracles: that is, an argument whose main premiss is that such and such remarkable events have occurred, and whose conclusion is that a god of the traditional sort both exists and intervenes, from time to time, in the ordinary world. . . .

[Here follows a brief exposition of Hume's essay "Of Miracles".]

(b) Hume's Argument—Discussion

What Hume has been expounding are the principles for the rational acceptance of testimony, the rules that ought to govern our believing or not believing what we are told. But the rules that govern people's actual acceptance of testimony are very different. We are fairly good at detecting dishonesty, insincerity, and lack of conviction, and we readily reject what we are told by someone who betrays these defects. But we are strongly inclined simply to accept, without question, statements that are obviously assured and sincere. As Hume would say, a firm association of ideas links someone else's saying, with honest conviction, that *p*, and its being the case that *p*, and we pass automatically from the perception of the one to belief in the other. Or, as he might also have said, there is an intellectual sympathy by which we tend automatically to share what we find to be someone else's belief, analogous to sympathy in the original sense, the tendency to share what we see to be someone else's feelings. And in general this is a useful tendency. People's beliefs about ordinary matters are right, or nearly right, more often than they are wildly wrong, so that intellectual sympathy enables fairly correct information to be passed on more smoothly than it could be if we were habitually cautious and constantly checked testimony against the principles for its rational acceptance. But what is thus generally useful can sometimes be misleading, and miracle reports are a special case where we need to restrain our instinctive acceptance of honest statements, and go back to the basic rational principles which determine whether a statement is really reliable or not. Even where we are cautious, and hesitate to accept what we are told—for example by a witness in a legal case—we often do not go beyond the question 'How intrinsically reliable is this witness?', or, in detail, 'Does he seem to be honest? Does he have a motive for misleading us? Is he the sort of person who might tell plausible lies? Or is he the sort of person who, in the circumstances, might have made a mistake?' If we are satisfied on all these scores, we are inclined to believe what the witness says, without weighing very seriously the question 'How intrinsically improbable is what he has told us?' But, as Hume insists, this further question is highly relevant. His general approach to the problem of when to accept testimony is certainly sound.

Hume's case against miracles is an epistemological argument: it does not try to show that miracles never do happen or never could happen, but only that we never have good reasons for believing that they have happened. It must be clearly distinguished from the suggestion that the very concept of a miracle is incoherent. That suggestion might be spelled out as follows. A miracle is, by definition, a violation of a law of nature, and a law of nature is, by definition, a regularity—or the statement of a regularity—about what happens, about the way the world works; consequently, if some event actually occurs, no regularity which its occurrence infringes (or, no regularity-statement which it falsifies) can really be a law of nature; so this event, however unusual or surprising, cannot after all be a miracle. The two definitions together entail that whatever happens is not a miracle, that is, that miracles never happen. This, be it noted, is not Hume's argument. If it were correct, it would make Hume's argument unnecessary. Before we discuss Hume's case, then, we should consider whether there is a coherent concept of a miracle which would not thus rule out the occurrence of miracles *a priori*.

If miracles are to serve their traditional function of giving spectacular support to religious claims—whether general theistic claims, or the authority of some specific religion or some particular sect or individual teacher—the concept must not be so weakened that anything at all unusual or remarkable counts as a miracle. We must keep in the definition the notion of a violation of natural law. But then, if it is to be even possible that a miracle should occur, we must modify the definition given above of a law of nature. What we want

to do is to contrast the order of nature with a possible divine or supernatural intervention. The laws of nature, we must say, describe the ways in which the world—including, of course, human beings—works when left to itself, when not interfered with. A miracle occurs when the world is not left to itself, when something distinct from the natural order as a whole intrudes into it.

This notion of ways in which the world works is coherent and by no means obscure. We know how to discover causal laws, relying on a principle of the uniformity of the course of nature—essentially the assumption that there are some laws to be found—in conjunction with suitable observations and experiments, typically varieties of controlled experiment whose underlying logic is that of Mill's 'method of difference'. Within the laws so established, we can further mark off basic laws of working from derived laws which hold only in a particular context or contingently upon the way in which something is put together. It will be a derived law that a particular clock, or clocks of a particular sort, run at such a speed, and this will hold only in certain conditions of temperature, and so on; but this law will be derived from more basic ones which describe the regular behaviour of certain kinds of material, in view of the way in which the clock is put together, and these more basic laws of materials may in turn be derived from yet more basic laws about sub-atomic particles, in view of the ways in which those materials are made up of such particles. In so far as we advance towards a knowledge of such a system of basic and derived laws, we are acquiring an understanding of ways in which the world works. As well as what we should ordinarily call causal laws, which typically concern interactions, there are similar laws with regard to the ways in which certain kinds of things simply persist through time, and certain sorts of continuous process just go on. These too, and in particular the more basic laws of these sorts, help to constitute the ways in which the world works. Thus there are several kinds of basic 'laws of working'. For our present purpose, however, it is not essential that we should even be approaching an understanding of how the world works; it is enough that we have the concept of such basic laws of working, that we know in principle what it would be to discover them. Once we have this concept, we have moved beyond the definition of laws of nature merely as (statements of) what always happens. We can see how, using this concept and using the assumption that there are some such basic laws of working to be found, we can hope to determine what the actual laws of working are by reference to a restricted range of experiments and observations. This opens up the possibility that we might determine that something *is* a basic law of working of natural objects, and yet also, independently, find that it was occasionally violated. An occasional violation does not in itself necessarily overthrow the independently established conclusion that this *is* a law of working.

Equally, there is no obscurity in the notion of intervention. Even in the natural world we have a clear understanding of how there can be for a time a closed system, in which everything that happens results from factors within that system in accordance with its laws of working, but how then something may intrude from outside it, bringing about changes that the system would not have produced of its own accord, so that things go on after this intrusion differently from how they would have gone on if the system had remained closed. All we need do, then, is to regard the whole natural world as being, for most of the time, such a closed system; we can then think of a supernatural intervention as something that intrudes into that system from outside the natural world as a whole.

If the laws by which the natural world works are deterministic, then the notion of a violation of them is quite clear-cut: such a violation would be an event which, given that the world was a closed system working in accordance with these laws, and given some actual earlier complete state of the world, simply could not have happened at all. Its occurrence would then be clear proof that either the supposed laws were not the real laws of working, or the earlier state was not as it was supposed to have been, or else the system was not closed after all. But if the basic laws of working are statistical or probabilistic, the notion of a violation of

them is less precise. If something happens which, given those statistical laws and some earlier complete state of the world, is extremely improbable—in the sense of physical probability: that is, something such that there is a strong propensity or tendency for it *not* to happen—we still cannot say firmly that the laws have been violated: laws of this sort explicitly allow that what is extremely improbable may occasionally come about. Indeed it is highly probable (both physically and epistemically) that some events, each of which is very improbable, will occur at rare intervals. If tosses of a coin were governed by a statistical law that gave a 50 per cent propensity to heads at each toss, a continuous run of ten heads would be a highly improbable occurrence; but it would be highly probable that there would be some such runs in a sequence of a million tosses. Nevertheless, we can still use the contrast between the way of working of the natural world as a whole, considered as a normally closed system, and an intervention or intrusion into it. This contrast does not disappear or become unintelligible merely because we lack decisive tests for its application. We can still define a miracle as an event which would not have happened in the course of nature, and which came about only through a supernatural intrusion. The difficulty is merely that we cannot now say with certainty, simply by reference to the relevant laws and some antecedent situation, that a certain event would not have happened in the course of nature, and therefore must be such an intrusion. But we may still be able to say that it is very probable—and this is now an epistemic probability— that it would not have happened naturally, and so is likely to be such an intrusion. For if the laws made it physically improbable that it would come about, this tends to make it epistemically improbable that it did come about through those laws, if there is any other way in which it could have come about and which is not equally improbable or more improbable. In practice the difficulty mentioned is not much of an extra difficulty. For even where we believe there to be deterministic laws and an earlier situation which together would have made an occurrence actually impossible in the course of nature, it is from our point of view at best epistemically very probable, not certain, that those are the laws and that that was the relevant antecedent situation.

Consequently, whether the laws of nature are deterministic or statistical, we can give a coherent definition of a miracle as a supernatural intrusion into the normally closed system that works in accordance with those laws, and in either case we can identify conceivable occurrences, and alleged occurrences, which if they were to occur, or have occurred, could be believed with high probability, though not known with certainty, to satisfy that definition.

However, the full concept of a miracle requires that the intrusion should be purposive, that it should fulfil the intention of a god or other supernatural being. This connection cannot be sustained by any ordinary causal theory; it presupposes a power to fulfil intentions directly, without physical means, which is highly dubious; so this requirement for a miracle will be particularly hard to confirm. On the other hand it is worth noting that successful prophecy could be regarded as a form of miracle for which there could in principle be good evidence. If someone is reliably recorded as having prophesied at t_1 an event at t_2 which could not be predicted at t_1 on any natural grounds, and the event occurs at t_2, then at any later time t_3 we can assess the evidence for the claims both that the prophecy was made at t_1 and that its accuracy cannot be explained either causally (for example, on the ground that it brought about its own fulfilment) or as accidental, and hence that it was probably miraculous.

There is, then, a coherent concept of miracles. Their possibility is not ruled out *a priori,* by definition. So we must consider whether Hume's argument shows that we never have good reason for believing that any have occurred.

Hume's general principle for the evaluation of testimony, that we have to weigh the unlikelihood of the event reported against the unlikelihood that the witness is mistaken or dishonest, is substantially correct. It is a corollary of the still more general principle of accepting whatever hypothesis gives the best overall explanation of all the available and relevant evidence. But some riders are

necessary. First, the likelihood or unlikelihood, the epistemic probability or improbability, is always relative to some body of information, and may change if additional information comes in. Consequently, any specific decision in accordance with Hume's principle must be provisional. Secondly, it is one thing to decide which of the rival hypotheses in the field at any time should be provisionally accepted in the light of the evidence then available; but it is quite another to estimate the weight of this evidence, to say how well supported this favoured hypothesis is, and whether it is likely that its claims will be undermined either by additional information or by the suggesting of further alternative hypotheses. What is clearly the best-supported view of some matter at the moment may still be very insecure, and quite likely to be overthrown by some further considerations. For example, if a public opinion poll is the only evidence we have about the result of a coming election, this evidence may point, perhaps decisively, to one result rather than another; yet if the poll has reached only a small sample of the electorate, or if it was taken some time before the voting day, it will not be very reliable. There is a dimension of reliability over and above that of epistemic probability relative to the available evidence. Thirdly, Hume's description of what gives support to a prediction, or in general to a judgement about an unobserved case that would fall under some generalization, is very unsatisfactory. He seems to say that if *all* so far observed As have been Bs, then this amounts to a 'proof' that some unobserved A will be (or is, or was) a B, whereas if some observed As have been Bs, but some have not, there is only a 'probability' that an unobserved A will be a B (pp. 110–12). This mixes up the reasoning *to* a generalization with the reasoning *from* a generalization to a particular case. It is true that the premises 'All As are Bs' and 'This is an A' constitute a proof of the conclusion 'This is a B', whereas the premises 'x per cent of As are Bs' and 'This is an A' yield—if there is no other relevant information—a probability of x per cent that this is a B: they *probabilify* the conclusion to this degree, or, as we can say, the probability of the conclusion 'This is a B' relative to that evidence is x per cent.

But the inductive argument from the observation 'All so far observed As have been Bs' to the generalization 'All As are Bs' is far from secure, and it would be most misleading to call this a proof, and therefore misleading also to describe as a proof the whole line of inference from 'All so far observed As have been Bs' to the conclusion 'This as yet unobserved A is a B'. Similarly, the inductive argument from 'x per cent of observed As have been Bs' to the statistical generalization 'x per cent of As are Bs' is far from secure, so that we cannot say that 'x per cent of observed As have been Bs' even probabilifies to the degree x per cent the conclusion 'This as yet unobserved A is a B'. A good deal of other information and background knowledge is needed, in either case, before the generalization, whether universal or statistical, is at all well supported, and hence before the stage is properly set for either proof or probabilification about an as yet unobserved A. It is harder than Hume allows here to arrive at well-supported generalizations of either sort about how the world works.

These various qualifications together entail that what has been widely and reasonably thought to be a law of nature may not be one, perhaps in ways that are highly relevant to some supposed miracles. Our present understanding of psychosomatic illness, for example, shows that it is not contrary to the laws of nature that someone who for years has seemed, to himself as well as to others, to be paralysed should rapidly regain the use of his limbs. On the other hand, we can still be pretty confident that it is contrary to the laws of nature that a human being whose heart has stopped beating for forty-eight hours in ordinary circumstances—that is, without any special life-support systems—should come back to life, or that what is literally water should without addition or replacement turn into what is literally good-quality wine.

However, any problems there may be about establishing laws of nature are neutral between the parties to the present debate, Hume's followers and those who believe in miracles; for both these parties need the notion of a well-established law of nature. The miracle advocate needs it in order to be able to say that the alleged occurrence is a miracle, a violation of natural law by supernatural intervention, no less than Hume needs it for his argument against believing that this event has actually taken place.

It is therefore not enough for the defender of a miracle to cast doubt (as he well might) on the certainty of our knowledge of the law of nature that seems to have been violated. For he must himself say that this *is* a law of nature: otherwise the reported event will not be miraculous. That is, he must in effect *concede* to Hume that the antecedent improbability of this event is as high as it could be, hence that, apart from the testimony, we have the strongest possible grounds for believing that the alleged event did not occur. This event must, by the miracle advocate's own admission, be contrary to a genuine, not merely a supposed, law of nature, and therefore maximally improbable. It is this maximal improbability that the weight of the testimony would have to overcome.

One further improvement is needed in Hume's theory of testimony. It is well known that the agreement of two (or more) *independent* witnesses constitutes very powerful evidence. Two independent witnesses are more than twice as good as each of them on his own. The reason for this is plain. If just one witness says that *p*, one explanation of this would be that it was the case that *p* and that he has observed this, remembered it, and is now making an honest report; but there are many alternative explanations, for example that he observed something else which he mistook for its being that *p*, or is misremembering what he observed, or is telling a lie. But if two witnesses who can be shown to be quite independent of one another both say that *p*, while again one explanation is that each of them has observed this and remembered it and is reporting honestly, the alternative explanations are not now so easy. They face the question 'How has there come about this *agreement* in their reports, if it was not the case that *p*? How have the witnesses managed to misobserve to the same effect, or to misremember in the same way, or to hit upon the same lie?' It is difficult for even a single liar to keep on telling a *consistent* false story; it is much harder for two or more liars to do so. Of course if there is any collusion between the witnesses, or if either has been influenced, directly or indirectly, by the other, or if both stories have a common source, this question is easily answered. That is why the independence of the witnesses is so important. This principle of the improbability of coincident error has two vital bearings upon the problem of miracles. On the one hand, it means that a certain sort of testimony can be more powerful evidence than Hume's discussion would suggest. On the other, it means that where we seem to have a plurality of reports, it is essential to check carefully whether they really are independent of one another; the difficulty of meeting this requirement would be an important supplement to the points made in Part II of Hume's essay. Not only in remote and barbarous times, but also in recent ones, we are usually justified in suspecting that what look like distinct reports of a remarkable occurrence arise from different strands of a single tradition between which there has already been communication.

We can now put together the various parts of our argument. Where there is some plausible testimony about the occurrence of what would appear to be a miracle, those who accept this as a miracle have the double burden of showing both that the event took place and that it violated the laws of nature. But it will be very hard to sustain this double burden. For whatever tends to show that it would have been a violation of natural law tends for that very reason to make it most unlikely that it actually happened. Correspondingly, those who deny the occurrence of a miracle have two alternative lines of defence. One is to say that the event may have occurred, but in accordance with the laws of nature. Perhaps there were unknown circumstances that made it possible; or perhaps what were thought to be the relevant laws of nature are not strictly laws; there may be as yet unknown kinds of natural causation through which this event might have come about. The other is to say that this event would indeed have violated natural law, but that for this very reason there is a very strong presumption against its having happened, which it is most unlikely that any testimony will be able to outweigh. Usually one of these defences will be stronger than the other. For many supposedly miraculous cures, the former will be quite a

likely sort of explanation, but for such feats as the bringing back to life of those who are really dead the latter will be more likely. But the *fork,* the disjunction of these two sorts of explanation, is as a whole a very powerful reply to any claim that a miracle has been performed.

However, we should distinguish two different contexts in which an alleged miracle might be discussed. One possible context would be where the parties in debate already both accept some general theistic doctrines, and the point at issue is whether a miracle has occurred which would enhance the authority of a specific sect or teacher. In this context supernatural intervention, though *prima facie* unlikely on any particular occasion, is, generally speaking, on the cards: it is not altogether outside the range of reasonable expectation for these parties. Since they agree that there is an omnipotent deity, or at any rate one or more powerful supernatural beings, they cannot find it absurd to suppose that such a being will occasionally interfere with the course of nature, and this *may* be one of these occasions. For example, if one were already a theist and a Christian, it would not be unreasonable to weigh seriously the evidence of alleged miracles as some indication whether the Jansenists or the Jesuits enjoyed more of the favour of the Almighty. But it is a very different matter if the context is that of fundamental debate about the truth of theism itself. Here one party to the debate is initially at least agnostic, and does not yet concede that there is a supernatural power at all. From this point of view the intrinsic improbability of a genuine miracle, as defined above, is very great, and one or other of the alternative explanations in our fork will always be much more likely—that is, either that the alleged event is not miraculous, or that it did not occur, that the testimony is faulty in some way.

This entails that it is pretty well impossible that reported miracles should provide a worthwhile argument for theism addressed to those who are initially inclined to atheism or even to agnosticism. Such reports can form no significant part of what, following Aquinas, we might call a *Summa contra Gentiles,* or what, following Descartes, we could describe as being addressed to infidels. Not only are such reports unable to carry any rational conviction on their own, but also they are unable even to contribute independently to the kind of accumulation or battery of arguments referred to in the Introduction. To this extent Hume is right, despite the inaccuracies we have found in his statement of the case.

One further point may be worth making. Occurrences are sometimes claimed to be literally, and not merely metaphorically, miracles, that is, to be genuine supernatural interventions into the natural order, which are not even *prima facie* violations of natural law, but at most rather unusual and unexpected, but very welcome. Thus the combination of weather conditions which facilitated the escape of the British army from Dunkirk in 1940, making the Luftwaffe less than usually effective but making it easy for ships of all sizes to cross the Channel, is sometimes called a miracle. However, even if we accepted theism, and could plausibly assume that a benevolent deity would have favoured the British rather than the Germans in 1940, this explanation would still be far less probable than that which treats it as a mere meteorological coincidence: such weather conditions can occur in the ordinary course of events. Here, even in the context of a debate among those who already accept theistic doctrines, the interpretation of the event as a miracle is much weaker than the rival natural explanation. *A fortiori,* instances of this sort are utterly without force in the context of fundamental debate about theism itself.

There is, however, a possibility which Hume's argument seems to ignore—though, as we shall see, he did not completely ignore it. The argument has been directed against the acceptance of miracles on testimony; but what, it may be objected, if one is not reduced to reliance on testimony, but has observed a miracle for oneself? Surprisingly, perhaps, this possibility does not make very much difference. The first of the above-mentioned lines of defence is still available: maybe the unexpected event that one has oneself observed did indeed occur, but in accordance with the laws of nature.

Either the relevant circumstances or the operative laws were not what one had supposed them to be. But at least a part of the other line of defence is also available. Though one is not now relying literally on another witness or other witnesses, we speak not inappropriately of the evidence of our senses, and what one takes to be an observation of one's own is open to questions of the same sort as is the report of some other person. I may have misobserved what took place, as anyone knows who has ever been fooled by a conjurer or 'magician', and, though this is somewhat less likely, I may be misremembering or deceiving myself after an interval of time. And of course the corroboration of one or more independent witnesses would bring in again the testimony of others which it was the point of this objection to do without. Nevertheless, anyone who is fortunate enough to have carefully observed and carefully recorded, for himself, an apparently miraculous occurrence is no doubt rationally justified in taking it very seriously; but even here it will be in order to entertain the possibility of an alternative natural explanation.

As I said, Hume does not completely ignore this possibility. The Christian religion, he says, cannot at this day be believed by any reasonable person without a miracle. 'Mere reason is insufficient to convince us of its veracity: And whoever is moved by *Faith* to assent to it, is conscious of a continued miracle in his own person, which subverts all the principles of his understanding . . .' (p. 131). But of course this is only a joke. What the believer is conscious of in his own person, though it may be a mode of thinking that goes against 'custom and experience', and so is contrary to the ordinary rational principles of the understanding, is not, as an occurrence, a violation of natural law. Rather it is all too easy to explain immediately by the automatic communication of beliefs between persons and the familiar psychological processes of wish fulfilment, and ultimately by what Hume himself was later to call 'the natural history of religion'.

V.4   Miracles: What if They Happen?

R I C H A R D   L .   P U R T I L L

Richard L. Purtill is professor of philosophy at Western Washington State University. In this reading he continues the critique of Hume begun by Swinburne and argues that a two-stage case for the occurrence of miracles can be made: first, an argument for the general possibilities of miracles, and second, an argument for the actuality of miracles. Comparing the laws of nature to the laws of a nation, Purtill argues that a miracle is analogous to an exception to the law of the land—for example, President Ford's pardoning of Richard Nixon after Watergate.

Regarding the question of whether we have evidence that a miracle ever took place, Purtill looks at various reports of miracles and sets up limiting criteria—for example, they must not be utterly fantastic, as fairy tales are; they must be interwoven into the larger fabric of the religion; there must be independent evidence for the truth of the religion. Purtill then examines the miracles of Christ in the light of those criteria and concludes that it is very likely that those miracles are genuine. If we already have reason to believe in a God who is active in human affairs, we should expect miracles; but if we do not have such independent reason to believe in God, we will be far less likely to believe in divine interventions.

"It's a miracle," said Mrs. Kennedy, sitting up in her bed, and even as Dr. Buchan put out a cautioning hand, he knew that yesterday she wouldn't have had the strength to sit up that far. "We call it a spontaneous remission," he replied, trying to make his voice as calm as possible. "They happen sometimes, we don't know why."

But Sarah Kennedy was sure she knew why and wasn't shy about saying so. "It's the power of prayer, Doctor," she said earnestly, "the prayers of my family and Father O'Sullivan and the good Sisters. . . ."

Despite himself, Buchan was drawn into arguing with her. "I presume that other people in the hospital are being prayed for just as hard, but they haven't had recoveries like yours," he snapped.

There were tears in Mrs. Kennedy's eyes now. "Ah, Doctor, it's a mystery of God," she said. "The Lord knows that I prayed as hard for my husband Michael, and for the daughter that died young, as anyone ever prayed. But prayer is just asking and sometimes God says no. It's no virtue of mine that He's spared me this time—maybe He has a job for me to do yet."

Buchan smiled a little coldly. "Very convenient," he said. "If you get well it's the power of prayer; if you don't it's the will of God. So whatever happens, you win."

He wondered if he'd gone too far, but he was reassured when he saw a trace of Mrs. Kennedy's old spirit in her grin. "Well, Doctor, tell me now," she said, "can *you* explain with all your great medical knowledge why a week ago I was at death's door and today I'm here taking the Mickey out of you?"

"No, I can't," he admitted, "but that isn't to say that we might not understand some day why things like this happen. The mind and body are related in ways we're only just beginning to understand."

But Mrs. Kennedy was not going to let him off so easily. "So it's faith healing, is it Doctor? But it's a funny kind of faith healing that can work on a person when she knows about as much of what's going on around her as a mackerel on ice."

Buchan got up from the edge of the bed where he had been, very unprofessionally, sitting. "No, Sarah, your case isn't faith healing and I'll admit that I don't know what it is. But these spontaneous remissions happen to people who don't pray as often as they occur to people that do, so you're not going to convert me to religion by getting up and dancing a jig. Don't overdo, and remember these things can get worse again as suddenly as they got better.''

Mrs. Kennedy lay back. "Ah, you're a terrible old heathen, Doctor, but you've been a good friend to me and mine. Go off to your pills and your laboratory tests, but you won't find any explanation in them for what's happened to me." And as Dr. Buchan slipped out the door wearing an indulgent smile, she muttered to herself, "And I'll pray for your conversion too, you old devil. Though that would be a bigger miracle than this one."

Some religious believers think that miracles continue to occur; others believe that they have occurred only at specific places and times, where extraordinary needs brought forth extraordinary help from God. But even if events which cannot be explained by science do occur in some religious contexts, what do such events prove?

One traditional way of providing a rational basis for religious belief begins with arguments for the existence of God and goes on to argue that a certain body of religious beliefs can be known to be a revelation from God because miracles have been worked in support of those religious beliefs. For example, a Christian of one traditional sort, when challenged as to the basis of one of his beliefs—say the Second Coming of Christ—would cite certain words said by Christ. When asked why we should believe these words of Christ, he would cite the miracles done by Christ, and especially His Resurrection, as evidence that Christ's words were backed up or authenticated by God. And when asked why he believed that those miracles had indeed occurred, the traditional Christian would argue that if God exists miracles cannot be ruled out, and that miracle is the best or only explanation for certain events recorded by history. If challenged as to the existence of God, he would try to give arguments based on reason and experience for God's existence.

Thus, this kind of traditional Christian, whom we might call a rationalistic believer, nowhere appeals to blind faith or personal experiences not shared by unbelievers, but bases his assent to particular doctrines on authority, his acceptance of authority on the evidence of miracles, and his acceptance of miracles on philosophical arguments for God and historical arguments for the actual occurrence of miracles.

Nowadays not only most nonbelievers but many people who would call themselves religious believers would challenge this way of providing a basis for religious belief. They would argue that accounts of miracles are not historically reliable and that a faith based on such accounts is open to historical and scientific objections. The traditional believer understands such objections from nonbelievers in God, but finds them puzzling from people calling themselves believers in God. For if God is the Creator and Ruler of the universe, then surely miracles are possible. Of course, if miracles were impossible, then any historical account which tells of the occurrence of miracles, as the Old and New Testaments plainly do, must be rejected as unhistorical. If miracles are tremendously improbable, then we must reject any account of them unless we get evidence of a kind which, in the nature of the case, history almost never gives us. But if God exists, miracles are not impossible, and unless we have some argument to show that they are improbable, then we cannot assume that they are. This undercuts most of the "historical" objections to miracles, for if we have no metaphysical objections, then we will have to examine the historical evidence on its merits. And if we do this we may find, as many reasonable and hardheaded men have found, that miracle is the best explanation for certain recorded events.

There may, of course, be historical objections to certain accounts of miracles—for example, one account may seem to be a mere imitation of another, or other historical evidence may render that particular supposed miracle improbable, and so on. But the general objection to miracles is not based on anything peculiar to history as such, but on philosophical grounds.

Another objection to miracles is the supposed objection from experience. Most versions of this objection trace back more or less indirectly to a famous objection by David Hume, which goes as follows:

> A miracle is a violation of the laws of nature; and as a firm and unalterable experience has established these laws, the proof against a miracle, from the very nature of the fact, is as entire as any argument from experience can possibly be imagined. . . . Nothing is esteemed a miracle, if it ever happens in the common course of nature. It is no miracle that a man, seemingly in good health, should die of a sudden; because such a kind of death, though more unusual than any other, has yet been frequently observed to happen. But it is a miracle that a dead man should come to life; because that has never been observed in any age or country. There must, therefore, be a uniform experience against every miraculous event, otherwise the event would not merit the appellation. And as a uniform experience amounts to a proof, there is here a direct and full proof, from the nature of the fact, against the existence of any miracle; nor can such a proof be destroyed, or the miracle rendered credible, but by an opposite proof, which is superior.[1]

Now obviously we must interpret Hume's objection in such a way that it is not an objection to any unique event. After all, up to a certain date, there was "uniform experience" against a man setting foot on the moon. It must, therefore, be a certain *class* or *kind* of events we are eliminating. But what class? Miracles? But this begs the whole question. As an "argument" against the statement that miracles occur, we have the assertion that there is uniform experience against miracles—in other words, the unsupported assertion that miracles don't happen!

Put in this way the point may seem obvious, but both in Hume's original account and in modern restatements of views like Hume's the point is often concealed. Instead of saying baldly that experience shows that miracles do not occur, which is obviously question-begging in the context of this argument, the class of events which "experience proves don't happen" is described in some other way—as events which "exhibit causal irregularity" or as events which "neither obey known scientific laws nor are taken as refuting alleged scientific laws," or some similar description. But looked at carefully, all such descriptions turn out

to be indirect ways of describing miracles. And to argue for the conclusion that miracles do not happen by assuming that miracles, under whatever description, don't happen is just to argue in a circle or beg the question.

This is not to deny that there could be some argument which concludes that miracles don't happen. But whatever that argument is, it must not have as one of its premises an assertion which amounts to saying that miracles don't happen, because that would be assuming what is supposed to be being proved.

Of course defenders of a Humean position would deny that they are arguing in a circle in this way. But to avoid the charge of circularity they must show that the class of events they are claiming experience rules out is not just an indirect description of the class of miracles. So far as I can see neither Hume's own argument or any neo-Humean argument can meet the challenge.

I think that the only respectable way of interpreting what Hume says here is to take him as arguing that past experience gives us some kind of assurance that laws of nature *cannot* be suspended. (If it merely alleges that they *have never been* suspended, it is just "miracles don't happen" in a new guise.) We interpret Hume, then, as saying that experience proves that natural laws are "unsuspendable." But how *could* experience show any such thing? Any such theory must be a philosophical interpretation of experience, not the direct result of experience. So before coming to any decision on this matter, we must look at the philosophical, as well as the historical, pros and cons with regard to the question of miracles. We can distinguish two separable arguments which need to be looked at in turn: the argument *for* (the possibility of) miracles, and the argument *from* miracles (for religious belief).

The argument for miracles consists of two stages—an argument for the general possibility of miracles, and an argument for the historical actuality of certain miracles. The first stage is philosophical and can be developed fairly completely within the limits of this chapter. The second stage is historical and we can only indicate the main lines of the argument. The argument *from* miracles for religious belief also has two stages—the first stage a philosophical consideration of the evidential value of miracles, and the second stage a historical consideration of what specific beliefs the evidence of miracles supports. Again, we will try to cover the philosophical stage as completely as we can and only indicate the general lines of the historical argument.

Let us begin, then, with a definition of miracle. By a miracle we will mean an exception to the natural order of things caused by the power of God. By this we will mean very much what people mean when they define miracle as a suspension or violation of natural law, but for reasons that will become clear "exception" is preferable to the terms "suspension" or "violation," and "natural order of things" is preferable to the term "natural law." Notice that by this definition no event which occurs as part of the natural order of things, no matter how improbable or how faith-inspiring, will count as a miracle. There may be a wider and looser sense of miracle in which striking coincidences which inspire religious belief are called "miracles," but they are not miracles in the stricter and narrower sense in which we are now using that term.

Before we can speak of exceptions to the natural order of things we must believe that there *is* a natural order of things. If anyone holds that there is no natural order, that the universe is chaotic, that the apparent order and understandability of the universe is an illusion, then that person can give no meaning to the idea of miracle, for that idea depends on contrast. Before there can be exceptions there must be rules or patterns for them to be exceptions to. The progress of science gives us an enormously strong argument against the idea that the universe is chaotic and without order and pattern, and we will assume in what follows that we can speak of the universe as genuinely orderly and intelligible. But if anyone really wished to challenge this, we would have to settle that issue before going on to any argument with him either for or from miracles.

Given that the universe is orderly and understandable, however, we can ask whether this or-

der can have exceptions and whether such exceptions could be due to the power of God. The answer to this question depends on the answer to another question. How can we account for the order and understandability of the universe? Ultimately there are only two possible answers to this question. We can account for the order of the universe by saying that the universe was made by a person, by a Being with knowledge and will, by someone who knows what he is doing and what he intends—in other words by God. And we can account for the understandability of the universe by saying that we are made in the image and likeness of the God who made the universe; our minds resemble His, however remotely. *Or* we can account for the order of the universe by saying that there is some inherent principle of order in the fundamental stuff of the universe, and account for our understanding that order by saying that our minds are the outcome of the unfolding of this inherent principle of order.

Either theory, if accepted, would have consequences. If we really accepted the idea that our minds were the accidental result of the workings of mindless forces, we should be haunted by doubts as to whether our apparent understanding of the universe is illusory. Dogmatic confidence of any kind, including dogmatic confidence that certain sorts of events "can't happen" is not what we should logically expect from a Universe Ultimate view. (Of course, insofar as dogmatism is often the outcome of a feeling of uncertainty, we might explain the dogmatism psychologically.) The consequences of the God theory are rather different. Our confidence in the understanding of the universe given to us by science would be considerable, but it would not be absolute. If the natural order is the result of God's action, then sometimes God might act in such a way as to make exceptions to the natural order.

In this view an exception to the natural order would be like the exceptions we sometimes make to established rules and procedures—for example, allowing an exceptionally gifted child to skip grades or enter college without graduating from high school, or declaring a holiday on a day that would normally be a working day. We can often see that not making exceptions to rules would be unreasonable or unkind. Exceptions must, of course, be rare if rules are to be generally relied upon, but we can live perfectly well with a system of rules or procedures which have occasional exceptions. We may or may not think President Ford's pardon of ex-President Nixon wise or fair, but occasional exceptions to legal procedures, such as presidential pardon, do not make our legal system chaotic or unreliable.

Furthermore, provided that God wished to give us strong evidence that a given message has His authority behind it, there would seem to be no better way than a miracle. If I claim to have authority in a certain organization, strong evidence of my authority would be an ability to suspend the rules or make exceptions to usual procedures. You might meditate on the problem of how a God who never interfered with the working of the universe could establish a message from Himself as authoritative.

The scientist, of course, *as a* scientist, ignores the possibility of miracles, just as the lawyer, *as a* lawyer, must ignore the possibility of a presidential pardon for his client, since there is nothing he can do *as a lawyer* which will ensure a presidential pardon. A pardon is a free action by the President, which cannot be guaranteed by any legal maneuver; a miracle is a free act by God which the scientist cannot bring within *his* procedures.

A presidential pardon is like a miracle in that though the *origin* of the pardon is outside ordinary legal procedures, a pardon once granted has legal consequences. A miracle, once it has occurred, has consequences which fit into the kind of patterns scientists study: Drinking too much of the wine Christ made from water at Cana in Galilee would make a wedding guest drunk, and if a scientist had been there with his instruments he could verify, though not explain, the change and measure the alcoholic content of the wine made from water.

It is important to note that a presidential pardon is not *il*legal: It does not violate any laws. Furthermore, it does not suspend the laws in the sense that at a given time or place some laws cease to operate in all cases—as if, for example, the laws of libel were suspended in Hannibal, Missouri on the first Sunday in March, so that no libels in that place or time were punishable. Rather, an individual exception is made to the law, so that of two men convicted of the same crime at the same time, one may be pardoned and the other not. Similarly, a miracle does not *violate* the laws of nature, nor suspend them for all events at a given time or place: The water in one jar might be changed to wine and that in an adjacent jar be unchanged. Lazarus may be raised and a man in an adjacent tomb who died at the same time may remain dead.

A presidential pardon cannot be compelled by any legal means; it can only be asked for. It is a free act of the President. Similarly, a miracle cannot be brought about by scientific means; it can only be prayed for. It is a free act of God. A presidential pardon cannot be predicted from the legal facts and it does not create a precedent: A pardon may be granted in one case, and in precisely similar circumstances another request may be denied. Similarly, a miracle cannot be predicted by scientific means and it gives no scientific grounds for prediction once it has occurred: The miracle at Cana in Galilee does not increase the probability that water will change to wine in similar circumstances.

To sum up: We can imagine a different legal system in which there were no pardons and so no exceptions to the rule of law. However, our system is not such a system but rather one in which certain exceptions to the legal order, called presidential pardons, sometimes occur. Lawyers as such have no concern with presidential pardons, for they cannot predict them, bring them about, or draw any precedents for them. A presidential pardon is, you might say, supralegal and therefore of no *legal* interest. Similarly, it could be that our universe was one in which there were no exceptions to the natural order, but if traditional religious believers are right, our universe is not such a universe, but one in which certain exceptions to the natural order, called miracles, sometimes occur. Scientists, as such, have no concern with miracles, for they cannot predict them, bring them about, or draw any conclusions about the future course of nature from them. A miracle is supernatural, and therefore of no scientific interest.

We could not settle whether presidential pardons are possible by looking at the day-to-day business of the courts; rather, we must ask what kind of legal system we live under. We cannot settle whether miracles occur by looking at the ordinary course of nature; we must ask what kind of universe we live in. This is a philosophical, not a scientific, question, and one very relevant philosophical consideration is that a universe made by God leaves room for confidence in human reason, whereas a universe of natural necessity does not.

If we come to the conclusion that miracles are possible, then we must consider miracle as one possible explanation of certain events recorded in history. Again, because most readers of this book will have been influenced to some extent by Christianity, we will consider Christian claims with regard to miracles. Early Christians claimed that the tomb of Christ was empty and that Christ had risen from the dead. The Roman and Jewish authorities did not refute this claim by producing the body, as they would certainly have done had *they* removed it from the tomb. The Apostles suffered persecution, hardship, and martyrdom to proclaim the message of Christ risen from the dead, which they surely would not have done if *they* had removed and hidden Christ's body. Christians claim that no naturalistic explanation which tries to explain the disappearance of the body and the confidence of the early Christians comes anywhere near accounting for all the facts.

If miracles were impossible, we should have to try to account for the data in some other way; but there is no good argument which shows that miracles are impossible. If miracles were tremendously improbable, many times more improbable than the most farfetched naturalistic explanation of the data, then it might be reasonable to accept an otherwise very implausible naturalistic explanation. But there seems to be no argument to show that miracles are tremendously improbable. It is not enough to say that they are rare and unusual—

an event may be rare and unusual but still to be expected in given circumstances. It is rare to have world records in athletic events broken, but it is to be expected at the Olympic Games. President Ford's pardon of ex-President Nixon was a rare and unusual event, but not unexpected in the very unusual circumstances which then prevailed. The Resurrection of Christ was a rare and unusual event, but in the context of His life and teaching, was it unexpected?

It is even possible to give some general idea of the circumstances in which miracles are to be expected. The first is extraordinary goodness or holiness on the part of the miracle worker. As the man born blind said to the Jews, "We know for certain that God does not answer the prayers of sinners." The second circumstance is the need to back up or authenticate a message from God. Christ was as good and holy the year before He began his public ministry as He was after He began it, but He did not begin to work miracles until He began to preach. There is, I think, a third condition: an openness and willingness to learn on the part of the audience. In some places Christ worked few miracles because of the hardness of heart of those in that place. Christ worked no miracles at Herod's request; He cast none of His pearls before that swine.

Let me pause here and make a parenthetical remark which is not directly relevant to my main theme, but has a connection with it. I have been mentioning as examples various miracles attributed to Christ in the Gospels, including the Fourth Gospel. This may seem to some to fly in the face of much recent biblical scholarship, which has argued that the miracles attributed to Christ are additions to the record of His life made by later generations of Christian believers rather than accounts of what actually happened at the time given by eyewitnesses. Now in some cases there may be reasons for doubting on purely textual grounds whether a certain part of the New Testament as we now have it was part of the original record, for example, in the debated case of the "long ending" of Mark's Gospel. But a careful examination of a good deal of "higher" criticism (as opposed to textual criticism) of the New Testament shows that it is not the case that the miraculous element is rejected because the text is doubtful, but rather that the text is regarded as doubtful because of a prior rejection of any miraculous element.

Insofar, then, as we can show by philosophical argument that neither science nor reason requires us to reject the possibility of miracles, we undermine the kind of doubt as to the reliability of our texts which is based on hostility to a miraculous or supernatural element in Scripture. We must entertain the possibility that Luke recounts the Virgin birth of Christ because it actually happened and not because the later Christian community borrowed elements from pagan mythology to enhance the importance of the founder of Christianity. To the unbiased eye the first hypothesis might seem much more plausible than the second. We might even be daring enough to entertain the hypothesis that the Fourth Gospel, which is full of eyewitness detail and local knowledge, was actually written by the Apostle John, and that its theological depth as compared to the other Gospels is due to the fact that John understood his Master better than some of the other disciples, rather than due to later interpretations by second-generation Christians. Plato's picture of Socrates is more profound than Xenophon's, at least partly because Plato was better fitted to understand Socrates than Xenophon was.

Do historical arguments based on the New Testament record, which argue that miracle is the only or best explanation of certain well-attested events amount to a *proof* that miracles have occurred? So long as we understand that the term "proof" means something different in historical studies than it does in mathematics or science or philosophy, it may well be that we do have adequate historical proof of miracles. But to show this in detail would involve getting down to the historical nitty-gritty, and I cannot do that here.

Let me turn, then, to the related question of what miracles prove. If it is granted, at least for the sake of argument, that God exists, that miracles are possible, and that we have good historical evidence that miracles marked the beginning of Christianity, does this prove the Christian claim to the truth of the revelation given to us by Christ?

Before we can decide this, we will have to examine three apparent difficulties.

The first difficulty is what we might call the problem of contradictory miracles. If it were the case that genuine miracles were worked in support of contradictory religious revelations, we would not know what to think. It would be like a witness whose integrity we were absolutely sure of giving contradictory testimony for both sides of a dispute. Something would have to give. We would have to conceive that the witness was not really honest, or deny that he actually gave the testimony on both sides, or find some way of showing that the contradiction was only apparent.

Similarly, if it were claimed that miracles are worked in support of contradictory religious revelations, we would have to give up the idea of miracles as proving a system of religion, unless we could show that the contradiction was only apparent, or that one set of opposed miracles was not genuine.

In some cases perhaps we can show that there is no genuine conflict. Many religious believers accept both Old Testament and New Testament miracles, and deny the claim (which has been made) that Old Testament miracles worked in the name of the One God of Judaism are in some ways incompatible with New Testament miracles worked in the name of God the Father, God the Son, and God the Holy Spirit. (This is, of course, because they would deny, on theological grounds, that Christian belief in the Trinity amounts to belief in three Gods.)

Many Christian religious believers would not even deny the possibility that God might have worked miracles for the "virtuous pagans" before Christ, to encourage them to emphasize those parts of their religion closest to the truth. If, for instance, God had worked a miracle for the Egyptian Pharaoh Amenhotep in support of his efforts to establish monotheism and overthrow the dark gods of old Egypt, they would find in this no challenge to Christianity, even though Amenhotep's monotheism might have been very crude and contained elements of untruth.

What would threaten the argument from miracles for the truth of Christianity would be genuine miracles worked in opposition to Christian claims or in support of incompatible claims. If, for instance, a Moslem holy man raised a man from the dead in order to persuade Christians that Mohammed's revelation had superseded that of Christ, this would be a case of genuine incompatibility. However, so far from any case of this kind being established, it is hard to show that any case of this kind has even been claimed. General statements are often made by opponents of Christianity that miracles are claimed by all religions, but leading cases of these alleged claims are hard to come by.

Certainly fairy-tale-like legends sometimes grow up around a figure like Buddha or Mohammed, but these have certain common characteristics. Such tales arise centuries after the time of their alleged occurrence. They contain strong elements of the fantastic (e.g., Mohammed riding his horse to the moon) and in their manner of telling they reveal their kinship to legend and myth. Compare any of these accounts with the accounts we find in the Gospels and the difference in atmosphere is at once apparent. Either the Gospel accounts are eyewitness accounts of real events occurring in genuine places, or the four writers we call Matthew, Mark, Luke, and John independently invented, out of the clear blue sky, a sort of realistic fantasy or science fiction which has no antecedents and no parallels in ancient literature. Those who have no metaphysical objections to miracles may find the hypothesis that the events really happened as they are related immensely more plausible than the other hypothesis.

It may be worthwhile to take a quick look, for purposes of comparison, at the closest thing we have around the time of the Gospels to an attempt at a realistic fantasy. This is the story of Appollonius of Tyana, written about A.D. 220 by Flavius Philostratus, which is sometimes referred to by controversialists as if it were a serious rival to the Gospel accounts of Christ's ministry and miracles. Penguin Classics publishes an excellent little paper back edition of this story, to which you may go for details, but let me note a few points in passing.

The story concerns a wandering sage who al-

legedly lived from the early years of the first century until about A.D. 96 or 98. Philostratus mentions some earlier sources for his work but at least some of these sources are probably his own invention. For one thing, Philostratus's account contains serious historical inaccuracies about things like dates of rulers, which seem to rule out reliance on any early source. The work was later used as anti-Christian propaganda, to discredit the uniqueness of Christ's miracles by setting up a rival miracle worker, as Socrates was sometimes set up as a rival to Christ as a martyr and teacher of virtue.

Still, there is some evidence that a neo-Pythagorean sage named Apollonius may really have lived, and thus Philostratus's work is a real example of what some have thought the Gospels to be: a fictionalized account of the life of a real sage and teacher, introducing miraculous events to build up the prestige of the central figure. It thus gives us a good look at what a real example of a fictionalized biography would look like, written at a time and place not too far removed from those in which the Gospels were written.

The first thing we notice is the fairy-tale atmosphere. There is a rather nice little vampire story, which inspired a minor poem by Keats, entitled *Lamia*. There are animal stories about, for instance, snakes in India big enough to drag off and eat an elephant. The sage wanders from country to country and wherever he goes he is likely to be entertained by the king or emperor, who holds long conversations with him and sends him on his way with camels and precious stones.

Interspersed with picturesque adventures there are occasional accounts of miracles, often involving prophecy or mind reading. A ruffian threatens to cut Apollonius's head off and the sage laughs and shouts out the name of a day three days hence; on that day the ruffian is executed for treason. Here is a typical passage about healing miracles:

> There came a man about thirty who was an expert lion-hunter but had been attacked by a lion and dislocated his hip, and so was lame in one leg. But the Wise Man massaged his hip and this restored the man

to an upright walk. Someone else who had gone blind went away with his sight fully restored, and another man with a paralysed arm left strong again. A woman too, who had had seven miscarriages was cured through the prayers of her husband as follows. The Wise Man told the husband, when his wife was in labor, to bring a live rabbit under his cloak to the place where she was, walk around her and immediately release the hare: for she would lose her womb as well as the baby if the hare was not immediately driven away (Bk. 3, Sec. 39).

Now the point is not that Appollonius is no serious rival to Christ; no one ever thought he was except perhaps a few anti-Christian polemicists about the time of some of the early persecutions of the Church. The point is that this is what you get when imagination goes to work on a historical figure in classical antiquity; you get miracle stories a little like those in the Gospels, but also snakes big enough to eat elephants, kings and emperors as supporting cast, travelers' tales, ghosts, and vampires. Once the boundaries of fact are crossed we wander into fairyland. And very nice, too, for amusement or recreation. But the Gospels are set firmly in the real Palestine of the first century, and the little details are not picturesque inventions but the real details that only an eyewitness or a skilled realistic novelist can give.

As against this, those who wish to eliminate miracles from the Gospels have not textual evidence, but theories. We do not have any trace of early sober narratives of the life of Christ without miracles and later versions in which miracles are added. What we have is a story with miracles woven into its very texture. Someone once made a shrewd point about this. Christ, say the Gospels, "went about doing good." Fine. But what good did He do? Did He clothe the naked, visit prisoners, counsel people on personal problems? No. He went about making the extravagant claim to forgive sins and backing this up by working miracles, mostly miracles of healing. Eliminate this element and, setting aside His preaching, what good did He go about doing?

The point is that the miraculous is interwoven with the primary story of Christianity in a way in which the miraculous is not interwoven with the primary story of Buddhism or Mohammedanism. Again, however, this is a matter for detailed inquiry into comparative religion and the history of religions.

The second major difficulty as to the evidential value of miracles which we will consider is the objection that what seems to us to be an exception to the natural order may just be the operation of some natural regularities which we do not yet understand. Perhaps, says this objection, Jesus was merely a rare type of charismatic personality who could arouse a faith response in people such that their minds acted on their bodies in a way that freed them from illness. After all, the relation of the mind and body in illness is a mysterious one, and some studies suggest that mental attitude has a great deal to do with illness. Thus we may someday understand scientifically, and even be able to reproduce, some of Christ's apparently miraculous cures.

The first comment to make on this line of objection is that, like any argument which depends on what science *may* be able to discover in the future, it is extremely weak. But we can also ask what range of illnesses and cures this theory is supposed to account for. For example, Christ might have cured a paralytic because the paralysis was hysterical and subject to psychosomatic healing. But what about the cure of leprosy? What about the cure of the man blind from birth? And it is no use saying that psychosomatic illnesses cured by the impact of a charismatic personality account for *some* of Christ's cures and that the rest are fictional, for this would be to pick and choose among the evidence in a blatant way. If I am allowed to pick which of the evidence I will explain and reject the rest, I can make almost any theory look plausible.

But, of course, the cases which are decisive against any theory of psychosomatic cures are the raisings from the dead reported in all four Gospels. A last-ditch attempt to explain these "naturally" might be to allege that the seemingly dead persons were only in a cataleptic state, but cases of this kind are so rare that to allege this as an explanation of the raising of the daughter of the Jairus, *and* of the son of the widow of Nain, *and* Lazarus, brings in coincidence to a fantastic degree. Each of these accounts is highly circumstantial, and none can be plausibly treated as a variation on one of the others.

In other words, the proponent of the view that Christ's cures were psychosomatic—"faith healing" in a limiting sense—must make up his mind whether or not he accepts the written records as factual or fictional, or whether he holds them to be a mixture of fact and fiction. If the records are fictional, no explanation of the cures is necessary. If the account is factual, all of the reported miracles must be accounted for, not just those which can be plausibly accounted for on naturalistic grounds. If it is alleged that there is a mixture of fact and fiction, there must be an independent standard of what is factual in the record and what is fictional. We cannot in logic allow the principle of choice: "What I can explain is fact, the rest is fiction." (Think what ex-President Nixon could have done to the Watergate story using that principle!)

If the proponent of an explanation by so far unknown laws of nature goes so far as to say that even raisings from the dead can be accounted for by these laws, he must again explain a tremendous implausibility: either that these laws operated coincidentally in the neighborhood of Jesus, or that an obscure provincial carpenter somehow was able to discover and make use of natural powers and possibilities that none of the wise sages or deep researchers had ever been able to master or control.

A final difficulty about the evidential value of miracles rests on the fear that some supernatural power less than that of God might account for the wonders worked by Christ—that Jesus did His works, if not by the powers of Beelzebub, then at least by the power of some spiritual being less than God. To say what power this might be, of course, would be in some sense to give a theological account of what powers greater than human there might be, and how they are related to one another.

Consider, however, a line of argument some-times heard from people influenced by certain sorts of Eastern religions, which goes something like this: Yes, of course Jesus was able to do apparently miraculous things; He was a Master, or Adept, and they can all do things of this sort. Jesus, living at the time and place that He did, tried to teach the Palestinian people a simple religion of love, put in terms of their own religious concepts, and this message has reached us in a distorted form. His real power lay in spiritual enlightenment, which you can learn by practicing Yoga (or going to Tibet, *or* studying with Mahatma X, or the like).

Again, there is a large blank check, drawn this time not on science, but on some sort of mystical religion. A friend of mine, arguing religion with opponents who seemed dogmatically sure of what God could or could not create, would challenge them, if they knew so much about creation, to create just one small rabbit—"to establish confidence." A similar challenge might be put to the exponents of "Eastern Wisdom" to duplicate even the least of Christ's miracles, to establish their claims. If they admit their own lack of power but claim others have performed some feats as great as Christ's, the problem simply reduces to one of the evidence for rival miracles discussed earlier.

In addition, there is a theological question as to whether a wise and loving God would allow people to be misled by permitting some lesser being to work apparent miracles. Real raising from the dead, creation of food or wine which is genuine and not illusory—such miracles seem by their nature to be the province of God only. But even if such things as the reading of thoughts or the manipulation of matter in scientifically inexplicable ways were possible to powers less than God, would God permit such occurrences in a context which gave rise to a false belief in men of good will, or seriously challenged the true beliefs of those already on the right path? A priori, it would seem not; and again, it does not seem that there is any reliable record of any such occurrences. (This is not to say that God may not sometimes permit "wonders" of this sort to be worked in order to refute them by His own power—for example, the story in Acts of the girl with the "prophetic spirit.")

The preceding comments, necessarily brief, give some indication of the lines along which the evidential value of miracles must be assessed. Are there indeed rival miracles? Can miracles be explained as due to powers less than God? If the answer to all these questions is no, then we are forced to grant that miracles give a strong argument for the existence of God.

Note

1. David Hume, *Enquiries*, ed. L. A. Selby-Bigge (Oxford: Oxford University Press, 1955), pp. 114–15.

V.5 Miracles and Revelation

RICHARD SWINBURNE

In our final reading in this section, Richard Swinburne takes up the matter of miracles where he left off in his previous article. There he argued, contra Hume, that miracles were possible. Here he argues that given the proviso that the existence of God is a plausible hypothesis or assumption, it is reasonable to expect that he would reveal himself in human history and that he would confirm the revelation by miracles (including predictive prophecy). Swinburne here sets forth the criteria that would have to be met were a religion to claim that it is that revelation. Although Swinburne later (in a section not included in this work) applies these criteria to Christianity, readers are free to use them to compare the revelations as they deem appropriate.

If a man concludes that it is probable that there is a God, it follows that he has a duty to worship and obey binding on him, and so he must investigate how best to fulfil it; and that involves investigating the claims of different creeds. However, I think that the expert or the person in a parental situation may still have a duty to compare creeds, even if on his evidence it is more probable than not that there

is no God. For his duty is to show to others how best to attain goals of supreme worth. He must investigate whether non-theistic ways to salvation are likely to attain that salvation. And also those dependent on him need to know as surely as they can, even if it is probable that there is no God and non-theistic ways are unlikely to attain their goal, which is the way most likely to attain its goal. Even if the agricultural biochemist believes that on balance it is improbable that more food can be got out of the land, if the people are very short of food, he still has a duty to investigate which method of fertilizing, irrigation, or crop rotation is more likely to produce an increase of yield (in the hope that his inquiries will show that one method is much more likely than any others to be successful). By analogy, if the religious investigator, who is an expert or in a parental situation, judges the goals of religion to be very worthwhile, it follows that he has a duty to pursue religious investigation even if he believes that it is not probable with respect to any one way that it will attain the goals of religion. So in these various circumstances it is a duty or at any rate a very worthwhile thing to investigate the relative probability of creeds, in order to produce a rational$_5$ belief about the relative probabilities of creeds, e.g., a belief that the Christian Creed is more probable than any rival creed which justifies a different religious way. The above conclusions about the duty to investigate the comparative probabilities of creeds hold, I urge, objectively for a man who has a certain belief about how probable it is that there is a God. If he does not support his beliefs about the comparative probabilities of creeds by proper investigation, they will not be rational. . . .

The process of showing the Christian Creed to be more probable than any rival creed which justifies a different religious way can be analysed as needing three steps: first, a demonstration that it is probable to some degree on reasonably believed evidence that there is a God; secondly, a demonstration that it is more probable, if there is a God, that the other items of the Christian Creed are true than that the other items of some rival theistic creed are true; and thirdly, a demonstration that it is more probable that the Christian Creed as a whole is true than that any non-theistic religious creed is true.

The first task is the traditional task of natural theology and is far too big a subject to be discussed here. It was the subject of my earlier volume, *The Existence of God.* I concluded there that it is more probable than not that there is a God. But all that is necessary for weak belief in the Christian Creed is a much less probable belief— say, putting it loosely, that there is a significant probability that there is a God. For, given that, there is quite a chance that salvation may be had by pursuing one of the religious ways of theistic religions, since the attainment of salvation according to these religions consists in God providing that salvation (e.g., forgiveness and life after death). The next stage is to show that if there is a God it is more likely that the other items of the Christian Creed are true than that the other items of some rival creed are true. For given that there is a God, then if the other items of the Christian Creed are more probable than the other items of rival theistic creeds, the Christian Creed as a whole (item common with other theistic creeds plus different items) will be more probable than any other theistic creed as a whole (common item plus different items). We need to show that it is more probable that God became incarnate in Christ than that Muhammad was his chief prophet; that the way to worship regularly is by attendance

at the Eucharist rather than by the five daily prayer-times, and so on. The choice between religious systems in these respects turns on a judgment about which is the true revelation of God. For the grounds for believing the other items of a theistic creed—that in this way God has intervened in history, that forgiveness is available in this way, that these are the fates for men in the after-life, that this is the way to live in this life— are normally that God has revealed these truths through the mouth of some human intermediary, whom we will call his prophet. I wish therefore now to discuss the kind of considerations which are relevant to assessing such claims to revelation. The discussion will be a brief discussion to indicate the kind of considerations which need to be investigated, rather than a thorough discussion of which is the true claim to revelation. I include the discussion to indicate the kind of investigation by which faith needs to be supported.

The Evidence of Revelation

A theistic religion claims that its prophet is a special messenger of God and that what he says about the nature of reality and how men ought to live is to believed because it comes from God. It is also sometimes claimed that the prophet and his actions have eternal significance because of his special status. The Christian claim that Jesus Christ was both God and man who by his sacrificial life redeemed the world is obviously such a claim— indeed it is by far the strongest claim for divine intervention in human history made by any of the great religions.

Theistic religions are normally prepared to allow that God has spoken to men in a limited way through prophets other than their own unique prophet. Thus Islam is prepared to allow that God spoke to men through Jesus Christ. But the point is that, according to each religion, there is truth and falsity mixed in the deliverances of prophets other than its own, and that where there is dispute the sayings of its own prophet take precedence—for what he says is true without qualification (and, perhaps also, what he does is of unrepeatable significance). If a religion claims that all prophets teach varying amounts of truth and falsity, and so purports to judge the worth of each prophet's teaching merely by considering what he says rather than the fact that he says it, that religion cannot be regarded in the traditional sense as a revealed religion, as teaching and supported by a revelation. For the grounds for believing any of what the religion asserts will not be that it has been revealed by God (for which in turn there is other evidence, including that other things which the prophet said are true); rather, the argument will always go the other way round—the grounds for believing that any of the things which a prophet teaches have been revealed by God are simply that they are true. A religion which claims a revelation in teaching claims that the prophet's message is to be believed, not because it can be known to be true independently of the prophet having said it, but because of the prophet's authority.

So then, what is the evidence for claims that some prophet is in this way a special messenger of God? The traditional view down the centuries, advocated among others by Aquinas, declared to be official Roman Catholic doctrine by the First Vatican Council and classically expounded by Paley, is that the evidence will be of various kinds but will include a central and crucial element of the miraculous.

In *Evidences of Christianity*, Paley argues that given that there is a God—who is, by definition, good—and that the human race lies in ignorance of things important for them to know, it is *a priori* to some extent to be expected that God would give a revelation to men. And what things are these important things? If the arguments of this book are correct, it is important for men to know the nature of the world and man's place in it, how they ought to live, how deep long-term happy well-being is to be achieved, how forgiveness is to be obtained from God, how God is to be worshipped and obeyed. A revelation such as the Christian revelation (as traditionally described) claims to provide knowledge on all these matters. Paley however stresses—to my mind totally disproportionately—the existence and nature of the

after-life at the expense of all other elements of revelation.

Yet knowledge of all these things has great value, other than its value in preparing men for the after-life. It is good that man should understand the world, know how to live in it and how to obtain the deepest well-being this Earth can provide; it is good too that man should know how to worship and obey God and obtain forgiveness from him—all this quite independently of the consequences in an after-life for man of his doing these things. But it is also good that man know how to obtain his eternal well-being.

Men are capable of receiving such knowledge. But much of it could not to all appearances be obtained by mere reflection on the natural world. That God is three persons in one substance could hardly, if true, be known to be true by such human reflection. I claimed, in *The Existence of God*, that various phenomena, including chiefly very general and publicly observable ones such as the orderliness of nature, show the dependence of the world on a creator God. We must, I argued, suppose him to be very powerful, wise, etc., if he is to be able to bring about the existence and orderliness of the world; and considerations of simplicity involve us inferring from 'very powerful . . . etc.' to 'infinitely powerful . . . etc.' But it is hard to see how any further details of his nature could be read off from the world. I have no conclusive proof that this cannot be done. I simply appeal to the apparent impossibility of seeing how it can be done; and to the fact that nobody today thinks that it can be done, and that very few people in the past ever thought that it could be done. Likewise, mere reflection on the natural world could hardly show the details of how men ought to worship God, e.g. in the Eucharist on Sundays; or how forgiveness from God is to be obtained—through pleading the Passion of Christ. And so on.

Other such purported knowledge as is conveyed in revelations such as the Christian revelation, is purported knowledge of matters about which men produce arguments of a general philosophical character arising out of reflection on the natural world. That God is omnipotent, omniscient, etc., is, as we have seen, the subject of such argument. So too are the general principles of morality, such as that men ought to tell the truth, keep their promises, and show compassion. Now maybe all such arguments fail; it needs a detailed discussion of each case to show whether they do or not. However, I have argued in *The Existence of God* that arguments to show that there is a God omnipotent, omniscient, and perfectly free do work. And plausibly, reason can help to show claims about morality to be justified.

However, if such knowledge of the omnipotence, omniscience, etc. of God and the general principles of morality can be obtained by natural means, it is evident that some men are too stupid to obtain the knowledge—the savage argues only to a much more lowly God—and some men will never reach that knowledge because of the climate of contrary opinion in which they grow up, the climate of an atheistic authority. It is sometimes through men yielding to bad desires, either to teach things which they do not really believe (in the interests of their state or party, church or career), or not to investigate further things which they are told on authority (through fear or laziness), that men come to hold beliefs and climates of opinion develop. Hence sin plays a role in moulding belief.

So the detailed truths of creeds will either not be known at all to men or (through men's stupidity, ignorance, and sin) be known only with difficulty. Yet these are the truths which are of crucial importance if men are to make themselves good men (true specimens of humanity), men worthy to obtain everlasting well-being. If there is a God (who is by definition good), he might to some degree be expected to intervene in history to reveal these truths which men could not discover for themselves and to give his authority to those to which reason pointed with insufficient force, for he has good reason to do this. There is also the reason to expect a revelation, not merely by teaching but by a human life, which the Christian tradition has always stressed but which Paley does not. Human sin and corruption need atonement. This is a primary reason why, on the traditional Christian doctrine, a revelation in the form of a person who lived a sacrificial life was to be expected.

So, given that there is good evidence that there is a God, there is some reason *a priori* to expect that there will be a revelation. What historical evidence would show that it had taken place on a certain occasion? It is a basic principle of confirmation theory that evidence confirms a hypothesis (i.e. adds to its probability) if and only if that evidence is more to be expected if the hypothesis is true than it would otherwise be. So given some prior probability that God would reveal himself in history, the evidence of history that he has done so will be such as is to be expected if the hypothesis is true, and not otherwise. The obvious kind of evidence, then, will be teaching such as God would be expected to give and actions such as God would be expected to do, of a kind and in circumstances in which they would not be expected to occur in the normal course of things.

What sort of teaching about the matters which man needs to know would God be expected to give through a prophet? Obviously teaching which is true and deep. Although the teaching itself must be true, it might however need to be embodied in the false historical and scientific presuppositions of the prophet's day if it is to be understood. For instance, suppose a prophet was teaching in a culture which believed that the world consisted of a flat and stationary earth surrounded by a heavenly dome in which Sun, Moon, planets, and stars moved. God wishes through the prophet to convey the message of the total dependence of the world on God. How is he to announce his message? There seem three possible ways. The prophet might say: 'It is God who holds the flat earth still and moves round it the heavenly lights.' Or he might say: 'Whatever the true scientific description of the world, it is God who brings about that state of affairs which that description describes.' Or he might begin by giving a true scientific account of the world and then say that God brings about that world. But if he is to announce his message in the third way, the religious truth can only be announced after a complete process of scientific education. And even if he is to announce it in the second way, the message will only be understood by a people who have done quite a lot of philosophical abstraction. They would have to have understood the possible falsity of most of their common-sense science, and have got used to the abstract concepts of states of affairs which might not be describable, and descriptions which might not apply to things. If the prophet's message is to be understood by a primitive culture, it is the first way of teaching which would have to be used. And unless one thinks that divine revelation can be given only to sophisticated peoples, that means that when a divine revelation is made to a primitive people, there is a distinction to be made between the prophet's message and the scientific and historical presuppositions in terms of which it is expressed. This distinction would need to be made by a later and less primitive society which knew a bit more about science and history, in order for it to see what was the religious message clothed in the false presuppositions. And of course if the later society was not sophisticated enough, it might fail to make the distinction, and so suppose the science and history to be part of the prophet's message. This could lead to its rejecting the message on the grounds that the science and history were false (the rational reaction); or, worse (the irrational reaction) adopting the old science and history (and rejecting the alleged advances here of more recent times) on the grounds that the prophet's message was true. It will, I hope, be unnecessary to give many historical examples of such reactions.

One all too sadly obvious modern one is the example of the different reactions to Darwin's theory of evolution. Christianity has regarded the Old Testament as in a sense and to a degree licensed by Christ. He took it largely for granted in his teaching, and the Church which he founded proclaimed it (with the exception of the laws about ritual and sacrifice) as God's message. The Old Testament in telling in Genesis 1 and 2 the Creation stories seems to presuppose that animal species came into being a few thousand years ago virtually simultaneously. The theory of evolution showed that they did not. So some rejected Christianity on the grounds that it taught what was scientifically false, and others rejected the theory of evolution on the grounds that it conflicted with true religion. But it seems odd to suppose that the

religious message of what is evidently a piece of poetry was concerned with the exact time and method of animal arrival on the Earth, or that that was what those who composed it were attempting to tell the world. Their message concerned, not the details of the time and method of animal arrival, but the ultimate cause of that arrival. To make the point that there is a distinction between a prophet's religious message and its scientific and historical presuppositions is not to deny that it may not always be easy to disentangle the message from the presuppositions, or to express it in more modern terms. One obvious step in going about this task is for the investigator to inquire into the circumstances of the prophet's utterance and see what he was denying, and contrast this with the assumptions about more mundane matters shared by the prophet and his opponents.

So then, with this qualification, the prophet must teach what is true. Must he teach only what is true? Can there be falsity mixed with his teaching? No: the whole body of what the prophet announces as his message must be true, for the reason given earlier: that it purports to be God's announcement to man of things beyond his power to discover for himself. However if a clear distinction could be made between the prophet's message and other things which he said but for which he did not claim any special authority, there is no reason to require that the latter be true.

The prophet's teaching must be, not merely true, but deep. Men need moral teaching and instruction about the nature of reality which is not readily available to them.

What would be the evidence that the prophet's teaching is true? First, none of what he teaches must be evidently false. His teaching on morality, for example, must not involve his telling men that they ought to do what is evidently morally wrong—the prophet who recommends cheating and child torture can be dismissed straight away. Likewise no factual teaching of the prophet must be proven false. If the prophet teaches that, whatever men do, the world will end in exactly thirty years time, and the world fails to end then; the prophet must be rejected. Secondly, such parts of the prophet's teaching as can be checked must be found to be true. Some of the prophet's moral teaching, for example, may coincide with our clear intuitions about morality. Thirdly, it may be that some parts of the prophet's teaching which do not appear obviously true to start with are found, through experience and reflection, to be true. One way in which subsequent experience could confirm a prophet's teaching would be if the sort of teaching about God, his nature, and action in history which the prophet gives makes sense of the investigator's own private and public experience, in the sense of making probable a course of experience which would not otherwise be probable. The course of a man's life, the answering of his prayers, and particular 'religious experiences' within that life might be such as the God proclaimed by the prophet would be expected to bring about. All that would be further evidence of the truth of the prophet's teaching.

All of this is independent evidence that some of what the prophet teaches is true. The fact that some of what the prophet teaches is seen to be true and deep is indeed some slight evidence that the other things which he said are true and deep. If a man says what is true on one deep matter, that is some evidence for supposing that he is a wise man, and so for supposing that what he says on other deep matters is true. But it is only slight evidence—many teachers who teach deep truths teach falsities also, and prophets who agree over one range of their teaching disagree over another range. That the moral teaching of Jesus Christ is true and deep is slender grounds for believing what he had to say about life after death.

Revelations include, and (as we have seen that Paley argued) can *a priori* be expected to include, things beyond human capacity independently to check. For example they typically assert the existence of a life after death; and they provide us with information about the sort of God who is to be worshipped in far more detail than a man could derive from examination of the created world, and they give us details of the way to worship him. Hence we need some evidence that what the prophet says is true when we cannot check independently whether it is or not. Analogy suggests the sort of evidence for which we ought to be looking. Suppose that in the days before wireless, telephones, and fast travel, a man claims to have visited a king of a distant country and to have brought back a message from him. What would show that the message comes from the king? First, the message may contain some prediction of an event of the future occurrence of which the messenger could have learnt only from the king; e.g. that the messenger's arrival would be followed by the arrival of some of the king's ships (the messenger having to all appearances travelled by land and so not having been able to meet such ships en route). Secondly, the messenger may bring some token which a man could only have obtained from the king, e.g. a precious stone of a kind only to be found in the king's country, and which is mined by the king alone and kept by him. The token might be the sort of token which people of the culture of those days traditionally gave to authenticate messages. By analogy, evidence that the prophet has his revelation from God and so is to be believed on deep matters where we have no independent means of checking, would be given, first, by his ability to predict some future event which he would have no means of predicting otherwise, i.e. by mere human powers. But any event in accordance with natural laws could be predicted by mere human powers. So this evidence needs to be evidence of an ability to predict events not in accordance with natural laws; and that, in a basically deterministic world, means violations of natural laws. The evidence would need also to suggest that the violations were brought about by God, and so were miracles. Secondly, evidence that the prophet had his revelation from God would be provided if the prophet's life was accompanied by events which, evidence suggested, were violations of natural laws produced by God in circumstances where such violations would naturally and by local convention be interpreted as vindicating the prophet's teaching. Both these further sources of evidence thus involve the occurrence of miracles.

Before taking the argument further, I need to spell out what I understand by a miracle and what would be evidence that an event was a miracle in my sense. I understand by a miracle a violation of the laws of nature, that is, a non-repeatable exception to the operation of these laws, brought about by God. Laws of nature have the form of universal statements 'all As are B', and state how bodies behave of physical necessity. Thus Kepler's three laws of planetary motion state how the planets move. The first law states that all planets move in ellipses with the sun at one focus. If this purported law is to be a law of nature, planets must in general move as it states.

What however is to be said about an isolated exception to a purported law of nature? Suppose that one day Mars moves out of its elliptical path for a brief period and then returns to the path. There are two possibilities. This wandering of Mars may occur because of some current condition of the Universe (e.g. the proximity of Jupiter drawing Mars out of its elliptical path), such that if that condition were to be repeated the event would happen again. In this case the phenomenon is an entirely regular phenomenon. The trouble is that what might have appeared originally to be a basic law of nature proves now not to be one. It proves to be a consequence of a more fundamental law that the original purported law normally holds, but that under circumstances describable in general terms (e.g. 'when planets are close to each other') there are exceptions to it. Such repeatable exceptions to purported laws merely show that the purported laws are not basic laws of nature. The other possibility is that the exception to the law was not caused by some current condition, in such a way that if the condition were to recur the event would happen again. In this case we have a non-repeatable exception to a law of nature. But how are we to describe this event further? There are two possible moves. We may say that if there occurs an exception to a purported law of nature, the purported law can be no law. If the purported law says 'all As are B' and there is an A which is not B, then 'all As are B' is no law. The trouble with saying that is that the purported law may be a very good device for giving accurate predictions in our field of study; it may be by far the best general formula for describing what happens in the field which there is. (I understand by a general formula a formula which describes what happens in all circumstances of a certain kind, but does not mention by name particular individuals, times, or places.) To deny that the purported law is a law, when there is no more accurate general formula, just because there is an isolated exception to its operation, is to ignore its enormous ability to predict what happens in the field.

For this reason it seems not unnatural to say that the purported law is no less a law for there being a non-repeatable exception to it; and then to describe the exception as a 'violation' of the law. At any rate this is a coherent way of talking, and I think that it is what those who use such expressions as 'violation' of a law of nature are getting at. In this case we must amend our understanding of what is a law of nature. To say that a generalization 'all As are B' is a universal law of nature is to say that being A physically necessitates being B, and so that any A will be B—apart from violations.

But how do we know that some event such as the wandering of Mars from its elliptical path is a non-repeatable rather than a repeatable exception to a purported law of nature? We have grounds for believing that the exception is non-repeatable in so far as any attempt to amend the purported law of nature so that it predicted the wandering of Mars as well as all the other observed positions of Mars, would make it so complicated and *ad hoc* that we would have no grounds for trusting its future predictions. It is no good for example amending the law so that it reads: 'all planets move in ellipses with the Sun at one focus, except in years when there is a competition for the World Chess Championship between two players both of whose surnames begin with K.' Why not? Because this proposed law mentions properties which have no other place in physics (no other physical law invokes this sort of property) and it mentions them in an *ad hoc* way (that is, the proposed new law has the form 'so-and-so holds except under such-and-such circumstances', when the only reason for adding the exceptive clause is that otherwise the law would be incompatible with observations; the clause does not follow naturally from the theory.) What we need if we are to have a more adequate law is a general formula, of which it is an entirely natural consequence that the exception to the original law occurs when it does.

In these ways we could have grounds for believing that an exception to a purported law was non-repeatable and so a violation of a natural law. Claims of this sort are of course corrigible—we could be wrong; what seemed inexplicable by natural causes might be explicable after all. But then we could be wrong about most things, including claims of the opposite kind. When I drop a piece of chalk and it falls to the ground, every one supposes that here is an event perfectly explicable by natural laws. But we could be wrong. Maybe the laws of nature are much more complicated than we suppose, and Newton's and Einstein's laws are mere approximations to the true laws of mechanics. Maybe the true laws of mechanics predict that almost always when released from the hand, chalk will fall to the ground, but not today because of a slightly abnormal distribution of distant galaxies. However although the true laws of nature predict that the chalk will rise, in fact it falls. Here is a stark violation of natural laws, but one which no one detects because of their ignorance of natural laws. 'You could be wrong' is a knife which cuts both ways. What seem to be perfectly explicable events might prove, when we come to know the laws of nature much better, to be violations. But of course this is not very likely. The reasonable man goes by the available evidence here, and also in the converse case. He supposes that what is, on all the evidence, a violation of natural laws really is one. There is good reason to suppose that events such as the following if they occurred would be violations of laws of nature: levitation, that is, a man rising in the air against gravity without the operation of magnetism or any other known physical force; resurrection from the dead of a man whose heart has not been beating for twenty-four hours and who counts as dead by other currently used criteria; water turning into wine without the assistance of chemical apparatus or catalysts; a man growing a new arm from the stump of an old one.

Since the occurrence of a violation of natural laws cannot be explained in the normal way, either it has no explanation or it is to be explained in a different way. The obvious explanation exists if there is a God who is responsible for the whole order of nature, including its conformity to natural laws, and who therefore can on occasion suspend the normal operation of natural laws and bring about or allow some one else to bring about events, not via this normal route. We should suppose that events have explanations if suggested explanations are at all plausible. If there is quite a bit of evidence that there is a God responsible for the natural order, then any violations are plausibly attributed to his agency and so plausibly recognized as miracles—at least so long as those violations are not ruled out by such evidence as we may have from other sources about God's character. God's permitting a law of nature to be violated is clearly necessary for this to occur if he is the author of Nature; and in the absence of evidence that any other agent had a hand in the miracle, it ought to be attributed to God's sole agency. But if there is evidence, say, that it happens after a command (as opposed to a request to God) for it to happen issued by another agent, then the miracle is to be attributed to a joint agency.

I have not considered here the kind of historical evidence needed to prove the occurrence of an event which if it occurred would be a violation, but clearly it will be of the same kind as the evidence for any other historical event. There is the evidence of one's own senses, the testimony of others (oral and written) and the evidence of traces (effects left by events, such as footprints, fingerprints, cigarette ash, etc.). I see no reason in principle why there should not be evidence of this kind to show the occurrence of a levitation or a resurrection from the dead.

Now I claimed earlier that two further kinds of evidence for the genuineness of a prophet's revelation would be provided if there was evidence of the prophet's ability to predict miracles, and if there was evidence that his teaching was vindicated by miracles. Christian theology has traditionally claimed both these further sources of evidence for the truth of what Christ said.

The life of Christ was, according to the Gospels, full of 'miracles'. Some of the 'miracle' stories are perhaps not intended to be taken literally, some of them are ill-authenticated, and some of the 'miracles' were not violations of natural laws (e.g. perhaps certain cures of the mentally deranged come into this category). Yet some of the Gospel 'miracles', in particular the stories of healings of the blind and dumb and lame, seem to me to be intended to be taken literally by the Gospel writers, to be moderately well authenticated, and to be violations of natural laws, if they occurred. But the story of one 'miracle' above all, of course, has dominated Christian teaching from the earliest days until the present—the story of the Resurrection of Christ. It seems to this writer that the writers of gospels and epistles intended their readers to believe that although Christ was killed on the Cross, he subsequently came to life (in a transformed body which left its tomb). If the events of the first Easter occurred in anything like the form recorded in the Gospels, there is a clear case of a violation of a natural law. As a violation of natural law, it would (for reasons already stated) be plausibly explained by the action of God intervening in human history.

Christian theology has claimed as evidence of the genuineness of Christ's revelation, his prophetic power in the sense of his ability to predict future events to be brought about by God, including Christ's crucifixion and resurrection, the establishment of the Church and the fall of Jerusalem. At any rate the resurrection, if it occurred, would have been, I have claimed, a miracle; and so if Christ had the ability to predict it, that would show some knowledge of God's purposes. I do not pronounce on the disputed issue of whether Christ did predict his Resurrection, or the other events, or whether there was anything miraculous in the latter.

Secondly, Christian theology has claimed that Christ's miracles, and above all the miracle of the Resurrection, marked God's vindication of Christ's teaching. The Resurrection meant that the sacrificial life of Jesus had not ended in disaster. If it occurred, it was the means of founding the Church and making the teaching of and about Jesus available to the world. Whatever is to be said about other purported miracles, the Resurrection (if it occurred) is for this reason reasonably interpreted

as involving the divine judgement that it is good that the teaching of Jesus triumph. Since that teaching involves showing men the way to salvation, if it is good that it triumph, that must be because the way which it shows men does lead to salvation. For although God may have good reason for allowing evil to triumph, if it occurs through the free choice of men—because it is good that men should make a difference to the world through their free choice, or in accord with natural processes—as a warning to men as to the consequences of allowing such natural processes to continue; he would seem to have no reason to intervene in nature to make it triumph. Apparently, miraculous triumphing is not to be expected but for divine action and approval and therefore plausibly signifies divine action and approval. Also, Jews of the first century AD would, I suggest, readily interpret miraculous intervention to secure the triumphing of Jesus's life and teaching as evidence of a divine 'signature' on that teaching and so of its truth (and perhaps also, if Christ's death was an atoning sacrifice, as the acceptance of that sacrifice). If God gives a message to men, the right interpretation of the message is (in the absence of other considerations) the way in which it would naturally be interpreted by those who received it. For any giver of messages uses such devices as, given the conventions of his audience, will be interpreted in the right way.

Similar considerations to those about a revelation via a prophet's teaching are relevant for assessing any claim that the prophet's life was in some sense God's life, viz. that the prophet was in some sense God incarnate (although claims to such revelation are not our main concern in this chapter). A primary issue here is whether the concept of an incarnation is a coherent one at all—whether there is not some internal contradiction in the suggestion that the same individual was both God and man. If there is not, then to any claim that God has become incarnate on a particular occasion, there are relevant, first, *a priori* considerations about whether God is likely to become incarnate and under what circumstances. I noted earlier the *a priori* considerations put forward in favour of expecting God to bring about a Christian-type atonement. Then there will be evidence of two further kinds relevant to showing that God has on a particular occasion become incarnate. There will, first, be the quality of a certain prophet's human life—that it shows the kind of pattern which God would be expected to show if he accepted human limitations. It needs much argument to show what that pattern would be. But clearly, to make an atonement of the kind earlier referred to, a holy and sacrificial life is needed. Moral reflection and reflection on the prophet's life may help the investigator to see in it depths of holiness and sacrifice which are not in evidence at first sight. Yet there are many sacrificial lives lived by men on Earth. The evidence that a particular one was divine would be the testimony of the prophet himself (shown to teach true teaching by the criteria previously considered) or his accredited representative (e.g., a church); that the prophet himself could work miracles at will (not merely pray successfully for them to happen); and that his life began and ended in a way which violated natural processes. For if through the prophet's life God entered and left the world in response to the current human condition, this would require some interruption of the operation of natural processes which are concerned with the created world and planned by God from the beginning of the created world. For if the prophet's coming into the world was a natural consequence of natural laws operative throughout human history (even if made so to operate by God's original choice), his coming into the world (and so also his leaving it) would not be the result of God's spontaneous response to the mess which men had made of their lives and of the Earth. So for more than one reason, incarnation requires to be accompanied by miracle; and evidence for such miracles in connection with a holy and sacrificial life is evidence of incarnation. Claims of an incarnation typically need to be backed up by a claim to revelation in teaching (e.g. the prophet or his accredited representative—a church—teaching that the prophet was God incarnate); and there are major religions (e.g. Judaism and Islam) which claim no incarnation and yet are to be compared with Christianity in respect of a revelation in teaching.

Brief though my discussion of revelation has been, I believe that it substantiates Paley's classical claim about revelation, especially revelation in teaching. Paley writes: 'In what way can a revelation be made, but by miracles? In none which we are able to conceive?' I have argued that Paley is right.

What a man needs to believe with respect to the claimed Christian revelation, if he is to pursue the Christian way is, we have seen, not that it is more probable than not that God revealed himself in Christ but that, if there is a God, it is more probable that he revealed himself in Christ than that he revealed himself through any other prophet with a conflicting message. If the argument of this chapter is correct, for another revelation to be more probable than the Christian revelation, it would have to be backed by a more evident miracle, or be backed by a miracle no less evident but containing more evidently true and deep teaching, or perhaps, be backed by a miracle somewhat less evident but containing teaching far more evidently true and deep. I shall come shortly to the question of how much investigation of comparative religion is necessary before a man can have a rational belief that this is so.

Paley's conclusion, after his investigation into this issue, was that no religion other than Christianity is backed by equally well-authenticated miracles. He claims that 'the only event in the history of the human species, which admits of comparison with the propagation of Christianity' is Islam. But he claims that 'Mahomet did not found his pretensions . . . upon proofs of supernatural agency, capable of being known and attested by others'.

I believe that, whatever the deficiencies of Paley's detailed historical arguments (and he wrote long before the great advances in biblical criticism in the late nineteenth century), the approach of the *Evidences* to these matters is correct. The evidence of a revelation is the plausibility to the reflective investigator of a prophet's teaching (and—if an incarnation is claimed—the holiness of his life); and some kind of miraculous divine signature symbolically affirming and forwarding the prophet's teaching and work. . . .

Bibliography for Part V

Broad, C. D. "Hume's Theory of the Credibility of Miracles." *Proceedings of the Aristotelian Society* 17 (1916–17). An insightful critique of Hume.

Flew, Antony. "Miracles." In *Encyclopedia of Philosophy*, edited by Paul Edwards. New York: Macmillan, 1966. A good survey of the problem, containing a Humean version of the attack on miracles.

Geisler, Norman L. *Miracles and Modern Thought*. Grand Rapids, Mich.: Zondervan, 1982. A clearly written apology for an evangelical position that comes to terms with major philosophical opponents. Valuable for its terse analyses, though tending to oversimplify the opposition.

Holland, R. F. "The Miraculous." *American Philosophical Quarterly* 2 (1965): 43–51. An elaborate study and defense of the possibility of miracles, containing important distinctions.

Lewis, C. S. *Miracles*. New York: Macmillan, 1947. A cogently and clearly argued defense of miracles.

Nowell-Smith, Patrick. "Miracles." In *New Essays in Philosophical Theology*, edited by Antony Flew and Alasdair MacIntyre. London: Macmillan, 1955. Attacks the concept of miracles as unscientific and, as such, incoherent.

Rowe, William. *Philosophy of Religion*. Chap. 9. Belmont: Wadsworth, 1978. A lucid introductory discussion of the overall problem.

Smart, Ninian. *Philosophers and Religious Truth*. Chap. 2. London: SCM, 1964. A defense of miracles against the charge that they are unscientific.

Swinburne, Richard. *The Concept of Miracle*. London: Macmillan, 1970. A development of the ideas contained in his articles in Part 5 of this volume.

PART VI

DEATH AND IMMORTALITY

Of all the many forms which natural religion has assumed none probably has exerted so deep and far-reaching an influence on human life as the belief in immortality and the worship of the dead; hence [a discussion] of this momentous creed and of the practical consequences which have been deduced from it can hardly fail to be at once instructive and impressive, whether we regard the record with complacency as a noble testimony to the aspiring genius of man, who claims to outlive the sun and the stars, or whether we view it with pity as a melancholy monument of fruitless labour and barren ingenuity expended in prying into that great mystery of which fools profess their knowledge and wise men confess their ignorance.*

$\mathbf{I}$s there life after death? Few questions have troubled humans as deeply as this one. Is this finite, short existence of three score and ten years all that we have? Or is there reason to hope for a blessed postmortem existence where love, justice, and peace, which we now experience in fragmented forms, will unfold in all their fullness and enable human existence to find fulfilment? Are we merely mortal or blessedly immortal?

Anthropological studies reveal a widespread and ancient sense of immortality. Prehistoric societies buried their dead with food so that the deceased would not be hungry in the next life. Most cultures and religions have some version of a belief in another life, whether it be in the form of a resurrected body, a transmigrated soul, reincarnation, or an ancestral spirit present with the tribe.

Let us begin by understanding what we mean by immortality. For our purposes we do not mean living on through our works or in the memories of our loved ones; we mean a conscious afterlife in which the individual continues to exist. As a definition the Catholic one will do: "that attribute in virtue of which a being is free from death. A being is incorruptible if it does not contain within itself a principle of dissolution; it is indestructible if it can resist every external power tending to destroy or annihilate it. If the inde-

---

* Sir James Frazier, *The Belief in Immortality*, vol. 1 (London: Macmillan, 1913), vii–viii.

structible and incorruptible being is endowed with life it is called immortal. Annihilation is always possible to God by the mere withdrawal of his conserving act."*

Death for most humans is the ultimate tragedy. It is the paramount evil, for it deprives us of all that we know and love on earth. Although there may be fates worse than death for some of us (living a completely evil life, being a heavy burden on others), our fear of death is profound. We want to live as long as possible (given a certain quality of life). We have a general craving for continued existence. The more life the better.

On the other hand, there is precious little direct evidence for life after death. After the brain ceases to function, a person cannot be resuscitated. We personally don't know of anyone who has come back from the dead to tell us about the next life.

So on the one hand we have a passionate longing to live again and be with our loved ones, and on the other hand there is little or no direct evidence that we shall live again. The grave seems the last environment for humankind. And yet we search for indirect evidence for immortality. We welcome any news from this possible distant clime as good news indeed, and we cannot but regard the promise of eternal life as an incentive to meet whatever a credible guide states as the necessary conditions for entry.

In the Western tradition three views have dominated this issue, one denying life after death and two affirming it. The negative view, going back to the ancient Greek atomist philosophers Democritus and Leucippus, holds that we are identical with our bodies (including our brains), so that when the body dies, so does the self. There is nothing more. We may call this view materialist monism, because it does not allow for the possibility of a soul or spiritual self that can live without the body. In our readings this view is set forth by Bertrand Russell, the eminent British philosopher who died in 1970. His argument is judged to be the most reasonable one by Antony Flew in his essay on survival.

The positive views divide into dualist and monist theories of life after death. The dualist views separate the body from the soul or self of the agent and affirm that it is the soul or self that lives forever. This view was held by the pre-Socratic philosopher Pythagoras (570–500 BC) and developed by Plato (427–347 BC). In modern philosophy it is represented by René Descartes (1596–1650). It is sometimes referred to as the Platonic-Cartesian view of immortality. These philosophers argue that we are essentially spiritual or mental beings and that our bodies are either unreal or not part of our essential selves. Death is merely the separation of our souls from our bodies, a sort of spiritual liberation. Although Plato has many arguments for this thesis, one of the most famous is found in the *Phaedo*, included in our first reading. One section is worth quoting in full:

When the soul employs the body in any inquiry, and makes use of sight, or hearing, or any other sense—for inquiry with the body must signify inquiry with the senses—she is dragged away by the body to the things which are imperma-

---

* *A Catholic Dictionary*, edited by D. Attwater (New York: Macmillan, 1941), 261.

nent, changing, and the soul wanders about blindly, and becomes confused and dizzy, like a drunken man, from dealing with things that are changing . . . . [But] when the soul investigates any question by herself, she goes away to the pure and eternal, and immortal and unchangeable, to which she is intrinsically related, and so she comes to be ever with it, as soon as she is by herself, and can be so; and then she rests from her wandering and dwells with it unchangingly, for she is related to what is unchanging. And is not this state of the soul called wisdom?*

The argument may be analyzed as follows:

1. If a person's soul while in the body is capable of any activity independently of the body, then it can perform that activity in separation from the body (i.e., after death, surviving death).
2. In pure or metaphysical thinking (i.e., in contemplating the forms and their interrelationships), a person's soul performs an activity independently of the body. No observation is necessary for this investigation.
3. Therefore, a person's soul can engage in pure or metaphysical thinking in separation from the body. That is, it can and must survive death.

This is a positive argument for the existence of the soul. Unfortunately, the second premise is dubious, for it could be the case that the mind's activity is epiphenomenal, that is, dependent on the brain. Although Plato is right in saying that we need not make an empirical examination of the world in order to think analytically or metaphysically, he has not shown that analytic and metaphysical thinking can go on without a body or brain.

As far as I know, no one has offered a sound argument to *prove* that we have a soul that succeeds our physical existence. However, this is not to say that there is no evidence for this point of view. We note some below.

The second positive view on immortality is associated with the Christian tradition, namely, St. Paul's statement in 1 Corinthians 15. It is interesting to note that there is very little mention made in the Old Testament of life after death. It is at best a shadowy existence in Sheol, the place under Jerusalem where the dead lie dormant or vaguely aware, a place comparable to Hades in Greek mythology. In the New Testament, although there are references to a spiritual existence, the soul (*psyche*) is not separated from the body (*soma*); rather, the person is a holistic, unified being with the soul or self being the form of the material body (in an almost Aristotelian sense). In death the soul is not liberated from the body as from a corpse, but rather a new, glorified *body* comes into being that is somehow related to our present earthly body. The classic passage is in Paul's first letter to the Corinthians. It reads as follows:

Now if Christ be preached that he rose from the dead, how say some among you that there is no resurrection of the dead? But if there be no resurrection of the dead, then is Christ not risen: And if Christ be not risen, then is our preaching in vain, and your faith is also in vain . . . . Ye are still in your sins. Then they which are fallen asleep in Christ are perished. If in this life only we have hope in Christ, we are of all men most miserable.

---

* *Phaedo*, 79 c–d, my translation.

But now is Christ risen from the dead, and become the first fruits of them that slept. For since by man came death by man also the resurrection of the dead . . . . For Christ must reign until he hath put all enemies under his feet. The last enemy that shall be destroyed is death.

But some man will say, How are the dead raised up? and with what body do they come? Thou fool, that which thou sowest is not quickened, except it die: and that which thou sowest, thou sowest not that body that shall be, but bare grain, it may chance of wheat, or so some other gain. But God giveth it a body as it hath pleased him, and to every seed his own body. All flesh is not the same flesh; but there is one kind of flesh of men, another flesh of beasts, another of fishes and another of birds. There are also celestial bodies, and bodies terrestrial: but the glory of the celestial is one, and the glory of the terrestrial is another. There is one glory of the sun, and another glory of the moon, and another glory of the stars: and one star differeth from another star in glory. So also is the resurrection of the dead. It is sown in dishonor; it is raised in glory: it is sown in weakness; it is raised in power: It is sown a natural body; it is raised a spiritual body. And so it is written, The first man Adam was made a living soul; the last Adam was made a quickening spirit. Howbeit that was not first which is spiritual, but that which is natural; and afterward that which is spiritual. The first man is of the earth, earthly: the second man is the Lord from heaven. As is the earthly, such are they also that are earthly: and as is the heavenly, such are they also that are heavenly. And as we have borne the image of the earthly, we shall also bear the image of the heavenly. Now this I say, brethren, that flesh and blood cannot inherit the kingdom of God; neither doth corruption inherit incorruption. Behold, I shew you a mystery; We shall not all sleep, but we shall all be changed. In a moment, in a twinkling of an eye, at the last trump: for the trumpet shall sound, and the dead shall be raised incorruptible, and we shall be changed. For this corruptible must put on incorruption, and this mortal must put on immortality.*

When I approach the subject of immortality in an undergraduate philosophy class, I poll the students to find out which they think is the Christian view of life after death—the view that in death the soul leaves the body and goes to heaven or the view that our bodies will be raised. Almost every student chooses the first view, which I then point out is basically Platonic and not Christian. This view is reflected in popular religion, not the least example being the bedtime prayer taught to children: "Now I lay me down to sleep, I pray the Lord my soul to keep. If I should die before I wake, I pray the Lord my soul to take." Of course, one could hold the view that there is an intermediate state in which the soul dwells disembodied, waiting for the resurrection day, at which time it will receive its new body.

Whether the notion of continued existence after death in either of these versions is a coherent thesis is a matter raised by Antony Flew and Jeffrey Olen in their analyses of immortality and personal identity. Olen's article is especially important, for it contains a serious discussion of the criteria of personal identity. Given the fact that we all undergo physical and mental change, under what conditions can we be said to be the *same* person over time (i.e., what gives us the right to say that some person P is the same person at t_2 as P was at some earlier time t_1)?

Olen and Flew examine two standard views on this matter, the one

---

* 1 Corinthians: 12–53, King James Version.

involving the psychological states criterion and the other involving the body (including the brain) criterion. The psychological states (or memory) criterion goes back to Locke and states that a person is the same person if and only if he or she is psychologically continuous in character, desires, and memories. There are at least three problems with this view. First, there is no way to distinguish *apparent* memories from *genuine* remembering, so that it could be the case that someone came among us detailing the events of Napoleon's life in such a way as to cause us to believe that he had somehow gotten hold of those memories. But we would probably be reluctant to say that this person was Napoleon, especially if we already knew him to be our uncle. A second problem is that our memories (and characters and desires, for that matter) could be duplicated in other persons, so that multiple subjects could have the same "memories." We would not be able to tell which of the persons was the rememberer. Finally, there is the problem of whether the concept of memory itself makes any sense apart from a body. What kind of existence would a purely mental existence be? Would it be in time and space? If it were in space, how would it as a nonsensory entity perceive anything at all? It seems that memory and character predicates are tied to a physical existence. This leads us to consider the body criterion as the proper criterion for personal identity.

The body criterion states that a person is the same person over time if he or she is continuous with his or her body. There are problems with this criterion too, for the body changes in ways that produce states far removed from their originals. Taking this criterion literally, we would have to conclude that when a zygote divides into identical twins during the first weeks of its existence, the two resulting entities are identical to each other (rather than being exactly similar). Furthermore, we can imagine situations in which the personality of one person is transferred to another. Locke illustrates this possibility in his story of the prince and the pauper, in which the body of the prince wakes up one day with the character and all the memories and desires of the pauper. We might be inclined to say that although the prince's body was before us, we were really speaking with the pauper. We can also imagine operations in the future in which our bodies and/or brains are divided and merged with prosthetic bodies or brains. The notions of continuity and uniqueness would conflict.

When we apply these two views of personal identity to the issue of immortality, the problems are compounded. The notion of a disembodied soul implies that one's existence as a person transcends one's embodiment such that the eventual corruption of one's body need not and will not involve the cessation of one's personal existence. One will live forever. But the notion of a disembodied soul suffers from the fact that our concept of experience seems to demand a body as a necessary condition for having experiences and for making sense of personal identity. It seems that memories and the ingredients are located in the physical brain, so one is at a loss to explain how the soul stores or reduplicates them.

The notion of resurrection (or reconstitution) states that you will continue to survive your death in a new glorified body. God will reconstitute you. This is eloquently (if grandiosely) stated on Benjamin Franklin's tombstone:

> This body of B. Franklin in Christ Church
>   cemetery,
> Printer, Like the Cover of an old Book,
> Its Contents torn out,
> And stript of its Lettering and Gilding,
> Lies here, Food for Worms.
> But the work shall not be lost;
> For it will, as he believed,
> Appear once more in a new and more
>   elegant Edition,
> Corrected and Improved by its Author.

But the resurrection view supposes that God will create a new being like yourself. The problem with this view, as is duly noted by Antony Flew in the fifth reading in this part, is that it does not seem all that comforting to learn that someday there will be someone just like you who will enjoy a blessed existence; for if there is no continuity between you and your future self, it is really not you but your successor (some one very similar, even exactly similar, to you, a sort of twin) who will enjoy eternal life.

Of course, many Christians believe that although there must be a body for one's full existence, it could be the case that the personality is preserved in an interim state of disembodiment between the first corruptible bodily existence and the second incorruptible bodily existence (see Richard Purtill, *Thinking About Religion,* chapter 9). But the problem remains of whether it makes sense to speak of a disembodied self.

Still, there is indirect evidence for the existence of a soul or the disembodied survival of the self. There is evidence of parapsychology and of out-of-the-body experiences. The first of these is discussed by John Hick in his article "Immortality and Resurrection" (our fourth reading). The best discussion of out-of-the-body (or near-death) experiences is found in James Moody's book *Life after Life,* in which he documents several cases of "clinically dead" persons who were revived and reported remarkably similar experiences. Moody sets down the outline of an ideal report in the following passage:

> A man is dying and, as he reaches the point of greatest physical distress, he hears himself pronounced dead by his doctor. He begins to hear an uncomfortable noise, a loud ringing or buzzing, and at the same time feels himself moving very rapidly through a long dark tunnel. After this, he suddenly finds himself outside of his own physical body, but still in the immediate physical environment, and he sees his own body from a distance, as though he is a spectator. He watches the resuscitation attempt from this unusual vantage point and is in a state of emotional upheaval.
>
> After a while, he collects himself and becomes more accustomed to his odd condition. He notices that he still has a "body," but one of a very different nature and with very different powers from the physical body he has left behind. Soon other things begin to happen. Others come to meet and to help him. He glimpses

the spirits of relatives and friends who have already died, and a loving, warm spirit of a kind he has never encountered before—a being of light—appears before him. This being asks him a question, nonverbally, to make him evaluate his life and helps him along by showing him a panoramic, instantaneous playback of the major events of his life. At some point he finds himself approaching some sort of barrier or border, apparently representing the limit between earthly life and the next life. Yet, he finds that he must go back to the earth, that the time for his death has not yet come. At this point he resists, for by now he is taken up with his experiences in the afterlife and does not want to return. He is overwhelmed by intense feelings of joy, love, and peace. Despite his attitude, though, he somehow reunites with his physical body and lives.*

This passage is not meant to represent any one person's report but is a model or composite of the common elements found in many stories. Moody himself makes no claims for the interpretation that the patients really experienced what they claim to have experienced. There could be neurological causes for the experiences, or they could be attributed to wish fulfillment. The point is, simply, that these experiences should be considered as part of the evidence to be examined carefully—and perhaps to be followed up with further research.

Returning to John Hick's article, we can say that the most important part of this essay is Hick's invitation to us to see the possibility of life after death. The case against immortality is not a clear-cut one. Hick invites us to consider a person, John Smith, who disappears from before the eyes of his friends in the United States. At the same moment an exact replica of him appears in India. Secondly, imagine that instead of reappearing, Smith dies, but at the moment of his death a Smith replica appears in India. We would probably say that he had been miraculously re-created in India. Finally, suppose that Smith died and his replica reappeared in a different world altogether, a resurrection world inhabited only by resurrected people.

Hick shows that the problems of identity and continuity of persons are not intractable. We can imagine coherent (logically possible) stories of reappearances in this life, so that it is not illogical to suppose a future life involving such a reappearance. Whether Hick is correct about this you may decide by closely examining these arguments.

Finally, you will want to look carefully at Jeffrey Olen's solution to the problem of personality and immortality, for although Olen accepts a materialist view of human personality, he also accepts a functionalist view of personhood. It is conceivable, according to his account, that we live on in another life through having another brain "programmed" with our personality and memory.

---

* *Life after Life* (New York: Bantam Books, 1976), 21f.

VI.1 Immortality of the Soul

PLATO

Plato (c. 427–347 BC), an Athenian and one of the most important philosophers who ever lived, believed that human beings were composed of two substances, a body and a soul. Of these, the true self is the soul, which lives on after the death of the body. All of Plato's writings are in the form of dialogues. In the first dialogue (from Alcibiades I*) Socrates argues with Alcibiades about the true self. The second dialogue (from the* Phaedo*) takes place in prison, where Socrates has been condemned to die. He is offered a way of escape but rejects it, arguing that it would be immoral to flee such a fate at this time and that he is certain of a better life after death.*

From *Alcibiades I*

Soc. And is self-knowledge an easy thing, and was he to be lightly esteemed who inscribed the text on the temple at Delphi? Or is self-knowledge a difficult thing, which few are able to attain?

Al. At times, I fancy, Socrates, that anybody can know himself; at other times, the task appears to be very difficult.

Soc. But whether easy or difficult, Alcibiades, still there is no other way; knowing what we are, we shall know how to take care of ourselves, and if we are ignorant we shall not know.

Al. That is true.

Soc. Well, then, let us see in what way the self-existent can be discovered by us; that will give us a chance to discovering our own existence, which without that we can never know.

Al. You say truly.

Soc. Come, now, I beseech you, tell me with whom you are conversing?—with whom but with me?

Reprinted from *Alcibiades I* and the *Phaedo,* translated by William Jowett (New York: Charles Scribner's Sons, 1889).

Al. Yes.

Soc. As I am with you?

Al. Yes.

Soc. That is to say, I, Socrates, am talking?

Al. Yes.

Soc. And I in talking use words?

Al. Certainly.

Soc. And talking and using words are, as you would say, the same?

Al. Very true.

Soc. And the user is not the same as the thing which he uses?

Al. What do you mean?

Soc. I will explain: the shoemaker, for example, uses a square tool, and a circular tool, and other tools for cutting?

Al. Yes.

Soc. But the tool is not the same as the cutter and user of the tool?

Al. Of course not.

Soc. And in the same way the instrument of the harper is to be distinguished from the harper himself?

Al. He is.

Soc. Now the question which I asked was whether you conceive the user to be always different from that which he uses?

Al. I do.

Soc. Then what shall we say of the shoemaker? Does he cut with his tools only or with his hands?

Al. With his hands as well.

Soc. He uses his hands too?

Al. Yes.

Soc. And does he use his eyes in cutting leather?

Al. He does.

Soc. And we admit that the user is not the same with the things which he uses?

Al. Yes.

Soc. Then the shoemaker and the harper are

to be distinguished from the hands and feet which they use?

Al. That is clear.

Soc. And does not a man use the whole body?

Al. Certainly.

Soc. And that which uses is different from that which is used?

Al. True.

Soc. Then a man is not the same as his own body?

Al. That is the inference.

Soc. What is he, then?

Al. I cannot say.

Soc. Nay, you can say that he is the user of the body.

Al. Yes.

Soc. And the user of the body is the soul?

Al. Yes, the soul.

Soc. And the soul rules?

Al. Yes.

Soc. Let me make an assertion which will, I think, be universally admitted.

Al. What is that?

Soc. That man is one of three things.

Al. What are they?

Soc. Soul, body, or the union of the two.

Al. Certainly.

Soc. But did we not say that the actual ruling principle of the body is man?

Al. Yes, we did.

Soc. And does the body rule over itself?

Al. Certainly not.

Soc. It is subject, as we were saying?

Al. Yes.

Soc. Then that is not what we are seeking?

Al. It would seem not.

Soc. But may we say that the union of the two rules over the body, and consequently that this is man?

Al. Very likely.

Soc. The most unlikely of all things: for if one of the members is subject, the two united cannot possibly rule.

Al. True.

Soc. But since neither the body, nor the union of the two, is man, either man has no real existence, or the soul is man?

Al. Just so.

Soc. Would you have a more precise proof that the soul is man?

Al. No; I think that the proof is sufficient.

Soc. If the proof, although not quite precise, is fair, that is enough for us; more precise proof will be supplied when we have discovered that which we were led to omit, from a fear that the inquiry would be too much protracted.

Al. What was that?

Soc. What I meant, when I said that absolute existence must be first considered; but now, instead of absolute existence, we have been considering the nature of individual existence, and that may be sufficient; for surely there is nothing belonging to us which has more absolute existence than the soul?

Al. There is nothing.

Soc. Then we may truly conceive that you and I are conversing with one another, soul to soul?

Al. Very true.

Soc. And that is just what I was saying—that I, Socrates, am not arguing or talking with the face of Alcibiades, but with the real Alcibiades; and that is with his soul.

Al. True. . . .

From the Phaedo

Socrates: What again shall we say of the actual acquirement of knowledge?—is the body, if invited to share in the inquiry, a hinderer or a helper? I mean to say, have sight and hearing any truth in them? Are they not, as the poets are always telling us, inaccurate witnesses? and yet, if even they are inaccurate and indistinct, what is to be said of the other senses?—for you will allow that they are the best of them?

Certainly, he replied.

Then when does the soul attain truth?—for in attempting to consider anything in company with the body she is obviously deceived.

Yes, that is true.

Then must not existence be revealed to her in thought, if at all?

Yes.

And thought is best when the mind is gathered into herself and none of these things trouble her—neither sounds nor sights nor pain nor any pleasure,—when she has as little as possible to do with the body, and has no bodily sense or feeling, but is aspiring after being?

That is true.

And in this the philosopher dishonors the body; his soul runs away from the body and desires to be alone and by herself?

That is true.

Well, but there is another thing, Simmias: Is there or is there not an absolute justice?

Assuredly there is.

And an absolute beauty and absolute good?

Of course.

But did you ever behold any of them with your eyes?

Certainly not.

Or did you ever reach them with any other bodily sense? (and I speak not of these alone, but of absolute greatness, and health, and strength, and of the essence or true nature of everything). Has the reality of them ever been perceived by you through the bodily organs? or rather, is not the nearest approach to the knowledge of their several natures made by him who so orders his intellectual vision as to have the most exact conception of the essence of that which he considers?

Certainly.

And he attains to the knowledge of them in their highest purity who goes to each of them with the mind alone, not allowing when in the act of thought the intrusion or introduction of sight or any other sense in the company of reason, but with the very light of the mind in her clearness penetrates into the very light of truth in each; he has got rid, as far as he can, of eyes and ears and of the whole body, which he conceives of only as a disturbing element, hindering the soul from the acquisition of knowledge when in company with her—is not this the sort of man who, if ever man did, is likely to attain the knowledge of existence?

There is admirable truth in that, Socrates, replied Simmias.

And when they consider all this, must not true philosophers make a reflection, of which they will speak to one another in such words as these: We have found, they will say, a path of speculation which seems to bring us and the argument to the conclusion, that while we are in the body, and while the soul is mingled with this mass of evil, our desire will not be satisfied, and our desire is of the truth. For the body is a source of endless trouble to us by reason of the mere requirement of food; and also is liable to diseases which overtake and impede us in the search after truth: and by filling us so full of loves, and lusts, and fears, and fancies, and idols, and every sort of folly, prevents our ever having, as people say, so much as a thought. From whence come wars, and fightings, and factions? whence but from the body and the lusts of the body? For wars are occasioned by the love of money, and money has to be acquired for the sake and in the service of the body; and in consequence of all these things the time which ought to be given to philosophy is lost. Moreover, if there is time and an inclination toward philosophy, yet the body introduces a turmoil and confusion and fear into the course of speculation, and hinders us from seeing the truth; and all experience shows that if we would have pure knowledge of anything we must be quit of the body, and the soul in herself must behold all things in themselves: then I suppose that we shall attain that which we desire, and of which we say that we are lovers, and that is wisdom; not while we live, but after death, as the argument shows; for if while in company with the body, the soul cannot have pure knowledge, one of two things seems to follow—either knowledge is not to be attained at all, or, if at all, after death. For then, and not till then, the soul will be in herself alone and without the body. In this present life, I reckon that we make the nearest approach to knowledge when we have the least possible concern or interest in the body, and are not saturated with the bodily nature, but remain pure until the hour when God himself is pleased to release us. And then the foolishness of the body will be cleared away and we shall be pure and hold converse with other pure souls, and know of ourselves the clear light everywhere; and this is surely the light of truth. For no impure thing is allowed to approach the pure. These are the sort of words, Simmias, which the true lovers of wisdom cannot help saying to one another, and thinking. You will agree with me in that?

Certainly, Socrates.

But if this is true, O my friend, then there is great hope that, going whither I go, I shall there be satisfied with that which has been the chief concern of you and me in our past lives. And now that the hour of departure is appointed to me, this is the hope with which I depart, and not I only, but every man who believes that he has his mind purified.

Certainly, replied Simmias.

And what is purification but the separation of the soul from the body, as I was saying before; the habit of the soul gathering and collecting herself into herself, out of all the courses of the body; the dwelling in her own place alone, as in another life, so also in this, as far as she can; the release of the soul from the chains of the body?

Very true, he said.

And what is that which is termed death, but this very separation and release of the soul from the body?

To be sure, he said.

And the true philosophers, and they only, study and are eager to release the soul. Is not the separation and release of the soul from the body their especial study?

That is true.

And as I was saying at first, there would be a ridiculous contradiction in men studying to live as nearly as they can in a state of death, and yet repining when death comes.

Certainly.

Then Simmias, as the true philosophers are ever studying death, to them, of all men, death is the least terrible. Look at the matter in this way: how inconsistent of them to have been always enemies of the body, and wanting to have the soul alone, and when this is granted to them, to be

trembling and repining; instead of rejoicing at their departing to that place where, when they arrive, they hope to gain that which in life they loved (and this was wisdom), and at the same time to be rid of the company of their enemy. Many a man has been willing to go to the world below in the hope of seeing there an earthly love, or wife, or son, and conversing with them. And will he who is a true lover of wisdom, and is persuaded in like manner that only in the world below he can worthily enjoy her, still repine at death? Will he not depart with joy? Surely, he will, my friend, if he be a true philosopher. For he will have a firm conviction that there only, and nowhere else, he can find wisdom in her purity. And if this be true, he would be very absurd, as I was saying, if he were to fear death.

. . . .

Socrates: And were we not saying long ago that the soul when using the body as an instrument of perception, that is to say, when using the sense of sight or hearing or some other sense (for the meaning of perceiving through the body is perceiving through the senses),—were we not saying that the soul too is then dragged by the body into the region of the changeable, and wanders and is confused; the world spins round her, and she is like a drunkard when under their influence?

Very true.

But when returning into herself she reflects; then she passes into the realm of purity, and eternity, and immortality, and unchangeableness, which are her kindred, and with them she ever lives, when she is by herself and is not let or hindered; then she ceases from her erring ways, and being in communion with the unchanging is unchanging. And this state of the soul is called wisdom?

That is well and truly said, Socrates, he replied.

And to which class is the soul more nearly alike and akin, as far as may be inferred from this argument, as well as from the preceding one?

I think, Socrates, that, in the opinion of every one who follows the argument, the soul will be infinitely more like the unchangeable,—even the most stupid person will not deny that.

And the body is more like the changing?

Yes.

Yet once more consider the matter in this light: When the soul and the body are united, then nature orders the soul to rule and govern, and the body to obey and serve. Now which of these two functions is akin to the divine? and which to the mortal? Does not the divine appear to you to be that which naturally orders and rules, and the mortal that which is subject and servant?

True.

And which does the soul resemble?

The soul resembles the divine, and the body the mortal,—there can be no doubt of that, Socrates.

Then reflect, Cebes: is not the conclusion of the whole matter this,—that the soul is in the very likeness of the divine, and immortal, and intelligible, and uniform, and indissoluble, and unchangeable; and the body is in the very likeness of the human, and mortal, and unintelligible, and multiform, and dissoluble, and changeable. Can this, my dear Cebes, be denied?

No indeed.

But if this is true, then is not the body liable to speedy dissolution? and is not the soul almost or altogether indissoluble?

Certainly.

And do you further observe, that after a man is dead, the body, which is the visible part of man, and has a visible framework, which is called a corpse, and which would naturally be dissolved and decomposed and dissipated, is not dissolved or decomposed at once, but may remain for a good while, if the constitution be sound at the time of death, and the season of the year favorable? For the body when shrunk and embalmed, as is the custom in Egypt, may remain almost entire through infinite ages; and even in decay, still there are some portions, such as the bones and ligaments, which are practically indestructible. You allow that?

Yes.

And are we to suppose that the soul, which is invisible, in passing to the true Hades, which like her is invisible, and pure, and noble, and on her way to the good and wise God, whither, if God will, my soul is also soon to go,—that the soul, I repeat, if this be her nature and origin, is blown away and perishes immediately on quitting the body, as the many say? That can never be, my dear Simmias and Cebes. The truth rather is, that the soul which is pure at departing draws after her no bodily taint, having never voluntarily had connection with the body, which she is ever avoiding, herself gathered into herself (for such abstraction has been the study of her life). And what does this mean but that she has been a true disciple of philosophy, and has practiced how to die easily? And is not philosophy the practice of death?

Certainly.

That soul, I say, herself invisible, departs to the invisible world,—to the divine and immortal and rational: thither arriving, she lives in bliss and is released from the error and folly of men, their fears and wild passions and all other human ills, and forever dwells, as they say of the initiated, in company with the gods? Is not this true, Cebes?

Yes, said Cebes, beyond a doubt.

VI.2   Skepticism over Immortality of the Soul

DAVID HUME

In this brief essay the Scottish Enlightenment philosopher David Hume (1711–1776) argues that there are several reasons for doubting that a person can survive death. He questions whether the notion of a 'soul' separate from the body is coherent and whether the moral argument—that the justice of God demands that there be an afterlife wherein we are rewarded for our deeds—makes much sense. On the contrary, the physical arguments from the analogy with nature strongly suggest that the soul is mortal. Hume's opening and closing paragraphs, which seem inconsistent with the tenor of the arguments, should be read with a touch of irony. Living in eighteenth-century Calvinist Scotland, where he suffered public opprobrium for his views, Hume often mischievously threw his reader off track with statements seeming to endorse the biblical doctrine of revelation.

By the mere light of reason it seems difficult to prove the immortality of the soul; the arguments for it are commonly derived either from metaphysical topics, or moral, or physical. But in reality it is the gospel, and the gospel alone, that has brought *life and immortality to light.*

I

Metaphysical topics suppose that the soul is immaterial, and that it is impossible for thought to belong to a material substance. But just metaphysics teach us, that the notion of substance is wholly confused and imperfect; and that we have no other idea of any substance, than as an aggregate of particular qualities inhering in an unknown something. Matter, therefore, and spirit, are at

Reprinted from David Hume, *Two Essays on Suicide and Immortality* (1777).

bottom equally unknown; and we cannot determine what qualities inhere in the one or in the other. They likewise teach us, that nothing can be decided à *priori* concerning any cause or effect; and that experience, being the only source of our judgments of this nature, we cannot know from any other principle, whether matter, by its structure or arrangement, may not be the cause of thought. Abstract reasonings cannot decide any question of fact or existence. But admitting a spiritual substance to be dispersed throughout the universe, like the ethereal fire of the Stoics, and to be the only inherent subject of thought, we have reason to conclude from *analogy,* that nature uses it after the manner she does the other substance, *matter.* She employs it as a kind of paste or clay; modifies it into a variety of forms and existences; dissolves after a time each modification, and from its substance erects a new form. As the same material substance may successively compose the bodies of all animals, the same spiritual substance may compose their minds: their consciousness or that system of thought which they formed during life, may be continually dissolved by death, and nothing interests them in the new modification. The most positive assertors of the mortality of the soul never denied the immortality of its substance; and that an immaterial substance, as well as a material, may lose its memory or consciousness, appears in part from experience, if the soul be immaterial. Reasoning from the common course of nature, and without supposing any new interposition of the Supreme Cause, which ought always to be excluded from philosophy, *what is incorruptible must also be ingenerable.* The soul therefore, if immortal, existed before our birth; and if the former existence noways concerned us, neither will the latter. Animals undoubtedly feel, think, love, hate, will, and even reason, though in a more imperfect manner than men: are their souls also immaterial and immortal?

II

Let us now consider the moral arguments, chiefly those derived from the justice of God, which is supposed to be further interested in the future punishment of the vicious and reward of the virtuous. But these arguments are grounded on the supposition that God has attributes beyond what he has exerted in this universe, with which alone we are acquainted. Whence do we infer the existence of these attributes? It is very safe for us to affirm, that whatever we know the Deity to have actually done is best; but it is very dangerous to affirm that he must always do what to us seems best. In how many instances would this reasoning fail us with regard to the present world? But if any purpose of nature be clear, we may affirm, that the whole scope and intention of man's creation, so far as we can judge by natural reason, is limited to the present life. With how weak a concern from the original inherent structure of the mind and passions, does he ever look further? What comparison either for steadiness or efficacy, betwixt so floating an idea and the most doubtful persuasion of any matter of fact that occurs in common life? There arise indeed in some minds some unaccountable terrors with regard to futurity; but these would quickly vanish were they not artificially fostered by precept and education. And those who foster them, what is their motive? Only to gain a livelihood, and to acquire power and riches in this world. Their very zeal and industry, therefore, are an argument against them.

What cruelty, what iniquity, what injustice in nature, to confine all our concern, as well as all our knowledge, to the present life, if there be another scene still waiting us of infinitely greater consequence? Ought this barbarous deceit to be ascribed to a beneficent and wise Being? Observe with what exact proportion the task to be performed, and the performing powers, are adjusted throughout all nature. If the reason of man gives him great superiority above other animals, his necessities are proportionably multiplied upon him: his whole time, his whole capacity, activity, courage, and passion, find sufficient employment in fencing against the miseries of his present condi-

tion; and frequently, nay, almost always, are too slender for the business assigned them. A pair of shoes, perhaps, was never yet wrought to the highest degree of perfection which that commodity is capable of attaining; yet it is necessary, at least very useful, that there should be some politicians and moralists, even some geometers, poets, and philosophers among mankind. The powers of men are no more superior to their wants, considered merely in this life, than those of foxes and hares are, compared to *their* wants and to their period of existence. The inference from parity of reason is therefore obvious.

On the theory of the soul's mortality, the inferiority of women's capacity is easily accounted for. Their domestic life requires no higher faculties either of mind or body. This circumstance vanishes and becomes absolutely insignificant on the religious theory: the one sex has an equal task to perform as the other; their powers of reason and resolution ought also to have been equal, and both of them infinitely greater than at present. As every effect implies a cause, and that another, till we reach the first cause of all, which is the Deity; every thing that happens is ordained by him, and nothing can be the object of his punishment or vengeance. By what rule are punishments and rewards distributed? What is the Divine standard of merit and demerit? Shall we suppose that human sentiments have place in the Deity? How bold that hypothesis! We have no conception of any other sentiments. According to human sentiments, sense, courage, good-manners, industry, prudence, genius, etc. are essential parts of personal merits. Shall we therefore erect an elysium for poets and heroes like that of ancient mythology? Why confine all rewards to one species of virtue? Punishment, without any proper end or purpose, is inconsistent with *our* ideas of goodness and justice; and no end can be served by it after the whole scene is closed. Punishment, according to *our* conception, should bear some proportion to the offence. Why then eternal punishment for the temporary offences of so frail a creature as man? Can any one approve of Alexander's rage, who intended to exterminate a whole nation because they had seized his favorite horse Bucephalus?[1]

Heaven and hell suppose two distinct species of men, the good and the bad; but the greatest part of mankind float betwixt vice and virtue. Were one to go round the world with an intention of giving a good supper to the righteous and a sound drubbing to the wicked, he would frequently be embarrassed in his choice, and would find the merits and demerits of most men and women scarcely amount to the value of either. To suppose measures of approbation and blame different from the human confounds every thing. Whence do we learn that there is such a thing as moral distinctions, but from our own sentiments? What man who has not met with personal provocation (or what good-natured man who has) could inflict on crimes, from the sense of blame alone, even the common, legal, frivolous punishments? And does any thing steel the breast of judges and juries against the sentiments of humanity but reflection on necessity and public interest? By the Roman law, those who had been guilty of parricide, and confessed their crime, were put into a sack along with an ape, a dog, and a serpent, and thrown into the river. Death alone was the punishment of those who denied their guilt, however fully proved. A criminal was tried before Augustus, and condemned after a full conviction; but the humane emperor, when he put the last interrogatory, gave it such a turn as to lead the wretch into a denial of his guilt. "You surely (said the prince) did not kill your father?"[2] This lenity suits our natural ideas of *right* even towards the greatest of all criminals, and even though it prevents so inconsiderable a sufferance. Nay, even the most bigoted priest would naturally without reflection approve of it, provided the crime was not heresy or infidelity; for as these crimes hurt himself in his *temporal* interest and advantages, perhaps he may not be altogether so indulgent to them. The chief source of moral ideas is the reflection on the interests of human society. Ought these interests, so short, so frivolous, to be guarded by punishments eternal and infinite? The damnation of one man is an infinitely greater evil in the universe than the subversion of a thousand millions of kingdoms. Nature has rendered human infancy peculiarly frail and mortal, as it were on purpose to refute the notion

of a probationary state; the half of mankind die before they are rational creatures.

III

The physical arguments from the analogy of nature are strong for the mortality of the soul; and are really the only philosophical arguments which ought to be admitted with regard to this question, or indeed any question of fact. Where any two objects are so closely connected that all alterations which we have ever seen in the one are attended with proportionable alterations in the other; we ought to conclude, by all rules of analogy, that, when there are still greater alterations produced in the former, and it is totally dissolved, there follows a total dissolution of the latter. Sleep, a very small effect on the body, is attended with a temporary extinction, at least a great confusion in the soul. The weakness of the body and that of the mind in infancy are exactly proportioned; their vigor in manhood, their sympathetic disorder in sickness, their common gradual decay in old age. The step further seems unavoidable; their common dissolution in death. The last symptoms which the mind discovers, are disorder, weakness, insensibility, and stupidity; the forerunners of its annihilation. The further progress of the same causes increasing, the same effects totally extinguish it. Judging by the usual analogy of nature, no form can continue when transferred to a condition of life very different from the original one in which it was placed. Trees perish in the water, fishes in the air, animals in the earth. Even so small a difference as that of climate is often fatal. What reason then to imagine, that an immense alteration, such as is made on the soul by the dissolution of its body, and all its organs of thought and sensation, can be effected without the dissolution of the whole? Every thing is in common betwixt soul and body. The organs of the one are all of them the organs of the other; the existence, therefore, of the one must be dependent on the other. The souls of animals are allowed to be mortal; and these bear so near a resemblance to the souls of men, that the analogy from one to the other forms a very strong argument. Their bodies are not more resembling, yet no one rejects the argument drawn from comparative anatomy. The Metempsychosis is therefore the only system of this kind that philosophy can hearken to.

Nothing in this world is perpetual; every thing, however, seemingly firm, is in continual flux and change: the world itself gives symptoms of frailty and dissolution. How contrary to analogy, therefore, to imagine that one single form, seeming the frailest of any, and subject to the greatest disorders, is immortal and indissoluble? What theory is that! how lightly, not to say how rashly, entertained! How to dispose of the infinite number of posthumous existences ought also to embarrass the religious theory. Every planet in every solar system, we are at liberty to imagine peopled with intelligent mortal beings, at least we can fix on no other supposition. For these then a new universe must every generation be created beyond the bounds of the present universe, or one must have been created at first so prodigiously wide as to admit of this continual influx of beings. Ought such bold suppositions to be received by any philosophy, and that merely on the pretext of a bare possibility? When it is asked, whether Agamemnon, Thersites, Hannibal, Varro, and every stupid clown that ever existed in Italy, Scythia, Bactria, or Guinea, are now alive; can any man think, that a scrutiny of nature will furnish arguments strong enough to anwer so strange a question in the affirmative? The want of argument without revelation sufficiently establishes the negative. *Quanto facilius,* says Pliny,[3] *certiusque sibi quemque credere, ac specimen securitatis antigene tali sumere experimento.* Our insensibility before the composition of the body seems to natural reason a proof of a like state after dissolution. Were our horrors of annihilation an original passion, not the effect of our general love of happiness, it would rather prove the mortality of the soul: for as nature does nothing in vain, she would never give us a horror against an impossible event. She may give us a horror against an unavoidable event, provided our endeavors, as in the present case, may often remove it to some distance. Death is in the end unavoidable; yet the human species could not be preserved had not nature inspired us with an aversion towards it. All doctrines are to be suspected which are favored by our passions; and the hopes and fears which gave rise to this doctrine are very obvious.

It is an infinite advantage in every controversy to defend the negative. If the question be out of the common experienced course of nature, this circumstance is almost if not altogether decisive. By what arguments or analogies can we prove any state of existence, which no one ever saw, and which no way resembles any that ever was seen? Who will repose such trust in any pretended philosophy as to admit upon its testimony the reality of so marvellous a scene? Some new species of logic is requisite for that purpose, and some new faculties of the mind, that they may enable us to comprehend that logic.

Nothing could set in a fuller light the infinite obligations which mankind have to Divine revelation, since we find that no other medium could ascertain this great and important truth.

Notes

1. Quintus Curtius [*History of Alexander,* VI. 5.]
2. Suetonius, *The Deified Augustus,* II. 3.
3. ["But how much easier and safer for each to trust in himself, and for us to derive our idea of future tranquillity from our experience of it before birth!" Pliny, *Natural History* VII. 55, tr. H. Rackham (Cambridge, Mass.: "Loeb Classical Library." 1947).]

VI.3   The Finality of Death

BERTRAND RUSSELL

In this brief essay the eminent British philosopher Bertrand Russell (1872–1970) outlines some of the major objections to the idea of life after death. He argues that it is not reasonable to believe that our personality and memories will survive the destruction of our bodies. He claims that the inclination to believe in immortality comes from emotional factors, notably the fear of death.

Before we can profitably discuss whether we shall continue to exist after death, it is well to be clear as to the sense in which a man is the same person as he was yesterday. Philosophers used to think that there were definite substances, the soul and the body, that each lasted on from day to day, that a soul, once created, continued to exist throughout all future time, whereas a body ceased temporarily from death till the resurrection of the body.

The part of this doctrine which concerns the present life is pretty certainly false. The matter of the body is continually changing by processes of nutriment and wastage. Even if it were not, atoms in physics are no longer supposed to have continuous existence; there is no sense in saying: this is the same atom as the one that existed a few minutes ago. The continuity of a human body is a matter of appearance and behavior, not of substance.

The same thing applies to the mind. We think and feel and act, but there is not, in addition to thoughts and feelings and actions, a bare entity, the mind or the soul, which does or suffers these occurrences. The mental continuity of a person is a continuity of habit and memory: there was yesterday one person whose feelings I can remember, and that person I regard as myself of yesterday;

From Bertrand Russell, *Why I Am Not a Christian* (London: George Allen & Unwin, 1957), pp. 88–93. Copyright © 1957 by Allen & Unwin. Reprinted by permission of Simon & Schuster and Allen & Unwin.

but, in fact, myself of yesterday was only certain mental occurrences which are now remembered and are regarded as part of the person who now recollects them. All that constitutes a person is a series of experiences connected by memory and by certain similarities of the sort we call habit.

If, therefore, we are to believe that a person survives death, we must believe that the memories and habits which constitute the person will continue to be exhibited in a new set of occurrences.

No one can prove that this will not happen. But it is easy to see that it is very unlikely. Our memories and habits are bound up with the structure of the brain, in much the same way in which a river is connected with the riverbed. The water in the river is always changing, but it keeps to the same course because previous rains have worn a channel. In like manner, previous events have worn a channel in the brain, and our thoughts flow along this channel. This is the cause of memory and mental habits. But the brain, as a structure, is dissolved at death, and memory therefore may be expected to be also dissolved. There is no more reason to think otherwise than to expect a river to persist in its old course after an earthquake has raised a mountain where a valley used to be.

All memory, and therefore (one may say) all minds, depend upon a property which is very noticeable in certain kinds of material structures but exists little if at all in other kinds. This is the property of forming habits as a result of frequent similar occurrences. For example: a bright light makes the pupils of the eyes contract; and if you repeatedly flash a light in a man's eyes and beat a gong at the same time, the gong alone will, in the end, cause his pupils to contract. This is a fact about the brain and nervous system—that is to say, about a certain material structure. It will be found that exactly similar facts explain our response to language and our use of it, our memories and the emotions they arouse, our moral or immoral habits of behavior, and indeed everything that constitutes our mental personality, except the part determined by heredity. The part determined by heredity is handed on to our posterity but cannot, in the individual, survive the disintegration of the body. Thus both the hereditary and the acquired parts of a personality are, so far as our experience goes, bound up with the characteristics of certain bodily structures. We all know that memory may be obliterated by an injury to the brain, that a virtuous person may be rendered vicious by encephalitis lethargica, and, that a clever child can be turned into an idiot by lack of iodine. In view of such familiar facts, it seems scarcely probable that the mind survives the total destruction of brain structure which occurs at death.

It is not rational arguments but emotions that cause belief in a future life.

The most important of these emotions is fear of death, which is instinctive and biologically useful. If we genuinely and wholeheartedly believed in the future life, we should cease completely to fear death. The effects would be curious, and probably such as most of us would deplore. But our human and subhuman ancestors have fought and exterminated their enemies throughout many geological ages and have profited by courage; it is therefore an advantage to the victors in the struggle for life to be able, on occasion, to overcome the natural fear of death. Among animals and savages, instinctive pugnacity suffices for this purpose; but at a certain stage of development, as the Mohammedans first proved, belief in Paradise has considerable military value as reinforcing natural pugnacity. We should therefore admit that militarists are wise in encouraging the belief in immortality, always supposing that this belief does not become so profound as to produce indifference to the affairs of the world.

Another emotion which encourages the belief in survival is admiration of the excellence of man. As the Bishop of Birmingham says, "His mind is a far finer instrument than anything that had appeared earlier—he knows right and wrong. He can build Westminster Abbey. He can make an airplane. He can calculate the distance of the sun. . . . Shall, then, man at death perish utterly? Does that incomparable instrument, his mind, vanish when life ceases?"

The Bishop proceeds to argue that "the universe has been shaped and is governed by an intelligent purpose," and that it would have been unintelligent, having made man, to let him perish.

To this argument there are many answers. In the first place, it has been found, in the scientific investigation of nature, that the intrusion of moral or aesthetic values has always been an obstacle to discovery. It used to be thought that the heavenly bodies must move in circles because the circle is the most perfect curve, that species must be immutable because God would only create what was perfect and what therefore stood in no need of improvement, that it was useless to combat epidemics except by repentance because they were sent as a punishment for sin, and so on. It has been found, however, that, so far as we can discover, nature is indifferent to our values and can only be understood by ignoring our notions of good and bad. The Universe may have a purpose, but nothing that we know suggests that, if so, this purpose has any similarity to ours.

Nor is there in this anything surprising. Dr. Barnes tells us that man "knows right and wrong." But, in fact, as anthropology shows, men's views of right and wrong have varied to such an extent that no single item has been permanent. We cannot say, therefore, that man knows right and wrong, but only that some men do. Which men? Nietzsche argued in favor of an ethic profoundly different from Christ's, and some powerful governments have accepted his teaching. If knowledge of right and wrong is to be an argument for immortality, we must first settle whether to believe Christ or Nietzsche, and then argue that Christians are immortal, but Hitler and Mussolini are not, or vice versa. The decision will obviously be made on the battlefield, not in the study. Those who have the best poison gas will have the ethic of the future and will therefore be the immortal ones.

Our feelings and beliefs on the subject of good and evil are, like everything else about us, natural facts, developed in the struggle for existence and not having any divine or supernatural origin. In one of Aesop's fables, a lion is shown pictures of huntsmen catching lions and remarks that, if he had painted them, they would have shown lions catching huntsmen. Man, says Dr. Barnes, is a fine fellow because he can make airplanes. A little while ago there was a popular song about the cleverness of flies in walking upside down on the ceiling, with the chorus: "Could Lloyd George do it? Could Mr. Baldwin do it? Could Ramsay Mac do it? Why, NO." On this basis a very telling argument could be constructed by a theologically-minded fly, which no doubt the other flies would find most convincing.

Moreover, it is only when we think abstractly that we have such a high opinion of man. Of men in the concrete, most of us think the vast majority very bad. Civilized states spend more than half their revenue on killing each other's citizens. Con-sider the long history of the activities inspired by moral fervor: human sacrifices, persecutions of heretics, witch-hunts, pogroms leading up to wholesale extermination by poison gases, which one at least of Dr. Barnes's episcopal colleagues must be supposed to favor, since he holds pacifism to be un-Christian. Are these abominations, and the ethical doctrines by which they are prompted, really evidence of an intelligent Creator? And can we really wish that the men who practiced them should live forever? The world in which we live can be understood as a result of muddle and accident; but if it is the outcome of deliberate purpose, the purpose must have been that of a fiend. For my part, I find accident a less painful and more plausible hypothesis.

VI.4   Immortality and Resurrection

J O H N   H I C K

John Hick, a British philosopher who now teaches at Claremont Graduate School, examines the Platonic notion of the immortality of the soul and argues that it is filled with problems. In its place he argues for the New Testament view of the re-creation of the psychophysical person, a holistic person who is body-soul in one. He then offers a thought experiment of "John Smith" reappearances to show that re-creation is conceivable and worthy of rational belief. In the last part of this essay Hick considers whether parapsychology can provide evidence for our survival of death.

The Immortality of the Soul

Some kind of distinction between physical body and immaterial or semimaterial soul seems to be as old as human culture; the existence of such a distinction has been indicated by the manner of

John H. Hick, *Philosophy of Religion,* 3d ed., copyright © 1983, pp. 122–32. Reprinted by permission of Prentice-Hall, Inc., Englewood Cliffs, N.J. Footnotes edited.

burial of the earliest human skeletons yet discovered. Anthropologists offer various conjectures about the origin of the distinction: perhaps it was first suggested by memories of dead persons; by dreams of them; by the sight of reflections of oneself in water and on other bright surfaces; or by meditation upon the significance of religious rites which grew up spontaneously in face of the fact of death.

It was Plato (428/7–348/7 B.C.), the philosopher who has most deeply and lastingly influenced Western culture, who systematically developed the body-mind dichotomy and first attempted to prove the immortality of the soul.[1]

Plato argues that although the body belongs to the sensible world,[2] and shares its changing and impermanent nature, the intellect is related to the unchanging realities of which we are aware when we think not of particular good things but of Goodness itself, not of specific just acts but of Justice itself, and of the other "universals" or eternal Ideas in virtue of which physical things and events have their own specific characteristics. Being related to this higher and abiding realm, rather than to the evanescent world of sense, reason or the soul is immortal. Hence, one who devotes his life to the contemplation of eternal realities rather than to the gratification of the fleeting desires of the body will find at death that whereas his body turns to dust, his soul gravitates to the realm of the unchanging, there to live forever. Plato painted an awe-inspiring picture, of haunting beauty and persuasiveness, which has moved and elevated the minds of men in many different centuries and lands. Nevertheless, it is not today (as it was during the first centuries of the Christian era) the common philosophy of the West; and a demonstration of immortality which presupposes Plato's metaphysical system cannot claim to constitute a proof for the twentieth-century disbeliever.

Plato used the further argument that the only things that can suffer destruction are those that are composite, since to destroy something means to disintegrate it into its constituent parts. All material bodies are composite; the soul, however, is simple and therefore imperishable. This argument was adopted by Aquinas and has become standard in Roman Catholic theology, as in the following passage from the modern Catholic philosopher, Jacques Maritain:

A spiritual soul cannot be corrupted, since it possesses no matter; it cannot be disintegrated, since it has no substantial parts; it cannot lose its individual unity, since it is self-subsisting, nor its internal energy, since it contains within itself all the sources of its energies. The human soul cannot die. Once it exists, it cannot disappear; it will necessarily exist for ever, endure without end. Thus, philosophic reason, put to work by a great metaphysician like Thomas Aquinas, is able to prove the immortality of the human soul in a demonstrative manner.[3]

This type of reasoning has been criticized on several grounds. Kant pointed out that although it is true that a simple substance cannot disintegrate, consciousness may nevertheless cease to exist through the diminution of its intensity to zero.[4] Modern psychology has also questioned the basic

premise that the mind is a simple entity. It seems instead to be a structure of only relative unity, normally fairly stable and tightly integrated but capable under stress of various degrees of division and dissolution. This comment from psychology makes it clear that the assumption that the soul is a simple substance is not an empirical observation but a metaphysical theory. As such, it cannot provide the basis for a general proof of immortality.

The body–soul distinction, first formulated as a philosophical doctrine in ancient Greece, was baptized into Christianity, ran through the medieval period, and entered the modern world with the public status of a self-evident truth when it was redefined in the seventeenth century by Descartes. Since World War II, however, the Cartesian mind–matter dualism, having been taken for granted for many centuries, has been strongly criticized by philosophers of the contemporary analytical school.[5] It is argued that the words that describe mental characteristics and operations— such as "intelligent," "thoughtful," "carefree," "happy," "calculating" and the like—apply in practice to types of human behavior and to behavioral dispositions. They refer to the empirical individual, the observable human being who is born and grows and acts and feels and dies, and not to the shadowy proceedings of a mysterious "ghost in the machine." Man is thus very much what he appears to be—a creature of flesh and blood, who behaves and is capable of behaving in a characteristic range of ways—rather than a nonphysical soul incomprehensibly interacting with a physical body.

As a result of this development much mid-twentieth-century philosophy has come to see man in the way he is seen in the biblical writings, not as an eternal soul temporarily attached to a mortal body, but as a form of finite, mortal, psychophysical life. Thus, the Old Testament scholar, J. Pedersen, says of the Hebrews that for them ". . . the body is the soul in its outward form."[6] This way of thinking has led to quite a different conception of death from that found in Plato and the neo-Platonic strand in European thought.

The Re-Creation of the Psychophysical Person

Only toward the end of the Old Testament period did after-life beliefs come to have any real importance in Judaism. Previously, Hebrew religious insight had focused so fully upon God's covenant with the nation, as an organism that continued through the centuries while successive generations lived and died, that the thought of a divine purpose for the individual, a purpose that transcended this present life, developed only when the breakdown of the nation as a political entity threw into prominence the individual and the problem of his personal destiny.

When a positive conviction arose of God's purpose holding the individual in being beyond the crisis of death, this conviction took the non-Platonic form of belief in the resurrection of the body. By the turn of the eras, this had become an article of faith for one Jewish sect, the Pharisees, although it was still rejected as an innovation by the more conservative Sadducees.

The religious difference between the Platonic belief in the immortality of the soul, and the Judaic-Christian belief in the resurrection of the body is that the latter postulates a special divine act of re-creation. This produces a sense of utter dependence upon God in the hour of death, a feeling that is in accordance with the biblical understanding of man as having been formed out of "the dust of the earth,"[7] a product (as we say today) of the slow evolution of life from its lowly beginnings in the primeval slime. Hence, in the Jewish and Christian conception, death is something real and fearful. It is not thought to be like walking from one room to another, or taking off an old coat and putting on a new one. It means sheer unqualified extinction—passing out from the lighted circle of life into "death's dateless night." Only through the sovereign creative love of God can there be a new existence beyond the grave.

What does "the resurrection of the dead" mean? Saint Paul's discussion provides the basic Christian answer to this question.[8] His conception of the general resurrection (distinguished from the unique resurrection of Jesus) has nothing to do with the resuscitation of corpses in a cemetery. It concerns God's re-creation or reconstitution of the human psychophysical individual, not as the organism that has died but as a *soma pneumatikon*, a "spiritual body," inhabiting a spiritual world as the physical body inhabits our present physical world.

A major problem confronting any such doctrine is that of providing criteria of personal identity to link the earthly life and the resurrection life. Paul does not specifically consider this question, but one may, perhaps, develop his thought along lines such as the following.[9]

Suppose, first, that someone—John Smith—living in the USA were suddenly and inexplicably to disappear from before the eyes of his friends, and that at the same moment an exact replica of him were inexplicably to appear in India. The person who appears in India is exactly similar in both physical and mental characteristics to the person who disappeared in America. There is continuity of memory, complete similarity of bodily features including fingerprints, hair and eye coloration, and stomach contents, and also of beliefs, habits, emotions, and mental dispositions. Further, the "John Smith" replica thinks of himself as being the John Smith who disappeared in the USA. After all possible tests have been made and have proved positive, the factors leading his friends to accept "John Smith" as John Smith would surely prevail and would cause them to overlook even his mysterious transference from one continent to another, rather than treat "John Smith," with all John Smith's memories and other characteristics, as someone other than John Smith.

Suppose, second, that our John Smith, instead of inexplicably disappearing, dies, but that at the moment of his death a "John Smith" replica, again complete with memories and all other characteristics, appears in India. Even with the corpse on our hands we would, I think, still have to accept this "John Smith" as the John Smith who died. We would have to say that he had been miraculously re-created in another place.

Now suppose, third, that on John Smith's death the "John Smith" replica appears, not in India, but as a resurrection replica in a different world altogether, a resurrection world inhabited only by resurrected persons. This world occupies its own space distinct from that with which we are now familiar. That is to say, an object in the resurrection world is not situated at any distance or in any direction from the objects in our present world, although each object in either world is spatially related to every other object in the same world.

This supposition provides a model by which one may conceive of the divine re-creation of the embodied human personality. In this model, the element of the strange and the mysterious has been reduced to a minimum by following the view of some of the early Church Fathers that the resurrection body has the same shape as the physical body,[10] and ignoring Paul's own hint that it may be as unlike the physical body as a full grain of wheat differs from the wheat seed.[11]

What is the basis for this Judaic-Christian belief in the divine recreation or reconstitution of the human personality after death? There is, of course, an argument from authority, in that life after death is taught throughout the New Testament (although very rarely in the Old Testament). But, more basically, belief in the resurrection arises as a corollary of faith in the sovereign purpose of God, which is not restricted by death and which holds man in being beyond his natural mortality. In the words of Martin Luther, "Anyone with whom God speaks, whether in wrath or in mercy, the same is certainly immortal. The Person of God who speaks, and the Word, show that we are creatures with whom God wills to speak, right into eternity, and in an immortal manner."[12] In a similar vein it is argued that if it be God's plan to create finite persons to exist in fellowship with himself, then it contradicts both his own intention and his love for the creatures made in his image if he allows men to pass out of existence when his purpose for them remains largely unfulfilled.

It is this promised fulfillment of God's purpose

for man, in which the full possibilities of human nature will be realized, that constitutes the "heaven" symbolized in the New Testament as a joyous banquet in which all and sundry rejoice together. As we saw when discussing the problem of evil, no theodicy can succeed without drawing into itself this eschatological[13] faith in an eternal, and therefore infinite, good which thus outweighs all the pains and sorrows that have been endured on the way to it.

Balancing the idea of heaven in Christian tradition is the idea of *hell*. This, too, is relevant to the problem of theodicy. For just as the reconciling of God's goodness and power with the fact of evil requires that out of the travail of history there shall come in the end an eternal good for man, so likewise it would seem to preclude man's eternal misery. The only kind of evil that is finally incompatible with God's unlimited power and love would be utterly pointless and wasted suffering, pain which is never redeemed and worked into the fulfilling of God's good purpose. Unending torment would constitute precisely such suffering; for being eternal, it could never lead to a good end beyond itself. Thus, hell as conceived by its enthusiasts, such as Augustine or Calvin, is a major part of the problem of evil! If hell is construed as eternal torment, the theological motive behind the idea is directly at variance with the urge to seek a theodicy. However, it is by no means clear that the doctrine of eternal punishment can claim a secure New Testament basis.[14] If, on the other hand, "hell" means a continuation of the purgatorial suffering often experienced in this life, and leading eventually to the high good of heaven, it no longer stands in conflict with the needs of theodicy. Again, the idea of hell may be deliteralized and valued as a *mythos*, as a powerful and pregnant symbol of the grave responsibility inherent in man's freedom in relation to his Maker.

Does Parapsychology Help?

The spiritualist movement claims that life after death has been proved by well-attested cases of communication between the living and the "dead." During the closing quarter of the nineteenth century and the decades of the present century this claim has been made the subject of careful and prolonged study by a number of responsible and competent persons.[15] This work, which may be approximately dated from the founding in London of the Society for Psychical Research in 1882, is known either by the name adopted by that society or in the United States by the name parapsychology.

Approaching the subject from the standpoint of our interest in this chapter, we may initially divide the phenomena studied by the parapsychologist into two groups. There are those phenomena that involve no reference to the idea of a life after death, chief among these being psychokinesis and extrasensory perception (ESP) in its various forms (such as telepathy, clairvoyance, and precognition). And there are those phenomena that raise the question of personal survival after death, such as the apparitions and other sensory manifestations of dead persons and the "spirit messages" received through mediums. This division is, however, only of preliminary use, for ESP has emerged as a clue to the understanding of much that occurs in the second group. We shall begin with a brief outline of the reasons that have induced the majority of workers in this field to be willing to postulate so strange an occurrence as telepathy.

Telepathy is a name for the mysterious fact that sometimes a thought in the mind of one person apparently causes a similar thought to occur to someone else when there are no normal means of communication between them, and under circumstances such that mere coincidence seems to be excluded.

For example, one person may draw a series of pictures or diagrams on paper and somehow transmit an impression of these to someone else in another room who then draws recognizable reproductions of them. This might well be a coincidence in the case of a single successful reproduction; but can a series consist entirely of coincidences?

Experiments have been devised to measure the probability of chance coincidence in supposed cases of telepathy. In the simplest of these, cards printed in turn with five different symbols are used. A pack of fifty, consisting of ten bearing each symbol, is then thoroughly shuffled, and the sender concentrates on the cards one at a time while the receiver (who of course can see neither sender nor cards) tries to write down the correct order of symbols. This procedure is repeated, with constant reshuffling, hundreds or thousands of times. Since there are only five different symbols, a random guess would stand one chance in five of being correct. Consequently, on the assumption that only "chance" is operating, the receiver should be right in about 20 per cent of his tries, and wrong in about 80 per cent; and the longer the series, the closer should be the approach to this proportion. However, good telepathic subjects are right in a far larger number of cases than can be reconciled with random guessing. The deviation from chance expectation can be converted mathematically into "odds against chance" (increasing as the proportion of hits is maintained over a longer and longer series of tries). In this way, odds of over a million to one have been recorded. J. B. Rhine (Duke University) has reported results showing "antichance" values ranging from seven (which equals odds against chance of 100,000 to one) to eighty-two (which converts the odds against chance to billions).[16] S. G. Soal (London University) has reported positive results for precognitive telepathy with odds against chance of $10^{35} \times 5$, or of billions to one.[17] Other researchers have also recorded confirming results.[18] In the light of these reports, it is difficult to deny that some positive factor, and not merely "chance," is operating. "Telepathy" is simply a name for this unknown positive factor.

How does telepathy operate? Only negative conclusions seem to be justified to date. It can, for example, be said with reasonable certainty that telepathy does not consist in any kind of physical radiation, analogous to radio waves. For, first, telepathy is not delayed or weakened in proportion to distance, as are all known forms of radiation; and, second, there is no organ in the brain or elsewhere that can plausibly be regarded as its sending or receiving center. Telepathy appears to be a purely mental occurrence.

It is not, however, a matter of transferring or transporting a thought out of one mind into another—if, indeed, such an idea makes sense at all. The telepathized thought does not leave the sender's consciousness in order to enter that of the receiver. What happens would be better described by saying that the sender's thought gives rise to a mental "echo" in the mind of the receiver. This "echo" occurs at the unconscious level, and consequently the version of it that rises into the receiver's consciousness may be only fragmentary and may be distorted or symbolized in various ways, as in dreams.

According to one theory that has been tentatively suggested to explain telepathy, our minds are separate and mutually insulated only at the conscious (and preconscious) level. But at the deepest level of the unconscious, we are constantly influencing one another, and it is at this level that telepathy takes place.[19]

How is a telepathized thought directed to one particular receiver among so many? Apparently the thoughts are directed by some link of emotion or common interest. For example, two friends are sometimes telepathically aware of any grave crisis or shock experienced by the other, even though they are at opposite ends of the earth.

We shall turn now to the other branch of parapsychology, which has more obvious bearing upon our subject. The *Proceedings of the Society for Psychical Research* contains a large number of carefully recorded and satisfactorily attested cases of the appearance of the figure of someone who has recently died to living people (in rare instances to more than one at a time) who were, in many cases, at a distance and unaware of the death. The S.P.R. reports also establish beyond reasonable doubt that the minds that operate in the mediumistic trance, purporting to be spirits of the departed, sometimes give personal information the medium could not have acquired by normal means and at times even give information, later verified, which had not been known to any living person.

On the other hand, physical happenings, such as the "materializations" of spirit forms in a visible

and tangible form, are much more doubtful. But even if we discount the entire range of physical phenomena, it remains true that the best cases of trance utterance are impressive and puzzling, and taken at face value are indicative of survival and communication after death. If, through a medium, one talks with an intelligence that gives a coherent impression of being an intimately known friend who has died and establishes identity by a wealth of private information and indefinable personal characteristics—as has occasionally happened—then we cannot dismiss without careful trial the theory that what is taking place is the return of a consciousness from the spirit world.

However, the advance of knowledge in the other branch of parapsychology, centering upon the study of extrasensory perception, has thrown unexpected light upon this apparent commerce with the departed. For it suggests that unconscious telepathic contact between the medium and his or her client is an important and possibly a sufficient explanatory factor. This was vividly illustrated by the experience of two women who decided to test the spirits by taking into their minds, over a period of weeks, the personality and atmosphere of an entirely imaginary character in an unpublished novel written by one of the women. After thus filling their minds with the characteristics of this fictitious person, they went to a reputable medium, who proceeded to describe accurately their imaginary friend as a visitant from beyond the grave and to deliver appropriate messages from him.

An even more striking case is that of the "direct voice" medium (i.e., a medium in whose séances the voice of the communicating "spirit" is heard apparently speaking out of the air) who produced the spirit of one "Gordon Davis" who spoke in his own recognizable voice, displayed considerable knowledge about Gordon Davis, and remembered his death. This was extremely impressive until it was discovered that Gordon Davis was still alive; he was, of all ghostly occupations, a real-estate agent, and had been trying to sell a house at the time when the séance took place![20]

Such cases suggest that genuine mediums are

simply persons of exceptional telepathic sensitiveness who unconsciously derive the "spirits" from their clients' minds.

In connection with "ghosts," in the sense of apparitions of the dead, it has been established that there can be "meaningful hallucinations," the source of which is almost certainly telepathic. To quote a classic and somewhat dramatic example: a woman sitting by a lake sees the figure of a man running toward the lake and throwing himself in. A few days later a man commits suicide by throwing himself into this same lake. Presumably, the explanation of the vision is that the man's thought while he was contemplating suicide had been telepathically projected onto the scene via the woman's mind.

In many of the cases recorded there is delayed action. The telepathically projected thought lingers in the recipient's unconscious mind until a suitable state of inattention to the outside world enables it to appear to his conscious mind in a dramatized form—for example, by a hallucinatory voice or vision—by means of the same mechanism that operates in dreams.

If phantoms of the living can be created by previously experienced thoughts and emotions of the person whom they represent, the parallel possibility arises that phantoms of the dead are caused by thoughts and emotions that were experienced by the person represented when he was alive. In other words, ghosts may be "psychic footprints," a kind of mental trace left behind by the dead, but not involving the presence or even the continued existence of those whom they represent.

These considerations tend away from the hopeful view that parapsychology will open a window onto another world. However, it is too early for a final verdict; and in the meantime one should be careful not to confuse absence of knowledge with knowledge of absence.

Notes

1. *Phaedo.*
2. The world known to us through our physical senses.

3. Jacques Maritain, *The Range of Reason* (London: Geoffrey Bles Ltd. and New York: Charles Scribner's Sons, 1953), p. 60.

4. Kant, *Critique of Pure Reason, Transcendental Dialectic*, "Refutation of Mendelessohn's Proof of the Permanence of the Soul."

5. Gilbert Ryle's *The Concept of Mind* (London: Hutchinson & Co., Ltd., 1949) is a classic statement of this critique.

6. *Israel* (London: Oxford University Press, 1926), I, 170.

7. Genesis 2:7; Psalm 103:14.

8. I Corinthians 15.

9. The following paragraphs are adapted, with permission, from a section of my article, "Theology and Verification," published in *Theology Today* (April, 1960) and reprinted in *The Existence of God* (New York: The Macmillan Company, 1964).

10. For example, Irenaeus, *Against Heresies*, Book II, Chap. 34, para. 1.

11. 1 Corinthians 15:37.

12. Quoted by Emil Brunner, *Dogmatics*, II, 69.

13. From the Greek *eschaton*, end.

14. The Greek word *aionios*, which is used in the New Testament and which is usually translated as "eternal" or "everlasting," can bear either this meaning or the more limited meaning of "for the aeon, or age."

15. The list of past presidents of the Society for Psychical Research includes the philosophers Henri Bergson, William James, Hans Driesch, Henry Sidgwick, F. C. S. Schiller, C. D. Broad, and H. H. Price; the psychologists William McDougall, Gardner Murphy, Franklin Prince, and R. H. Thouless; the physicists Sir William Crookes, Sir Oliver Lodge, Sir William Barrett, and Lord Rayleigh; and the classicist Gilbert Murray.

16. J. B. Rhine, *Extrasensory Perception* (Boston: Society for Psychical Research, 1935), Table XLIII, p. 162. See also Rhine, *New Frontiers of the Mind* (New York: Farrar and Rinehart, Inc., 1937), pp. 69f.

17. S. G. Soal, *Proceedings of the Society for Psychical Research*, XLVI, 152–98 and XLVII, 21–150. See also S. G. Soal's *The Experimental Situation in Psychical Research* (London: The Society for Psychical Research, 1947).

18. For surveys of the experimental work, see Whately Carrington, *Telepathy* (London: Methuen & Co. Ltd., 1945); G. N. M. Tyrrell, *The Personality of Man* (London: Penguin Books Ltd., 1946); S. G. Soal and F. Bateman, *Modern Experiments in Telepathy* (London: Faber & Faber Ltd. and New Haven, Conn.: Yale University Press, 1954); and for important Russian work, L. L. Vasiliev, *Experiments in Mental Suggestion*, 1962 (Church Crookham: Institute for the Study of Mental Images, 1963—English translation).

19. Whately Carrington, *Telepathy* (London: Methuen & Co. Ltd., 1945), Chaps. 6–8.

20. S. G. Soal, "A Report of Some Communications Received through Mrs. Blanche Cooper," Sec. 4, *Proceedings of the Society for Psychical Research,* XXXV, 560–89.

VI.5   Against Survival

ANTONY FLEW

Antony Flew, a British philosopher now teaching at York University in Ontario, Canada, here considers three ways in which we could survive our death: (1) the Platonic-Cartesian way of the disembodied soul; (2) the astral body way; and (3) the biblical reconstitution way. He rejects the Platonic-Cartesian way as incoherent, for we cannot understand what it is to have experiences without a body. He rejects the reconstitution way, for what is re-created is not us but simply something like us. The view that he finds most logical is the idea of an astral body. In this view we already have a duplicate ethereal body, "a soul in bodily shape . . . in form resembling that of a human being in every respect," which continues to exist after we die. Although this idea is logically possible, there is no reason to believe such a far-fetched doctrine.

Bertrand Russell once wrote: "All the questions which have what is called a human interest—such, for example, as the question of a future life—belong, at least in theory, to special sciences and are capable, at least in theory, of being decided by empirical evidence . . . a genuinely scientific philosophy cannot hope to appeal to any except those who have the wish to understand, to escape from intellectual bewilderment . . . it does not offer, or attempt to offer, a solution to the problem of human destiny, or of the destiny of the Universe."

Reprinted from Antony Flew, *God, Freedom, and Immortality* (Buffalo, N.Y.: Prometheus Books, 1976) by permission of the author and the publisher. Footnotes deleted.

1. The Enormous Initial Obstacle

There is a huge obstacle which lies across the path of any doctrine of personal survival or personal immortality. This enormous initial obstacle is perfectly obvious and perfectly familiar. Nevertheless, in order to put the whole discussion into the correct perspective, it is useful to begin by actually stating what it is. For only when this has been done shall we fully appreciate for what they are the three main sorts of ways of trying to circumvent or to overcome the obstacle; and only when this is appreciated shall we be able adequately to assess the success or failure of any such attempt.

Yet the vocabulary available for describing the obstacle may well be felt unfairly to prejudice the question against the believer in personal survival or personal immortality. To meet this difficulty I propose first to say and, hopefully, later to show that it is certainly not my intention to prejudge issues in this or any other way.

This huge obstacle lying across the path of any doctrine of personal survival or personal immortality is the familiar fact that—with the possible exceptions of the prophet Elijah and Mary the mother of Jesus bar Joseph—all men die and are in more or less short order buried, cremated, or otherwise disposed of. This universal fact of death is what leads us normally to distinguish after a shipwreck or an air crash, exclusively and exhaustively, between the Dead and the Survivors, with no third category of Both or Neither. This is the fact which gave the proposition 'All men are mortal' its hallowed status as the first premise of the stock traditional example of a valid syllogism; which proceeds from this and the further premise that 'Socrates is (or was) a man', to the true if unexciting conclusion that 'Socrates is (or was) mortal'.

2. Survival and Immortality

Confronted by such an obstacle how is any such doctrine to get started? Before trying to suggest an answer I wish to make a sharp, simplifying move. I propose from now on to speak only of survival, without qualification, rather than of personal survival and personal immortality. I shall thus be taking it for granted, first, that what we are interested in is our personal post-mortem futures, if any. 'Survival' through our children and our children's children after we ourselves are irrecoverably dead, 'immortality' through the memories of others thanks to our great works, or even our immersion in some universal world-soul—whatever that might mean—may be as much as, or much more than, most of us will in fact be getting. And it may be lamentably self-centred, albeit humanly altogether understandable, that we should be concerned about more than these thin substitutes. But, for better or for worse, what we are discussing now is the possibility of our post-mortem survival as persons identifiable as those we are here and now.

I shall also be taking it for granted, second, that survival is the necessary though of course not the sufficient condition of immortality. We can and shall concentrate on survival because this is pre-eminently a case where it is the first step which counts. Immortality is just more of the same—survival for ever. This may seem another point too obvious to be worth making. I sympathise with this impatient reaction. But it is wrong. For consider that the Roman Catholic Professor R. F. Holland could write, in reviewing C. B. Martin's path-breaking study *Religious Belief*, in *Mind* for 1961: "Christians believe that they are to be resurrected. . . . They believe that they are in for damnation or salvation. . . . The notion of 'looking forward to life after death as a means of settling questions concerning the existence and nature of God' . . . smacks of Spiritualism . . . rather than Christianity" (p. 572).

3. Three Ways for Survival

We shall, therefore, have in mind always and only personal survival; and we shall be concentrating on survival rather than on immortality inasmuch as the former is the necessary but not the sufficient first step to the latter. So, now, back to the question of how, granted the undeniable fact that we shall all die, anyone can possibly maintain that some or all of us will nevertheless survive. I distinguish three sorts of ways in which attempts can be, and have been, made to overcome this enormous initial obstacle.

(i) The first and most familiar I call the Platonic or Platonic-Cartesian way. This consists in two moves, not one. The first move is to maintain that what is ordinarily thought of as a person in fact consists of two radically disparate elements: the one, the body, earthy, corporeal, and perishable; the other, the soul, incorporeal, invisible, intangible, and perhaps imperishable. The second move in the Platonic or Platonic-Cartesian way consists in the contention that it is the second of these two elements which is the real, essential person. It is obvious that if this way will go, then what I call the enormous initial obstacle is really no obstacle at all: the death of the body is not necessarily the death of the soul, which is the true person; and such an essentially incorporeal entity cannot in principle be touched by the earthy corruptions of the graveyard or the inferno of the crematorium. The case where this soul is stipulated to be not incorporeal but corporeal I classify as a special case of the second way, the way of the astral body.

(ii) This second suggestion, like the first, consists in two moves, not one. The first move is to claim that inside and, so to speak, shadowing what is ordinarily thought of as the person is another being of the same form. And the second move is, as before, to maintain that this shadow being is the real person. The crucial difference between the Platonic-Cartesian way and the way of the astral body is that, whereas in the former the soul is supposed to be essentially incorporeal, in the latter the astral body is equally essentially in its own way corporeal—albeit, of course, necessarily constituted of a different and somehow more shadowy and ethereal sort of stuff than familiar, workaday matter. Strictly speaking, it could not make sense to ask of a Platonic-Cartesian soul any such everyday and down-to-earth questions as 'What is it?', 'How big is it?', 'How broad and long is it?'. Of the astral body, on the other hand, at least some such questions must be sensibly askable even if not in practice answerable, or what would be the point of talking of an astral body and not simply of a Platonic-Cartesian soul?

Once this crucial distinguishing point is grasped, the best method of increasing one's sympathetic understanding of the way of the astral body is to think of those stock cinematic representations—as long ago in the movie version of Noël Coward's *Blithe Spirit*—in which a shadow person, visible only sometimes and only to some of the characters, detaches itself from a person shown as dead and thereafter continues to participate in the developing action, at one time discernibly and at another time not.

This second way is not, I think, nowadays given the attention which it deserves. Part of the reason for this is that people familiar with the materials of psychical research have been persuaded to adopt a different interpretation of those apparitions of the living, the dying, and the dead which have to others seemed to provide the main prop for an astral body view (Tyrrell, *passim*). But partly, I suspect, the way of the astral body is simply ruled out of court as unacceptably crude or intolerably materialist; and this hasty dismissal is made all the easier by the assumption—which I shall soon be challenging—that there are no serious theoretical objections to the Platonic-Cartesian way.

(iii) The third of the three sorts of ways which I want to distinguish and label finds its traditional home in religion rather than in psychical research. This is the one which I call the reconstitutionist way. The nature of this third way cannot be better

shown than by quoting an epitaph composed for himself by Benjamin Franklin, Founding Father and Signer of the American Declaration of Independence. This epitaph has been erected not on but near his grave in Christ Church cemetery, Philadelphia, by the Poor Richard Society of that his city: "The body of B. Franklin, Printer, Like the Cover of an old Book, Its Contents torn out, And stript of its Lettering and Gilding, Lies here, Food for Worms. But the work shall not be lost; for it will, as he believ'd, appear once more in a new and more elegant Edition Corrected and improved By the Author."

4. Difficulties of the Reconstitutionist Way

The great, and surely quite decisive, difficulty here may be christened the Replica Objection. Consider a short but most revealing passage from Chapter XVII 'The Night Journey' in the *Koran*. As usual it is Allah speaking: "Thus shall they be rewarded: because they disbelieved our revelations and said, 'When we are turned to bones and dust shall we be raised to life?' Do they not see that Allah, who has created the heavens and the earth, has power to create their like? Their fate is preordained beyond all doubt. Yet the wrongdoers persist in unbelief."

Certainly Allah the omnipotent must have "power to create their like." But in making Allah talk in these precise terms of what He might indeed choose to do, the Prophet was speaking truer than he himself appreciated. For thus to produce even the most indistinguishably similar object after the first one has been totally destroyed and disappeared is to produce not the same object again, but a replica. To punish or to reward a replica, reconstituted on Judgement Day, for the sins or the virtues of the old Antony Flew dead and cremated in 1984 is as inept and as unfair as it would be to reward or to punish one identical twin for what was in fact done by the other. Again and similarly, the Creator might very well choose to issue a Second Edition—"Corrected and improved by the Author"—of Benjamin Franklin.

But that Second Edition, however welcome, would by the same token not be the original Signer.

It was partly, though of course only partly, because he appreciated the force of this Replica Objection that Aquinas mixed a strong Platonic element into his version of the reconstitutionist way. The soul which could, and in his view did, survive death and wait for the reconstitution of the whole person on Judgement Day was for Aquinas only an incomplete fragment and not, as it was for Plato, the real and essential person. Yet this incomplete Thomist soul should, hopefully, be just enough to bridge the gap between now and then, and to provide sufficient necessary continuity between the Flew you see and the reconstituted Flew of Judgement Day to overcome the otherwise fatal Replica Objection.

In Section 3 I deliberately distinguished all my three ways in ideal purity. But when we come to real cases we often find that the protagonist of what is predominantly one has been pressed by some difficulty to admit at least some element of another. Thus the primarily reconstitutionist Aquinas is driven to become in part a Platonist also. Later we shall see both how Plato himself, against all his wishes and intentions, lapses into an astral body view; and how the spokesman for an astral body in his turn may find himself so qualifying the nature of his elusive hypothesised body that it must become indistinguishable from a Platonic-Cartesian incorporeal soul.

5. Difficulties of the Platonic Way

The first thing with which we must try to come to terms here is that the assumptions of the Platonic-Cartesian way, which in some contexts we find it so easy to make, are nevertheless both extraordinary and extraordinarily questionable.

(i) To appreciate how easy it is in some contexts to make these Platonic-Cartesian assumptions, consider a paper by the late Professor C. J. Ducasse, 'What would constitute conclusive evidence of survival after death?'. It was published in the *Journal of the Society for Psychical Research* for 1962. Ducasse supposes that our friend John Doe has been on board an aircraft which crashed in the ocean, and no survivors have been found. Our phone rings " and (a) a voice we recognise as John Doe's is heard and a conversation with it held which convinces us that the speaker is really John Doe . . . or (b) the voice heard is not John Doe's but that of some other person seemingly relaying his words to us and ours to him; and that the conversation so held does convince us that the person with whom we are conversing through that intermediary is John Doe" (p. 401). Ducasse continues: "Obviously, the two imagined situations (a) and (b) are, in all essentials, analogues of cases where a person is conversing with the purported surviving spirit of a deceased friend who either, in case (a), 'possesses' for the time being parts at least of the body of a medium . . . or else who, in case (b), employs the medium only as intermediary . . ." (pp. 401–402).

Now certainly this constitutes as clear and vivid a description as could be desired of the model in terms of which mediums and their sitters usually think of the proceedings of the seance room. Yet it is neither obvious nor true that "the two imagined situations . . . are, in all essentials, analogues" of the seance situation. The crucial difference lies in the fact that in the case of the imaginary plane crash we know only "that no survivors have been found," whereas in the seance case we presumably know, beyond any possibility of doubt, that our friend has indeed died, and that his remains have been duly buried, cremated, or in some other way consumed. Now Ducasse, in his own way, appreciated all this perfectly well. The reason why he did not see it as representing any difficulty at all for 'the survival hypothesis' is that here he, like almost everyone else when considering what is in psychical research called 'the survival evidence', took for granted a Platonic-Cartesian view of man.

These Platonic-Cartesian assumptions are made explicit a little later, when Ducasse continues: "Thus, because the John Doe case and the case of conversation through a medium are complete analogues, the particular kind of content of the conversation that would be adequate to prove or make positively probable that John Doe had survived the crash would likewise be adequate to prove or make positively probable that the mind of our deceased friend has survived the death of his body" (p. 402). This possibly surviving mind of Ducasse's is—as he himself, again in his own fashion, emphasizes—for our purposes nothing else but the Platonic-Cartesian soul: for it is an incorporeal entity which inhabits the body; and it is the real, essential person. Ducasse continues: "When the question of survival is formulated thus in terms not of 'spirits' but of *minds* then the allegation that the survival explanation makes gratuitously . . . four assumptions . . . is seen to be erroneous. For (a) that there are minds is not an assumption but a known fact; (b) that minds are capable of remembering is likewise not an assumption but is known; (c) that minds are capable of 'possessing' living human bodies is also a known fact, for 'possession' is but the name of the *normal* relation of a mind to its living body. *Paranormal* 'possession' would be possession in the very same sense, but only temporary, and of a living body by a mind other than its own—that other mind either being one which had been that of a body now dead; or being a mind temporarily wandering from its own living body. And (d) that telepathic communication between minds is possible is also a known fact" (p. 403: italics and inverted commas original).

(ii) Having shown by reference to Ducasse how easy and natural it is to make Platonic-Cartesian assumptions in the context of what is usually described as the survival evidence, the next thing is to challenge both these assumptions. What I shall now be doing is to develop, in a philosopher's way, a suggestion made many years ago by a leading American psychologist and psychical researcher, Gardner Murphy. Writing on 'Difficulties confronting the survival hypothesis' in the *Journal of the American Society for Psychical Research* for 1945 Murphy spoke of the "fact that bodies are the vehicles of personality, and that most people have no conception of personality except in such terms . . .". He challenged "the reader to try for a few minutes to imagine what his

personal existence would be like if he were deprived of every device for making contact with his environment, except through the hypothetical use of continuous telepathy to and from other invisible minds" (p. 71).

I think that Murphy understated his case. For, surely, 'personality' is a term which has to be defined in terms of persons. My personality is some sort of function of my characteristics and my dispositions; and it could make no more sense to talk of my personality surviving my dissolution—of these characteristics existing without a me for them to be the characteristics of—than it would to talk of the grin of Carroll's Cheshire Cat outlasting the face of which it was one possible configuration. Nor is it just "most people," as Murphy modestly puts it, it is all of us whose conceptions of personality are grounded in the corporeal. For, as I have just said, personality is essentially some sort of function of persons; and persons are—surely equally essentially—corporeal.

Consider, for instance, how you would teach the meaning of any person word to a child. This is done, and I think could only be done, by some sort of direct or indirect pointing at members of that very special class of living physical objects to which we one and all belong. Or again, and slightly more subtly, consider some of the things which we easily and regularly say about people, and think how few, if any, of these things could be intelligibly said about incorporeal entities. We meet people, we shake hands with them, eat with them, see them, hear them; they get up, go to bed, sit down, smile, laugh, cry. All these activities, and many, many more, could only be predicated intelligibly of corporeal creatures.

Now look again at what Ducasse called the "known facts," and what I still want to call his Platonic-Cartesian assumptions. I agree, of course, that there are minds, provided that by this we mean only that such statements as that he has a first-rate mind, or that the child is developing a mind of his own, are often true. But these statements are, in the interpretation in which we know that they are often true, statements about the capacities and dispositions of flesh and blood people. They must not be misconstrued to imply that the people in question already possess, or are in the process of acquiring, important incorporeal components; much less that these—or any—people actually are incorporeal beings.

It is also perfectly true and much to the point to insist that all normal people are capable of a certain amount of remembering. But, to say that minds are the possessors of these capacities is either an oddly artificial and, it appears, highly misleading way of stating a fact about people, or else a speculative suggestion about a possible explanation of that same fact in terms of a hypothetical and, presumably, corporeal entity.

(iii) Suppose we were to grant that ESP is a reality, there is still absolutely no experimental reason to describe it as communication between minds or souls rather than as communication between people. Indeed, I believe that something even stronger and much more interesting might be said—something at which Murphy was perhaps hinting when he spoke a shade disrespectfully of "the hypothetical use of continuous telepathy to and from other invisible minds." For could such bodiless beings, necessarily lacking all conventional sensory equipment, properly be said to communicate with one another by ESP, or even singly to possess any ESP capacity? And, if they could, could they be said to know that they were thus communicating, or that they did possess such a capacity?

These questions arise—although I cannot recall having heard them put before—because the term 'ESP' is, whether implicitly or explicitly, defined negatively by reference to the absence or neglect of all ordinary and ultimately perceptual methods of acquiring and communicating information; and because it is only by reference at some stage to the conventional sources that we become able to identify authentic ESP experiences or performances as being truly such; and thus to distinguish these both from acquisitions of information through normal channels and from such autonomous features of our own lives as our spontaneous and not significantly veridical imaginings. We never should forget, what too often is forgotten, that 'ESP' is not the name of some directly identifiable means of information transfer. Indeed,

despite the close resemblance between the words 'telepathy' and 'telephony', any performance depending on telephony or any other such known and normal means is for that very reason at once disqualified as a case of telepathy; and the same applies, with appropriate alterations, as regards clairvoyance. Nor can authentic ESP experiences be picked out as such simply by reference to the strong conviction of the subject that this is the real thing. It is, or should be, notorious that subjective conviction is not a sufficient condition of either normal or paranormal knowledge: I may with complete confidence and absolute sincerity claim either to know normally or to have exercised my supposed ESP capacity, and yet in fact be totally mistaken. We must, therefore, distinguish: between (a) in fact possessing or exercising some ESP capacity, whether or not you believe or know that you do or are; (b) believing that you possess or are exercising an ESP capacity, whether or not you in fact do or are; and (c) genuinely knowing—as opposed to believing with however little warrant or however mistakenly—that you do possess or perhaps actually are exercising such a capacity.

Suppose now that in the light of these reminders we try to apply ESP concepts to these putative incorporeal subjects of experiences. Suppose further that it is a fact that there actually is some close correspondence between the mental contents of two such hypothetical bodiless beings, although such a fact would not, surely, be known by any normal means by anyone—whether bodied or bodiless. Now how could either of these bodiless beings have, how indeed could there even be, any reason for saying that this close correspondence must point to some information transfer from one to the other? How could either of these bodiless beings have—indeed how could there even be—any reason for holding that some of its mental contents must have been intruded by, or otherwise correspond with, some of those of another similarly bodiless being; and some particular one, at that? How could either have, indeed how could there be, any good reason for picking out some if its mental contents as—so to speak—messages received, for taking these but not those as the expressions of an exercise not of imagination but of ESP? Fundamentally similar difficulties arise when we attempt to apply ESP concepts to the different cases of information transfer between an ordinary person and a supposed bodiless being, and between material things and such a being (telepathy from the living to a spirit, that is, and clairvoyance by a spirit). The upshot appears to be that the concepts of ESP are essentially parasitical upon everyday and this-worldly notions; that where there could not be the normal, there could not be ESP as the exception to that rule.

It is too often and too easily assumed that ESP capacities could be, or even must be, the attributes of something altogether immaterial and incorporeal; partly for no better reason than that they do indeed seem to be non-physical in the entirely different sense of being outside the range of today's physical theories. Yet the truth appears to be that the very concepts of ESP are just as much involved with the human body as are those of other human capacities. It was this point which Wittgenstein was making, with regard to our normal and known attributes and capacities rather than anything putative or paranormal, when he said gnomically: "The human body is the best picture of the human soul" (Wittgenstein (2), p. 178).

(iv) We have no business, therefore, simply to take a Platonic-Cartesian view of man for granted; and to proceed at once to the question of whether the so-called survival evidence is in fact sufficient to establish that we, in our putative essential natures as incorporeal souls, do survive death and the dissolution of our bodies. Before we can possibly become entitled to begin to construe that material as evidence for this conclusion a great deal of work will have to be done to show: (a) that there can be a coherent notion of an incorporeal personal being; and (b) that a being of this sort could significantly and truly be said to be the same person as he was when he was a creature of flesh and blood.

My own conviction is that no amount of work can turn these two tricks. It is surely significant that Plato himself—an imaginative writer of genius as well as the Founding Father of philosophy—when he came at the end of his *Republic* to describe in the Myth of Er the life of supposedly incorporeal souls, was quite unable to say anything about them which did not presuppose that they must be, after all, in some fashion corporeal. So, against all his wishes and intentions, Plato there lapsed from his own eponymous position into what was in effect an astral body view.

(v) But, suppose we take Plato's own failure in the Myth of Er—as, surely, he would have done had it been pointed out to him—as showing only that our vocabulary and our imagination are deplorably limited by our present, but temporary, enmeshment in the body. And suppose we concede—as surely we must—that the person words of our present vocabulary do not refer to incorporeal souls, but to creatures of all too solid flesh. Can we not develop a new and coherent concept of an incorporeal being to whom at least some of the characteristics presently ascribed to people could also significantly be attributed? I do not think that we can. The basic difficulties are, first, to provide a principle of individuation by which one such being could, at least in theory, be distinguished from another such being; and, second, to provide a principle of identity to permit us to say that one such being at a later time is the same as that being at an earlier time.

This is difficult ground, though we can get much help by considering the unsuccessful labours of Descartes and his successors. Since they mistook it that people are incorporeal subjects of experience, our problem appeared to them not as one of developing a coherent new notion, but as that of giving an account of our present notion of a person. But this does not make their efforts any less relevant to us. The first thing which emerges is that such an incorporeal personal being will have to be conceived as consisting of a series of conscious experiences—along, no doubt, with some dispositions, inclinations, and capacities. In the light of what has been argued already in a previous subsection (5 (iii)), we have to add that unless we can solve the theoretical problem of attributing ESP and other putative paranormal capacities to such a being, these dispositions and so on will have to refer exclusively to actual or possible members of the same series of experiences. We now have a choice between two options: either, with Descartes, we attribute these experiences to an incorporeal spiritual substance—the I in Descartes' claim "I am a thinking substance"; or else, with Hume, we say that we can make nothing of the idea of such a substance and then go on to say that such an incorporeal being must simply consist in a series of experiences.

Neither alternative shows promise. Take the second first. Whatever difficulties there may be about the idea of a substance characterised as incorporeal, it should be easy to see why some substance is required. The word 'substance' is being used here in its main—not, alas, its only—philosophical sense. In this sense a substance is that which can significantly be said to exist separately and in its own right, so to speak. Any experience requires a substance to be the experience of in exactly the same way that a grin requires a face to be the grin of. Since it makes no sense to talk of a pain or a joy or any other sort of awareness without an owner, Hume's suggestion in the *Treatise* (I (iv) 6) that a person might simply and solely consist in a collection of such "loose and separate" experiences must be rated as, strictly, nonsense.

Hume himself never seems to have realised that and why this suggestion cannot do. But he did soon see, and confessed in the Appendix, that there is no available string, no uniting principle, to bind any such collection together and to distinguish it from any other. The obvious candidate might seem to be memory, as Locke had suggested earlier in his *Essay* (II (xxvii)). For, surely, we are inclined to think, the person himself must always be able—if only he would tell us, and would tell us true—to say whether it was in fact he or another who had the thought or did the deed. But this, as we shall see in Chapter Ten, will not work.

Expressed in modern terms, there is no possibility of giving an account of the self-identity and individuation of incorporeal collections of experiences in terms of their memory capacities. Certainly if I truly remember, and do not merely seem to remember, doing the deed, then necessarily I must be the same person as did that deed: true memory thus presupposes true personal identity. But what I remember is that I am the same person

as did the deed. That I do so remember is not, and cannot be, itself what it is for me to be the same person as did it.

So what about the Cartesian alternative? Can we accept that an incorporeal person would be the incorporeal substance which enjoyed or suffered certain experiences, and was endowed with certain capacities? The principle of individuation would then be a matter of being, or belonging to, one such substance rather than to another; and the principle of self-identity would be a matter of being, or belonging to, the same such substance.

But now, before we discuss the qualifications of this candidate, can we be told who (or what) he (or it) is? For when we were dealing with regular or conventional (corporeal) persons, there was no difficulty in saying—indeed, in showing—what was the substance to which we were attributing the experiences, the dispositions, etc.: they were the experiences, the dispositions, or whatever, of a flesh and blood person. But what positive characterisation can we give to these postulated incorporeal substances? Can we say anything to differentiate such an incorporeal substance from an imaginary, an unreal, a non-existent substance?: "Beyond the wholly empty assurance that it is a metaphysical principle which guarantees continuing identity through time, or the argument that since we know that identity persists some such principle must hold in default of others, no content seems available for the doctrine. Its irrelevance . . . is due to its being merely an alleged identity-guaranteeing condition of which no independent characterisation is forthcoming" (Penelhum, p. 76).

6. Difficulties in the Way of the Astral Body

The great, and in my view insuperable, difficulties of the Platonic way, the assumptions of which have so often been taken for granted or even asserted as known facts, should now lead us to look with a new interest and respect at the way of the astral body.

In the context of this more sympathetic approach, it begins to emerge that many of those who have been thought of as—and who probably thought themselves—Platonic-Cartesians have really been believers in astral bodies. There is, for instance, some reason to think that the Latin Father Tertullian, who certainly held the soul to be corporeal, was also inclined to think of it as of human shape; and what is this but an astral body? See Chapter IX of his *de Anima,* in which he cites the visions of the good sister who saw "a soul in bodily shape . . . in form resembling that of a human being in every respect." Tertullian then goes on to argue that such an object must have a colour, which could be no other than an "ethereal transparent one."

Since we come to examine this notion of an astral body so soon after deploying the objection to the candidate notion of incorporeal spiritual substance, it will be easy to see what the problem for the protagonist is going to be. It is, obviously, to find some positive characterisation for an astral body: such that an astral body really would be a sort of body in a way in which an imaginary body, or a non existent body, or an incorporeal body are not sorts of body; and at the same time such that the hypothesis that we have, or are, astral bodies is not shown to be false by any presently available facts. Confronted by this problem, the danger for the protagonist of an astral body view is that in his concern to avoid immediate falsification by presently known facts he may so qualify the nature of the body which he wants to hypothesize that it becomes in effect not a body, albeit elusive, but instead an incorporeal Platonic-Cartesian soul: "A fine brash hypothesis may thus be killed by inches, the death by a thousand qualifications."

In principle these dangers could, I think, be escaped fairly easily. We should need only to postulate the detectability of astral bodies by an instrument of a kind not yet invented. But such an utterly arbitrary postulation would invite the comment made by Bertrand Russell in another connection: "The method of 'postulating' what we want has many advantages; they are the same as the advantages of theft over honest toil" (Russell (2),

p. 21). Such a drastic postulation would be warranted only if we thought—or think—that the survival evidence cannot be interpreted in terms of various ESP ongoings among ordinary corporeal people, and if we also believe—as I have been arguing that we should—that the Platonic-Cartesian way will not go. It would also be much encouraged if evidence for levitating, apporting, and generally rip-roaring physical mediumship were better than it is.

7. Tentative Conclusions on the Substantive Question

Certainly I cannot myself recommend the reckless postulation which would be required in order to proceed along the way of the astral body. For I remain persuaded by the sort of considerations deployed so long ago by Professor E. R. Dodds in his 'Why I do not believe in survival', in the *Proceedings of the Society for Psychical Research* for 1934. The crux of this landmark paper, which ought to be reprinted in some more accessible and more widely circulating form, is that the so-called survival evidence can be adequately, and therefore better interpreted in terms of more or less elaborate and unconscious normal and paranormal transactions among the living—without postulating any surviving entities at all. Substantially the same conclusion was reached by Murphy in the paper mentioned in Section 5 (ii). If, however, I were to take the opposite view to that of Dodds and Murphy on this issue, as many do, then I should have to postulate some sort of astral body; and that notwithstanding the rather formidable difficulties indicated in the previous Section 6. For these difficulties, unlike those of the supposed hypothesis of disembodied survival, do not necessarily reduce the proposed postulate to incoherence. My conclusion is, therefore, that if there is to be a case for individual and personal survival, what survives must be some sort of astral body; but that, in the present state of the evidence, we have no need of that hypothesis.

VI.6 Personal Identity and Life after Death

J E F F R E Y   O L E N

Jeffrey Olen, who teaches philosophy at the University of Wisconsin at Stevens Point, discusses the criteria of personal identity in order to determine what would have to survive our death if we were to be able to say that it is truly we who survive. Through some intriguing thought experiments Olen builds a case for the possibility of survival. Olen has a functionalist view of personhood, believing that "the human brain is analogous to a computer." In this view, a given brain state is also a given mental state because it performs the appropriate function in the appropriate "program." That is, the human brain embodies certain abstract descriptions. Olen argues that just as different computers can process the same information, so we could survive after death in another body as long as our personalities and memories were preserved intact.

It is Sunday night. After a long night of hard drinking, John Badger puts on his pajamas, lowers the heat in his Wisconsin home to fifty-five degrees and climbs into bed beneath two heavy blankets. Meanwhile, in Florida, Joe Everglade kisses his wife goodnight and goes to sleep.

The next morning, two very confused men wake up. One wakes up in Wisconsin, wondering where he is and why he is wearing pajamas, lying under two heavy blankets, yet shivering from the cold. He looks out the window and sees nothing but pine trees and snow. The room is totally unfamiliar. Where is his wife? How did he get to this cold, strange place? Why does he have such a terrible hangover? He tries to spring out of bed with his usual verve but feels an unaccustomed aching in his joints. Arthritis? He wanders unsurely through the house until he finds the bath-

room. What he sees in the mirror causes him to spin around in sudden fear. But there is nobody behind him. Then the fear intensifies as he realizes that it was his reflection that had stared back at him. But it was the reflection of a man thirty years older than himself, with coarser features and a weather-beaten face.

In Florida, a man awakens with a young woman's arm around him. When she too awakens, she snuggles against him and wishes him good morning. "Who are you?" he asks. "What am I doing in your bed?" She just laughs, then tells him that he will have to hurry if he is going to get in his ten miles of jogging. From the bathroom she asks him about his coming day. None of the names or places she mentions connect with anything he can remember. He climbs out of bed, marveling at the ease with which he does so, and looks first out the window and then into the mirror over the dresser. The sun and swimming pool confound him. The handsome young man's reflection terrifies him.

Then the phone rings. The woman answers it. It is the man from Wisconsin. "What happened last night, Mary? How did I get here? How did I get to look this way?"

"Who is this?" she asks.

"Don't you recognize my voice, Mary?" But he knew that the voice was not his own. "It's Joe."

"Joe who?"

"Your husband."

She hangs up, believing it to be a crank call. When she returns to the bedroom, the man in her husband's robe asks how he got there from Wisconsin, and why he looks as he does.

Personal Identity

What happened in the above story? Who woke up in Joe Everglade's bed? Who woke up in John Badger's? Which one is Mary's husband? Has

Badger awakened with Everglade's memories and Everglade with Badger's? Or have Badger and Everglade somehow switched bodies? How are we to decide? What considerations are relevant?

To ask such questions is to raise the problem of *personal identity.* It is to ask what makes a person the same person he was the day before. It is to ask how we determine that we are dealing with the same person that we have dealt with in the past. It is to ask what constitutes personal identity over time. It is also to ask what we mean by the *same person.* And to answer this question, we must ask what we mean by the word "person."

Persons

In the previous chapter, we asked what a human being is. We asked what human beings are made of, what the nature of the human mind is, and whether human beings are part of nature or distinct from it.

To ask what a *person* is, however, is to ask a different question. Although we often use the terms "person" and "human being" interchangeably, they do not mean the same thing. If we do use them interchangeably, it is only because all the persons we know of are human beings, and because, as far as we know, whenever we are confronted with the same human being we are confronted with the same person.

But the notion of a human being is a *biological* notion. To identify something as a human being is to identify it as a member of *Homo sapiens,* a particular species of animal. It is a type of organism defined by certain physical characteristics.

The notion of a person, on the other hand, is *not* a biological one. Suppose, for instance, that we find life on another planet, and that this life is remarkably like our own. The creatures we discover communicate through a language as rich as our own, act according to moral principles, have a legal system, and engage in science and art. Suppose also that despite these cultural similarities, this form of life is biologically different from human life. In that case, these creatures would be persons, but not humans. Think, for example, of the alien in *E.T.* Since he is biologically different

from us, he is not human. He is, however, a person.

What, then, is a person? Although philosophers diagree on this point, the following features are relatively noncontroversial.

First, a person is an intelligent, rational creature. Second, it is a creature capable of a peculiar sort of consciousness—self-consciousness. Third, it not only has beliefs, desires, and so forth, but it has beliefs *about* its beliefs, desires, and so forth. Fourth, it is a creature to which we ascribe moral responsibility. Persons are responsible for their actions in a way that other things are not. They are subject to moral praise and moral blame. Fifth, a person is a creature that we treat in certain ways. To treat something as a person is to treat it as a member of our own moral community. It is to grant it certain rights, both moral and legal. Sixth, a person is a creature capable of reciprocity. It is capable of treating us as members of the same moral community. Finally, a person is capable of verbal communication. It can communicate by means of a *language,* not just by barks, howls, and tail-wagging.

Since, as far as we know, only human beings meet the above conditions, only human beings are considered to be persons. But once we recognize that to be a person is not precisely the same thing that it is to be a human being, we also recognize that other creatures, such as the alien in *E.T.* is also a person. We also recognize that perhaps not all human beings are persons—human fetuses, for example, as some have argued. Certainly, in the American South before the end of the Civil War, slaves were not considered to be persons. We might also mention a remark of D'Artagnan, in Richard Lester's film version of *The Three Musketeers.* Posing as a French nobleman, he attempted to cross the English Channel with a companion. When a French official remarked that his pass was only for one person, D'Artagnan replied that he was only one person—his companion was a servant.

Moreover, once we recognize the distinction between human beings and persons, certain questions arise. Can one human being embody more than one person, either at the same time or successive times? In the example we introduced at the beginning of this chapter, has Badger's body become Everglade's and Everglade's Badger's? Can the person survive the death of the human being? Is there personal survival after the death of the body?

Concerning identity through time in general, two issues must be distinguished. First, we want to know how we can *tell* that something is the same thing we encountered previously. That is, we want to know what the *criteria* are for establishing identity through time. Second, we want to know what *makes* something the same thing it was previously. That is, we want to know what *constitutes* identity through time.

Although these issues are related, they are not the same, as the following example illustrates. We can *tell* that someone has a case of the flu by checking for certain symptoms, such as fever, lack of energy, and sore muscles. But having these symptoms does not *constitute* having a case of the flu. It is the presence of a flu virus—not the symptoms—that makes an illness a case of the flu.

We commonly use two criteria for establishing personal identity. The first is the *bodily criterion,* the second the *memory criterion.* How do we apply them?

We apply the bodily criterion in two ways. First, we go by physical resemblance. If I meet someone on the street who looks, walks, and sounds just like Mary, I assume that it is Mary. Since the body I see resembles Mary's body exactly, I assume that the person I see is Mary. But that method can sometimes fail us, as in the case of identical twins. In such cases, we can apply the bodily criterion in another way. If I can discover that there is a continuous line from one place and time to another that connects Mary's body to the body I now see, I can assume that I now see Mary. Suppose, for example, that Mary and I went to the beach together, and have been together all afternoon. In that case, I can say that the person I am now with is the person I began the day with.

There are, however, times when the bodily criterion is not available. If Mary and Jane are identical twins, and I run across one of them on the street, I may have to ask who it is. That is, I

may have to rely on Mary's memory of who she is. And, if I want to make sure that I am not being fooled, I may ask a few questions. If Mary remembers things that I believe only Mary can remember, and if she remembers them as happening to *her,* and not to somebody else, then I can safely say that it really is Mary.

Generally, the bodily criterion and the memory criterion do not conflict, so we use whichever is more convenient. But what happens if they do conflict? That is what happened in our imagined story. According to the bodily criterion, each person awoke in his own bed, but with the memories of someone else. According to the memory criterion, each person awoke in the other's bed with the body of someone else. Which criterion should we take as decisive? Which is fundamental, the memory criterion or the bodily criterion?

The Constitution of Personal Identity

To ask the above questions is to ask what *constitutes* personal identity. What is it that makes me the same person I was yesterday? What makes the author of this book the same person as the baby born to Sam and Belle Olen in 1946? Answers to these questions will allow us to say which criterion is fundamental.

Perhaps the most widely discussed answer to our question comes from John Locke (1632–1704), whose discussion of the topic set the stage for all future discussions. According to Locke, the bodily criterion cannot be fundamental. Since the concept of a person is most importantly the concept of a conscious being who can be held morally and legally responsible for past actions, it is *continuity of consciousness* that constitutes personal identity. The bodily criterion is fundamental for establishing sameness of *animal,* but not sameness of *person.*

Suppose, for instance, that John Badger had been a professional thief. If the person who awoke in Badger's bed could never remember any of Badger's life as his own, but had only Everglade's memories and personality traits, while the man who awoke in Everglade's bed remembered all of

Badger's crimes as his own, would we be justified in jailing the man who awoke in Badger's bed while letting the man who awoke in Everglade's go free? Locke would say no. The person who awoke in Badger's bed was not Badger.

If we agree that it is sameness of consciousness that constitutes personal identity, we must then ask what constitutes sameness of consciousness. Some philosophers have felt that it is sameness of *mind,* where the mind is thought of as a continuing nonphysical substance. Although Locke did not deny that minds are nonphysical, he did not believe that sameness of nonphysical substance is the same thing as sameness of consciousness. If we can conceive of persons switching *physical* bodies, we can also conceive of persons switching *non*physical ones.

Then what does Locke take to be crucial for personal identity? *Memory.* It is my memory of the events of Jeffrey Olen's life as happening to *me* that makes me the person those events happened to. It is my memory of his experiences as *mine* that makes them mine.

Although Locke's answer seems at first glance a reasonable one, many philosophers have considered it inadequate. One reason for rejecting Locke's answer is that we don't remember everything that happened to us. If I don't remember anything that happened to me during a certain period, does that mean that whoever existed "in" my body then was not me? Hardly.

Another reason for rejecting Locke's answer is that memory is not always accurate. We often sincerely claim to remember things that never happened. There is a difference, then, between *genuine* memory and *apparent* memory. What marks this difference is the *truth* of the memory claim. If what I claim to remember is not true, it cannot be a case of genuine memory.

But that means that memory cannot constitute personal identity. If I claim to remember certain experiences as being my experiences, that does not make them mine, because my claim may be a case of apparent memory. If it is a case of genuine memory, that is because it is true that the remembered experiences are mine. But the memory does

not *make* them mine. Rather, the fact that they *are* mine makes it a case of genuine memory. So Locke has the situation backward. But if memory does not constitute personal identity, what does?

Some philosophers have claimed that, regardless of Locke's views, it *must* be sameness of mind, where the mind is thought of as a continuing nonphysical entity. This entity can be thought of as the self. It is what makes us who we are. As long as the same self continues to exist, the same person continues to exist. The major problem with this answer is that it assumes the truth of mind-body dualism, a position we found good reason to reject in the previous chapter. But apart from that, there is another problem.

In one of the most famous passages in the history of philosophy, David Hume (1711–1776) argued that there is no such self—for reasons that have nothing to do with the rejection of dualism. No matter how hard we try, Hume said, we cannot discover such a self. Turning inward and examining our own consciousness, we find only individual experiences—thoughts, recollections, images, and the like. Try as we might, we cannot find a continuing self. In that case, we are justified in believing only that there are *experiences*—not that there is a continuing *experiencer.* Put another way, we have no reason to believe that there is anything persisting through time that underlies or unifies these experiences. There are just the experiences themselves.

But if we accept this view, and still require a continuing nonphysical entity for personal identity, we are forced to the conclusion that there is no such thing as personal identity. We are left, that is, with the position that the idea of a person existing through time is a mere fiction, however useful in daily life. And that is the position that Hume took. Instead of persons, he said, there are merely "bundles of ideas."

Thus, the view that personal identity requires sameness of mind can easily lead to the view that there is no personal identity. Since this conclusion seems manifestly false, we shall have to look elsewhere? But where?

The Primacy of the Bodily Criterion

If neither memory nor sameness of mind constitutes personal identity, perhaps we should accept the view that sameness of *body* does. Perhaps it is really the bodily criterion that is fundamental.

If we reflect on the problem faced by Locke's theory because of the distinction between genuine and apparent memory, it is tempting to accept the primacy of the bodily criterion. Once again, a sincere memory claim may be either genuine memory or apparent memory. How can we tell whether the claim that a previous experience was mine is genuine memory? By determining whether I was in the right place in the right time to have it. And how can we determine that? By the bodily criterion. If my *body* was there, then *I* was there. But that means that the memory criterion must rest on the bodily criterion. Also, accepting the primacy of the bodily criterion gets us around Hume's problem. The self that persists through and has the experiences I call mine is my physical body.

This answer also has the advantage of being in keeping with materialism, a view accepted in the previous chapter. If human beings are purely physical, then persons must also be purely physical, whatever differences there may be between the notion of a person and the notion of a human being. But if persons are purely physical, what makes me the same person I was yesterday is no different in kind from what makes my typewriter the same typewriter it was yesterday. In both cases, we are dealing with a physical object existing through time. In the latter case, as long as we have the same physical materials (allowing for change of ribbon, change of keys, and the like) arranged in the same way, we have the same typewriter. So it is with persons. As long as we have the same physical materials (allowing for such changes as the replacement of cells) arranged in the same way, we have the same person.

Although this answer is a tempting one, it is not entirely satisfactory. Suppose that we could manage a brain transplant from one body to another. If we switched two brains, so that all the memories and personality traits of the persons involved were also switched, wouldn't we conclude that the persons, as well as their brains, had switched bodies? When such operations are performed in science-fiction stories, they are described this way.

But this possibility does not defeat the view that the bodily criterion is fundamental. It just forces us to hold that the bodily criterion must be applied to the brain, rather than the entire body. Personal identity then becomes a matter of brain identity. Same brain, same person. Unfortunately, even with this change, our answer does not seem satisfactory. Locke still seems somehow right. Let us see why.

Badger and Everglade Reconsidered

Returning to our tale of Badger and Everglade, we find that some troubling questions remain. If Mrs. Everglade continues to live with the man who awoke in her bed, might she not be committing adultery? Shouldn't she take in the man who awoke in Badger's bed? And, once again assuming that Badger was a professional thief, would justice really be served by jailing the man who awoke in his bed? However we answer these questions, one thing is certain—the two men would always feel that they had switched bodies. So, probably, would the people who knew them. Furthermore, whenever we read science-fiction stories describing such matters, we invariably accept them as stories of switched bodies. But if we accept the bodily criterion as fundamental, we are accepting the impossible, and the two men in our story, Mrs. Everglade, and their friends are mistaken in their beliefs. How, then, are we to answer our questions?

If we are unsure, it is because such questions become very tricky at this point. Their trickiness seems to rest on two points. First, cases like the Badger-Everglade case do not happen in this world. Although we are prepared to accept them in science-fiction tales, we are totally unprepared to deal with them in real life.

Second, and this is a related point, we need

some way of *explaining* such extraordinary occurrences. Unless we know how the memories of Badger and Everglade came to be reversed, we will be unable to decide the answers to our questions. In the movies, it is assumed that some nonphysical substance travels from one body to another, or that there has been a brain transplant of some sort. On these assumptions, we are of course willing to describe what happens as a change of body. This description seems to follow naturally from such explanations.

What explains what happened to Badger and Everglade? We can rule out change of nonphysical substance, because of what was said in the previous chapter and earlier in this chapter. If we explain what happened as the product of a brain switch, then the bodily criterion applied to the brain allows us to say that Badger and Everglade did awaken in each other's bed, and that Mrs. Everglade would be committing adultery should she live with the man who awoke in her bed.

Are there any other possible explanations? One that comes readily to mind is hypnotism. Suppose, then, that someone had hypnotized Badger and Everglade into believing that each was the other person. In that case, we should not say that there had been a body switch. Badger and Everglade awoke in their own beds, and a wave of the hypnotist's hand could demonstrate that to everyone concerned. Their memory claims are not genuine memories, but apparent ones.

But suppose it was not a case of hypnotism? What then? At this point, many people are stumped. What else could it be? The strong temptation is to say nothing. Without a brain transplant or hypnotism or something of the sort, the case is impossible.

Suppose that we accept this conclusion. If we do, we may say the following: The memory criterion and the bodily criterion cannot really conflict. If the memories are genuine, and not apparent, then whenever I remember certain experiences as being mine, it is possible to establish that the same brain is involved in the original experiences and the memory of them. Consequently, the memory criterion and the bodily criterion are equally fundamental. The memory criterion is fundamental in

the sense that consciousness determines what part of the body is central to personal identity. Because sameness of consciousness requires sameness of brain, we ultimately must apply the bodily criterion to the brain. But the bodily criterion is also fundamental, because we assume that some physical object—the brain—must remain the same if the person is to remain the same.

Multiple Personality

In recent years there have been two well-known books, both made into films, each about a woman having several radically distinct personalities—*The Three Faces of Eve* and *Sybil*. Based on actual cases, the books give detailed and fascinating accounts of the lives of the two women.

Each personality had its own memories, its own values, its own behavior patterns, even its own name. At any given time, Eve or Sybil would assume one of these personalities. Whatever happened to her during that time would be remembered as happening only to that personality. When Eve or Sybil assumed another personality, she would either claim not to know of these experiences or claim that they had happened to someone else. The other personalities were thought of and spoken of in the third person.

Unlike science fiction and fantasy cases, the multiple-personality phenomenon is something that happens in the real world. What are we to say about it? On the one hand, we are tempted to say that each woman embodied several persons. Very often their psychiatrists spoke as though that were true. On the other hand, there is an equally strong temptation to say that each woman embodied only one person, somehow split into different personalities. Thus, we sometimes call such cases instances of *split* personality, rather than of *multiple* personality.

The first temptation is due to the fact that each woman seems to embody several distinct streams of consciousness. That is, we are led to view each woman as consisting of several persons by the *memory criterion*. The second temptation is due to the fact that each woman has only one body. That is, we are led to view each woman as one person by the *bodily criterion*. Which criterion should we accept? If there is one body but several streams of consciousness, how many persons are there? When discussing the Badger-Everglade case, we said that our answer must depend on our explanation of what happened. I think that the same thing holds for the Eve and Sybil cases.

How are such cases explained? At present, they are generally given psychoanalytic explanations. A typical psychoanalytic explanation might go like this. All of us have various aspects to our personalities. Sometimes we are forced to repress some of these aspects for one reason or another. Perhaps one of them arouses deep feelings of guilt in us; perhaps we feel we must repress it to win the love of our parents. If the repressed aspect is strong enough, and if we are unwilling to recognize it as being ours, it can cause an inner conflict resulting in a case of split or multiple personality.

This type of explanation seems to require that there is one person managing the various aspects of his or her personality. It makes the phenomenon of multiple personality seem like a strategy unconsciously adopted by *one* person to resolve inner conflict. Thus, if we accept this type of explanation, it seems that we should accept the view that the phenomenon involves one badly fractured person, rather than several persons ''in'' one body. So when dealing with Eve and Sybil, we should rely on the bodily criterion, not the memory criterion.

The Memory Criterion Revisited

Although the answer given above is a tidy one, it may still seem unsatisfactory. Perhaps it is a cheap trick just to dismiss the Badger-Everglade case as mere fantasy and then ignore it. After all, if we can meaningfully describe such cases in books and films, don't we have to pay some attention to them? As long as we can imagine situations in which two persons can switch bodies without a brain transplant, don't we need a theory of personal identity to cover them?

Philosophers are divided on this point. Some

think that a theory of personal identity has to account only for what can happen in this world, while others think it must account for whatever can happen in any conceivable world. Then again, some do not believe that there is any conceivable world in which two persons could change bodies without a brain switch, while there are others who are not sure that such things are impossible in the actual world.

Without trying to decide the matter, I can make the following suggestion for those who demand a theory of personal identity that does not rely on the assumption that genuine memory is tied to a particular brain.

In the previous chapter, I concluded that functionalism is the theory of mind most likely to be true. To have a mind, I said, is to embody a psychology. I also said that we don't merely move our bodies, but write poetry, caress the cheek of someone we love, and perform all sorts of human actions. I might have expressed this point by saying that we are not just human beings, but persons as well. What makes a human being a person? We are persons because we embody a psychology.

If that is true, then it may also be true that we are the persons we are because of the psychologies we embody. If it is a psychology that makes a human being a person, then it is a particular psychology that makes a particular human being a particular person. Sameness of psychology constitutes sameness of person. In that case, we can agree with this much of Locke's theory—it is continuity of consciousness that constitutes personal identity. But what is continuity of consciousness, if not memory?

An answer to this question is provided by the contemporary British philosopher Anthony Quinton. At any moment, we can isolate a number of mental states belonging to the same momentary consciousness. Right now, for instance, I am simultaneously aware of the sound and sight and feel of my typewriter, plus the feel and taste of my pipe, plus a variety of other things. Such *momentary* consciousnesses belong to a continuous *series*. Each one is linked to the one before it and the one following it by certain similarities and recollections. This series is my own *continuity* of consciousness, my own *stream* of consciousness. It is this stream of consciousness that makes me the same person I was yesterday.

If we accept Quinton's theory, we can then say that the memory criterion, not the bodily criterion, is fundamental. We can also say that, even if in this world continuity of consciousness requires sameness of brain, we can conceive of worlds in which it does not. To show this, let us offer another possible explanation of the Badger-Everglade situation.

Suppose a mad computer scientist has discovered a way to reprogram human beings. Suppose that he has found a way to make us the embodiment of any psychology he likes. Suppose further that he decided to experiment on Badger and Everglade, giving Badger Everglade's psychology and Everglade Badger's and that is why the events of our story occurred. With this explanation and the considerations of the previous paragraphs, we can conclude that Badger and Everglade did change bodies. By performing his experiment, the mad scientist has made it possible for a continuing stream of consciousness to pass from one body to another. He has, in effect, performed a body transplant. . . .

Should we accept Quinton's theory? There seems to be no good reason not to. In fact, there are at least two good reasons for accepting it. First, it seems consistent with a functionalist theory of the mind. Second, it allows us to make sense of science-fiction stories while we continue to believe that in the real world to be the same person we were yesterday is to have the same brain.

Life After Death

Is it possible for the person to survive the death of the body? Is there a sense in which *we* can continue to live after our bodies have died? Can there be a personal life after death?

According to one popular conception of life after death, at the death of the body the soul leaves the body and travels to a realm known as heaven. Of course, this story must be taken as metaphori-

cal. Does the soul literally leave the body? How? Out of the mouth? Ears? And how does it get to heaven? By turning left at Mars? Moreover, if the soul remains disembodied, how can it perceive anything? What does it use as sense organs? And if all souls remain disembodied, how can one soul recognize another? What is there to recognize?

As these questions might suggest, much of this popular story trades on a confusion. The soul is thought of as a translucent physical substance, much like Casper the ghost, through which other objects can pass as they do through air or water. But if the soul is *really* nonphysical, it can be nothing like that.

If this story is not to be taken literally, is there some version of it that we can admit as a possibility? Is there also the possibility of personal survival through reincarnation as it is often understood—the re-embodiment of the person without memory of the former embodiment?

Materialism and the Disembodied Soul

So far, we have considered both the mind and the body as they relate to personal identity. Have we neglected the soul? It may seem that we have, but philosophers who discuss the mind-body question and personal identity generally use the terms "mind" and "soul" interchangeably. Is the practice legitimate, or is it a confusion?

The practice seems to be thoroughly legitimate. If the soul is thought to be the crucial element of the person, it is difficult to see how it could be anything but the mind. If it is our character traits, personality, thoughts, likes and dislikes, memories, and continuity of experience that makes us the persons we are, then they must belong to the soul. If they are taken to be crucial for one's personal identity, then it seems impossible to separate them from one's soul.

Moreover, people who accept some version of the popular conception of life after death noted above believe in certain continuities between earthly experiences and heavenly ones. In heaven, it is believed, we remember our earthly lives, we recognize friends and relatives, our personalities are like our earthly personalities, and we are judged by God for our actions on earth. But if we believe any of this, we must also believe that the soul cannot be separated from the mind.

If that is the case, it is difficult to accept the continued existence of a disembodied soul. Once we accept some form of materialism, we seem compelled to believe that the soul must be embodied. Does that rule out the possibility of any version of the popular story being true?

Some philosophers think that it does. Suppose, for instance, that the mind-brain identity theory is true. In that case, when the brain dies, so does the mind. Since the mind is the repository of memory and personality traits, it is identical with the soul. So when the brain dies, so does the soul.

This is a powerful argument, and it has convinced a number of people. On the other hand, it has also kept a number of people from accepting materialism of any sort. If it is felt that materialism and life after death are incompatible, and if one is firmly committed to the belief in life after death, then it is natural for one to reject materialism.

Is there a way of reconciling materialism and life after death? I think so.

Although it seems necessary that persons must be embodied, it does not seem necessary that the same person must be embodied by the same body. In our discussion of personal identity, we allowed that Badger and Everglade might have changed bodies, depending on our explanation of the story. Let us try a similar story.

Mary Brown is old and sick. She knows she will die within a couple of weeks. One morning she does die. At the same time, in some other world, a woman wakes up believing herself to be Mary. She looks around to find herself in a totally unfamiliar place. Someone is sitting next to her. This other woman looks exactly like Mary's mother, who died years earlier, and believes herself to be Mary's mother. Certainly, she knows everything about Mary that Mary's mother would know.

Before the woman believing herself to be Mary can speak, she notices some surprising things about herself. She no longer feels old or sick. Her pains are gone, and her mind is as sharp as ever. When she asks where she is, she is told heaven.

She is also told that her husband, father, and numerous old friends are waiting to see her. All of them are indistinguishable from the persons they claim to be. Meanwhile, back on earth, Mary Brown is pronounced dead. Is this woman in "heaven" really Mary Brown? How could we possibly explain the phenomenon?

Suppose we put the story in a religious context. Earlier, we saw that one possible explanation of the Badger-Everglade case is that some mad computer scientist had reprogrammed the two so that each embodied the psychology of the other. Suppose we replace the mad scientist with God, and say that God had kept a body in heaven for the purpose of embodying Mary's psychology when she died, and that the person believing herself to be Mary is the new embodiment of Mary's psychology. Would this count as a genuine case of life after death?

If we accept the Badger-Everglade story, appropriately explained, as a case of two persons switching bodies, there seems no reason to deny that Mary has continued to live "in" another body. But even if we are unsure of the Badger-Everglade case, we can approach Mary Brown's this way. What is it that we want to survive after death? Isn't it our memories, our consciousness of self, our personalities, our relations with others? What does it matter whether there is some nonphysical substance that survives? If that substance has no memories of a prior life, does not recognize the soul of others who were important in that earlier life, what comfort could such a continuing existence bring? In what sense would it be the survival of the *person*? How would it be significantly different from the return of the lifeless body to the soil?

If we assume that our story is a genuine case of personal survival of the death of the body, we may wonder about another point. Is it compatible with Christian belief? According to John Hick, a contemporary British philosopher who imagined a similar story, the answer is yes. In I Corinthians 15, Paul writes of the resurrection of the body—not of the physical body, but of some spiritual body. Although one *can* think of this spiritual body as a translucent ghost-like body that leaves the physical body at death, Hick offers another interpretation.

The human being, Hick says, becomes extinct at death. It is only through God's intervention that the spiritual body comes into existence. By the resurrection of this spiritual body, we are to understand a *recreation* or *reconstitution* of the person's body in heaven. But that is precisely what happened in our story.

Thus, a materialist view of the nature of human beings is not incompatible with the Christian view of life after death. Nor, for that matter, is it incompatible with the belief that the spiritual body is nonphysical. If we can make sense of the claim that there might be such things as nonphysical bodies, then there is no reason why a nonphysical body could not embody a psychology. Remember—according to functionalism, an abstract description such as a psychology is independent of any physical description. Just as we can play chess using almost anything as chess pieces, so can a psychology be embodied by almost anything, assuming that it is complex enough. So if there can be nonphysical bodies, there can be nonphysical persons. Of course, nothing said so far assures us that the Christian story—or any other story of life after death—is true. That is another matter, to be considered in Part VII.

Reincarnation

Much of what has been said so far does, however, rule out the possibility of reincarnation as commonly understood. If human beings are purely physical, then there is no nonphysical substance that is the person that can be reincarnated in another earthly body. Moreover, even if there were such a substance, it is difficult to see how its continued existence in another body could count as the reincarnation of a particular person, *if* there is no other continuity between the old life and the new one. Once again, personal survival requires some continuity of consciousness. It is not sameness of *stuff* that constitutes personal identity, but sameness of consciousness. This requirement is often overlooked by believers in reincarnation.

But suppose that there is some continuity of consciousness in reincarnation. Suppose that memories and the rest do continue in the next incarnation, but that they are not easily accessible. Suppose, that is, that the slate is not wiped completely clean, but that what is written on it is hard to recover. In that case, the passage of the soul into a new incarnation would count as personal survival *if* there were such a soul to begin with.

Assuming, again, that there is not, what can we say about the possibility of reincarnation? To conceive of such a possibility, we must conceive of some very complicated reprogramming by God or some mad scientist or whatever. I shall leave it to you to come up with such a story, but I shall say this much. There does not seem to be any good reason to think that any such story is remotely plausible, least of all true.

The Final Word?

In this chapter we looked at two closely related questions: What constitutes personal identity? And is it possible for a person to survive the death of her own body?

The answer to the second question depended on the first. If we had concluded that the basis of personal identity is sameness of body, then we would have been forced to conclude that life after death is impossible. And there did seem to be good reason to come to these conclusions. How, we asked, could we assure that any memory claim is a case of genuine memory? Our answer was this. In the cases likely to confront us in our daily lives, we must establish some physical continuity between the person who had the original experience and the person who claims to remember it.

But the problem with this answer is that it is too limited. Because we can imagine cases like the Everglade-Badger example, and because our science-fiction tales and religious traditions offer stories of personal continuity without bodily continuity, we can say the following. Regardless of what happens in our daily lives, our concept of a person is a concept of something that does not seem tied to a particular body. Rather, our concept of a person seems to be tied to a particular stream of consciousness. If there is one continuing stream of consciousness over time, then there is one continuing person. Our question, then, was whether we can give a coherent account of continuity of consciousness from one body to another.

The answer was yes. Using the computer anal-ogy of the functionalist, we can explain such continuity in terms of programming. If it is possible to "program" another brain to have the same psychology as the brain I now have, then it is possible for me to change bodies. And if it is possible for me to change bodies, then it is also possible for me to survive the death of my body.

Bibliography for Part VI

Ducasse, Curt John. *A Critical Examination of the Belief in Life after Death.* Springfield, Ill.: Thomas, 1961. One of the most comprehensive defenses of the Platonic-Cartesian view of immortality.

Geach, Peter. *God and the Soul.* London: Routledge & Kegan Paul, 1969. An examination of the concept of the soul.

Flew, Antony. "Immortality." In *Encyclopedia of Philosophy,* edited by Paul Edwards. New York: Free Press, 1965. A helpful survey of the history of the notion of immortality and the arguments connected with it.

Lamont, Corliss. *The Illusion of Immortality.* New York: The Philosophical Library, 1965. A strong attack on several arguments for immortality.

Penelhum, Terrence. *Survival and Disembodied Existence.* London: Routledge & Kegan Paul, 1970. A fine-tuned examination of the key concepts and arguments associated with both the Platonic and the reconstitution views of survival.

Perry, John. *Personal Identity and Immortality.* Indianapolis: Hackett, 1979. An excellent dialogue on the subject.

Purtill, Richard. *Thinking about Religion.* Chaps. 9 and 10. Englewood Cliffs, N.J.: Prentice-Hall, 1978. A fascinating defense of the Christian notion of life after death.

Quinton, Anthony. "The Soul." *Journal of Philosophy* 59 (1962): 393–409. A good survey and analysis of concepts and arguments associated with the notion of the soul.

FAITH AND REASON

One of the most important issues in the philosophy of religion is the relationship of faith to reason. Is religious belief rational? Or is faith essentially an irrational activity, or, at least, an arational one? If we cannot prove the claims of religious belief, is it nevertheless reasonable to believe these claims? For example, even if we do not have a deductive proof for the existence of God, is it nevertheless reasonable to believe that God exists? In the debate over faith and reason two opposing positions have dominated the field. The first position asserts that faith and reason are commensurable (i.e., it is rational to believe in God). The second position denies this assertion. Those holding to the first position differ among themselves over the extent of the compatibility between faith and reason. Most adherents follow Thomas Aquinas in relegating the compatibility to the 'preambles of faith' (e.g., concerning the existence of God and his nature) over against the 'articles of faith' (e.g., the doctrine of the incarnation). Few have gone as far as Immanuel Kant, who maintained complete harmony between reason and faith, that is, religious belief within the realm of reason alone.

The second position divides into two subpositions. One asserts that faith is opposed to reason and belongs in the area of irrationality (those who hold to this belief include such unlikely bedfellows as David Hume and Søren Kierkegaard). The second asserts that faith is higher than reason, is transrational. John Calvin and Karl Barth assert that a natural theology is inappropriate because it seeks to meet unbelief on its own ground (ordinary, finite reason). Revelation, however, is "self-authenticating," "carrying with it its own evidence." We may call this position the 'transrational' view of faith. Faith is not against reason but above and beyond it in its own proper domain. Actually, Kierkegaard shows that the two subpositions are compatible, for he holds that faith is both above reason (superior to it) and against reason (because human reason has been affected by sin). The irrationalist and transrationalist positions are sometimes hard to separate in the incommensurabilist's argument. Faith gets such a high value that reason seems to end up looking not simply inadequate but culpable. To use reason where faith claims the field is not only inappropriate but irreverent and faithless.

The readings in this part of our work exemplify the positions that we have just described. The part is divided into four sections. The first section simply introduces some of the main problems in the debate. Sections B through D are more elaborate discussions of issues central to the debate. Section B deals with pragmatic arguments for religious belief. The question asked here is, Is it sometimes morally permissible purposefully to get one-self to believe what the evidence alone doesn't warrant? Section C deals with the issue of fideism, that is, whether religious belief is a separate form of life wherein external judgments are precluded and objective reason plays a very limited role. Section D deals with a broader notion of the role of reason in assessing religious claims and centers on recent developments in the debate, namely, whether religious belief is properly basic, needing no further defense. There is considerable overlap between sections C and D, and the discussion in C is to a large degree continued in D.

VII.A Challenges to Faith and Responses

We begin section A with a brief debate between three Oxford University philosophers that took place in 1948. Antony Flew challenges theists to state the conditions under which they would give up their faith, arguing that unless one can state what would 'falsify' one's belief, one does not have a meaningful belief. If nothing *could* count against the belief, it does not make a serious assertion. Serious truth claims need to be tested. R. M. Hare responds by arguing that this is the wrong way of describing faith, for religious faith consists of a set of profoundly unfalsifiable assumptions—which he calls *bliks*—that govern all of a person's other beliefs. There are insane and sane *bliks*, but we cannot help having some *bliks* about the world. Religion is not subject to rational scrutiny but is beyond (and possibly against) reason. Basil Mitchell opts for a compromise position. Rational considerations enter into the debate on religious faith, but no one can say exactly when a gradual accumulation of evidence comes to count sufficiently against a believed proposition that the believer feels obliged to give it up. Rational considerations count against religious belief, but the believer will strive to see to it that they do not count decisively against it.

Our second reading is Michael Scriven's "The Presumption of Atheism." Scriven argues that unless theism can assemble reasonably clear evidence to support the thesis that God exists, rational people cannot respond even with agnosticism, let alone faith. The only proper response is atheism. Rationally, 'faith' should mean faithfulness to a reasonable commitment; and 'agnosticism' is rational only when a hypothesis and its denial both have some support, that is, when the evidence is balanced so that the thesis is about 50 percent probable. Since Scriven claims elsewhere that the arguments for the existence of God fail to give significant support, he judges theism to be wholly unfounded. The challenge of Scriven's argument to the believer is to explain how religious belief can be justified if the traditional arguments fail.

Our third reading is C. S. Lewis's "On Obstinacy in Belief." Lewis takes up the argument where Basil Mitchell leaves off in his response to Antony Flew. Lewis distinguishes between the logic of entering into a faith relationship and the logic of fidelity once one has entered into it. There is room for speculative thinking and doubt when one is first making the decision, but once one begins to experience the relationship with God, a "logic of personal relationship" takes over. This logic may make doubt an inappropriate attitude, a sort of unfaithful suspicion that a paranoic lover may have in wondering whether to trust someone who has done nothing but good to the beloved. Lewis argues that the evidence that gradually accumulates in the believer's life is as overwhelming and self-authenticating as it is intangible and difficult to communicate to an unbeliever.

Can faith be rationally justified? Is it rationally acceptable to believe in God? This is the challenge that rationalists put to religion. Can it and should it be met? The rest of Part 7 centers around this challenge.

VII.A.1   Theology and Falsification

ANTONY FLEW, R. M. HARE, AND BASIL MITCHELL

Antony Flew is professor of philosophy at York University in Canada. R. M. Hare and Basil Mitchell are professors of philosophy at Oxford University. In this 1948 Oxford University symposium, Flew challenges theists to state the conditions under which they would give up their faith. He contends that unless one can state what would falsify one's belief, one does not have a meaningful belief. If nothing could count against the belief, it does not make a serious assertion, for serious truth claims must be ready to undergo rational scrutiny. R. M. Hare responds by arguing that this is the wrong way of describing faith, for religious faith consists of a set of profoundly unfalsifiable assumptions—which he calls bliks—*that govern all of a person's other beliefs. There are insane and sane* bliks, *but we cannot escape having them. Even the scientist has such fundamental assumptions. Hence religion should not be subject to the kind of rational scrutiny that Flew urges. Basil Mitchell opts for a compromise position. Rational considerations enter into the debate on faith, but no one can say exactly when a gradual accumulation of evidence becomes sufficient to overthrow religious belief. Although rational considerations count against faith, the believer will not let them count decisively against it.*

Antony Flew

Let us begin with a parable. It is a parable developed from a tale told by John Wisdom in his haunting and revelatory article 'Gods.'[1] Once upon a time two explorers came upon a clearing in the jungle. In the clearing were growing many flowers and many weeds. One explorer says,

From *New Essays in Philosophical Theology,* edited by Antony Flew and Alasdair MacIntyre (London: SCM Press, 1955), pp. 96–108. Copyright © 1953 by SCM Press Ltd. Reprinted by permission of Macmillan Publishing Company. Footnotes edited.

"Some gardener must tend this plot." The other disagrees, "There is no gardener." So they pitch their tents and set a watch. No gardener is ever seen. "But perhaps he is an invisible gardener." So they set up a barbed-wire fence. They electrify it. They patrol with bloodhounds. (For they remember how H. G. Wells's *The Invisible Man* could be both smelt and touched though he could not be seen.) But no shrieks ever suggest that some intruder has received a shock. No movements of the wire ever betray an invisible climber. The bloodhounds never give cry. Yet still the Believer is not convinced. "But there is a gardener, invisible, intangible, insensible to electric shocks, a gardener who has no scent and makes no sound, a gardener who comes secretly to look after the garden which he loves." At last the Sceptic despairs, "But what remains of your original assertion? Just how does what you call an invisible, intangible, eternally elusive gardener differ from an imaginary gardener or even from no gardener at all?"

In this parable we can see how what starts as an assertion, that something exists or that there is some analogy between certain complexes of phenomena, may be reduced step by step to an altogether different status, to an expression perhaps of a "picture preference." The Sceptic says there is no gardener. The Believer says there is a gardener (but invisible, etc.). One man talks about sexual behaviour. Another man prefers to talk of Aphrodite (but knows that there is not really a superhuman person additional to, and somehow responsible for, all sexual phenomena). The process of qualification may be checked at any point before the original assertion is completely withdrawn and something of that first assertion will remain (Tautology). Mr. Wells's invisible man could not, admittedly, be seen, but in all other respects he was a man like the rest of us. But though the process of qualification may be, and of course usually is, checked in time, it is not always judiciously so halted. Someone may dissipate his assertion completely without noticing that he has done so. A fine brash hypothesis may thus be killed by inches, the death by a thousand qualifications.

And in this, it seems to me, lies the peculiar danger, the endemic evil, of theological utterance. Take such utterances as "God has a plan," "God created the world," "God loves us as a father loves his children." They look at first sight very much like assertions, vast cosmological assertions. Of course, this is no sure sign that they either are, or are intended to be, assertions. But let us confine ourselves to the cases where those who utter such sentences intend them to express assertions. (Merely remarking parenthetically that those who intend or interpret such utterances as crypto-commands, expressions of wishes, disguised ejaculations, concealed ethics, or as anything else but assertions, are unlikely to succeed in making them either properly orthodox or practically effective).

Now to assert that such and such is the case is necessarily equivalent to denying that such and such is not the case. Suppose then that we are in doubt as to what someone who gives vent to an utterance is asserting, or suppose that, more radically, we are sceptical as to whether he is really asserting anything at all, one way of trying to understand (or perhaps it will be to expose) his utterance is to attempt to find what he would regard as counting against, or as being incompatible with, its truth. For if the utterance is indeed an assertion, it will necessarily be equivalent to a denial of the negation of that assertion. And anything which would count against the assertion, or which would induce the speaker to withdraw it and to admit that it had been mistaken, must be part of (or the whole of) the meaning of the negation of that assertion. And to know the meaning of the negation of an assertion, is as near as makes no matter, to know the meaning of that assertion. And if there is nothing which a putative assertion denies then there is nothing which it asserts either: and so it is not really an assertion. When the Sceptic in the parable asked the Believer, "Just how does what you call an invisible, intangible, eternally elusive gardener differ from an imaginary gardener or even from no gardener at all?" he was suggesting that the Believer's earlier statement had been

eroded by qualification that it was no longer as assertion at all.

Now it often seems to people who are not religious as if there was no conceivable event or series of events the occurrence of which would be admitted by sophisticated religious people to be a sufficient reason for conceding "There wasn't a God after all" or "God does not really love us then." Someone tells us that God loves us as a father loves his children. We are reassured. But then we see a child dying of inoperable cancer of the throat. His earthly father is driven frantic in his efforts to help, but his Heavenly Father reveals no obvious sign of concern. Some qualification is made—God's love is "not a merely human love" or it is "an inscrutable love," perhaps—and we realize that such sufferings are quite compatible with the truth of the assertion that "God loves us as a father (but, of course, . . .)." We are reassured again. But then perhaps we ask: what is this assurance of God's (appropriately qualified) love worth, what is this apparent guarantee really a guarantee against? Just what would have to happen not merely (morally and wrongly) to tempt but also (logically and rightly) to entitle us to say "God does not love us" or even "God does not exist?" I therefore put to the succeeding symposiasts the simple central questions, "What would have to occur or to have occurred to constitute for you a disproof of the love of, or of the existence of, God?"

R. M. Hare

I wish to make it clear that I shall not try to defend Christianity in particular, but religion in general—not because I do not believe in Christianity, but because you cannot understand what Christianity is, until you have understood what religion is.

I must begin by confessing that, on the ground marked out by Flew, he seems to me to be completely victorious. I therefore shift my ground by relating another parable. A certain lunatic is convinced that all dons want to murder him. His friends introduce him to all the mildest and most respectable dons that they can find, and after each of them has retired, they say, "You see, he doesn't really want to murder you; he spoke to you in a most cordial manner; surely you are convinced now?" But the lunatic replies "Yes, but that was only his diabolical cunning; he's really plotting against me the whole time, like the rest of them; I know it I tell you." However many kindly dons are produced, the reaction is still the same.

Now we say that such a person is deluded. But what is he deluded about? About the truth or falsity of an assertion? Let us apply Flew's test to him. There is no behaviour of dons that can be enacted which he will accept as counting against his theory; and therefore his theory, on this test, asserts nothing. But it does not follow that there is no difference between what he thinks about dons and what most of us think about them—otherwise we should not call him a lunatic and ourselves sane, and dons would have no reason to feel uneasy about his presence in Oxford.

Let us call that in which we differ from this lunatic, our respective *bliks*. He has an insane *blik* about dons; we have a sane one. It is important to realize that we have a sane one, not no *blik* at all; for there must be two sides to any argument—if he has a wrong *blik*, then those who are right about dons must have a right one. Flew has shown that a *blik* does not consist in an assertion or system of them; but nevertheless it is very important to have the right *blik*.

Let us try to imagine what it would be like to have different *bliks* about other things than dons. When I am driving my car, it sometimes occurs to me to wonder whether my movements of the steering-wheel will always continue to be followed by corresponding alterations in the direction of the car. I have never had a steering failure, though I have had skids, which must be similar. Moreover, I know enough about how the steering of my car is made, to know the sort of thing that would have to go wrong for the steering to fail— steel joints would have to part, or steel rods break, or something—but how do I know that this won't happen? The truth is, I don't know; I just have a *blik* about steel and its properties, so that normally I trust the steering of my car; but I find it not at all difficult to imagine what it would be like to lose

this *blik* and acquire the opposite one. People would say I was silly about steel; but there would be no mistaking the reality of the difference between our respective *bliks*—for example, I should never go in a motor-car. Yet I should hesitate to say that the difference between us was the difference between contradictory assertions. No amount of safe arrivals or bench-tests will remove my *blik* and restore the normal one: for my *blik* is compatible with any finite number of such tests.

It was Hume who taught us that our whole commerce with the world depends upon our *blik* about the world; and that differences between *bliks* about the world cannot be settled by observation of what happens in the world. That was why, having performed the interesting experiment of doubting the ordinary man's *blik* about the world, and showing that no proof could be given to make us adopt one *blik* rather than another, he turned to backgammon to take his mind off the problem. It seems, indeed, to be impossible even to formulate as an assertion the normal *blik* about the world which makes me put my confidence in the future reliability of steel joints, in the continued ability of the road to support my car, and not gape beneath it revealing nothing below; in the general nonhomicidal tendencies of dons; in my own continued well-being (in some sense of that word that I may not now fully understand) if I continue to do what is right according to my lights; in the general likelihood of people like Hitler coming to a bad end. But perhaps a formulation less inadequate than most is to be found in the Psalms: "The earth is weak and all the inhabiters thereof: I bear up the pillars of it."

The mistake of the position which Flew selects for attack is to regard this kind of talk as some sort of *explanation,* as scientists are accustomed to use the word. As such, it would obviously be ludicrous. We no longer believe in God as an Atlas— *nous n'avons pas besoin de cette hypothèse.* But it is nevertheless true to say that, as Hume saw, without a *blik* there can be no explanation; for it is by our *bliks* that we decide what is and what is not an explanation. Suppose we believed that everything that happened, happened by pure chance. This would not of course be an assertion; for it is compatible with anything happening or not happening, and so, incidentally, is its contradictory. But if we had this belief, we should not be able to explain or predict or plan anything. Thus, although we should not be *asserting* anything different from those of a more normal belief, there would be a great difference between us; and this is the sort of difference that there is between those who really believe in God and those who really disbelieve in him.

The word "really" is important, and may excite suspicion. I put it in, because when people have had a good Christian upbringing, as have most of those who now profess not to believe in any sort of religion, it is very hard to discover what they really believe. The reason why they find it so easy to think that they are not religious, is that they have never got into the frame of mind of one who suffers from the doubts to which religion is the answer. Not for them the terrors of the primitive jungle. Having abandoned some of the more picturesque fringes of religion, they think that they have abandoned the whole thing—whereas in fact they still have got, and could not live without, a religion of a comfortably substantial, albeit highly sophisticated, kind, which differs from that of many "religious people" in little more than this, that "religious people" like to sing Psalms about theirs—a very natural and proper thing to do. But nevertheless there may be a big difference lying behind—the difference between two people who, though side by side, are walking in different directions. I do not know in what direction Flew is walking; perhaps he does not know either. But we have had some examples recently of various ways in which one can walk away from Christianity, and there are any number of possibilities. After all, man has not changed biologically since primitive times; it is his religion that has changed, and it can easily change again. And if you do not think that such changes make a difference, get acquainted with some Sikhs and some Mussulmans of the same Punjabi stock; you will find them quite different sorts of people.

There is an important difference between Flew's parable and my own which we have not yet noticed. The explorers do not *mind* about their garden; they discuss it with interest, but not with concern. But my lunatic, poor fellow, minds about dons; and I mind about the steering of my car; it often has people in it that I care for. It is because I mind very much about what goes on in the garden in which I find myself, that I am unable to share the explorers' detachment.

Basil Mitchell

Flew's article is searching and perceptive, but there is, I think, something odd about his conduct of the theologian's case. The theologian surely would not deny that the fact of pain counts against the assertion that God loves men. This very incompatibility generates the most intractable of theological problems—the problem of evil. So the theologian *does* recognize the fact of pain as counting against Christian doctrine. But it is true that he will not allow it—or anything—to count decisively against it; for he is committed by his faith to trust in God. His attitude is not that of the detached observer, but of the believer.

Perhaps this can be brought out by yet another parable. In time of war in an occupied country, a member of the resistance meets one night a stranger who deeply impresses him. They spend that night together in conversation. The Stranger tells the partisan that he himself is on the side of the resistance—indeed that he is in command of it, and urges the partisan to have faith in him no matter what happens. The partisan is utterly convinced at that meeting of the Stranger's sincerity and constancy and undertakes to trust him.

They never meet in conditions of intimacy again. But sometimes the Stranger is seen helping members of the resistance, and the partisan is grateful and says to his friends, "He is on our side."

Sometimes he is seen in the uniform of the police handing over patriots to the occupying power. On these occasions his friends murmur against him: but the partisan still says, "He is on our side." He still believes that, in spite of appearances, the Stranger did not deceive him. Sometimes he asks the Stranger for help and receives it.

He is then thankful. Sometimes he asks and does not receive it. Then he says, "The Stranger knows best." Sometimes his friends, in exasperation, say "Well, what *would* he have to do for you to admit that you were wrong and that he is not on our side?" But the partisan refuses to answer. He will not consent to put the Stranger to the test. And sometimes his friends complain, "Well, if *that's* what you mean by his being on our side, the sooner he goes over to the other side the better."

The partisan of the parable does not allow anything to count decisively against the proposition "The Stranger is on our side." This is because he has committed himself to trust the Stranger. But he of course recognizes that the Stranger's ambiguous behaviour *does* count against what he believes about him. It is precisely this situation which constitutes the trial of his faith.

When the partisan asks for help and doesn't get it, what can he do? He can (a) conclude that the stranger is not on our side or; (b) maintain that he is on our side, but that he has reasons for withholding help.

The first he will refuse to do. How long can he uphold the second position without its becoming just silly?

I don't think one can say in advance. It will depend on the nature of the impression created by the Stranger in the first place. It will depend, too, on the manner in which he takes the Stranger's behaviour. If he blandly dismisses it as of no consequence, as having no bearing upon his belief, it will be assumed that he is thoughtless or insane. And it quite obviously won't do for him to say easily, "Oh, when used of the Stranger the phrase 'is on our side' *means* ambiguous behavior of this sort." In that case he would like the religious man who says blandly of a terrible disaster "It is God's will." No, he will only be regarded as sane and reasonable in his belief, if he experiences in himself the full force of the conflict.

It is here that my parable differs from Hare's. The partisan admits that many things may and do count against his belief: whereas Hare's lunatic who has a *blik* about dons doesn't admit that anything counts against his *blik*. Nothing *can* count against *bliks*. Also the partisan has a reason for

having in the first instance committed himself, viz. the character of the Stranger; whereas the lunatic has no reason for his *blik* about dons—because, of course, you can't have reasons for *bliks*.

This means that I agree with Flew that theological utterances must be assertions. The partisan is making an assertion when he says, "The Stranger is on our side."

Do I want to say that the partisan's belief about the Stranger is, in any sense, an explanation? I think I do. It explains and makes sense of the Stranger's behaviour: it helps to explain also the resistance movement in the context of which he appears. In each case it differs from the interpretation which the others put upon the same facts.

"God loves men" resembles "the Stranger is on our side" (and many other significant statements, e.g. historical ones) in not being conclusively falsifiable. They can both be treated in at least three different ways: (1) As provisional hypotheses to be discarded if experience tells against them; (2) As significant articles of faith; (3) As vacuous formulae (expressing, perhaps, a desire for reassurance) to which experience makes no difference and which make no difference to life.

The Christian, once he has committed himself, is precluded by his faith from taking up the first attitude: "Thou shalt not tempt the Lord thy God." He is in constant danger, as Flew has observed, of slipping into the third. But he need not; and, if he does, it is a failure in faith as well as in logic.

Antony Flew

It has been a good discussion: and I am glad to have helped to provoke it. But now—at least in *University*—it must come to an end: and the Editors of *University* have asked me to make some concluding remarks. Since it is impossible to deal with all the issues raised or to comment separately upon each contribution, I will concentrate on Mitchell and Hare, as representative of two very different kinds of response to the challenge made in "Theology and Falsification."

The challenge, it will be remembered, ran like this. Some theological utterances seem to, and are intended to, provide explanations or express assertions. Now an assertion, to be an assertion at all, must claim that things stand thus and thus; *and not otherwise*. Similarly an explanation, to be an explanation at all, must explain why this particular thing occurs; *and not something else*. Those last clauses are crucial. And yet sophisticated religious people—or so it seemed to me—are apt to overlook this, and tend to refuse to allow, not merely that anything actually does occur, but that anything conceivably could occur, which would count against their theological assertions and explanations. But in so far as they do this their supposed explanations are actually bogus, and their seeming assertions are really vacuous.

Mitchell's response to this challenge is admirably direct, straightforward, and understanding. He agrees "that theological utterances must be assertions." He agrees that if they are to be assertions, there must be something that would count against their truth. He agrees, too, that believers are in constant danger of transforming their would-be assertions into "vacuous formulae." But he takes me to task for an oddity in my "conduct of the theologian's case. The theologian surely would not deny that the fact of pain counts against the assertion that God loves men. This very incompatibility generates the most intractable of theological problems, the problem of evil." I think he is right. I should have made a distinction between two very different ways of dealing with what looks like evidence against the love of God: the way I stressed was the expedient of qualifying the original assertion; the way the theologian usually takes, at first, is to admit that it looks bad but to insist that there is—there must be—some explanation which will show that, in spite of appearances, there really is a God who loves us. His difficulty, it seems to me, is that he has given God attributes which rule out all possible saving explanations. In Mitchell's parable of the Stranger it is easy for the believer to find plausible excuses for ambiguous behaviour: for the Stranger is a man. But suppose the Stranger is God. We cannot say that he would like to help but cannot: God is omnipotent. We cannot say that he would help if he only knew: God is omniscient. We cannot say that he is not responsible for the

wickedness of others: God creates those others. Indeed an omnipotent, omniscient God must be an accessory before (and during) the fact to every human misdeed; as well as being responsible for every non-moral defect in the universe. So, though I entirely concede that Mitchell was absolutely right to insist against me that the theologian's first move is to look for an *explanation*, I still think that in the end, if relentlessly pursued, he will have to resort to the avoiding action of *qualification*. And there lies the danger of that death by a thousand qualifications, which would, I agree, constitute "a failure in faith as well as in logic."

Hare's approach is fresh and bold. He confesses that "on the ground marked out by Flew, he seems to me to be completely victorious." He therefore introduces the concept of *blik*. But while I think that there is room for some such concept in philosophy, and that philosophers should be grateful to Hare for his invention, I nevertheless want to insist that any attempt to analyse Christian religious utterances as expressions or affirmations of a *blik* rather than as (at least would-be) assertions about the cosmos is fundamentally misguided. *First*, because thus interpreted they would be entirely unorthodox. If Hare's religion really is a *blik*, involving no cosmological assertions about the nature and activities of a supposed personal creator, then surely he is not a Christian at all? *Second*, because thus interpreted, they could scarcely do the job they do. If they were not even intended as assertions then many religious activities would become fraudulent, or merely silly. If "You ought *because* it is God's will" asserts no more than "You ought," then the person who prefers the former phraseology is not really giving a reason, but a fraudulent substitute for one, a dialectical dud cheque. If "My soul must be immortal *because* God loves his children, etc." asserts no more than "My soul must be immortal," then the man who reassures himself with theological arguments for immortality is being as silly as the man who tries to clear his overdraft by writing his bank a cheque on the same account. (Of course neither of these utterances would be distinctively Christian: but this discussion never pretended to be so confined.) Religious utterances may indeed express false or even bogus assertions: but I simply do not believe that they are not both intended and interpreted to be or at any rate to presuppose assertions, at least in the context of religious practice; whatever shifts may be demanded, in another context, by the exigencies of theological apologetic.

One final suggestion. The philosophers of religion might well draw upon George Orwell's last appalling nightmare *1984* for the concept of *doublethink*. "*Doublethink* means the power of holding two contradictory beliefs simultaneously, and accepting both of them. The party intellectual knows that he is playing tricks with reality, but by the exercise of *doublethink* he also satisfies himself that reality is not violated" (*1984*, p. 220). Perhaps religious intellectuals too are sometimes driven to doublethink in order to retain their faith in a loving God in face of the reality of a heartless and indifferent world. But of this more another time, perhaps.

Note

1. *P.A.S.*, 1944-5, reprinted as Ch. X of *Logic and Language*, Vol. I (Blackwell, 1951), and in his *Philosophy and Psychoanalysis* (Blackwell, 1953).

VII.A.2   The Presumption of Atheism

MICHAEL SCRIVEN

Michael Scriven is professor of philosophy at the University of California at Berkeley. In this article he argues that unless theism can assemble reasonably clear evidence to support the thesis that God exists, rational people cannot respond even with agnosticism, let alone faith. The only proper response is atheism. Rationally, 'faith' should mean faithfulness to a reasonable commitment; and 'agnosticism' is rational only when a hypothesis and its denial both have some support, that is, when the evidence is balanced so that the thesis is about 50 percent probable. Since Scriven claims elsewhere that the arguments for the existence of God fail to give significant support, he judges theism to be wholly unfounded. The challenge of Scriven's argument to the believer is to explain how religious belief can be justified if the traditional arguments fail.

Faith and Reason

We must now contend with the suggestion that reason is irrelevant to the commitment to theism because this territory is the domain of another faculty: the faculty of faith. It is sometimes even hinted that it is morally wrong and certainly foolish to suggest we should be reasoning about God. For this is the domain of faith or of the "venture of faith," of the "knowledge that passeth understanding," of religious experience and mystic insight.

Now the normal meaning of *faith* is simply "confidence"; we say that we have great faith in someone or in some claim or product, meaning that we believe and act as if they were very reliable. Of such faith we can properly say that it is well founded or not, depending on the evidence for whatever it is in which we have faith. So there is no incompatibility between this kind of faith and reason; the two are from different families and can make a very good marriage. Indeed if they do not join forces, then the resulting ill-based or inadequate confidence will probably lead to disaster. So faith, in this sense, means only a high degree of belief and may be reasonable or unreasonable.

But the term is sometimes used to mean an *alternative to reason* instead of something that should be founded on reason. Unfortunately, the mere use of the term in this way does not demonstrate that faith is a possible route to truth. It is like using the term "winning" as a synonym for "playing" instead of one possible outcome of playing. This is quaint, but it could hardly be called a satisfactory way of proving that we are winning; any time we "win" by changing the meaning of winning, the victory is merely illusory. And so it proves in this case. To use "faith" *as if* it were an alternative way to the truth cannot by-pass the crucial question whether such results really have any likelihood of being true. A rose by any other name will smell the same, and the inescapable facts about "faith" in the new sense are that it is still *applied* to a belief and is still supposed to imply *confidence in* that belief: the belief in the existence and goodness of God. So we can still ask the same old question about that belief: Is the confidence justified or misplaced? To say we "take it on faith" does not get it off parole.

Suppose someone replies that theism is a kind of belief that does not need justification by evidence. This means either that no one cares whether it is correct or not or that there is some other way of checking that it is correct besides looking at the evidence for it, that is, giving reasons for believing it. But the first alternative is false since very many people care whether there is a God or not; and the second alternative is false because any method of showing that belief is likely to be true is, by definition, a justification of that belief, that is, an appeal to reason. You certainly cannot show that a belief in God is likely to be true just by having confidence in it and by saying this is a case of knowledge "based on" faith, any more than you can win a game just by playing it and by calling that winning.

It is psychologically possible to have faith in something without any basis in fact, and once in a while you will turn out to be lucky and to have backed the right belief. This does not show you "really knew all along"; it only shows you cannot be unlucky all the time. But, in general, beliefs without foundations lead to an early grave or to an accumulation of superstitions, which are usually troublesome and always false beliefs. It is hardly possible to defend this approach just by *saying* that you have decided that in this area confidence is its own justification.

Of course, you might try to *prove* that a feeling of great confidence about certain types of propositions is a reliable indication of their truth. If you succeeded, you would indeed have shown that the belief was justified; you would have done this by justifying it. To do this you would have to show what the real facts were and show that when someone had the kind of faith we are now talking about, it usually turned out that the facts were as he believed, just as we might justify the claims of the telepath. The catch in all this is simply that you have got to show what the real facts are in some way *other* than by appealing to faith, since that would simply be assuming what you are trying to prove. And if you can show what the facts are in this other way, you do not need faith in any new sense at all; you are already perfectly entitled to confidence in any belief that you have shown to be well supported.

How are you going to show what the real facts are? You show this by any method of investigation that has itself been tested, the testing being done by still another tested method, etc., through a series of tested connections that eventually terminates in our ordinary everyday reasoning and testing procedures of logic and observation.

Is it not prejudiced to require that the validation of beliefs always involves ultimate reference to our ordinary logic and everyday-plus-scientific knowledge? May not faith (religious experience, mystic insight) give us access to some new domain of truth? It is certainly possible that it does this. But, of course, it is also possible that it lies. One can hardly accept the reports of those with faith or, indeed, the apparent revelations of one's own religious experiences on the ground that they *might* be right. So *might* be a fervent materialist who saw his interpretation as a revelation. Possibility is not veracity. Is it not of the very greatest importance that we should try to find out whether we really can justify the use of the term "truth" or "knowledge" in describing the content of faith? If it is, then we must find something in that content that is known to be true in some other way, because to get off the ground we must first push off against the ground—we cannot lift ourselves by our shoelaces. If the new realm of knowledge is to be a realm of knowledge and not mythology, then it must tell us something which relates it to the kind of case that gives meaning to the term "truth." If you want to use the old word for the new events, you must show that it is applicable.

Could not the validating experience, which religious experience must have if it is to be called true, be the experience of others who also have or have had religious experiences? The religious community could, surely, provide a basis of agreement analogous to that which ultimately underlies scientific truth. Unfortunately, agreement is not the only requirement for avoiding error, for all may be in error. The difficulty for the religious community is to show that its agreement is not simply agreement about a shared mistake. If agreement were the only criterion of truth, there could never be a shared mistake; but clearly either the atheist group or the theist group shares a mistake. To decide which is wrong must involve appeal to something other than mere agreement. And, of course, it is clear that particular religious beliefs are mistaken, since religious groups do not all agree and they cannot all be right.

Might not some or all scientific beliefs be wrong too? This is conceivable, but there are crucial differences between the two kinds of belief. In the first place, any commonly agreed religious beliefs concern only one or a few entities and their properties and histories. What for convenience we are here calling "scientific belief" is actually the sum total of all conventionally founded human knowledge, much of it not part of any science, and it embraces billions upon billions of facts, each of them perpetually or frequently subject to checking by independent means, each connected with a million others. The success of *this* system of knowledge shows up every day in everything we do: we eat, and the food is not poison; we read, and the pages do not turn to dust; we slip, and the gravity does not fail to pull us down. We are not just relying on the existence of agreement about the interpretation of a certain experience among a small part of the population. We are relying directly on our extremely reliable, nearly universal, and independently tested senses, and each of us is constantly obtaining independent confirmation for claims based on these, many of these confirmations being obtained for many claims, independently of each other. It is the wildest flight of fancy to suppose that there is a body of common religious beliefs which can be set out to exhibit this degree of repeated checking by religious experiences. In fact, there is not only gross disagreement on even the most fundamental claims in the creeds of different churches, each of which is supported by appeal to religious experience or faith, but where there is agreement by many people, it is all too easily open to the criticism that it arises from the common cultural exposure of the child or the adult convert and hence is not independent in the required way.

This claim that the agreement between judges is spurious in a particular case because it only reflects previous common indoctrination of those in agreement is a serious one. It must always be met by direct disproof whenever agreement is appealed to in science, and it is. The claim that the food is not poison cannot be explained away as a myth of some subculture, for anyone, even if told nothing about the eaters in advance, will judge that the people who ate it are still well. The whole methodology of testing is committed to the doctrine that any judges who could have learned what they are expected to say about the matter they are judging are completely valueless. Now anyone exposed to religious teaching, whether a believer or not, has long known the standard for such experiences, the usual symbols, the appropriate circumstances, and so on. These suggestions are usually very deeply implanted, so that they cannot be avoided by good intentions, and consequently members of our culture are rendered entirely incapable of being independent observers. Whenever observers are not free from previous contamination in this manner, the only way to support their claims is to examine independently testable *con-*

sequences of the novel claims, such as predictions about the future. In the absence of these, the religious-experience gambit, whether involving literal or analogical claims, is wholly abortive.

A still more fundamental point counts against the idea that agreement among the religious can help support the idea of faith as an alternative path to truth. It is that every sane theist also believes in the claims of ordinary experience, while the reverse is not the case. Hence, the burden of proof is on the theist to show that the *further step* he wishes to take will not take him beyond the realm of truth. The two positions, of science and religion, are not symmetrical; the adherent of one of them suggests that we extend the range of allowable beliefs and yet is unable to produce the same degree of acceptance or "proving out" in the ordinary field of human activities that he insists on before believing in a new instrument or source of information. The atheist obviously cannot be shown his error in the way someone who thinks that there are no electrons can be shown his, *unless some of the arguments for the existence of God are sound*. Once again, we come back to these. If some of them work, the position of religious knowledge is secure; if they do not, nothing else will make it secure.

In sum, the idea of separating religious from scientific knowledge and making each an independent realm with its own basis in experience of quite different kinds is a counsel of despair and not a product of true sophistication, for one cannot break the connection between everyday experience and religious claims, for purposes of defending the latter, without eliminating the consequences of religion for everyday life. There is no way out of this inexorable contract: if you want to support your beliefs, you must produce some experience which can be shown to be a reliable indicator of truth, and that can be done only by showing a connection between the experience and what we know to be true in a previously established way.

So, if the criteria of religious truth are not connected with the criteria of everyday truth, then they are not criteria of truth at all and the beliefs they "establish" have no essential bearing on our lives, constitute no explanation of what we see around us, and provide no guidance for our course through time.

The Consequences if the Arguments Fail

The arguments are the only way to establish theism, and they must be judged by the usual standards of evidence—this we have argued. It will now be shown that if they fail, there is no alternative to atheism.

Against this it has commonly been held that the absence of arguments *for* the existence of something is not the same as the presence of arguments *against* its existence; so agnosticism or an option remains when the arguments fail. But insofar as this is true, it is irrelevant. It is true only if we restrict "arguments for the existence of something" to highly specific demonstrations which attempt to establish their conclusion as beyond all reasonable doubt. The absence of these is indeed compatible with the conclusion's being quite likely, which would make denial of its existence unjustified. But if we take arguments for the existence of something to include all the evidence which supports the existence claim to any significant degree, i.e., makes it at all probable, then the evidence means there is no likelihood of the existence of the entity. And this, of course, is a complete justification for the claim that the entity does not exist, provided that the entity is not one which might leave no traces (a God who is impotent or who does not care for us), and provided that we have comprehensively examined the area where such evidence would appear if there were any. Now justifying the claim that something does not exist is not quite the same as proving or having arguments that it doesn't, but it is what we are talking about. That is, we need not have a proof that God does not exist in order to justify atheism. Atheism is obligatory in the absence of any evidence for God's existence.

Why do adults not believe in Santa Claus? Simply because they can now explain the phenomena for which Santa Claus's existence is invoked without any need for introducing a novel entity. When we were very young and naively believed our parents' stories, it was hard to see how the presents could get there on Christmas morning since the doors were locked and our parents were asleep in bed. Someone *must* have brought them down the chimney. And how could that person get to the roof without a ladder and with all those presents? Surely only by flying. And then there is a great traditional literature of stories and songs which immortalize the entity and his (horned) attendents; surely these cannot all be just products of imagination? Where there is smoke, there must be fire.

Santa Claus is not a bad hypothesis at all for six-year-olds. As we grow up, no one comes forward to *prove* that such an entity does not exist. We just come to see that there is not the least reason to think he *does* exist. And so it would be entirely foolish to assert that he does, or believe that he does, or even think it likely that he does. Santa Claus is in just the same position as fairy godmothers, wicked witches, the devil, and the ether. Each of these entities has some supernatural powers, i.e., powers which contravene or go far beyond the powers that we know exist, whether it be the power to levitate a sled and reindeer or the power to cast a spell. Now even belief in something for which there is no evidence, i.e., a belief which goes *beyond* the evidence, although a lesser sin than belief in something which is *contrary* to well-established laws, is plainly irrational in that it simply amounts to attaching belief where it is not justified. So the proper alternative, when there is no evidence, is not mere suspension of belief, for example, about Santa Claus, it is *disbelief*. It most certainly is not faith.

The situation is slightly different with the Abominable Snowman, sea serpents, or even the Loch Ness monster. No "supernatural" (by which, in this context, we only mean wholly unprecedented) kinds of powers are involved. Previous discoveries have been made of creatures which had long seemed extinct, and from these we can immediately derive some likelihood of further discoveries. Footprints or disturbances for which no fully satisfactory alternative explanation has yet been discovered (although such an explanation is by no means impossible) have been seen in the Himalayan snow and the Scottish lochs. It would be credulous for the layman to believe firmly in the existence of these entities. Yet it would be equally inappropriate to say it is certain they do not exist. Here is a domain for agnosticism (though perhaps an agnosticism inclined toward skepticism). For the agnostic does not believe that a commitment either way is justified, and he is surely right about strange creatures which, while of a new *appearance*, have powers that are mere extensions, proportional to size, of those with which we are already familiar on this earth. There is some suggestive, if by no means conclusive, evidence for such entities; and the balance of general considerations is not heavily against them.

But when the assertion is made that something exists with powers that strikingly transcend the well-established generalizations we have formulated about animal capacities or reasonable extrapolations from them, then we naturally expect correspondingly better evidence before we concede that there is a serious likelihood of having to abandon those generalizations. It is entirely appropriate to demand much stronger support for claims of telepathy or levitation or miraculous cures than for new sports records or feats of memory in which previous levels of performance are merely bettered to some degree, in a way that is almost predictable. On the other hand, it is entirely prejudiced to reject all such evidence on the ground that it *must* be deceptive because it contravenes previously established generalizations. This is simply to deify the present state of science; it is the precise opposite of the experimental attitude. It is right to demand a stronger case to overthrow a strong case and to demand very strong evidence to demonstrate unprecedented powers. It is irrational to require that the evidence of these powers be just as commonplace and compelling as for the previously known powers of man or beast: one cannot legislate the exceptional into the commonplace.

We can now use a set of distinctions that

would previously have seemed very abstract. First, let us distinguish a belief which is wholly without general or particular evidential support from one which can be directly disproved. The claim that a race of men lives on the moons of Jupiter or that a certain cola causes cancer of the colon is entirely unfounded but not totally impossible. The view that the ratio of a circle's circumference to its diameter can be expressed as a fraction is demonstrably untenable, as is the view that some living men are infinitely strong, or that any man is or has been unbeatable at chess, or that the FBI has wiped out the Mafia. We normally say that a claim is *well founded* if there is evidence which is best explained by this claim. We may say it is *provable* if the evidence is indubitable and the claim is very clearly required. If there is no evidence which points to this particular claim, although some general background considerations make it not too unlikely that something like this should be true (Loch Ness monster, mile record broken twice in 1980), we would say there is *some general support* for the claim. We shall say it is *wholly unfounded* (or *wholly unsupported*) if there is no evidence for it in particular and no general considerations in its favor, and *disprovable* if it implies that something would be the case that definitely is not the case.

Of course it is foolish to believe a claim that is disproved, but it is also foolish to believe a wholly unsupported claim, and it is still foolish even to treat such a claim as if it were worth serious consideration. A claim for which there is some general or some particular support cannot be dismissed, but neither can it be treated as established. The connection between evidential support and the appropriate degree of belief can be demonstrated as shown in the diagram that follows, which is quite unlike the oversimplified idea that the arrangement should be:

Provable   Theism
Disprovable   Atheism
Neither   Agnosticism

The crucial difference is that both "unfounded" and "disprovable" correlate with atheism, just as the two corresponding types of provability corre-

late with theism; hence the agnostic's territory is smaller than he often supposes.

Recalling that to get even a little evidential support for the existence of a Being with supernatural powers will require that the little be of very high quality (*little* does not mean "dubious"), we see that the failure of all the arguments, that is, of all the evidence, will make even agnosticism in the wide sense an indefensible exaggeration of the evidential support. And agnosticism in the narrow sense will be an exaggeration unless the arguments are strong enough to establish about a 50 per cent probability for the claim of theism. Apart from the wide and narrow senses of agnosticism there is also a distinction between a positive agnostic and a negative agnostic.

A *positive agnostic* maintains that the evidence is such as to make his position the correct one and those of the theist and atheist incorrect. *Negative agnosticism* is simply the position of not accepting either theism or atheism; it does not suggest that they are both wrong—it may be just an expression of felt indecision or ignorance. The difference between negative and positive agnosticism is like the difference between a *neutral* who says, "I don't know who's right—maybe one of the disputants, or maybe neither," and a *third force* who says, "Neither is right, and I have a third alternative which *is* right." Obviously, the negative agnostic has not progressed as far in his thinking as the positive agnostic, in one sense, because he has not been able to decide which of the three possible positions is correct. The view of the negative agnostic cannot be right, but his position may be the right position for someone who has not thought the matter through or who lacks the capacity to do so.

In practice, an agnostic's position is often the product of an untidy mixture of factors. He may never have happened to come across an argument for either theism or atheism which struck him as compelling; a rough head counting has revealed intelligent people on either side; his nose for social stigmas indicates a slight odor of intellectual deficiency attached to theism by contemporary intellectuals and a suggestion of unnecessary boat rocking or perhaps rabid subversion attached to

Evidential Situation	Appropriate Attitude	Name for Appropriate Attitude in Theism Case	
1. Strictly disprovable, i.e., demonstrably incompatible with the evidence. 2. Wholly unfounded, i.e., wholly lacking in general or particular support.	Rejection	Atheism	
3. Possessing some general or particular support; still improbable.	Skepticism but recognition as a real *possibility;* not to be wholly disregarded in comprehensive planning out to be bet *against.*	Skepticism	
4. Possessing substantial support but with substantial alternatives still open; a balance of evidence for and against; about 50 per cent probable.	Suspension of judgment. Make no commitment either way; treat each alternative as approximately equally serious.	Agnosticism (narrow sense)	Agnosticism (wide sense)
5. Possessing powerful evidential support; some difficulties of inadequacies or significant alternatives remaining; probable.	Treat as probably true; be *on.*	Pragmatic theism	
6. Possessing overwhelming particular support and no basis for alternative views; beyond reasonable doubt; provable in the usual sense. 7. Strictly provable, i.e., as a demonstrably necessary result of indubitable facts.	Acceptance	Theism	

atheism. This makes the agnostic fence look pretty attractive; so up he climbs, to sit on top. But now we put the challenge to him. Is he incapable of thinking out an answer for himself? If so, he is intellectually inferior to those below; if not, he must descend and demonstrate the failings of the contestants before he is entitled to his perch. Agnosticism as a position is interesting and debatable; agnosticism as the absence of a position is simply a sign of the absence of intellectual activity or capacity.

Combining and Separating Arguments and Evidence

There used to be a standing joke in the Rationalist Club at Melbourne University about the theologian who said: "None of the arguments is any good by itself, but taken together they constitute an overwhelming proof." Alas for the simple approach; the instinct of the theologian was better than the formal training of the rationalists, although the error is not easily stated. There used to be a small book on the market which contained 200 "proofs" that $-1 = +1$; entertaining though these are, they do not make it one bit more likely that -1 really does equal $+1$, for they are all invalid. If you knew nothing about mathematics, even about elementary arithmetic, and the only way you could find out whether $+1$ equaled -1 was by counting the number of alleged proofs in each direction, you might reasonably conclude that it did. But if you were seriously concerned with the truth of the matter, you would want to investigate the validity of the proofs for yourself; and you would find that they were all unsound. So there is no advantage in numbers, *as far as mathematical proofs go.* They either do the whole trick or nothing at all.

The situation is different with scientific proofs, whereby we hope to do no more than show that one conclusion is so probable as to be beyond reasonable doubt. Let us suppose you are investigating a murder case. There are three clues. The first one points most strongly at North as the suspect; the second, at East; the third, at West. Obviously, you could not argue that South had been shown to be the culprit from a consideration of any one of these clues by itself. Yet there are circumstances in which you can put them all together and conclude that South was, *without any doubt,* the murderer. Here we have a number of "proofs" (items of evidence) which separately do nothing to establish a particular conclusion but which add up to a good proof of that conclusion. How is this possible? The point about probability proofs is that they do not make the alternative explanations completely impossible and may indicate a second-best hypothesis. So, although the first clue is North's handkerchief at the scene of the crime, you also know that South is North's roommate and may have borrowed his handkerchief, while no one else could have done so without considerable difficulty. And although the second clue is that East very frequently had violent arguments with the victim and had been heard to threaten him with injury, it was also true that South stood to gain by the victim's death since he

inherited his job in a public relations firm. And West's professional skill at judo, which ties in well with the victim's curiously broken neck, is not such as to make South's army training in basic karate blows an irrelevant consideration. So South is by a long way the most likely murderer. In the same way, with respect to those arguments for the existence of God which are of the probability-increasing kind, we shall have to consider not only whether they make God's existence likely on their own but whether some of them make it a sufficiently good alternative explanation so that when we take all the arguments together it is the best overall explanation.

Obviously this can happen only if the *same hypothesis* receives support as an alternative in each case, for example, the hypothesis that South is the murderer. It would not work at all if the first clue made a secondary suspect of one man called South and the next of a cousin of the first suspect, also called South. After looking at all the arguments in this kind of situation, we would not have any one candidate who was better qualified than any other; we could not even say that it was probably someone from the family of South, for as a matter of fact this is less likely than that it was one of the other three, North, East, and West.

It could be argued that the greatest confidence trick in the history of philosophy is the attempt to make the various arguments for the existence of God support each other by using the same term for the entity whose existence each is supposed to establish. In fact, almost all of them bear on entities of apparently quite different kinds, ranging from a Creator to a moral Lawgiver. The proofs must, therefore, be supplemented with a further proof or set of proofs that shows these apparently different entities to be the same if the combination trick is to work. Otherwise the arguments must be taken separately, in which case they either establish or fail to establish the existence of a number of remarkable but unrelated entities.

It can sometimes be argued that considerations of simplicity require one to adopt the hypothesis that only a single entity is involved, when the alternative is to introduce several special entities.

But the circumstances in which this is legitimate are quite limited; we do not, for example, argue that simplicity requires us to assume that the murderer South is also the unknown person who stole some bonds from a bank the day before the murder. We would have to show some connection through means, opportunity, motive, or *modus operandi,* before the identification could be made at all plausible. Simplicity is a fine guide to the best hypothesis if one can only decide which hypothesis is the simpler. Although there is a greater simplicity in terms of the number of entities involved if we say, for example, that the Creator is the moral Lawgiver, there is a greater complexity in terms of the number of explanations required, since now we must explain why and how one entity could perform these two functions. In short, we have really got to give a plausible specific reason before we can identify the two criminals or the two theological entities, since simplicity is now clearly gained by either alternative, and until we do so, any commitment to such an identification is wholly unfounded.

If only a very weak case can be made for the claim that the same entity is involved in the different arguments, the "linkage proof," it will mean that the separate arguments must be much stronger (though they need not be individually adequate) for the conclusion that God exists.

Instead of attempting to establish monotheism, one can, of course, frankly accept the arguments as separate proofs of the existence of separate beings. Roughly speaking, such a polytheist loses one god for each argument that fails and in this sense has a more vulnerable position. But the monotheist may still lose one property or power of his God for each argument that fails and thus fail altogether to establish the existence of the Being he has defined as God, Who has *all* these properties.

It is possible that monotheism owes some of its current support to the feeling that few if any of the separate arguments are without defect and hence *must* be combined for strength. But if this is so, it is surprising that more attention has not been paid to the linkage arguments, which then become crucial.

Another factor acting in favor of monotheism is the feeling that it is less difficult, in the face of the increasing success of naturalistic science, to postulate one supernatural being than several. (But it may be that only the *combination* of properties is supernatural.) To this extent there is a kind of negative justification for the widespread and curious claim that Christianity was in some sense the precursor of modern science with its allegedly unifying theories, but the causal relation is reversed. Christian theology may have been fleeing into monotheism from the shadow cast ahead of the development of Babylonian and Greek science.

VII.A.3   On Obstinacy in Belief

C. S. LEWIS

C. S. Lewis (1898–1963) was a British philosopher, theologian, and literary critic who taught at Oxford and Cambridge Universities. In this selection he traces how assent moves from the logic of speculation, in which inquiry and doubt are appropriate, to the logic of personal relationship within faith, in which religious experience becomes self-confirming and overwhelming, making doubt a sort of inattentiveness or infidelity.

Reprinted from C. S. Lewis, *The World's Last Night,* copyright © 1960 by C. S. Lewis. Reprinted by permission of Harcourt Brace Jovanovich, Inc.

Papers have more than once been read to the Socratic Club at Oxford in which a contrast was drawn between a supposedly Christian attitude and a supposedly scientific attitude to belief. We have been told that the scientist thinks it his duty to proportion the strength of his belief exactly to the evidence; to believe less as there is less evidence and to withdraw belief altogether when reliable adverse evidence turns up. We have been told that, on the contrary, the Christian regards it as positively praiseworthy to believe without evidence, or in excess of the evidence, or to maintain his belief unmodified in the teeth of steadily increasing evidence against it. Thus a "faith that has stood firm," which appears to mean a belief immune from all the assaults of reality, is commended.

If this were a fair statement of the case, then the co-existence within the same species of such scientists and such Christians, would be a very staggering phenomenon. The fact that the two classes appear to overlap, as they do, would be quite inexplicable. Certainly all discussion between creatures so different would be hopeless. The purpose of this essay is to show that things are really not quite so bad as that. The sense in which scientists proportion their belief to the evidence and the sense in which Christians do not, both need to be defined more closely. My hope is that when this has been done, though disagreement between the two parties may remain, they will not be left staring at one another in wholly dumb and desperate incomprehension.

And first, a word about belief in general. I do not see that the state of "proportioning belief to evidence" is anything like so common in the scientific life as has been claimed. Scientists are mainly concerned not with believing things but with finding things out. And no one, to the best of my knowledge, uses the word "believe" about things he has found out. The doctor says he "believes" a man was poisoned before he has examined the body; after the examination, he says the man was poisoned. No one says that he believes the multiplication table. No one who catches a thief red-handed says he believes that man was stealing. The scientist, when at work, that is, when he is a scientist, is labouring to escape from belief and unbelief into knowledge. Of course he uses hypotheses or supposals. I do not think these are beliefs. We must look, then, for the scientist's be-

haviour about belief not to his scientific life but to his leisure hours.

In actual modern English usage the verb "believes," except for two special usages, generally expresses a very weak degree of opinion. "Where is Tom?" "Gone to London, I believe." The speaker would be only mildly surprised if Tom had not gone to London after all. "What was the date?" "430 B.C., I believe." The speaker means that he is far from sure. It is the same with the negative if it is put in the form "I believe not." ("Is Jones coming up this term?" "I believe not.") But if the negative is put in a different form it then becomes one of the special usages I mentioned a moment ago. This is of course the form "I don't believe it," or the still stronger "I don't believe you." "I don't believe it" is far stronger on the negative side than "I believe" is on the positive. "Where is Mrs. Jones?" "Eloped with the butler, I believe." "I don't believe it." This, especially if said with anger, may imply a conviction which in subjective certitude might be hard to distinguish from knowledge by experience. The other special usage is "I believe" as uttered by a Christian. There is no great difficulty in making the hardened materialist understand, however little he approves, the sort of mental attitude which this "I believe" expresses. The materialist need only picture himself replying, to some report of a miracle, "I don't believe it," and then imagine this same degree of conviction on the opposite side. He knows that he cannot, there and then, produce a refutation of the miracle which would have the certainty of mathematical demonstration; but the formal possibility that the miracle might after all have occurred does not really trouble him any more than a fear that water might not be H and O. Similarly, the Christian does not necessarily claim to have demonstrative proof; but the formal possibility that God might not exist is not necessarily present in the form of the least actual doubt. Of course there are Christians who hold that such demonstrative proof exists, just as there may be materialists who hold that there is demonstrative disproof. But then, whichever of them is right (if either is) while he retained the proof or disproof would be not believing or disbelieving but knowing. We are speaking of belief and disbelief in the strongest degree but not of knowledge. Belief, in this sense, seems to me to be assent to a proposition which we think so overwhelmingly probable that there is a psychological exclusion of doubt, though not a logical exclusion of dispute.

It may be asked whether belief (and of course disbelief) of this sort ever attaches to any but theological propositions. I think that many beliefs approximate to it; that is, many probabilities seem to us so strong that the absence of logical certainty does not induce in us the least shade of doubt. The scientific beliefs of those who are not themselves scientists often have this character, especially among the uneducated. Most of our beliefs about other people are of the same sort. The scientist himself, or he who was a scientist in the laboratory, has beliefs about his wife and friends which he holds, not indeed without evidence, but with more certitude than the evidence, if weighed in the laboratory manner, would justify. Most of my generation had a belief in the reality of the external world and of other people—if you prefer it, a disbelief in solipsism—far in excess of our strongest arguments. It may be true, as they now say, that the whole thing arose from category mistakes and was a pseudo-problem; but then we didn't know that in the twenties. Yet we managed to disbelieve in solipsism all the same.

There is, of course, no question so far of belief without evidence. We must beware of confusion between the way in which a Christian first assents to certain propositions and the way in which he afterwards adheres to them. These must be carefully distinguished. Of the second it is true, in a sense, to say that Christians do recommend a certain discounting of apparent contrary evidence, and I will later attempt to explain why. But so far as I know it is not expected that a man should assent to these propositions in the first place without evidence or in the teeth of the evidence. At any rate, if anyone expects that, I certainly do not. And in fact, the man who accepts Christianity always thinks he had good evidence; whether, like Dante, *fisici e metafisici argomenti,* or historical evidence, or the evidence of religious experience, or authority, or all these together. For of course

authority, however we may value it in this or that particular instance, is a kind of evidence. All of our historical beliefs, most of our geographical beliefs, many of our beliefs about matters that concern us in daily life, are accepted on the authority of other human beings, whether we are Christians, Atheists, Scientists, or Men-in-the Street.

It is not the purpose of this essay to weigh the evidence, of whatever kind, on which Christians base their belief. To do that would be to write a full-dress *apologia.* All that I need do here is to point out that, at the very worst, this evidence cannot be so weak as to warrant the view that all whom it convinces are indifferent to evidence. The history of thought seems to make this quite plain. We know, in fact, that believers are not cut off from unbelievers by any portentous inferiority of intelligence or any perverse refusal to think. Many of them have been people of powerful minds. Many of them have been scientists. We may suppose them to have been mistaken, but we must suppose that their error was at least plausible. We might indeed, conclude that it was, merely from the multitude and diversity of the arguments against it. For there is not one case against religion, but many. Some say, like Capaneus in Statius, that it is a projection of our primitive fears, *primus in orbe deos fecit timor:* others, with Euhemerus, that it is all a "plant" put up by wicked kings, priests, or capitalists; others, with Tylor, that it comes from dreams about the dead; others, with Frazer, that it is a by-product of agriculture; others, like Freud, that it is a complex; the moderns that it is a category mistake. I will never believe that an error against which so many and various defensive weapons have been found necessary was, from the outset, wholly lacking in plausibility. All this "post haste and rummage in the land" obviously implies a respectable enemy.

There are of course people in our own day to whom the whole situation seems altered by the doctrine of the concealed wish. They will admit that men, otherwise apparently rational, have been deceived by the arguments for religion. But they will say that they have been deceived first by their own desires and produced the arguments afterwards as a rationalisation: that these arguments have never been intrinsically even plausible, but have seemed so because they were secretly weighted by our wishes. Now I do not doubt that this sort of thing happens in thinking about religion as in thinking about other things: but as a general explanation of religious assent it seems to me quite useless. On that issue our wishes may favour either side or both. The assumption that every man would be pleased, and nothing but pleased, if only he could conclude that Christianity is true, appears to me to be simply preposterous. If Freud is right about the Oedipus complex, the universal pressure of the wish that God should not exist must be enormous, and atheism must be an admirable gratification to one of our strongest suppressed impulses. This argument, in fact, could be used on the theistic side. But I have no intention of so using it. It will not really help either party. It is fatally ambivalent. Men wish on both sides: and again, there is fear-fulfilment as well as wish-fulfilment, and hypochondriac temperaments will always tend to think true what they most wish to be false. Thus instead of the one predicament on which our opponents sometimes concentrate there are in fact four. A man may be a Christian because he wants Christianity to be true. He may be an atheist because he wants atheism to be true. He may be an atheist because he wants Christianity to be true. He may be a Christian because he wants atheism to be true. Surely these possibilities cancel one another out? They may be of some use in analysing a particular instance of belief or disbelief, where we know the case history, but as a general explanation of either they will not help us. I do not think they overthrow the view that there is evidence both for and against the Christian propositions which fully rational minds, working honestly, can assess differently.

I therefore ask you to substitute a different and less tidy picture for that with which we began. In it, you remember, two different kinds of men, scientists, who proportioned their belief to the evidence, and Christians, who did not, were left facing one another across a chasm. The picture I should prefer is like this. All men alike, on questions which interest them, escape from the region of belief into that of knowledge when they can,

and if they succeed in knowing, they no longer say they believe. The questions in which mathematicians are interested admit of treatment by a particularly clear and strict technique. Those of the scientist have their own technique, which is not quite the same. Those of the historian and the judge are different again. The mathematician's proof (at least so we laymen suppose) is by reasoning, the scientist's by experiment, the historian's by documents, the judge's by concurring sworn testimony. But all these men, as men, on questions outside their own disciplines, have numerous beliefs to which they do not normally apply the methods of their own disciplines. It would indeed carry some suspicion of morbidity and even of insanity if they did. These beliefs vary in strength from weak opinion to complete subjective certitude. Specimens of such beliefs at their strongest are the Christian's "I believe" and the convinced atheist's "I don't believe a word of it." The particular subject-matter on which these two disagree does not, of course, necessarily involve such strength of belief and disbelief. There are some who moderately opine that there is, or is not, a God. But there are others whose belief or disbelief is free from doubt. And all these beliefs, weak or strong, are based on what appears to the holders to be evidence; but the strong believers or disbelievers of course think they have very strong evidence. There is no need to suppose stark unreason on either side. We need only suppose error. One side has estimated the evidence wrongly. And even so, the mistake cannot be supposed to be of a flagrant nature; otherwise the debate would not continue.

So much, then, for the way in which Christians come to assent to certain propositions. But we have now to consider something quite different; their adherence to their belief after it has once been formed. It is here that the charge of irrationality and resistance to evidence becomes really important. For it must be admitted at once that Christians do praise such an adherence as if it were meritorious; and even, in a sense, more meritorious the stronger the apparent evidence against their faith becomes. They even warn one another that such apparent contrary evidence—such "trials to faith" or "temptations to doubt"—may be expected to occur, and determine in advance to resist them. And this is certainly shockingly unlike the behaviour we all demand of the scientist or the historian in their own disciplines. There, to slur over or ignore the faintest evidence against a favourite hypothesis, is admittedly foolish and shameful. It must be exposed to every test; every doubt must be invited. But then I do not admit that a hypothesis is a belief. And if we consider the scientist not among his hypotheses in the laboratory but among the beliefs in his ordinary life, I think the contrast between him and the Christian would be weakened. If, for the first time, a doubt of his wife's fidelity crosses the scientist's mind, does he consider it his duty at once to entertain this doubt with complete impartiality, at once to evolve a series of experiments by which it can be tested, and to await the result with pure neutrality of mind? No doubt it may come to that in the end. There are unfaithful wives; there are experimental husbands. But is such a course what his brother scientists would recommend to him (all of them, I suppose, except one) as the first step he should take and the only one consistent with his honour as a scientist? Or would they, like us, blame him for a moral flaw rather than praise him for an intellectual virtue if he did so?

This is intended, however, merely as a precaution against exaggerating the difference between Christian obstinacy in belief and the behaviour of normal people about their non-theological beliefs. I am far from suggesting that the case I have supposed is exactly parallel to the Christian obstinacy. For of course evidence of the wife's infidelity might accumulate, and presently reach a point at which the scientist would be pitiably foolish to disbelieve it. But the Christians seem to praise an adherence to the original belief which holds out against any evidence whatever. I must now try to show why such praise is in fact a logical conclusion from the original belief itself.

This can be done best by thinking for a moment of situations in which the thing is reversed. In Christianity such faith is demanded of us; but there are situations in which we demand it of others. There are times when we can do all that a fellow creature needs if only he will trust us. In

getting a dog out of a trap, in extracting a thorn from a child's finger, in teaching a boy to swim or rescuing one who can't, in getting a frightened beginner over a nasty place on a mountain, the one fatal obstacle may be their distrust. We are asking them to trust us in the teeth of their senses, their imagination, and their intelligence. We ask them to believe that what is painful will relieve their pain and that what looks dangerous is their only safety. We ask them to accept apparent impossibilities: that moving the paw farther back into the trap is the way to get it out—that hurting the finger very much more will stop the finger hurting—that water which is obviously permeable will resist and support the body—that holding on to the only support within reach is not the way to avoid sinking—that to go higher and on to a more exposed ledge is the way not to fall. To support all these *incredibilia* we can rely only on the other party's confidence in us—a confidence certainly not based on demonstration, admittedly shot through with emotion, and perhaps, if we are strangers, resting on nothing but such assurance as the look of our face and the tone of our voice can supply, or even, for the dog, on our smell. Sometimes, because of their unbelief, we can do no mighty works. But if we succeed, we do so because they have maintained their faith in us against apparently contrary evidence. No one blames us for demanding such faith. No one blames them for giving it. No one says afterwards what an unintelligent dog or child or boy that must have been to trust us. If the young mountaineer were a scientist, it would not be held against him, when he came up for a fellowship, that he had once departed from Clifford's rule of evidence by entertaining a belief with strength greater than the evidence logically obliged him to.

Now to accept the Christian propositions is *ipso facto* to believe that we are to God, always, as that dog or child or bather or mountain climber was to us, only very much more so. From this it is a strictly logical conclusion that the behaviour which was appropriate to them will be appropriate to us, only very much more so. Mark: I am not saying that the strength of our original belief must by psychological necessity produce such behaviour. I am saying that the content of our original belief by logical necessity entails the proposition that such behaviour is appropriate. If human life is in fact ordered by a beneficent being whose knowledge of our real needs and of the way in which they can be satisfied infinitely exceeds our own, we must expect *a priori* that His operations will often appear to us far from beneficent and far from wise, and that it will be our highest prudence to give Him our confidence in spite of this. This expectation is increased by the fact that when we accept Christianity we are warned that apparent evidence against it will occur—evidence strong enough "to deceive if possible the very elect." Our situation is rendered tolerable by two facts. One is that we seem to ourselves, besides the apparently contrary evidence, to receive favourable evidence. Some of it is in the form of external events: as when I go to see a man, moved by what I felt to be a whim, and find he has been praying that I should come to him that day. Some of it is more like the evidence on which the mountaineer or the dog might trust his rescuer—the rescuer's voice, look, and smell. For it seems to us (though you, on your premises, must believe us deluded) that we have something like a knowledge-by-acquaintance of the Person we believe in, however imperfect and intermittent it may be. We trust not because "a God" exists, but because *this* God exists. Or if we ourselves dare not claim to "know" Him, Christendom does, and we trust at least some of its representatives in the same way: because of the sort of people they are. The second fact is this. We think we can see already why, if our original belief is true, such trust beyond the evidence, against much apparent evidence, has to be demanded of us. For the question is not about being helped out of one trap or over one difficult place in a climb. We believe that His intention is to create a certain personal relation between Himself and us, a relation really *sui generis* but analogically describable in terms of filial or of erotic love. Complete trust is an ingredient in that relation—such trust as could have no room to grow except where there is also room for doubt. To love involves trusting the beloved beyond the evidence, even against much evidence. No man is our friend who believes in our good intentions only when they are proved. No man is our friend who will not be very slow to accept evidence against them. Such confidence, between one man and another, is in fact almost universally praised as a moral beauty, not blamed as a logical error. And the suspicious man is blamed for a meanness of character, not admired for the excellence of his logic.

There is, you see, no real parallel between Christian obstinacy in faith and the obstinacy of a bad scientist trying to preserve a hypothesis although the evidence has turned against it. Unbelievers very pardonably get the impression that an adherence to our faith is like that, because they meet Christianity, if at all, mainly in apologetic works. And there, of course, the existence and beneficence of God must appear as a speculative question like any other. Indeed, it is a speculative question as long as it is a question at all. But once it has been answered in the affirmative, you get quite a new situation. To believe that God—at least *this* God—exists is to believe that you as a person now stand in the presence of God as a Person. What would, a moment before, have been variations in opinion, now becomes variations in your personal attitude to a Person. You are no longer faced with an argument which demands your assent, but with a Person who demands your confidence. A faint analogy would be this. It is one thing to discuss *in vacuo* whether So-and-So will join us tonight, and another to discuss this when So-and-So's honour is pledged to come and some great matter depends on his coming. In the first case it would be merely reasonable, as the clock ticked on, to expect him less and less. In the second, a continued expectation far into the night would be due to our friend's character if we had found him reliable before. Which of us would not feel slightly ashamed if one moment after we had given him up he arrived with a full explanation of his delay? We should feel that we ought to have known him better.

Now of course we see, quite as clearly as you, how agonisingly two-edged all this is. A faith of this sort, if it happens to be true, is obviously what we need, and it is infinitely ruinous to lack it. But there can be faith of this sort where it is wholly ungrounded. The dog may lick the face of the man who comes to take it out of the trap; but the man may only mean to vivisect it in South Parks Road when he has done so. The ducks who come to the call "Dilly, dilly, come and be killed" have confidence in the farmer's wife, and she wrings their necks for their pains. There is that famous French story of the fire in the theatre. Panic was spreading, the spectators were just turning from an audience into a mob. At that moment a huge bearded man leaped through the orchestra on to the stage, raised his hand with a gesture full of nobility, and cried, *"Que chacun regagne sa place."* Such was the authority of his voice and bearing that everyone obeyed him. As a result they were all burned to death, while the bearded man walked quietly out through the wings to the stage door, took a cab which was waiting for someone else, and went home to bed.

That demand for our confidence which a true friend makes of us is exactly the same that a confidence trickster would make. That refusal to trust, which is sensible in reply to a confidence trickster, is ungenerous and ignoble to a friend, and deeply damaging to our relation with him. To be forewarned and therefore forearmed against apparently contrary appearance is eminently rational if our belief is true; but if our belief is a delusion, this same forewarning and forearming would obviously be the method whereby the delusion rendered itself incurable. And yet again, to be aware of these possibilities and still to reject them is clearly the precise mode, and the only mode, in which our personal response to God can establish itself. In that sense the ambiguity is not something that conflicts with faith so much as a condition which makes faith possible. When you are asked for trust you may give it or withhold it; it is senseless to say that you will trust if you are given demonstrative certainty. There would be no room for trust if demonstration were given. When demonstration is given what will be left will be simply the sort of relation which results from having trusted, or not having trusted, before it was given.

The saying "Blessed are those that have not seen and have believed" has nothing to do with our original assent to the Christian propositions. It was not addressed to a philosopher inquiring whether God exists. It was addressed to a man who already believed that, who already had long acquaintance with a particular Person, and evidence that that Person could do very odd things, and who then refused to believe one odd thing more, often predicted by that Person and vouched for by all his closest friends. It is a rebuke not to scepticism in the philosophic sense but to the psychological quality of being "suspicious." It says in effect, "You should have known me better." There are cases between man and man where we should all, in our different way, bless those who have not seen and have believed. Our relation to those who trusted us only after we were proved innocent in court cannot be the same as our relation to those who trusted us all through.

Our opponents, then, have a perfect right to dispute with us about the grounds of our original assent. But they must not accuse us of sheer insanity if, after the assent has been given, our adherence to it is no longer proportioned to every fluctuation of the apparent evidence. They cannot of course be expected to know on what our assurance feeds, and how it revives and is always rising from its ashes. They cannot be expected to see how the *quality* of the object which we think we are beginning to know by acquaintance drives us to the view that if this were a delusion then we should have to say that the universe had produced no real thing of comparable value and that all explanations of the delusion seemed somehow less important than the thing explained. That is knowledge we cannot communicate. But they can see how the assent, of necessity, moves us from the logic of speculative thought into what might perhaps be called the logic of personal relations. What would, up till then, have been variations simply of opinion become variations of conduct by a person to a Person. *Credere Deum esse* turns into *Credere in Deum.* And *Deum* here is this God, the increasingly knowable Lord.

VII.B Pragmatic Justification of Religious Belief

In this section we have three readings dealing with the *practical* reasonableness of religious belief. That is, even if we cannot find good evidence for religious beliefs, would it perhaps be in our interest to get ourselves to believe in these propositions anyway? And would such believing be morally permissible? In the first reading, "The Wager," the renowned French physicist and mathematician Blaise Pascal (1623–1662) argues that if we do a cost-benefit analysis of the matter, we find that it is eminently reasonable to get ourselves to believe that God exists regardless of whether we have good evidence for that belief. The argument goes something like this: Regarding the proposition 'God exists' reason is neutral. It can neither prove nor disprove it. But we must make a choice on this matter, for not to choose for God is in effect to choose against him and lose the possible benefits that belief would bring. Since these benefits promise to be infinite and the loss equally infinite, we might set forth the possibilities shown in Figure 1

There is some sacrifice of earthly pleasures involved in belief in God, but by multiplying the various combinations we find that there is an incommensurability between A and C, on the one hand, and B and D on the other. For no matter how enormous the *finite* gain, the mere possibility of *infinite* gain will always make the latter preferable to the former. So the only relevant possibilities are A and C. Since A (believing in God) promises infinite happiness and C (not believing in God) infinite unhappiness, a rational cost-benefit analysis leaves no doubt about what we should do. We have a clear self-interested reason for believing in God.

The reader should go over this argument closely. Are there any weaknesses in it? Does it demonstrate that we all should do whatever is necessary to come to believe that God exists? Is such a belief necessary and sufficient for eternal happiness?

In the second reading in this section, "The Ethics of Belief," the British philosopher W. K. Clifford (1845–1879) assembles reason's roadblock to such pragmatic justifications for religious belief. Clifford argues that there is an ethics to belief that makes immoral all believing without sufficient evidence. Pragmatic justifications are not justifications at all but counterfeits of genuine justifications, which must always be based on evidence.

Clifford illustrates his thesis with the example of a ship owner who sends an emigrant ship to sea. He knows that the ship is old and not well built, but he fails to have the ship inspected. Dismissing from his mind all doubts and suspicions that the vessel is not seaworthy, he trusts in Providence to care for his ship. He acquires a sincere and comfortable conviction in this way and collects his insurance money without a trace of guilt after the ship sinks and all the passengers drown.

Clifford comments that although the ship owner sincerely believed that all was well with the ship, his sincerity in no way exculpates him because "he had no right to believe on such evidence as was before him." One has an obligation to get oneself in a position in which one will believe propositions only on sufficient evidence. Furthermore, it is not a valid objection to say that the ship owner had an obligation to *act*

Figure 1		*God exists*	*God does not exist*
	I believe	A. Infinite gain with minimal finite loss	B. Overall finite loss in terms of sacrifice of earthly goods
	I do not believe	C. Infinite loss with finite gain	D. Overall finite gain

in a certain way (viz., inspect the ship), not *believe* in a certain way. The ship owner does have an obligation to inspect the ship, but the objection overlooks the function of believing in guiding action. "No man holding a strong belief on one side of a question, or even wishing to hold a belief on one side, can investigate it with such fairness and completeness as if he were really in doubt and unbiassed; so that the existence of a belief not founded on fair inquiry unfits a man for the performance of this necessary duty." The general conclusion is that it is always wrong for anyone to believe anything on insufficient evidence.

The classic response to Clifford's ethics of belief is William James's "The Will to Believe" (1896), the last reading in this section. James argues that life would be greatly impoverished if we confined our beliefs to such a Scrooge-like epistemology as Clifford proposes. In everyday life, where the evidence for important propositions is often unclear, we must live by faith or cease to act at all. Although we may not make leaps of faith just anywhere, sometimes practical considerations force us to make decisions about propositions that do not have their truth value written on their faces.

In "The Sentiment of Rationality" (1879) James defines 'faith' as "a belief in something concerning which doubt is still theoretically possible; and as the test of belief is willingness to act, one may say that faith is the readiness to act in a cause the prosperous issue of which is not certified to us in advance." In "The Will to Believe" he speaks of 'belief' as a live, momentous optional hypothesis on which we cannot avoid a decision, for not to choose is in effect to choose against the hypothesis.

There is a good illustration of this notion of faith in "The Sentiment of Rationality." A mountain climber in the Alps finds himself in a position from which he can escape only by means of an enormous leap. If he tries to calculate the evidence, believing only on sufficient evidence, he will be paralyzed by emotions of fear and mistrust and hence will be lost. With-

out evidence that he is capable of performing this feat successfully, the climber would be better off getting himself to believe that he can and will make the leap. "In this case . . . the part of wisdom clearly is to believe what one desires; for the belief is one of the indispensable preliminary conditions of the realization of its object. *There are then cases where faith creates its own verification.*"

James claims that religion may be such an optional hypothesis for many people, and in this case one has the right to believe the better story rather than the worse. To do so, one must will to believe what the evidence alone is inadequate to support.

There are two questions, one descriptive and the other normative, that you should keep in mind when you are reading these essays. The first is whether it is possible to believe propositions at will. In what sense can we get ourselves to believe propositions that the evidence doesn't force upon us. Surely we can't believe that the world is flat or that two plus two equals five simply by willing to do so, but which propositions (if any) are subject to volitional influences? Is it psychologically impossible to make the kinds of moves that Pascal and James advise? Does it involve self-deception? If we know that the only cause for our belief in a religious proposition is our desire to believe, can we rationally continue to believe that proposition? Is there something self-defeating about volitional projects?

The second question involves the ethics of belief, stressed by Clifford. Supposing that we can get ourselves to believe or disbelieve propositions, is this morally permissible? What are the arguments for and against integrity of belief?

Note that Pascal's volitionalism is indirect, whereas James's might be interpreted as direct. In Pascal's case one must will to believe the proposition *p*, discover the best means to get into that state (e.g., going to church, participating in Mass, taking holy water, etc.), and act in such a way as to make the acquisition of the belief likely. In direct volitionalism one supposes that one can obtain some beliefs simply by fiat of the will.

Note that there are two different types of cases here. In one type, the truth of the proposition is something we have no control over. In the other type, the truth of the proposition is something that still has not been decided, but believing in it might help bring about the desired state of affairs (the case of the mountain climber is an example of this type). Should we have a different attitude about each of these types of cases?

You may also consider whether pragmatic justification allows one to believe decisively, in an absolute way. Many think that such belief is necessary for authentic religious faith, but pragmatic grounds alone seem to prevent complete confidence in what is assented to.

VII.B.1   The Wager

BLAISE PASCAL

In our first reading, the renowned French physicist and mathematician Blaise Pascal (1623–1662) argues that if we do a cost-benefit analysis of the matter, we find that it is eminently reasonable to get ourselves to believe that God exists regardless of whether we have good evidence for that belief. The argument goes something like this: Regarding the proposition 'God exists' reason is neutral. It can neither prove nor disprove it. But we make a choice on this matter, for not to choose for God is in effect to choose against him and lose the possible benefits that belief would bring. Since these benefits of faith promise to be infinite and the loss equally infinite, we must take a gamble on faith.

Infinite—nothing.—Our soul is cast into a body, where it finds number, time, dimension. Thereupon it reasons, and calls this nature, necessity, and can believe nothing else.

Unity joined to infinitely adds nothing to it, no more than one foot to an infinite measure. The finite is annihilated in the presence of the infinite, and becomes a pure nothing. So our spirit before

Reprinted from Blaise Pascal, *Thoughts,* translated by W. F. Trotter (New York: Collier & Son, 1910).

God, so our justice before divine justice. There is not so great disproportion between our justice and that of God, as between unity and infinity.

The justice of God must be vast like His compassion. Now, justice to the outcast is less vast, and ought less to offend our feelings than mercy towards the elect.

We know that there is an infinite, and are ignorant of its nature. As we know it to be false that numbers are finite, it is therefore true that there is an infinity in number. But we do not know what it is. It is false that it is even, it is false that it is odd; for the addition of a unit can make no change in its nature. Yet it is a number, and every number is odd or even (this is certainly true of every finite number). So we may well know that there is a God without knowing what He is. Is there not one substantial truth, seeing there are so many things which are not the truth itself?

We know then the existence and nature of the finite, because we also are finite and have extension. We know the existence of the infinite, and are ignorant of its nature, because it has extension like us, but not limits like us. But we know neither the existence nor the nature of God, because He has neither extension nor limits.

But by faith we know His existence; in glory we shall know His nature. Now, I have already shown that we may well know the existence of a thing, without knowing its nature.

Let us now speak according to natural lights.

If there is a God, He is infinitely incomprehensible, since, having neither parts nor limits, He has no affinity to us. We are then incapable of knowing either what He is or if He is. This being so, who will dare to undertake the decision of the question? Not we, who have no affinity to Him.

Who then will blame Christians for not being able to give a reason for their belief, since they profess a religion for which they cannot give a reason? They declare, in expounding it to the world, that it is a foolishness, *stultitiam;* and then you complain that they do not prove it! If they proved it, they would not keep their words; it is in lacking proofs, that they are not lacking in sense. "Yes, but although this excuses those who offer it as such, and take away from them the blame of putting it forward without reason, it does not excuse those who receive it." Let us then examine this point, and say, "God is, or He is not." But to which side shall we incline? Reason can decide nothing here. There is an infinite chaos which separates us. A game is being played at the extremity of this infinite distance where heads or tails will turn up. What will you wager? According to reason, you can do neither the one thing nor the other; according to reason, you can defend neither of the propositions.

Do not then reprove for error those who have made a choice; for you know nothing about it. "No, but I blame them for having made, not this choice, but a choice; for again both he who chooses heads and he who chooses tails are equally at fault, they are both in the wrong. The true course is not to wager at all."

—Yes; but you must wager. It is not optional. You are embarked. Which will you choose then; Let us see. Since you must choose, let us see which interests you least. You have two things to lose, the true and the good; and two things to stake, your reason and your will, your knowledge and your happiness; and your nature has two things to shun, error and misery. Your reason is no more shocked in choosing one rather than the other, since you must of necessity choose. This is

one point settled. But your happiness? Let us weigh the gain and the loss in wagering that God is. Let us estimate these two chances. If you gain, you gain all; if you lose, you lose nothing. Wager them without hesitation that He is.—"That is very fine. Yes, I must wager; but I may perhaps wager too much."—Let us see. Since there is an equal risk of gain and of loss, if you had only to gain two lives, instead of one, you might still wager. But if there were three lives to gain, you would have to play (since you are under the necessity of playing), and you would be imprudent, when you are forced to play, not to chance your life to gain three at a game where there is an equal risk of loss and gain. But there is an eternity of life and happiness. And this being so, if there were an infinity of chances, of which one only would be for you, you would still be right in wagering one to win two, and you would act stupidly, being obliged to play, by refusing to stake one life against three at a game in which out of an infinity of an infinitely happy life to gain. But there is here an infinity of an infinitely happy life to gain, a chance of gain against a finite number of chances of loss, and what you stake is finite. It is all divided; wherever the infinite is and there is not an infinity of chances of loss against that of gain, there is no time to hesitate, you must give all. And thus, when one is forced to play, he must renounce reason to preserve his life, rather than risk it for infinite gain, as likely to happen as the loss of nothingness.

For it is no use to say it is uncertain if we will gain, and it is certain that we risk, and that the infinite distance between the *certainty* of what is staked and the *uncertainty* of what will be gained, equals the finite good which is certainly staked against the uncertain infinite. It is not so, as every player stakes a certainty to gain an uncertainty, and yet he stakes a finite certainty to gain a finite uncertainty, without transgressing against reason. There is not an infinite distance between the certainty staked and the uncertainty of the gain; that is untrue. In truth, there is an infinity between the certainty of gain and the certainty of loss. But the uncertainty of the gain is proportioned to the certainty of the stake according to the proportion of the chances of gain and loss. Hence it comes that, if there are as many risks on one side as on the other, the course is to play even; and then the certainty of the stake is equal to the uncertainty of the gain, so far is it from the fact that there is an infinite distance between them. And so our proposition is of infinite force, when there is the finite to stake in a game where there are equal risks of gain and of loss, and the infinite to gain. This is demonstrable; and if men are capable of any truths, this is one.

"I confess it, I admit it. But still is there no means of seeing the faces of the cards?"—Yes, Scripture and the rest, &c.—"Yes, but I have my hands tied and my mouth closed; I am forced to wager, and am not free. I am not released, and am so made that I cannot believe. What then would you have me do?"

"True. But at least learn your inability to believe, since reason brings you to this, and yet you cannot believe. Endeavour then to convince yourself, not by increase of proofs of God, but by the abatement of your passions. You would like to attain faith, and do not know the way; you would like to cure yourself of unbelief, and ask the remedy for it. Learn of those who have been bound like you, and who now stake all their possessions. These are people who know the way which you would follow, and who are cured of an ill of which you would be cured. Follow the way by which they began; by acting as if they believe, taking the holy water, having masses said, &c. Even this will naturally make you believe, and deaden your acuteness.—"But this is what I am afraid of."—And why? What have you to lose?

But to show you that this leads you there, it is this which will lessen the passions, which are your stumbling-blocks.

The end of this discourse.—Now what harm will befall you in taking this side? You will be faithful, honest, humble, grateful, generous, a sincere friend, truthful. Certainly you will not have those poisonous pleasures, glory and luxury; but will you not have others? I will tell you that you will thereby gain in this life, and that, at each step you take on this road, you will see so great certainty of gain, so much nothingness in what you risk, that you will at last recognize that you have wagered for something certain and infinite, for which you have given nothing.

"Ah! This discourse transports me, charms me," &c.

If this discourse pleases you and seems impressive, know that it is made by a man who has knelt, both before and after it, in prayer to that Being, infinite and without parts, before whom he lays all he has, for you also to lay before Him all you have for your own good and for His glory, so that strength may be given to lowliness.

VII.B.2 The Ethics of Belief

W. K. CLIFFORD

In this reading the British philosopher W. K. Clifford (1845–1879) assembles reason's roadblock to pragmatic (or "wager") justifications for religious belief of the sort Pascal proposes. Clifford argues that there is an ethics to belief that makes immoral all believing without sufficient evidence. Pragmatic justifications are not justifications at all but counterfeits of genuine justifications, which must always be based on evidence.

Clifford illustrates his thesis with the example of a ship owner who sends an emigrant ship to sea. He knows that the ship is old and not well built, but he fails to have the ship inspected. Dismissing from his mind all doubts and suspicions that the vessel is not seaworthy, he trusts in Providence to care for his ship. He acquires a sincere and comfortable conviction in this way and collects his

Reprinted from W. K. Clifford, *Lectures and Essays* (London: Macmillan, 1879).

insurance money without a trace of guilt after the ship sinks and all the passengers drown. Clifford argues that although the ship owner sincerely believed that all was well with the ship, his sincerity in no way exculpates him because "he had no right to believe on such evidence as was before him." One has an obligation to get oneself in a position in which one will believe propositions only on sufficient evidence. His general conclusion is that it is always wrong for anyone to believe anything on insufficient evidence.

A shipowner was about to send to sea an emigrant ship. He knew that she was old, and not over-well built at the first; that she had seen many seas and climes, and often had needed repairs. Doubts had been suggested to him that possibly she was not seaworthy. These doubts preyed upon his mind and made him unhappy; he thought that perhaps he ought to have her thoroughly overhauled and refitted, even though this should put him to great expense. Before the ship sailed, however, he succeeded in overcoming these melancholy reflections. He said to himself that she had gone safely through so many voyages and weathered so many storms that it was idle to suppose she would not come safely home from this trip also. He would put his trust in Providence, which could hardly fail to protect all these unhappy families that were leaving their fatherland to seek for better times elsewhere. He would dismiss from his mind all ungenerous suspicions about the honesty of builders and contractors. In such ways he acquired a sincere and comfortable conviction that his vessel was thoroughly safe and seaworthy; he watched her departure with a light heart, and benevolent wishes for the success of the exiles in their strange new home that was to be; and he got his insurance money when she went down in midocean and told no tales.

What shall we say of him? Surely this, that he was verily guilty of the death of those men. It is admitted that he did sincerely believe in the soundness of his ship; but the sincerity of his conviction can in no wise help him, because he had no right to believe on such evidence as was before him. He had acquired his belief not by honestly earning it in patient investigation, but by stifling his doubts. And although in the end he may have felt so sure about it that he could not think otherwise, yet inasmuch as he had knowingly and willingly worked himself into that frame of mind, he must be held responsible for it.

Let us alter the case a little, and suppose that the ship was not unsound after all; that she made her voyage safely, and many others after it. Will that diminish the guilt of her owner? Not one jot. When an action is once done, it is right or wrong forever; no accidental failure of its good or evil fruits can possibly alter that. The man would not have been innocent, he would only have been not found out. The question of right or wrong has to do with the origin of his belief, not the matter of it; not what it was, but how he got it; not whether it turned out to be true or false, but whether he had a right to believe on such evidence as was before him.

There was once an island in which some of the inhabitants professed a religion teaching neither the doctrine of original sin nor that of eternal punishment. A suspicion got abroad that the professors of this religion had made use of unfair means to get their doctrines taught to children. They were accused of wresting the laws of their country in such a way as to remove children from the care of their natural and legal guardians; and even of stealing them away and keeping them concealed from their friends and relations. A certain number of men formed themselves into a society for the purpose of agitating the public about this matter. They published grave accusations against individual citizens of the highest position and character, and did all in their power to injure those citizens in the exercise of their professions. So great was the noise they made, that a Commission was appointed to investigate the facts; but after the Commission had carefully inquired into all the evidence that could be got, it appeared that the accused were innocent. Not only had they been accused on insufficient evidence, but the evidence of their innocence was such as the agitators might easily have obtained, if they had attempted a fair inquiry. After these disclosures the inhabitants of that country looked upon the members of the agitating society, not only as persons whose judgment was to be distrusted, but also as no longer to be counted honorable men. For although they had sincerely and conscientiously believed in the charges they had made, yet they had no right to believe on such evidence as was before them. Their sincere convictions, instead of being honestly earned by patient inquiring, were stolen by listening to the voice of prejudice and passion.

Let us vary this case also, and suppose, other things remaining as before, that a still more accurate investigation proved the accused to have been really guilty. Would this make any difference in the guilt of the accusers? Clearly not; the question is not whether their belief was true or false, but whether they entertained it on wrong grounds. They would no doubt say, "Now you see that we were right after all; next time perhaps you will believe us." And they might be believed, but they would not thereby become honorable men. They would not be innocent, they would only be not found out. Every one of them, if he chose to examine himself *in foro conscientiae,* would know that he had acquired and nourished a belief, when he had no right to believe on such evidence as was before him; and therein he would know that he had done a wrong thing.

It may be said, however, that in both of these supposed cases it is not the belief which is judged to be wrong, but the action following upon it. The shipowner might say, "I am perfectly certain that my ship is sound, but still I feel it my duty to have her examined, before trusting the lives of so many people to her." And it might be said to the agitator, "However convinced you were of the justice of your cause and the truth of your convictions, you ought not to have made a public attack upon any man's character until you had examined the evidence on both sides with the utmost patience and care."

In the first place, let us admit that, so far as it goes, this view of the case is right and necessary; right, because even when a man's belief is so fixed that he cannot think otherwise, he still has a choice in regard to the action suggested by it, and so cannot escape the duty of investigating on the ground of the strength of his convictions; and necessary, because those who are not yet capable of controlling their feelings and thoughts must have a plain rule dealing with overt acts.

But this being premised as necessary, it becomes clear that it is not sufficient, and that our previous judgment is required to supplement it. For it is not possible so to sever the belief from the action it suggests as to condemn the one without condemning the other. No man holding a strong belief on one side of a question, or even wishing to hold a belief on one side, can investigate it with such fairness and completeness as if he were really in doubt and unbiassed; so that the existence of a belief not founded on fair inquiry unfits a man for the performance of this necessary duty.

Nor is that truly a belief at all which has not some influence upon the actions of him who holds it. He who truly believes that which prompts him to an action has looked upon the action to lust after it, he has committed it already in his heart. If a belief is not realized immediately in open deeds, it is stored up for the guidance of the future. It goes to make a part of that aggregate of beliefs which is the link between sensation and action at every moment of all our lives, and which is so organized and compacted together that no part of it can be isolated from the rest, but every new addition modifies the structure of the whole. No real belief, however trifling and fragmentary it may seem, is ever truly insignificant; it prepares us to receive more of its like, confirms those which resembled it before, and weakens others; and so gradually it lays a stealthy train in our inmost thoughts, which may some day explode into overt action, and leave its stamp upon our character forever.

And no one man's belief is in any case a private matter which concerns himself alone. Our lives are guided by that general conception of the course of things which has been created by society for social purposes. Our words, our phrases, our forms and processes and modes of thought, are common property, fashioned and perfected from age to age; an heirloom which every succeeding generation inherits as a precious deposit and a sacred trust to be handed on to the next one, not unchanged but enlarged and purified, with some clear marks of its proper handiwork. Into this, for good or ill, is woven every belief of every man who has speech of his fellows. An awful privilege, and an awful responsibility, that we should help to create the world in which posterity will live.

In the two supposed cases which have been considered, it has been judged wrong to believe on insufficient evidence, or to nourish belief by suppressing doubts and avoiding investigation. The reason of this judgment is not far to seek: it is that in both these cases the belief held by one man was of great importance to other men. But for as much as no belief held by one man, however seemingly trivial the belief, and however obscure the believer, is ever actually insignificant or without its effect on the fate of mankind, we have no choice but to extend our judgment to all cases of belief whatever. Belief, that sacred faculty which prompts the decisions of our will, and knits into harmonious working all the compacted energies of our being, is ours not for ourselves, but for humanity. It is rightly used on truths which have been established by long experience and waiting toil, and which have stood in the fierce light of free and fearless questioning. Then it helps to bind men together, and to strengthen and direct their common action. It is desecrated when given to unproved and unquestioned statements, for the solace and private pleasure of the believer; to add a tinsel splendor to the plain straight road of our life and display a bright mirage beyond it; or even to drown the common sorrows of our kind by a self-deception which allows them not only to cast down, but also to degrade us. Whoso would deserve well of his fellows in this matter will guard the purity of his belief with a very fanaticism of jealous care, lest at any time it should rest on an unworthy object, and catch a stain which can never be wiped away.

It is not only the leader of men, statesman, philosopher, or poet, that owes this bounden duty to mankind. Every rustic who delivers in the village alehouse his slow, infrequent sentences, may help to kill or keep alive the fatal superstitions which clog his race. Every hard-worked wife of an artisan may transmit to her children beliefs which shall knit society together, or rend it in pieces. No

simplicity of mind, no obscurity of station, can escape the universal duty of questioning all that we believe.

It is true that this duty is a hard one, and the doubt which comes out of it is often a very bitter thing. It leaves us bare and powerless where we thought that we were safe and strong. To know all about anything is to know how to deal with it under all circumstances. We feel much happier and more secure when we think we know precisely what to do, no matter what happens, than when we have lost our way and do not know where to turn. And if we have supposed ourselves to know all about anything, and to be capable of doing what is fit in regard to it, we naturally do not like to find that we are really ignorant and powerless, that we have to begin again at the beginning, and try to learn what the thing is and how it is to be dealt with—if indeed anything can be learned about it. It is the sense of power attached to a sense of knowledge that makes men desirous of believing, and afraid of doubting.

This sense of power is the highest and best of pleasures when the belief on which it is founded is a true belief, and has been fairly earned by investigation. For then we may justly feel that it is common property, and holds good for others as well as for ourselves. Then we may be glad, not that *I* have learned secrets by which I am safer and stronger, but that *we men* have got mastery over more of the world; and we shall be strong, not for ourselves, but in the name of Man and in his strength. But if the belief has been accepted on insufficient evidence, the pleasure is a stolen one. Not only does it deceive ourselves by giving us a sense of power which we do not really possess, but it is sinful, because it is stolen in defiance of our duty to mankind. That duty is to guard ourselves from such beliefs as from a pestilence, which may shortly master our own body and then spread to the rest of the town. What would be thought of one who, for the sake of a sweet fruit, should deliberately run the risk of bringing a plague upon his family and his neighbors?

And, as in other such cases, it is not the risk only which has to be considered; for a bad action is always bad at the time when it is done, no matter what happens afterwards. Every time we let ourselves believe for unworthy reasons, we weaken our powers of self-control, of doubting, of judicially and fairly weighing evidence. We all suffer severely enough from the maintenance and support of false beliefs and the fatally wrong actions which they lead to, and the evil born when one such belief is entertained is great and wide. But a greater and wider evil arises when the credulous character is maintained and supported, when a habit of believing for unworthy reasons is fostered and made permanent. If I steal money from any person, there may be no harm done by the mere transfer of possession; he may not feel the loss, or it may prevent him from using the money badly. But I cannot help doing this great wrong towards Man, that I make myself dishonest. What hurts society is not that it should lose its property, but that it should become a den of thieves; for then it must cease to be society. This is why we ought not to do evil that good may come; for at any rate this great evil has come, that we have done evil and are made wicked thereby. In like manner, if I let myself believe anything on insufficient evidence, there may be no great harm done by the mere belief; it may be true after all, or I may never have occasion to exhibit it in outward acts. But I cannot help doing this great wrong toward Man, that I make myself credulous. The danger to society is not merely that it should believe wrong things, though that is great enough; but that it should become credulous, and lose the habit of testing things and inquiring into them; for then it must sink back into savagery.

The harm which is done by credulity in a man is not confined to the fostering of a credulous character in others, and consequent support of false beliefs. Habitual want of care about what I believe leads to habitual want of care in others about the truth of what is told to me. Men speak the truth to one another when each reveres the truth in his own mind and in the other's mind; but how shall my friend revere the truth in my mind when I myself am careless about it, when I believe things because I want to believe them, and because they

are comforting and pleasant? Will he not learn to cry, "Peace," to me, when there is no peace? By such a course I shall surround myself with a thick atmosphere of falsehood and fraud, and in that I must live. It may matter little to me, in my cloud-castle of sweet illusions and darling lies; but it matters much to Man that I have made my neighbors ready to deceive. The credulous man is father to the liar and the cheat; he lives in the bosom of this his family, and it is no marvel if he should become even as they are. So closely are our duties knit together, that whoso shall keep the whole law, and yet offend in one point, he is guilty of all.

To sum up: it is wrong always, everywhere, and for anyone, to believe anything upon insufficient evidence.

If a man, holding a belief which he was taught in childhood or persuaded of afterwards, keeps down and pushes away any doubts which arise about it in his mind, purposely avoids the reading of books and the company of men that call in question or discuss it, and regards as impious those questions which cannot easily be asked without disturbing it—the life of that man is one long sin against mankind.

If this judgment seems harsh when applied to those simple souls who have never known better, who have been brought up from the cradle with a horror of doubt, and taught that their eternal welfare depends on what they believe, then it leads to the very serious question, Who hath made Israel to sin? . . .

Inquiry into the evidence of a doctrine is not to be made once for all, and then taken as finally settled. It is never lawful to stifle a doubt; for either it can be honestly answered by means of the inquiry already made, or else it proves that the inquiry was not complete.

"But," says one, "I am a busy man; I have no time for the long course of study which would be necessary to make me in any degree a competent judge of certain questions, or even able to understand the nature of the arguments." Then he should have no time to believe. . . .

VII.B.3 The Will to Believe

WILLIAM JAMES

The classic response to Clifford's ethics of belief is William James's ''The Will to Believe'' (1896), in which James argues that life would be greatly impoverished if we confined our beliefs to such a Scrooge-like epistemology as Clifford proposes. In everyday life, where the evidence for important propositions is often unclear, we must live by faith or cease to act at all. Although we may not make leaps of faith just anywhere, sometimes practical considerations force us to make decisions regarding propositions that do not have their truth value written on their faces. 'Belief' is defined as a live, momentous optional hypothesis on which we cannot avoid a decision, for not to choose is in effect to choose against the hypothesis. James claims that religion may be such an optional hypothesis for many people, and in this case one has the right to believe the better story rather than the worse. To do so, one must will to believe what the evidence alone is inadequate to support.

I

Let us give the name of hypothesis to anything that may be proposed to our belief; and just as the electricians speak of live and dead wires, let us speak of any hypothesis as either *live* or *dead*. A live hypothesis is one which appeals as a real possibility to him to whom it is proposed. If I ask you to believe in the Mahdi, the notion makes no electric connection with your nature—it refuses to scintillate with any credibility at all. As an hypothesis it is completely dead. To an Arab, however (even if he be not one of the Mahdi's followers), the hypothesis is among the mind's possibilities: It is alive. This shows that deadness and liveness in an hypothesis are not intrinsic properties, but relations to the individual thinker. They are measured

Reprinted from William James, *The Will to Believe* (New York: Longmans, Green & Co., 1897).

by his willingness to act. The maximum of liveness in an hypothesis means willingness to act irrevocably. Practically, that means belief; but there is some believing tendency wherever there is willingness to act at all.

Next, let us call the decision between two hypotheses an *option*. Options may be of several kinds. They may be first, *living* or *dead*; secondly, *forced* or *avoidable*; thirdly, *momentous* or *trivial*; and for our purposes we may call an option a *genuine* option when it is of a forced, living, and momentous kind.

1. A living option is one in which both hypotheses are live ones. If I say to you: ''Be a theosophist or be a Mohammedan,'' it is probably a dead option, because for you neither hypothesis is likely to be alive. But if I say: ''Be an agnostic or be a Christian,'' it is otherwise: trained as you are, each hypothesis makes some appeal, however small, to your belief.

2. Next, if I say to you: ''Choose between going out with your umbrella or without it,'' I do not offer you a genuine option, for it is not forced. You can easily avoid it by not going out at all. Similarly, if I say, ''Either love me or hate me,'' ''Either call my theory true or call it false,'' your option is avoidable. You may remain indifferent to me, neither loving nor hating, and you may decline to offer any judgment as to my theory. But if I say, ''Either accept this truth or go without it,'' I put on you a forced option, for there is no standing place outside of the alternative. Every dilemma based on a complete logical disjunction, with no possibility of not choosing, is an option of this forced kind.

3. Finally, if I were Dr. Nansen and proposed to you to join my North Pole expedition, your option would be momentous; for this would probably be your similar opportunity, and your choice now would either exclude you from the North Pole sort of immortality alto-

gether or put at least the chance of it into your hands. He who refuses to embrace a unique opportunity loses the prize as surely as if he tried and failed. *Per contra,* the option is trivial when the opportunity is not unique, when the stake is insignificant, or when the decision is reversible if it later prove unwise. Such trivial options abound in the scientific life. A chemist finds an hypothesis live enough to spend a year in its verification: he believes in it to that extent. But if his experiments prove inconclusive either way, he is quit for his loss of time, no vital harm being done.

It will facilitate our discussion if we keep all these distinctions well in mind.

II

The next matter to consider is the actual psychology of human opinion. When we look at certain facts, it seems as if our passional and volitional nature lay at the root of all our convictions. When we look at others, it seems as if they could do nothing when the intellect had once said its say. Let us take the latter facts up first.

Does it not seem preposterous on the very face of it to talk of our opinions being modifiable at will? Can our will either help or hinder our intellect in its perceptions of truth? Can we, by just willing it, believe that Abraham Lincoln's existence is a myth, and that the portraits of him in *McClure's Magazine* are all of some one else? Can we, by any effort of our will, or by any strength of wish that it were true, believe ourselves well and about when we are roaring with rheumatism in bed, or feel certain that the sum of the two one-dollar bills in our pocket must be a hundred dollars? We can *say* any of these things, but we are absolutely impotent to believe them; and of just such things is the whole fabric of the truths that we do believe in made up—matters of fact, immediate or remote, as Hume said, and relations between ideas, which are either there or not there for us if we see them so, and which if not there cannot be put there by any action of our own.

In Pascal's *Thoughts* there is a celebrated passage known in literature as Pascal's wager. In it he tries to force us into Christianity by reasoning as if our concern with truth resembled our concern with the stakes in a game of chance. Translated freely his words are these: You must either believe or not believe that God is—which will you do? Your human reason cannot say. A game is going on between you and the nature of things which at the day of judgment will bring out either heads or tails. Weigh what your gains and your losses would be if you should stake all you have on heads, or God's existence: if you win in such case, you gain eternal beatitude; if you lose, you lose nothing at all. If there were an infinity of chances, and only one for God in this wager, still you ought to stake your all on God; for though you surely risk a finite loss by this procedure, any finite loss is reasonable, even a certain one is reasonable, if there is but the possibility of infinite gain. Go, then, and take holy water, and have masses said; belief will come and stupefy your scruples. . . . Why should you not? At bottom, what have you to lose?

You probably feel that when religious faith expresses itself thus, in the language of the gaming-table, it is put to its last trumps. Surely Pascal's own personal belief in masses and holy water had far other springs; and this celebrated page of his is but an argument for others, a last desperate snatch at a weapon against the hardness of the unbelieving heart. We feel that a faith in masses and holy water adopted wilfully after such a mechanical calculation would lack the inner soul of faith's reality; and if we were ourselves in the place of the Deity, we should probably take particular pleasure in cutting off believers of this pattern from their infinite reward. It is evident that unless there be some preexisting tendency to believe in masses and holy water, the option offered to the will by Pascal is not a living option. Certainly no Turk ever took to masses and holy water on its account; and even to us Protestants these means of salvation seem such foregone impossibilities that Pascal's logic, invoked for them specifically, leaves us unmoved. As well might the Mahdi write to us, saying, "I am the Expected One whom God has created in his effulgence. You shall be infinitely happy if you confess me; otherwise you shall be cut off from the light of the sun. Weigh, then, your infinite gain if I am genuine against your finite sacrifice if I am not!'' His logic would be that of Pascal; but he would vainly use it on us, for the hypothesis he offers us is dead. No tendency to act on it exists in us to any degree.

The talk of believing by our volition seems, then, from one point of view, simply silly. From another point of view it is worse than silly, it is vile. When one turns to the magnificent edifice of the physical sciences, and sees how it was reared; what thousands of disinterested moral lives of men lie buried in its mere foundations; what patience and postponement, what choking down of preference, what submission to the icy laws of outer fact are wrought into its very stones and mortar; how absolutely impersonal it stands in its vast august-ness—then how besotted and contemptible seems every little sentimentalist who comes blowing his voluntary smoke-wreaths, and pretending to decide things from out of his private dream! Can we wonder if those bred in the rugged and manly school of science should feel like spewing such subjectivism out of their mouths? The whole system of loyalties which grow up in the schools of science go dead against its toleration; so that it is only natural that those who have caught the scientific fever should pass over to the opposite extreme, and write sometimes as if the incorruptibly truthful intellect ought positively to prefer bitterness and unacceptableness to the heart in its cup.

It fortifies my soul to know
That though I perish, Truth is so

sings Clough, while Huxley exclaims: "My only consolation lies in the reflection that, however bad our posterity may become, so far as they hold by the plain rule of not pretending to believe what they have no reason to believe, because it may be to their advantage so to pretend [the word 'pretend' is surely here redundant], they will not have reached the lowest depth of immorality." And that delicious *enfant terrible* Clifford writes: "Belief is desecrated when given to unproved and unquestioned statements for the solace and private plea-

sure of the believer. . . . Whoso would deserve well of his fellows in this matter will guard the purity of his belief with a very fanaticism of jealous care, lest at any time it should rest on an unworthy object, and catch a stain which can never be wiped away. . . . If [a] belief has been accepted on insufficient evidence [even though the belief be true, as Clifford on the same page explains] the pleasure is a stolen one. . . . It is sinful because it is stolen in defiance of our duty to mankind. That duty is to guard ourselves from such beliefs as from a pestilence which may shortly master our own body and then spread to the rest of the town. . . . It is wrong always, everywhere, and for every one, to believe anything upon insufficient evidence."

III

All this strikes one as healthy, even when expressed, as by Clifford, with somewhat too much of robustious pathos in the voice. Free will and simple wishing do seem, in the matter of our credences, to be only fifth wheels to the coach. Yet if any one should thereupon assume that intellectual insight is what remains after wish and will and sentimental preference have taken wing, or that pure reason is what then settles our opinions, he would fly quite as directly in the teeth of the facts.

It is only our already dead hypotheses that our willing nature is unable to bring to life again. But what has made them dead for us is for the most part a previous action of our willing nature of an antagonistic kind. When I say "willing nature," I do not mean only such deliberate volitions as may have set up habits of belief that we cannot now escape from—I mean all such factors of belief as fear and hope, prejudice and passion, imitation and partisanship, the circumpressure of our caste and set. As a matter of fact we find ourselves believing, we hardly know how or why. Mr. Balfour gives the name of "authority" to all those influences, born of the intellectual climate, that make hypotheses possible or impossible for us, alive or dead. Here in this room, we all of us believe in molecules and the conservation of energy, in democracy and necessary progress, in Protestant Christianity and the duty of fighting for "the doctrine of the immortal Monroe," all for no reasons worthy of the name. We see into these matters with no more inner clearness, and probably with much less, than any disbeliever in them might possess. His unconventionality would probably have some grounds to show for its conclusions; but for us, not insight, but the *prestige* of the opinions, is what makes the spark shoot from them and light up our sleeping magazines of faith. Our reason is quite satisfied, in nine hundred and ninety-nine cases out of every thousand of us, if it can find a few arguments that will do to recite in case our credulity is criticized by some one else. Our faith is faith in some one else's faith, and in the greatest matters this is the most the case. . . .

Evidently, then, our non-intellectual nature does influence our convictions. There are passional tendencies and volitions which run before and others which come after belief, and it is only the latter that are too late for the fair; and they are not too late when the previous passional work has been already in their own direction. Pascal's argument, instead of being powerless, then seems a regular clincher, and is the last stroke needed to make our faith in masses and holy water complete. The state of things is evidently far from simple; and pure insight and logic, whatever they might do ideally, are not the only things that really do produce our creeds.

IV

Our next duty, having recognized this mixedup state of affairs, is to ask whether it be simply reprehensible and pathological, or whether, on the contrary, we must treat it as a normal element in making up our minds. The thesis I defend is, briefly stated, this: *Our passional nature not only lawfully may, but must, decide an option between propositions, whenever it is a genuine option that cannot by its nature be decided on intellectual grounds; for to say, under such circumstances, "Do not decide, but leave the question open," is itself a passional decision—just like deciding yes*

or no—and is attended with the same risk of losing the truth. . . .

VII

One more point, small but important, and our preliminaries are done. There are two ways of looking at our duty in the matter of opinion—ways entirely different, and yet ways about whose difference the theory of knowledge seems hitherto to have shown very little concern. *We must know the truth;* and *we must avoid error*—these are our first and great commandments as would-be knowers; but they are not two ways of stating an identical commandment, they are two separable laws. Although it may indeed happen that when we believe the truth A, we escape as an incidental consequence from believing the falsehood B, it hardly ever happens that by merely disbelieving B we necessarily believe A. We may in escaping B fall into believing other falsehoods, C or D, just as bad as B; or we may escape B by not believing anything at all, not even A.

Believe truth! Shun error!—these, we see, are two materially different laws; and by choosing between them we may end by coloring differently our whole intellectual life. We may regard the chase for truth as paramount, and the avoidance of error as secondary; or we may, on the other hand, treat the avoidance of error as more imperative, and let truth take its chance. Clifford, in the instructive passage which I have quoted, exhorts us to the latter course. Believe nothing, he tells us, keep your mind in suspense forever, rather than by closing it on insufficient evidence incur the awful risk of believing lies. You, on the other hand, may think that the risk of being in error is a very small matter when compared with the blessings of real knowledge, and be ready to be duped many times in your investigation rather than postpone indefinitely the chance of guessing true. I myself find it impossible to go with Clifford. We must remember that these feelings of our duty about either truth or error are in any case only expressions of our passional life. Biologically considered, our minds are as ready to grind out falsehood as veracity, and he who says, ''Better go without belief forever than believe a lie!'' merely shows his own preponderant private horror of becoming a dupe. He may be critical of many of his desires and fears, but this fear he slavishly obeys. He cannot imagine any one questioning its binding force. For my own part, I have also a horror of being duped; but I can believe that worse things than being duped may happen to a man in this world: so Clifford's exhortation has to my ears a thoroughly fantastic sound. It is like a general informing his soldiers that it is better to keep out of battle forever than to risk a single wound. Not so are victories either over enemies or over nature gained. Our errors are surely not such awfully solemn things. In a world where we are so certain to incur them in spite of all our caution, a certain lightness of heart seems healthier than this excessive nervousness on their behalf. At any rate, it seems the fittest thing for the empiricist philosopher.

VIII

And now, after all this introduction, let us go straight at our question. I have said, and now repeat it, that not only as a matter of fact do we find our passional nature influencing us in our opinions, but that there are some options between opinions in which this influence must be regarded both as an inevitable and as a lawful determinant of our choice.

I fear here that some of you my hearers will begin to scent danger, and lend an inhospitable ear. Two first steps of passion you have indeed had to admit as necessary—we must think so as to avoid dupery, and we must think so as to gain truth; but the surest path to those ideal consummations, you will probably consider, is from now onwards to take no further passional step.

Well, of course, I agree as far as the facts will allow. Wherever the option between losing truth and gaining it is not momentous, we can throw the chance of *gaining truth* away, and at any rate save ourselves from any chance of *believing falsehood,* by not making up our minds at all till objective evidence has come. In scientific questions, this is

almost always the case; and even in human affairs in general, the need of acting is seldom so urgent that a false belief to act on is better than no belief at all. Law courts, indeed, have to decide on the best evidence attainable for the moment, because a judge's duty is to make law as well as to ascertain it, and (as a learned judge once said to me) few cases are worth spending much time over: the great thing is to have them decided on *any* acceptable principle, and got out of the way. But in our dealings with objective nature we obviously are recorders, not makers, of the truth; and decisions for the mere sake of deciding promptly and getting on to the next business would be wholly out of place. Throughout the breadth of physical nature facts are what they are quite independently of us, and seldom is there any such hurry about them that the risks of being duped by believing a premature theory need be faced. The questions here are always trivial options, the hypotheses are hardly living (at any rate not living for us spectators), the choice between believing truth or falsehood is seldom forced. The attitude of sceptical balance is therefore the absolutely wise one if we would escape mistakes. What difference, indeed, does it make to most of us whether we have or have not a theory of the Röntgen rays, whether we believe or not in mind-stuff, or have a conviction about the causality of conscious states? It makes no difference. Such options are not forced on us. On every account it is better not to make them, but still keep weighing reasons *pro et contra* with an indifferent hand.

I speak, of course, here of the purely judging mind. For purposes of discovery such indifference is to be less highly recommended, and science would be far less advanced than she is if the passionate desires of individuals to get their own faiths confirmed had been kept out of the game. See for example the sagacity which Spencer and Weismann now display. On the other hand, if you want an absolute duffer in an investigation, you must, after all, take the man who has no interest whatever in its results: he is the warranted incapable, the positive fool. The most useful investigator, because the most sensitive observer, is always he whose eager interest in one side of the question is balanced by an equally keen nervousness lest he become deceived.[1] Science has organized this nervousness into a regular *technique,* her so-called method of verification; and she has fallen so deeply in love with the method that one may even say she has ceased to care for truth by itself at all. It is only truth as technically verified that interests her. The truth of truths might come in merely affirmative form, and she would decline to touch it. Such truth as that, she might repeat with Clifford, would be stolen in defiance of her duty to mankind. Human passions, however, are stronger than technical rules. "*Le coeur a ses raisons,*" as Pascal says, "*que la raison ne connait pas*";[2] and however indifferent to all but the bare rules of the game the umpire, the abstract intellect, may be, the concrete players who furnish him the materials to judge of are usually, each one of them, in love with some pet "live hypothesis" of his own. Let us agree, however, that wherever there is no forced option, the dispassionately judicial intellect with no pet hypothesis, saving us, as it does, from dupery at any rate, ought to be our ideal.

The question next arises: Are there not somewhere forced options in our speculative questions, and can we (as men who may be interested at least as much in positively gaining truth as in merely escaping dupery) always wait with impunity till the coercive evidence shall have arrived? It seems *a priori* improbable that the truth should be so nicely adjusted to our needs and powers as that. In the great boarding-house of nature, the cakes and the butter and the syrup seldom come out so even and leave the plates so clean. Indeed, we should view them with scientific suspicion if they did.

IX

Moral questions immediately present themselves as questions whose solution cannot wait for sensible proof. A moral question is a question not of what sensibly exists, but of what is good, or would be good if it did exist. Science can tell us what exists; but to compare the *worths,* both of what exists and of what does not exist, we must consult not science, but what Pascal calls our heart. . . . .

Turn now from these wide questions of good to a certain class of questions of fact, questions concerning personal relations, states of mind between one man and another. *Do you like me or not?*—for example. Whether you do or not depends, in countless instances, on whether I meet you halfway, am willing to assume that you must like me, and show you trust and expectation. The previous faith on my part in your liking's existence is in such cases what makes your liking come. But if I stand aloof, and refuse to budge an inch until I have objective evidence, until you shall have done something apt, as the absolutists say, *ad extorquendum assensum meum,* ten to one your liking never comes. How many women's hearts are vanquished by the mere sanguine insistence of some man that they *must* love him! He will not consent to the hypothesis that they cannot. The desire for a certain kind of truth here brings about that special truth's existence; and so it is in innumerable cases of other sorts. . . . *And where faith in a fact can help create the fact,* that would be an insane logic which should say that faith running ahead of scientific evidence is the "lowest kind of immorality" into which a thinking being can fall. Yet such is the logic by which our scientific absolutists pretend to regulate our lives!

X

In truths dependent on our personal action, then, faith based on desire is certainly a lawful and possibly an indispensable thing.

But now, it will be said, these are all childish human cases, and have nothing to do with great cosmical matters, like the question of religious faith. Let us then pass on to that. Religions differ so much in their accidents that in discussing the religious question we must make it very generic and broad. What then do we now mean by the religious hypothesis? Science says things are; morality says some things are better than other things; and religion says essentially two things.

First, she says that the best things are the more eternal things, the overlapping things, the things in the universe that throw the last stone, so to speak, and say the final word. "Perfection is eternal"—this phrase of Charles Secrétan seems a good way of putting this first affirmation of religion, an affirmation which obviously cannot yet be verified scientifically at all.

The second affirmation of religion is that we are better off even now if we believe her first affirmation to be true.

Now, let us consider what the logical elements of this situation are *in case the religious hypothesis in both its branches be really true.* (Of course, we must admit that possibility at the outset. If we are to discuss the question at all, it must involve a living option. If for any of you religion be a hypothesis that cannot, by any living possibility, be true, then you need go no farther. I speak to the "saving remnant" alone.) So proceeding, we see, first, that religion offers itself as a *momentous* option. We are supposed to gain, even now, by our belief, and to lose by our non-belief, a certain vital good. Secondly, religion is a *forced* option, so far as that good goes. We cannot escape the issue by remaining sceptical and waiting for more light, because, although we do avoid error in that way *if religion be untrue,* we lose the good, *if it be true,* just as certainly as if we positively chose to disbelieve. It is as if a man should hesitate indefinitely to ask a certain woman to marry him because he was not perfectly sure that she would prove an angel after he brought her home. Would he not cut himself off from that particular angel-possibility as decisively as if he went and married some one else? Scepticism, then, is not avoidance of option; it is option of a certain particular kind of risk. *Better risk loss of truth than chance of error*—that is your faith-vetoer's exact position. He is actively playing his stake as much as the believer is; he is backing the field against the religious hypothesis, just as the believer is backing the religious hypothesis against the field. To preach scepticism to us as a duty until "sufficient evidence" for religion be found, is tantamount therefore to telling us, when in presence of the religious hypothesis, that to yield to our fear of its being error is wiser and better than to yield to our hope that it may be true. It is not intellect against all passions, then; it is only intellect with one passion laying down its

law. And by what, forsooth, is the supreme wisdom of this passion warranted? Dupery for dupery, what proof is there that dupery through hope is so much worse than dupery through fear? I, for one, can see no proof; and I simply refuse obedience to the scientist's command to imitate his kind of option, in a case where my own stake is important enough to give me the right to choose my own form of risk. If religion be true and the evidence for it be still insufficient, I do not wish, by putting your extinguisher upon my nature (which feels to me as if it had after all some business in this matter), to forfeit my sole chance in life of getting upon the winning side—that chance depending, of course, on my willingness to run the risk of acting as if my passional need of taking the world religiously might be prophetic and right.

All this is on the supposition that it really may be prophetic and right, and that, even to us who are discussing the matter, religion is a live hypothesis which may be true. Now, to most of us religion comes in a still further way that makes a veto on our active faith even more illogical. The more perfect and more eternal aspect of the universe is represented in our religions as having personal form. The universe is no longer a mere *It* to us, but a *Thou*, if we are religious; and any relation that may be possible from person to person might be possible here. For instance, although in one sense we are passive portions of the universe, in another we show a curious autonomy, as if we were small active centers on our own account. We feel, too, as if the appeal of religion to us were made to our own active goodwill, as if evidence might be forever withheld from us unless we met the hypothesis halfway to take a trivial illustration: just as a man who in a company of gentlemen made no advances, asked a warrant for every concession, and believed no one's word without proof, would cut himself off by such churlishness from all the social rewards that a more trusting spirit would earn—so here, one who should shut himself up in snarling logicality and try to make the gods extort his recognition willy-nilly, or not get it at all, might cut himself off forever from his only opportunity of making the gods' acquaintance. This feeling, forced on us we know not whence that by obstinately believing that there are gods (although not to do so would be so easy both for our logic and our life) we are doing the universe the deepest service we can, seems part of the living essence of the religious hypothesis. If the hypothesis *were* true in all its parts, including this one, then pure intellectualism, with its veto on our making willing advances, would be an absurdity; and some participation of our sympathetic nature would be logically required. I therefore, for one, cannot see my way to accepting the agnostic rules for truth-seeking, or wilfully agree to keep my willing nature out of the game. I cannot do so for this plain reason, that *a rule of thinking which would absolutely prevent me from acknowledging certain kinds of truth if those kinds of truth were really there, would be an irrational rule.* That for me is the long and short of the formal logic of the situation, no matter what the kinds of truth might materially be.

I confess I do not see how this logic can be escaped. But sad experience makes me fear that some of you may still shrink from radically saying with me, *in abstracto,* that we have the right to believe at our own risk any hypothesis that is live enough to tempt our will. I suspect, however, that if this is so, it is because you have got away from the abstract logical point of view altogether, and are thinking (perhaps without realizing it) of some particular religious hypothesis which for you is dead. The freedom to "believe what we will" you apply to the case of some patent superstition; and the faith you think of is the faith defined by the schoolboy when he said, "Faith is when you believe something that you know ain't true." I can only repeat that this is misapprehension. *In concreto,* the freedom to believe can only cover living options which the intellect of the individual cannot by itself resolve; and living options never seem absurdities to him who has them to consider. When I look at the religious question as it really puts itself to concrete men, and when I think of all the possibilities which both practically and theoretically it involves, then this command that we shall put a stopper on our heart, instincts, and courage, and *wait*—acting of course meanwhile more or less as if religion were not true[3]—till doomsday, or till such time as our intellect and senses working together may have raked in evidence enough—this command, I say, seems to me the queerest idol ever manufactured in the philosophic cave. Were we scholastic absolutists, there might be more excuse. If we had an infallible intellect with its objective certitudes, we might feel ourselves disloyal to such a perfect organ of knowledge in not trusting to it exclusively, in not waiting for its releasing word. But if we are empiricists, if we believe that no bell in us tolls to let us know for certain when truth is in our grasp, then it seems a piece of idle fantasticality to preach so solemnly our duty of waiting for the bell. Indeed we *may* wait if we will—I hope you do not think that I am denying that—but if we do so, we do so at our peril as much as if we believed. In either case we *act,* taking our life in our hands. No one of us ought to issue vetoes to the other, nor should we bandy words of abuse. We ought, on the contrary, delicately and profoundly to respect one another's mental freedom: then only shall we bring about the intellectual republic; then only shall we have that spirit of inner tolerance without which all our outer tolerance is soulless, and which is empiricism's glory; then only shall we live and let live, in speculative as well as in practical things.

I began by a reference to Fitz-James Stephen; let me end by a quotation from him. "What do you think of yourself? What do you think of the world? . . . These are questions with which all must deal as it seems good to them. They are riddles of the Sphinx, and in some way or other we must deal with them. . . . In all important transactions of life we have to take a leap in the dark. . . . If we decide to leave the riddles unanswered, that is a choice; if we waver in our answer, that, too, is a choice: but whatever choice we make, we make it at our peril. If a man chooses to turn his back altogether on God and the future, no one can prevent him; no one can show beyond reasonable doubt that he is mistaken. If a man thinks otherwise and acts as he thinks, I do not see that any one can prove that he is mistaken. Each must act as he thinks best; and if he is wrong, so much the worse for him. We stand on a mountain pass in the midst of whirling snow and blinding mist, through which we get glimpses now and then of paths which may be deceptive. If we stand still we shall be frozen to death. If we take the wrong road we shall be dashed to pieces. We do not certainly know whether there is any right one. What must we do? 'Be strong and of a good courage.' Act for the best, hope for the best, and take what comes.

. . . If death ends all, we cannot meet death better.''

Notes

1. Compare Wilfrid Ward's Essay "The Wish to Believe," in his *Witnesses to the Unseen* (Macmillan & Co., 1893).

2. "The heart has its reasons which reason does not know."

3. Since belief is measured by action, he who forbids us to believe religion to be true, necessarily also forbids us to act as we should if we did believe it to be true. The whole defence of religious faith hinges upon action. If the action required or inspired by the religious hypothesis is in no way different from that dictated by the naturalistic hypothesis, then religious faith is a pure superfluity, better pruned away, and controversy about its legitimacy is a piece of idle trifling, unworthy of serious minds. I myself believe, of course, that the religious hypothesis gives to the world an expression which specifically determines our reactions, and makes them in a large part unlike what they might be on a purely naturalistic scheme of belief.

VII.C   Fideism: Faith Without/Against Reason

Fideism may be called the position that holds that objective reason is simply inappropriate for religious belief. Faith does not need reason for its justification, and the attempt to apply rational categories to religion is completely out of place. Faith creates its own justification, its own criteria of internal assessment. Perhaps there are two versions of fideism. The first states that religion is bound to appear absurd when judged by the standards of theoretical reason. The second merely says that religion is an activity in which reason is properly inoperative. It is not so much against reason as above reason. The two positions are compatible. The third-century theologian Tertullian seemed to hold that religious faith was both against and beyond human reason (and perhaps St. Paul holds the same in 1 Corinthians, chapter 1), but many fideists, such as Calvin, would subscribe only to the latter position.

The Danish philosopher Søren Kierkegaard (1813–1855), father of existentialism, seems to hold to both versions of fideism. For him, faith, not reason, is the highest virtue a human can reach; faith is necessary for the deepest human fulfillment. If Kant, the rationalist, adhered to a "religion within the limits of reason alone," Kierkegaard adhered to "reason within the limits of religion alone." He unashamedly proclaimed faith to be higher than reason in the development of essential humanness, that alone which promised eternal happiness. In a more everyday sense, Kierkegaard thought that we all live by simple faith in plans, purposes, and people. It is rarely the case in ordinary life that reason is our basic guide. Paraphrasing Hume, he might have said that "reason is and ought to be a slave to faith," for we all have an essential faith in something, and reason comes in largely as an afterthought in order to rationalize our intuitions and commitments.

No one writes more passionately about faith nor values it more highly than Kierkegaard.

Whereas his predecessors had largely viewed it as a necessary evil, a distant cousin to the princely knowledge, Kierkegaard reversed the order. Knowledge about metaphysical issues is not really desirable, because it prevents the kind of human striving that is essential for our fullest development. For him, faith is the highest virtue precisely because it is objectively uncertain; for personal growth into selfhood depends on uncertainty, risk, venturing forth over seventy thousand fathoms of ocean water. Faith is the lover's loyalty to the beloved when all the evidence is against her. Faith is the soul's deepest yearnings and hopes, which the rational part of us cannot fathom. Even if we had direct proof for theism or Christianity, we would not want it, for such objective certainty would take the venture out of the religious pilgrimage, reducing it to a set of dull mathematical certainties.

According to Kierkegaard, genuine theistic faith appears when reason reaches the end of its tether, when the individual sees that without God there is no purpose to life.

> In this manner God becomes a postulate, but not in the otiose manner in which this word is commonly understood. It becomes clear rather that the only way in which an existing individual comes into relation with God, is when the dialectical contradiction brings his passion to the point of despair, and helps him to embrace God with the "category of despair" (faith). Then the postulate is so far from being arbitrary that it is precisely a life-necessity. It is then not so much that God is a postulate, as that the existing individual's postulation of God is necessary.

In the selection from *Concluding Unscientific Postscript* (1846), "Subjectivity is Truth," included in this section, Kierkegaard argues that there is something fundamentally misguided in trying to base one's religious faith on objective evidence or reason. It is both useless (it won't work) and a bad thing (it detracts one from the essential task of growing in faith). He then goes on to develop a theory of subjectivity wherein faith finds an authentic home.

In our second reading, Robert M. Adams examines three of Kierkegaard's arguments against objective reason in religion (found in our first reading). Although he appreciates the depth of Kierkegaard's insight, he argues that the sort of fideism embraced by Kierkegaard has problems. The three arguments that Adams identifies may be described as follows:

1. The approximation argument
   A. All historical inquiry gives, at best, only approximate results.
   B. Approximate results are inadequate for religious faith (which demands certainty).
   C. Therefore, all historical inquiry is inadequate for religious faith.

2. The postponement argument
   A. One cannot have an authentic religious faith without being totally committed to the belief in question.
   B. One cannot be totally committed to any belief based on an inquiry in which one recognizes the possibility of a future need to revise the results.
   C. Therefore, authentic religious faith cannot be based on any inquiry in which one recognizes the possibility of a future need to revise the results.
   D. Since all rational inquiry recognizes the contingency of future revision, no authentic religious faith can be based on it.

3. The passion argument
   A. The most essential and valuable trait of religious faith is passion, a passion of the greatest possible intensity.
   B. An infinite passion requires objective improbability.
   C. Therefore, that which is most essential and valuable in religious faith requires objective improbability.

You should pay special attention to Adams's discussion of these points in order to determine whether his contentions undermine Kierkegaard's points. It should be noted that

Adams is sympathetic to the motivation that led Kierkegaard to set forth the arguments that he did, and he recognizes that Kierkegaard's conclusion does follow from an appealing conception of religion, although Adams himself sees no need to accept that conception. Adams's article is important both for its insight into Kierkegaard's thought and for Adams's ability to translate Kierkegaard's difficult style into clear argument form.

In our third reading, we turn to the leading type of fideism in contemporary philosophy of religion. We begin with a short piece from Ludwig Wittgenstein's "Lectures on Religious Belief." Wittgenstein argues that there is something *sui generis* or special about the very linguistic framework of believers, so that the concepts they use cannot be adequately grasped by outsiders. One has to share in a form of life in order to understand the way the various concepts function in that language game. Wittgenstein ridicules one Father O'Hara for giving the impression that there is a nonperspectival, impartial way of assessing the truth value of religious assertions. Such a view, Wittgenstein believes, is absurd.

A particularly lucid interpreter and adherent of Wittgensteinian fideism is Norman Malcolm, whose article "The Groundlessness of Belief" is included as the fourth reading in this section. Malcolm contends that religious belief is in no sense a hypothesis, for it cannot be and ought not to be justified rationally. It is essentially a groundless belief like other beliefs that do not need further support, such as our belief that things don't just vanish, our belief in the uniformity of nature, and our knowledge of our own intentions.

Like other fundamental assumptions religious beliefs are not derived from other beliefs but themselves form the support for all our other beliefs. They form the framework of our inquiry on which the very process of justification depends. Hence, it does not make sense to ask for a justification of religious claims or a refutation of them from a point outside the religious framework. Science and religion are just two different language games. "Neither stands in need of justification, the one no more than the other."

Finally, Gary Gutting offers a dialogue among a Catholic rationalist, a Calvinist transrationalist, and a Wittgensteinian fideist in which a critical discussion of fideism takes place. There are two separate points at issue in the discussion: (1) whether nonbelievers can understand religious language and (2) whether reason can adjudicate the truth claims of religion. Gutting challenges you to come to your own conclusion on the strengths and weaknesses of fideism. The discussion is continued in the fourth section of this part.

VII.C.1   Subjectivity is Truth

SØREN KIERKEGAARD

Our first reading is taken from the Concluding Unscientific Postscript *by Danish philosopher Søren Kierkegaard (1813–1855), father of existentialism. Kierkegaard represents a radical version of fideism in which faith not only is higher than reason but, in a sense, opposes it. Faith, not reason, is the highest virtue a human can reach; faith is necessary for the deepest human fulfilment. Kierkegaard argues that there is something fundamentally misguided in trying to base one's religious faith on objective evidence or reason. It is both useless (it won't work) and a bad thing (it detracts one from the essential task of growing in faith). He then goes on to develop a theory of subjectivity wherein faith finds an authentic home. Even if we had direct proof for theism or Christianity, we would not want it, for such objective certainty would take the venture out of the religious pilgrimage, reducing it to a set of dull mathematical certainties.*

The problem we are considering is not the truth of Christianity but the individual's relation to Christianity. Our discussion is not about the scholar's systematic zeal to arrange the truths of Christianity in nice tidy categories but about the individual's personal relationship to this doctrine, a relation-ship which is properly one of infinite interest to him. Simply stated, "I, Johannes Climacus, born in this city, now thirty years old, a decent fellow like most folk, suppose that there awaits me, as it awaits a maid and a professor, a highest good, which is called an eternal happiness. I have heard that Christianity is the way to that good, and so I ask, how may I establish a proper relationship to Christianity?"

I hear an intellectual's response to this, "What outrageous presumption! What egregious egoistic vanity in this theocentric and philosophically enlightened age, which is concerned with global history, to lay such inordinate weight on one's petty self."

I tremble at such a reproof and had I not already inured myself to these kinds of responses, I would slink away like a dog with his tail between his legs. But I have no guilt whatsoever about what I am doing, for it is not I who is presumptuous, but, rather, it is Christianity itself which compels me to ask the question in this way. For Christianity places enormous significance on my little self, and upon every other self however insignificant it may seem, in that it offers each self eternal happiness on the condition that a proper relationship between itself and the individual is established.

Although I am still an outsider to faith, I can see that the only unpardonable sin against the majesty of Christianity is for an individual to take his relationship to it for granted. However modest

From *Concluding Unscientific Postscript to the Philosophical Fragments* (1844), translated by Louis Pojman. This selection and translation has been made for this volume.

it may seem to relate oneself in this way, Christianity considers such a casual attitude to be imprudent. So I must respectfully decline all theocentric helpers and the helpers' helpers who would seek to help me through a detached relationship to this doctrine. I would rather remain where I am with my infinite concern about my spiritual existence, with the problem of how I may become a Christian. For while it is not impossible for one with an infinite concern for his eternal happiness to achieve salvation, it is entirely impossible for one who has lost all sensitivity to the relationship to achieve such a state.

The objective problem is: Is Christianity true? The subjective problem is: What is the individual's relationship to Christianity? Quite simply, how may I, Johannes Climacus, participate in the happiness promised by Christianity? The problem concerns myself alone; partly because, if it is properly set forth, it will concern everyone in exactly the same way; and partly because all the other points of view take faith for granted, as trivial.

In order to make my problem clear, I shall first describe the objective problem and show how it should be treated. In this way the historical aspect will be given its due. After this I shall describe the subjective problem.

The Objective Problem of the Truth of Christianity. From an objective point of view Christianity is a historical fact whose truth must be considered in a purely objective manner, for the modest scholar is far too objective not to leave himself outside—though as a matter of fact, he may count himself as a believer. 'Truth' in this objective sense may mean either (1) historical truth or (2) philosophical truth. As historical truth, the truth claims must be decided by a critical examination of the various sources in the same way we determine other historical claims. Considered philosophically, the doctrine that has been historically verified must be related to the eternal truth.

The inquiring, philosophical, and learned researcher raises the question of the truth, but not the subjective truth, that is, the truth as appropriated. The inquiring researcher is interested, but he

is not infinitely, personally, and passionately interested in a way that relates his own eternal happiness to this truth. Far be it for the objective person to be so immodest, so presumptuous as that!

Such an inquirer must be in one of two states. Either he is already in faith convinced of the truth of Christianity—and in such a relationship he cannot be infinitely interested in the objective inquiry, since faith itself consists in being infinitely concerned with Christianity and regards every competing interest as a temptation; or he is not in faith but objectively considering the subject matter, and as such not in a condition of being infinitely interested in the question.

I mention this in order to draw your attention to what will be developed in the second part of this work, namely, that the problem of the truth of Christianity is never appropriately set forth in this objective manner, that is, it does not arise at all, since Christianity lies in decision. Let the scholarly researcher work with indefatigable zeal even to the point of shortening his life in devoted service to scholarship. Let the speculative philosopher spare neither time nor effort. They are nevertheless not personally and passionately concerned. On the contrary, they wouldn't want to be but will want to develop an objective and disinterested stance. They are only concerned about objective truth, so that the question of personal appropriation is relatively unimportant, something that will follow their findings as a matter of course. In the last analysis what matters to the individual is of minor significance. Herein precisely lies the scholar's exalted equanimity as well as the comedy of his parrotlike pedantry.

The Historical Point of View. When Christianity is considered through its historical documents, it becomes vital to get a trustworthy account of what Christian doctrine really is. If the researcher is infinitely concerned with his relationship to this truth, he will immediately despair, because it is patently clear that in historical matters the greatest certainty is still only an approximation, and an approximation is too weak for one to build his eternal happiness upon, since its incommensurability with eternal happiness prevents it from obtaining.

So the scholar, having only a historical interest in the truth of Christianity, begins his work with tremendous zeal and contributes important research until his seventieth year. Then just fourteen days before his death he comes upon a new document that casts fresh light over one whole side of his inquiry. Such an objective personality is the antithesis of the restless concern of the subject who is infinitely interested in eternal happiness and who surely deserves to have a decisive answer to the question concerning that happiness.

When one raises the historical question of the truth of Christianity or of what is and what is not Christian truth, we come directly to the Holy Scriptures as the central document. The historical investigation focuses first on the Bible.

The Holy Scriptures. It is very important that the scholar secure the highest possible reliability in his work. In this regard it is important for me not to pretend that I have learning or show that I have none, for my purpose here is more important. And that is to have it understood and remembered that even with the most impressive scholarly credentials and persistence, even if all the intelligence of all the critics met in one single head, still one would get no further than an approximation. We could never show more than that there is an incommensurability between the infinite personal concern for one's eternal happiness and the reliability of the documents.

When the Scriptures are considered as the ultimate arbiter, which determines what is and what is not Christian, it becomes imperative to secure their reliability through a critical historical investigation. So we must deal here with several issues: the canonicity of each book of the Bible, their authenticity, their integrity, the trustworthiness of the authors, and finally, we must assume a dogmatic guarantee: inspiration. When one thinks of the prodigious labors that the English are devoting to digging the tunnel under the Thames, the incredible expenditure of time and effort, and how a little accident can upset the whole project for a long time, one may be able to get some idea of what is involved in the undertaking that we are describing. How much time, what diligence, what

glorious acumen, what remarkable scholarship from generation to generation have been requisitioned to accomplish this work of supreme wonder! And yet a single little dialectical doubt can suddenly touch the foundations and for a long time disturb the whole project, closing the underground way to Christianity, which one has tried to establish objectively and scientifically, instead of approaching the problem as it should be approached, above ground—subjectively.

But let us assume first that the critics have established everything that scholarly theologians in their happiest moments ever dreamed to prove about the Bible. These books and no others belong to the canon. They are authentic, complete, their authors are trustworthy—it is as though every letter were divinely inspired (one cannot say more than this, for inspiration is an object of faith and is qualitatively dialectical. It cannot be reached by a quantitative increment). Furthermore, there is not the slightest contradiction in these holy writings. For let us be careful in formulating our hypothesis. If there is even a word that is problematic, the parenthesis of uncertainty begins again, and the critical philological enterprise will lead one astray. In general, all that is needed to cause us to question our findings is a little circumspection, the renunciation of every learned middle-term, which could in a twinkle of the eye degenerate into a hundred-year parenthesis.

And so it comes to pass that everything we hoped for with respect to the Scriptures has been firmly established. What follows from this? Has anyone who didn't previously have faith come a single step closer to faith? Of course not, not a single step closer. For faith isn't produced through academic investigations. It doesn't come directly at all, but, on the contrary, it is precisely in objective analysis that one loses the infinite personal and passionate concern that is the requisite condition for faith, its ubiquitous ingredient, wherein faith comes into existence.

Has anyone who had faith gained anything in terms of faith's strength and power? No, not the least. Rather, his prodigious learning which lies like a dragon at faith's door, threatening to devour it, will become a handicap, forcing him to put forth an even greater prodigious effort in fear and trembling in order not to fall into temptation and confuse knowledge with faith. Whereas faith had uncertainty as a useful teacher, it now finds that certainty is its most dangerous enemy. Take passion away and faith disappears, for certainty and passion are incompatible. Let an analogy throw light on this point. He who believes that God exists and providentially rules the world finds it easier to preserve his faith (and not a fantasy) in an imperfect world where passion is kept awake, than in an absolutely perfect world; for in such an ideal world faith is unthinkable. This is the reason that we are taught that in eternity faith will be annulled.

Now let us assume the opposite, that the opponents have succeeded in proving what they desired to establish regarding the Bible and did so with a certainty that transcended their wildest hopes. What then? Has the enemy abolished Christianity? Not a whit. Has he harmed the believer? Not at all. Has he won the right of being free from the responsibility of becoming a believer? By no means. Simply because these books are not by these authors, are not authentic, lack integrity, do not seem to be inspired (though this cannot be demonstrated since it is a matter of faith), it in no way follows that these authors have not existed, and above all it does not follow that Christ never existed. In so far as faith perdures, the believer is at liberty to assume it, just as free (mark well!); for if he accepted the content of faith on the basis of evidence, he would now be on the verge of giving up faith. If things ever came this far, the believer is somewhat to blame, for he invited the procedure and began to play into the hands of unbelief by attempting to prove the content of faith.

Here is the heart of the matter, and I come back to learned theology. For whose sake is the proof sought? Faith does not need it. Yes, it must regard it as an enemy. But when faith begins to feel ashamed, when like a young woman for whom love ceases to suffice, who secretly feels ashamed of her lover and must therefore have it confirmed by others that he really is quite remarkable, so likewise when faith falters and begins to

lose its passion, when it begins to cease to be faith, then proof becomes necessary in order to command respect from the side of unbelief.

So when the subject of faith is treated objectively, it becomes impossible for a person to relate himself to the decision of faith with passion, let alone with infinitely concerned passion. It is a self-contradiction and as such comical to be infinitely concerned about what at best can only be an approximation. If in spite of this, we still preserve passion, we obtain fanaticism. For the person with infinite passionate concern every relevant detail becomes something of infinite value. The error lies not in the infinite passion but in the fact that its object has become an approximation.

As soon as one takes subjectivity away—and with it subjectivity's passion—and with passion the infinite concern—it becomes impossible to make a decision—either with regard to this problem or any other; for every decision, every genuine decision, is a subjective action. A contemplator (i.e., an objective subject) experiences no infinite urge to make a decision and sees no need for a commitment anywhere. This is the falsity of objectivity and this is the problem with the Hegelian notion of mediation as the mode of transition in the continuous process, where nothing endures and where nothing is infinitely decided because the movement turns back on itself and again turns back; but the movement itself is a chimera and philosophy becomes wise afterwards. Objectively speaking, this method produces results in great supply, but it does not produce a single decisive result. This is as is expected, since decisiveness inheres in subjectivity, essentially in passion and maximally in the personal passion that is infinitely concerned about one's eternal happiness.

Christianity is spirit, spirit is inwardness, inwardness is subjectivity, subjectivity is essentially passion and at its maximum infinite personal and passionate concern about one's eternal happiness.

Becoming Subjective. Objectively we only consider the subject matter, subjectively we consider the subject and his subjectivity, and, behold, subjectivity is precisely our subject matter. It must constantly be kept in mind that the subjective problem is not about some other subject matter but simply about subjectivity itself. Since the problem is about a decision, and all decisions lie in subjectivity, it follows that not a trace of objectivity remains, for at the moment that subjectivity slinks away from the pain and crisis of decision, the problem becomes to a degree objective. If the Introduction still awaits another work before a judgment can be made on the subject matter, if the philosophical system still lacks a paragraph, if the speaker still has a final argument, the decision is postponed. We do not raise the question of the truth of Christianity in the sense that when it has been decided, subjectivity is ready and willing to accept it. No, the question is about the subject's acceptance of it, and it must be regarded as an infernal illusion or a deceitful evasion which seeks to avoid the decision by taking an objective treatment of the subject matter and assumes that a subjective commitment will follow from the objective deliberation as a matter of course. On the contrary, the decision lies in subjectivity and an objective acceptance is either a pagan concept or one devoid of all meaning.

Christianity will give the single individual eternal happiness, a good that cannot be divided into parts but can only be given to one person at a time. Although we presuppose that subjectivity is available to be appropriated, a possibility that involves accepting this good, it is not a subjectivity without qualification, without a genuine understanding of the meaning of this good. Subjectivity's development or transformation, its infinite concentration in itself with regard to an eternal happiness—this highest good of Infinity, an eternal happiness—this is subjectivity's developed possibility. As such, Christianity protests against all objectivity and will infinitely concern itself only with subjectivity. If there is any Christian truth, it first arises in subjectivity. Objectively it does not arise at all. If its truth is only in a single person, then Christianity exists in him alone, and there is greater joy in heaven over this one than over all world history and philosophical systems which, as objective forces, are incommensurable with the Christian idea.

Philosophy teaches that the way to truth is to become objective, but Christianity teaches that the way is to become subjective, that is, to become a subject in truth. Lest we seem to be trading on ambiguities, let it be said clearly that Christianity aims at intensifying passion to its highest pitch; but passion is subjectivity and does not exist objectively at all.

Subjective Truth, Inwardness; Truth is Subjectivity. For an objective reflection the truth becomes an object, something objective, and thought points away from the subject. For subjective reflection the truth becomes a matter of appropriation, of inwardness, of subjectivity, and thought must penetrate deeper and still deeper into the subject and his subjectivity. Just as in objective reflection, when objectivity had come into being, subjectivity disappeared, so here the subjectivity of the subject becomes the final stage, and objectivity disappears. It is not for an instant forgotten that the subject is an existing individual, and that existence is a process of becoming, and that therefore the idea of truth being an identity of thought and being is a chimera of abstraction; this is not because the truth is not such an identity but because the believer is an existing individual for whom the truth cannot be such an identity as long as he exists as a temporal being.

If an existing subject really could transcend himself, the truth would be something complete for him, but where is this point outside of himself? The I = I is a mathematical point that does not exist, and insofar as one would take this standpoint, he will not stand in another's way. It is only momentarily that the existential subject experiences the unity of the infinite and the finite, which transcends existence, and that moment is the moment of passion. While scribbling modern philosophy is contemptuous of passion, passion remains the highest point of existence for the individual who exists in time. In passion the existential subject is made infinite in imagination's eternity, and at the same time he is himself.

All essential knowledge concerns existence, or only that knowledge that relates to existence is essential, is essential knowledge. All knowledge that is not existential, that does not involve inward reflection, is really accidental knowledge, its degree and compass are essentially a matter of no importance. This essential knowledge that relates itself essentially to the existing individual is not to be equated with the above-mentioned abstract identity between thought and being. But it means that knowledge must relate itself to the knower, who is essentially an existing individual, and therefore all essential knowledge essentially relates itself to existence, to that which exists. But all ethical and all ethical-religious knowledge has this essential relationship to the existence of the knower.

In order to elucidate the difference between the objective way of reflection and the subjective way, I shall now show how subjective reflection makes its way back into inwardness. The highest point of inwardness in an existing person is passion, for passion corresponds to truth as a paradox, and the fact that the truth becomes a paradox is grounded in its relation to an existing individual. The one corresponds to the other. By forgetting that we are existing subjects, we lose passion and truth ceases to be a paradox, but the knowing subject begins to lose his humanity and becomes fantastic and the truth likewise becomes a fantastic object for this kind of knowledge.

When the question of truth is put forward in an objective manner, reflection is directed objectively to the truth as an object to which the knower is related. The reflection is not on the relationship but on whether he is related to the truth. If that which he is related to is the truth, the subject is in the truth. When the question of truth is put forward in a subjective manner, reflection is directed subjectively to the individual's relationship. If the relation's HOW is in truth, the individual is in truth, even if the WHAT to which he is related is not true.

We may illustrate this by examining the knowledge of God. Objectively the reflection is on whether the object is the true God; subjectively reflection is on whether the individual is related to a *what* in such a way that his relationship in truth is a God-relationship. On which side does the truth lie? Ah, let us not lean towards mediation and say, it is on neither side but in the mediation of both of them.

The existing individual who chooses the objective way enters upon the entire approximation process that is supposed to bring God into the picture. But this in all eternity cannot be done because God is Subject and therefore exists only for the subjective individual in inwardness. The existing individual who chooses the subjective way comprehends instantly the entire dialectical difficulty involved in having to use some time, perhaps a long time, in order to find God objectively. He comprehends this dialectical difficulty in all its pain because every moment without God is a moment lost—so important is the matter of being related to God. In this way God certainly becomes a postulate but not in the useless sense in which it is often taken. It becomes the only way in which an existing individual comes into a relation with God—when the dialectical contradiction brings passion to the point of despair and helps him embrace God with the category of despair (faith). Now the postulate is far from being arbitrary or optional. It becomes a life-saving necessity, so that it is no longer simply a postulate, but rather the individual's postulation of the existence of God is a necessity.

Now the problem is to calculate on which side there is the most truth: *either* the side of one who seeks the true God objectively and pursues the approximate truth of the God-idea *or* the side of one who is driven by infinite concern for his relationship to God. No one who has not been corrupted by science can have any doubt in the matter.

If one who lives in a Christian culture goes up to God's house, the house of the true God, with a true conception of God, with knowledge of God and prays—but prays in a false spirit; and one who lives in an idolatrous land prays with the total passion of the infinite, although his eyes rest on the image of an idol; where is there most truth? The one prays in truth to God, although he worships an idol. The other prays in untruth to the true God and therefore really worships an idol.

When a person objectively inquires about the

problem of immortality and another person embraces it as an uncertainty with infinite passion, where is there most truth, and who really has the greater certainty? The one has entered into an inexhaustible approximation, for certainty of immortality lies precisely in the subjectivity of the individual. The other is immortal and fights against his uncertainty.

Let us consider Socrates. Today everyone is playing with some proof or other. Some have many, some fewer. But Socrates! He put the question objectively in a hypothetical manner: "*if* there is immortality." Compared to the modern philosopher with three proofs for immortality, should we consider Socrates a doubter? Not at all. On this little *if* he risks his entire life, he dares to face death, and he has directed his life with infinite passion so that the *if* is confirmed—*if* there is immortality. Is there any better proof for life after death? But those who have the three proofs do not at all pattern their lives in conformity with the idea. If there is an immortality, it must feel disgust over their lackadaisical manner of life. Can any better refutation be given of the three proofs? These crumbs of uncertainty helped Socrates because they hastened the process along, inciting the passions. The three proofs that that others have are of no help at all because they are dead to the spirit, and the fact that they need three proofs proves that they are spiritually dead. The Socratic ignorance that Socrates held fast with the entire passion of his inwardness was an expression of the idea that eternal truth is related to an existing individual, and that this will be in the form of a paradox as long as he exists; and yet it is just possible that there is more truth in Socratic ignorance than is contained in the "objective truth" of the philosophical systems, which flirts with the spirit of the times and cuddles up to associate professors.

The objective accent falls on *what* is said; the subjective accent falls on *how* it is said. This distinction is valid even for aesthetics and shows itself in the notion that what may be objectively true may in the mouth of certain people become false. This distinction is illustrated by the saying that the difference between the older days and our day is

that in the old days only a few knew the truth while in ours all know it, except that the inwardness towards it is in inverse proportion to the scope of its possession. Aesthetically the contradiction that the truth becomes error in certain mouths is best understood comically. In the ethical-religious domain the accent is again on the *how*. But this is not to be understood as referring to decorum, modulation, delivery, and so on, but to the individual's relationship to the proposition, the way he relates himself to it. Objectively it is a question simply about the content of the proposition, but subjectively it is a question of inwardness. At its maximum this inward *how* is the passion of infinity and the passion of the infinite is itself the truth. But since the passion of the infinite is exactly subjectivity, subjectivity is the truth. Objectively there is no infinite decision or commitment, and so it is objectively correct to annul the difference between good and evil as well as the law of noncontradiction and the difference between truth and untruth. Only in subjectivity is there decision and commitment, so that to seek this in objectivity is to be in error. It is the passion of infinity that brings forth decisiveness, not its content, for its content is precisely itself. In this manner the subjective *how* and subjectivity are the truth.

But the *how* that is subjectively emphasized because the subject is an existing individual is also subject to a temporal dialectic. In passion's decisive moment, where the road swings off from the way to objective knowledge, it appears that the infinite decision is ready to be made. But in that moment the existing individual finds himself in time, and the subjective *how* becomes transformed into a striving, a striving that is motivated by and is repeatedly experienced in the decisive passion of the infinite. But this is still a striving.

When subjectivity is truth, subjectivity's definition must include an expression for an opposition to objectivity, a reminder of the fork in the road, and this expression must also convey the tension of inwardness. Here is such a definition of truth: *the objective uncertainty, held fast in an appropriation process of the most passionate inward-*

ness is the truth, the highest truth available for an *existing* person. There where the way swings off (and where that is cannot be discovered objectively but only subjectively), at that place objective knowledge is annulled. Objectively speaking he has only uncertainty, but precisely there the infinite passion of inwardness is intensified, and truth is precisely the adventure to choose objective uncertainty with the passion of inwardness.

When I consider nature in order to discover God, I do indeed see his omnipotence and wisdom, but I see much more that disturbs me. The result of all this is objective uncertainty, but precisely here is the place for inwardness because inwardness apprehends the objective uncertainty with the entire passion of infinity. In the case of mathematical statements objectivity is already given, but because of the nature of mathematics, this truth is existentially indifferent.

Now the above definition of truth is an equivalent description of faith. Without risk there is no faith. Faith is precisely the contradiction between the infinite passion of inwardness and objective uncertainty. If I can grasp God objectively, I do not believe, but because I cannot know God objectively, I must have faith, and if I will preserve myself in faith, I must constantly be determined to hold fast to the objective uncertainty, so as to remain out upon the ocean's deep, over seventy thousand fathoms of water, and still believe.

In the sentence 'subjectivity, inwardness is truth', we see the essence of Socratic wisdom, whose immortal service is exactly to have recognized the essential meaning of existence, that the knower is an *existing* subject, and for this reason in his ignorance Socrates enjoyed the highest relationship to truth within the paganism. This is a truth that speculative philosophy unhappily again and again forgets: that the knower is an existing subject. It is difficult enough to recognize this fact in our objective age, long after the genius of Socrates.

When subjectivity, inwardness, is the truth, the truth becomes objectively determined as a paradox, and that it is paradoxical is made clear by the fact that subjectivity is truth, for it repels objectivity, and the expression for the objective repul-

sion is the intensity and measure of inwardness. The paradox is the objective uncertainty, which is the expression for the passion of inwardness, which is precisely the truth. This is the Socratic principle. The eternal, essential truth, that is, that which relates itself essentially to the individual because it concerns his existence (all other knowledge is, Socratically speaking, accidental, its degree and scope being indifferent), is a paradox. Nevertheless, the eternal truth is not essentially in itself paradoxical, but it becomes so by relating itself to an existing individual. Socratic ignorance is the expression of this objective uncertainty, the inwardness of the existential subject is the truth. To anticipate what I will develop later, Socratic ignorance is an analogy to the category of the absurd, only that there is still less objective certainty in the absurd, and therefore infinitely greater tension in its inwardness. The Socratic inwardness that involves existence is an analogy to faith, except that this inwardness is repulsed not by ignorance but by the absurd, which is infinitely deeper. Socratically the eternal, essential truth is by no means paradoxical in itself, but only by virtue of its relation to an existing individual.

Subjectivity, inwardness, is the truth. Is there a still more inward expression for this? Yes, there is. If subjectivity is seen as the truth, we may posit the opposite principle: that subjectivity is untruth, error. Socratically speaking, subjectivity is untruth if it fails to understand that subjectivity is truth and desires to understand itself objectively. But now we are presupposing that subjectivity in becoming the truth has a difficulty to overcome in as much as it is in untruth. So we must work backwards, back to inwardness. Socratically, the way back to the truth takes place through recollection, supposing that we have memories of that truth deep within us.

Let us call this untruth of the individual 'sin'. Seen from eternity the individual cannot be in sin, nor can he be eternally presupposed as having been in sin. So it must be that he becomes a sinner by coming into existence (for the beginning point is that subjectivity is untruth). He is not born as a sinner in the sense that he is sinful before he is born, but he is born in sin and as a sinner. We shall call this state *original sin*. But if existence has acquired such power over him, he is impotent to make his way back to eternity through the use of his memory (supposing that there is truth in the Platonic idea that we may discover truth through recollection). If it was already paradoxical that the eternal truth related itself to an existing individual, now it is absolutely paradoxical that it relates itself to such an individual. But the more difficult it is for him through memory to transcend existence, the more inwardness must increase in intense passion, and when it is made impossible for him, when he is held so fast in existence that the back door of recollection is forever closed to him through sin, then his inwardness will be the deepest possible.

Subjectivity is truth. Through this relationship between the eternal truth and the existing individual the paradox comes into existence. Let us now go further and suppose that the eternal truth is essentially a paradox. How does this paradox come into existence? By juxtaposing the eternal, essential truth with temporal existence. When we set them together within the truth itself, the truth becomes paradoxical. The eternal truth has come into time. This is the paradox. If the subject is hindered by sin from making his way back to eternity by looking inward through recollection, he need not trouble himself about this, for now the eternal essential truth is no longer behind him, but it is in front of him, through its being in existence or having existed, so that if the individual does not *existentially* get hold of the truth, he will never get hold of it.

It is impossible to accentuate existence more than this. When the eternal truth is related to an existing individual, truth becomes a paradox. The paradox repels the individual because of the objective uncertainty and ignorance towards inwardness. But since this paradox in itself is not paradoxical, it does not push the spirit far enough. For without risk there is no faith, and the greater the risk the greater the faith, and the more objective reliability, the less inwardness (for inwardness is precisely subjectivity). Indeed, the less objective reliability, the deeper becomes the possible inwardness. When the paradox is in itself paradoxical, it repels the individual by the power of the

absurd, and the corresponding passion, which is produced in the process, is faith. But subjectivity, inwardness, is truth, for otherwise we have forgotten the Socratic contribution; but there is no more striking expression for inwardness than when the retreat from existence through recollection back to eternity is made impossible; and when the truth as paradox encounters the individual who is caught in the vice-grip of sin's anxiety and suffering, but who is also aware of the tremendous risk involved in faith—when he nevertheless makes the leap of faith—this is subjectivity at its height.

When Socrates believed in the existence of God, he held fast to an objective uncertainty in passionate inwardness, and in that contradiction, in that risk faith came into being. Now it is different. Instead of the objective uncertainty, there is objective certainty about the object—certainty that it is absurd, and it is, again, faith that holds fast to that object in passionate inwardness. Compared with the gravity of the absurd, Socratic ignorance is a joke, and compared with the strenuosity of faith in believing the paradox, Socratic existential inwardness is a Greek life of leisure.

What is the absurd? The absurd is that the eternal truth has entered time, that God has entered existence, has been born, has grown, and so on, has become precisely like any other human being, quite indistinguishable from other humans. The absurd is precisely by its objective repulsion the measure of the inwardness of faith. Suppose there is a man who desires to have faith. Let the comedy begin. He desires to obtain faith with the help of objective investigation and what the approximation process of evidential inquiry yields. What happens? With the help of the increment of evidence the absurd is transformed to something else; it becomes probable, it becomes more probable still, it becomes perhaps highly and overwhelmingly probable. Now that there is respectable evidence for the content of his faith, he is ready to believe it, and he prides himself that his faith is not like that of the shoemaker, the tailor, and the simple folk, but comes after a long investigation. Now he prepares himself to believe it. Any proposition that is almost probable, reasonably probable, highly and overwhelmingly probable, is something that is almost known and as good as known, highly and overwhelmingly known—but it is not believed, not through faith; for the absurd is precisely faith's object and the only positive attitude possible in relation to it is faith and not knowledge.

Christianity has declared itself to be the eternal that has entered time, that has proclaimed itself as the *paradox* and demands faith's inwardness in relation to that which is a scandal to the Jews and folly to the Greeks—and as absurd to the understanding. It is impossible to say this more strongly than by saying: subjectivity is truth, and objectivity is repelled by it—by virtue of the absurd.

Subjectivity culminates in passion. Christianity is the paradox; paradox and passion belong together as a perfect match, and the paradox is perfectly suited to one whose situation is to be in the extremity of existence. Indeed, there never has been found in all the world two lovers more suited

to each other than passion and paradox, and the strife between them is a lover's quarrel, when they argue about which one first aroused the other's passion. And so it is here. The existing individual by means of the paradox has come to the extremity of existence. And what is more wonderful for lovers than to be granted a long time together with each other without anything disturbing their relation except that which makes it more inwardly passionate? And this is what is granted to the unspeculative understanding between the passion and paradox, for they will dwell harmoniously together in time and be changed first in eternity.

But the speculative philosopher views things altogether differently. He believes but only to a certain degree. He puts his hand to the plow but quickly looks about for something to know. From a Christian perspective it is hard to see how he could reach the highest good in this manner.

VII.C.2   Kierkegaard's Arguments Against Objective Reasoning in Religion

ROBERT MERRIHEW ADAMS

In our second reading, Robert Merrihew Adams, professor of philosophy at the University of California at Los Angeles, examines three of Kierkegaard's arguments against objective reason in religion (found in our first reading). Although he appreciates the depth of Kierkegaard's insight, he argues that the sort of fideism embraced by Kierkegaard has several problems. The three arguments that Adams identifies are called the approximation argument, the postponement argument, and the passion argument.

It is sometimes held that there is something in the nature of religious faith itself that renders it useless or undesirable to reason objectively in support of such faith, even if the reasoning should happen to have considerable plausibility. Søren Kierkegaard's *Concluding Unscientific Postscript* is probably the document most commonly cited as representative of this view. In the present essay I shall discuss three arguments for the view. I call them the Approximation Argument, the Postponement Argument, and the Passion Argument; and I suggest they can all be found in the *Postscript*. I shall try to show that the Approximation Argument is a bad argument. The other two will not be so easily disposed of, however. I believe they show that Kierkegaard's conclusion, or something like it, does indeed follow from a certain conception of religiousness—a conception which has some ap-

Reprinted from *The Monist*, vol. 60, no. 2 (1977), by permission of the author and The Hegeler Institute, La Salle, Ill. Footnotes edited.

peal, although for reasons which I shall briefly suggest, I am not prepared to accept it.

Kierkegaard uses the word "objective" and its cognates in several senses, most of which need not concern us here. We are interested in the sense in which he uses it when he says, "it is precisely a misunderstanding to seek an objective assurance," and when he speaks of "an objective uncertainty held fast in the appropriation-process of the most passionate inwardness" (pp. 41, 182).[1] Let us say that a piece of reasoning, *R*, is *objective reasoning* just in case every (or almost every) intelligent, fair-minded, and sufficiently informed person would regard *R* as showing or tending to show (in the circumstances in which *R* is used, and to the extent claimed in *R*) that *R*'s conclusion is true or probably true. Uses of "objective" and "objectively" in other contexts can be understood from their relation to this one; for example, an objective uncertainty is a proposition which cannot be shown by objective reasoning to be certainly true.

I. The Approximation Argument

"Is it possible to base an eternal happiness upon historical knowledge?" is one of the central questions in the *Postscript,* and in the *Philosophical Fragments* to which it is a "postscript." Part of Kierkegaard's answer to the question is that it is not possible to base an eternal happiness on objective reasoning about historical facts.

> For nothing is more readily evident than that the greatest attainable certainty with respect to anything historical is merely an *approximation*. And an approximation, when viewed as a basis for an eternal happiness, is wholly inadequate, since the incommensurability makes a result impossible. [p. 25]

Kierkegaard maintains that it is possible, however, to base an eternal happiness on a belief in historical facts that is independent of objective evidence for them, and that that is what one must do in order to be a Christian. This is the Approximation Argument for the proposition that Christian faith cannot be based on objective reasoning. (It is assumed that some belief about historical facts is an essential part of Christian faith, so that if religious faith cannot be based on objective historical reasoning, then Christian faith cannot be based on objective reasoning at all.) Let us examine the argument in detail.

Its first premise is Kierkegaard's claim that "the greatest attainable certainty with respect to anything historical is merely an approximation." I take him to mean that historical evidence, objectively considered, never completely excludes the possibility of error. "It goes without saying," he claims, "that it is impossible in the case of historical problems to reach an objective decision so certain that no doubt could disturb it" (p. 41). For Kierkegaard's purposes it does not matter how small the possibility of error is, so long as it is finitely small (that is, so long as it is not literally infinitesimal). He insists (p. 31) that his Approximation Argument makes no appeal to the supposition that the objective evidence for Christian historical beliefs is weaker than the objective evidence for any other historical belief. The argument turns on a claim about *all* historical evidence. The probability of error in our belief that there was an American Civil War in the nineteenth century, for instance, might be as small as $10(1/2,000,000)$; that would be a large enough chance of error for Kierkegaard's argument.

It might be disputed, but let us assume for the sake of argument that there is some such finitely small probability of error in the objective grounds for all historical beliefs, as Kierkegaard held. This need not keep us from saying that we "know," and it is "certain," that there was an American Civil War. For such an absurdly small possibility of error is as good as no possibility of error at all, "for all practical intents and purposes," as we might say. Such a possibility of error is too small to be worth worrying about.

But would it be too small to be worth worrying about if we had an *infinite* passionate interest in the question about the Civil War? If we have an infinite passionate interest in something, there is no limit to how important it is to us. (The nature of such an interest will be discussed more fully in section 3 below.) Kierkegaard maintains that in relation to an infinite passionate interest *no* possibility of error is too small to be worth worrying about. "In relation to an eternal happiness, and an infinite passionate interest in its behalf (in which latter alone the former can exist), an iota is of importance, of infinite importance . . ." (p. 28). This is the basis for the second premise of the Approximation Argument, which is Kierkegaard's claim that "an approximation, when viewed as a basis for an eternal happiness, is wholly inadequate" (p. 25). "An approximation is essentially incommensurable with an infinite personal interest in an eternal happiness" (p. 26).

At this point in the argument it is important to have some understanding of Kierkegaard's conception of faith, and the way in which he thinks faith excludes doubt. Faith must be decisive; in fact it seems to consist in a sort of decision-making. "The conclusion of belief is not so much a conclusion as a resolution, and it is for this reason that belief excludes doubt." The decision of faith is a decision to disregard the possibility of error—to act on what is believed, without hedging one's bets to take account of any possibility of error.

To disregard the possibility of error is not to be unaware of it, or fail to consider it, or lack anxiety about it. Kierkegaard insists that the believer must be keenly *aware* of the risk of error. "If I wish to preserve myself in faith I must constantly be intent upon holding fast the objective uncertainty, so as to remain out upon the deep, over seventy thousand fathoms of water, still preserving my faith" (p. 182).

For Kierkegaard, then, to ask whether faith in a historical fact can be based on objective reasoning is to ask whether objective reasoning can justify one in disregarding the possibility of error which (he thinks) historical evidence always leaves. Here another aspect of Kierkegaard's conception of faith plays its part in the argument. He thinks that in all genuine religious faith the believer is *infinitely* interested in the object of his faith. And he thinks it follows that objective reasoning cannot justify him in disregarding *any* possibility of error about the object of faith, and therefore cannot lead him all the way to religious faith where a historical fact is concerned. The farthest it could

lead him is to the conclusion that *if* he had only a certain finite (though very great) interest in the matter, the possibility of error would be too small to be worth worrying about and he would be justified in disregarding it. But faith disregards a possibility of error that *is* worth worrying about, since an infinite interest is involved. Thus faith requires a "leap" beyond the evidence, a leap that cannot be justified by objective reasoning (cf. p. 90).

There is something right in what Kierkegaard is saying here, but his Approximation Argument is a bad argument. He is right in holding that grounds of doubt which may be insignificant for most practical purposes can be extremely troubling for the intensity of a religious concern, and that it may require great decisiveness, or something like courage, to overcome them religiously. But he is mistaken in holding that objective reasoning could not justify one in disregarding any possibility of error about something in which one is infinitely interested.

The mistake, I believe, lies in his overlooking the fact that there are at least two different reasons one might have for disregarding a possibility of error. The first is that the possibility is too small to be worth worrying about. The second is that the risk of not disregarding the possibility of error would be greater than the risk of disregarding it. Of these two reasons only the first is ruled out by the infinite passionate interest.

I will illustrate this point with two examples, one secular and one religious. A certain woman has a very great (though not infinite) interest in her husband's love for her. She rightly judges that the objective evidence available to her renders it 99.9 per cent probable that he loves her truly. The intensity of her interest is sufficient to cause her some *anxiety* over the remaining 1/1,000 chance that he loves her not; for her this chance is not too small to be worth worrying about. (Kierkegaard uses a similar example to support his Approximation Argument; see p. 511.) But she (very reasonably) wants to *disregard* the risk of error, in the sense of not hedging her bets, if he does love her. This desire is at least as strong as her desire not to be deceived if he does not love her. Objective reasoning should therefore suffice to bring her to the conclusion that she ought to disregard the risk of error, since by not disregarding it she would run 999 times as great risk of frustrating one of these desires.

Or suppose you are trying to base your eternal happiness on your relation to Jesus, and therefore have an infinite passionate interest in the question whether he declared Peter and his episcopal successors to be infallible in matters of religious doctrine. You want to be committed to whichever is the true belief on this question, disregarding any possibility of error in it. And suppose, just for the sake of argument, that objective historical evidence renders it 99 per cent probable that Jesus did declare Peter and his successors to be infallible—or 99 per cent probable that he did not—for our present discussion it does not matter which. The one per cent chance of error is enough to make you *anxious,* in view of your infinite interest. But objective reasoning leads to the conclusion that you ought to commit yourself to the more probable opinion, *disregarding* the risk of error, if your strongest desire in the matter is to be so committed to the true opinion. For the only other way to satisfy this desire would be to commit yourself to the less probable opinion, disregarding the risk of error in it. The first way will be successful if and only if the more probable opinion is true, and the second way if and only if the less probable opinion is true. Surely it is prudent to do what gives you a 99 per cent chance of satisfying your strong desire, in preference to what gives you only a one per cent chance of satisfying it.

In this argument your strong desire to be committed to the true opinion is presupposed. The reasonableness of this desire may depend on a belief for which no probability can be established by purely historical reasoning, such as the belief that Jesus is God. But any difficulties arising from this point are distinct from those urged in the Approximation Argument, which itself presupposes the infinite passionate interest in the historical question.

There is some resemblance between my arguments in these examples and Pascal's famous Wager argument. But whereas Pascal's argument turns on weighing an infinite interest against a finite one, mine turn on weighing a large chance of success against a small one. An argument closer to Pascal's will be discussed in section 4 below.

The reader may well have noticed in the foregoing discussion some unclarity about what sort of justification is being demanded and given for religious beliefs about historical facts. There are at least two different types of question about a proposition which I might try to settle by objective reasoning: (1) Is it probable that the proposition is true? (2) In view of the evidence which I have for and against the proposition, and my interest in the matter, is it prudent for me to have faith in the truth of the proposition, disregarding the possibility of error? Correspondingly, we may distinguish two ways in which a belief can be *based on* objective reasoning. The proposition believed may be the conclusion of a piece of objective reasoning, and accepted because it is that. We may say that such a belief is *objectively probable.* Or one might hold a belief or maintain a religious faith because of a piece of objective reasoning whose conclusion is that it would be prudent, morally right, or otherwise desirable for one to hold that belief or faith. In this latter case let us say that the belief is *objectively advantageous.* It is clear that historical beliefs can be objectively probable; and in the Approximation Argument, Kierkegaard does not deny Christian historical beliefs can be objectively probable. His thesis is, in effect, that in view of an infinite passionate interest in their subject matter, they cannot be objectively advantageous, and therefore cannot be fully justified objectively, even if they are objectively probable. It is this thesis that I have attempted to refute. I have not been discussing the question whether Christian historical beliefs are objectively probable.

2. The Postponement Argument

The trouble with objective historical reasoning, according to the Approximation Argument, is that it cannot yield complete certainty. But that is not Kierkegaard's only complaint against it as a basis for religious faith. He also objects that objective historical inquiry is never completely finished, so that one who seeks to base his faith on it postpones his religious commitment forever. In the process of historical research "new difficulties arise and are overcome, and new difficulties again arise. Each generation inherits from its predecessor the illusion that the method is quite impeccable, but the learned scholars have not yet succeeded . . . and so forth. . . . The infinite personal passionate interest of the subject . . . vanishes more and more, because the decision is postponed, and postponed as following directly upon the result of the learned inquiry" (p. 28). As soon as we take "an historical document" as "our standard for the determination of Christian truth," we are "involved in a parenthesis whose conclusion is everlastingly prospective" (p. 28)—that is, we are involved in a religious digression which keeps religious commitment forever in the future.

Kierkegaard has such fears about allowing religious faith to rest on *any* empirical reasoning. The danger of postponement of commitment arises not only from the uncertainties of historical scholarship, but also in connection with the design argument for God's existence. In the *Philosophical Fragments* Kierkegaard notes some objections to the attempt to prove God's existence from evidence of "the wisdom in nature, the goodness, the wisdom in the governance of the world," and then says, "even if I began I would never finish, and would in addition have to live constantly in suspense, lest something so terrible should suddenly happen that my bit of proof would be demolished." What we have before us is a quite general sort of objection to the treatment of religious beliefs as empirically testable. On this point many analytical philosophers seem to agree with Kierkegaard. Much discussion in recent analytical philosophy of religion has proceeded from the supposition that religious beliefs are not empirically testable. I think it is far from obvious that that supposition is correct; and it is interesting to consider arguments that may be advanced to support it.

Kierkegaard's statements suggest an argument that I call the Postponement Argument. Its first premise is that one cannot have an authentic religious faith without being totally committed to it. In order to be totally committed to a belief, in the relevant sense, one must be determined not to abandon the belief under any circumstances that one recognizes as epistemically possible.

The second premise is that one cannot yet be totally committed to any belief which one bases on an inquiry in which one recognizes any possibility of a future need to revise the results. Total commitment to any belief so based will necessarily be postponed. I believe that this premise, suitably interpreted, is true. Consider the position of someone who regards himself as committed to a belief on the basis of objective evidence, but who recognizes some possibility that future discoveries will destroy the objective justification of the belief. We must ask how he is disposed to react in the event, however unlikely, that the objective basis of his belief is overthrown. Is he prepared to abandon the belief in that event? If so, he is not totally committed to the belief in the relevant sense. But if he is determined to cling to his belief even if its objective justification is taken away, then he is not basing the belief on the objective justification—or at least he is not basing it solely on the justification.

The conclusion to be drawn from these two premises is that authentic religious faith cannot be based on an inquiry in which one recognizes any possibility of a future need to revise the results. We ought to note that this conclusion embodies two important restrictions on the scope of the argument.

In the first place, we are not given an argument that authentic religious faith cannot *have* an objective justification that is subject to possible future revision. What we are given is an argument that the authentic believer's holding of his religious belief cannot *depend* entirely on such a justification.

In the second place, this conclusion applies only to those who *recognize* some epistemic possibility that the objective results which appear to support their belief may be overturned. I think it would be unreasonable to require, as part of total commitment, a determination with regard to one's response to circumstances that one does not rec-ognize as possible at all. It may be, however, that one does not recognize such a possibility when one ought to.

Kierkegaard needs one further premise in or-der to arrive at the conclusion that authentic reli-gious faith cannot without error be based on any objective empirical reasoning. This third premise is that in every objective empirical inquiry there is always, objectively considered, some epistemic possibility that the results of the inquiry will need to be revised in view of new evidence or new reasoning. I believe Kierkegaard makes this as-sumption; he certainly makes it with regard to his-torical inquiry. From this premise it follows that one is in error if in any objective empirical inquiry one does not recognize any possibility of a future need to revise the results. But if one does recog-nize such a possibility, then according to the con-clusion already reached in the Postponement Ar-gument, one cannot base an authentic religious faith on the inquiry.

Some philosophers might attack the third premise of this argument; and certainly it is con-troversial. But I am more inclined to criticize the first premise. There is undoubtedly something plausible about the claim that authentic religious faith must involve a commitment so complete that the believer is resolved not to abandon his belief under any circumstances that he regards as episte-mically possible. If you are willing to abandon your ostensibly religious beliefs for the sake of ob-jective inquiry, mightn't we justly say that objec-tive inquiry is your real religion, the thing to which you are most deeply committed?

There is also something plausible to be said on the other side, however. It has commonly been thought to be an important part of religious ethics that one ought to be humble, teachable, open to correction, new inspiration, and growth of insight, even (and perhaps especially) in important reli-gious beliefs. That view would have to be dis-carded if we were to concede to Kierkegaard that the heart of commitment in religion is an uncondi-tional determination not to change in one's impor-tant religious beliefs. In fact I think there is some-thing radically wrong with this conception of

religious commitment. Faith ought not to be thought of as unconditional devotion to a belief. For in the first place the object of religious devo-tion is not a belief or attitude of one's own, but God. And in the second place it may be doubted that religious devotion to God can or should be completely unconditional. God's love for sinners is sometimes said to be completely unconditional, not being based on any excellence or merit of theirs. But religious devotion to God is generally thought to be based on His goodness and love. It is the part of the strong, not the weak, to love uncon-ditionally. And in relation to God we are weak.

3. The Passion Argument

In Kierkegaard's statements of the Approximation Argument and the Postponement Argument it is assumed that a system of religious beliefs might be objectively probable. It is only for the sake of argu-ment, however, that Kierkegaard allows this as-sumption. He really holds that religious faith, by its very nature, needs objective *im*probability. "Anything that is almost probable, or probable, or extremely and emphatically probable, is some-thing [one] can almost know, or as good as know, or extremely and emphatically almost *know*—but it is impossible to *believe*" (p. 189). Nor will Kierkegaard countenance the suggestion that reli-gion ought to go beyond belief to some almost-knowledge based on probability. "Faith is the highest passion in a man. There are perhaps many in every generation who do not even reach it, but no one gets further." It would be a betrayal of religion to try to go beyond faith. The suggestion that faith might be replaced by "probabilities and guarantees" is for the believer "a temptation to be resisted with all his strength" (p. 15). The attempt to establish religious beliefs on a foundation of objective probability is therefore no service to reli-gion, but inimical to religion's true interests. The approximation to certainty which might be af-forded by objective probability is rejected, not only for the reasons given in the Approximation Argument and Postponement Argument, but also from a deeper motive, "since on the contrary it behooves us to get rid of introductory guarantees of security, proofs from consequences, and the whole mob of public pawnbrokers and guarantors, so as to permit the absurd to stand out in all its clarity—in order that the individual may believe if he wills it; I merely say that it must be strenuous in the highest degree so to believe" (p. 190).

As this last quotation indicates, Kierkegaard thinks that religious belief ought to be based on a strenuous exertion of the will—a passionate striving. His reasons for thinking that objective probability is religiously undesirable have to do with the place of passion in religion, and constitute what I call the Passion Argument. The first premise of the argument is that the most essential and the most valuable feature of religiousness is passion, indeed an infinite passion, a passion of the greatest possible intensity. The second premise is that an infinite passion requires objective improbability. And the conclusion therefore is that that which is most essential and most valuable in religiousness requires objective improbability.

My discussion of this argument will have three parts. (a) First I will try to clarify, very briefly, what it is that is supposed to be objectively improbable. (b) Then we will consider Kierkegaard's reasons for holding that infinite passion requires objective improbability. In so doing we will also gain a clearer understanding of what a Kierkegaardian infinite passion is. (c) Finally I will discuss the first premise of the argument—although issues will arise at that point which I do not pretend to be able to settle by argument.

(a) What are the beliefs whose improbability is needed by religious passion? Kierkegaard will hardly be satisfied with the improbability of just any one belief; it must surely be at least an important belief. On the other hand it would clearly be preposterous to suppose that every belief involved in Christianity must be objectively improbable. (Consider, for example, the belief that the man Jesus did indeed live.) I think that what is demanded in the Passion Argument is the objective improbability of at least one belief which must be true if the goal sought by the religious passion is to be attained.

(b) We can find in the *Postscript* suggestions of several reasons for thinking that an infinite passion needs objective improbability. The two that seem to me most interesting have to do with (i) the risks accepted and (ii) the costs paid in pursuance of a passionate interest.

(i) One reason that Kierkegaard has for valuing objective improbability is that it increases the *risk* attaching to the religious life, and risk is so essential for the expression of religious passion that "without risk there is no faith" (p. 182). About the nature of an eternal happiness, the goal of religious striving, Kierkegaard says "there is nothing to be said . . . except that it is the good which is attained by venturing everything absolutely" (p. 382).

> But what then does it mean to venture? A venture is the precise correlative of an uncertainty; when the certainty is there the venture becomes impossible. . . . If what I hope to gain by venturing is itself certain, I do not risk or venture, but make an exchange. . . . No, if I am in truth resolved to venture, in truth resolved to strive for the attainment of the highest good, the uncertainty must be there, and I must have room to move, so to speak. But the largest space I can obtain, where there is room for the most vehement gesture of the passion that embraces the infinite, is uncertainty of knowledge with respect to an eternal happiness, or the certain knowledge that the choice is in the finite sense a piece of madness: now there is room, now you can venture! [pp. 380–82]

How is it that objective improbability provides the largest space for the most vehement gesture of infinite passion? Consider two cases. (A) You plunge into a raging torrent to rescue from drowning someone you love, who is crying for help. (B) You plunge into a raging torrent in a desperate attempt to rescue someone you love, who appears to be unconscious and *may* already have drowned. In both cases you manifest a passionate interest in saving the person, risking your own life in order to do so. But I think Kierkegaard would say there is more passion in the second case than in the first. For in the second case you risk your life in what is, objectively considered, a smaller chance that you will be able to save your loved one. A greater passion is required for a more desperate attempt.

A similar assessment may be made of the following pair of cases. (A') You stake everything on your faith in the truth of Christianity, knowing that it is objectively 99 per cent probable that Christianity is true. (B') You stake everything on your faith in the truth of Christianity, knowing that the truth of Christianity is, objectively, possible but so improbable that its probability is, say, as small as 10(1/2,000,000). There is passion in both cases, but Kierkegaard will say that there is more passion in the second case than in the first. For to venture the same stake (namely, everything) on a much smaller chance of success shows greater passion.

Acceptance of risk can thus be seen as a *measure* of the intensity of passion. I believe this provides us with one way of understanding what Kierkegaard means when he calls religious passion "infinite." An *infinite* passionate interest in *x* is an interest so strong that it leads one to make the greatest possible sacrifices in order to obtain *x*, on the smallest possible chance of success. The infinity of the passion is shown in that there is no sacrifice so great one will not make it, and no chance of success so small one will not act on it. A passion which is infinite in this sense requires, by its very nature, a situation of maximum risk for its expression.

It will doubtless be objected that this argument involves a misunderstanding of what a passionate interest is. Such an interest is a disposition. In order to have a great passionate interest it is not necessary actually to make a great sacrifice with a small chance of success; all that is necessary is to have such an intense interest that one *would* do so if an appropriate occasion should arise. It is therefore a mistake to say that there *is* more passion in case (B) than in case (A), or in (B') than in (A'). More passion is *shown* in (B) than in (A), and in (B') than in (A'); but an equal passion may exist in cases in which there is no occasion to show it.

This objection may well be correct as regards what we normally mean by "passionate interest." But that is not decisive for the argument. The crucial question is what part dispositions, possibly unactualized, ought to play in religious devotion. And here we must have a digression about the position of the *Postscript* on this question—a posi-

tion that is complex at best and is not obviously consistent.

In the first place I do not think that Kierkegaard would be prepared to think of passion, or a passionate interest, as primarily a disposition that might remain unactualized. He seems to conceive of passion chiefly as an intensity in which one actually does and feels. "Passion is momentary" (p. 178), although capable of continual repetition. And what is momentary in such a way that it must be repeated rather than protracted is presumably an occurrence rather than a disposition. It agrees with this conception of passion that Kierkegaard idealizes a life of "persistent striving," and says that the religious task is to "exercise" the God-relationship and to give "existential expression" to the religious choice (pp. 110, 364, 367).

All of this supports the view that what Kierkegaard means by "an infinite passionate interest" is a pattern of actual decision-making, in which one continually exercises and expresses one's religiousness by making the greatest possible sacrifices on the smallest possible chance of success. In order to actualize such a pattern of life one needs chances of success that are as small as possible. That is the room that is required for "the most vehement gesture" of infinite passion.

But on the other hand Kierkegaard does allow a dispositional element in the religious life, and even precisely in the making of the greatest possible sacrifices. We might suppose that if we are to make the greatest possible sacrifices in our religious devotion, we must do so by abandoning all worldly interests and devoting all our time and attention to religion. That is what monasticism attempts to do, as Kierkegaard sees it; and (in the *Postscript,* at any rate) he rejects the attempt, contrary to what our argument to this point would have led us to expect of him. He holds that "resignation" (pp. 353, 367) or "renunciation" (pp. 362, 386) of *all* finite ends is precisely the first thing that religiousness requires; but he means a renunciation that is compatible with pursuing and enjoying finite ends (pp. 362–71). This renunciation is the practice of a sort of detachment; Kierkegaard uses the image of a dentist loosening the soft tissues around a tooth, while it is still in place, in preparation for pulling it (p. 367). It is partly a matter of not treating finite things with a desperate seriousness, but with a certain coolness or humor, even while one pursues them (pp. 368, 370).

This coolness is not just a disposition. But the renunciation also has a dispositional aspect. "Now if for any individual an eternal happiness is his highest good, this will mean that all finite satisfactions are volitionally relegated to the status of what may have to be renounced in favor of an eternal happiness" (p. 350). The volitional relegation is not a disposition but an act of choice. The object of this choice, however, appears to be a dispositional state—the state of being such that one *would* forgo any finite satisfaction *if it were* religiously necessary or advantageous to do so.

It seems clear that Kierkegaard, in the *Post-script,* is willing to admit a dispositional element at one point in the religious venture, but not at another. It is enough in most cases, he thinks, if one is *prepared* to cease for the sake of religion from pursuing some finite end; but it is not enough that one *would* hold to one's belief in the face of objective improbability. The belief must actually be improbable, although the pursuit of the finite need not actually cease. What is not clear is a reason for this disparity. The following hypothesis, admittedly somewhat speculative as interpretation of the text, is the best explanation I can offer.

The admission of a dispositional element in the religious renunciation of the finite is something to which Kierkegaard seems to be driven by the view that there is no alternative to it except idolatry. For suppose one actually ceases from all worldly pursuits and enters a monastery. In the monastery one would pursue a number of particular ends (such as getting up in the middle of the night to say the offices) which, although religious in a way ("churchy," one might say), are still finite. The absolute *telos* or end of religion is no more to be identified with them than with the ends pursued by an alderman (pp. 362–71). To pretend otherwise would be to make an idolatrous identification of the absolute end with some finite end. An existing person cannot have sacrificed everything by actually having ceased from pursuing *all* finite ends. For as long as he lives and acts he is pursuing some finite end. Therefore his renouncing *everything* finite must be at least partly dispositional.

Kierkegaard does not seem happy with this position. He regards it as of the utmost importance that the religious passion should come to expression. The problem of finding an adequate expression for a passion for an infinite end, in the face of the fact that in every concrete action one will be pursuing some finite end, is treated in the *Postscript* as the central problem of religion (see especially pp. 386–468). If the sacrifice of everything finite must remain largely dispositional, then perhaps it is all the more important to Kierkegaard that the smallness of the chance for which it is sacrificed should be fully actual, so that the infinity of the religious passion may be measured by an actuality in at least one aspect of the religious venture.

(ii) According to Kierkegaard, as I have argued, the intensity of a passion is measured in part by the smallness of the chances of success that one acts on. It can also be measured in part by its *costliness*—that is, by how much one gives up or suffers in acting on those chances. This second measure can also be made the basis of an argument for the claim that an infinite passion requires objective improbability. For the objective improbability of a religious belief, if recognized, increases the costliness of holding it. The risk involved in staking everything on an objectively improbable belief gives rise to an anxiety and mental suffering whose acceptance is itself a sacrifice. It seems to follow that if one is not staking everything on a belief one sees to be objectively improbable, one's passion is not infinite in Kierkegaard's sense, since one's sacrifice could be greater if one did adhere to an improbable belief.

Kierkegaard uses an argument similar to this. For God to give us objective knowledge of Himself, eliminating paradox from it, would be "to lower the price of the God-relationship."

And even if God could be imagined willing, no man with passion in his heart could desire it. To a maiden genuinely in love it could never occur to that she had bought her happiness too dear, but rather that she had not bought it dear enough. And just as the passion of the infinite was itself the truth, so in the case of the highest value it holds true that the price is the value, that a low price means a poor value. . . . [p. 207]

Kierkegaard here appears to hold, first, that an increase in the objective probability of religious belief would reduce its costliness, and second, that the value of a religious life is measured by its cost. I take it his reason for the second of these claims is that passion is the most valuable thing in a religious life and passion is measured by its cost. If we grant Kierkegaard the requisite conception of an infinite passion, we seem once again to have a plausible argument for the view that objective improbability is required for such a passion.

(c) We must therefore consider whether infinite passion, as Kierkegaard conceives of it, ought to be part of the religious ideal of life. Such a passion is a striving, or pattern of decision-making, in which, with the greatest possible intensity of feeling, one continually makes the greatest possible sacrifices on the smallest possible chance of success. This seems to me an impossible ideal. I doubt that any human being could have a passion of this sort, because I doubt that one could make a sacrifice so great that a greater could not be made, or have a (nonzero) chance of success so small that a smaller could not be had.

But even if Kierkegaard's ideal is impossible, one might want to try to approximate it. Intensity of passion might still be measured by the greatness of sacrifices made and the smallness of chances of success acted on, even if we cannot hope for a greatest possible or a smallest possible here. And it could be claimed that the most essential and valuable thing in religiousness is a passion that is very intense (though it cannot be infinite) by this standard—the more intense the better. This claim will not support an argument that objective improbability is absolutely required for religious passion. For a passion could presumably be very intense, involving great sacrifices and risks of some other sort, without an objectively improbable belief. But it could still be argued that objectively improbable religious beliefs enhance the value of the religious life by increasing its sacrifices and diminishing its chances of success, whereas objective probability

detracts from the value of religious passion by diminishing its intensity.

The most crucial question about the Passion Argument, then, is whether maximization of sacrifice and risk are so valuable in religion as to make objective improbability a desirable characteristic of religious beliefs. Certainly much religious thought and feeling places a very high value on sacrifice and on passionate intensity. But the doctrine that it is desirable to increase without limit, or to the highest possible degree (if there is one) the cost and risk of a religious life is less plausible (to say the least) than the view that *some* degree of cost and risk may add to the value of a religious life. The former doctrine would set the religious interest at enmity with all other interests, or at least with the best of them. Kierkegaard is surely right in thinking that it would be impossible to live without pursuing some finite ends. But even so it would be possible to exchange the pursuit of better finite ends for the pursuit of worse ones—for example, by exchanging the pursuit of truth, beauty, and satisfying personal relationships for the self-flagellating pursuit of pain. And a way of life would be the costlier for requiring such an exchange. Kierkegaard does not, in the *Postscript,* demand it. But the presuppositions of his Passion Argument seem to imply that such a sacrifice would be religiously desirable. Such a conception of religion is demonic. In a tolerable religious ethics some way must be found to conceive of the religious interest as inclusive rather than exclusive of the best of other interests—including, I think, the interest in having well-grounded beliefs.

4. Pascal's Wager and Kierkegaard's Leap

Ironically, Kierkegaard's views about religious passion suggest a way in which his religious beliefs could be based on objective reasoning—not on reasoning which would show them to be objectively probable, but on reasoning which shows them to be objectively advantageous. Consider the situation of a person whom Kierkegaard would regard as a genuine Christian believer. What would such a person want most of all? He would want above all else to attain the truth through Christianity. That is, he would desire both that Christianity be true and that he himself be related to it as a genuine believer. He would desire that state of affairs (which we may call *S*) so ardently that he would be willing to sacrifice everything else to obtain it, given only the smallest possible chance of success.

We can therefore construct the following argument, which has an obvious analogy to Pascal's Wager. Let us assume that there is, objectively, some chance, however small, that Christianity is true. This is an assumption which Kierkegaard accepts (p. 31), and I think it is plausible. There are two possibilities, then: either Christianity is true, or it is false. (Others might object to so stark a disjunction, but Kierkegaard will not.) If Christianity is false it is impossible for anyone to obtain *S*, since *S* includes the truth of Christianity. It is only if Christianity is true that anything one does will help one or hinder one in obtaining *S*. And if Christianity is true, one will obtain *S* just in case one becomes a genuine Christian believer. It seems obvious that one would increase one's chances of becoming a genuine Christian believer by becoming one now (if one can), even if the truth of Christian beliefs is now objectively uncertain or improbable. Hence it would seem to be advantageous for anyone who can to become a

genuine Christian believer now, if he wants *S* so much that he would be willing to sacrifice everything else for the smallest possible chance of obtaining *S*. Indeed I believe that the argument I have given for this conclusion is a piece of objective reasoning, and that Christian belief is therefore *objectively* advantageous for anyone who wants *S* as much as a Kierkegaardian genuine Christian must want it.

Of course this argument does not tend at all to show that it is objectively probable that Christianity is true. It only gives a practical, prudential reason for believing, to someone who has a certain desire. Nor does the argument do anything to prove that such an absolutely overriding desire for *S* is reasonable. It does show, however, that just as Kierkegaard's position has more logical structure than one might at first think, it is more difficult than he probably realized for him to get away entirely from objective justification.

Note

1. Søren Kierkegaard, *Concluding Unscientific Postscript*, translated by David F. Swenson; introduction, notes, and completion of translation by Walter Lowrie (Princeton: Princeton University Press, 1941). Page references in parentheses in the body of the present paper are to this work.

VII.C.3   A Lecture on Religious Belief

LUDWIG WITTGENSTEIN

In our third reading, we turn to the leading type of fideism in contemporary philosophy of religion. Ludwig Wittgenstein (1889–1951), an Austrian-British philosopher who taught at Cambridge University, may be the most influential philosopher of the twentieth century. In this selection from his

"Lectures on Religious Belief" he argues that there is something sui generis *or special about the very linguistic framework of believers, so that the concepts they use cannot be adequately grasped by outsiders. One has to share in a form of life in order to understand the way the various concepts function in that language game. Wittgenstein ridicules one Father O'Hara for giving the impression that there is a nonperspectival, impartial way of*

Reprinted from *Lectures and Conversations*, edited by Cyril Barrett (Berkeley: University of California Press, 1966), pp. 53–59, by permission of the publisher.

assessing the truth value of religious assertions. Such a view, Wittgenstein believes, is absurd.

An Austrian general said to someone: "I shall think of you after my death, if that should be possible." We can imagine one group who would find this ludicrous, another who wouldn't.

[During the war, Wittgenstein saw consecrated bread being carried in chromium steel. This struck him as ludicrous.]

Suppose that someone believed in the Last Judgement, and I don't, does this mean that I believe the opposite to him, just that there won't be such a thing? I would say: "not at all, or not always."

Suppose I say that the body will rot, and another says "No. Particles will rejoin in a thousand years, and there will be a Resurrection of you."

If some said: "Wittgenstein, do you believe in this?" I'd say: "No." "Do you contradict the man?" I'd say: "No."

If you say this, the contradiction already lies in this.

Would you say: "I believe the opposite", or "There is no reason to suppose such a thing"? I'd say neither.

Suppose someone were a believer and said: "I believe in a Last Judgement," and I said: "Well, I'm not so sure. Possibly." You would say that there is an enormous gulf between us. If he said "There is a German aeroplane overhead," and I said "Possibly. I'm not so sure," you'd say we were fairly near.

It isn't a question of my being anywhere near him, but on an entirely different plane, which you could express by saying: "You mean something altogether different, Wittgenstein."

The difference might not show up at all in any explanation of the meaning.

Why is it that in this case I seem to be missing the entire point?

Suppose somebody made this guidance for this life: believing in the Last Judgement. Whenever he does anything, this is before his mind. In a way, how are we to know whether to say he believes this will happen or not?

Asking him is not enough. He will probably say he has proof. But he has what you might call an unshakeable belief. It will show, not by reasoning or by appeal to ordinary grounds for belief, but rather by regulating for in all his life.

This is a very much stronger fact—foregoing pleasures, always appealing to this picture. This in one sense must be called the firmest of all beliefs, because the man risks things on account of it which he would not do on things which are by far better established for him. Although he distinguishes between things well-established and not well-established.

Lewy: Surely, he would say it is extremely well-established.

First, he may use "well-established" or not use it at all. He will treat this belief as extremely well-established, and in another way as not well-established at all.

If we have a belief, in certain cases we appeal again and again to certain grounds, and at the same time we risk pretty little—if it came to risking our lives on the ground of this belief.

There are instances where you have a faith—where you say "I believe"—and on the other hand this belief does not rest on the fact on which our ordinary everyday beliefs normally do rest.

How should we compare beliefs with each other? What would it mean to compare them?

You might say: "We compare the states of mind."

How do we compare states of mind? This obviously won't do for all occasions. First, what you say won't be taken as the measure for the firmness of a belief? But, for instance, what risks you would take?

The strength of a belief is not comparable with the intensity of a pain.

An entirely different way of comparing beliefs is seeing what sorts of grounds he will give.

A belief isn't like a momentary state of mind. "At 5 o'clock he had a very bad toothache."

Suppose you had two people, and one of them, when he had to decide which course to take, thought of retribution, and the other did not. One person might, for instance, be inclined to take everything that happened to him as a reward or punishment, and another person doesn't think of this at all.

If he is ill, he may think: "What have I done to deserve this?" This is one way of thinking of retribution. Another way is, he thinks in a general way whenever he is ashamed of himself: "This will be punished."

Take two people, one of whom talks of his behaviour and of what happens to him in terms of retribution, the other one does not. These people think entirely differently. Yet, so far, you can't say they believe different things.

Suppose someone is ill and he says: "This is a punishment," and I say: "If I'm ill, I don't think of punishment at all." If you say: "Do you believe the opposite?"—you can call it believing the opposite, but it is entirely different from what we would normally call believing the opposite.

I think differently, in a different way. I say different things to myself. I have different pictures.

It is this way: if someone said: "Wittgenstein, you don't take illness as punishment, so what do you believe?"—I'd say: "I don't have any thoughts of punishment."

There are, for instance, these entirely different ways of thinking first of all—which needn't be expressed by one person saying one thing, another person another thing.

What we call believing in a Judgement Day or not believing in a Judgement Day—The expression of belief may play an absolutely minor role.

If you ask me whether or not I believe in a Judgement Day, in the sense in which religious people have belief in it, I wouldn't say: "No. I don't believe there will be such a thing." It would seem to me utterly crazy to say this.

And then I give an explanation: "I don't believe in . . .", but then the religious person never believes what I describe.

I can't say. I can't contradict that person.

In one sense, I understand all he says—the English words "God", "separate", etc. I understand. I could say: "I don't believe in this," and this would be true, meaning I haven't got these thoughts or anything that hangs together with them. But not that I could contradict the thing.

You might say: "Well, if you can't contradict

him, that means you don't understand him. If you did understand him, then you might." That again is Greek to me. My normal technique of language leaves me. I don't know whether to say they understand one another or not.

These controversies look quite different from any normal controversies. Reasons look entirely different from normal reasons.

They are, in a way, quite inconclusive.

The point is that if there were evidence, this would in fact destroy the whole business.

Anything that I normally call evidence wouldn't in the slightest influence me.

Suppose, for instance, we knew people who foresaw the future; make forecasts for years and years ahead; and they described some sort of a Judgement Day. Queerly enough, even if there were such a thing, and even if it were more convincing than I have described but, belief in this happening wouldn't be at all a religious belief.

Suppose that I would have to forego all pleasures because of such a forecast. If I do so and so, someone will put me in fires in a thousand years, etc. I wouldn't budge. The best scientific evidence is just nothing.

A religious belief might in fact fly in the face of such a forecast, and say "No. There it will break down."

As it were, the belief as formulated on the evidence can only be the last result—in which a number of ways of thinking and acting crystallize and come together.

A man would fight for his life not to be dragged into the fire. No induction. Terror. That is, as it were, part of the substance of the belief.

That is partly why you don't get in religious controversies, the form of controversy where one person is *sure* of the thing, and the other says: 'Well, possibly.'

You might be surprised that there hasn't been opposed to those who believe in Resurrection those who say "Well, possibly."

Here believing obviously plays much more this role: suppose we said that a certain picture might play the role of constantly admonishing me, or I always think of it. Here, an enormous difference would be between those people for whom the picture is constantly in the foreground, and the others who just didn't use it at all.

Those who said: "Well, possibly it may happen and possibly not" would be on an entirely different plane.

This is partly why one would be reluctant to say: "These people rigorously hold the opinion (or view) that there is a Last Judgement". "Opinion" sounds queer.

It is for this reason that different words are used: 'dogma', 'faith'.

We don't talk about hypothesis, or about high probability. Nor about knowing.

In a religious discourse we use such expressions as: "I believe that so and so will happen," and use them differently to the way in which we use them in science.

Although, there is a great temptation to think we do. Because we do talk of evidence, and do talk of evidence by experience.

We could even talk of historic events.

It has been said that Christianity rests on an historic basis.

It has been said a thousand times by intelligent people that indubitability is not enough in this case. Even if there is as much evidence as for Napoleon. Because the indubitability wouldn't be enough to make me change my whole life.

It doesn't rest on an historic basis in the sense that the ordinary belief in historic facts could serve as a foundation.

Here we have a belief in historic facts different from a belief in ordinary historic facts. Even, they are not treated as historical, empirical, propositions.

Those people who had faith didn't apply the doubt which would ordinarily apply to *any* historical propositions. Especially propositions of a time long past, etc.

What is the criterion of reliability, dependability? Suppose you give a general description as to when you say a proposition has a reasonable weight of probability. When you call it reasonable, is this *only* to say that for it you have such and such evidence, and for others you haven't?

For instance, we don't trust the account given of an event by a drunk man.

Father O'Hara[1] is one of those people who make it a question of science.

Here we have people who treat this evidence in a different way. They base things on evidence which taken in one way would seem exceedingly flimsy. They base enormous things on this evidence. Am I to say they are unreasonable? I wouldn't call them unreasonable.

I would say, they are certainly not *reasonable,* that's obvious.

'Unreasonable' implies, with everyone, rebuke.

I want to say: they don't treat this as a matter of reasonability.

Anyone who reads the Epistles will find it said: not only that it is not reasonable, but that it is folly.

Not only is it not reasonable, but it doesn't pretend to be.

What seems to me ludicrous about O'Hara is his making it appear to be *reasonable.*

Why shouldn't one form of life culminate in an utterance of belief in a Last Judgement? But I couldn't either say "Yes" or "No" to the statement that there will be such a thing. Nor "Perhaps," nor "I'm not sure."

It is a statement which may not allow of any such answer.

If Mr. Lewy is religious and says he believes in a Judgement Day, I won't even know whether to say I understand him or not. I've read the same things as he's read. In a most important sense, I know what he means.

If an atheist says: "There won't be a Judgement Day, and another person says there will," do they mean the same?—Not clear what criterion of meaning the same is. They might describe the same things. You might say, this already shows that they mean the same.

We come to an island and we find beliefs there, and certain beliefs we are inclined to call religious. What I'm driving at is, that religious beliefs will not . . . They have sentences, and there are also religious statements.

These statements would not just differ in respect to what they are about. Entirely different connections would make them into religious beliefs, and there can easily be imagined transitions where we wouldn't know for our life whether to call them religious beliefs or scientific beliefs.

You may say they reason wrongly.

In certain cases you would say they reason wrongly, meaning they contradict us. In other cases you would say they don't reason at all, or "It is an entirely different kind of reasoning." The first, you would say in the case in which they reason in a similar way to us, and make something corresponding to our blunders.

Whether a thing is a blunder or not—it is a blunder in a particular system. Just as something is a blunder in a particular game and not in another.

You could also say that where we are reasonable, they are not reasonable—meaning they don't use *reason* here.

If they do something very like one of our blunders, I would say, I don't know. It depends on further surroundings of it.

It is difficult to see, in cases in which it has all the appearances of trying to be reasonable.

I would definitely call O'Hara unreasonable. I would say, if this is religious belief, then it's all superstition.

But I would ridicule it, not by saying it is based on insufficient evidence. I would say: here is a man who is cheating himself. You can say: this man is ridiculous because he believes, and bases it on weak reasons.

The word 'God' is amongst the earliest learnt—pictures and catechisms, etc. But not the same consequences as with pictures of aunts. I wasn't shown [that which the picture pictured].

The word is used like a word representing a person. God sees, rewards, etc.

"Being shown all these things, did you understand what this word meant?" I'd say, "Yes and no. I did learn what it didn't mean. I made myself understand. I could answer questions, understand questions when they were put in different ways—and in that sense could be said to understand."

If the question arises as to the existence of a god or God, it plays an entirely different role to that of the existence of any person or object I ever heard of. One said, had to say, that one *believed* in the existence, and if one did not believe, this was regarded as something bad. Normally if I did not believe in the existence of something no one would think there was anything wrong in this. . . .

Note

1. Contribution to a Symposium on *Science and Religion* (Lond: Gerald Howe, 1931, pp. 107–116).

VII.C.4   The Groundlessness of Belief

NORMAN MALCOLM

Norman Malcolm is a particularly lucid interpreter and adherent of Wittgensteinian fideism. Until his recent retirement Malcolm taught philosophy at Cornell University. In this reading he contends that religious belief is in no sense a hypothesis, for it cannot be and ought not to be justified rationally. It is essentially a groundless belief like other beliefs that do not need further support, such as our belief that things don't just vanish, our belief in the uniformity of nature, and our knowledge of our own intentions.

Like other fundamental assumptions religious beliefs are not derived from other beliefs but themselves form the support for all our other beliefs. They form the framework of our inquiry on which the very process of justification depends. Hence, it

Reprinted from *Reason and Religion,* edited by Stuart C. Brown. Copyright © 1977 by The Royal Institute of Philosophy. Used by permission of the publisher, Cornell University Press.

does not make sense to ask for a justification of religious claims or a refutation of them from a point outside the religious framework. Science and religion are just two different language games. "Neither stands in need of justification, the one no more than the other."

I

In his final notebooks Wittgenstein wrote that it is difficult "to realize the groundlessness of our believing."[1] He was thinking of how much mere acceptance, on the basis of no evidence, forms our lives. This is obvious in the case of small children. They are told the names of things. They accept what they are told. They do not ask for grounds. A child does not demand a proof that the person who feeds him is called "Mama." Or are we to suppose that the child reasons to himself as follows: "The others present seem to know this person who is feeding me, and since they call her 'Mama' that probably is her name"? It is obvious on reflection that a child cannot consider evidence or even doubt anything until he has already learned much. As Wittgenstein puts it: "The child learns by believing the adult. Doubt comes *after* belief" (*OC*, 160).

What is more difficult to perceive is that the lives of educated, sophisticated adults are also formed by groundless beliefs. I do not mean eccentric beliefs that are out on the fringes of their lives, but fundamental beliefs. Take the belief that familiar material things (watches, shoes, chairs) do not cease to exist without some physical explanation. They don't "vanish in thin air." It is interesting that we do use that very expression: "I *know* I put the keys right here on this table. They must have vanished in thin air!" But this exclamation is hyperbole; we are not speaking in literal seriousness. I do not know of any adult who would consider, in all gravity, that the keys might have inexplicably ceased to exist.

Yet it is possible to imagine a society in which it was accepted that sometimes material things do go out of existence without having been crushed, melted, eroded, broken into pieces, burned up, eaten, or destroyed in some other way. The difference between those people and ourselves would not consist in their *saying* something that we don't say ("It vanished in thin air"), since we say it too. I conceive of these people as acting and thinking differently from ourselves in such ways as the following: If one of them could not find his wallet he would give up the search sooner than you or I would; also he would be less inclined to suppose that it was stolen. In general, what we would regard as convincing circumstantial evidence of theft those people would find less convincing. They would take fewer precautions than we would to protect their possessions against loss or theft. They would have less inclination to save money, since it too can just disappear. They would not tend to form strong attachments to material things, animals, or other people. Generally, they would stand in a looser relation to the world than we do. The disappearance of a desired object, which would provoke us to a frantic search, they would be more inclined to accept with a shrug. Of course, their scientific theories would be different; but also their attitude toward experiment, and inference from experimental results, would be more tentative. If the repetition of a familiar chemical experiment did not yield the expected result this *could* be because one of the chemical substances had vanished.

The outlook I have sketched might be thought to be radically incoherent. I do not see that this is so. Although those people consider it to be possible that a wallet might have inexplicably ceased to exist, it is also true that they regard that as unlikely. For things that are lost usually do turn up later; or if not, their fate can often be accounted for. Those people use pretty much the same criteria of identity that we do; their reasoning would resemble ours quite a lot. Their thinking would not be incoherent. But it would be different, since they would leave room for some possibilities that we exclude.

If we compare their view that material things do sometimes go out of existence inexplicably, with our own rejection of that view, it does not appear to me that one position is supported by *better evidence* than is the other. Each position is compatible with ordinary experience. On the one hand it is true that familiar objects (watches, wallets, lawn chairs) occasionally disappear without any adequate explanation. On the other hand it happens, perhaps more frequently, that a satisfying explanation of the disappearance is discovered.

Our attitude in this matter is striking. We would not be willing to consider it as even improbable that a missing lawn chair had "just ceased to exist." We would not entertain such a suggestion. If anyone proposed it we would be sure he was joking. It is no exaggeration to say that this attitude is part of the foundations of our thinking. I do not want to say that this attitude is *unreasonable*; but rather that it is something that we do not *try* to support with grounds. It could be said to belong to "the framework" of our thinking about material things.

Wittgenstein asks: "Does anyone ever test whether this table remains in existence when no one is paying attention to it?" (*OC*, 163). The answer is: Of course not. Is this because we would not call it "a table" if that were to happen? But we do call it "a table" and none of us makes the test. Doesn't this show that we do not regard that occurrence as a possibility? People who did so regard it would seem ludicrous to us. One could imagine that they made ingenious experiments to decide the question; but this research would make us smile. Is this because experiments were conducted by our ancestors that settled the matter once and for all? I don't believe it. The principle that material things do not cease to exist without physical cause is an unreflective part of the framework within which physical investigations are made and physical explanations arrived at.

Wittgenstein suggests that the same is true of what might be called "the principle of the continuity of nature":

Think of chemical investigations. Lavoisier makes experiments with substances in his laboratory and now concludes that this and that takes place when there is burning. He does not say that it might happen otherwise another time. He has got hold of a world-picture—not of course one that he invented: he learned it as a child. I say world-picture and not

hypothesis, because it is the matter-of-course (*selbst-verständliche*) foundation for his research and as such also goes unmentioned (*OC*, 167).

But now, what part is played by the presupposition that a substance A always reacts to a substance B in the same way, given the same circumstances? Or is that part of the definition of a substance? (*OC*, 168).

Framework principles such as the continuity of nature or the assumption that material things do not cease to exist without physical cause belong to what Wittgenstein calls a "system." He makes the following observation, which seems to me to be true: "All testing, all confirmation and disconfirmation of a hypothesis takes place already within a system. And this system is not a more or less arbitrary and doubtful point of departure for all our arguments: no, it belongs to the nature of what we call an argument. The system is not so much the point of departure, as the element in which arguments have their life" (*OC*, 105).

A "system" provides the boundaries within which we ask questions, carry out investigations, and make judgments. Hypotheses are put forth, and challenged, *within* a system. Verification, justification, the search for evidence, occur *within* a system. The framework propositions of the system are not put to the test, not backed up by evidence. This is what Wittgenstein means when he says: "Of course there is justification; but justification comes to an end" (*OC*, 192); and when he asks: "Doesn't testing come to an end?" (*OC*, 164); and when he remarks that "whenever we test anything we are already presupposing something that is not tested" (*OC*, 163).

That this is so is not to be attributed to human weakness. It is a conceptual requirement that our inquiries and proofs stay within boundaries. Think, for example, of the activity of calculating a number. Some steps in a calculation we will check for correctness, but others we won't: for example, that $4 + 4 = 8$. More accurately, some beginners might check it, but grown-ups won't. Similarly, some grown-ups would want to determine by calculation whether $25 \times 25 = 625$, whereas others would regard that as laughable. Thus the boundaries of the system within which *you* calculate may not be exactly the same as *mine*. But we do calculate; and, as Wittgenstein remarks, "In certain circumstances . . . we regard a calculation as sufficiently checked. What gives us a right to do so? . . . Somewhere we must be finished with justification, and then there remains the proposition that *this* is how we calculate" (*OC*, 212). If someone did not accept any boundaries for calculating this would mean that he had not learned *that* language-game: "If someone supposed that *all* our calculations were uncertain and that we could rely on none of them (justifying himself by saying that mistakes are always possible) perhaps we would say he was crazy. But can we say he is in error? Does he not just react differently? We rely on calculations, he doesn't; we are sure, he isn't" (*OC*, 217). We are taught, or we absorb, the systems within which we raise doubts, make inquiries, draw conclusions. We grow into a framework. We don't question it. We accept it trustingly. But this acceptance is not a consequence of reflection. We do not decide to accept framework propositions. We do not decide that we live on the earth, any more than we decide to learn our native tongue. We do come to adhere to a framework proposition, in the sense that it forms the way we think. The framework propositions that we accept, grow into, are not idiosyncrasies but common ways of speaking and thinking that are pressed on us by our human community. For our acceptances to have been withheld would have meant that we had not learned how to count, to measure, to use names, to play games, or even *to talk*. Wittgenstein remarks that "a language-game is only possible if one trusts something." Not *can*, but *does* trust something (*OC*, 509). I think he means by this trust or acceptance what he calls belief "in the sense of religious belief" (*OC*, 459). What does he mean by belief "in the sense of religious belief"? He explicitly distinguishes it from *conjecture* (*Vermutung*: ibid.) I think this means that there is nothing tentative about it; it is not adopted as a hypothesis that might later be withdrawn in the light of new evidence. This also makes explicit an important feature of Wittgenstein's understanding of belief, in the sense of "religious belief," namely, that it does not rise or fall on the basis of evidence or grounds: it is "groundless."

II

In our Western academic philosophy, religious belief is commonly regarded as unreasonable and is viewed with condescension or even contempt. It is said that religion is a refuge for those who, because of weakness of intellect or character, are unable to confront the stern realities of the world. The objective, mature, *strong* attitude is to hold beliefs solely on the basis of *evidence*.

It appears to me that philosophical thinking is greatly influenced by this veneration of evidence. We have an aversion to statements, reports, declarations, beliefs, that are not based on grounds. There are many illustrations of this philosophical bent.

For example, in regard to a person's report that he has an image of the Eiffel Tower we have an inclination to think that the image must *resemble* the Eiffel Tower. How else could the person declare so confidently what his image is *of*? *How could he know*?

Another example: A memory-report or memory-belief must be based, we think, on some mental *datum* that is equipped with various features to match the corresponding features of the memory-belief. This datum will include an image that provides the *content* of the belief, and a peculiar feeling that makes one refer the image to a *past* happening, and another feeling that makes one believe that the image is an *accurate* portrayal of the past happening, and still another feeling that informs one that it was *oneself* who witnessed the past happening. The presence of these various features makes memory-beliefs thoroughly reasonable.

Another illustration: If interrupted in speaking one can usually give a confident account, later on, of what one had been *about* to say. How is this possible? Must not one remember *a feeling of tendency to say just those words*? This is one's basis for knowing what one had been about to say. It justifies one's account.

Still another example: After dining at a friend's house you announce your intention to go home. How do you know your intention? One theory proposes that you are presently aware of a particular mental state or bodily feeling which, as you recall from your past experience, has been highly correlated with the behavior of going home; so you infer that *that* is what you are going to do now. A second theory holds that you must be aware of some definite mental state or event which reveals itself, not by experience but *intrinsically*, as the intention to go home. Your awareness of that mental item *informs* you of what action you will take.

Yet another illustration: This is the instructive case of the man who, since birth, has been immune to sensations of bodily pain. On his thirtieth birthday he is kicked in the shins and for the first time he responds by crying out, hopping around on one foot, holding his leg, and exclaiming, "The pain is terrible!" We have an overwhelming inclination to wonder, "How could he tell, *this first time,* that what he felt was *pain?*" Of course, the implication is that *after* the first time there would be *no* problem. Why not? Because his first experience with pain would provide him with a sample that would be preserved in memory; thereafter he would be equipped to determine whether any sensation he feels is or isn't pain; he would just compare it with the memory-sample to see whether the two match! Thus he will have a justification for believing that what he feels is pain. But the *first time* he will not have this justification. This is why the case is so puzzling. Could it be that this first time he *infers* that he is in pain from his own behavior?

A final illustration: Consider the fact that after a comparatively few examples and bits of instruction a person can go on to carry out a task, apply a word correctly in the future, continue a numerical series from an initial segment, distinguish grammatical from ungrammatical constructions, solve arithmetical problems, and so on. These correct performances will be dealing with new and different examples, situations, combinations. The performance output will be far more varied than the instruction input. How is this possible? What car-

ries the person from the meager instruction to his rich performance? The explanation has to be that an effect of his training was that he abstracted the Idea, perceived the Common Nature, "internalized" the Rule, grasped the Structure. What else could bridge the gap between the poverty of instruction and the wealth of performance? Thus we postulate an intervening mental act or state which removes the inequality and restores the balance.

My illustrations belong to what could be called the *pathology* of philosophy. Wittgenstein speaks of a "general disease of thinking" which attempts to explain occurrences of discernment, recognition, or understanding, by postulating mental states or processes from which those occurrences flow "as from a reservoir" (*BB,* p. 143). These mental intermediaries are assumed to contribute to the causation of the various cognitive performances. More significantly for my present purpose, they are supposed to *justify* them; they provide our *grounds* for saying or doing this rather than that; they *explain how we know.* The Image, or Cognitive State, or Feeling, or Idea, or Sample, or Rule, or Structure, *tells* us. It is like a road map or a signpost. It guides our course.

What is "pathological" about these explanatory constructions and pseudoscientific inferences? Two things at least. First, the movement of thought that demands these intermediaries is circular and empty, unless it provides criteria for determining their presence and nature *other than* the occurrence of the phenomena they are postulated to explain—and, of course, no such criteria are forthcoming. Second, there is the great criticism by Wittgenstein of this movement of philosophical thought: namely, his point that no matter what kind of state, process, paradigm, sample, structure, or rule, is conceived as giving us the necessary guidance, *it* could be taken, or understood, as indicating a *different* direction from the one in which we actually did go. The assumed intermediary Idea, Structure, or Rule, does not and cannot reveal that because of it we went in the only direction it was reasonable to go. Thus the internalized intermediary we are tempted to invoke to bridge the gap between training and performance, as being that which shows us what we must do or say if we are to be rational, cannot do the job it was invented to do. It cannot fill the epistemological gap. It cannot provide the bridge of justification. It cannot put to rest the How-do-we-know? question. Why not? Because it cannot tell us how *it itself* is to be taken, understood, applied. Wittgenstein puts the point briefly and pwerfully: "Don't always think that you read off your words from facts; that you portray these in words according to rules. For even so you would have to apply the rule in the particular case without guidance" (*PI*, 292). Without guidance! Like Wittgenstein's signpost arrow that cannot tell us whether to go in the direction of the arrow tip or in the opposite direction, so too the Images, Ideas, Cognitive Structures, or Rules, that we philosophers imagine as devices for guidance, cannot interpret themselves to us. The signpost does not tell the traveler how to read it. A second signpost might tell him how to read the first one; we can imagine such a case. But this can't go on. If the traveler is to continue his journey he will have to do something on his own, without guidance.

The parable of the traveler speaks for *all* of the language-games we learn and practice; even those in which there is the most disciplined instruction and the most rigorous standards of conformity. Suppose that a pupil has been given thorough training in some procedure, whether it is drawing patterns, building fences, or proving theorems. But then he has to carry on by himself in new situations. How does he know what to do? Wittgenstein presents the following dialogue: "'However you instruct him in the continuation of a pattern—how can he *know* how he is to continue by himself?'—Well, how do *I* know?—If that means 'Have I grounds?', the answer is: the grounds will soon give out. And then I shall act, without grounds'' (*PI*, 211). Grounds come to an end. Answers to How-do-we-know? questions come to an end. Evidence comes to an end. We must speak, act, live, without evidence. This is so, not just on the fringes of life and language, but at the center of our most regularized activities. We do learn rules and learn to follow them. But our training was in the past! We had to leave it behind and proceed on our own.

It is an immensely important fact of nature that as people carry on an activity in which they have received a common training, they do largely *agree* with one another, accepting the same examples and analogies, taking the same steps. We agree in what to say, in how to apply language. We agree in our responses to particular cases.

As Wittgenstein says: "That is not agreement in opinions but in form of life" (*PI*, 241). We cannot explain this agreement by saying that we are just doing what the rules tell us—for our agreement in applying rules, formulae, and signposts is what gives them their *meaning*.

One of the primary pathologies of philosophy is the feeling that we must *justify* our language-games. We want to establish them as well-grounded. But we should consider here Wittgenstein's remark that a language-game "is not based on grounds. It is there—like our life" (*OC*, 559).

Within a language-game there is justification and lack of justification, evidence and proof, mistakes and groundless opinions, good and bad reasoning, correct measurements and incorrect ones. One cannot properly apply these terms to a language-game itself. It may, however, be said to be "groundless," not in the sense of a groundless opinion, but in the sense that we accept it, we live it. We can say, "This is what we do. This is how we are."

In this sense religion is groundless; and so is chemistry. Within each of these two systems of thought and action there is controversy and argument. Within each there are advances and recessions of insight into the secrets of nature or the spiritual condition of humankind and the demands of the Creator, Savior, Judge, Source. Within the framework of each system there is criticism, explanation, justification. But we should not expect that there might be some sort of rational justification of the framework itself.

A chemist will sometimes employ induction. Does he have evidence for a Law of Induction? Wittgenstein observes that it would strike him as nonsense to say, "I know that the Law of Induction is true." ("Imagine such a statement made in a law court.") It would be more correct to say, "I believe in the Law of Induction" (*OC*, 500). This way of putting it is better because it shows that the attitude toward induction is belief in the sense of "religious" belief—that is to say, an acceptance which is not conjecture or surmise and for which there is no reason—it is a groundless acceptance.

It is intellectually troubling for us to conceive that a whole system of thought might be groundless, might have no rational justification. We realize easily enough, however, that grounds soon give out—that we cannot go on giving reasons for our reasons. There arises from this realization the conception of a reason that is *self-justifying*—something whose credentials as a reason cannot be questioned.

This metaphysical conception makes its presence felt at many points—for example, as an explanation of how a person can tell what his mental image is *of*. We feel that the following remarks, imagined by Wittgenstein, are exactly right: "'The image must be more similar to its object than any picture. For however similar I make the picture to what it is supposed to represent, it can always be the picture of something else. But it is essential to the image that it is the image of *this* and of nothing else'" (*PI*, 389). A pen and ink drawing represents the Eiffel Tower; but it could represent a mine shaft or a new type of automobile jack. Nothing prevents this drawing from being taken as a representation of something other than the Eiffel Tower. But my mental image of the Eiffel Tower is *necessarily* an image of the Eiffel Tower. Therefore it must be a "remarkable" kind of picture. As Wittgenstein observes: "Thus one might come to regard the image as a super-picture" (*ibid.*). Yet we have no intelligible conception of how a super-picture would differ from an ordinary picture. It would seem that it has to be a *super-likeness*—but what does this mean?

There is a familiar linguistic practice in which one person *tells* another what his image is of (or what he intends to do, or what he was about to say) and no question is raised of how the first one *knows* that what he says is true. This question is imposed from outside, artificially, by the philosophical craving for justification. We can see here the significance of these remarks: "It isn't a question of explaining a language-game by means of

our experiences, but of noting a language-game" (*PI*, 655). "Look on the language-game as the *primary* thing" (*PI*, 656). Within a system of thinking and acting there occurs, *up to a point*, investigation and criticism of the reasons and justifications that are employed in that system. This inquiry into whether a reason is good or adequate cannot, as said, go on endlessly. We stop it. We bring it to an end. We come upon something that *satisfies* us. It is as if we made a decision or issued an edict: "*This* is an adequate reason!" (or explanation, or justification). Thereby we fix a boundary of our language-game.

There is nothing wrong with this. How else could we have disciplines, systems, games? But our fear of groundlessness makes us conceive that we are under some logical compulsion to terminate at *those particular* stopping points. We imagine that we have confronted the self-evident reason, the self-justifying explanation, the picture or symbol whose meaning cannot be questioned. This obscures from us the *human* aspect of our concepts—the fact that what we call "a reason," "evidence," "explanation," "justification," is what appeals to and satisfies *us*.

III

The desire to provide a rational foundation for a form of life is especially prominent in the philosophy of religion, where there is an intense preoccupation with purported proofs of the existence of God. In American universities there must be hundreds of courses in which these proofs are the main topic. We can be sure that nearly always the critical verdict is that the proofs are invalid and consequently that, up to the present time at least, religious belief has received no rational justification.

Well, of course not! The obsessive concern with the proofs reveals the assumption that in order for religious belief to be intellectually respectable it *ought* to have a rational justification. *That* is the misunderstanding. It is like the idea that we are not justified in relying on memory until memory has been proved reliable.

Roger Trigg makes the following remark: "To say that someone acts in a certain way because of his belief in God does seem to be more than a redescription of his action. . . . It is to give a *reason* for it. The belief is distinct from the commitment which may follow it, and is the justification for it."[2] It is evident from other remarks that by "belief in God" Trigg means "belief in the existence of God" or "belief that God exists." Presumably by the *acts* and *commitments* of a religious person Trigg refers to such things as prayer, worship, confession, thanksgiving, partaking of sacraments, and participation in the life of a religious group.

For myself I have great difficulty with the notion of belief in *the existence* of God, whereas the idea of belief *in* God is to me intelligible. If a man did not ever pray for help or forgiveness, or have any inclination toward it; nor ever felt that it is "a good and joyful thing" to thank God for the blessings of this life; nor was ever concerned about his failure to comply with divine commandments— then, it seems clear to me, he could not be said to believe in God. Belief in God is not an all or none thing; it can be more or less; it can wax and wane. But belief in God in any degree does require, as I understand the words, some religious action, some commitment, or if not, at least a bad conscience.

According to Trigg, if I take him correctly, a man who was entirely devoid of any inclination toward religious action or conscience, might believe in *the existence* of God. What would be the marks of this? Would it be that the man knows some theology, can recite the Creeds, is well-read in Scripture? Or is his belief in the existence of God something different from this? If so, what? What would be the difference between a man who knows some articles of faith, heresies, scriptural writings, and in addition believes in the existence of God, and one who knows these things but does not believe in the existence of God? I assume that both of them are indifferent to the acts and commitments of religious life.

I do not comprehend this notion of belief in *the existence* of God which is thought to be distinct from belief *in* God. It seems to me to be an artificial construction of philosophy, another illustration of the craving for justification.

Religion is a form of life; it is language embedded in action—what Wittgenstein calls a "language-game." Science is another. Neither stands in need of justification, the one no more than the other.

Present-day academic philosophers are far more prone to challenge the credentials of religion than of science, probably for a number of reasons. One may be the illusion that science can justify its own framework. Another is the fact that science is a vastly greater force in our culture. Still another may be the fact that by and large religion is to university people an alien form of life. They do not participate in it and do not understand what it is all about.

Their nonunderstanding is of an interesting nature. It derives, at least in part, from the inclination of academics to suppose that their employment as scholars demands of them the most severe objectivity and dispassionateness. For an academic philosopher to become a religious believer would be a stain on his professional competence! Here I will quote from Nietzsche, who was commenting on the relation of the German scholar of his day to religious belief; yet his remarks continue to have a nice appropriateness for the American and British scholars of our own day:

> Pious or even merely church-going people seldom realize *how much* good will, one might even say wilfulness, it requires nowadays for a German scholar to take the problem of religion seriously; his whole trade . . . disposes him to a superior, almost good-natured merriment in regard to religion, sometimes mixed with a mild contempt directed at the "uncleanliness" of spirit which he presupposes wherever one still belongs to the church. It is only with the aid of history (thus *not* from his personal experience) that the scholar succeeds in summoning up a reverent seriousness and a certain shy respect towards religion; but if he intensifies his feelings towards it even to the point of feeling grateful to it, he has still in his own person not got so much as a single step closer to that which still exists as church or piety; perhaps the reverse. The practical indifference to religious things in which he was born and raised is as a rule sublimated in him into a caution and cleanliness which avoids contact with religious people and things: . . . Every age has its own divine kind of naïvety for the invention of

which other ages may envy it—and how much naïvety, venerable, childlike and boundlessly stupid naïvety there is in the scholar's belief in his superiority, in the good conscience of his tolerance, in the simple unsuspecting certainty with which his instinct treats the religious man as an inferior and lower type which he himself has grown beyond and *above*.[3]

Notes

1. Ludwig Wittgenstein, *On Certainty*, ed. G. E. M. Anscombe and G. H. von Wright; English translation by D. Paul and G. E. M. Anscombe (Oxford, 1969), para-graph 166. Henceforth I include references to this work in the text, employing the abbreviation "*OC*" followed by paragraph number. References to Wittgenstein's *The Blue and Brown Books* (Oxford, 1958) are indicated in the text by "*BB*" followed by page number. References to his *Philosophical Investigations,* ed. G. E. M. Anscombe and R. Rhees; English translation by Anscombe (Oxford, 1967) are indicated by "*PI*" followed by paragraph number. In *OC* and PI, I have mainly used the translations of Paul and Anscombe but with some departures.

2. *Reason and Commitment* (Cambridge, 1973), p. 75.

3. Friedrich Nietzsche, *Beyond Good and Evil,* trans. R. J. Hollingdale, para. 58.

VII.C.5   A Dialogue on Wittgensteinian Fideism

G A R Y   G U T T I N G

In our final reading in this section, Gary Gutting, who teaches philosophy at the University of Notre Dame, offers a dialogue among a Catholic rationalist, a Calvinist transrationalist, and a Wittgensteinian fideist in which a critical discussion of fideism takes place. The Wittgensteinian (abbreviated "W") agrees with the Calvinist that faith is above reason, but he wants to agree with the Catholic in saying that, in a sense, faith is still rational. There are two separate points at issue in the discussion: (1) whether nonbelievers can understand religious language and (2) whether reason can adjudicate the truth claims of religion.

Introduction

The following dialogue is a continuation of an earlier piece, "The Catholic and the Calvinist: A Dialogue on Faith and Reason."* In the earlier discussion, the Catholic argues that religious belief needs to be "strongly rational" (i.e., needs to be justified in a way that makes not believing irratio-

nal). The Calvinist claims that the most reason can do is show that religious belief is "weakly rational" (i.e., justified in a way that allows for the rationality of nonbelief as well as belief). He maintains that nonbelief is wrong, but not because it violates any rational norms. The Catholic cannot see that there could be anything wrong with a nonbelief that was rational. Their concluding exchange is this:

Calvinist: You're assuming that the believer's experience must be expressible in the categories of rational thought. My point is that it can't be. I see now that all this talk of justification and grounds of belief is an implicit reductionism. It denies the utterly unique, supernatural character of religious faith and tries to derive faith from natural conditions and considerations. All this philosophy of religion leads only to an idolatry of reason.

Catholic: I don't accept the either/or between being reasonable and being religious. Though I don't entirely see how to do it, I won't be content until I can see my way to a faith that is strongly rational.

The present selection introduces a new character, the Wittgensteinian, who tries to mediate the dispute between the Catholic and the Calvinist. This character's views are often very similar to those philosophers of religion influenced by Wittgen-

This article has been commissioned for this volume and appears for the first time in print here.

* *Faith and Philosophy* 2 (1985): 236–56.

stein (e.g., Norman Malcolm and, especially, D. Z. Phillips, whose writings are the source of much of what the Wittgensteinian says). But neither this character's views nor the views of the other two characters should be identified with those of any actual person.

Wittgensteinian (W) My basic idea derives from something Wittgenstein has taught us: that talk of justifying belief makes sense only within the framework of a given mode of discourse—within, as he would say, a given "language-game." Within such a framework, we can, of course, ask whether or not having a certain belief is a mistake—for example, whether it's adequately supported by the relevant evidence. But there's no sense to asking whether the framework itself is mistaken, since the framework defines the standards that determine whether something's a mistake. There's no meaning for the term *mistake* without the framework. The analogy with ordinary games is instructive here. I can make a mistake in playing chess by, say, moving a bishop from a white to a black square; this is a mistake because it's contrary to the rules of chess. But suppose someone asked whether chess itself—the rules that define the game—is a mistake. Obviously, such a question just reflects a misunderstanding of what is meant by a mistake.

Cath. But what does this have to do with religious belief?

W. Well, religion can be thought of as a mode of discourse, a language-game.

Cal. One small emendation. I think it would be better to say that, in Wittgensteinian terms, a religion is a form of life—an interrelated group of beliefs and practices—that includes a characteristic mode of discourse.

W. Fine. In any case, the religious mode of discourse defines its own standards of justification, its own criteria for what is and what is not a mistaken belief. Accordingly, it makes no sense to ask for a justification of religion itself, that is, to ask if religion itself is a mistake. This is why the idea of giving a rational justification of religious belief is, as our Calvinist friend says, entirely out of the question. On the other hand, this doesn't mean that religious belief is irrational, contrary to reason. It's not, but not because religious belief *is* rationally justified. Rather, it's beyond justification because it defines the standards for justification.

Cath. For what sort of justification does the religious mode of discourse define the standards?

W. For the justification of religious beliefs, of course.

Cath. Well, then, why do you say that there's no sense to questions about the justification of religious beliefs?

W. We need to distinguish between fundamental religious beliefs and derivative ones. Take the analogous case of science. Wittgenstein made the same point about it that he made about religion. He said that "those philosophers who asked for a 'justification' of science were like the Ancients who felt there must be an Atlas to support the Earth on his shoulders."

Cath. Just what is that supposed to mean?

W. Well, I take Wittgenstein to be talking about the demand—often made by philosophers who have misunderstood Hume—for a justification of the most basic assumptions of the scientific enterprise.

Cal. What would that involve?

W. Presumably, it would mean establishing, first, the reality of the physical world that is the subject-matter of science and, second, the validity of the methods (e.g., induction) whereby scientists develop accounts of the physical world. It seems to me that there's simply no sense to asking for justifications of such fundamental claims. It is like asking for a proof that the rules of chess are right. Similarly, it seems to me senseless to ask for a justification of the most fundamental claims of religion.

Cath. But of course this doesn't mean that no scientific claim need be justified. On the contrary, there is no *specific* scientific claim—no particular assertion about what there is in the physical world and how it behaves—for which it's not appropriate to ask a justification. Any particular hypothesis or theory or even observation statement can be challenged and needs vindicating by the appropriate scientific procedures.

W. Of course. And the justification is carried out in terms of the standards defined by the scientific framework. But what are you driving at?

Cath. I want you to see that Wittgenstein's point about limits to requests for justification applies at best only to the general enterprises of science and religion. Just as there's no basis for saying that any particular scientific theory—even one of great generality such as quantum mechanics or general relativity—is beyond justification, so too there's no basis for saying that any specific religious viewpoint—such as Catholicism or even generic Christianity—is beyond justification. So suppose we agree with your Wittgensteinian point about religion. What does it amount to? As in the case of science, we could say that the most fundamental assumptions of the religious viewpoint are not open to questions of justification. But what are these assumptions? First, that there is a divine reality and, second, that this reality has revealed itself to humanity in some special way. Anything more, such as identification of special characteristics of the divine reality or of the particular ways that it has revealed itself, will go beyond the general religious viewpoint to the claims of some specific religion. Now, while the analogy with science may suggest that these two fundamental assumptions can't be and need not be justified, it also strongly suggests that any other religious claims—including all the characteristic doctrines of the major world religions—are open to and require justification.

Cal. If so, our friend's attempt at mediation is a failure, since in fact no one believes simply that there is some sort of divine reality and that it has somehow revealed itself to us. We believe in the God and the revelation of some specific religion. It's these specific beliefs that I claim should be believed without rational justification.

W. I agree there may be difficulties about specific doctrinal beliefs. Of course most such beliefs can be justified in a religious framework by appealing to the revelation accepted by the religion in question. The problem is how to justify the claim that a particular purported revelation does indeed come from God. I don't pretend to have a solution to this problem. Perhaps an adequate re-

sponse will require a better understanding of the nature and function of special revelations. There are various possibilities. It may turn out that the apparently competing claims of different religions are just different modes of expressing the fundamental truths of the divine reality and its presence in the world. Or perhaps an adequate understanding of these fundamental truths, which define the religious mode of discourse and are beyond justification, will provide a basis for evaluating claims to special revelations. In any case, I think we make an important advance if we get clear about the epistemic status of fundamental religious truths.

Cath. Well, I think that Wittgenstein may well be right in general about the limits of demands for justification. But from the fact that there are such limits it doesn't follow that fundamental religious beliefs fall beyond them. The axioms of, say, the general theory of relativity require justification, even though they are the fundamental principles of a mode of theoretical discourse.

W. But that's because general relativistic discourse isn't autonomous. It—including its fundamental principles—is part of scientific discourse in general and so subject to its criteria of justification.

Cath. It seems to me that the same can be said of religious discourse. Its fundamental claims are factual ones about what there is (God, souls) and what has happened (God's revelation as a historical event). Consequently, these claims are made in the framework of factual discourse and must be justified the way any other factual claims must be—from arguments based on observed facts. And this is just what the tradition of positive apologetics has tried to do: show that God must exist as the only good explanation of certain basic facts about our world—its existence, its order—and show from historical evidence that this God has revealed himself in time. I admit that this project has not been entirely successful, but it seems to me that some such effort is essential if religious belief is to be rational.

W. That's because you totally misunderstand the significance of religious beliefs. You take them to be factual claims, on a par with those of empirical science. Surely you don't really expect to prove God's existence from laboratory experiments or by deductions from some scientific theory.

Cath. You really needn't caricature my position quite that grossly. I didn't say that religious claims are scientific assertions. They're obviously not formulated in the precise mathematical way that scientific statements are. But I think it's obvious—not absurd—that religious beliefs are factual claims about what there is and what has happened and so need to be supported by the sort of evidence appropriate to any factual claim. Surely you don't deny that Christians think it's a fact that God exists and that he revealed himself in Christ?

W. It's a fact in the extremely generic sense that any truth is a fact. But it's not a fact in the ordinary specific sense of a contingent truth about the world. God doesn't just happen to exist—he's not a thing among other things. He's an *eternal* being, one that must exist. As such, truths about him are of an entirely different order from truths about the contingent, temporal things of our world. Maybe you don't make "God exists" a scientific claim in the strict sense, but you certainly do make it a *hypothesis* for which we must seek evidence pro and con.

Cath. What's wrong with that?

W. It ignores the fact that God isn't the sort of entity that might or might not exist. I don't endorse the ontological argument as a proof of God's existence, but I do think it shows that God either must exist or can't exist. "God exists" isn't a hypothesis that might or might not be true.

Cath. I think you're confusing a metaphysical point with an epistemological one. It's true that in reality God either necessarily exists or else necessarily doesn't exist. If a hypothesis is a claim that is at best contingently true, then of course "God exists" isn't a hypothesis. But it can also be proper to call even a necessary truth or falsehood a hypothesis if we don't *know* whether or not it's true. We can rightly say that, as far as we know, a claim may or may not be true—even if it's either necessarily true or necessarily false. Even mathematicians, who deal only with the necessary, speak of conjectures and hypotheses in this sense. So just

because a claim is not contingent, it doesn't follow that we can't inquire about its truth or falsity or that such inquiry doesn't need to base itself on evidence and arguments.

W. But "God exists" is no more a mathematical theorem than it is a scientific hypothesis. It's an entirely *sui generis* assertion that simply can't be evaluated by the criteria of any other modes of discourse. When I emphasize the necessity of God's existence, I don't mean to assimilate it to the truths of formal discourses such as logic and mathematics. I'm rather emphasizing that God's reality is something that is entirely independent of the world of contingent things—its existence, its nature, its history. His reality is not something that can be in any way derived from that of creatures. Any such derivation would compromise God's transcendence.

Cath. It seems to me that you're once again confusing the metaphysical and the epistemological. God's existence as a transcendent reality can't derive from creatures, of course; he can't be causally dependent on them. But we can derive the truth that he exists from causal facts about creatures. Metaphysically, God can't derive from creatures; but, epistemologically, knowledge of the truth that he exists as their cause can derive from knowledge about creatures.

W. I can't make any sense of saying that God causes the contingent world. Causality is a relation among entities within the world. It's unintelligible to speak of its holding between the world and something outside it. I should think that, after Hume and Kant, this is utterly clear.

Cal. I think you're overoptimistic about the durability of their conclusions. But, in any case, I don't see how a Christian can agree that there's no sense in which God causes the world. That's as much as to say that he's not our creator.

W. But why do we need to understand creation in terms of causality? I can well imagine someone coming to believe that there is an ultimate cause of the world and saying, "So what?" as far as his personal life is concerned. There's nothing religious about a First Cause. I think we should rather understand God's creation as a matter of his being the meaning of the world. When I say God is the Creator of the world, I've adopted a new and transforming way of making sense of the world; I see it from the standpoint of eternity rather than of time.

Cath. Just what do you mean by that?

W. Our ordinary, temporal, worldly view sees the value of things as depending on the use to which they can be put. We take our happiness—as individuals or as a community—as the ultimate goal and judge the value of things and events in the world on the basis of their efficiency as means to that goal. But to see the world as God's creation is to see that things have an intrinsic value quite apart from their uses as means to our happiness. They are good in themselves simply because they exist and are what they are. Loving God is precisely loving what there is for its own sake, without regard for what it can do for us.

Cath. Why do you say that seeing things this way is taking the standpoint of eternity?

W. Because no matter how things go for us in worldly terms—and we can, at any moment, lose all our happiness—there is always this intrinsic worth of things, always this basis for loving and accepting our world, no matter what it has done to us. This is the viewpoint that allows us to say, as Socrates did, that even though literally anything can happen to us, nonetheless all is well.

Cath. The view you're presenting strikes me as a supernatural escapism. It turns away from the temporal reality of things and says that only their eternal meaning has any importance. I don't think that's a properly Christian attitude.

W. Neither do I. Holding to the eternal—that is, loving God—can never be an escape from the temporal. We live in time and there is no getting away from it. On the other hand, it's wrong to think that the eternal has nothing to do with the temporal, to hold a two kingdoms view of religion and the world, each autonomous in its own place. Rather—and this, I think, is the core of the Christian message—a sense of the eternal must have a decisive effect on my life in the world.

Cath. How?

W. By making me realize that there is an absolute value, an inviolability in worldly things—particularly in persons—that must always inform and,

at crucial points, limit my struggle with the world, my efforts to maximize contingent goods. The morality of the world is a morality of rights and duties, all geared to achieving temporal happiness. There are irreducible temporal goods and evils that rightly have immense significance for us. But there are limits to temporal values: on the one hand, their incompleteness and contingency, and, on the other hand, the underlying eternal values, the worth of things and especially persons in themselves, apart from their contribution to happiness. Further, these limits are not just the boundaries defining an autonomous realm. They have consequences for the way we conduct our temporal affairs (how we act morally); and they provide a dimension of good that is always present to us, come what may.

Cal. Just what do you have in mind as the consequences of the viewpoint of eternity for morality?

W. Moral actions can be thought of in terms of projects designed to bring about certain goods, for example, the projects of raising a family, building a friendship, eradicating a disease, attaining certain truths. The eternal can have significance for these moral projects in various ways. For example, in terms of a project's outcome, the eternal helps us come to terms with failure by making us aware of a dimension of value even in our failures. Thus, if my children have disappointed me, there may be no good they have done for which I can love them as I hoped to; but they remain valuable and lovable just as themselves. Losses are real and may be almost impossible to bear; but, for someone who can hold to the viewpoint of the eternal, everything is never lost. The eternal also makes a difference for successful projects. It reminds us that our gains are not everything either.

Cal. That's all fine and very Christian as far as it goes. But I thought you saw the eternal as imposing limits on our moral behavior.

W. I do. The eternal limits the means that may be used in carrying out projects by requiring an ultimate respect for the intrinsic value of persons and of things affected by what we do. There may be no simple way of determining these limits, but they're always there. There are some things that a

Christian can't do no matter what the temporal good to be attained. This would be my way of reconciling the consequentialist and the deontological approaches to ethics: The former is valid as long as we don't encroach on the eternal values protected by the latter.

Cath. The attitude you've sketched is interesting, even attractive. And I don't deny that it expresses much of the ethical messages of Christianity. But it's merely an ethical attitude and doesn't include the essential claims of Christianity about the reality of God. Christians may well think about the world in the way you've suggested; but they do so because they believe that it has been created by a transcendent, eternal, all-good God. That's what we might call a metaphysical foundation of their ethical attitudes. You assert the attitudes but omit any mention of the foundation.

W. I'm not sure what you mean. I most certainly assert the reality of God. To view the world from what I've called the standpoint of eternity is precisely to love God, and you can't love what you don't think exists.

Cal. But what you call "loving God" is actually just an attitude toward the world. You said earlier that God is the meaning of the world. That's true for the Christian in the sense that God is a being other than the world who made it and thereby gave it its meaning. But you don't mean that when you say God is the meaning of the world. You mean merely that the world has an intrinsic value apart from its uses for us. You just focus on one aspect of the world as you see it—its meaning as intrinsically valuable—and call that God. But you're not saying there is anything other than the world, you're not asserting God's existence as a transcendent being, which is what Christianity does.

W. I'm not saying, of course, that God is another thing to be added on to all the other things of the world. That's not the Christian view. God isn't just another thing—even a particularly impressive one.

Cal. Excuse me, but that just evades the issue. It's possible to speak of God as transcendent, existing apart from the world, and still not imply that he's just another thing to be added to the world.

Of course his reality is of a different order from that of creatures—he's an infinite being—and of course that reality is the source of the meaning of creaturely reality. But God also exists as a concrete individual in his own right, an infinite substance, independent of all finite substances. On your account, God has no such independent reality. He is actually just an aspect of the world, an ethical value that it has. You keep the word *God* but you eliminate the reality.

W. I think it's rather you who eliminate the divine reality. You make God a substance, a concrete existent, that has causally produced everything else that exists. To my mind, this is making God just another thing, even though an infinitely superior one. But, in any case, if God is as you say, then how can we rightly believe in him without the sort of rational basis our Catholic friend is demanding? In asserting the existence of God, we're doing essentially the same thing that we are when we assert the existence of any causal power that acts on the things of the world. Surely, then, we need the same sort of rational basis for believing in God as we would need for believing in Zeus, fairies, extraterrestials, or any other powerful entities that people have claimed exist.

Cath. But aren't you too eliminating God by making talk of him just talk about the world?

W. There I think you both have been misunderstanding me. In one sense, of course, all we have ever encountered are the things of the world, the individual, temporal existents that causally interact with us and with one another. If we believe only in this temporal world, what meaning can we find in our lives? Only the meaning corresponding to our achievement of happiness by means of temporal things. If things go well—if I'm healthy, have a sufficient amount of enjoyment and success—then my life is happy and meaningful. But if fate isn't kind, I may suffer, I may lose everything important to my happiness; then my life is unhappy and meaningless. This is the view of things we take if we believe in nothing beyond the temporal world, if we think of the world solely in its own terms. It's a common view, the one expressed, for example, by the old Greek insistence that we can call no man happy until he's dead—

until, that is, we've found out what fate has in store for him. Christians, however, don't share this view. They take a view of the temporal world other than that required of those who believe only in the temporal world. They see this world as having an eternal value—something they could never see if they accepted that world on its own terms. In this sense, they reject the world; that is, they reject the ultimacy of the world's own system of values and see the world *sub specie aeternitatis*—as something of eternal value. This other-than-worldly viewpoint is precisely the viewpoint of God, and it's in this sense that God is other than the world.

Cal. But surely the viewpoint you are talking about is just a subjective attitude that we happen to take. It may be other than the ordinary human view, but it's still *our* view. So aren't you just identifying God with a certain attitude of human beings?

W. Believing is, of course, a matter of *our* taking a certain attitude toward the world. But the attitude isn't just arbitrarily assumed. We take it because we see it as the objectively right way of looking at things, quite apart from what we feel or want. Moreover, it's an attitude that sees things in their eternal aspect rather than in their mere temporality. That's why we say it's God's attitude.

Cal. But you still have nothing more than an objective truth about the eternal significance of worldly things. You don't believe in anything more than the temporal world.

W. If I believed in only the temporal world, I wouldn't believe in its eternal significance. To believe only in the world is to be a Protagorean: to see nothing beyond the flux of time and hence to assign things value and meaning only in relation to human purposes. But I believe in the eternal, which is to believe in God.

Cal. Well, perhaps you believe in God as some sort of abstract principle—eternal value—in which temporal things participate. But you certainly don't believe in the personal God of Christianity.

W. Of course I don't believe that God is a person like you and me: a substantial agent acting in time. But Christianity doesn't require any such anthropomorphic superstition. On the contrary, it has always insisted that human conceptions must fall short of the mystery of the divine reality. Accordingly, when Christianity tells us that God is a person, it would be a great mistake to think this means we can simply apply to him the concept of personhood we use in thinking about ourselves. It is rather a matter of realizing that the language we use to speak of persons is less inadequate in speaking of God than are other languages we might employ (the language of abstract entities, the language of inanimate things, etc.). Now I certainly don't deny that God is a person in this analogous sense. For one thing, the experience of the eternal value of things affects us so deeply, transforms our consciousness so fundamentally, that it can only be compared to our love of persons. To speak of God as an inanimate object or an abstract entity would be entirely inappropriate to express the depth of our religious experience. On the other hand, it is equally inappropriate to think of God in many of the ways we think of ourselves and other persons—as needing to be persuaded (e.g., by prayer) to act for the good, as being angry at our sins and demanding reparation for them, as displaying his power by miraculous interventions in the course of nature, and so on. Personifying God in such a way introduces an anthropomorphic, superstitious notion of the divine that has no place in true Christian belief.

Cal. I like the way you brush aside the beliefs of the vast majority of Christians throughout history as superstitions.

W. I don't mean to be dismissive of sincerely held beliefs, and I recognize that much of what we now find inappropriate in speaking of God may well have played an essential role in developing a more adequate conception of the divine. But quite apart from the question of adequacy to the Christian message, it seems to me that the view of God that I've called superstitious—that is, the view of him as causally active in the world—is indefensible. A causally active God can be known from his effects; and if belief in him can't be justified by arguments from these effects, then we're not entitled to it. But I take it as clear from several centuries of philosophical discussion that there are no good arguments for a causally active God.

Cath. It is interesting that, for all your talk of the inappropriateness of demands to justify religious belief, you yourself make such demands for the sort of beliefs that many, if not most, religious people hold. You say "superstitious" beliefs should be rejected because they're unjustified. But why not say the same thing of your allegedly more enlightened beliefs?

W. The beliefs I call superstitious are really no different in principle from the causal explanatory hypotheses of scientific theories. They are claims that there are powers at work in the world that produce certain effects. Why believe such things unless they're proven on the basis of the alleged effects? By contrast, the religious view, as I conceive it, is by no means a hypothesis about how effects are produced in the world. It is rather the expression of a way of regarding the world and its value entirely apart from what its contingent course might be. It's not a matter of seeing that certain facts are true of the world and drawing conclusions from them; it's a matter of seeing all the facts of the world in a new perspective, as having a new sort of significance. Superstitious belief accepts the framework of our ordinary, temporal vision of the world and tries to introduce God as a further feature of the world so conceived. True religious belief is something much more radical: It's a transformation of the very conceptual framework in terms of which we view the world, a revolution in the way we see things. You might even say that, whereas superstitious belief believes in God as a new item in the same old (prereligious) world, properly religious belief believes in a new world.

Cath. So, roughly, your view is that, since questions of justification can be raised only within a framework or—to use your earlier terminology—a mode of discourse, they can't be raised about religion taken precisely as belief in a new framework.

W. Yes. The mistake made by philosophical critics of religious belief and by superstitious believers is to think that religious claims are made within a preestablished framework—for example, that of empirical science or, more broadly, that of our everyday conception of the world as a nexus of causal powers—when in fact they are constitutive of an entirely new, distinctively religious framework. It's this that makes questions about the rational justification of religious beliefs inappropriate.

Cal. There's a lot I dislike in your view: It dilutes religious belief and it doesn't recognize the real tension that exists between faith and reason. But there's one consequence of it that I strongly endorse. It entails the senselessness of the project, so dear to our Catholic friend, of positive apologetics—the project of rationally showing nonbelievers that they ought to believe.

Cath. Why so?

W. I should think the point is quite obvious. Such apologetics necessarily misrepresent the nature of religious belief. The apologetic effort can take either of two directions. It might try to establish the value of believing, or it might try to establish the truth of what is believed. In either case, it would have to employ arguments (premises and modes of inference) that are shared by believers and nonbelievers. With the first approach—that of showing the value of belief—this would mean showing that belief in God has value as a means to achieving certain nonreligious (worldly) goals, for example, human happiness. But this contradicts the religious view that God and belief in him are absolute and eternal values, not means to temporal goods. The second approach—showing the truth of belief—can proceed only by treating God's existence as a hypothesis about a thing that exists in addition to the other things of this world. This is necessary since the nonbeliever, who must be convinced on the basis of premises he accepts, is precisely one who sees reality as merely a matter of causal activity in the world. He sees power as the necessary mark of the real. But God is precisely a reality that is not of that sort. He does not make a causal difference in the world. So any being whose existence could be demonstrated to a nonbeliever wouldn't be God.

Cath. I don't think the point's at all obvious. For one thing, you're assuming that, because believers and nonbelievers see the world in fundamentally different ways, they have no common ground that allows them to discuss their differences. That would be so only if the religious viewpoint were an entirely closed system, with no significance for anything outside itself.

W. I certainly don't think of religion in that way. It's not a self-contained, esoteric game. It provides responses to fundamental questions and concerns that are shared by everybody: love, death, guilt, . . .

Cath. Well, then, why can't these common questions and concerns be a basis for communication between believers and nonbelievers? Why, in particular, can't believers show that their answers to questions about love, death, guilt, and so on are more satisfactory than any others?

W. From the fact that nonbelievers understand the questions religious belief is responding to, it doesn't follow that they can understand the answers it gives. How can they? To have the requisite understanding is already to be in the framework of faith.

Cal. I don't see how that follows. It seems to me that there are those who perfectly well understand what faith is saying but refuse to accept it.

W. I agree that there is such a thing as religious revolt, the rejection of grace. Such revolt occurs within the framework of religion. In one sense, the rebel does see things in a religious way. He believes that there is a God, that God is calling him to a certain sort of life; but he simply refuses to bend his will to the truth he perceives. His rebellion is a matter of refusing to live as he realizes he ought. He has faith in a minimal sense but refuses the consolations of hope and the obligations of charity. This sort of disbelief is one way of adopting a religious perspective.

Cath. But it seems to me you're ignoring a deeper sense of revolt, one for which it's not a matter of a rebel, like Satan, acknowledging the truth of a religion but refusing to live in accord with it. It's also possible to appreciate thoroughly what a religion claims and offers—hence to understand it from the inside—but still refuse to believe that it's true. I agree that atheism and agnosticism are often attitudes based on a simple failure to grasp what religion is about. But I think there are also forms of doubt and even denial that are themselves genuinely religious phenomena because they arise precisely from an understanding of what religion is saying. Certainly, it is absurd to say that those who have been deeply committed believers and later give up their faith don't understand what they're giving up.

W. I'm not so sure. They will typically say that belief doesn't mean anything to them any more.

Cath. But surely that can refer to a loss of importance for religion in their lives, rather than to a literal loss of comprehension. To make a simple comparison, a person whose entire life centered around soccer in his youth may well, as he develops more mature interests, say that soccer no longer means anything to him. But that doesn't mean he no longer knows the rules of the game or that he couldn't play it if he wanted to or even that he can't empathize with those whose lives do center on it. Similarly, a reformed gambler or alcoholic entirely understands the form of life that he's abandoned. I admit that it's easy to misunderstand a view that has no appeal to us. D. Z. Phillips has shown how observers of alien cultures have often caricatured their practices as blatant superstitions. For example, the custom of placing the mouth of an infant on that of its dying mother has been said to derive from the silly belief that the soul is literally in the breath and can be physically passed from one person to another. Phillips shows that this is an unfair interpretation and explains how the practice may have an entirely natural and sensible symbolic meaning. But what I want to emphasize is that, although Phillips clearly provides us with a proper understanding of another culture's religion, neither he nor we accept that religion. If we can understand religions of other cultures without accepting them, surely a person raised in a Christian culture can understand Christianity without believing in it.

W. Well, perhaps it's too strong to say that nonbelievers simply don't understand what believers hold, but I still think there are important differences between the kind of understanding believers and nonbelievers have of religion. In any case, I don't see how this issue affects my main point: Rational justification can occur only within a given framework, and questions about religious belief are questions about which framework to adopt. Hence they can't be answered with rational justification. I agree that religion is a genuine answer to questions that concern both believers and nonbelievers, but religious answers are of the sort that fundamentally transform our understanding of the questions they answer. Nonbelievers, for example, are obviously concerned with suffering; they want to know why it occurs, how we should react to it. They of course ask such questions in the framework of temporal goods, a framework that leads them to expect answers that present suffering as an indirect means of furthering our happiness. But what then will they make of a Christian answer to the question of suffering such as the one Simone Weil puts forward: "If I thought that God sends me suffering by an act of His will and for my good, I should think I was something, and I should miss the chief use of suffering, which is to teach me that I am nothing." To accept *this* as an answer to his question about suffering, the nonbeliever would have to give up the temporal framework in terms of which he has posed the question and reformulate it in the Christian framework of eternity.

Cath. But people can be led to radical transformations of viewpoint.

W. Of course, but not by processes of rational persuasion. We can say various things on behalf of belief to nonbelievers; they may find them convincing or not. What we can't do is *rationally* persuade them. There isn't sufficient common ground between them and us to provide the premises for a compelling argument. In that sense, belief and nonbelief are, as Thomas Kuhn says of rival scientific paradigms,* incommensurable. Kuhn is no doubt too extreme in thinking that rival paradigms correspond to differences so great that they can't be bridged by rational argument. Scientific paradigms are ultimately commensurable, since otherwise science couldn't be the rational enterprise it

obviously is. But I think the sort of account Kuhn wrongly endorses for science is correct for religion. Believers and nonbelievers see the world in ways sufficiently different to make impossible rational arguments for moving from one view to the other. Of course, there's some common ground among believers and nonbelievers—as there is among all human beings; and that's why religion is relevant to the concerns of nonbelievers. But there's not sufficient common ground to support a rational bridge from one standpoint to the other. In this sense, belief and nonbelief are incommensurable.

Cath. I think you misunderstand both Kuhn and religion, and the reason is that you have too limited a view of what can be involved in rational persuasion. You're looking at it as entirely a matter of argument from antecedently accepted premises that deductively or inductively support a conclusion. That's one form of rational persuasion, and it's prominent in such enterprises as Kuhnian normal science. But to use Stephen Toulmin's distinction, you're making the mistake of identifying logicality with rationality. You're ignoring the fact that there are modes of rational persuasion other than logical argument from antecedently shared premises, and this leads you to miss Kuhn's point about scientific revolutions. You think he's saying that, because rival paradigms are incommensurable, changes of paradigm are not rational. His point, in fact, is that such changes *are* rational and that their occurrence requires us to broaden our conception of rationality. It seems to me that, ironically, you're making the same sort of reductionist mistake about the nature of religious rationality that you've accused others of making about the nature of religious beliefs. You've condemned those who think all meaningful statements about reality—including religious ones—must be taken as empirical hypotheses, confirmed by scientific observation. In other words, you've rejected the positivist mistake of reducing reality to empirical reality. But now you've fallen into a similar positivist trap yourself by reducing rationality to logicality.

W. Far be it from me to commit the sin of reductionism. But I'm not convinced that there's any content to your suggestion that persuasion can

---

* *The Structure of Scientific Revolutions* (Chicago: Univ. of Chicago Press, 1962).

be rational without being logical. If what I say does not logically entail or make probable my conclusion, how can I claim to have made a rationally convincing case?

Cath. As a matter of fact, there's nothing more common than rationality without logicality. All sorts of our everyday conclusions are arrived at in this way. Who of us, for example, does or could construct a good argument showing that the car we've decided to buy is the one that in fact best suits our desires or that we've chosen the best school for our children or cast the right vote in an election? In all such cases, there are numerous conflicting considerations, and the issue could be decided by argument only if there were some non-problematic way of ordering or weighing the considerations. Should the inconvenience of the two-door car count more than its slightly lower price and, if so, by how much? Should the certainty that my child will get a better grounding in mathematics at a private school outweigh the probability that he will feel inferior in a group of wealthy children? Do Jones's sincerity and intelligence compensate for his lack of administrative experience? Ordinarily, I can't assign precise weights or orderings to such considerations and so cannot construct an argument that will tell me what I should do. The only option is to survey all the relevant considerations, think long and hard about how they interrelate, and then make a final judgment. My point is that, if I've thought the matter through responsibly, there's every reason to say that this judgment is rational, even though it isn't derived from a logical argument. And, if Kuhn is right, this is also the sort of rationality at work in changes in scientific paradigms.

Cal. But aren't such judgments rational only in the weak sense—which you've rejected as an inadequate ground of religious belief—of my having a right but not an obligation to judge as I do?

Cath. I don't think so. It seems to me that if, after the most careful consideration, my judgment clearly favors a given conclusion, then I'd be irrational not to accept that conclusion. Surely, in the case of science, when the community of scientists has judged that a certain paradigm is the best available, it would be irrational of them nonetheless to endorse some other paradigm.

Cal. Yes, but there you have another factor operating—the consensus of a scientific community. That means that there's been a convergence to the same conclusion in the judgments of many, indeed, almost all, qualified individuals. But what about the case, which is that of religious belief, where there is no such consensus? Then, it seems to me, each person is epistemically entitled to his or her opinion, but there's no reason to say that any opinion is rationally preferable to another. I'm rational in accepting my judgment, but so are those who make a contrary one. But that's precisely the weak rationality we agreed isn't a sufficient basis for religious belief.

Cath. All right. But at any rate what I've said at least still tells against our Wittgensteinian friend's suggestion that it's inappropriate to speak of justifying fundamental religious beliefs. That suggestion was based on the assumption that rational justification could only take the form of logical argument. My examples from everyday life—as well as Kuhn's discussion of science—show that there are other forms of rational justification, that we shouldn't reduce rationality to logicality. I agree that, without a conclusive logical argument, my own judgment alone provides only a weakly rational justification. We need some sort of consensus to say that a judgment is strongly rational. But there's no reason in principle why religious beliefs couldn't be the object of such a consensus. If they were, they'd be rationally justified in the strong sense; it would be irrational not to hold them.

Cal. Yes, but in fact there's no such consensus, and so reason says it's perfectly all right not to believe. Faith says otherwise, so we're still left with the choice between faith and reason. You know my decision.

Cath. I know it, but I could never live with it myself.

VII.D Rationality and Justified Religious Belief

In this section we are concerned with the contemporary discussion of the relationship of reason to religious belief. In the theoretical or epistemological sense (over against the pragmatic sense) of rationality, is it rational to believe religious propositions? Specifically, is it rational to believe that God exists? These readings offer various interpretations of the notion of rationality and show how they apply to theistic belief.

In the first reading, "Rational Theistic Belief without Proof," John Hick continues the debate about the relevancy of the proofs or arguments for theistic belief that we studied in Part 1, section D. Hick agrees with Cahn in viewing the proofs as largely irrelevant to religion. They are neither sufficient nor necessary for the religious life. Not only do the so-called proofs for the existence of God fail to accomplish what they set out to do, but even if they did demonstrate what they purported to demonstrate, this would at best only force our notional assent. They would not bring about the deep devotion and sense of worship necessary for a full religious life. Furthermore, they are not necessary because believers have something *better*, an intense, coercive, indubitable experience, which convinces them of the reality of the being in question. For believers, God is not a hypothesis brought in ex machina to explain the world but a living presence, closer to them than the air they breathe.

Nonetheless, believers are not irrational in believing in God. Hick describes a notion of person-relativeness of evidence, such that it might be rational for one person, A, on the evidence E_1, which A has, to believe some proposition p, whereas it may be clearly irrational for B to believe that same p given the evidence E_2, which B has. Religious individuals base their belief upon certain evidence that comes through religious experience that nonreligious individuals do not have as part of their data. Although the believers cannot demonstrate that they are right, they can show that it is reasonable for them to believe that God exists, given their experience.

At this point Hick develops a notion of religious experience analogous to our claim that we experience an external world. Neither proposition can be proved, but both are natural beliefs. The main difference between the two kinds of experience is that virtually everyone agrees on the reality of an external world, but only a relatively small minority of humankind experience compelling religious experience. Should this undermine the argument from religious experience? Not necessarily, for it may be the case that the few have access to a higher reality. They cannot easily be dismissed as insane or simply hallucinating, for the "general intelligence and exceptionally high moral quality of the great religious figures clashes with any analysis of their experience in terms of abnormal psychology."

At the end of his article Hick applies his thesis about the sense of the presence of God to the problem of the plurality of religions. He suggests that there is a convergence of religious experience, indicating the existence of a common higher reality.

In our next reading, Alvin Plantinga carries on Hick's argument, arguing that the evidentialist objections to theism (such as those put forth by W. K. Clifford earlier in this volume) fail to make their case, for the evidentialists have yet to set forth unambiguous criteria to account for all the clear cases of justified beliefs that would exclude the belief in God. Plantinga outlines the position of the foundationalist-evidentialist as one that claims that all justified beliefs must either be properly basic by virtue of fulfilling certain criteria or be based on other beliefs. This eventually results in a treelike construction with properly basic beliefs resting at the bottom, or the foundation. According to classic foundationalism,

A proposition *p* is properly basic for a person *S* if and only if *p* is either self-evident to *S* or incorrigible for *S* or evident to the senses for *S*.

Self-evident propositions are those that a person just sees as true immediately, such as that one plus two equals three or that a contradiction cannot be true. Incorrigible propositions are those about one's states of consciousness in which one cannot mistakenly believe what is not true, such as 'I think, therefore I am' or 'I am in pain'. Aquinas and Locke add a third type of proposition, that which is evident to the senses, such as 'I see a tree'. The goal of the classical foundationalist is to protect our belief systems from error by allowing only solid or absolutely certain beliefs to make up the foundation of our belief systems. Plantinga shows that there are many beliefs that we seem to be justified in holding that do not fit into any of these three categories, such as memory beliefs (e.g., 'I ate breakfast this morning'), belief in an external world, and belief in other minds. These beliefs are not dependent on other beliefs, yet neither are they self-evident, incorrigible, or evident to the senses.

Having shown the looseness of what we can accept as properly basic, Plantinga next shows that the Protestant Reformers saw belief in God as properly basic. He asks us to consider this as a legitimate option and examines possible objections to it. His claim is that belief in God is properly basic and that none of the objections to this view succeed. Note that although Plantinga's position may resemble the fideist position in that it does not appeal to evidence to support theism, it differs from it in being open to consideration of the claims of reason. If the atheologian could assemble a clear and cogent case against theism, the rational believer would have to revise his or her religious beliefs. In this sense, Plantinga's reformed epistemology might be considered a version of soft rationalism, a type of rationalism that makes no claims to having exact criteria for what is to count as

rationally acceptable but is open to evidence and argument.

In the next reading, "In Search of the Foundations of Theism," Philip Quinn criticizes Plantinga's arguments, claiming (1) that Plantinga has failed to show that the criteria for proper basicality that he rejects are in any way defective and (2) that Plantinga's procedure for justifying criteria for proper basicality provides no advantage over a criterion wherein no theistic propositions are properly basic. Although Quinn believes that Plantinga's argument is unsound, he is open to the possibility that some propositions that self-evidently entail that God exists could be properly basic. In the second part of his paper Quinn argues that, even if this were so, being properly basic would be relatively unimportant and such propositions would seldom be properly basic for intellectually sophisticated adult theists in our culture.

Alvin Plantinga's response to Philip Quinn's critique appears in *Faith and Philosophy*, vol. 3, no. 3 (July 1986).

Finally, in the last reading in this section, "Can Religious Belief Be Rational?", I argue that a coherentist approach to religion may have a better chance of justifying religious belief than a foundationalist approach. That is, rather than view our beliefs in terms of the foundationalist model, in which one belief is supported by more basic beliefs until we get to foundational beliefs for which there is no further evidence, it might be better to see our belief systems in terms of a web or network of beliefs mutually supporting each other. Although some beliefs may be privileged or more self-evident than others, few beliefs can be sustained independently of the whole system or large parts of it.

Furthermore, there is a certain person-relativeness in every person's noetic structure. Each of us has had a different, complex history of evidence gathering and belief formation, so that intersubjective belief comparison and evaluation becomes difficult. What is rational for you to believe, given your framework, may not be rational for me to believe, given my framework. That is, we find ourselves assessing evidence within various world views, from interpretive perspectives, so that it is difficult to communicate across world views. Nevertheless, there are core experiences and criteria of rationality that are common to all (or nearly all) humans and that can provide a common measure for attempting to arrive at optimally rational positions. That is, although it is difficult

to be critically rational about religious beliefs and experiences, it is possible, and the rationally religious person seeks to scrutinize all of his or her beliefs and revise those beliefs as fresh experience is made available. So communication and a sharing of our reasons for our various belief systems is possible in spite of the high degree of relativity in those systems.

VII.D.1   Rational Theistic Belief without Proof

J O H N   H I C K

In this reading John Hick, professor of philosophy at Claremont Graduate School, argues that the so-called proofs for the existence of God are largely irrelevant to religion. They are neither sufficient nor necessary for the religious life. Not only do they fail to accomplish what they set out to do, but even if they did accomplish it, this would at best only force our notional assent. They would not bring about the deep devotion and sense of worship necessary for a full religious life. Furthermore, they are not necessary because believers have something better, an intense, coercive, indubitable experience, which convinces them of the reality of the being in question. For believers, God is not a hypothesis brought in ex machina to explain the world but a living presence, closer to them than the air they breathe.

Nonetheless, believers are not irrational in believing in God. Hick describes a notion of person-relativeness of evidence, so that it might be rational for one person, A, on the evidence E_1, which A has, to believe some proposition p, whereas it may be clearly irrational for B to believe that same p given the evidence E_2, which B has. Religious individuals base their belief upon

certain evidence that comes through religious experience that nonreligious individuals do not have as part of their data.

Hick goes on to develop a notion of religious experience analogous to our claim that we experience an external world. At the end of his article Hick applies his thesis about the sense of the presence of God to the problem of the plurality of religions. He suggests that there is a convergence of religious experience, indicating the existence of a common higher reality.

(a) The religious rejection of the theistic arguments

We have seen that the major theistic arguments are all open to serious philosophical objections. Indeed we have in each case concluded, in agreement with the majority of contemporary philosophers, that these arguments fail to do what they profess to do. Neither those which undertake strictly to demonstrate the existence of an absolute Being, nor those which profess to show divine existence to be probable, are able to fulfil their promise. We have seen that it is impossible to demonstrate the reality of God by a priori reasoning, since such reasoning is confined to the realm of concepts; impossible to demonstrate it by a pos-

Reprinted from John Hick, *Arguments for the Existence of God* (Macmillan, London and Basingstoke, 1971) by permission of the publisher. Footnotes edited.

teriori reasoning, since this would have to include a premise begging the very question at issue; and impossible to establish it as in a greater or lesser degree probable, since the notion of probability lacks any clear meaning in this context. A philosopher unacquainted with modern developments in theology might well assume that theologians would, *ex officio,* be supporters of the theistic proofs and would regard as a fatal blow this conclusion that there can be neither a strict demonstration of God's existence nor a valid probability argument for it. In fact however such an assumption would be true only of certain theological schools. It is true of the more traditional Roman Catholic theology, of sections of conservative Protestantism, and of most of those Protestant apologists who continue to work within the tradition of nineteenth-century idealism. It has never been true, on the other hand, of Jewish religious thought; and it is not true of that central stream of contemporary Protestant theology which has been influenced by the 'neo-orthodox' movement, the revival of Reformation studies and the 'existentialism' of Kierkegaard and his successors; or of the most significant contemporary Roman Catholic thinkers, who are on this issue (as on so many others) in advance of the official teaching of the magisterium. Accordingly we have now to take note of this theological rejection of the theistic proofs, ranging from a complete lack of concern for them to a positive repudiation of them as being religiously irrelevant or even harmful. There are several different considerations to be evaluated.

1. It has often been pointed out that for the man of faith, as he is depicted in the Bible, no theistic proofs are necessary. Philosophers in the rationalist tradition, holding that to know means to be able to prove, have been shocked to find that in the Bible, which is supposed to be the basis of Western religion, no attempt whatever is made to demonstrate the existence of God. Instead of professing to establish the divine reality by philosophical reasoning the Bible throughout takes this for granted. Indeed to the biblical writers it would have seemed absurd to try to establish by logical argumentation that God exists. For they were convinced that they were already having to do with him and he with them in all the affairs of their lives. They did not think of God as an inferred entity but as an experienced reality. Many of the biblical writers were (sometimes, though doubtless not at all times) as vividly conscious of being in God's presence as they were of living in a material world. It is impossible to read their pages without realising that to them God was not a proposition completing a syllogism, or an idea adopted by the mind, but the supreme experiential reality. It would be as sensible for a husband to desire a philosophical proof of the existence of the wife and family who contribute so much of the meaning and value of his life as for the man of faith to seek for a proof of the existence of the God within whose purpose he believes that he lives and moves and has his being.

As Cook Wilson wrote:

If we think of the existence of our friends; it is the 'direct knowledge' which we want: merely inferential knowledge seems a poor affair. To most men it would be as surprising as unwelcome to hear it could not be directly known whether there were such existences as their friends, and that it was only a matter of (probable) empirical argument and inference from facts which are directly known. And even if we convince ourselves on reflection that this is really the case, our actions prove that we have a confidence in the existence of our friends which can't be derived from an empirical argument (which can never be certain) for a man will risk his life for his friend. We don't want merely inferred friends. Could we possibly be satisfied with an inferred God?

In other words the man of faith has no need of theistic proofs; for he has something which for him is much better. However it does not follow from this that there may not be others who do need a theistic proof, nor does it follow that there are in fact no such proofs. All that has been said about the irrelevance of proofs to the life of faith may well be true, and yet it might still be the case that there are valid arguments capable of establishing the existence of God to those who stand outside the life of faith.

2. It has also often been pointed out that the God whose existence each of the traditional theistic proofs professes to establish is only an abstrac-

tion from and a pale shadow of the living God who is the putative object of biblical faith. A First Cause of the Universe might or might not be a deity to whom an unqualified devotion, love and trust would be appropriate; Aquinas's *Et hoc omnes intelligunt Deum* ('and this all understand to be God') is not the last step in a logical argument but merely an exercise of the custom of over-looking a gap in the argument at this point. A Necessary Being, and indeed a being who is meta-physically absolute in every respect—omnipotent, omniscient, eternal, uncreated—might be morally good or evil. As H. D. Aitken has remarked, 'Logi-cally, there is no reason why an almighty and om-niscient being might not be a perfect stinker.' A divine Designer of the world whose nature is read off from the appearances of nature might, as Hume showed, be finite or infinite, perfect or im-perfect, omniscient or fallible, and might indeed be not one being but a veritable pantheon. It is only by going beyond what is proved, or claimed to have been proved, and identifying the First Cause, Necessary Being, or Mind behind Nature with the God of biblical faith that these proofs could ever properly impel to worship. By them-selves and without supplementation of content and infusion of emotional life from religious tradi-tions and experiences transcending the proofs themselves they would never lead to the life of faith.

The ontological argument on the other hand is in this respect in a different category. If it succeeds it establishes the reality of a being so perfect in every way that no more perfect can be conceived. Clearly if such a being is not worthy of worship none ever could be. It would therefore seem that, unlike the other proofs, the ontological argument, if it were logically sound, would present the rela-tively few persons who are capable of appreciat-ing such abstract reasoning with a rational ground for worship. On the other hand, however, whilst this is the argument that would accomplish most if it succeeded it is also the argument which is most absolutely incapable of succeeding; for it is, as we have seen, inextricably involved in the fallacy of professing to deduce existence from a concept.

3. It is argued by some religious writers that a logical demonstration of the existence of God would be a form of coercion and would as such be incompatible with God's evident intention to treat his human creatures as free and responsible per-sons. A great deal of twentieth-century theology emphasises that God as the infinite personal real-ity, having made man as person in his own image, always treats men as persons, respecting their rela-tive freedom and autonomy. He does not override the human mind by revealing himself in over-whelming majesty and power, but always ap-proaches us in ways that leave room for an un-compelled response of human faith. Even God's own entry into our earthly history, it is said, was in an 'incognito' that could be penetrated only by the eyes of faith. As Pascal put it, 'willing to appear openly to those who seek him with all their heart, and to be hidden from those who flee from him with all their heart, he so regulates the knowledge of himself that he has given indications of himself which are visible to those who seek him and not to those who do not seek him. There is enough light for those to see who only desire to see, and enough obscurity for those who have a contrary disposition.' God's self-revealing actions are ac-cordingly always so mediated through the events of our temporal experience that men only become aware of the divine presence by interpreting and responding to these events in the way which we call religious faith. For if God were to disclose himself to us in the coercive manner in which our physical environment obtrudes itself we should be dwarfed to nothingness by the infinite power thus irresistibly breaking open the privacy of our souls. Further, we should be spiritually blinded by God's perfect holiness and paralysed by his infinite en-ergy; 'for human kind cannot bear very much real-ity.' Such a direct, unmediated confrontation breaking in upon us and shattering the frail auton-omy of our finite nature would leave no ground for a free human response of trust, self-commitment and obedience. There could be no call for a man to venture upon a dawning consciousness of God's reality and thus to receive this conscious-ness as an authentic part of his own personal exis-tence precisely because it has not been injected

into him or clamped upon him by magisterial exercise of divine omnipotence.

The basic principle invoked here is that for the sake of creating a personal relationship of love and trust with his human creatures God does not force an awareness of himself upon them. And (according to the view which we are considering) it is only a further application of the same principle to add that a logically compelling demonstration of God's existence would likewise frustrate this purpose. For men—or at least those of them who are capable of following the proof—could then be forced to know that God is real. Thus Alasdair MacIntyre, when a Christian apologist, wrote: 'For if we could produce logically cogent arguments we should produce the kind of certitude that leaves no room for decision; where proof is in place, decision is not. We do not decide to accept Euclid's conclusions; we merely look to the rigour of his arguments. If the existence of God were demonstrable we should be as bereft of the possibility of making a free decision to love God as we should be if every utterance of doubt or unbelief was answered by thunderbolts from heaven.' This is the 'religious coercion' objection to the theistic proofs.

To what extent is it a sound objection? We may accept the theological doctrine that for God to force men to know him by the coercion of logic would be incompatible with his purpose of winning the voluntary response and worship of free moral beings. But the question still remains whether the theistic proofs could ever do this. Could a verbal proof of divine existence compel a consciousness of God comparable in coerciveness with a direct manifestation of his divine majesty and power? Could anyone be moved and shaken in their whole being by the demonstration of a proposition, as men have been by a numinous experience of overpowering impressiveness? Would the things that have just been said about an overwhelming display of divine glory really apply to verbal demonstrations—that infinite power would be irresistibly breaking in upon the privacy of our souls and that we should be blinded by God's perfect holiness and paralysed by his infinite energy? Indeed could a form of words, culmi-

nating in the proposition that 'God exists', ever have power by itself to produce more than what Newman calls a notional assent in our minds?

It is of course true that the effect of purely rational considerations such as those which are brought to bear in the theistic proofs are much greater in some minds than in others. The more rational the mind the more considerable is the effect to be expected. In many persons—indeed taking mankind as a whole, in the great majority—the effect of a theistic proof, even when no logical flaw is found in it, would be virtually nil! But in more sophisticated minds the effect must be greater, and it is at least theoretically possible that there are minds so rational that purely logical considerations can move them as effectively as the evidence of their senses. It is therefore conceivable that someone who is initially agnostic might be presented with a philosophical proof of divine existence—say the ontological argument, with its definition of God as that than which no more perfect can be conceived—and might as a result be led to worship the being whose reality has thus been demonstrated to him. This seems to be possible; but I believe that even in such a case there must, in addition to an intelligent appreciation of the argument, be a distinctively religious response to the idea of God which the argument presents. Some propensity to respond to unlimited perfection as holy and as rightly claiming a response of unqualified worship and devotion must operate, over and above the purely intellectual capacity for logical calculation. For we can conceive of a purely or merely logical mind, a kind of human calculating machine, which is at the same time devoid of the capacity for numinous feeling and worshipping response. Such a being might infer that God exists but be no more existentially interested in this conclusion than many people are in, say, the fact that the Shasta Dam is 602 feet high. It therefore seems that when the acceptance of a theistic proof leads to worship, a religious reaction occurs which turns what would otherwise be a purely abstract conclusion into an immensely significant and moving fact. In Newman's terminology, when a notional assent to the proposition that

God exists becomes a real assent, equivalent to an actual living belief and faith in God, there has been a free human response to an idea which could instead have been rejected by being held at the notional level. In other words, a verbal proof of God's existence cannot by itself break down our human freedom; it can only lead to a notional assent which has little or no positive religious value or substance.

I conclude, then, that the theological objections to the theistic proofs are considerably less strong than the philosophical ones; and that theologians who reject natural theology would therefore do well to do so primarily on philosophical rather than on theological grounds. These philosophical reasons are, as we have seen, very strong; and we therefore now have to consider whether, in the absence of any theistic proofs, it can nevertheless be rational to believe in the existence of God.

(b) Can there be rational theistic belief without proofs?

During the period dominated by the traditional theistic arguments the existence of God was often treated by philosophers as something to be discovered through reasoning. It was seen as the conclusion of an inference; and the question of the rationality of the belief was equated with that of the soundness of the inference. But from a religious point of view, as we have already seen, there has always been something very odd about this approach. The situation which it envisages is that of people standing outside the realm of faith, for whom the apologist is trying to build a bridge of rational inference to carry them over the frontier into that realm. But of course this is not the way in which religious faith has originally or typically or normally come about. When the cosmological, ontological, teleological and moral arguments were developed, theistic belief was already a functioning part of an immemorially established and developing form of human life. The claims of religion are claims made by individuals and communities on the basis of their experience—and experience which is none the less their own for occuring within an inherited framework of ideas. We

are not dealing with a merely conceivable metaphysical hypothesis which someone has speculatively invented but which hardly anyone seriously believes. We are concerned, rather, with convictions born out of experience and reflection and living within actual communities of faith and practice. Historically, then, the philosophical 'proofs' of God have normally entered in to support and confirm but not to create belief. Accordingly the proper philosophical approach would seem to be a probing of the actual foundations and structure of a living and operative belief rather than of theoretical and non-operative arguments subsequently formulated for holding those beliefs. The question is not whether it is possible to prove, starting from zero, that God exists; the question is whether the religious man, given the distinctively religious form of human existence in which he participates, is properly entitled as a rational person to believe what he does believe?

At this point we must consider what we mean by a rational belief. If by a belief we mean a proposition believed, then what we are to be concerned with here are not rational beliefs but rational believings. Propositions can be well-formed or ill-formed, and they can be true or false, but they cannot be rational or irrational. It is *people* who are rational or irrational, and derivatively their states and their actions, including their acts and states of believing. Further, apart from the believing of analytic propositions, which are true by definition and are therefore rationally believed by anyone who understands them, the rationality of acts (or states) of believing has to be assessed separately in each case. For it is a function of the relation between the proposition believed and the evidence on the basis of which the believer believes it. It might conceivably be rational for Mr X to believe p but not rational for Mr Y to believe p, because in relation to the data available to Mr. X p is worthy of belief but not in relation to the date available to Mr Y. Thus the question of the rationality of belief in the reality of God is the question of the rationality of a particular person's believing, given the data that he is using; or that of the believing of a class of people who share the same body of data. Or putting the same point the other way round, any assessing of the belief-worthiness of the proposition that God exists must be an assessing of it in relation to particular ranges of data.

Now there is one area of data or evidence which is normally available to those who believe in God, and that provides a very important part of the ground of their believing, but which is normally not available to and therefore not taken into account by those who do not so believe; and this is religious experience. It seems that the religious man is in part basing his believing upon certain data of religious experience which the non-religious man is not using because he does not have them. Thus our question resolves itself into one about the theist's right, given his distinctively religious experience, to be certain that God exists. It is the question of the rationality or irrationality, the well-groundedness or ill-groundedness, of the religious man's claim to know God. The theist cannot hope to prove that God exists; but despite this it may nevertheless be possible for him to show it to be wholly reasonable for him to believe that God exists.

What is at issue here is not whether it is rational for someone else, who does not participate in the distinctively religious mode of experience, to believe in God on the basis of the religious man's reports. I am not proposing any kind of 'argument from religious experience' by which God is inferred as the cause of the special experiences described by mystics and other religious persons. It is not the non-religious man's theoretical use of someone else's reported religious experience that is to be considered, but the religious man's own practical use of it. The question is whether he is acting rationally in trusting his own experience and in proceeding to live on the basis of it.

In order to investigate this question we must consider what counts as rational belief in an analogous case. The analogy that I propose is that between the religious person's claim to be conscious of God and any man's claim to be conscious of the physical world as an environment, existing independently of himself, of which he must take account.

In each instance a realm of putatively cognitive experience is taken to be veridical and is acted upon as such, even though its veridical character cannot be logically demonstrated. So far as sense experience is concerned this has emerged both from the failure of Descartes' attempt to provide a theoretical guarantee that our senses relate us to a real material environment, and from the success of Hume's attempt to show that our normal non-solipsist belief in an objective world of enduring objects around us in space is neither a product of, nor justifiable by, philosophical reasoning but is what has been called in some expositions of Hume's thought (though the term does not seem to have been used by Hume himself) a natural belief. It is a belief which naturally and indeed inevitably arises in the normal human mind in response to normal human perceptual experience. It is a belief on the basis of which we live and the rejection of which, in favour of a serious adoption of the solipsist alternative, would so disorient our relationship to other persons within a common material environment that we should be accounted insane. Our insanity would consist in the fact that we should no longer regard other people as independent centres of consciousness, with their own purposes and wills, with whom interpersonal relationships are possible. We should instead be living in a one-person world.

It is thus a basic truth in, or a presupposition of, our language that it is rational or sane to believe in the reality of the external world that we inhabit in common with other people, and irrational or insane not to do so.

What are the features of our sense experience in virtue of which we all take this view? They would seem to be twofold: the givenness or the involuntary character of this form of cognitive experience, and the fact that we can and do act successfully in terms of our belief in an external world. That is to say, being built and circumstanced as we are we cannot help initially believing as we do, and our belief is not contradicted, but on the contrary continuously confirmed, by our continuing experience. These characteristics jointly constitute a sufficient reason to trust and live on the basis of our perceptual experience in the absence of any positive reason to distrust it; and our inability to exclude the theoretical possibility of our experience as a whole being purely subjective does not constitute such a reason. This seems to be the principle on which, implicitly, we proceed. And it is, by definition, rational to proceed in this way. That is to say, this is the way in which all human beings do proceed and have proceeded, apart from a very small minority who have for that very reason been labelled by the majority as insane. This habitual acceptance of our perceptual experience is thus, we may say, part of our operative concept of human rationality.

We can therefore now ask whether a like principle may be invoked on behalf of a parallel response to religious experience. 'Religious experience' is of course a highly elastic concept. Let us restrict attention, for our present purpose, to the theistic 'sense of the presence of God', the putative awareness of a transcendent divine Mind within whose field of consciousness we exist and with whom therefore we stand in a relationship of mutual awareness. This sense of 'living in the divine presence' does not take the form of a direct vision of God, but of experiencing events in history and in our own personal life as the medium of God's dealings with us. Thus religious differs from non-religious experience, not as the awareness of a different world, but as a different way of experiencing the same world. Events which can be experienced as having a purely natural significance are experienced by the religious mind as having also and at the same time religious significance and as mediating the presence and activity of God.

It is possible to study this type of religious experience either in its strongest instances, in the primary and seminal religious figures, or in its much weaker instances in ordinary adherents of the traditions originated by the great exemplars of faith. Since we are interested in the question of the claims which religious experience justifies it is appropriate to look at that experience in its strongest and purest forms. A description of this will accordingly apply only very partially to the ordinary rank-and-file believer either of today or in the past.

If then we consider the sense of living in the divine presence as this was expressed by, for example, Jesus of Nazareth, or by St Paul, St Francis,

St Anselm or the great prophets of the Old Testament, we find that their 'awareness of God' was so vivid that he was as indubitable a factor in their experience as was their physical environment. They could no more help believing in the reality of God than in the reality of the material world and of their human neighbours. Many of the pages of the Bible resound with the sense of God's presence as a building might reverberate from the tread of some gigantic being walking through it. God was known to the prophets and apostles as a dynamic will interacting with their own wills; a sheerly given personal reality, as inescapably to be reckoned with as destructive storm and life-giving sunshine, the fixed contours of the land, or the hatred of their enemies and the friendship of their neighbours.

Our question concerns, then, one whose 'experience of God' has this compelling quality, so that he is no more inclined to doubt its veridical character than to doubt the evidence of his senses. Is it rational for him to take the former, as it is certainly rational for him to take the latter, as reliably cognitive of an aspect of his total environment and thus as knowledge in terms of which to act? Are the two features noted above in our sense experience—its givenness, or involuntary character, and the fact that we can successfully act in terms of it—also found here? It seems that they are. The sense of the presence of God reported by the great religious figures has a similar involuntary and compelling quality; and as they proceed to live on the basis of it they are sustained and confirmed by their further experiences in the conviction that they are living in relation, not to illusion, but to reality. It therefore seems prima facie, that the religious man *is* entitled to trust his religious experience and to proceed to conduct his life in terms of it.

The analogy operating within this argument is between our normal acceptance of our sense experience as perception of an objective external world, and a corresponding acceptance of the religious experience of 'living in God's presence' as the awareness of a divine reality external to our own minds. In each case there is a solipsist alternative in which one can affirm *solus ipse* to the exclusion of the transcendent—in the one case denying a physical environment transcending our own private consciousness and in the other case denying a divine Mind transcending our own private consciousness. It should be noted that this analogy is not grounded in the perception of particular material objects and does not turn upon the contrast between veridical and illusory sense perceptions, but is grounded in our awareness of an objective external world as such and turns upon the contrast between this and a theoretically possible solipsist interpretation of the same stream of conscious experience.

(c) Religious and perceptual belief

Having thus set forth the analogy fairly boldly and starkly I now want to qualify it by exploring various differences between religious and sensory experience. The resulting picture will be more complex than the first rough outline presented so far; and yet its force as supporting the rationality of theistic faith will not, I think, in the end have been undermined.

The most obvious difference is that everyone has and cannot help having sense experiences, whereas not everyone has religious experiences, at any rate of the very vivid and distinct kind to which we have been referring. As bodily beings existing in a material environment, we cannot help interacting consciously with that environment. That is to say, we cannot help 'having' a stream of sense experiences; and we cannot help accepting this as the perception of a material world around us in space. When we open our eyes in daylight we cannot but receive the visual experiences that come to us; and likewise with the other senses. And the world which we thus perceive is not plastic to our wishes but presents itself to us as it is, whether we like it or not. Needless to say, our senses do not coerce us in any sense of the word 'coerce' that implies unwillingness on our part, as when a policeman coerces an unwilling suspect to accompany him to the police station. Sense experience is coercive in the sense that we cannot when sane believe that our material environment is not broadly as we perceive it to be, and that if we did momentarily persuade ourselves

that what we experience is not there we should quickly be penalised by the environment and indeed, if we persisted, destroy by it.

In contrast to this we are not obliged to interact consciously with a spiritual environment. Indeed it is a commonplace of much contemporary theology that God does not force an awareness of himself upon mankind but leaves us free to know him by an uncompelled response of faith. And yet once a man has allowed himself freely to become conscious of God—it is important to note—that experience is, at its top levels of intensity, coercive. It creates the situation of the person who *cannot help* believing in the reality of God. The apostle, prophet or saint may be so vividly aware of God that he can no more doubt the veracity of his religious awareness than of his sense experience. During the periods when he is living consciously in the presence of God, when God is to him the divine Thou, the question whether God exists simply does not arise. Our cognitive freedom in relation to God is not to be found at this point but at the prior stage of our coming to be aware of him. The individual's own free receptivity and responsiveness plays an essential part in his dawning consciousness of God; but once he *has* become conscious of God that consciousness can possess a coercive and indubitable quality.

It is a consequence of this situation that whereas everyone perceives and cannot help perceiving the physical world, by no means everyone experiences the presence of God. Indeed only rather few people experience religiously in the vivid and coercive way reported by the great biblical figures. And this fact immediately suggests a sceptical question. Since those who enjoy a compelling religious experience form such a small minority of mankind, ought we not to suspect that they are suffering from a delusion comparable with that of the paranoiac who hears threatening voices from the walls or the alcoholic who sees green snakes?

This is of course a possible judgment to make. But this judgement should not be made *a priori,* in the absence of specific grounds such as we have in the other cases mentioned. And it would in fact be difficult to point to adequate evidence to support

VII.D.1 *Rational Theistic Belief without Proof* **451**

this hypothesis. On the contrary the general intelligence and exceptionally high moral quality of the great religious figures clashes with any analysis of their experience in terms of abnormal psychology. Such analyses are not indicated, as is the parallel view of paranoiacs and alcoholics, by evidence of general disorientation to reality or of incapacity to live a productive and satisfying life. On the contrary, Jesus of Nazareth, for example, has been regarded by hundreds of millions of people as the fulfilment of the ideal possibilities of human nature. A more reasonable negative position would therefore seem to be the agnostic one that whilst it is proper for the religious man himself, given his distinctive mode of experience, to believe firmly in the reality of God, one does not oneself share that experience and therefore has no ground upon which to hold that belief. Theism is then not positively denied, but is on the other hand consciously and deliberately not affirmed. This agnostic position must be accepted by the theist as a proper one. For if it is reasonable for one man, on the basis of his distinctively religious experience, to affirm the reality of God it must also be reasonable for another man, in the absence of any such experience, not to affirm the reality of God.

The next question that must be raised is the closely connected one of the relation between rational belief and truth. I suggested earlier that, strictly, one should speak of rational believings rather than of rational beliefs. But nevertheless it is sometimes convenient to use the latter phrase, which we may then understand as follows. By a rational belief we shall mean a belief which it is rational for the one who holds it to hold, given the data available to him. Clearly such beliefs are not necessarily or always true. It is sometimes rational for an individual to have, on the basis of incomplete data, a belief which is in fact false. For example, it was once rational for people to believe that the sun revolves round the earth; for it was apparently perceived to do so, and the additional theoretical and observational data were not yet available from which it has since been inferred that it is the earth which revolves round the sun. If, then, a belief may be rational and yet false, may not the

religious man's belief be of this kind? May it not be that when the data of religious experience are supplemented in the believer's mind by further data provided by the sciences of psychology or sociology, it ceases to be rational for him to believe in God? Might it not then be rational for him instead to believe that his 'experience of the presence of God' is to be understood as an effect of a buried infancy memory of his father as a benevolent higher power; or of the pressure upon him of the human social organism of which he is a cell; or in accordance with some other naturalistic theory of the nature of religion?

Certainly this is possible. Indeed we must say, more generally, that all our beliefs, other than our acceptance of logically self-certifying propositions, are in principle open to revision or retraction in the light of new data. It is always conceivable that something which it is now rational for us to believe, it may one day not be rational for us to believe. But the difference which this general principle properly makes to our present believing varies from a maximum in relation to beliefs involving a considerable theoretical element, such as the higher-level hypotheses of the sciences, to a minimum in relation to perceptual beliefs, such as the belief that I now see a sheet of paper before me. And I have argued that so far as the great primary religious figures are concerned, belief in the reality of God is closer to the latter in that it is analogous to belief in the reality of the perceived material world. It is not an explanatory hypothesis, logically comparable with those developed in the sciences, but a perceptual belief. God was not, for Amos or Jeremiah or Jesus of Nazareth, an inferred entity but an experienced personal presence. If this is so, it is appropriate that the religious man's belief in the reality of God should be no more provisional than his belief in the reality of the physical world. The situation is in each case that, given the experience which he has and which is part of him, he cannot help accepting as 'there' such aspects of his environment as he experiences. He cannot help believing either in the reality of the material world which he is conscious of inhabiting, or of the personal divine presence which is overwhelmingly evident to him and to which his mode of living is a free response. And I have been suggesting that it is *as* reasonable for him to hold and to act upon the one belief as the other.

(d) The problem of conflicting religious beliefs

We must now take note of another circumstance which qualifies and threatens to erode our analogy. What are we to make of the immense variety of the forms of religious experience, giving rise as they do to apparently incompatible beliefs? In contrast to this, human sense experience reveals a world which is public in that normally the perceptions of any two individuals can readily be correlated in terms of the hypothesis of a common world which they jointly inhabit.

The variety commonly brought under the name of religion is indeed as wide as the range of man's cultural and psychological diversities. By no means all religious experience is theistic; ultimate reality is apprehended as non-personal and as multi-personal as well as unipersonal. And if we choose to extend the notion of religious experience, as Abraham Maslow has recently done by his concept of peak-experiences, the variety is multiplied again. But even apart from this last expansion of the field it is clearly true that religious experience is bewilderingly varied in content and that the different reports to which it gives rise cannot easily be correlated as alternative accounts of the same reality. And therefore since one could restate the argument of the earlier part of this chapter from the point of view of many different religions, with their different forms of religious experience and belief, the question arises whether the argument does not prove too much. In establishing the rationality of the Judaic-Christian theist's belief in the reality of God, must it not also and equally establish the rationality of the Buddhist's belief, arising out of *his* own coercive religious experience, and likewise of Hindu belief and of Islamic belief, and so on?

We need, I think, have no hesitation in accepting this implication. The principle which I have used to justify as rational the faith of a Christian who on the basis of his own religious experience cannot help believing in the reality of 'the God and Father of our Lord Jesus Christ', also operates to justify as rational the faith of a Muslim who on the basis of *his* religious experience cannot help believing in the reality of Allah and his providence; and the faith of the Buddhist who on the basis of *his* religious experience cannot help accepting the Buddhist picture of the universe; and so on.

But this is not the end of the matter. Various possibilities now open before us. I can only in conclusion attempt a small-scale map of the different paths that may be taken, showing in what direction they each lead and forecasting to some extent the kind of difficulties that are to be expected if one chooses to travel along them.

The first fork in the road is constituted by the alternative possibilities that the truth concerning the nature of the universe will, and that it will not, ultimately be a matter of public knowledge. The question is whether there will eventually be a situation in which all rational persons will find themselves obliged to agree, on the basis of a common body of experience, that the universe has this or that specific character. The issue, in other words, is that of the ultimate public verifiability and falsifiability of religious faiths.

On the one hand, in one conceivable picture of the universe it is possible for adherents of different and incompatible faiths to remain, so long as they continue to exist and to hold beliefs, under the impression that their own understanding of the universe is true; for they never meet an experiential crux which either verifies or falsifies their faith. This is a not always acknowledged feature of the pictures adopted both by the non-eschatological religions and by most atheistic and naturalistic theories. On the other hand, in another possible picture of the universe, or rather family of pictures painted by the different eschatological religions, the future development of human experience will narrow down the options until eventually only one faith is compatible with the facts and it becomes irrational to hold any contrary view. Thus it is affirmed in Christianity, in Islam, in one type of Judaism and perhaps in one type of Buddhism that the universe has a certain definite structure and is moving towards a certain definite fulfilment such that in the light of that fulfilment it will be beyond rational doubt that the universe has the particular character that it has.

Both types of universe are logically possible. If Christianity is true we are living in a universe of the latter type, in which religious faith is ultimately verified; and since we are now investigating the rationality of the Christian belief in God we shall want at this first fork to take the verifiability-of-faiths option in order to explore it further and to see where it leads.

Travelling along this path, then, we now meet a second fork in the road, offering two rival conceptions of the relations between the different religions. Along one path we affirm the ultimate compatibility of the plurality of religious faiths, whilst along the other path we deny this. The latter, incompatibility thesis leads us to the following picture: it is at the moment rational for adherents of different religions, whose experience is such that they cannot help believing as they do, to hold their respective beliefs. But—still assuming the verifiability-of-faiths thesis—it will eventually cease to be possible for rational persons to adhere to rival and incompatible understandings of the universe. For according to this option in its strongest form, there is one true faith and many false ones—this view corresponding of course to the traditional dogmatic stances of the eschatological religions, such as Christianity and Islam. There is however a specifically Christian reason for abandoning this stance. This is that belief in the redeeming love of God for all his human creatures makes it incredible that the divine activity in relation to mankind should have been confined to those within the reach of the influence of the Christian revelation. The majority of the human beings who have existed since man began have lived either before or outside the historical influence of Jesus of Nazareth. Thus the doctrine that there is no salvation outside historic Christianity would in effect deny the universal love and redeeming activity of God.

Any modification of that traditional claim soon leads us over onto the alternative path, at the end of which lies the conclusion that the different forms of religious experience, giving rise to the different religions of the world, are properly to be understood as experiences of different aspects of one immensely complex and rich divine reality. If this is so, the beliefs of the different religions will be related to a larger truth as the experiences which gave rise to those beliefs are related to a larger reality.

The further exploration of this possibility would take us beyond our present necessarily limited inquiry. I have argued that when on the basis of his own compelling religious experience someone believes in the reality of God, he is believing rationally; and I have added the rider that when we set alongside this argument the fact of the plurality of religions and their forms of religious experience, we are led to postulate a divine reality of which the different religions of the world represent different partial experiences and partial knowledge. This latter possibility remains, however, to be adequately developed and examined.

VII.D.2   Religious Belief without Evidence

ALVIN PLANTINGA

Alvin Plantinga, professor of philosophy at the University of Notre Dame, argues that it is rational to believe in God in spite of the lack of evidence for such belief. Those (like W. K. Clifford) who insist that we must have evidence for all our beliefs simply fail to make their case, for the evidentialists have yet to set forth unambiguous criteria to account for all the clear cases of justified beliefs that would exclude the belief in God. Plantinga outlines the position of the foundationalist-evidentialist as one that claims that all justified beliefs must either be properly basic by virtue of fulfilling certain criteria or be based on other beliefs. This eventually results in a treelike construction with properly basic beliefs resting at the bottom.

Plantinga shows that there are many beliefs that we seem to be justified in holding that do not fit into the foundationalist framework, such as memory beliefs (e.g., 'I ate breakfast this morning'), belief in an external world, and belief in other minds. These beliefs are not dependent on other beliefs, yet neither are they self-evident, incorrigible, or evident to the senses.

Having shown the looseness of what we can accept as properly basic, Plantinga next shows that the Protestant Reformers saw belief in God as properly basic. He asks us to consider this as a legitimate option and examines possible objections to it.

What I mean to discuss, in this paper, is the question, Is belief in God rational? That is to say, I wish to discuss the question "Is it rational, or reasonable, or rationally acceptable, to believe in God?"

This article consists of selections from *Rationality and Religious Belief*, edited by C. F. Delaney, copyright © 1979, and *Faith and Rationality*, edited by Alvin Plantinga and Nicholas Wolterstorff, copyright © 1983, by permission of the publisher, the University of Notre Dame Press, and the author. Footnotes deleted.

I mean to *discuss* this question, not answer it. My initial aim is not to argue that religious belief *is* rational (although I think it is) but to try to understand this question.

The first thing to note is that I have stated the question misleadingly. What I really want to discuss is whether it is rational to believe that God exists—that there is such a person as God. Of course there is an important difference between believing that God exists and believing *in* God. To believe that God exists is just to accept a certain proposition—the proposition that there really is such a person as God—as true. According to the book of James (2:19) the devils believe this proposition, and they tremble. To believe *in* God, however, is to trust him, to commit your life to him, to make his purposes your own. The devils do not do that. So there is a difference between believing in God and believing that he exists; for purposes of economy, however, I shall use the phrase 'belief in God' as a synonym for 'belief that God exists'.

Our question, therefore, is whether belief in God is rational. This question is widely asked and widely answered. Many philosophers—most prominently, those in the great tradition of natural theology—have argued that belief in God *is* rational; they have typically done so by providing what they took to be *demonstrations* or *proofs* of God's existence. Many others have argued that belief in God is *irrational*. If we call those of the first group 'natural theologians', perhaps we should call those of the second 'natural atheologians'. (That would at any rate be kinder than calling them 'unnatural theologians'.) J. L. Mackie, for example, opens his statement of the problem of evil as follows: "I think, however, that a more telling criticism can be made by way of the traditional problem of evil. Here it can be shown, not merely that religious beliefs lack rational support, but that they are positively irrational. . . ." And a very large number of philosophers take it that a central question—perhaps *the* central question—

of philosophy of religion is the question whether religious belief in general and belief in God in particular is rationally acceptable.

Now an apparently straightforward and promising way to approach this question would be to take a definition of rationality and see whether belief in God conforms to it. The chief difficulty with this appealing course, however, is that no such definition of rationality seems to be available. If there *were* such a definition, it would set out some conditions for a belief's being rationally acceptable—conditions that are severally necessary and jointly sufficient. That is, each of the conditons would have to be met by a belief that is rationally acceptable; and if a belief met all the conditions, then it would follow that it is rationally acceptable. But it is monumentally difficult to find any non-trivial necessary conditions at all. Surely, for example, we cannot insist that *S*'s belief that *p* is rational only if it is *true*. For consider Newton's belief that if *x*, *y* and *z* are moving colinearly, then the motion of *z* with respect to *x* is the sum of the motions of *y* with respect to *x* and *z* with respect to *y*. No doubt Newton was rational in accepting this belief; yet it was false, at least if contemporary physicists are to be trusted. And if they aren't—that is, if they are wrong in contradicting Newton—then *they* exemplify what I'm speaking of; they rationally believe a proposition which, as it turns out, is false.

Nor can we say that a belief is rationally acceptable only if it is possibly true, not necessarily false in the broadly logical sense. For example, I might do the sum $735 + 421 + 9,216$ several times and get the same answer: $10,362$. I am then rational in believing that $735 + 421 + 9,216 = 10,362$, even though the fact is I've made the same error each time—failed to carry a '1' from the first column—and thus believe what is necessarily false. Or I might be a mathematical neophyte who hears from his teacher that every continuous function if differentiable. I need not be irrational in believing this, despite the fact that it is necessarily false. Examples of this sort can be multiplied.

So this question presents something of an initial enigma in that it is by no means easy to say what it is for a belief to be rational. And the fact is those philosophers who ask this question about belief in God do not typically try to answer it by giving necessary and sufficient conditions for rational belief. Instead, they typically ask whether the believer has *evidence* or *sufficient evidence* for his belief; or they may try to argue that in fact there is sufficient evidence for the proposition that there is *no* God; but in any case they try to answer this question by finding evidence for or against theistic belief. Philosophers who think there are sound arguments for the existence of God—the natural theologians—claim there is good evidence *for* this proposition; philosophers who believe that there are sound arguments for the non-existence of God naturally claim that there is evidence *against* this proposition. But they concur in holding that belief in God is rational only if there is, on balance, a preponderance of evidence for it—or less radically, only if there is not, on balance, a preponderance of evidence against it.

The nineteenth-century philosopher W. K. Clifford provides a splendid if somewhat strident example of the view that the believer in God must have evidence if he is not to be irrational. Here he does not discriminate against religious belief; he apparently holds that a belief of any sort at all is rationally acceptable only if there is sufficient evidence for it. And he goes on to insist that it is wicked, immoral, monstrous, and perhaps even impolite to accept a belief for which one does not have sufficient evidence:

> Whoso would deserve well of his fellows in this matter will guard the purity of his belief with a very fanaticism of jealous care, lest at any time it should rest on an unworthy object, and catch a stain which can never be wiped away.

He adds that if a

> belief has been accepted on insufficient evidence, the pleasure is a stolen one. Not only does it deceive ourselves by giving us a sense of power which we do not really possess, but it is sinful, because it is stolen in defiance of our duty to mankind. That duty is to guard ourselves from such beliefs as from a pestilence which may shortly master our body and spread to the rest of the town.

And finally:

> To sum up: it is wrong always, everywhere, and for anyone to believe anything upon insufficient evidence.

(It is not hard to detect, in these quotations, the "tone of robustious pathos" with which William James credits him.) Clifford finds it utterly obvious, furthermore, that those who believe in God do indeed so believe on insufficient evidence and thus deserve the above abuse. A believer in God is, on his view, at best a harmless pest and at worst a menace to society; in either case he should be discouraged.

Now there are some initial problems with Clifford's claim. For example, he doesn't tell us how *much* evidence is sufficient. More important, the notion of evidence is about as difficult as that of rationality: What is evidence? How do you know when you have some? How do you know when you have sufficient or enough? Suppose, furthermore, that a person thinks he has sufficient evidence for a proposition *p* when in fact he does not—would he then be irrational in believing *p*? Presumably a person can have sufficient evidence for what is false—else either Newton did not have sufficient evidence for his physical beliefs or contemporary physicists don't have enough for *theirs.* Suppose, then, that a person has sufficient evidence for the false proposition that he has sufficient evidence for *p.* Is he then irrational in believing *p*? Presumably not; but if not, having sufficient evidence is not, contrary to Clifford's claim, a necessary condition for believing *p* rationally.

But suppose we temporarily concede that these initial difficulties can be resolved and take a deeper look at Clifford's position. What is essential to it is the claim that we must evaluate the rationality of belief in God by examining its relation to *other* propositions. We are directed to estimate its rationality by determining whether we have *evidence* for it—whether we know, or at any rate rationally believe, some other propositions which stand in the appropriate relation to the proposition in question. And belief in God is rational, or reasonable, or rationally acceptable, on

this view, only if there are other propositions with respect to which it is thus evident.

According to the Cliffordian position, then, there is a set of propositions *E* such that my belief in God is rational if and only if it is evident with respect to *E*—if and only if *E* constitutes, on balance, evidence for it. But what propositions are to be found in *E*? Do we know that belief in God is not itself in *E*? If it *is,* of course, then it is certainly evident with respect to *E*. How does a proposition get into *E* anyway? How do we decide which propositions are the ones such that my belief in God is rational if and only if it is evident with respect to them? Should we say that *E* contains the propositions that I *know*? But then, for our question to be interesting, we should first have to argue or agree that I don't know that God exists—that I only *believe* it, whether rationally or irrationally. This position is widely taken for granted, and indeed taken for granted by theists as well as others. But why should the latter concede that he doesn't know that God exists—that at best he rationally believes it? The Bible regularly speaks of *knowledge* in this context—not just rational or well-founded belief. Of course it is true that the believer has *faith*—faith in God, faith in what He reveals, faith that God exists—but this by no means settles the issue. The question is whether he doesn't also *know* that God exists. Indeed, according to the Heidelberg Catechism, knowledge is an essential element of faith, so that one has true faith that *p* only if he knows that *p:*

> True faith is not only a certain (i.e., sure) knowledge whereby I hold for truth all that God has revealed in His word, but also a deep-rooted assurance created in me by the Holy Spirit through the gospel that not only others but I too have had my sins forgiven, have been made forever right with God and have been granted salvation. (Q 21)

So from this point of view a man has true faith that *p* only if he knows that *p* and also meets a certain further condition: roughly (where *p* is a universal proposition) that of accepting the universal instantiation of *p* with respect to himself. Now of course the theist may be unwilling to concede that he does not have true faith that God exists; accordingly he may be unwilling to concede—initially, at any rate—that he does not know, but only believes that God exists.

[After a discussion of others' attacks on theism from an evidentialist perspective, Plantinga turns to the foundationalist theory of knowledge, beginning with the classical version of that doctrine, held by Aquinas, Descartes, Locke, Clifford, and many others.]

[Both] Aquinas and the evidentialist objector [to theism] concur in holding that belief in God is rationally acceptable only if there is evidence for it—if, that is, it is probable with respect to some body of propositions that constitutes the evidence. And here we can get a better understanding of Aquinas and the evidentialist objector if we see them as accepting some version of *classical foundationalism*. This is a *picture* or total way of looking at faith, knowledge, justified belief, rationality, and allied topics. This picture has been enormously popular in Western thought; and despite a substantial opposing groundswell, I think it remains the dominant way of thinking about these topics. According to the foundationalist some propositions are properly basic and some are not; those that are not are rationally accepted only on the basis of *evidence,* where the evidence must trace back, ultimately, to what *is* properly basic. The existence of God, furthermore, is not among the propositions that are properly basic; hence a person is rational in accepting theistic belief only if he has evidence for it. The vast majority of those in the western world who have thought about our topic have accepted some form of classical foundationalism. The evidentialist objection to belief in God, furthermore, is obviously rooted in this way of looking at things. So suppose we try to achieve a deeper understanding of it.

Earlier I said the first thing to see about the evidentialist objection is that it is a *normative* contention or claim. The same thing must be said about foundationalism: this thesis is a normative thesis, a thesis about how a system of beliefs *ought* to be structured, a thesis about the properties of a correct, or acceptable, or rightly structured system of beliefs. According to the foundationalist there are norms, or duties, or obligations with respect to belief just as there are with respect to actions. To conform to these duties and obligations is to be rational; to fail to measure up to them is to be irrational. To be rational, then, is to exercise one's epistemic powers *properly*—to exercise them in such a way as to go contrary to none of the norms for such exercise. . . .

I think we can understand foundationalism more fully if we introduce the idea of a *noetic structure.* A person's noetic structure is the set of propositions he believes, together with certain epistemic relations that hold among him and these propositions. As we have seen, some of my beliefs may be based upon others; it may be that there are a pair of propositions A and B such that I believe B, and believe A *on the basis of B.* An account of a person's noetic structure, then, would specify which of his beliefs are basic and which nonbasic. Of course it is abstractly possible that *none* of his beliefs is basic; perhaps he holds just three beliefs, A, B, and C, and believes each of them on the basis of the other two. We might think this improper or irrational, but that is not to say it could not be done. And it is also possible that *all* of his beliefs are basic; perhaps he believes a lot of propositions but does not believe any of them on the basis of any others. In the typical case, however, a noetic structure will include both basic and nonbasic beliefs. It may be useful to give some examples of beliefs that are often basic for a person. Suppose I seem to see a tree; I have that characteristic sort of experience that goes with perceiving a tree. I may then believe the proposition that I see a tree. It is *possible* that I believe that proposition *on the basis of* the proposition that I seem to see a tree; in the typical case, however, I will not believe the former on the basis of the latter because in the typical case I will not believe the latter at all. I will not be paying any attention to my experience but will be concentrating on the tree. Of course I *can* turn my attention to my experience, notice how things look to me, and acquire the belief that I seem to see something that looks like *that;* and if you challenge my claim that I see a tree, perhaps I *will* thus turn my attention to my experience. But in the typical case I will not believe that I see a tree on the basis of a proposition about my experience; for I believe A on the basis of B only if I believe B, and in the typical case where I perceive a tree I do not believe (or entertain) any propositions about my experience. Typically I take such a proposition as basic. Similarly, I believe I had breakfast this morning; this too is basic for me. I do not believe this proposition on the basis of some proposition about my experience—for example, that I seem to remember having had breakfast. In the typical case I will not have even considered *that* question—the question whether I *seem* to remember having had breakfast; instead I simply believe that I had breakfast; I take it as basic.

Second, an account of a noetic structure will include what we might call an index of *degree of* belief. I hold some of my beliefs much more firmly than others. I believe both that 2 + 1 = 3 and that London, England, is north of Saskatoon, Saskatchewan; but I believe the former more resolutely than the latter. Some beliefs I hold with maximum firmness; others I do in fact accept, but in a much more tentative way. . . .

Third, a somewhat vaguer notion: an account of S's noetic structure would include something like an index of *depth of ingression*. Some of my beliefs are, we might say, on the periphery of my noetic structure. I accept them, and may even accept them firmly, but I could give them up without much change elsewhere in my noetic structure. I believe there are some large boulders on the top of the Grand Teton. If I come to give up this belief (say by climbing it and not finding any), that change need not have extensive reverberations throughout the rest of my noetic structure; it could be accommodated with minimal alteration elsewhere. So its depth of ingression into my noetic structure is not great. On the other hand, if I were to come to believe that there simply is no such thing as the Grand Teton, or no mountains at all, or no such thing as the state of Wyoming, that would have much greater reverberations. And suppose I were to come to think there had not been much of a past (that the world was created just five minutes ago, complete with all its appar-

ent memories and traces of the past) or that there were not any other persons: these changes would have even greater reverberations; these beliefs of mine have great depth of ingression into my noetic structure. . . .

Now foundationalism is best construed, I think, as a thesis about *rational* noetic structures. A noetic structure is rational if it could be the noetic structure of a person who was completely rational. To be completely rational, as I am here using the term, is not to believe only what is true, or to believe all the logical consequences of what one believes, or to believe all necessary truths with equal firmness, or to be uninfluenced by emotion in forming belief; it is, instead, to do the right thing with respect to one's believings. It is to violate no epistemic duties. From this point of view, a rational person is one whose believings meet the appropriate standards; to criticize a person as irrational is to criticize her for failing to fulfill these duties or responsibilities, for failing to conform to the relevant norms or standards. To draw the ethical analogy, the irrational is the impermissible; the rational is the permissible. . . .

A rational noetic structure, then, is one that could be the noetic structure of a wholly rational person; and foundationalism, as I say, is a thesis about such noetic structures. We may think of the foundationalist as beginning with the observation that some of our beliefs are based upon others. According to the foundationalist a rational noetic structure will *have a foundation*—a set of beliefs not accepted on the basis of others; in a rational noetic structure some beliefs will be basic. Nonbasic beliefs, of course, will be accepted on the basis of other beliefs, which may be accepted on the basis of still other beliefs, and so on until the foundations are reached. In a rational noetic structure, therefore, every nonbasic belief is ultimately accepted on the basis of basic beliefs. . . .

According to the foundationalist, therefore, every rational noetic structure has a foundation, and all nonbasic beliefs are ultimately accepted on the basis of beliefs in the foundations. But a belief cannot properly be accepted on the basis of just *any* other belief; in a rational noetic structure, A will be accepted on the basis of B only if B supports A or is a member of a set of beliefs that together support A. It is not clear just what this relation—call it the "supports" relation—is; and different foundationalists propose different candidates. Presumably, however, it lies in the neighborhood of *evidence;* if A supports B, then A is evidence for B, or makes B evident; or perhaps B is likely or probable with respect to B. This relation admits of degrees. My belief that Feike can swim is supported by my knowledge that nine out of ten Frisians can swim and Feike is a Frisian; it is supported more strongly by my knowledge that the evening paper contains a picture of Feike triumphantly finishing first in the fifteen-hundred meter freestyle in the 1980 summer Olympics. And the foundationalist holds, sensibly enough, that in a rational noetic structure the strength of a nonbasic belief will depend upon the degree of support from foundational beliefs. . . .

By way of summary, then, let us say that according to foundationalism: (1) in a rational noetic structure the believed-on-the-basis-of relation is asymmetric and irreflexive, (2) a rational noetic structure has a foundation, and (3) in a rational noetic structure nonbasic belief is proportional in strength to support from the foundations.

Conditions on Proper Basicality

Next we note a further and fundamental feature of classic varieties of foundationalism: they all lay down certain conditions of proper basicality. From the foundationalist point of view not just any kind of belief can be found in the foundations of a rational noetic structure; a belief to be properly basic (that is, basic in a rational noetic structure) must meet certain conditions. It must be capable of functioning foundationally, capable of bearing its share of the weight of the whole noetic structure. Thus Thomas Aquinas, as we have seen, holds that a proposition is properly basic for a person only if it is self-evident to him or "evident to the senses."

Suppose we take a brief look at self-evidence. Under what conditions does a proposition have it? What kinds of propositions are self-evident? Examples would include very simple arithmetical truths such as

(1) 2 + 1 = 3;

simple truths of logic such as

(2) No man is both married and unmarried;

perhaps the generalizations of simple truths of logic, such as

(3) For any proposition *p* the conjunction of *p* with its denial is false;

and certain propositions expressing identity and diversity; for example,

(4) Redness is distinct from greenness,
(5) The property of being prime is distinct from the property of being composite,

and

(6) The proposition *all men are mortal* is distinct from the proposition *all mortals are men.*

. . . .

Still other candidates—candidates which may be less than entirely uncontroversial—come from many other areas; for example,

(7) If *p* is necessarily true and *p* entails *q,* then *q* is necessarily true,
(8) If e^1 occurs before e^2 and e^2 occurs before e^3, then e^1 occurs before e^3,

and

(9) It is wrong to cause unnecessary (and unwanted) pain just for the fun of it.

What is it that characterizes these propositions? According to the tradition the outstanding characteristic of a self-evident proposition is that one simply sees it to be true upon grasping or understanding it. Understanding a self-evident proposition is sufficient for apprehending its truth. Of course this notion must be relativized to *persons;* what is self-evident to you might not be to me. Very simple arithmetical truths will be self-evident to nearly all of us, but a truth like 17 + 18 = 35 may be self-evident only to some. And of course a proposition is self-evident to a person only if he does in fact grasp it, so a proposition will not be self-evident to those who do not apprehend the concepts it involves. As Aquinas says, some propositions are self-evident only to the learned; his example is the truth that immaterial substances do not occupy space. Among those propositions whose concepts not everyone grasps, some are such that anyone who *did* grasp them would see their truth; for example,

(10) A model of a first-order theory T assigns truth to the axioms of T.

Others — $17 + 13 = 30$, for example—may be such that some but not all of those who apprehend them also see that they are true.

But how shall we understand this "seeing that they are true"? Those who speak of self-evidence explicitly turn to this visual metaphor and expressly explain self-evidence by reference to vision. There are two important aspects to the metaphor and two corresponding components to the idea of self-evidence. First, there is the *epistemic* component: a proposition *p* is self-evident to a person *S* only if *S* has *immediate* knowledge of *p*—that is, knows *p*, and does not know *p* on the basis of his knowledge of other propositions. Consider a simple arithmetic truth such as $2 + 1 = 3$ and compare it with one like $24 \times 24 = 576$. I know each of these propositions, and I know the second but not the first on the basis of computation, which is a kind of inference. So I have immediate knowledge of the first but not the second.

But there is also a phenomenological component. Consider again our two propositions; the first but not the second has about it a kind of luminous aura or glow when you bring it to mind or consider it. Locke speaks, in this connection, of an "evident luster"; a self-evident proposition, he says, displays a kind of "clarity and brightness to the attentive mind." Descartes speaks instead of "clarity and distinctness"; each, I think, is referring to the same phenomenological feature. And this feature is connected with another: upon understanding a proposition of this sort one feels a strong inclination to accept it; this luminous obviousness seems to compel or at least impel assent. Aquinas and Locke, indeed, held that a person, or at any rate a normal, well-formed human being, finds it impossible to withhold assent when con-

sidering a self-evident proposition. The phenomenological component of the idea of self-evidence, then, seems to have a double aspect: there is the luminous aura that $2 + 1 = 3$ displays, and there is also an experienced tendency to accept or believe it. Perhaps, indeed, the luminous aura *just is* the experienced impulsion toward acceptance; perhaps these are the very same thing. In that case the phenomenological component would not have the double aspect I suggested it did have; in either case, however, we must recognize this phenomenological aspect of self-evidence.

Aquinas therefore holds that self-evident propositions are properly basic. I think he means to add that propositions "evident to the senses" are also properly basic. By this latter term I think he means to refer to *perceptual* propositions—propositions whose truth or falsehood we can determine by looking or employing some other sense. He has in mind, I think, such propositions as

(11) There is a tree before me,
(12) I am wearing shoes,

and

(13) That tree's leaves are yellow.

So Aquinas holds that a proposition is properly basic if and only if it is either self-evident or evident to the senses. Other foundationalists have insisted that propositions basic in a rational noetic structure must be *certain* in some important sense. Thus it is plausible to see Descartes as holding that the foundations of a rational noetic structure include, not such propositions as (25)–(27), but more cautious claims—claims about one's own mental life; for example,

(14) It seems to me that I see a tree,
(15) I seem to see something green,

or, as Professor Chisholm puts it,

(16) I am appeared greenly to.

Propositions of this latter sort seem to enjoy a kind of immunity from error not enjoyed by those of the former. I could be mistaken in thinking I see a pink rat; perhaps I am hallucinating or the victim of an illusion. But it is at the least very much harder to see that I could be mistaken in believing that I *seem* to see a pink rat, in believing that I am appeared pinkly (or pink ratly) to. Suppose we say that a proposition with respect to which I enjoy this sort of immunity from error is incorrigible for me; then perhaps Descartes means to hold that a proposition is properly basic for *S* only if it is either self-evident or incorrigible for *S*.

By way of explicit definition:

(17) *p* is incorrigible for *S* if and only if (a) it is not possible that *S* believe *p* and *p* be false, and (b) it is not possible that *S* believe ~*p* and *p* be true.

· ·

Here we have a further characteristic of foundationalism: the claim that not just any proposition is properly basic. Ancient and medieval foundationalists tended to hold that a proposition is properly basic for a person only if it is either self-evident or evident to the senses: modern foundationalists—Descartes, Locke, Leibniz, and the like—tended to hold that a proposition is properly basic for *S* only if either self-evident or incorrigible for *S*. Of course this is a historical generalization and is thus perilous; but perhaps it is worth the risk. And now let us say that a *classical foundationalist* is any one who is either an ancient and medieval or a modern foundationalist.

The Collapse of Foundationalism

Now suppose we return to the main question: Why should not belief in God be among the foundations of my noetic structure? The answer, on the part of the classical foundationalist, was that even if this belief is *true*, it does not have the characteristics a proposition must have to deserve a place in the foundations. There is no room in the foundations for a proposition that can be rationally accepted only on the basis of other propositions. The only properly basic propositions are those that are self-evident or incorrigible or evident to the senses. Since the proposition that God exists is none of the above, it is not properly basic for any-

one; that is, no well-formed, rational noetic structure contains this proposition in its foundations. But now we must take a closer look at this fundamental principle of classical foundationalism:

(18) A proposition *p* is properly basic for a person *S* if and only if *p* is either self-evident to *S* or incorrigible for *S* or evident to the senses for *S*.

(18) contains two claims: first, a proposition is properly basic *if* it is self-evident, incorrigible, or evident to the senses, and, second, a proposition is properly basic *only if* it meets this condition. The first seems true enough; suppose we concede it. But what is to be said for the second? Is there any reason to accept it? Why does the foundationalist accept it? Why does he think the theist ought to?

We should note first that if this thesis, and the correlative foundationalist thesis that a proposition is rationally acceptable only if it follows from or is probable with respect to what is properly basic—if these claims are true, then enormous quantities of what we all in fact believe are irrational. One crucial lesson to be learned from the development of modern philosophy—Descartes through Hume, roughly—is just this: relative to propositions that are self-evident and incorrigible, most of the beliefs that form the stock in trade of ordinary everyday life are not probable—at any rate there is no reason to think they are probable. Consider all those propositions that entail, say, that there are enduring physical objects, or that there are persons distinct from myself, or that the world has existed for more than five minutes: none of these propositions, I think, is more probable than not with respect to what is self-evident or incorrigible for me; at any rate no one has given good reason to think any of them is. And now suppose we add to the foundations propositions that are evident to the senses, thereby moving from modern to ancient and medieval foundationalism. Then propositions entailing the existence of material objects will of course be probable with respect to the foundations, because included therein. But the same cannot be said either for propositions about the past or for propositions entailing the existence of persons distinct from myself; as before, these will not be probable with respect to what is properly basic.

And does not this show that the thesis in question is false? The contention is that

(19) *A* is properly basic for me only if *A* is self-evident or incorrigible or evident to the senses for me.

But many propositions that do not meet these conditions *are* properly basic for me. I believe, for example, that I had lunch this noon. I do not believe this proposition on the basis of other propositions; I take it as basic; it is in the foundations of my noetic structure. Furthermore, I am entirely rational in so taking it, even though this proposition is neither self-evident nor evident to the senses nor incorrigible for me. Of course this may not convince the foundationalist; he may think that in fact I do *not* take that proposition as basic, or perhaps he will bite the bullet and maintain that if I really *do* take it as basic, then the fact is I *am*, so far forth, irrational.

Perhaps the following will be more convincing. According to the classical foundationalist (call him *F*) a person *S* is rational in accepting (19) only if either (19) is properly basic (self-evident or incorrigible or evident to the senses) for him, or he believes (19) on the basis of propositions that are properly basic for him and support (19). Now presumably if *F* knows of some support for (19) from propositions that are self-evident or evident to the senses or incorrigible, he will be able to provide a good argument—deductive, inductive, probabilistic or whatever—whose premises are self-evident or evident to the senses or incorrigible and whose conclusion is (19). So far as I know, no foundationalist has provided such an argument. It therefore appears that the foundationalist does not know of any support for (19) from propositions that are (on his account) properly basic. So if he is to be rational in accepting (19), he must (on his own account) accept it as basic. But according to (19) itself, (19) is properly basic for *F* only if (19) is self-evident or incorrigible or evident to the senses for him. Clearly (19) meets none of these condi-

tions. Hence it is not properly basic for *F*. But then *F* is self-referentially inconsistent in accepting (19); he accepts (19) as basic, despite the fact that (19) does not meet the condition for proper basicality that (19) itself lays down.

Furthermore, (19) is either false or such that in accepting it the foundationalist is violating his epistemic responsibilities. For *F* does not know of any argument or evidence for (19). Hence if it is true, he will be violating his epistemic responsibilities in accepting it. So (19) is either false or such that *F* cannot rationally accept it. Still further, if the theist were to accept (19) at the foundationalist's urging but without argument, he would be adding to his noetic structure a proposition that is either false or such that in accepting it he violates his noetic responsibilities. But if there is such a thing as the ethics of belief, surely it will proscribe believing a proposition one knows to be either false or such that one ought not to believe it. Accordingly, I ought not to accept (19) in the absence of argument from premises that meet the condition it lays down. The same goes for the foundationalist: if he cannot find such an argument for (19), he ought to give it up. Furthermore, he ought not to urge and I ought not to accept any objection to theistic belief that crucially depends upon a proposition that is true only if I ought not believe it. . . .

Now we could canvass revisions of (19), and later I shall look into the proper procedure for discovering and justifying such criteria for proper basicality. It is evident, however, that classical foundationalism is bankrupt, and insofar as the evidentialist objection is rooted in classical foundationalism, it is poorly rooted indeed.

Of course the evidentialist objection *need* not presuppose classical foundationalism; someone who accepted quite a different version of foundationalism could no doubt urge this objection. But in order to evaluate it, we should have to see what criterion of proper basicality was being invoked. In the absence of such specification the objection remains at best a promissory note. So far as the present discussion goes, then, the next move is up to the evidentialist objector. He must specify a criterion for proper basicality that is free from self-referential difficulties, rules out belief in God as properly basic, and is such that there is some reason to think it is true. . . .

The Reformed Objection to Natural Theology

Suppose we think of natural theology as the attempt to prove or demonstrate the existence of God. This enterprise has a long and impressive history—a history stretching back to the dawn of Christendom and boasting among its adherents many of the truly great thinkers of the Western world. One thinks, for example, of Anselm, Aquinas, Scotus, and Ockham, of Descartes, Spinoza, and Leibniz. Recently—since the time of Kant, perhaps—the tradition of natural theology has not been as overwhelming as it once was; yet it continues to have able defenders both within and without officially Catholic philosophy.

Many Christians, however, have been less than totally impressed. In particular Reformed or Calvinist theologians have for the most part taken a dim view of this enterprise. A few Reformed thinkers—B. B. Warfield, for example—endorse the theistic proofs, but for the most part the Reformed attitude has ranged from tepid endorsement, through indifference, to suspicion, hostility, and outright accusations of blasphemy. And this stance is initially puzzling. It looks a little like the attitude some Christians adopt toward faith healing: it can't be done, but even if it could it shouldn't be. What exactly, or even approximately, do these sons and daughters of the Reformation have against proving the existence of God? What *could* they have against it? What could be less objectionable to any but the most obdurate atheist?

The Objection Initially Stated

By way of answering this question, I want to consider three representative Reformed thinkers. Let us begin with the nineteenth-century Dutch theologian Herman Bavinck:

A distinct natural theology, obtained apart from any revelation, merely through observation and study of the universe in which man lives, does not exist. . . .

Scripture urges us to behold heaven and earth, birds and ants, flowers and lilies, in order that we may see and recognize God in them. "Lift up your eyes on high, and see who hath created these." Is. 40:26. Scripture does not reason in the abstract. It does not make God the conclusion of a syllogism, leaving it to us whether we think the argument holds or not. But it speaks with authority. Both theologically and religiously it proceeds from God as the starting point.

We receive the impression that belief in the existence of God is based entirely upon these proofs. But indeed that would be "a wretched faith, which, before it invokes God, must first prove his existence." The contrary, however, is the truth. There is not a single object the existence of which we hesitate to accept until definite proofs are furnished. Of the existence of self, of the world round about us, of logical and moral laws, etc., we are so deeply convinced because of the indelible impressions which all these things make upon our consciousness that we need no arguments or demonstration. Spontaneously, altogether involuntarily: without any constraint or coercion, we accept that existence. Now the same is true in regard to the existence of God. The so-called proofs are by no means the final grounds of our most certain conviction that God exists. This certainty is established only by faith; that is, by the spontaneous testimony which forces itself upon us from every side.

According to Bavinck, then, belief in the existence of God is not based upon proofs or arguments. By "argument" here I think he means arguments in the style of natural theology—the sort given by Aquinas and Scotus and later by Descartes, Leibniz, Clarke, and others. And what he means to say, I think, is that Christians do not *need* such arguments. Do not need them for what?

Here I think Bavinck means to hold two things. First, arguments or proofs are not, in general, the source of the believer's confidence in God. Typically the believer does not believe in God on the basis of arguments; nor does he believe such truths as that God has created the world on the basis of arguments. Second, argument is not needed for *rational justification;* the believer is entirely within his epistemic right in believing, for example, that God has created the world, even if he has no argument at all for that conclusion. The believer does not need natural theology in order to achieve rationality or epistemic propriety in believing; his belief in God can be perfectly rational even if he knows of no cogent argument, deductive or inductive, for the existence of God—indeed, even if there is no such argument.

Barvinck has three further points. First he means to add, I think, that we cannot come to knowledge of God on the basis of argument; the arguments of natural theology just do not work. (And he follows this passage with a more or less traditional attempt to refute the theistic proofs, including an endorsement of some of Kant's fashionable confusions about the ontological argument.) Second, Scripture "proceeds from God as the starting point," and so should the believer. There is nothing by way of proofs or arguments for God's existence in the Bible; that is simply presupposed. The same should be true of the Christian believer then; he should *start* from belief in God rather than from the premises of some argument whose conclusion is that God exists. What is it that makes those premises a better starting point anyway? And third, Bavinck points out that belief in God relevantly resembles belief in the existence of the self and of the external world—and, we might add, belief in other minds and the past. In none of these areas do we typically *have* proof or arguments, or *need* proofs or arguments.

Suppose we turn next to John Calvin, who is as good a Calvinist as any. According to Calvin God has implanted in us all an innate tendency, or nisus, or disposition to believe in him:

'There is within the human mind, and indeed by natural instinct, an awareness of divinity.' This we take to be beyond controversy. To prevent anyone from taking refuge in the pretense of ignorance, God himself has implanted in all men a certain understanding of his divine majesty. Ever renewing its memory, he repeatedly sheds fresh drops. Since, therefore, men one and all perceive that there is a God and that he is their Maker, they are condemned by their own testimony because they have failed to honor him and to consecrate their lives to his will. If ignorance of God is to be looked for anywhere, surely one is most likely to find an example of it among the more backward

folk and those more remote from civilization. Yet there is, as the eminent pagan says, no nation so barbarous, no people so savage, that they have not a deep-seated conviction that there is a God. So deeply does the common conception occupy the minds of all, so tenaciously does it inhere in the hearts of all! Therefore, since from the beginning of the world there has been no region, no city, in short, no household, that could do without religion, there lies in this a tacit confession of a sense of deity inscribed in the hearts of all.

Indeed, the perversity of the impious, who though they struggle furiously are unable to extricate themselves from the fear of God, is abundant testimony that this conviction, namely, that *there is some God*, is naturally inborn in all, and is fixed deep within, as it were in the very marrow. . . . From this we conclude *that it is not a doctrine that must first be learned in school*, but one of which each of us is master from his mother's womb and which nature itself permits no one to forget.

Calvin's claim, then, is that God has created us in such a way that we have a strong tendency or inclination toward belief in him. This tendency has been in part overlaid or suppressed by sin. Were it not for the existence of sin in the world, human beings would believe in God to the same degree and with the same natural spontaneity that we believe in the existence of other persons, an external world, or the past. This is the natural human condition; it is because of our presently unnatural sinful condition that many of us find belief in God difficult or absurd. The fact is, Calvin thinks, one who does not believe in God is in an epistemically substandard position—rather like a man who does not believe that his wife exists, or thinks she is like a cleverly constructed robot and has no thoughts, feelings, or consciousness.

Although this disposition to believe in God is partially suppressed, it is nonetheless universally present. And it is triggered or actuated by a widely realized condition:

Lest anyone, then, be excluded from access to happiness, he not only sowed in men's minds that seed of religion of which we have spoken, but revealed himself and daily discloses himself in the whole workmanship of the universe. As a consequence, men cannot open their eyes without being compelled to see him.

Like Kant, Calvin is especially impressed in this connection, by the marvelous compages of the starry heavens above:

> Even the common folk and the most untutored, who have been taught only by the aid of the eyes, cannot be unaware of the excellence of divine art, for it reveals itself in this innumerable and yet distinct and well-ordered variety of the heavenly host.

And Calvin's claim is that one who accedes to this tendency and in these circumstances accepts the belief that God has created the world—perhaps upon beholding the starry heavens, or the splendid majesty of the mountains, or the intricate, articulate beauty of a tiny flower—is entirely within his epistemic rights in so doing. It is not that such a person is justified or rational in so believing by virtue of having an implicit argument—some version of the teleological argument, say. No; he does not need any argument for justification or rationality. His belief need not be based on any other propositions at all; under these conditions he is perfectly rational in accepting belief in God in the utter absence of any argument, deductive or inductive. Indeed, a person in these conditions, says Calvin, *knows* that God exists.

Elsewhere Calvin speaks of "arguments from reason" or rational arguments:

> The prophets and apostles do not boast either of their keenness or of anything that obtains credit for them as they speak; nor do they dwell upon rational proofs. Rather, they bring forward God's holy name, that by it the whole world may be brought into obedience to him. Now we ought to see how apparent it is not only by plausible opinion but by clear truth that they do not call upon God's name heedlessly or falsely. If we desire to provide in the best way for our consciences—that they may not be perpetually beset by the instability of doubt or vacillation, and that they may not also boggle at the smallest quibbles—we ought to seek our conviction in a higher place than human reasons, judgments, or conjectures, that is, in the secret testimony of the Spirit. (book 1, chapter 7, p. 78)

Here the subject for discussion is not belief in the existence of God, but belief that God is the author of the Scriptures; I think it is clear, however, that Calvin would say the same thing about belief in God's existence. The Christian does not *need* natural theology, either as the source of his confidence or to justify his belief. Furthermore, the Christian *ought* not to believe on the basis of argument; if he does, his faith is likely to be "unstable and wavering," the "subject of perpetual doubt." If my belief in God is based on argument, then if I am to be properly rational, epistemically responsible, I shall have to keep checking the philosophical journals to see whether, say, Anthony Flew has finally come up with a good objection to my favorite argument. This could be bothersome and time-consuming; and what do I do if someone does find a flaw in my argument? Stop going to church? From Calvin's point of view believing in the existence of God on the basis of rational argument is like believing in the existence of your spouse on the basis of the analogical argument for other minds—whimsical at best and unlikely to delight the person concerned. . . .

Karl Barth joins Calvin and Bavinck in holding that the believer in God is entirely within his epistemic rights in believing as he does even if he does not know of any good theistic argument. They all hold that belief in God is *properly basic*—that is, such that it is rational to accept it without accepting it on the basis of any other proposition or beliefs at all. In fact, they think the Christian ought not to accept belief in God on the basis of argument; to do so is to run the risk of a faith that is unstable and wavering, subject to all the wayward whim and fancy of the latest academic fashion. What the Reformers held was that a believer is entirely rational, entirely within his epistemic rights, in *starting with* belief in God, in accepting it as basic, and in taking it as premise for argument to other conclusions.

In rejecting natural theology, therefore, these Reformed thinkers mean to say first of all that the propriety or rightness of belief in God in no way depends upon the success or availability of the sort of theistic arguments that form the natural theologian's stock in trade. I think this is their central claim here, and their central insight. As these Reformed thinkers see things, one who takes belief in God as basic is not thereby violating any epistemic duties or revealing a defect in his noetic structure; quite the reverse. The correct or proper way to believe in God, they thought, was not on the basis of arguments from natural theology or anywhere else; the correct way is to take belief in God as basic.

I spoke earlier of classical foundationalism, a view that incorporates the following three theses:

(1) In every rational noetic structure there is a set of beliefs taken as basic—that is, not accepted on the basis of any other beliefs,

(2) In a rational noetic structure nonbasic belief is proportional to support from the foundations,

and

(3) In a rational noetic structure basic beliefs will be self-evident or incorrigible or evident to the senses.

Now I think these three Reformed thinkers should be understood as rejecting classical foundationalism. They may have been inclined to accept (1); they show no objection to (2); but they were utterly at odds with the idea that the foundations of a rational noetic structure can at most include propositions that are self-evident or evident to the senses or incorrigible. In particular, they were prepared to insist that a rational noetic structure can include belief in God as basic. As Bavinck put it, "Scripture . . . does not make God the conclusion of a syllogism, leaving it to us whether we think the argument holds or not. But it speaks with authority. Both theologically and religiously it proceeds from God as the starting point." And of course Bavinck means to say that we must emulate Scripture here.

In the passages I quoted earlier, Calvin claims the believer does not need argument—does not need it, among other things, for epistemic respectability. We may understand him as holding, I think, that a rational noetic structure may very well contain belief in God among its foundations. Indeed, he means to go further, and in two separate directions. In the first place he thinks a Christian *ought* not believe in God on the basis of other propositions; a proper and well-formed Christian noetic structure will *in fact* have belief in God among its foundations. And in the second place Calvin claims that one who takes belief in God as

basic can *know* that God exists. Calvin holds that one can *rationally accept* belief in God as basic; he also claims that one can *know* that God exists even if he has no argument, even if he does not believe on the basis of other propositions. A foundationalist is likely to hold that some properly basic beliefs are such that anyone who accepts them *knows* them. More exactly, he is likely to hold that among the beliefs properly basic for a person *S*, some are such that if *S* accepts them, *S* knows them. He could go on to say that *other* properly basic beliefs cannot be known if taken as basic, but only rationally believed; and he might think of the existence of God as a case in point. Calvin will have none of this; as he sees it, one needs no arguments to know that God exists. . . .

Is Belief in God Properly Basic?

The Great Pumpkin Objection

It is tempting to raise the following sort of question. If belief in God is properly basic, why cannot *just any* belief be properly basic? Could we not say the same for any bizarre aberration we can think of? What about voodoo or astrology? What about the belief that the Great Pumpkin returns every Halloween? Could I properly take *that* as basic? Suppose I believe that if I flap my arms with sufficient vigor, I can take off and fly about the room; could I defend myself against the charge of irrationality by claiming this belief is basic? If we say that belief in God is properly basic, will we not be committed to holding that just anything, or nearly anything, can properly be taken as basic, thus throwing wide the gates to irrationalism and superstition?

Certainly not. According to the Reformed epistemologist certain beliefs are properly basic in certain circumstances; those same beliefs may *not* be properly basic in other circumstances. Consider the belief that I see a tree: this belief is properly basic in circumstances that are hard to describe in detail, but include my being appeared to in a certain characteristic way; that same belief is not properly basic in circumstances including, say, my knowledge that I am sitting in the living room listening to music with my eyes closed. What the Reformed epistemologist holds is that there are widely realized circumstances in which belief in God is properly basic; but why should that be thought to commit him to the idea that just about *any* belief is properly basic in any circumstances, or even to the vastly weaker claim that for any belief there are circumstances in which it is properly basic? Is it just that he rejects the criteria for proper basicality purveyed by classical foundationalism? But why should *that* be thought to commit him to such tolerance of irrationality? Consider an analogy. In the palmy days of positivism the positivists went about confidently wielding their verifiability criterion and declaring meaningless much that was clearly meaningful. Now suppose someone rejected a formulation of that criterion—the one to be found in the second edition of A. J. Ayer's *Language, Truth and Logic,* for example. Would that mean she was committed to holding that

(1) T' was brillig; and the slithy toves did gyre and gymble in the wabe,

contrary to appearances, makes good sense? Of course not. But then the same goes for the Reformed epistemologist: the fact that he rejects the criterion of proper basicality purveyed by classical foundationalism does not mean that he is committed to supposing just anything is properly basic.

But what then is the problem? Is it that the Reformed epistemologist not only rejects those criteria for proper basicality but seems in no hurry to produce what he takes to be a better substitute? If he has no such criterion, how can he fairly reject belief in the Great Pumpkin as properly basic?

This objection betrays an important misconception. How *do* we rightly arrive at or develop criteria for meaningfulness, or justified belief, or proper basicality? Where do they come from? Must one have such a criterion before one can sensibly make any judgments—positive or negative—about proper basicality? Surely not. Suppose I do not know of a satisfactory substitute for the criteria proposed by classical foundationalism; I am nevertheless entirely within my epistemic

rights in holding that certain propositions in certain conditions are not properly basic.

Some propositions seem self-evident when in fact they are not; that is the lesson of some of the Russell paradoxes. Nevertheless it would be irrational to take as basic the denial of a proposition that seems self-evident to you. Similarly, suppose it seems to you that you see a tree; you would then be irrational in taking as basic the proposition that you do not see a tree or that there are no trees. In the same way, even if I do not know of some illuminating criterion of meaning, I can quite properly declare (1) (above) meaningless.

And this raises an important question—one Roderick Chisholm has taught us to ask. What is the status of criteria for knowledge, or proper basicality, or justified belief? Typically these are universal statements. The modern foundationalist's criterion for proper basicality, for example, is doubly universal:

(2) For any proposition *A* and person *S*, *A* is properly basic for *S* if and only if *A* is incorrigible for *S* or self-evident to *S*.

But how could one know a thing like that? What are its credentials? Clearly enough, (2) is not self-evident or just obviously true. But if it is not, how does one arrive at it? What sorts of arguments would be appropriate? Of course a foundationalist might find (2) so appealing he simply takes it to be true, neither offering argument for it nor accepting it on the basis of other things he believes. If he does so, however, his noetic structure will be self-referentially incoherent. (2) itself is neither self-evident nor incorrigible; hence if he accepts (2) as basic, the modern foundationalist violates in accepting it the condition of proper basicality he himself lays down. On the other hand, perhaps the foundationalist will try to produce some argument for it from premises that are self-evident or incorrigible: it is exceeding hard to see, however, what such an argument might be like. And until he has produced such arguments, what shall the rest of us do—we who do not find (2) at all obvious or compelling? How could he use (2) to show us that belief in God, for example, is not properly basic? Why should we believe (2) or pay it any attention?

The fact is, I think, that neither (2) nor any other revealing necessary and sufficient condition for proper basicality follows from clearly self-evident premises by clearly acceptable arguments. And hence the proper way to arrive at such a criterion is, broadly speaking, *inductive*. We must assemble examples of beliefs and conditions such that the former are obviously properly basic in the latter, and examples of beliefs and conditions such that the former are obviously *not* properly basic in the latter. We must then frame hypotheses as to the necessary and sufficient conditions of proper basicality and test these hypotheses by reference to those examples. Under the right conditions, for example, it is clearly rational to believe that you see a human person before you: a being who has thoughts and feelings, who knows and believes things, who makes decisions and acts. It is clear, furthermore, that you are under no obligation to reason to this belief from others you hold; under those conditions that belief is properly basic for you. But then (2) must be mistaken; the belief in question, under those circumstances, is properly basic, though neither self-evident nor incorrigible for you. Similarly, you may seem to remember that you had breakfast this morning, and perhaps you know of no reason to suppose your memory is playing you tricks. If so, you are entirely justified in taking that belief as basic. Of course it is not properly basic on the criteria offered by classical foundationalists, but that fact counts not against you but against those criteria. . . .

Accordingly, criteria for proper basicality must be reached from below rather than above; they should not be presented *ex cathedra* but argued to and tested by a relevant set of examples. But there is no reason to assume, in advance, that everyone will agree on the examples. The Christian will of course suppose that belief in God is entirely proper and rational; if he does not accept this belief on the basis of other propositions, he will conclude that it is basic for him and quite properly so. Followers of Bertrand Russell and Madelyn Murray O'Hare may disagree; but how is that relevant? Must my criteria, or those of the Christian community, conform to their examples? Surely not. The Christian community is responsible to *its* set of examples, not to theirs. . . .

So, the Reformed epistemologist can properly hold that belief in the Great Pumpkin is not properly basic, even though he holds that belief in God is properly basic and even if he has no full-fledged criterion of proper basicality. Of course he is committed to supposing that there is a relevant *difference* between belief in God and belief in the Great Pumpkin if he holds that the former but not the latter is properly basic. But this should prove no great embarrassment; there are plenty of candidates. These candidates are to be found in the neighborhood of the conditions that justify and ground belief in God—conditions I shall discuss in the next section. Thus, for example, the Reformed epistemologist may concur with Calvin in holding that God has implanted in us a natural tendency to see his hand in the world around us; the same cannot be said for the Great Pumpkin, there being no Great Pumpkin and no natural tendency to accept beliefs about the Great Pumpkin.

VII.D.3   In Search of the Foundations of Theism

PHILIP QUINN

Philip Quinn is a philosopher at the University of Notre Dame. In this reading he criticizes the arguments of Alvin Plantinga (see previous reading), claiming (1) that Plantinga has failed to show that the criteria for proper basicality that he rejects are in any way defective and (2) that Plantinga's procedure for justifying criteria for proper basicality provides no advantage over a criterion wherein no theistic propositions are properly basic. Although Quinn believes that Plantinga's argument is unsound, he is open to the possibility that some propositions that self-evidently entail that God exists could be properly basic. In the second part of his paper Quinn argues that, even if this were so, being properly basic would be relatively unimportant and such propositions would seldom be properly basic for intellectually sophisticated adult theists in our culture.

Foundationalism comes in two varieties. Descriptive foundationalism is a thesis about the structure of a body of beliefs, and normative foundationalism is a thesis about the structure of epistemic justification for a body of beliefs. Both varieties partition a body of beliefs into two subclasses, a foundational class and a founded class. For descriptive foundationalism, the foundational class is the class of basic beliefs. A belief is basic for a person at a time provided it is accepted by that person at that time but is not accepted by that person at that time on the basis of any of his or her other beliefs at that time. For normative foundationalism, the foundational class is the class of properly basic beliefs. A belief is properly basic for a person at a time just in case it is basic for the person at the time and its being basic for the person at the time is contrary to no correct canon of epistemic propriety and results from no epistemic

Reprinted from *Faith and Philosophy* (October 1985) by permission of the author and editor.

deficiency on his or her part at that time. For descriptive foundationalism, the founded class is the class of beliefs based on basic beliefs, and for normative foundationalism, the founded class is the class of beliefs properly based on properly basic beliefs.

It surely is possible that, for some human persons at some times, certain propositions that self-evidently entail that God exists are basic. But is it also possible that, for some human persons at some times, certain propositions that self-evidently entail that God exists are *properly* basic? In other words, could such propositions *be*, or at least *be among*, the normative foundations of theism, at least for some people at some times? The answers to these questions depend, of course, on what the correct criteria for proper basicality turn out to be.

Recently Alvin Plantinga has been arguing that it is in order for a religious epistemologist to return affirmative answers to these questions.[1] There are two prongs to Plantinga's argument. The first is destructive: It is an attempt to show that certain criteria for proper basicality, according to which propositions that self-evidently entail the existence of God could not be properly basic, are seriously defective and must be rejected. The second is constructive: It is an attempt to elaborate a procedure for justifying criteria for proper basicality that will allow that some propositions self-evidently entailing that God exists could turn out to be properly basic.

This paper has two aims. The first is to criticize Plantinga's argument. In the first section of the paper, I argue for two claims: (1) that Plantinga has failed to show that the criteria for proper basicality he proposes to reject are in any way defective; and (2) that Plantinga's procedure for justifying criteria for proper basicality provides no better reason for adopting criteria according to which some propositions that self-evidently entail the existence of God can be properly basic than for adopting a criterion according to which no such propositions can be properly basic. The paper's second aim is exploratory. Although Plantinga's argument is unsuccessful, it may nevertheless be true that some propositions that self-evidently entail that God exists could be properly basic. And so, in the second section of the paper, I go on to argue, on the hypothesis that this is true, for two additional claims: (1) that actually being properly basic would be a relatively unimportant feature of such propositions because they would be at least as well justified if properly based on other properly basic propositions and could always be so based; and (2) that such propositions would seldom, if ever, be properly basic for intellectually sophisticated adult theists in our culture.

Critique of Plantinga

The criteria for proper basicality Plantinga proposes to reject are those of classical foundationalism. Classical foundationalism is the disjunction of ancient or medieval foundationalism and modern foundationalism. The criterion for proper basicality of ancient or medieval foundationalism is the triply universal claim:

(1) For any proposition p, person S, and time t, p is properly basic for S at t if and only if p is self-evident to S at t or is evident to the senses of S at t.

And the criterion for proper basicality of modern foundationalism is this triply universal claim:

(2) For any proposition p, person S, and time t, p is properly basic for S at t if and only if p is incorrigible for S at t or is self-evident to S at t.

Although Plantinga thinks the propositions expressed by both (1) and (2) should be rejected on grounds of self-referential incoherence, he actually discusses only the latter proposition at any length. However, it is clear that if his argument for self-referential incoherence succeeds against the proposition expressed by (2), a similar argument will, *mutatis mutandis,* work equally well against the proposition expressed by (1). But what exactly

is the argument? And how must does it really prove?

Consider the proposition expressed by (2). What place does it have in the modern foundationalist's own structure of epistemic justification? Is it in the foundational class? Does the modern foundationalist suppose that it is ever properly basic for anyone? If he or she does, then he or she must hold that for someone at some time it is either incorrigible or self-evident. Plantinga believes it to be "neither self-evident nor incorrigible."[2] I agree. I think the proposition expressed by (2) is never incorrigible for or self-evident to me. Are Plantinga and I idiosyncratic in this respect? Could the modern foundationalist claim with any plausibility that we are just plain mistaken on this point? I think the answer to these questions has to be negative. It seems to me perfectly clear that the proposition expressed by (2) is never incorrigible for or self-evident to anyone. Hence, no one, not even a modern foundationalist, is entitled to suppose that the proposition expressed by (2) is ever properly basic for anyone.

Does this suffice to show that modern foundationalism is self-referentially incoherent? Obviously it does not. What would be self-referentially incoherent would be to affirm the proposition expressed by (2), to assert that it is itself never incorrigible for or self-evident to anyone, and also to claim that it is itself properly basic for someone at some time. But this leaves the modern foundationalist with the option of continuing to affirm the proposition expressed by (2) while conceding that it is itself never properly basic for anyone. For all that has been said so far, the proposition expressed by (2), though never properly basic for anyone, is for some people at some times properly based on propositions that, by its own lights, are properly basic for those people at those times. In discussion, Plantinga has claimed that no modern foundationalist has ever given a good argument for the view that the proposition expressed by (2) is, for some people at some times, properly based on propositions that by its own lights, are properly basic for them then. Maybe this is so. But, even if it is, this does not show that modern foundationalism is self-referentially incoherent. All it shows is that the modern foundationalist has so far not completed the task of justifying the proposition expressed by (2) in the only way that remains open to him or her, namely, by showing how it can, for some people at some times, be properly based on propositions that are, by its own lights, properly basic for them at those times. Can this be done, and, if so, how? More generally, how could any criterion for proper basicality be justified?

Plantinga offers us an explicit answer to the more general question. He says:

> . . . the proper way to arrive at such a criterion is, broadly speaking, *inductive*. We must assemble examples of beliefs and conditions such that the former are obviously properly basic in the latter, and examples of beliefs and conditions such that the former are obviously *not* properly basic in the latter. We must then frame hypotheses as to the necessary and sufficient conditions of proper basicality and test these hypotheses by reference to those examples.[3]

As I understand the proposed procedure, it requires that we do two things. First, we are to assemble the data upon which the induction will be based. A datum may be represented as an ordered pair whose first member is a belief and whose second member is a condition. Positive data are data such that the beliefs that are their first members are obviously properly basic in the conditions that are their second members; negative data are data such that the beliefs that are their first members are obviously not properly basic in the conditions that are their second members. Call the set of data, presumably finite, so assembled 'the initial set'. Second, we are to frame hypotheses stating necessary and sufficient conditions for proper basicality and test them against the data in the initial set. A hypothesis will pass the test posed by the data in the initial set if and only if all of the positive data in the initial set and none of the negative data in that set satisfy its necessary and sufficient conditions for proper basicality. So far, so good.

However, two questions about this procedure quickly arise. First, how do we know that there will be *any* hypothesis at all stating nontrivial necessary and sufficient conditions for proper basicality that will pass the test posed by the data in the initial set? Maybe the initial set will itself be inconsistent or in some other way subtly incoherent. So perhaps we should be allowed to throw data out of the initial set should we discover that it is in some fashion incoherent. But, second, how do we know that there will be *only one* hypothesis stating nontrivial necessary and sufficient conditions for proper basicality that will pass the test posed by the data in the initial set? If the initial set is finite and our hypotheses are universally quantified, as the classical foundationalist's criteria are, then the data in the initial set will underdetermine the truth of hypotheses. In that case, there may very well be several interesting hypotheses that all pass the test posed by the data in the initial set and yet disagree radically about the proper basicality of examples outside the initial set. So perhaps we should also be allowed to add data to the initial set if this will help us to eliminate at least some of those hypotheses that have passed the test posed by the data in the initial set. These considerations make one thing very clear. Plantinga has so far given us only the rough outlines of the first stage of a broadly inductive procedure for arriving at a uniquely justified criterion of proper basicality. Many more details would need to be filled in before we could have any rational assurance that correct application of the procedure would yield exactly one hypothesis about conditions necessary and sufficient for proper basicality inductively best supported by, or most firmly based upon, the data in the initial set in some suitable revision of the initial set.

But, rough though it be, Plantinga's sketch of the first stage of a procedure for justifying criteria of proper basicality is nonetheless well enough developed to permit us to see that it confronts at the outset at least one important difficulty. This is because, as Plantinga himself acknowledges, there is no reason to assume in advance that everyone will agree on what is to go into the initial set. Plantinga says:

> The Christian will of course suppose that belief in God is entirely proper and rational; if he doesn't accept this belief on the basis of other propositions, he will conclude that it is basic for him and quite properly so. Followers of Bertrand Russell and Madelyn Murray O'Hare (*sic!*) may disagree, but how is

that relevant! Must my criteria, or those of the Christian community, conform to their examples? Surely not. The Christian community is responsible to *its* set of examples, not to theirs.[4]

The difficulty is, of course, that this is a game any number can play. Followers of Muhammed, followers of Buddha, and even followers of the Reverend Moon can join in the fun. Even the modern foundationalist can play. When a modern foundationalist, under optimal conditions for visual perception, seems to see a green beach ball in front of her, she can claim that one thing that is obviously properly basic for her then is this:

(3) I am being appeared to greenly.

And one thing that is obviously not properly basic for her then, she can say, is this:

(4) I am seeing a green beachball.

After all, as she sees it, the proposition expressed by the latter sentence is for her then properly based, at least in part, on the proposition expressed by the former. And she can then mimic Plantinga's own argument in this fashion: "Followers of G. E. Moore and Alvin Plantinga may disagree, but how is that relevant? Must my criteria, or those of the community of modern foundationalists, conform to their examples? Surely not. The community of modern foundationalists is responsible to *its* set of examples, not to theirs." It would seem that what is sauce for Russell's goose should also be sauce for Plantinga's gander. Turn about *is,* in this case, fair play.

Ad hominem arguments to one side, the problem is that fidelity to the data in an initial set constructed from intuitions about what is obvious is a very weak constraint on the justification of a criterion for proper basicality. The modern foundationalist can easily choose the data in his or her initial set so that his or her criterion for proper basicality passes the test they pose by making sure (1) that the only beliefs that nearly everyone would admit are, in the associated conditions, incorrigible or self-evident are the first members of positive data, and (2) that all beliefs that nearly everyone would, in the associated conditions, not consider incorrigible or self-evident are either the first

members of negative data or outside the initial set altogether. How is this to be accomplished?

Suppose a modern foundationalist is contemplating believing that she is being appeared to redly in conditions optimal for visual experience in which she is being appeared to redly. Surely she can plausibly say that it is self-evident to her that that belief would be properly basic for her in those conditions, and clearly she can also reasonably claim that it is self-evident to her that that belief would be self-evident to her in those conditions. Now suppose the same modern foundationalist is contemplating believing that Jove is expressing disapproval in conditions optimal for auditory experience in which she is being appeared to thunderously. Surely she can plausibly say that it is self-evident to her that that belief would not be properly basic for her in those conditions, and clearly she can also reasonably claim that it is self-evident to her that that belief would be neither incorrigible nor self-evident to her in those conditions. After having assembled a rich initial set of positive and negative data by ringing the changes on these two thought experiments, the modern foundationalist is then in a position to claim and properly so, that his or her criterion, though not itself properly basic, is properly based, in accord with what Plantinga has told us about proper procedures for justifying criteria for proper basicality, on beliefs that are properly basic by its own lights.

It is important to understand that the data I am supposing the modern foundationalist might use to justify his or her criterion of proper basicality derive from thought experiments about hypothetical situations. My claim is not that when, for instance, a person in fact believes that Jove is expressing disapproval in conditions optimal for auditory experience in which she is being appeared to thunderously, it will then in fact be self-evident to her that that belief is not properly basic for her in those conditions. After all, she may not even wonder whether that belief is properly basic for her in those conditions when she happens to have the belief in the conditions. Rather my claim is that when a modern foundationalist contemplates the hypothetical situation of believing that Jove is expressing disapproval in conditions optimal for auditory experience in which she is being appeared to thunderously, then she can with plausibility maintain that it is self-evident to her that that belief would not in those conditions be properly basic for her. Because I hold that our intuitions about such hypothetical situations often provide the ultimate and decisive test of philosophical generalizations, I think the role of such beliefs about hypothetical situations in confirming or disconfirming philosophical generalizations is best explained on the supposition that they can be, in the right circumstances, self-evident.

In discussion, Plantinga has objected to this line of argument. If I understand his objection, it goes as follows. To say that a belief is properly basic in a set of circumstances is to say, among other things, that in those circumstances a person could accept the belief without displaying some kind of noetic defect. But what constitutes a noetic defect depends upon what constitutes the proper working of one's noetic equipment. So a proposition to the effect that a certain person on a certain occasion is displaying no such defect cannot possibly be self-evident because it cannot be self-evident to one that all one's noetic equipment is in proper working order. Hence, a proposition to the effect that a certain belief is properly basic on a certain occasion cannot possibly be self-evident either.

I concede, of course, that it is not usually self-evident to one that all one's noetic equipment is in proper working order. But if Plantinga's objection is to have any force against my argument, it must apply to the particular hypothetical case I have described above. I believe it does not. Our modern foundationalist is supposed to be contemplating believing that she is being appeared to redly in conditions optimal for visual experience in which she is being appeared to redly. It seems quite clear to me that it could be self-evident to her that she would display no noetic defect in accepting that belief in those conditions. To be sure, her noetic equipment might then have some defects of which she was unaware. She might then, for example, not be able to recognize the taste of ordinary table salt. But that is irrelevant provided she would display none of these defects in accepting the belief

that she is being appeared to redly in the specified circumstances. For all that is required is that it could be self-evident to her that she would display no such defect in accepting that belief in those circumstances. Because I believe this requirement can be met, I conclude that Plantinga's objection fails. In short, it can be self-evident to one that one is displaying no noetic defect in accepting a certain belief on a certain occasion without it also being self-evident to one then that all one's noetic equipment is in proper working order.

I do not expect that this reply will bring Plantinga's objections to an end. I suspect Plantinga will continue to think the modern foundationalist has made some mistake if he or she proceeds in this fashion to justify his or her criterion for proper basicality. But it is not obvious that this is so; nor is it obvious what precisely the mistake might be. After all, one of the rules of the game specifies that the community of modern foundationalists is permitted to be responsible to *its* set of examples. Hence, absent a good argument by Plantinga that establishes that a mistake must occur in such a procedure, I think we are entitled to hold that Plantinga's own procedure for justifying criteria for proper basicality provides no better reason for adopting criteria according to which some propositions that self-evidently entail the existence of God can be properly basic than for adopting a criterion, namely, the one proposed by the modern foundationalist, according to which no such propositions can be properly basic.

Of course, nothing I have said rules out the possibility that Plantinga could use the inductive procedure he advocates to justify a criterion of proper basicality according to which some propositions that self-evidently entail that God exists can be properly basic. Indeed, if, as his talk about being responsible to the examples of the Christian community suggests, he would take some such propositions to be the first members of positive data in his initial set and thereafter not delete all such positive data in revising his initial set, it is pretty obvious that Plantinga can succeed in this task, though success at so cheap a price may be thought by some to come uncomfortably close to question begging. But if Plantinga does succeed in performing this exercise, then I think the conclusion we should draw is that his fight with classical foundationalism has resulted in a standoff.

What If Belief in God Could Be Properly Basic?

If my critique of Plantinga has been successful, I have shown that he fails to prove that belief in propositions that self-evidently entail God's existence could ever be properly basic for anyone. But it might be true that belief in such propositions could be properly basic, even if Plantinga has not proved it. And if it were, what would be the consequences for religious epistemology? I now turn to an exploration of this issue.

Plantinga's examples of beliefs that could be properly basic in the right conditions include the following items:

(5) God is speaking to me.
(6) God disapproves of what I have done.

and

(7) God forgives me for what I have done.

And according to Plantinga, the right conditions include a component that is, broadly speaking, experiential. He says,

Upon reading the Bible, one may be impressed with a deep sense that God is speaking to him. Upon having done what I know is cheap, or wrong, or wicked I may feel guilty in God's sight and form the belief that *God disapproves of what I've done.* Upon confession and repentence, I may feel forgiven, forming the belief *God forgives me for what I've done.*[5]

It strikes me that part of what makes the suggestion that beliefs like those expressed by (5)–(7) could be properly basic in conditions like those partially described in the quoted passage seem attractive is an analogy with an extremely plausible view about how certain Moorean commonsense beliefs are often justified. When I have the experience of seeming to see a hand in front of me in the right conditions, I may be justified in believing that

(8) I see a hand in front of me.

This justification may be direct in the sense of being grounded directly in the experience itself without passing through the intermediary of a belief about the way I am being appeared to such as

(9) It seems to me that I see a hand in front of me.

For I may not in the circumstances have entertained, much less accepted, the proposition expressed by (9), but, on the view under consideration, my justification for believing the proposition expressed by (8) is in no way defective on that account. Hence, the proposition expressed by (8) may be basic, and quite properly so, in the right conditions. And if this is, as I believe it to be, an attractive view about how believing the proposition expressed by (8) can be, and sometimes is, justified, then there is an argument from analogy for supposing that propositions like those expressed by (5)–(7) may also be properly basic in conditions that include an experiential component of the right sort for grounding such beliefs. To be sure, there are significant disanalogies. The direct justification of the belief expressed by (8) is grounded in a mode of sensory experience that is now generally believed by nonskeptical epistemologists to be reliable in the right conditions. By contrast, the direct justification of the beliefs expressed by (5)–(7) is grounded in a mode of experience that, though it may be reliable in the right conditions, is not now generally believed by nonskeptical epistemologists to be so. But, although such considerations might be taken to show that the analogical argument is not very strong, it does not deprive the positive analogy of heuristic and explanatory capabilities. I am going to make use of these capabilities in the remainder of the discussion.

When I have the experience of seeming to see a hand in front of me in the right conditions, though the proposition expressed by (8) could then be properly basic for me, it could instead be the case that the proposition expressed by (9) is then properly basic for me and the proposition expressed by (8) is then properly based, at least in part, on the proposition expressed by (9). For when I have that experience in those conditions, I might well be attending mainly to the qualitative aspects of my visual experience with the result that the proposition expressed by (9) is then basic for me. If this happens, the proposition expressed by (9) would clearly be properly basic for me. I might well also then base the proposition expressed by (8) in part on the proposition expressed by (9). And, if this too happens, then the proposition expressed by (8) would be properly based, in part, on the proposition expressed by (9) because the latter proposition does nothing more than serve to articulate that part of the content of my visual experience that is relevant to justifying the former. If the proposition expressed by (8) were indirectly justified by being properly based on the proposition expressed by (9), it would be no less well justified than if it were directly justified by being directly grounded in visual experience. Since, by hypothesis, my visual experience in those conditions suffices to confer a certain degree of justification on the proposition expressed by (8), the amount of justification that reaches the proposition expressed by (8) from that experience will not be less in those conditions if it passes by way of the proposition expressed by (9) than if it is transmitted directly without intermediary. But neither would its justification be any better if indirect in this way. Moreover, it could happen that at a certain time the proposition expressed by (8) is properly basic for me and at a later time it is no longer properly basic, though still justified, for me because in the interval it has come to be properly based on the proposition expressed by (9). For in the interval I might, for example, have come to wonder whether I was justified in believing the proposition expressed by (8) and as a result come to believe the proposition expressed by (9) and to base properly on this belief my belief in the proposition expressed by (8). And if such a process did occur, I think the degree to which the proposition expressed by (8) was justified for me would, other things remaining unaltered, stay constant through it.

By analogy, similar things seem true of the examples that are Plantinga's prime candidates for religious beliefs that could be properly basic. When I am impressed with a deep sense that God is speaking to me, if the proposition expressed by

(5) could then be properly basic for me, then it could instead be the case that some other proposition is among those then properly basic for me and the proposition expressed by (5) is then properly based in part on it. Such a proposition is:

(10) It seems to me that God is speaking to me.

If the proposition expressed by (5) were indirectly justified for me by being properly based on the proposition expressed by (10), its justification would be no better, and no worse, than if it were properly basic and directly justified for me by being directly grounded in my experiential sense that God is speaking to me, other things remaining the same. And it could happen that in the course of time the proposition expressed by (5) changes from being properly basic for me to being properly based in part for me on the proposition expressed by (10) without gain or loss of degree of justification.

So, oddly enough, if certain propositions that self-evidently entail the existence of God can be properly basic for a person at a time, it is epistemically unimportant whether such propositions actually are properly basic for that person at that time. Without loss of degree of justification, such theistic propositions can just as well be properly based, at least in part, on others that are descriptive of the person's experience at the time and are then properly basic for the person. Although such theistic propositions would not need to be based on the evidence of other propositions, they always could be so based. So the cautious philosopher who did so base them would be every bit as justified in believing in the existence of God as the reckless mystic who did not.

There is another salient feature of directly justified Moorean beliefs like the one expressed by (8) which would have an analogue in the case of religious beliefs like those expressed by (5)–(7) if they could be properly basic in the right conditions. This is that the kind of justification conferred on such Moorean beliefs by direct grounding in experience of the right sort is defeasible. So, for example, a potential defeater for the proposition expressed by (8) is this:

(11) I am now hallucinating a hand.

If propositions such as (8) are taken to be properly basic in the right conditions, then a full specification of those conditions must include reference to the status of potential defeaters such as (11). What would it be reasonable to say about potential defeaters when specifying in fuller detail the right conditions for proper basicality of the proposition expressed by (8)? Several possibilities come to mind.

It might be suggested that conditions are right for the proposition expressed by (8) to be properly basic for me only if none of its potential defeaters is true. This suggestion clearly misses the mark. When I have the experience of seeming to see a hand in front of me, it may be that the proposition expressed by (8) is true and the proposition expressed by (11) is false, and yet I am justified in rejecting the former and accepting the latter because, for instance, I remember taking a large dose of some hallucinogen only an hour ago and hallucinating wildly in the interval. Merely to insist that potential defeaters be false in order for conditions to be right for proper basicality is to require much too little.

Alternatively, it might be suggested that conditions are right for the proposition expressed by (8) to be properly basic for me only if each of its potential defeaters is such that I have some reason to think it is false. Clearly this suggestion errs in the direction of demanding too much. I have never exhaustively enumerated the potential defeaters of the proposition expressed by (8), and I am inclined to doubt that I would ever complete such a task if I began it. I have certainly never mobilized or acquired a reason against each of them. No one I know has ever tried to do such a thing in defense of all of his or her Moorean commonsense beliefs. So if such beliefs frequently are properly basic in virtue of being directly grounded in sensory experience, as I think they are, conditions are often right for proper basicality without such an elaborate structure of reasons for the falsity of potential defeaters having been mobilized.

It does, however, seem initially plausible to suppose that conditions are right for the proposition expressed by (8) to be properly basic for me only if I have no sufficiently substantial reasons to

think that any of its potential defeaters is true and this is not due to epistemic negligence on my part. Two features of this claim require a bit of explanation. First, if the only reason I have to think that some potential defeater of the proposition expressed by (8) is true is, for instance, that I remember once, long ago, having mistaken a tree's branches for a hand, then that will not usually suffice to undermine the *prima facie* justification the proposition expressed by (8) has in the right experiential conditions to such an extent that that proposition is not properly basic. More generally, since *prima facie* justification comes in degrees, although any good reason one has for thinking one of a proposition's potential defeaters is true will undermine that proposition's *prima facie* justification to some degree, slight reasons will usually not singly undermine it to the extent that it is no longer *prima facie* justified. Instead, it will usually remain *prima facie* justified in the presence of one or a few such reasons but to a lesser degree than it would be in their absence. It takes a sufficiently substantial reason for thinking one of its potential defeaters is true to rob a proposition of proper basicality in conditions in which it would otherwise be properly basic.[6] Second, if I happen to lack sufficiently substantial reasons to think that any potential defeater of the proposition expressed by (8) is true merely because, for example, I have negligently failed to recall that I ingested some hallucinogenic substance only an hour ago and have been hallucinating wildly in the interval, then clearly conditions are not right for the proposition expressed by (8) to be properly basic for me, even though it may in fact be basic for me. More generally, a proposition is not *prima facie* justified if one negligently ignores good reasons for thinking one of its potential defeaters is true that would be sufficiently substantial to undermine the proposition's *prima facie* justification to such an extent that it would not be *prima facie* justified. Such epistemic negligence would constitute an epistemic deficiency.

By analogy, it also seems initially plausible to say that conditions are right for the propositions expressed by (5)–(7) to be properly basic for me only if I have no sufficiently substantial reason to think that any of their potential defeaters is true and this is not due to epistemic negligence on my part. But there is the rub. A potential defeater of the propositions expressed by (5)–(7) is this:

(12) God does not exist.

And, unfortunately, I do have very substantial reasons for thinking that the proposition expressed by (12) is true. My reasons derive mainly from one of the traditional problems of evil. What I know, partly from experience and partly from testimony, about the amount and variety of nonmoral evil in the universe confirms highly for me the proposition expressed by (12). Of course, this is not indefeasible confirmation of the proposition expressed by (12). It could be defeated by other things I do not know. Perhaps it is not even undefeated confirmation. Maybe it even is defeated by other things I do know. Nevertheless, it does furnish me with a very substantial reason for thinking that the proposition expressed by (12) is true. Moreover, I dare say that many, perhaps most, intellectually sophisticated adults in our culture are in an epistemic predicament similar to mine. As I see it, an intellectually sophisticated adult in our culture would have to be epistemically negligent not to have very substantial reasons for thinking that what (12) expresses is true. After all, nontrivial atheological reasons, ranging from various problems of evil to naturalistic theories according to which theistic belief is illusory or merely projective, are a pervasive, if not obtrusive, component of the rational portion of our cultural heritage.

But, even if such reasons are very substantial, are they sufficiently substantial to make it the case that the propositions expressed by (5)–(7) would no longer be properly basic in conditions of the sort described by Plantinga in which, we are supposing, they could have been properly basic but for the presence of such substantial reasons? On reflection, I am convinced that such reasons are, taken collectively, sufficiently substantial, though I confess with regret that I cannot at present back up my intuitive conviction with solid arguments. But I conjecture than many, perhaps most, intellectually sophisticated adults in our culture will share my intuitive conviction on this point. And so

I conclude that many, perhaps most, intellectually sophisticated adult theists in our culture are seldom, if ever, in conditions that are right for propositions like those expressed by (5)–(7) to be properly basic for them.

It does not follow from this conclusion that intellectually sophisticated adult theists in our culture cannot be justified in believing propositions like those expressed by (5)–(7). For all that I have said, some such propositions are such that, for every single one of their potential defeaters that is such that there is some very substantial reason to think it is true, there is an even better reason to think it is false. And so, for all I know, some intellectually sophisticated adult theists in our culture could be, or perhaps even are, in the fortunate position, with respect to some such propositions and their potential defeaters, of having, for each potential defeater that some epistemically nonnegligent, intellectually sophisticated adult in our culture has a very substantial reason to think is true, an even better reason to think it is false. But if there are such fortunate theists in our culture, they are people who have already accomplished at least one of the main tasks traditionally assigned to natural theology. Although they may know of no proof of the existence of God, they possess reasons good enough to defend some proposition that self-evidently entails the existence of God against all of its potential defeaters that epistemically nonnegligent, intellectually sophisticated adults in our culture have very substantial reasons to believe. I tend to doubt that many intellectually sophisticated adult theists in our culture are in this fortunate position for any appreciable portion of their lives.

But suppose someone were in this fortunate position. Such a person would have reasons good enough to defend theistic belief against all of its potential defeaters that epistemically nonnegligent, intellectually sophisticated adults in our culture have very substantial reasons to believe, and such reasons would be parts of such a person's total case for the rationality of theistic belief. But would such a person's theistic belief have to be based on such reasons? That depends, of course, on exactly what is involved in basing one belief on others. Plantinga is prudently reticent about describing the basing relation; he says only that, "although this relation isn't easy to characterize in a revealing and nontrivial fashion, it is nonetheless familiar."[7] On the basis of the examples Plantinga gives, I once conjectured in discussion that he thinks the relation is characterized by something like the following principle:

(13) For any person *S* and distinct propositions *p* and *q*, *S* believes *q* on the basis of *p* only if *S* entertains *p*, *S* accepts *p*, *S* infers *q* from *p*, and *S* accepts *q*.[8]

If Plantinga does have in mind some such narrow conception of the basing relation, then our hypothetical fortunate person's theistic belief clearly need not be based on all the reasons, including defenses against potential defeaters that have very substantial support, in the person's total case for the rationality of theistic belief. After all, some such defenses may consist only of considerations that show that certain atheological arguments are unsound or otherwise defective, and our fortunate person's belief need not be based, in this narrow sense, on such considerations. Indeed, for all I know, it is possible that all our fortunate person's successful defenses against potential defeaters that have substantial support are of this sort. Hence, for all I know, our fortunate person could have a successful total case for the rationality of theistic belief made up entirely of reasons such that belief in some proposition that self-evidently entails the existence of God needs none of them for a basis. Thus, for all I know, on this narrow conception of the basing relation, our fortunate person's theistic belief might be properly basic in the right conditions.

If I were to endorse some such narrow conception of the basing relation, I would have to revise my earlier proposal about when it is plausible to suppose conditions are right for propositions to be properly basic for me. I am inclined to believe that the appropriate thing to say, in light of the line of reasoning developed in the previous paragraph, is that it seems plausible to suppose that conditions are right for propositions like those expressed by

(5)–(7) to be, in the narrow sense, properly basic for me only if (i) either I have no sufficiently substantial reason to think that any of their potential defeaters is true, or I do have some such reasons but, for each such reason I have, I have an even better reason for thinking the potential defeater in question is false, and (ii), in either case, my situation involves no epistemic negligence on my part. I could then put the point I am intent on pressing by saying that, depending on which of the two disjuncts in the first clause of this principle one imagines my satisfying, I would have to be nonnegligently either rather naive and innocent or quite fortunate and sophisticated in order for conditions to be right for propositions like those expressed by (5)–(7) to be, in the narrow sense, properly basic for me. When I examine my epistemic predicament, I find myself forced to conclude that I am in neither of those extreme situations. Since I have very substantial reasons for thinking the proposition expressed by (12) is true, innocence has been lost. But, because I have not yet done enough to defend theistic belief against potential defeaters that have substantial support, I have not reached the position of our hypothetical fortunate person. Innocence has not, so to speak, been regained. Hence, conditions are not now right for propositions like those expressed by (5)–(7) to be, in the narrow sense, properly basic for me. My conjecture is that many, perhaps most, intellectually sophisticated persons in our culture are in an epistemic predicament similar to mine in this respect for most of their adult lives.

There is, of course, nothing wrong with construing the basing relation in some such narrow fashion provided one is tolerably clear about what one is doing. Surely there is such a relation, and Plantinga is free to use it in his theories if he wishes. But I think it may be more perspicuous, or at least equally illuminating, to look at matters in a slightly different way. Consider again our hypothetical fortunate person who has reasons good enough to defend theistic belief against all of its potential defeaters that epistemically nonnegligent, intellectually sophisticated adults in our culture have very substantial reasons to believe. I would say that, for such a person, theistic belief would be based, in a broad sense, on all the reasons that are parts of the person's total case for the rationality of theistic belief. In employing this broad conception of the basing relation, I am aiming to draw attention to the fact that, if the person did not have all those reasons and were like many, perhaps most, intellectually sophisticated adults in our culture, theistic belief would not be rational for the person, or at least its rationality would be diminished to an appreciable extent if some of those reasons were absent. On this broad conception of the basing relation, I would not need to revise the principle concerning the right conditions for certain propositions to be, in the broad sense, properly basic for me, to which I had ascribed initial plausibility, in order to accommodate the hypothetical fortunate person, for the fortunate person's theistic belief would be, in the broad sense, properly based on all the reasons that comprise his or her total case for the rationality of theistic belief. Reasons that are, in the broad sense, part of a basis for theistic belief need not be related to a proposition that self-evidently entails the existence of God in the same way that the premises of an inference are related to its conclusion. They may instead provide part of a basis for theistic belief roughly in the same way a physicist's demonstration that the so-called "clock paradox" does not reveal an inconsistency in special relativity provides part of a basis for special relativity. Or, to cite what may be a more helpful analogy in the present context, they may provide part of a basis for theistic belief in much the same way Richard Swinburne's argument in *The Coherence of Theism* that the claim that God exists is not demonstrably incoherent provides part of the basis for Swinburne's claim in *The Existence of God* that God's existence is more probable than not.[9] And if I am right about the epistemic predicament of many, perhaps most, intellectually sophisticated adult theists in our culture, for them theistic belief stands in need of at least some basis of this kind if it is to be rational. This may, in the end, be a point on which Plantinga and I have a disagreement that is not merely verbal. I would insist, and Plantinga, for all I know, might not, that many, perhaps most, intellectually sophisticated adult theists in

our culture must, if their belief in God is to be rational, have a total case for the rationality of theistic belief that includes defenses against defeaters that have very substantial support.

Conclusion

If theistic belief can be *prima facie* justified by experience at all, then there may be less difference between Plantinga and his opponents than one might at first have thought.[10] Plantinga locates a proper doxastic foundation for theistic belief at the level of propositions like that expressed by (5); a modern foundationalist would wish to claim that there is a subbasement in the truly proper doxastic structure at the level of propositions like that expressed by (10).

Plantinga's view has the advantage of psychological realism. I doubt that most theists generate their doxastic structures by first entertaining and accepting propositions like that expressed by (10) and then inferring from them, together perhaps with some epistemic principles, propositions like that expressed by (5). Nonetheless, I think there is something to be said on behalf of what I take to be an important insight captured by the modern foundationalist's position, though perhaps not perfectly articulated there. Although it may be a mistake to suppose that a phenomenological belief like the one expressed by (10) must always mediate between experience and a belief like the one expressed by (5) in a properly constructed structure of *prima facie* justification for a belief like the one expressed by (5), experience of the sort that could serve to ground a belief like the one expressed by (5) is itself so thoroughly shaped and penetrated by conceptual elements that, if it grounds a belief like the one expressed by (5) directly, then that belief is based on a cognitive state of the believer, even if that state is not an explicit belief with a phenomenological proposition for its object. Perhaps it is at the level of such cognitive states that we may hope to discover the real evidential foundations in experience for theistic belief.[11]

Notes

1. Alvin Plantinga, "Is Belief in God Properly Basic?" *Nous* 15 (1981). Additional discussion related to the charge that modern foundationalism is self-referentially incoherent may be found in Alvin Plantinga, "Is Belief in God Rational?" *Rationality and Religious Belief*, edited by C. F. Delaney (Notre Dame: Univ. of Notre Dame Press, 1979). Material from both these papers has subsequently been incorporated into Alvin Plantinga, "Rationality and Religious Belief," *Contemporary Philosophy of Religion*, edited by Steven M. Cahn and David Shatz (New York: Oxford Univ. Press, 1982). And some of the same themes are further amplified in Alvin Plantinga, "Reason and Belief in God," *Faith and Rationality*, edited by Alvin Plantinga and Nicholas Wolterstorff (Notre Dame: Univ. of Notre Dame Press, 1983).

2. Plantinga, "Is Belief in God Properly Basic?" 49.

3. Ibid., 50.

4. Idem.

5. Ibid., 46.

6. I came to appreciate this point as a result of reflecting on comments by Jonathan Malino and William P. Alston.

7. Plantinga, "Is Belief in God Properly Basic?" 41.

8. In a more thorough treatment, it would be important to worry about the temporal references in this principle. If I have just looked up the spelling of *umbrageous* in my dictionary, then my belief about how that word is spelled may now be based on my belief about what *my* dictionary says. But if I last looked up its spelling many months ago, then my belief about how *umbrageous* is spelled may now only be based on my belief that I seem to remember seeing it spelled that way in *some dictionary or other.* Presumably bases of the sort specified by this principle can and sometimes do shift with time.

9. See Richard Swinburne, *The Coherence of Theism* (Oxford: Clarendon Press, 1977) and Richard Swinburne, *The Existence of God* (Oxford: Clarendon Press, 1979).

10. A recent defense of the view that theistic belief can be *prima facie* justified by experience of certain kinds may be found in William P. Alston, "Religious Experience and Religious Belief," *Nous* 16 (1982).

11. Some of the material in this paper was included in comments on Plantinga's "Is Belief in God Properly Basic?" I read at the 1981 meeting of the Western Division of the American Philosophical Association. Robert Audi was the other commentator on Plantinga's paper. Earlier versions of the present paper were read in 1984 at the Greensboro Symposium on the Logic of Religious Concepts, where Jonathan Malino was my commentator, and at the University of Notre Dame, where Alvin Plantinga was my commentator. In making various revisions, I have profited by the comments of Audi, Malino, and Plantinga and also by written criticism from William P. Alston, Roderick M. Chisholm, George I. Mavrodes, and Ernest Sosa.

VII.D.4   Can Religious Belief Be Rational?

LOUIS POJMAN

In this essay I argue for a thoroughly rationalist conception of faith within a coherentist framework. First I outline an ethics of belief that makes rational believing a duty, and then I explain a person-relative notion of belief using a coherentist model. Rather than view our beliefs in terms of the foundationalist model, in which one belief is supported by more basic beliefs until we get to foundational beliefs for which there is no further evidence, it might be better to see our belief systems in terms of a web or network of beliefs mutually supporting each other. Although some beliefs may be more self-evident than others, few beliefs can be sustained independently of the whole system or large parts of it. Furthermore, there is a certain person-relativeness in every person's noetic structure. Each of us has had a different, complex history of evidence gathering and belief formation, so that intersubjective belief comparison and evaluation becomes difficult. Nevertheless, there are core experiences and criteria of rationality that are common to all humans and that can provide a common measure for attempting to arrive at optimally rational positions.

This is a revised version of an article that will appear soon in a Festschrift for John Macquarrie.

Introduction

In this essay I argue for a thoroughly rationalistic faith. I argue that religious faith has a moral dimension underlying it, so that any faith that is not rational for a person to hold may also be immoral. I outline a notion of an ethics of belief that makes rational believing a *prima facie* moral duty and casts moral censure at leaps of faith beyond the evidence. Then I outline a coherentist strategy for justifying religious belief within the bounds of reason.

Nearly every Christian theologian has demurred from the idea of a wholly rational faith. The Catholic tradition, stemming from Thomas Aquinas, avers that the subset of doctrines, the preambles, are in accordance with reason but that such doctrines as the incarnation and the trinity are beyond its pale. On the other side of the spectrum we have the antirationalists, who believe that the key to religious belief is a miracle of faith "which subverts all the principles of understanding," as Hume skeptically but Hamann and Kierkegaard approvingly put it. (It's a fascinating intellectual anecdote in the history of philosophy that Hamann discovered Hume's dictum and set it forth in his writings as the essence of faith, where it was read by Kierkegaard, who thought Hamann had originated it and applauded him for his brilliant insight.) For Tertullian, Hamann, Kierkegaard, and Shestov the very irrationality of Christianity is reason for embracing it. If God is wholly other, we should expect his truth to seem contradictory to sinful human minds. Modern fideists, following some remarks by Wittgenstein, claim that religious belief is groundless and not subject to rational scrutiny. Somewhere in between these opposing positions is the reformed view (that of Calvin, Warfield, and Bavinck) of natural theology as somehow an irreverent activity. As Barth puts it, to reason about faith is to assume the standpoint of unbelief; it "makes reason a judge over Christ." Most recently, a well-argued version of this position has been developed by Alvin Plantinga, which claims that belief in God may be properly basic to the foundations of one's noetic structure, as justified as our belief that there are other minds

or as any of our immediate empirical or memory beliefs (e.g., the memory belief that I had breakfast this morning).[1]

Although I have learned much from Plantinga and have sympathy for a great deal in his position, especially since he has modified it lately to include the notion that reason could infirm faith's stance, I find two problems with his position, which I have tried to remedy:

(1) The criteria of proper basicality for Plantinga seem so open-ended that virtually any world view, no matter how implausible to thoughtful people, could be justified. Although honest people will certainly differ about what is properly basic, one should suspect or even not fully accept one's own beliefs as basic if they fail to win support from the consensus of rationally informed people or epistemologists as basic or evidential. There are limits to what can count as properly basic, and although exact criteria are hard to come by, not everything can properly be part of the foundations of a noetic structure. As far as I understand the logic of Plantinga's position, there are no epistemically neutral criteria that would eliminate anyone's favorite insane belief. Here his position reminds one of Hare's famous paranoid student who had a *blik* (read "properly basic belief") that all dons were out to harm him.

(2) Secondly, I doubt that theoretical beliefs such as the existence of a divine creator of the universe fit as well into a foundationalist view of epistemology as they do into a coherentist framework. Would we believe in God if the concept had no support at all from our beliefs about the world's having a cause, a design or order, if we didn't have testimony of various encounters with the divine, if there were no claims to miraculous events confirming divine authority? Theistic belief does not stand unsupported, alone and in isolation, but as part and parcel of many other considerations that together helps us make sense of the world. Although a great many of our core beliefs cannot easily be traced back to their origins or justificatory basis, we can still offer considerations for them, showing that they are supported by other beliefs in an all-encompassing network of beliefs. Our noetic structure may well be more in the met-

aphorical shape of a web than in the shape of a house with a foundation. It is the very foundational metaphor that makes Plantinga's views so implausible to some of us.

The Ethics of Belief

First let me state why there are ethical duties to believe according to the best evidence available. Often the beliefs that we have affect the well-being of others. Suppose that you are a physician who is consulted about certain symptoms. You prescribe a drug that you have a hunch will help the patient, but your diagnosis is wrong and the patient dies. When examiners inquire into the situation, they discover that you hadn't kept up on your medicine and that your mistake would have been easily prevented had you been aware of side effects of the drug in question (and had you not misdiagnosed the symptoms). Since you could have had correct beliefs about these matters had you read the latest literature in the area, which was abundantly available, you are rightly judged to be culpably ignorant. You had an obligation to keep up with the literature. At bottom, an ethic of belief may reduce to an ethic of investigation and openness to criticism, but the point is that we are responsible for many of the beliefs that we have and that, as guides to actions, eventually result in action that may harm or help our fellow humans.

Of course, the duty to believe according to the best evidence is not our only moral duty, and perhaps there are times when another duty overrides it, but it is a duty that ought to be taken with the utmost seriousness, more than most thinkers have afforded it. Besides, how confident can we be of our beliefs if we know deep down that they are not backed up by good evidence?

If we apply this to religious belief, we can see that it is also important that we follow the best reasons in forming our belief states. Since the best justified beliefs have the best chance of being true and hence reliable, we should seek to justify even our most personal religious beliefs or doubt them. It would seem that a morally good God who created us as rational would honor doxastic honesty even if it led to unbelief.[2]

Rationality and Conceptual Frameworks

Sometimes it is claimed that we use a clear-cut decision-making process, similar to the one used in mathematics and empirical science, when we arrive at justified belief or truth. A person has a duty to believe exactly according to the available evidence. Hence there is no excuse for anyone to believe anything on insufficient evidence. Such is the case of Descartes and logical positivism, which is echoed in Clifford's classical formula, "It is wrong always, everywhere, and for anyone to believe anything on insufficient evidence." Laying aside the criticism that the statement itself is self-referentially incoherent (it doesn't give us sufficient evidence for believing itself), the problem is that different data will count as evidence to different degrees according to the background beliefs a person has. The contribution of Polanyi, Popper, and Wittgenstein has been to demonstrate the power of perspectivism, the thesis that the way we evaluate or even pick out evidence is determined by our prior picture of the world, which itself is made up of a loosely connected and mutually supporting network of propositions. Do the farmer, the real estate dealer, and the landscape artist on looking at a field see the same field?

The nonperspectivist position, seen in Plato, Aquinas, Descartes, Locke, Clifford, and Chisholm, seems damaged beyond repair. However, the reaction has been to claim that since what is basic is the conceptual (fiduciary) framework, no interchange between world views is possible. As Karl Barth says, "Belief can only preach to unbelief." No argument is possible. We may call this reaction to the postcritical critique of rationalism "hard-perspectivism."

The nonperspectivist writes as though arriving at the truth were a matter of impartial evaluation of the evidence, and the hard-perspectivist writes as though no meaningful communication were possible. The world views (*Weltanschauungen*) are discontinuous. As fideists often say, "The believer and unbeliever live in different worlds."[3] There is an infinite qualitative distinction existing between various forms of life that no amount of argument or discussion can bridge. For hard-perspectivists, including Wittgensteinian fideists, reason can only have intramural significance. There are no bridges between world views.

However, hard-perspectivism is not the only possible reaction to the postcritical revolution. One may accept the insight that our manner of evaluating evidence is strongly affected by our conceptual frameworks without opting for a view that precludes communication across world views. One may recognize the depth of a conceptual framework and still maintain that communication between frameworks is possible and that reason may have an intermural as well as intramural significance in the process. Such a view has been called soft-perspectivist. The soft-perspectivist is under no illusion regarding the difficulty of effecting a massive shift in the total evaluation of an immense range of data, of producing new patterns of feeling and acting in persons, but he or she is confident that the program is viable. One of the reasons given in support of this is that there is something like a core rationality common to every human culture, especially with regard to practical life. Certain rules of inference (deductive and inductive) have virtually universal application. Certain assumptions (basic beliefs) seem common to every culture (e.g., that there are other minds, that there is time, that things move, that perceptions are generally to be trusted, and so on). Through sympathetic imagination one can attain some understanding of another's conceptual system; through disappointment one can begin to suspect weakness in one's own world view and thus seek for a more adequate explanation. It is not my purpose here to produce a full defense of a soft-perspective position, but only to indicate its plausibility. The assumption on which this essay is written is that the case for soft-perspectivism can be made. And if it is true, then it is possible for reason to play a significant role in the examination, revi-

sion, and rejection of one's current beliefs and in the acquisition of new beliefs.

Does Rationality Imply a Neutrality That Is Incompatible with Religious Faith?

We may say that postcritical rationalists of the soft-perspectivist variety are individuals who seek to support all their beliefs (especially their convictions)[4] with good reasons. They attempt to evaluate the evidence as impartially as possible, to accept the challenge of answering criticisms, and to remain open to the possibility that they might be wrong and may need to revise, reexamine, or reject any one of their beliefs (at least those not involving broadly logical necessity). This character description of the rationalist is often interpreted to mean that rationalists must be neutral and detached with regard to their beliefs.[5] This is a mistake. It is a confusion between *impartiality* and *neutrality*. Both concepts imply conflict situations (e.g., war, a competitive sport, a legal trial, an argument), but to be neutral signifies not taking sides, doing nothing to influence the outcome, remaining passive in the fray; whereas impartiality *involves* one in the conflict in that it calls for a judgment in favor of the party that is right. To the extent that one party is right or wrong (measured by objective criteria) neutrality and impartiality are incompatible concepts. To be neutral is to detach oneself from the struggle; to be impartial (rational) is to commit oneself to a position—though not partially (i.e., unfairly or arbitrarily) but in accordance with an objective standard. The model of the neutral person is an atheist who is indifferent about football watching a game between Notre Dame and Southern Methodist. The model of the partial or prejudiced person is the coach who, on any given dispute, predictably judges his team to be in the right and the other to be in the wrong and for whom it is an axiom that any judgment by a referee against his team is, at best, of dubious merit. The model of the impartial person is the referee in the game, who, knowing that his wife has just bet their life savings on the underdog, Southern Methodist, still manages to call what any reasonable spectator would judge to be a fair game. He does not let his wants or self-interest enter into the judgment he makes.

To be rational does not lessen the passion involved in religious beliefs. Rational believers, who believe that they have good grounds for believing that a perfect being exists, are not less likely to trust that being absolutely than believers who do not think that they have reasons. Likewise, persons who live in hope of God's existence may be as passionate about their commitment as persons who entertain no doubts. In fact the rational hoper or believer will probably judge it to be irrational not to be absolutely committed to such a being. Hence the charge leveled against the rationalist by Kierkegaard and others that rational inquiry cools the passions seems unfounded.

However, nonrationalists have a slightly different but related argument at hand. They may argue that if there were sufficient evidence available, it might be the case that one might be both religious and rational. But there is not sufficient evidence; hence the very search for evidence simply detracts believers from worship and passionate service, leading them on a wild-goose chase for evidence that does not exist. The believer is involved in cool calculation instead of passionate commitment, questioning instead of obeying.

There are at least two responses to this charge. First of all, how does the nonrationalist know that there is not sufficient evidence for a religious claim? How does the nonrationalist know that not merely a demonstrative proof but even a cumulative case with some force is impossible? It would seem reasonable to expect that a good God would not leave his creatures wholly in the dark about so important a matter. The nonrationalist's answer (that of Calvin and Kierkegaard, and suggested by Plantinga) that sin has destroyed the use of reason or our ability to see God seem unduly ad hoc and inadequate. It would seem that little children in nontheistic cultures should manifest some theistic tendencies on this view, for which there is no evidence. Second, why cannot the search for truth itself be a way of worshipping God? A passionate

act of service? Again one would expect the possession of well-founded beliefs to be God's will for us. Is the person who in doubt prays, "God, if you exist, please show me better evidence," any less passionate a worshipper than the person who worships without doubts?

A word is in order about the relation of the emotions and passions to religious belief. The claims of a religion cannot but move a person. Anyone who does not see the importance of its claims either does not have a sense of selfhood or does not understand what is being said, for a religion claims to explain who and why one is and what one can expect to become. It claims to make sense out of the world. For example, to entertain the proposition that a personal, loving Creator exists is to entertain a proposition whose implications affect every part of a person's understanding of self and world. If the proposition is true, the world is personal rather than mechanistic, friendly rather than strange, purposeful rather than simply a vortex of chance and necessity. If it is not true, a different set of entailments follow that are likely to lead to different patterns of feeling and action. If Judeo-Christian theism is accepted, the believer has an additional reason for being a moral person, for treating fellow humans with equal respect. It is because God has created all persons in his image, as infinitely precious, destined to enjoy his fellowship forever. Theism can provide a more adequate metaphysical basis for morality. Hence it can be both descriptively and prescriptively significant.

Towards a Theory of Rationality

It is often said that rational persons tailor the strength of their beliefs to the strength of the evidence. The trouble with this remark is that it is notoriously difficult to give sense to any discussion of discovering objective criteria for what is to count as evidence and to what extent it is to count. One of my criticisms of Swinburne's usually perceptive work is that he tries to apply the concept of probabilities to world views, as though we somehow could identify evidential wholes without comparing them to other outcomes.

Deciding *what* is to count as evidence for something else in part depends on a whole network of other considerations, and deciding *to what extent* something is to count as evidence involves weighing procedures that are subjective. Two judges may have the same evidence before them and come to different verdicts. Two equally rational persons may have the same evidence about the claims of a religion and still arrive at different conclusions in the matter. It would seem that the prescription to tailor one's beliefs according to the evidence is either empty or a shorthand for something more complex. I think that it is the latter. Let me illustrate what I think it signifies.

Consider any situation in which our self-interest may conflict with the truth. Take the case of three German wives who are suddenly confronted with evidence that their husbands have been unfaithful. Their surnames are Uberglaubig, Misstrauisch, and Wahrnehmen. Each is disturbed about the evidence and makes further inquiries. Mrs. Uberglaubig is soon finished and finds herself rejecting all the evidence, maintaining resolutely her husband's fidelity. Others, even relatives of Mr. Uberglaubig, are surprised by her credulity, for the evidence against Mr. Uberglaubig is the sort that would lead most people to conclude that he was unfaithful. No matter how much evidence is adduced, Mrs. Uberglaubig is unchanged in her judgment. She seems to have a fixation about her husband's fidelity. Mrs. Misstrauisch seems to suffer from an opposite weakness. If Mrs. Uberglaubig overbelieves, she seems to underbelieve. She suspects the worst and even though others who know Mr. Misstrauisch deem the evidence against him weak (especially in comparison to the evidence presented against Mr. Uberglaubig), she is convinced that her husband is unfaithful. No evidence seems to be sufficient to reassure her. It is as though the very suggestion of infidelity were enough to stir up doubts and disbelief. Mrs. Wahrnehmen also considers the evidence, which is considerable, and comes to a judgment, though with some reservations. Suppose she finds herself believing that her husband is faithful. Others may differ in their assessment of the situation, but Mrs. Wahrnehmen is

willing and able to discuss the matter, gives her grounds, and considers the objections of others. Perhaps we can say that she is more self-aware, more self-controlled, and more self-secure than the other women. She seems to have the capacity to separate her judgment from her hopes, wants, and fears in a way that the other two women do not.

This should provide some clue to what it means to be rational. It does not necessarily mean having true beliefs (though we would say that rationality tends toward truth), for it might just turn out that by luck Mr. Wahrnehmen is indeed an adulterer and Mr. Uberglaubig innocent. Still, we would want to say that Mrs. Wahrnehmen was justified in her beliefs but Mrs. Uberglaubig was not.

What does characterize rational judgment are two properties, one being *intentional* and the other being *capacity-behavioral*. First, rationality involves an intention to seek the truth or the possession of a high regard for the truth, especially when there may be a conflict between it and one's wishes. It involves a healthy abhorrence of being deceived combined with a parallel desire to have knowledge in matters vital to one's life. Mrs. Wahrnehmen and Mrs. Misstrauisch care about the truth in a way that Mrs. Uberglaubig does not. But secondly, it involves a skill or behavioral capacity to judge impartially, to examine the evidence objectively, to know what sort of things count in coming to a considered judgment. It is as though Mrs. Wahrnehmen alone were able to see clearly through the fog of emotion and self-interest, focusing on some ideal standard of evidence. Of course, there is no such simple standard of evidence, any more than there is for the art critic in making a judgment on the authenticity of a work of art. Still, the metaphor of the ideal standard may be useful. It draws attention to the objective feature in rational judgment, a feature that is internalized in the person of the expert. Like learning to discriminate between works of art or with regard to criminal evidence, rationality is a learned trait that calls for a long apprenticeship (a lifetime?) under the cooperative tutelage of other rational persons. Some people with little formal education seem to learn this better than some "well-educated" people, but despite this uncomfortable observation, I would like to believe that it is the job of education to train people to judge impartially over a broad range of human experience.

As a skill combined with an intention, rationality may seem to be in a shaky situation. How do we decide who has the skill or who has the right combination of traits? There is no certain way, but judge we must in this life, and the basis of our judgment will be manifestations of behavior that we classify as truth directed, noticing that persons with this skill seek out evidence and pay attention to criticism and counterclaims, that they usually support their judgment with recognizable good reasons, that they revise and reject their beliefs in the light of new information. These criteria are not foolproof, and it seems impossible to give an exact account of the process involved in rational decision or belief, but this seems to be the case with any skill. In the end rationality seems more like a set of trained intuitions than anything else.

Let us carry our story a little further. Suppose now Mrs. Wahrnehmen receives some new information to the effect that her husband has been unfaithful. Suppose it becomes known to others who were previously convinced by her arguments acquiting her husband, and suppose that the new evidence infirms many of those arguments, so that the third parties now come to believe that Mr. Wahrnehmen is an adulterer. Should Mrs. Wahrnehmen give up her belief? Perhaps not. At least, it may not be a good thing to give it up at once. If she has worked out a theory to account for a great many of her husband's actions, she might better cling to her theory and work out some ad hoc hypotheses to account for this evidence. This principle of clinging to one's theory in spite of adverse evidence is what Peirce debunkingly and Lakatos approvingly call the principle of tenacity.[6] It receives special attention in Lakatos's treatment of a progressive research program. In science, theoretical change often comes as a result of persevering with a rather vaguely formulated hypothesis (a core hypothesis), which the researcher will hold on to in spite of a good many setbacks. Scientists

must be ready to persevere (at least for a time) even in the face of their own doubts and their recognition of the validity of their opponents' objections. If maximum fruitfulness of the experiment is to be attained, it must endure through many modifications as new evidence comes in. As Basil Mitchell has pointed out, a scientific thesis is like a growing infant, which "could be killed by premature antisepsis." The biographies of eminent scientists and scholars are replete with instances of going it alone in the face of massive intellectual opposition and finally overturning a general verdict. Hence researchers cushion the core hypothesis against the blows and shocks that might otherwise force them to give it up. They invent ad hoc explanations in the hope of saving the core hypothesis. They surround the core hypothesis with a battery of such hypotheses, and as the ad hoc hypotheses fall, they invent new ones. Mitchell compares this process to a criminal network, in which the mastermind (core hypothesis) always manages to escape detection and punishment "by sacrificing some of his less essential underlings, unless or until the final day of reckoning comes and his entire empire collapses."[7]

Admittedly, each ad hoc hypothesis weakens the system, but the core hypothesis may nevertheless turn out to approximate a true or adequate theory. But the more ad hoc hypotheses it becomes necessary to invent, the less plausibility attaches to the core hypothesis, until the time comes when the researcher is forced to give up the core hypothesis and conclude that the whole project has outlived its usefulness. In Lakatos's words, it has become a "degenerative research project."[8] No one can say exactly when that time comes in a particular project, but every experimental scientist fears it and, meanwhile, lives in hope that the current project will bear fruit.

Let us apply this paradigm to rational religious believers. Once they find themselves with a deep conviction, they have a precedent or model in science for clinging to it tenaciously, experimenting with it, drawing out all its implications, and surrounding it with tentative ad hoc or auxilliary explanations in order to cushion it from premature antisepsis. Nevertheless, if the analogy with the scientist holds, they must recognize that the time may come when they are forced to abandon their conviction because of the enormous accumulation of counterevidence. Such rational persons probably cannot say exactly when and how this might happen, and they do not expect it to happen, but they acknowledge the possibility of its happening. There is no clear decision procedure that tells us when we have crossed over the fine line between plausibility and implausibility, but suddenly the realization hits us that we now disbelieve theory *A* and believe theory *B,* whereas up to this point the reverse was true. Conversions or paradigm switches occur every day in the minds of both the highly rational and the less rational. There is also a middle zone where a person considering two seemingly incompatible explanatory theories can find something plausible in each of them, so that the person cannot be said to believe either one. Still, such individuals may place their hope in one theory and live by it in an experimental faith, keeping themselves open to new evidence and maintaining the dialogue with those who differ so as not to slip into a state of self-deception. The whole matter of double vision and experimental faith is quite complicated, but often we can see the world in more than one way and yet find our moral bearings. What I want to emphasize is the Kierkegaardian point (used in an un-Kierkegaardian manner) that more important than *what* one believes is the manner in which one believes, the *how* of believing, the openness of mind, the willingness to discuss the reasons for one's belief, the carefulness of one's examination of new and conflicting evidence, one's commitment to follow the argument and not simply one's emotions, one's training as a rational person that enables one to recognize what is to count as a good argument.

This leads me to say a few things about the role and mode of argument in rationality. One of the problems that has plagued discussion in philosophy of religion through the ages is that the way philosophers have written has implied that unless one had a deductive proof for a religious thesis, one had no justification for it. The result of this narrow view of argument in religious matters has

pushed those who believe in religion to the point of conceding too much, that is, that religion is not rational. This is one of the main reasons for the incommensurabilist position. I think that this is a mistake. Our concept of argument must be broadened from mere deductive and strict inductive argument to include non–rule-governed judgments. What I have in mind is the sort of intuitive judgment illustrated by the art critic in assessing an authentic work of art, the chicken sexer in identifying the sex of the baby chicks without knowing or being able to tell us how he knows the chick's sexual identity, or the water diviner in discovering underground springs without knowing how he does so. Another example of non–rule-governed reasoning is a child's invention of new sentences. The child follows rules, which seem to be programed into her, but she does not do it consciously and cannot tell us what the rules are. Later, however, she may be able to do so.

Perhaps even more typical of everyday non–rule-governed reasoning is the process whereby judges or juries make judgments when the evidence is ambiguous or there is considerable evidence on both sides of an issue. In weighing pros and cons and assessing conflicting evidence, the judge or jury does not normally go through standard logical procedures to arrive at a verdict. They rely on intangible and intuitive weighing procedures. It is hard to see how the deductive and strict inductive schemes of argument can account for our judgments when we have good reasons for and against a conclusion. Nor is it easy to see how deductive and strict inductive reasoning account for the decisions experts make in distinguishing the valuable from the mediocre. They cannot formalize their judgment, and we may not be able to offer an account of it, but we would still recognize it as valid and importantly rational. Perhaps we ought generally to aim at formalizing our judgments as carefully as possible, using the traditional forms of reasoning, but it is not always necessary or possible to do this. We can be said to be rational because we typically arrive at decisions and judgments that other rational creatures would regard as a fair estimation of the evidence (this excuses the occasional idiosyncratic judgment); because we attempt to face the challenge of our opponent with the grounds of our beliefs; and because we are honest about the deficiencies of our positions. It is a whole family of considerations that leads us to an overall conclusion about whether another person is rational and not simply whether or not the person is able to provide sound deductive or inductive arguments. Of course, induction plays a strong role in our relying on another's judgments. It is because we have generally found that people of this sort usually make reliable judgments in cases of such-and-such a type that we are ready to take their intuitions as credible.

A great deal more needs to be said about non–rule-governed judgments, but this discussion at least shows that something broader than the standard moves is needed in an account of rational argument. There is a need to recognize the important role that intuition plays in reasoning itself or, at least, in the reasoning of the trained person. This is what the Greeks called *phronesis* ("wise insight") and *ortho logos* ("correct thinking"), and it should be given greater emphasis in modern philosophy.

Is a Rational Account of Religion Compatible with the Biblical Picture of Faith?

Let me turn finally to the important objection that the position that I have outlined distorts the biblical notion of faith. Biblical faith is, the critic affirms, believing against or without sufficient evidence. As Hick points out, there is little deductive reasoning in the Scriptures, but the Holy of Holies is taken as the starting point of all thinking.[9]

But the claim that this is the sole meaning of faith in the Bible seems an unwarranted generalization. Actually, several different but related concepts of faith are found in the Bible, including loyalty, trust, fear, and obedience, as well as propositional belief. What we have called rational faith seems duly accounted for in the miracles and prophecy of the Bible, especially the Old Testament, which in part serve as evidence for the He-

brew faith. When Elijah, in 1 Kings 18, competes with the priests of Baal on Mt. Carmel to determine which god is more powerful, we are given a concrete scientific testing of competing hypotheses. When John the Baptist's disciples come to ask Jesus if he is the Messiah, Jesus does not rebuke them for seeking grounds for their beliefs but immediately "cures many diseases and plagues and evil spirits" and opens the eyes of the blind; only after this does he answer them, "Go and tell John what you have seen and heard: the blind receive their sight, the lame walk, lepers are cleansed, and the deaf hear, the dead are raised up, the poor have the good news preached to them" (Luke 7:20–22). When Jesus does chide his disciples for unbelief it seems to be for good reasons. "Don't you remember what the Scriptures demand? Don't you trust me in spite of my being with you so long and having proved my reliability over and over?" What the Scriptures deny is *sight*. We cannot see God directly and live, for there is another dimension to his reality, but we can see him *indirectly* through his works (Rom. 1:20f). When Thomas doubts good evidence (viz., the witness of his fellow disciples and the words of Jesus' prophecy), he is given evidence, the point being not that evidence is contrary to faith but that dependence on too much outward evidence may get in the way of inward discernment. There is just enough evidence to satisfy a person passionately concerned but not enough to produce a comfortable proof.

Usually, nonrationalists make their point about the antipathy between faith and reason in the Bible by pointing to Abraham's reliance on God even to the point of being willing to kill his son, Isaac. Abraham, the father of faith, is put forth as the paradigm of believing against all evidence. As Kierkegaard puts it, "Abraham believed by virtue of the absurd," despite the impossibility of the promise to give him a son when he was old or to bring him back after he was sacrificed. He believed God would somehow bring it about that Isaac would live in spite of the fact that he was going to kill him. The reader will recall the story. God tells Abraham to go to Mt. Moriah and sacrifice Isaac in order to prove his love for God. Abraham proceeds to carry out the command, but at the last moment an angel stops him, showing him a lamb in the thicket to be used for the offering. The story of Abraham and Isaac has usually been taken as the height of religious faith: believing God when it really affects one's deepest earthly commitments. It is taken to prove that faith is irrational, that faith involves believing against all standards of rationality.

Of course, many Old Testament scholars dismiss the literalness of the story and interpret it within the context of Middle Eastern child sacrifice. The story, according to these scholars, provides the pictorial grounds for breaking with the custom. But even leaving aside this plausible explanation, we might contend that Abraham's action can be seen as rational given his noetic framework. One can imagine him replying to a friendly skeptic years after the incident in the following manner:

I heard a voice. It was the same voice (or so I believed) that commanded me years before to leave my country, my kindred, and my father's house to venture forth into the unknown. It was the same voice that promised me that I would prosper. I hearkened, and though the evidence seemed weak, the promise was fulfilled. It was the same voice that promised me a son in my old age and Sarah's old age, when childbearing was thought to be impossible. Yet it happened. My trust was vindicated. My whole existence has been predicated on the reality of that voice. I already became an exception by hearkening unto it the first time. I have never regretted it. This last call was in a tone similar to the other calls. The voice was unmistakable. To deny its authenticity would be to deny the authenticity of the others. In doing so, I should be admitting that my whole life has been founded on an illusion. But I don't believe that it has, and I prefer to take the risk of obeying what I take to be the voice of God and disobey certain norms than to obey the norms and miss the possibility of any absolute relation to the Absolute. And what's more,

I'm ready to recommend that all people who feel so called by a higher power do exactly as I have done.

It seems to me that even if we accept the story of Abraham's offering his son as a sacrifice at face value, we can give it an interpretation not inconsistent with the commensurabilist's position. Abraham has had inductive evidence that following the voice is the best way to live. We can generalize the principle on which Abraham acted to be as follows:

If one acts on a type of intuition I in an area of experience E, over a period of time t and with remarkable success, and no other information is relevant or overriding, one can be said to have good reason for following that intuition (I_n, an instance of type I) the next time it presents itself in an E-type situation.

Given the cultural context of Abraham's life, his actions seem amenable to a rationalist account. Of course, what this shows is that given enough background data, almost any proposition could be considered *rational* for an individual believer. Irrationality would occur if Abraham neglected counterevidence at his disposal.

My point in all this has not been to prove that the Bible contains a fully developed philosophy of faith and reason but simply to indicate that it seems far closer to the commensurabilist's position than the fideist might imagine. My impression is that the Scriptures pay a great deal of attention to evidence, acts of deliverance, and the testimony of the saints and prophets who hear God's voice and sometimes even get a vision of his splendor.

Let me end this article on a conciliatory note. I can appreciate the criticism of someone who feels that my approach overemphasizes the rational and intellectual aspects of believing at the expense of the emotional and volitional aspects, the feelings of divine presence and inner certainty and devotion. I do not want to deny the importance of these feelings. My point has been simply that they are compatible with a rationalist perspective. Further thought on the matter may reveal that my approach to religion as an experimental faith in a viable hypothesis fails to get at the heart of religious commitment. But even so, the general quest for justification may not be inappropriate. Complex as religious phenomena are, profound as the feelings are, at some point religious experience needs to be scrutinized honestly and carefully by the believer him- or herself. When Barth and Bultmann protest that God does not need to justify himself before man, the proper response is to echo Karl Jasper's reply to Bultmann: "I do not say that God has to justify himself, but that everything that appears in the world and claims to be God's word, God's act, God's revelation, has to justify itself."[10] This outline of a commensurabilist position with regard to religious belief is intended as a small step in doing just that.

Notes

1. The most complete version of Plantinga's views is his essay "Reason and Belief in God," in *Faith and Rationality*, edited by Alvin Plantinga and Nicholas Wolterstorff (Notre Dame: Univ. of Notre Dame Press, 1983).

2. See my book, *Religious Belief and the Will* (London: Routledge & Kegan Paul, forthcoming), part 2, chap. 2.

3. Alvin Plantinga suggests that the believer and the unbeliever have different conceptions of reason. Op. cit., 91.

4. I follow McClendon and Smith's definition of *conviction* here as "a persistent belief such that if *X* has a conviction, it will not be easily relinquished without making *X* a significantly different person than before." James McClendon and James Smith, *Understanding Religious Convictions* (Notre Dame: Univ. of Notre Dame Press, 1975), 7.

5. Even McClendon and Smith make this mistake in their usually reliable work. Ibid., 108.

6. Basil Mitchell, "Faith and Reason: A False Antithesis?" *Religious Studies* 16 (June 1980); I. Lakatos, "Falsification and Methodology of Scientific Research Programs," in *Criticism and the Growth of Knowledge*, edited by I. Lakatos and A. Musgrave (Cambridge: Cambridge Univ. Press, 1970) 91–196.

7. Mitchell, op. cit.

8. Lakatos, op. cit., 118.

9. John Hick, *Arguments for the Existence of God* (New York: Macmillan, 1971), chap. 7.

10. Quoted in John Macquarrie, *Twentieth Century Religious Thought* (New York: Harper & Row, 1966), 334.

Bibliography for Part VII

Crosson, Frederick, ed. *The Autonomy of Religious Belief.* Notre Dame: Univ. of Notre Dame Press, 1981. A valuable set of articles on fideism, especially those of Phillips and Nielsen.

Delaney, C. F., ed. *Rationality and Religious Belief.* Notre Dame: Univ. of Notre Dame Press, 1978. A good collection of essays on faith and reason.

Flew, Antony. *The Presumption of Atheism.* New York: Harper & Row, 1976. Part 1, chapters 1, 2, and 5 are relevant to the discussion.

Kellenberger, J. *Religious Discovery, Faith and Knowledge.* Englewood Cliffs, N.J.: Prentice-Hall, 1972. A lucid defense of a moderate fideist position.

Mackie, J. L. *The Miracle of Theism: Arguments for and against the Existence of God.* Oxford: Clarendon Press, 1982. Probably the best defense of atheism in recent years, taking into consideration every major argument in the field.

Mavrodes, George. *Belief in God.* New York: Random House, 1970. A clear presentation of religious epistemology.

Mitchell, Basil. *The Justification of Religious Belief.* London: Macmillan, 1973. A good discussion of the cumulative case for theism.

Phillips, D. Z. *Religion without Explanation.* Oxford: Basil Blackwell, 1976. A valuable study by one of the foremost Wittgensteinian philosophers.

Swinburne, Richard. *Faith and Reason.* Oxford: Clarendon Press, 1981. One of the best studies of the subject in recent years.

PART VIII

RELIGION AND ETHICS

In examining the relationship of religion to ethics, we find two problems, which are indicated by the following questions: (1) Does morality depend on religion? and (2) Are religious ethics essentially different from secular ethics? These questions are related, but they are not the same. Unlike many religions of the ancient world, Judaism and Christianity are ethical monotheisms. They not only promise salvation to the faithful but tie ethical responsibility into the matrix of salvation in a very close way, by making the moral life either a necessary condition for God's favor or a consequence of it.

The question is whether moral standards themselves depend on God for their validity or whether there is an autonomy of ethics so that even God is subject to the moral order. As Socrates asks in our first reading, taken from the *Euthyphro*, "Do the gods love holiness because it is holy, or is it holy because the gods love it?" According to one theory, called the divine command theory, ethical principles are simply the commands of God. They derive their validity from God's commanding them, and they *mean* 'commanded by God'. Without God, there would be no universally valid morality. As Dostoevsky wrote in *The Brothers Karamazov*, "If God doesn't exist, everything is permissible." Many interpret the writings of Nietzsche as representing such a nihilistic ethics, a world view in which there is no God (or in which he is "dead," irrelevant to life).

The opposing viewpoint is that ethical values are autonomous and that even God must keep the moral law, which exists independently of him—as logical laws do. God, of course, *knows* what is right—better than we do— but in principle we act morally for the same reasons that God does. We both follow moral reasons that are independent of God. If there is no God, on this account, nothing is changed. Morality is left intact, and if we choose to be moral, we have the very same duties we would have as theists. This point of view is presented by Jonathan Harrison in our readings.

The motivation for the divine command theory is to preserve or do justice to the omnipotence or sovereignty of God. God somehow is thought to be less sovereign or necessary to our lives if he is not the source of morality. When the believer asks what the will of God is, it is a direct appeal to a personal will, not to an independently existing rule.

One problem with the divine command theory is that it would seem to make the attribution of 'goodness' to God redundant. When we say 'God is good', we think that we are stating a property to God, but if 'good' simply meant 'what God commands or wills', then we are not attributing any property to God. Our statement merely means 'God wills what God wills', which is a tautology. A second problem is that if God's arbitrary fiat (in the sense of not being based on reasons) is the sole arbiter of right and wrong, it would seem to be logically possible for such "heinous" acts as rape, killing of the innocent for the fun of it, and gratuitous cruelty to become morally good actions—if God suddenly decided to command us to do these things. But then, wouldn't morality be reduced to the right of the powerful, Nietzsche's 'might makes right'? This argument is developed by Jonathan Harrison. Baruch A. Brody and Robert Merrihew Adams respond to this criticism in their contributions, trying to neutralize its force.

The second problem in the relationship between religion and morality is the degree to which religious morality and nonreligious morality are in *content* and *form* similar to each other. According to Kant, who held to the autonomy of ethics, there could be no difference between valid religious ethics and valid philosophical ethics. God and humanity each have to obey the same rational principles, and reason is sufficient to guide us to these principles. But some utilitarians, such as Patrick Nowell-Smith in our readings, have argued that religious ethics are essentially deontological (based on rules without decisive regard for consequences), whereas secular ethics, at their best, are teleological, based on what will produce the best overall consequences. Nowell-Smith argues that this shows the superiority of secular ethics over religious ethics, but Brody and Adams, who agree that religious ethics are in fact different from secular ethics, contend that a position like Nowell-Smith's is too simple and that religious ethics add something rich and vital to the moral life.

Brody argues that we have a special relation to God as our creator that entails certain rights on his part towards all of his creation, including us, and certain obligations on our part towards God. In this sense, morality is based on divine commands but in such a way as to avoid any arbitrariness on the part of God. Brody uses the injunction against suicide to illustrate how a religious morality generates different principles than a purely secular morality does.

Adams attempts to meet the standard criticisms against the divine command theory by modifying it so as to take into account the nature of God as loving. Although it is not logically impossible for God to command us to do what is gratuitously cruel, he would not do so because of his love.

The question is, Does this move, which makes love a necessary property of God, undermine Adams's thesis? The opponent might argue as follows: Instead of saying that God must prohibit gratuitous cruelty because it is evil, Adams suggests that God must prohibit it because it is unloving. But does this not still refer to a standard outside of God, that is, the standard of love?

And does not the notion of love simply replace the notion of an external moral order as the meter against which even God's commands must be judged?

Finally, Adams's essay contains a valuable section detailing the ways in which secular and religious morality are different and the ways in which they are similar.

VIII.1   Morality and Religion

P L A T O

We have already encountered the writings of Plato (427–347 BC) in our readings on immortality. Here we see his mentor, Socrates, engaged in a dialogue with the self-righteously religious Euthyphro, who is going to court to report his father for having killed a slave. In the course of the discussion Socrates raises the question that is known as the question of the divine command theory of ethics: Is the good good because God loves it, or does God love the good because it is good?

Socrates. But shall we . . . say that whatever all the gods hate is unholy, and whatever they all love is holy: while whatever some of them love, and others hate, is either both or neither? Do you wish us now to define holiness and unholiness in this manner?

Euthyphro. Why not, Socrates?

Socr. There is no reason why I should not, Euthyphro. It is for you to consider whether that definition will help you to instruct me as you promised.

Euth. Well, I should say that holiness is what all the gods love, and that unholiness is what they all hate.

Socr. Are we to examine this definition, Euthyphro, and see if it is a good one? Or are we to be content to accept the bare assertions of other men, or of ourselves, without asking any questions? Or must we examine the assertions?

Euth. We must examine them. But for my part I think that the definition is right this time.

Socr. We shall know that better in a little while, my good friend. Now consider this question. Do the gods love holiness because it is holy, or is it holy because they love it?

Euth. I do not understand you, Socrates.

Socr. I will try to explain myself: we speak of a thing being carried and carrying, and begin led and leading, and being seen and seeing; and you understand that all such expressions mean different things, and what the difference is.

Euth. Yes, I think I understand.

Socr. And we talk of a thing being loved, and, which is different, of a thing loving?

Euth. Of course.

Socr. Now tell me: is a thing which is being carried in a state of being carried, because it is carried, or for some other reason?

Euth. No, because it is carried.

Socr. And a thing is in a state of being led, because it is led, and of being seen, because it is seen?

Euth. Certainly.

Socr. Then a thing is not seen because it is in a state of being seen; it is in a state of being seen because it is seen: and a thing is not led because it is in a state of being led; it is in a state of being led because it is led: and a thing is not carried because it is in a state of being carried; it is in a state of being carried because it is carried. Is my meaning clear now, Euthyphro? I mean this: if anything becomes, or is affected, it does not become because it is in a state of becoming; it is in a state of becoming because it becomes; and it is not affected because it is in a state of being affected: it is in a state of being affected because it is affected. Do you not agree?

Euth. I do.

Socr. Is not that which is being loved in a state, either of becoming, or of being affected in some way by something?

Euth. Certainly.

Socr. Then the same is true here as in the former cases. A thing is not loved by those who love it because it is in a state of being loved. It is in a state of being loved because they love it.

Reprinted from the *Euthyphro,* translated by William Jowett (New York: Charles Scribner's Sons, 1889).

Euth. Necessarily.

Socr. Well, then, Euthyphro, what do we say about holiness? Is it not loved by all the gods, according to your definition?

Euth. Yes.

Socr. Because it is holy, or for some other reason?

Euth. No, because it is holy.

Socr. Then it is loved by the gods because it is holy: it is not holy because it is loved by them?

Euth. It seems so.

Socr. But then what is pleasing to the gods is pleasing to them, and is in a state of being loved by them, because they love it?

Euth. Of course.

Socr. Then holiness is not what is pleasing to the gods, and what is pleasing to the gods is not holy, as you say, Euthyphro. They are different things.

Euth. And why, Socrates?

Socr. Because we are agreed that the gods love holiness because it is holy: and that it is not holy because they love it. Is not this so?

Euth. Yes.

Socr. And that what is pleasing to the gods because they love it, is pleasing to them by reason of this same love: and that they do not love it because it is pleasing to them.

Euth. True.

Socr. Then, my dear Euthyphro, holiness, and what is pleasing to the gods, are different things. If the gods had loved holiness because it is holy, they would also have loved what is pleasing to them because it is pleasing to them; but if what is pleasing to them had been pleasing to them because they loved it, then holiness too would have been holiness, because they loved it. But now you see that they are opposite things, and wholly different from each other. For the one is of a sort to be loved because it is loved: while the other is loved, because it is of a sort to be loved. My question, Euthyphro, was, What is holiness? But it turns out that you have not explained to me the essence of holiness; you have been content to mention an attribute which belongs to it, namely, that all the gods love it. You have not yet told me what is its essence. Do not, if you please, keep from me what holiness is; begin again and tell me that. Never mind whether the gods love it, or whether it has other attributes: we shall not differ on that point. Do your best to make it clear to me what is holiness and what is unholiness.

VIII.2 Morality: Religious and Secular

PATRICK NOWELL-SMITH

Patrick Nowell-Smith is a British philosopher who teaches at York University in Canada. He is a utilitarian—that is, he believes that ethics ought to maximize the welfare of society or happiness in it. He argues in this section that religious ethics are essentially deontological (based on rules without decisive regard for consequences), whereas secular ethics, at their best (viz., utilitarianism), are teleological and aim at producing the best overall consequences. Nowell-Smith argues that this shows the superiority of secular ethics over religious ethics.

Reprinted from "Morality: Religious and Secular," in *The Rationalist Annual*, 1961 (London: Pemberton Publishing Co., 1961) by permission of the author.

The central thesis of this paper is that religious morality is infantile. I am well aware that this will sound absurd. To suggest that Aquinas and Kant—to say nothing of millions of Christians of lesser genius—never grew up is surely to put oneself out of court as a philosopher to be taken seriously. My thesis is not so crude as that; I shall try to show that, in the moralities of adult Christians, there are elements which can be set apart from the rest and are, indeed, inconsistent with them, that these elements can properly be called "religious" and that just these elements are infantile.

I shall start by making some assumptions that I take to be common ground between Christians and secular humanists. I propose to say almost nothing about the *content* of morality; that love, sympathy, loyalty, and consideration are virtues, and that their opposites, malice, cruelty, treachery, and callousness, are vices, are propositions that I shall assume without proof. One can't do everything at the same time, and my job now is not to refute Thrasymachus. Secondly, I propose to occupy, as common ground, some much more debatable territory; I shall assume in broad outline the metaphysical view of the nature of man that we have inherited from Plato and Aristotle. The basis of this tradition is that there is something called "Eudaimonia" or "The Good Life," that this consists in fulfilling to the highest possible degree the nature of Man, and that the nature of Man is to be a rational, social animal. Love, I shall assume, is the supreme virtue because the life of love is, in the end, the only life that is fully rational and fully social. My concern will be, not with the content of morality, but with its form or structure, with the ways in which the manifold concepts and affirmations of which a moral system is composed hang together; not with rival views of what conduct is moral and what is immoral, but with rival views of what morality *is*.

This contrast between form and content is not difficult to grasp, but experience has taught me that it is often ignored. When they discover that I have moral views but no religious beliefs, people often ask me this question: "Where do you get your moral ideas from?" Faced with this question, my habit is to take it literally and to answer it truthfully. "From my father and mother," I say, "from the companions of my boyhood and manhood, from teachers and from books, from my own reflections on the experience I have had of the sayings and doings of myself and others, an experience similar in countless ways to that of other people born of middle-class English parents some forty-five years ago, but in its totality

unique." This boring and autobiographical answer never satisfies the questioner; for, though it is the right answer to the question he actually asked, it is not, as I very well knew, the answer to the question he really had in mind. He did not want to know *from whom* I learnt my moral views; he wanted to know what *authority* I have for holding them. But why, if this is what he wanted to know, did he not ask me? He has confused two different questions; and it is natural enough that he should have confused them, since it is often the case that to point to the source of an opinion or claim is to show the authority on which it is based. We appeal to the dictionary to vindicate an assertion about the spelling of a word, and the policeman's production of a warrant signed by a magistrate is a necessary and sufficient condition of his authority to enter my house. But even a dictionary can make mistakes, and one may doubt whether one *ought* to admit the policeman even after his legal title to enter has been satisfactorily made out. "He certainly has a legal right," one might say, "but even so, things being as they are, ought I to admit him?"

Those who put this question to me have made an assumption that they have not examined because they have not reflected sufficiently on the form of morality. They have simply assumed that just as the legal propriety of an action is established by showing it to emanate from an authoritative source, so also the moral propriety of an action must be established in the same way; that legal rightness has the same form as moral rightness, and may therefore be used to shed light on it. This assumption made, they naturally suppose that, even when I agree with them—for example, about the immorality of murder—I have no right to hold this impeccable view unless I can show that I have received it from an authoritative source. My autobiographical answer clearly fails to do this. My parents may have had a right to my obedience, but no right to make the moral law. Morality, on this view, is an affair of being commanded to behave in certain ways by some person who has a right to issue such commands; and, once this premise is granted, it is said with some reason that only God has such a right. Morality must be based on religion, and a morality not so based, or one based on the wrong religion, lacks all validity.

It is this premise, that being moral consists in obedience to commands, that I deny. There is an argument, familiar to philosophers but of which the force is not always appreciated, which shows that this premise cannot be right. Suppose that I have satisfied myself that God has commanded me to do this or that thing—in itself a large supposition, but I will waive objections on this score in order to come quickly to the main point—it still makes *sense* for me to ask whether or not I *ought* to do it. God, let us say, is an omnipotent, omniscient creator of the universe. Such a creator might have evil intentions and might command me to do wrong; and if that were the case though it would be imprudent to disobey, it would not be wrong. There is nothing in the idea of an omnipotent, omniscient creator which, by itself, entails his goodness or his right to command, unless we are prepared to assent to Hobbes' phrase, "God, who by right, *that is by irresistible power,* commandeth all things." Unless we accept Hobbes' consistent but repugnant equation of God's right with his might, we must be persuaded *independently* of his goodness before we admit his right to command. We must judge for ourselves whether the Bible is the inspired word of a just and benevolent God or a curious amalgam of profound wisdom and gross superstition. To judge this is to make a moral decision, so that in the end, so far from morality being based on religion, religion is based on morality.

Before passing to my main theme, I must add two cautions about what this argument does *not* prove. It does not prove that we should in no case take authority as a guide. Suppose that a man's aim is to make money on the Stock Exchange. He decides that it would be most profitable to invest his money in company A; but his broker prefers company B. He will usually be well advised to accept the verdict of his broker, even if the broker is, as they often are, inarticulate in giving his reasons. He might decide to put all his financial affairs in the hands of a broker, and to do nothing but what the broker tells him to do. But *this* decision, even if it is the only financial decision he ever makes in his life, is still his own. In much the

same way, a man might decide to put his conscience wholly into the hands of a priest or a Church, to make no moral decisions of his own but always to do what the priest tells him. Even he, though he makes but one moral decision in his life, must make and continually renew that one. Those who accept the authority of a priest or a Church on what to do are, in accepting that authority, deciding for themselves. They may not fully comprehend that this is so; but that is another matter.

Secondly, to deny that morality need or can have an external nonmoral basis on which to stand is by no means to deny that it can have an internal basis, in the sense of one or a few moral beliefs that are fundamental to the other beliefs of the system. A man's views on gambling or sex or business ethics may (though they need not) form a coherent system in which some views are held *because* certain others views are held. Utilitarianism is an example of such a system in which all moral rules are to be judged by their tendency to promote human happiness. A moral system of this kind is like a system of geometry in which some propositions appear as axioms, others as theorems owing their place in the system to their derivability from the axioms. Few of us are so rationalistic as to hold all our moral beliefs in this way, but to move towards this goal is to begin to think seriously about morals.

2. In any system of morality we can distinguish between its content and its form. By its "content" I mean the actual commands and prohibitions it contains, the characteristics it lists as virtues and as vices; by its "form" I mean the sort of propositions it contains and the ways in which these are thought of as connected with each other. The basic distinction here is between a teleological morality in which moral rules are considered to be subordinate to ends, to be rules *for* achieving ends and consequently to be judged by their tendency to promote those ends, and a deontological system in which moral rules are thought of as absolute, as categorical imperatives in no way depending for their validity on the good or bad consequences of obedience, and in which moral

goodness is thought to lie in conformity to these rules for their own sake. The first of these ways of looking at morality as a whole derives from the Greeks, so I shall call it the Greek view of morality; it can be summed up in the slogan "the Sabbath was made for man, not man for the Sabbath." The second, deriving from Jewish sources, I shall call the Hebrew view. This involves a serious oversimplification, since we find deontological elements in the Greek New Testament and teleological elements in the Hebrew Old Testament; but, taken broadly, the contrast between the deontological character of the Old and the teleological character of the New Testaments is as striking as the difference of language. I shall also indulge in another serious oversimplification in speaking of Christianity as a morality of the Hebrew type while it is, of course, an amalgam of both with different elements predominating in different versions. This oversimplification would be quite unjustifiable if my task were to give an account of Christian morality; but it is legitimate here because my task is to contrast those elements in the Christian tradition which secular humanists accept with those which they reject, and these are broadly coterminous with the Greek and the Hebrew elements in Christianity respectively.

How there can be these two radically different ways of looking at morality, one which sees it as a set of recipes to be followed for the achievement of ends, the other which sees it as a set of commands to be obeyed, can best be understood if we consider the way in which we learn what it is to be moral. For a man's morality is a set of habits of choice, of characteristic responses to his environment, in particular to his social environment, the people among whom he lives; and habits are learnt in childhood. Growing up morally is learning to cope with the world into which we find ourselves pitched, and especially to cope with our relations with other human beings. In the course of living we learn to reflect on our responses, to find in some of them sources of satisfaction, in others of regret, and "coping with the world" means coping with it in a manner ultimately satisfactory to ourselves. Philosophers such as Aristotle and Hobbes who boldly and crudely identified

"good" with "object of desire" may have made a technical mistake; but they were certainly on the right lines. If men had no desires and aversions, if they felt no joy and no remorse, if they were totally indifferent to everything in the universe, there would be no such thing as choice and we should have no concept of morality, of good and evil.

The baby is born with some desires, not many; others it acquires as time goes on. Learning to cope with the world is learning how to satisfy and to modify these desires in a world that is partly propitious and partly hostile. For the world does not leap to gratify my desires like an assiduous flunkey; I do not get fed by being hungry. My desires are incompatible with each other and they come into conflict with those of other people. We have to learn both to bend the world to our wills and to bend our wills to the world. A man's morality is the way in which, in important matters, he does this.

Men are by nature rational and social animals, but only potentially so; they become actually rational and social only in a suitable environment, an environment in which they learn to speak a language. Learning how to cope with one's environment goes on side by side with learning to talk. The child's concepts, the meanings which, at every stage, words have for him, change as his horizon becomes wider, as he learns to grasp ideas that are more and more complicated, more and more remote from the primitive actions and passions that initially constitute his entire conscious life. It is not therefore surprising that the *form* of his morality, the meanings which moral words have and the ways in which they hang together, reflect at each stage the kind of experience he has. To babies who cannot yet talk we cannot, without serious error, attribute any thoughts at all; but though they cannot think, they can certainly feel, experience pleasure and pain, satisfaction and frustration. It is in these preverbal experiences that the origin of the ideas of "good" and "bad," even of "right" and "wrong," must be found; for their later development I turn to Piaget. My case for saying that religious morality is infantile cannot be conclusively made out without a much more detailed study of Piaget's researches than I have space for; I shall concentrate on a few points that seem to me to bear directly on the issue between the religious morality of law and the secular morality of purpose.

Piaget made a detailed study of the attitudes of children of different ages to the game of marbles, and he found three distinct stages. A very small child handles the marbles and throws them about as his humor takes him; he is playing, but not playing a *game;* for there are no rules governing his actions, no question of anything being done right or wrong. Towards the end of this stage he will, to some extent, be playing according to rules; for he will imitate older children who are playing a rule-governed game. But the child himself is not conscious of obeying rules; he has not yet grasped the concept of a "rule," of what a rule *is.* We may call this the premoral attitude to rules.

The second type of attitude is exhibited by children from five to nine. During this stage, says Piaget, "the rules are regarded as sacred and inviolable, emanating from adults and lasting for ever. Every suggested alteration in the rules strikes the child as a transgression." Piaget calls this attitude to rules "heteronomous" to mark the fact that the children regard the rules as coming, as indeed they do, from the outside, as being imposed on them by others. We might also call this the "deontological stage," to mark the fact that the rules are not questioned; they just *are* the rules of marbles, and that's that. At this stage the child has the concept of a rule, he knows what a rule is; but he has not yet asked what a rule is *for.* This deontological character is obviously connected with the unchangeability of the rules. Like laws in a primitive society, they are thought of as having been handed down from time immemorial, as much a part of the natural order of things as sunrise and sunset. The child may chafe at obedience and may sometimes disobey; but he does not question the authority of the rules.

Finally, at the third stage, the child begins to learn what the rules are for, what the point of having any rules is, and why it is better to have this rule rather than that. "The rule," says Piaget, "is now looked upon as a law due to mutual consent, which you must respect if you want to be loyal,

but which it is permissible to alter on condition of enlisting the general opinion on your side." He calls this type of attitude "autonomous" to mark the fact that the children now regard themselves, collectively, as the authors of the rules. This is not to say that they falsely suppose themselves to have invented them; they know well enough that they received them from older children. But they are the authors in the sense of being the final authorities; what tradition gave them they can change; from "this is how we learnt to play" they no longer pass unquestioningly to "this is how we ought to play." We might also call this stage "teleological" to mark the fact that the rules are no longer regarded as sacred, as worthy of obedience simply because they are what they are, but as serving a purpose, as rules for playing a game that they want to play. Rules there must certainly be; and in one sense they are sacred enough. Every player must abide by them; he cannot pick and choose. But in another sense there is nothing sacred about them; they are, and are known to be, a *mere* device, to be molded and adapted in the light of the purpose which they are understood by all the players to serve.

To illustrate the transition between the second and the third stages I should like to refer to a case from my own experience. Last summer I was with one other adult and four children on a picnic, and the children wanted to play rounders. We had to play according to the rules they had learnt at school because those just were the rules of rounders. This involved having two teams, and you can well imagine that, with only three players in each team, the game quickly ran on the rocks. When I suggested adapting the rules to our circumstances all the children were scandalized at first. But the two older children soon came round to the idea that, situated as we were, we should have to change the rules or not play at all and to the idea that it would not be wicked to change the rules. The two younger children were troubled, one might say, in their consciences about the idea of changing the rules. In Piaget's words, they thought of an alteration of rules as a transgression against them, having as yet no grasp of the distinction between an alteration of the rules by common consent to achieve a common purpose and the unilateral breach or defiance of them. In the eyes of these younger children we were not proposing to play a slightly different game, one better adapted to our situation; we were proposing to play the old game, but to play it wrong, almost dishonestly.

In another of Piaget's researches, this time directly concerned with moral attitudes, he told the children pairs of stories in each of which a child does something in some sense "bad" and asked which of the children was naughtier, which deserved most punishment. In one such story a child accidentally breaks fifteen cups while opening a door, and in the companion story breaks one cup while stealing jam. The replies of the very young children are mixed, some saying that the first child was naughtier; older children are unanimous in calling the second child naughtier. They have got beyond the primitive level of assessing moral guilt by the extent of the damage done.

Some of the youngest children do not recognize an act as wrong unless it is actually found out and punished, and we may call these last two points taken together "moral realism," because they display an attitude of mind that makes questions of morality questions of external fact. The inner state of the culprit—his motives and intentions—have nothing to do with it. To break crockery is wrong; therefore to break more crockery is more wrong. Moral laws are like laws of Nature, and Nature gives no marks for good or bad intentions and accepts no excuses. The fire will burn you if you touch it, however careful you were to avoid it. But if you are careless and, by good luck, avoid it, you will not be burnt; for Nature gives no bad marks for carelessness either. In the same way, if you lie and are punished, that is bad; but if you lie and are not punished, that is not bad at all. The fact that retribution did not follow *shows* that the lie was not, in this case, wrong.

3. I want now to compare the religious with the secular attitude towards the moral system which, in its content, both Christians and Humanists accept. I shall try to show that the religious

attitude retains these characteristics of deontology, heteronomy and realism which are proper and indeed necessary in the development of a child, but not proper to an adult: But I must repeat the caution with which I began. The views which I called "moral realism," which make intentions irrelevant, were expressed by very young children. No doubt many of these children were Christians and I do not wish to suggest that they never grew up, that they never adopted a more mature and enlightened attitude. This would be absurd. My thesis is rather that these childish attitudes survive in the moral attitudes of adult Christians—and of some secular moralists—as an alien element, like an outcrop of igneous rock in an alluvial plain. When Freud says of someone that he is fixated at the oral stage of sexuality he does not mean that he still sucks his thumb; he means rather that some of his characteristic attitudes and behavior patterns can be seen as an adult substitute for thumb sucking. In the same way, I suggest that some elements characteristic of Christian morality are substitutes for childish attitudes. In the course of this comparison I shall try to show how these infantile attitudes belong to a stage that is a *necessary* stage on the way to the fully adult, a stage which we must have passed through in order to reach maturity.

It needs little reflection to see that deontology and heteronomy are strongly marked features of all religious moralities. First for deontology. For some Christians the fundamental sin, the fount and origin of all sin, is disobedience to God. It is not the nature of the act of murder or of perjury that makes it wrong; it is the fact that such acts are transgressions of God's commands. On the other hand, good acts are not good in themselves, good in their own nature, but good only *as acts of obedience to God. "I give no alms only to satisfy the hunger of my brother, but to accomplish the will and command of my God; I draw not my purse for his sake that demands it, but his that enjoined it" (Sir Thomas Browne, *Religio Medici* II, 2). Here charity itself is held to be good *only because* God has told us to be charitable. It is difficult not to see in this a reflection of the small child's attitude towards his parents and the other authorities from whom he learns what it is right to do. In the first instance little Tommy learns that it is wrong to pull his sister's hair, not because it hurts her, but because Mummy forbids it.

The idea of heteronomy is also strongly marked in Christian morality. "Not as I will, but as thou wilt." The demand made by Christianity is that of surrendering self, not in the ordinary sense of being unselfish, of loving our neighbor and even our enemy. It is the total surrender of the *will* that is required; Abraham must be prepared to sacrifice Isaac at God's command, and I take this to mean that we must be prepared to sacrifice our most deeply felt moral concerns if God should require us to do so. If we dare to ask why, the only answer is "Have faith"; and faith is an essentially heteronomous idea; for it is not a reasoned trust in someone in whom we have good grounds for reposing trust; it is blind faith, utter submission of our own reason and will.

Now, to the small child morality is necessarily deontological and heteronomous in form; he must learn *that* certain actions are right and others wrong before he can begin to ask *why* they are, and he learns this from other people. The child has his own spontaneous springs of action; there are things he wants to do off his own bat; morality is a curb, at first nothing but a curb on his own volition. He comes up against parental discipline, even if only in the form of the giving and withdrawing of love, long before he can have any compassion, long before he has any conception of others as sentient beings. When he begins to learn language, words like "bad" must mean simply "what hurts me; what I don't like"; through the mechanism of parental discipline they come to mean "what adults forbid and punish me for." It is only because actions which cause suffering to others figure so largely among parental prohibitions that the child learns to connect the word "bad" with them at all.

If we consider the foundations of Christian ethics in more detail we shall find in them moral realism as well. Christianity makes much of charity and the love of our neighbor; but it does not say, as the Greeks did, that this is good because it is what befits the social animal, Man. We ought to be charitable because this is laid on us as a duty and because this state of the soul is the proper state for it during its transient mortal life. We must be charitable because (we are told) only so can we arrive at the soul's goal, the right relation to God. This fundamental isolation of the individual soul with God seems clearly to reflect what one supposes must be the state of mind of the small baby for whom, at the dawn of consciousness, there is only himself on the one side and the collective world of adults, represented largely by his parents, on the other, for whom the idea of others as individuals, as beings like himself, does not yet exist.

This impression is increased when we consider some accounts of what this right relationship between the soul and God is. Granted that to achieve this is the object of right living, just *what* relationship is it that we are to try to achieve? The terms of the relation are an omnipotent creator and his impotent creature, and between such terms the only relation possible is one of utter one-sided dependence, in which the only attitude proper to the creature must be one of adoration, a blend of love and fear. Surely this is just how the world must appear to the young child; for he really *is* impotent, wholly dependent on beings whose ways he cannot understand, beings sometimes loving, sometimes angry, but always omnipotent, always capricious—in short, gods. "As for Dr. Wulicke himself personally, he had all the awful mystery, duplicity, obstinacy, and jealousy of the Old Testament God. He was as frightful in his smiles as in his anger."[1]

Consider in this connection the ideas of original sin and grace. Every son of Adam is, of his own nature, utterly corrupt, redeemable only by divine grace. Once more, the conditions in which the child learns morality provide an obvious source for this remarkable conception. Parents are not only omniscient and omnipotent; they are also necessarily and always morally in the right. This must be so, since they are, as the child sees it, the authors of the moral law. Morality, the idea of something being right or wrong, enters the horizon of the child only at those points at which he has, so to speak, a dispute with authority, only on those occasions on which he is told or made to do something that he does not spontaneously want to do. From these premises that, at the time when the meanings of "right" and "wrong" are being learnt, the child must disagree with its parents and that they must be right he naturally passes to the conclusion that he must always be wrong. To have the sense of actual sin is to have the sense that one has, on this occasion, done wrong; to have the sense of original sin is simply to feel that one must be always and inevitably wrong. This sense of sin has often been deliberately and cruelly fostered; John Bunyan is not the only man to have left on record the agony of his childhood; but the point I wish to make is that the infantile counterpart of the sense of sin is a necessity at a certain stage of moral development, the stage at which moral words are being learnt and moral rules accepted as necessarily what parents say they are.

On the other side of the picture there is the doctrine of grace. Each individual soul is either saved or damned; but its fate, at least according to some versions, is wholly out of its own control. In these extreme versions, grace is absolutely necessary and wholly sufficient for salvation; and grace is the *free* gift of God. As far as the creature is concerned, there is absolutely nothing that he can do or even try to do either to merit or to obtain it.[2] From his point of view the giving or withholding of the means of salvation must be wholly capricious.

Once more, this is how parental discipline must seem to the child who cannot yet understand its aims and motives. Consider, for example, how even the most careful and consistent parents react towards what they call the clumsiness of a child. He knocks things over; he fumbles with his buttons. Though most parents do not think of themselves as punishing a child for such things, their behavior is, from the child's point of view, indistinguishable from punishment. They display more irritation when the child knocks over a valuable vase than when he knocks over a cheap cup, when the button-fumbling happens to occur at a moment when they are in a hurry than when it

does not. If a father takes from a small child something that is dangerous to play with or stops him hurting himself by a movement necessarily rough, that to the child is indistinguishable from punishment; it is a thwarting of his inclination for no reason that he can see. Children often say things that they know to be untrue; sometimes they are reprimanded for lying, sometimes complimented on their imagination. How can the child know under which heading, the good or the bad, a piece of invention will come, except by observing whether it is punished or rewarded? The child, by this time, is beginning to make efforts to try to please his parents, to do what, in his childish mind, he thinks right. The parents, not being expert child psychologists, will often fail to notice this; more often they will disregard it. To the child, therefore, there is little correlation between his own intentions and the reactions he evokes from the adult world. Salvation in the form of parental smiles and damnation in the form of parental frowns will come to him, like grace, in a manner that both seems and is wholly unconnected with any inwardly felt guilt. The mystery of God's ways to Man is the mystery of a father's ways to his children.

This characterization of religious morality as essentially infantile may seem to be unnecessary; for do not Christians themselves liken their relationship to God as that of child to father? In so doing they do not seem to me always to realize how incompatible this father-child relationship is with the Greek conception of the good life which they recognize as one of the sources of their moral doctrine. Aristotle says that children, like animals, have no share in the good life (a remark which always sounds so odd when people translate it as "children have no share in happiness"), and the reason he gives is that children do not *act*. This is a deep furrow to begin to plough at this stage—what is meant by "action"; but briefly it is motion that is self-initiated and responsible. The prime difference between the adult and the child is that the adult has freedom to choose for himself and has, what goes with freedom, responsibility for his actions. In the life of a child there is always, in the last resort, the parent or some substitute for a parent to turn to. The father is responsible at law for the actions of his child; he will undo what harm the child has done; he will put things right, will save the child from the consequences of his mistakes. To pass from childhood into adulthood is essentially to pass from dependence into freedom, and the price we pay is responsibility. As adults we make our own choices and must accept their consequences; the shield that in our childish petulance we once thought so irksome is no longer there to protect us. To many of us this is a matter of life-long regret, and we search endlessly for a father substitute. Surely "they" will get us out of the mess; there ought to be a law; why doesn't somebody. . . . These, in this godless age, are the common secular substitutes; religion, when it is not a patent substitute, is only a more profound, a more insinuating one.

4. The postulation of a god as the author of the moral law solves no more problems in ethics than the postulation of a god as first cause solves problems in metaphysics. Nor need we base morality, as I have done, on the metaphysical conception of Man as a rational, social animal, though we shall do so if we care to maintain the link with the old meaning of the word "humanist." To me, as a philosopher, some systematic view of the whole of my experience, some metaphysic, is essential, and this conception of the nature of Man makes more sense of my experience than any other I know. But I certainly should not argue that *because* the species Man has such and such a nature, *therefore* each and every man ought to act in such and such ways. In trying to sketch a humanist morality I shall start simply with the idea that a morality is a set of habits of choice ultimately determined by the question "What life is most satisfactory to me as a whole?" and I start with this because I simply do not *understand* the suggestion that I ought to do anything that does not fit into this conception. Outside this context the word "ought" has for me no meaning; and here at least I should expect Christians to agree with me.

If we start in this way, inquiries into my own nature and into the nature of Man at once become relevant. For my nature is such that there are some things that are impossible for me to do. Some hopes must be illusory, and nothing but frustration could come of indulging them. I could not, for example, become an operatic tenor or a test cricketer. Inquiries into the nature of Man are relevant in two ways; first, because I have to live as a man among men, secondly, because all men are to some degree alike and some of my limitations are common to us all. None of us can fly or witness past events. It is only insofar as men are alike that we can even begin to lay down rules as to how they should (all) behave; for it is only insofar as they are alike that they will find satisfaction and frustration in the same things. Prominent among the similarities among men are the animal appetites, the desire for the love and companionship of their own species, and the ability to think; and it is these three similarities that make us all "moral" beings. Morality consists largely, if not quite wholly, in the attempt to realize these common elements in our nature in a coherent way, and we have found that this cannot be done without adopting moral rules and codes of law. Humanism does not imply the rejection of all moral rules, but it does imply the rejection of a deontological attitude towards them. Even Piaget's older children could not have played marbles without rules; but they treated them as adaptable, as subservient to the purpose of playing a game, which is what they wanted to do. They treated the rules as a wise man treats his motor car, not as an object of veneration but as a convenience.

This, I suggest, is how we, as adults, should regard moral rules. They are necessary, in the first place, because one man's aim in life often conflicts with the aims of others and because most of our aims involve the cooperation of others, so that, even for purely selfish reasons, we must conform to rules to which others also conform. Most moral rules, from that prohibiting murder to that enjoining punctuality, exist for this purpose. But morality is not wholly an affair of regulating our dealings with others; each man has within himself desires of many different kinds which cannot all be fully satisfied; he must establish an order of priorities. Here I think almost all moralists, from Plato to D. H. Lawrence, have gone astray; for they have overemphasized the extent to which men are like each other and consequently been led to embrace the illusory concept of a "best life" that is the same for all of us. Plato thought this was a life dominated by the pursuit of knowledge, Lawrence one dominated by the pursuit of sensual experience and animal activity. I do not happen to enjoy lying naked on the grass; but I should not wish to force my preference for intellectual endeavor on anyone who did. Why should we not, within the framework of uniformity required for any life to be satisfactory to anyone at all, seek satisfaction in our own different ways?

The word "morality" is usually understood in a sense narrower than that in which I have been using it, to refer to just this necessary framework, to the rules to which we must all conform in order to make our aims, however diverse, realizable in a world which we all have to share. In Hobbes' words, the sphere of morality is limited to "those qualities of mankind that concern their living together in peace and unity" (*Leviathan*, ch. xi). If this is the purpose of moral rules, we must be willing to keep them under review and to discard or modify those that, in the light of experience, we find unnecessary or obstructive. But they must retain a certain inflexibility, since, in our casual contacts, it is important that people should be reliable, should conform so closely to a publicly agreed code that, even if we do not know them as individuals, we know what to expect of them. "That men perform their covenants made" is an adequate summary of morality in this limited sense.

But, though morality in this sense is necessary, it is not all. Rules belong to the superficial periphery of life. Like the multiplication table and other thought-saving dodges, they exist to free us for more important activities. It is beyond the power of any man to regulate all his dealings with all the people with whom he comes in casual contact by love; for love requires a depth of understanding

that cannot be achieved except in close intimacy. Rules have no place in marriage or in friendship. This does not mean that a man must keep his word in business but may break promises made to his wife or to a friend; it is rather that the notion of keeping a promise made to a wife or friend from a sense of duty is utterly out of place, utterly foreign to the spirit of their mutual relationship. For what the sense of duty requires of us is always the commission or omission of specific acts.

That friends should be loyal to one another I take for granted; but we cannot set out a list of acts that they should avoid as disloyal with the sort of precision (itself none too great) with which we could list the things a man should not do in business. Too much will depend on the particular circumstances and the particular natures of the people concerned. Rules must, of their very nature, be general; that is their virtue and their defect. They lay down what is to be done or not done in *all* situations of a certain general kind, and they do this because their function is to ensure reliability in the absence of personal knowledge. But however large we make the book of rules, however detailed we try to make its provisions, its complexity cannot reach to that of a close personal relationship. Here what matters is not the commission or omission of specific acts but the spirit of the relationship as a whole. A man thinks, not of what his obligation to his wife or his friend requires of him, but of what it is best for his wife or his friend that he should do. A personal relationship does indeed consist of specific acts; the spirit that exists between husband and wife or between friends is nothing over and above the specific things they do together. But each specific act, like each brush stroke in a picture or each note in a symphony, is good or bad only as it affects the quality of the relationship as a whole. The life of love is, like a work of art, not a means to an end, but an end in itself. For this reason in all close human relationships there should be a flexibility in our attitude to rules characteristic to the expert artist, craftsman, or games player.

The expert moves quickly, deftly, and, to the

untutored eye, even carelessly. It takes me hours to prune an apple tree, and I have to do it book in hand; the expert goes over the tree in a few minutes, snipping here and slashing there, with the abandonment of a small boy who has neither knowledge of pruning nor intention to prune. Indeed, to someone who does not know what he is about, his movements must seem more like those of Piaget's youngest children who just threw the marbles about. But the similarity is superficial. For one thing, the master craftsman's movements do mostly follow the book for all that he never refers to it; and for another he does know what he is about and it is just this knowledge that entitles him to flout the rules when it is suitable to do so. No apple tree is exactly like the drawing in the book, and expertise lies in knowing when and how to deviate from its instructions.

This analogy must not be pressed too far. The conduct of life is more complicated and more difficult than any such task as pruning a tree and few of us could claim, without improper pride, the master craftsman's licence. But I should like to press it some way, to suggest that, in all important matters, our chief consideration should be, not to conform to any code of rules, but simply how we can produce the best results; that we should so act that we can say in retrospect, not "I did right," but "I did what befitted the pattern of life I have set myself as a goal."

As a philosopher, I cannot but speak in abstract generalities, and it is central to my thesis that at this point the philosopher must give way to the novelist. Tolstoy, Thomas Mann, and Forster have given us many examples of the contrast between the rule-bound and the teleological attitudes to life. But I should like to end by descending one level, not to the particular, but to the relatively specific, and to consider as an example one moral rule, the prohibition of adultery.

By "adultery" I understand the act of sexual intercourse with someone other than one's spouse. It is expressly forbidden in the Bible, absolutely and without regard to circumstances; it is a crime in some countries and many would make it

a crime in this. Until very recently it was almost the only ground for civil divorce. A marriage is supposed to be a life-long union. It could be entirely devoid of love—some married couples have not spoken to each other for years, communicating by means of a blackboard; yet no grounds for divorce existed. Or the husband might insist on sexual intercourse with his wife against her will and yet commit no sin. But let him once go out, get drunk, and have a prostitute and the whole scene changes. He has sinned; his wife has a legal remedy and, in the eyes of many who are not Christians but have been brought up in a vaguely Christian tradition, he has now done a serious wrong. This is a rule-and-act morality according to which what is wrong is a specific act; and it is wrong in all circumstances even, for example, if the wife is devoid of jealousy or so devoid of love that she would rather have her husband lie in any bed but hers.

If we look at this rule against adultery from a teleological standpoint it must appear wholly different. A humanist may, of course, reject the whole conception of monogamy; but if, like myself, he retains it, he will do so only because he believes that the life-long union of a man and a woman in the intimacy of marriage is a supreme form of love. Copulation has its part to play in such a union; but, for the species Man, it cannot be its essence. If someone who holds this view still thinks adultery is wrong, he will do so because it appears to him to be an act of disloyalty, an act likely to break the union which he values. Two consequences follow from this. The first is that if a marriage is, for whatever reason, devoid of love, there is now no union to break; so neither adultery nor any other act can break it. The second is that since adultery is now held to be wrong, not in itself, but only *as an act of disloyalty*, it will not *be* wrong when it is *not* an act of disloyalty. An adultery committed with the full knowledge and consent of the spouse will not be wrong at all. A so-called "platonic" friendship, even too assiduous an attendance at the local pub or sewing circle, anything that tends to weaken the bonds of love between the partners will be far more damaging to the marriage and consequently far more deeply immoral. Just *what* specific acts are immoral must, on this view, depend on the particular circumstances and the particular people concerned. Christians also insist on the uniqueness of individual people; but since law is, of its nature, general, this insistence seems wholly incompatible with the morality of law to which they are also committed.

Notes

1. Thomas Mann, *Buddenbrooks*, referring to the headmaster whom Hanno and Kai nicknamed "The Lord God." The whole chapter, Part XI, ch. 2, illustrates this point.

2. This is, I know, heretical; yet I cannot see in the subtle palliatives offered by Catholic theologians anything but evasions, vain attempts to graft a more enlightened moral outlook on to a theological tree which will not bear them. The reformers seem to me to have been right in the sense that they were restoring the original doctrine of the Church.

VIII.3   Morality and Religion Reconsidered

BARUCH A. BRODY

Baruch A. Brody is professor of philosophy at Rice University and the Baylor College of Medicine in Houston. In this reading Brody argues that we have a special relation to God as our creator that entails certain rights on his part towards all of his creation, including us, and certain obligations on our part towards God. In this sense, morality is based on divine commands but in such a way as to avoid any arbitrariness on the part of God. Brody uses the injunction against suicide to illustrate how a religious morality generates different principles than a purely secular morality does.

There are many people who believe that, in one way or another, morality needs a religious backing. One of the many things that might be meant by this vague and ambiguous claim[1] is the following: there are certain moral truths that are true only because of the truth of certain religious truths. In particular, the truth of certain claims about the rightness (wrongness) of a given action is

dependent upon the truth of certain religious claims to the effect that God wants us to do (refrain from doing) that action. This belief, in effect, bases certain parts of morality upon the will of God.

Philosophers have not commonly agreed with such claims. And there is an argument, whose ancestor is an argument in the *Euthyphro*, that is supposed to show that such claims are false. It runs as follows: the proponents of the claim in question have reversed the order of things. Doing a given action *A* is not right (wrong) because God wants us to do (refrain from doing) *A*; rather, God wants us to do (refrain doing doing) *A* because of some other reason which is the real reason why *A* is right (wrong) for us to do. For, if the situation were the way it is depicted by the proponents of the claim in question, we would have moral truths based upon the arbitrary desires of God as to what we should do (refrain from doing), and this is objectionable.

I would like to reexamine this issue and to show that the situation is far more complicated than philosophers normally imagine it to be. I should like to show (a) that the general argument suggested by the *Euthyphro* is not as persuasive as it is ordinarily thought to be, and (b) that it is even less persuasive when we see the religious claim applied to specific moral issues, and that this is so

From Baruch A. Brody, "Morality and Religion Reconsidered," in *Readings in the Philosophy of Religion: An Analytic Approach*, edited by Baruch A. Brody, copyright © 1974, pp. 592–603. Reprinted by permission of Prentice-Hall, Inc., Englewood Cliffs, N.J. Footnotes edited.

because the claims about the will of God can be supplemented by additional theological claims.

I

Let us begin by looking at the argument more carefully. We shall formulate it as follows:

(1) Let us suppose that it is the case that there is some action A that is right (wrong) only because God wants us to do (refrain from doing) it.

(2) There must be some reason for God's wanting us to do (refrain from doing) A, some reason that does not involve God's wanting us to do (refrain from doing) it.

(3) Therefore, that reason must also be a reason why A is right (wrong).

(4) So we have a contradiction, (1) is false, and either there are no actions that are right (wrong) because God wants us to do (refrain from doing) them or, if there are such actions, that is not the only reason why those actions are right (wrong).

What can be said by way of defense on (2)? The basic idea behind it seems to be the following: if God wanted us to do (refrain from doing) A, but he had no reason for that want that was independent of his act of wanting, then his act of wanting would be an arbitrary act, one that entails some imperfection in him. But God is a perfect being. Therefore, he must have some reason for wanting us to do (refrain from doing) A, some reason that is, of course, independent of that want of his. Now it is not entirely clear that this argument is sound, for it is not clear that the performance by an agent of an arbitrary act (even an arbitrary act of willing) entails some imperfection in the agent.[2] But we shall let that issue pass for now and focus, for the moment, on the crucial step (3).

It is clear that step (3) must rest upon some principle like the following:

(Trans.) If p because of q and q because of r, then p because of r.

There are two things that should be noted about

this principle. The first is that if we are to use it in our context we will have to take it as ranging over different types of cases in which we say "because." After all, there are significant differences between cases in which we make claims of the form "A is right (wrong) because God wants us to do (refrain from doing) A" and cases in which we make claims of the form "God wants us to do (refrain from doing) A because r," for it is only in the latter type of case that we have the reason-for-wanting, "because." The second point is that there are real problems with this principle. While Joe may go home because his wife wants him to do so, and she may want him to do so because she wants to have it out with him, it may well not be the case that he goes home because she wants to have it out with him. So the principle is going to need some modifying, and it is not clear how one is to do this while still preserving the inference from (1) and (2) to (3).

Still, let us suppose that this can be done. Our argument faces the following further objection: God's wanting us to do (refrain from doing) A is not the whole of the reason why the action is right (wrong); the additional part of the reason is that he is our creator to whom we owe obedience. And when we take into account the full reason, the argument collapses. After all, the *Euthyphro* argument would then run as follows:

(1') Let us suppose that there is some action A that is right (wrong) only because God wants us to do (refrain from doing) A and he is our creator to whom we owe obedience.

(2') There must be some reason for God's wanting us to do (refrain from doing) A, some reason that does not involve God's wanting us to do (refrain from doing) A.

(3') Therefore, that reason must also be a reason why A is right (wrong).

(4') So we have a contradiction, (1') is false, and either there are no actions that are right (wrong) because God, who is our creator and to whom we owe obedience, wants us to do (refrain from doing) them, or, if there are such actions, that is not the only reason why those actions are right (wrong).

And even supposing that (Trans.) is true, (3′) would not follow from (1′) and (2′).

It is clear that the proponents of the *Euthyphro* argument have got to block this move. How might they do so? The most straightforward move is to deny the moral relevance of the fact that God is our creator, to claim that even if he is, we have no obligation to obey his wishes and that, therefore, the reason advanced in (1′) cannot be a reason why *A* is right (wrong).

Is this move acceptable? Consider, for a moment, our special obligation to obey the wishes of our parents.[3] Why do we have that obligation? Isn't it because they created us? And since this is so, we seem to have an obligation, in at least some cases, to follow their wishes. So, *x*'s being our creator can be part of a reason for doing (refraining from doing) an action *A* if the other part is that that is *x*'s wish. And if this is so in the case of our parents, why shouldn't it also be so in the case of God? How then can the defendents of the *Euthyphro* argument say that the fact that God created us cannot, together with some facts about his wishes, be a reason for doing (refraining from doing) some action *A*?

The proponents of the *Euthyphro* argument have a variety of ways, of differing plausibilities, of objecting to this defense of (1′). They might claim: (a) that we have no special obligations at all to our parents; (b) that it is no part of the special obligations that we have to our parents to do (refrain from doing) what they want us to do (refrain from doing); (c) that our special obligations to our parents are due to something that they do other than merely creating us, something that God does not do, so the whole question of our special obligations to our parents has nothing to do with the truth of (1′).[4]

But there is another move open to the proponents of the *Euthyphro* argument. Rather than attempting to object to (1′), they might construct the following alternative argument against it, one that has the additional merit of not depending upon (Trans.):

(1′) Let us suppose that there is some action *A* that is right (wrong) only because God wants us to do (refrain from doing) *A* and he is our creator to whom we owe obedience.

(2′*) There must be some reason for God's wanting us to do (refrain from doing) *A*, some reason that does not involve God's wanting us to do (refrain from doing) *A*, and some reason that is, by itself, a reason why *A* is right (wrong).

(4′) So we have a contradiction, (1′) is false, and either there are no actions that are right (wrong) because God, who is our creator and to whom we owe obedience, wants us to do (refrain from doing) them, or, if there are such actions, that is not the only reason why those actions are right (wrong).

The trouble with this move, of course, is that it rests upon the extremely strong assumption (2′*), and even if, to avoid the problem with arbitrary acts of willing, we are prepared to grant (2′), there seems to be little reason to grant this stronger (2′*) with its extra assumption about what are the types of reasons that God has for his acts of willing.

In short, then, the traditional argument that the rightness or wrongness of an action cannot depend upon the will of God rests upon some dubious premises, and things get worse when we add the idea that we have an obligation to follow God's wishes because he is our creator. There is, however, more to say about this issue, for there are reasons to suppose that some particular moral truths may depend in a special way upon the idea that God is the creator. We turn, therefore, to a consideration of these special cases.

II

Let us begin by considering a set of issues surrounding the idea of property rights. What is involved in one's owning a piece of property, in one's having a right to it? It seems to mean, in part, that while one may not use that property so as to infringe upon the rights of others, one may, if one wants, use it in such a way as to benefit while others lose. No doubt this distinction is unclear for there are cases in which it is difficult to say whether someone's rights have been infringed upon or whether he has simply lost out. But the distinction is clear enough for our purposes.

How does one come to own a piece of property? One intuitively attractive picture runs as follows: if there is a physical object that belongs to no one, and if some person comes along and does something with it (mixes his labor with it), then the object in question belongs to that person. He may then, in one way or another, transfer that property to someone else, who then has property rights in that object. Indeed, transference is now the most prevalent way of acquiring property. But all property rights are ultimately based, in this picture, upon these initial acts of acquisition through the mixing of one's labor with unowned objects. This picture certainly faces some familiar objections. To begin with, what right does a person have to appropriate the ownerless piece of property for himself, thereby depriving all of us of the right to use it? And secondly, does the act of mixing his labor with it give him ownership rights over the initial, ownerless object or simply over the products (if any) of his interaction with it? But we shall leave aside these worries for now and suppose that something like this account is correct, for the question that we want to consider is whether or not it would have to be modified in light of any theological truths.

This picture clearly presupposes that, if there is such a thing as property owned by human beings, then there was, at least at one point in human history, such a thing as ownerless property, property that one could acquire if one mixed one's labor with it. But suppose that the universe was created by a personal God. Then, it might well be argued, he owns the whole universe, and there is not, and never has been, such a thing as ownerless property. Now suppose further that this creator allows men to use for their purposes the property that they mix their labor with, but he does so with the restriction that they must not use it in such a way as to cause a great loss to other people (even though the rights of these people are not infringed upon). That is to say, suppose that this creator allows people to take his property only if they follow certain of his wishes. Then, don't they have

an obligation to do so, or, at least, an obligation to either return the property or to do so? So, in short, if God, the creator, does wish us not to use the things of the world in certain ways, this will entail certain moral restrictions on property rights that might not be present otherwise.

Let us, at this point, introduce the idea of stewardship over property. We shall say that someone has stewardship over a piece of property just in case they own that piece of property subject to certain restrictions as to how they may use it and/or subject to certain requirements as to how they must use it, restrictions and/or requirements that were laid down by some previous owner of that piece of property. Now, what I have been arguing for is the idea that, if certain theological beliefs (that God created the universe but allows man to appropriate the property in it subject to certain restrictions and requirements that he lays down) are true, then men will have rights of stewardship, and not property rights, over the property that they possess. And if this is so, then there will be moral truths (about restrictions and requirements that property-possessors must follow) that might not be true if these theological beliefs were false. So we have here a set of moral claims whose truth or falsehood might depend upon the truth or falsehood of certain theological claims.

The question that we must now consider is whether or not the *Euthyphro* argument, even if sound in general, could be used against the claim we are now considering. How would it run in this context? Presumably, it would run as follows:

(1″) Let us suppose that there are certain restrictions on property rights and that they exist only because God, from whom we get our stewardship over the earth, has imposed them.

(2″) There must be some reason why God has imposed these restrictions, a reason that does not involve his wanting us to follow them.

(3″) Therefore, that reason must also be a reason why we should follow those restrictions.

(4″) So we have a contradiction, (1″) is false, and either there are no such restrictions or there is some additional reason as to why they exist.

As we saw in the last section, when we considered (1')–(4'), even if we grant (2") and (Trans.), (3") doesn't follow from (1") and (2"). Now even if we grant what we are reluctant to grant in the last section, viz., that (1') is objectionable because the mere fact that someone created us gives us no moral reason for following his wishes, we would still have no reason for independently objecting to (1"). For if we have mere stewardship over the property we possess, then surely we do have an obligation to follow the wishes of him from whom we got our stewardship, and if God did create the world, then it certainly looks as though our property possession is a property stewardship gotten ultimately from God.

This point can also be put as follows. Neither (3') nor (3") follows from the previous steps in their respective arguments, even if we grant the truth of (Trans.), because the reasons they provide for the moral claims in question involve some other theological facts besides God's willing certain things. Now the defenders of the *Euthyphro* argument may try to attack (1") on independent grounds, but it is difficult to see the grounds that they would have. So it looks then as though certain theological claims are relevant to certain moral truths having to do with the existence and extent of rights over property.

To be sure, the defenders of the *Euthyphro* argument might, in desperation, trot out the following argument:

(1") Let us suppose that there are certain restrictions on property rights and that they exist only because God, from whom we get our stewardship over the earth, has imposed them.

(2"*) There must be some reason why God has imposed these restrictions, a reason that does not involve his wanting us to follow them, and one that is, by itself, a reason why we should follow these restrictions.

(4") So we have a contradiction, (1") is false, and either there are no such restrictions or there is some additional reason as to why they exist.

But like step (2'*) of the previous section, step (2"*) has little to recommend it. Even if a perfect God has to have reasons for wanting us to behave in certain ways, and, a fortiori, for imposing restrictions on our behavior, it is unclear why they must meet the very strong final requirement laid down by (2"*).

III

In the previous section, we have discussed the implications of the theological idea that God, the creator, owns the universe for the issue of property rights. It is sometimes felt that this idea also has implications for the moral issue of the permissibility of suicide. We will, in this section, explore that possibility.

The liberal argument for the permissibility of suicide is stated very clearly early on in the *Phaedo*:

> . . . sometimes and for some people death is better than life. And it probably seems strange to you that it should not be right for those to whom death would be an advantage to benefit themselves, but that they should have to await the services of someone else. [62A]

It will do no good, of course, to object that the person might have some extremely important obligations that he would leave unfulfilled if he committed suicide, and this is why it is wrong for him to do so, because we could easily confine the discussions to cases in which he has no such obligations or to cases in which he could arrange for the executors of his estate to fulfill them. And moreover, such an argument would really only show that one should not be remiss in fulfilling one's obligations, it would not really show that there was something particularly wrong with the way the person who committed suicide did that.

Plato himself does not accept this argument for suicide (although he does think one can accede in being condemned to death), and he is opposed to suicide on the grounds that we are the possessions of the gods. His argument runs as follows:

If one of your possessions were to destroy itself without intimation from you that you wanted it to die, wouldn't you be angry with it and punish it, if you had any means of doing so . . . so if you look at it this way, I suppose it is not unreasonable to say that we must not put an end to ourselves until God sends more compulsions like the one we are facing now. [62C]

Leaving aside the peculiarity of the idea that one ought, if one can, to punish those who succeed in destroying themselves—as opposed to the more reasonable idea that one ought to punish those who merely try,—the idea that Plato is advancing is that the gods' property rights extend to us, and that we therefore have no right to destroy ourselves unless they give their permission.

There are cases in which many religious people want to allow that suicide is permissible. One such case is that of the person who commits suicide rather than face being compelled to do some very evil act. Thus, in a great many religious traditions, it would even be thought to be a meritorious act to commit suicide rather than face being tortured into committing acts of apostasy. Another such case is that of the person who commits suicide rather than reveal under torture secrets that would lead to the destruction of many innocent people. Can these exceptions be reconciled with the argument against suicide that we have been considering? It seems to me that they can. After all, the crucial objection to our destroying ourselves is that we have no right to do so without the permission of our owner, God, and the religious person might well add the additional claim that God has (perhaps in a revelation) already given his permission in these cases.

Obviously, the *Euthyphro* argument cannot be raised against the claim that we are considering. After all, the crucial first premise would be the claim that

(1″) Let us suppose that we cannot take our own lives only because we are the property of God, who created us, and he does not want us to destroy this piece of his property.

Then even if we add

(2‴) There must be some reason why he doesn't want us to do so, some reason that does not involve this want of his.

we will not, even assuming (Trans.), get the crucial

(3‴) Therefore, that reason must also be a reason why we should not take our own lives.

We can, no doubt, consider using

(2‴*) There must be some reason why he doesn't want us to do so, some reason that does not involve this want of his, and which is, by itself, a reason why we should not take our own lives.

instead of (2‴), but it is no more plausible than (2′*) and (2″*). Nor can we easily object to (1‴) in the way that we did to (1′). Even if we have no obligation to listen to the wishes of him who has created us, just because he has created us, we do have an obligation not to destroy someone else's property, and, if God created us, then perhaps we are God's property.

Having said this, we can now see that more is at stake here than a mere prohibition of suicide. For if we are the property of God, then perhaps we just have an obligation to do whatever he says, and then perhaps we can return to our initial general claims about morality and consider the possible claim that

(1′#) actions are right (wrong) for us to do just in case and only because God, who has created us and owns us and whom we therefore have an obligation to follow, wants us to do (refrain from doing) them.

So a great deal hinges on this point.

Despite all that we have seen, it is unclear that this argument against suicide (and, a fortiori, the more general claim just considered) will do. In the case of property rights, the crucial idea was that God, who created the world, owns all property, and this claim seemed a coherent one. But here, in (1‴), the crucial idea is that God, because he created us, owns us. And perhaps one can object directly to (1‴) that it is incoherent. Does it make sense, after all, to talk of an all-just being owning or possessing a human being? Isn't doing that an unjust act, one that cannot meaningfully be ascribed to an all-just being?

It is difficult to assess this objection. There is no doubt that the objection to the institution of slavery is exactly that we think it unjust for one human being to own another human being, to have another human being as his possession. But is it unjust for God, who is vastly superior to us and is our creator, to possess human beings? To put this question another way, is slavery unjust because it is wrong for one human being to possess another (in which case, both the argument against suicide and the general claim, with their supposition that we are the possessions of God, can stand) or because it is wrong that a human being be a possession, a piece of property (in which case, both collapse on the grounds of incoherence)? Religious people have, very often, opted for the former alternative,[5] and as it is difficult to see an argument to disprove their contentions; we have, probably, to conclude that theological claims might make a difference to the truth or falsity of moral claims concerning suicide, and perhaps to a great many other issues as well.

IV

There is still one final issue about which it is often claimed that theological beliefs about the will of a God who created the world are relevant to the truth of moral beliefs about that issue. This is the moral issue raised by vegetarians. At least some vegetarians argue as follows: we normally suppose that it is wrong, except in certain very special cases, to take the life of an innocent human being. But we normally have no objections to taking the life of members of many other species to obtain from their bodies food, clothing, etc. Let us call these normal moral views the conventional consciousness. Now, argues the vegetarian, it is difficult to defend the conventional consciousness. What characteristics are possessed by all human

beings, but by no members of any other species, and are such as to justify such a sharp moral distinction as the one drawn by the conventional consciousness?

I think that no one would deny that there is a gradation of development between different species, and most would concede that this gives rise to a gradation of rights. While few would object to killing a mosquito if it is being a minor nuisance, many would object to killing a dog on the same grounds. The interesting point, says the vegetarian, is that when we get to the case of human beings, the conventional consciousness accords to them many rights (including the strong right to life) even though there is not a sufficiently dramatic biological difference between these species to justify such a sharp moral difference. Therefore, concludes the vegetarian, we should reject the conventional consciousness and accord more of these rights (especially the right to life) to members of more species of animals.

This vegetarian argument draws further support from the fact that the intuitions embedded in the conventional consciousness are about species. After all, there are a variety of extreme cases (newly born infants, severely retarded individuals, people who are near death) in which many of the subtler features of human beings are not present but in which the conventional consciousness accords to the people in question far more rights than those normally accorded to animals. This makes it far more difficult to believe that there are some characteristics (a) possessed by all human beings, (b) not possessed by all animals, and (c) which justify the moral distinctions drawn by the conventional consciousness. So, the vegetarian concludes, we must reject the conventional consciousness.

There is a religious response to this vegetarian argument which runs as follows: when God created the world, he intended that man should use certain other species for food, clothing, etc. God did not, of course, give man complete freedom to do what he wants with these creatures. They are not, for example, to be treated cruelly. But, because that was God's intention, man can, and should use these creatures to provide him with food, clothing, etc. This view is embodied in the following Talmudic story:

> A calf was being taken to the slaughter, when it broke away, hid his head under Rabbi's skirts, and lowed in terror. *Go, said he, for this wast thou created.* [B. Metzia, 85a]

It is pretty clear, once more, that the *Euthyphro* argument will not do against the claim we are considering. It is

(1'''') Man can take the lives of animals so that he can obtain from their bodies food, clothing, etc., only because God, who created the world and owns everything in it, intended that he do so.

and even if we grant

(2'''') There is some reason why he intended things that way, some reason that does not involve that intention.

and (Trans.), we do not get the crucial

(3'''') This must also be a reason why it is permissible for us to take the lives of animals for the sake of obtaining food, clothing, etc.

The crucial objection to this claim has to do with the coherency of (1''''). Let us suppose that we are not troubled by the religious claims discussed in the previous section; let us suppose that we find nothing objectionable with the idea that God owns us. Then, presumably, even if we are impressed with the vegetarian argument, we will still find nothing objectionable with the idea that God owns animals as well. But we may still find (1'''') objectionable. For it, in effect, supposes that God's property rights extend so far as to allow the life of the piece of property in question to be taken by others, indeed, to so order things that this is done. And is this compatible with the idea of an all-just being? After all, even enlightened systems of slavery did not allow the slave-owner to take (or to have taken) the life of his slave. Does God's majesty really mean then that he can do even this?

We are straining here with the limits of the idea that everything is God's property because he is the creator of everything. When we applied the

idea to inanimate objects, we saw that it could have important implications for the question of property rights. If we didn't object to applying it to human beings, we saw that it could (at least) have important applications for the question of the permissibility of suicide. If we are now prepared to take it to further extremes, it could serve as a response to the vegetarian's argument about animals and their right to life.

V

In a way, this essay can be seen as a gloss on the Psalmist's remarks that "the earth and all that fill it belong to God." We have tried to show that this idea may have important moral implications, and that it would therefore be wrong to suppose that there are no moral claims whose truth or falsehood may depend upon the truth or falsehood of theological claims. But it is, of course, clear that this is not the only theological belief that may have moral consequences. On other occasions, we shall look at other such theological beliefs.

Notes

1. Other things that might be meant are: (a) we know that certain moral truths are true because we know the truth of certain religious truths (perhaps, that God has revealed to us that the action is right), and (b) we have a reason to do what is right because of the truth of certain religious truths (perhaps, that God will reward us if we do). We will not discuss these claims in this paper.

2. This is a claim that would certainly be denied by writers in the Calvinist tradition. Thus, Jonathan Edwards, writes as follows in connection with the question of salvation and damnation:

> It is meet that God should order all these things according to his own pleasure. By reason of his greatness and glory, by which he is infinitely above all, he is worthy to be sovereign, and that his pleasure should in all things take place. [*Jonathan Edwards* (Hill and Wang: 1935) p. 119]

3. This analogy between our obeying the will of God and the will of our parents is based upon the Talmudic discussion (in *Tractate Kedushin*, 30b) of the obligation to honor one's parents.

4. Of the three moves, the third seems most plausible. But religious people might well respond to it as follows: let us grant that our special obligations to our parents are due to additional facts about the parent-child relationship (e.g., the way parents raise and sustain their children, etc.). God has those additional relations to all of his creations, and they therefore still have to him the special obligation of obedience.

5. This is evidenced in the Talmudic idea (*Kedushin,* 22[b]) that it is wrong for man to sell himself into slavery because God would object on the grounds that "they are my slaves, and not the slaves of slaves."

VIII.4   God's Commands and Man's Duties

JONATHAN HARRISON

Jonathan Harrison teaches philosophy at the University of Nottingham in England. In this reading he distinguishes three interpretations of the relationship between God's commands and humanity's duties: (1) Because he is omniscient, God knows what is right and what is wrong, and because he is good, he wants us to do what is right and so commands us to do it; (2) God's command is what makes an action right and his prohibition is what makes an action wrong. Before he commands them, no actions are right or wrong; (3) 'right' means commanded by God and 'wrong' means prohibited by God. Harrison examines these distinctions and opts for the first one as the most satisfactory.

When we consider the relation between God's commands and man's duties, it seems to be a fairly good rough approximation to the truth to say that there are three possible views about the nature of this relation. In the *first* place, it is possible to say that God, since he is omniscient, always knows what is right and wrong, and, since he is perfectly good, always commands us to do what is right and prohibits us from doing what is wrong; he is pleased with us when we obey his commands, and do what is right, and displeased with us when we disobey his commands, and do what is wrong. On this view, God's will is determined by his knowledge of right and wrong. *Secondly,* it is possible to say that what makes right actions right and what makes wrong actions wrong is that God has commanded the right actions and prohibited the wrong ones, and that being commanded by God is the *only* thing which makes an action right and being prohibited by God is the *only* thing which makes an action wrong. On this view, it is impossible for God, in commanding some actions and prohibiting others, to be guided by the fact that the actions he commands are right and the actions he prohibits are wrong, because, before he has commanded them, no actions are right, and before he has prohibited them, no actions are wrong. The *third* possible view is that there are not two pairs of different facts, being commanded by God and being right, and being prohibited by God and being wrong: to say that an action is right just *means* that it is commanded by God, and to say that an action is wrong just *means* that it is prohibited by God. Hence it is impossible to raise the question, which the first view answered in one way and the second view in another, whether it is the fact that an action is right that causes God to command it or whether, conversely it is the fact that an action is commanded by God that makes it right. On the third view there are not two different facts, being commanded by God and being right, such that we can ask whether the first is dependent upon the second or whether the second is dependent upon the first. There is just one single fact, which may be put indifferently by saying either that God has commanded something or that it is right.

Reprinted from Jonathan Harrison, *Our Knowledge of Right and Wrong* (London: George Allen & Unwin, 1971) by permission of the publisher. Footnotes edited.

Which of these three theories one holds does not necessarily make any difference to what one thinks is right and wrong. It is perfectly possible, for example, for theologians who hold each of these three theories to agree that it is right for us to love one another, but the first kind of theologian will think that, though loving actions are both right and commanded by God, they are commanded by God because they are right. The second kind of theologian will think that though loving actions are both commanded by God and right, they are right because God has commanded them. The third theologian will think that, though it is true to say of loving actions that they are commanded by God and true to say of them that they are right, to say these things is not to make two different statements about loving actions, but to make one and the same statement in two different ways.

However, though which of these three theories one holds *need* not make any difference to what actions one actually thinks are right and wrong, there is one possible circumstance in which it *will* make a very great deal of difference. If there is no God, then, if you accept the second theory, that only what God commands is right, you are logically bound to say that there are no right and wrong actions, for, according to your theory, only one thing can make an action right, namely, that God commands it, and, if there is no God, nothing can be commanded by him. If you hold the third theory, and think that to say that an action is right just *means* that God has commanded it and that to say that an action is wrong just *means* that God has prohibited it, you will also, if you think that there is no God, be logically committed to holding that nothing is right and nothing is wrong, for, of course, if there is no God there will be no actions which God commands and no actions which he prohibits. If, however, you hold the first theory, it is possible for you to think both that there is no God and also to think that some actions are right and others wrong. Since, on this view, actions are right for some reason other than that God commands them—though God does command or prohibit them in fact—it is possible for actions which are right to go on being right, even if there is no God.

The three theories, though they need not make any difference to one's views about what actions are right and wrong, are nevertheless very different kinds of theory. One might describe the first as a sort of *psychological* theory about God's policy of action. It states that it is God's policy, in directing the behaviour of his creatures, always to command right actions and to prohibit wrong ones. The second theory is not a psychological theory about what makes God command some actions and prohibit others. It says nothing about what causes God to command a certain class of action, but simply says that, if God does command any class of action, it is right for us to perform actions of this class. Hence it is a theory not about God's policy of action, but a *moral* theory about what makes right actions right. The third theory says nothing about what makes actions right or wrong, nor anything about what makes God command some actions and prohibit others. It is simply a *linguistic* theory about the meanings of the words 'right' and 'wrong.' It says that the word 'right' simply means 'commanded by God,' and that the word 'wrong' simply means 'prohibited by God.' Hence these three theories, though they do not necessarily—while they may—make any difference to one's views about what actions are right and what actions are wrong, are theories of very different kinds. . . . Odd though it may seem, there is even no logical connection between which of these three views one holds and whether one believes that there actually is a God or not, though perhaps the first of the three is the most *natural* view for an atheist or an agnostic, since it is the only one of the three which can be adopted by someone who both wants to hold that some things are right and wrong and at the same time wants to hold that there is no God—and most atheists and agnostics do appear to wish to hold that some things are right and others wrong. One can hold the second view or the third and at the same time believe that there is not a God, provided, of course, one is prepared to embrace the logical conclusion that, in that event, nothing is right and nothing is wrong. It is presumably partly extreme reluctance to accept that nothing is right and wrong which has driven most who think that there is no God, or that it cannot be decided whether there is a God or not, to embrace the first of the three views we have distinguished. . . .

Whether one holds the first view or the second, though it may not make any difference to the actions one thinks are right and wrong, does make a difference to whether one thinks that one finds out *first* what God commands, or whether one thinks that one finds out *first* what is right or wrong. If the second view is correct, one must find out first what God commands, and then argue that, since everything God commands is right, this kind of thing, which God is supposed to command, is right. It is not, on the second view, possible to find out what is right or wrong first, without previously having determined whether or not God commands it; hence, on the second view, ignorance of God's commands or of his existence must imply an equal degree of ignorance concerning what actions are right and what wrong.

On the first view it is perfectly possible to argue from an antecedent knowledge of right and wrong as a premise to a conclusion about what God commands or prohibits. We may, on this view, argue that, since it is wrong for us to harm one another, and since God forbids us to perform any action which is wrong, God must forbid us to harm one another, or more accurately, that if he exists at all, he must forbid us to harm one another. That, if God exists (and there is a right and wrong which neither consists in the fact that he commands some things and forbids others, nor is *determined* by the fact that he commands some things and forbids others) he always commands what is right and forbids what is wrong would seem to follow from the fact that God is, by definition, perfectly good. If he sometimes commanded what was wrong or forbade what is right, this would be inconsistent with the way in which we would expect a perfectly good being to behave.

There are difficulties with each of these three views. The first view has difficulty in explaining how, if it is true, God can be omnipotent. If we accept the first view, we must suppose that God's will, and in particular what actions God commands men to perform and what actions he commands them to refrain from performing, is deter-

mined by a moral law which is not identical with his commands, as it is on the third view, nor determined by his commands, as it would be on the second view. This seems to imply that the fact that certain things are wrong and other things are right is something over which God has no control. If he could control it, then it would be extremely odd to suppose that his will was subsequently determined by what he had himself brought about. It would be a very extraordinary situation if, though God's will was determined by the moral law, he himself decided what the moral law which determined his actions should be. God's will might just as well not be determined by any law at all, as be determined by a law which he himself decided upon. . . .

The second and third views apparently have no difficulty in accounting for God's omnipotence. On the second view, God, by deciding what actions he will command and what actions he will prohibit, actually decides what the moral law shall be, for whatever he commands becomes right for us, and whatever he prohibits becomes wrong. On the third view, he decides what shall be right for us and what wrong, for the fact that something is right just is the fact that he commands it, and the fact that it is wrong just is the fact that he prohibits it, and, presumably, he commands and prohibits what he pleases.

The difficulty the second and third view have is to explain how God can be good at all, let alone how he can be perfectly good. For one thing, the conclusion, which each of these two veiws entails, that whatever God were to command would be right for us, even if he commanded homicide, cannibalism or incest, is one which many people find shocking. For another thing, it seems reasonable to ask how, if the second or third views are true, can it even make sense to raise the question whether God is good or not, for, to say that a rational being is good is to say that his will accords with the moral law. God, however, could be neither good nor not good in this sense, for the moral law, on both the second view and the third, is something which he himself lays down or determines; hence his will could not be determined by the moral law, for there simply is no moral law, independent of what he himself decides, to determine it. Though there is nothing immoral in his commanding anything he pleases—for he himself determines what shall and shall not be immoral—many find the idea that God is in that way above morality repulsive.

Quite apart from the fact that there is nothing, however outrageous human beings may find it, which God may not, so far as moral considerations go, do, there is also a logical difficulty involved in saying that God is perfectly good on these two views. For God cannot be perfectly good, in the sense that whatever he does is right, if what he does is not determined by his knowledge of what is right, as it would be on the first of the three views. Indeed, it may be argued that it is even circular to define God as a being who is, among other things, perfectly good, if we also want to say that a being is good if he does what is right, and that he does what is right if he does what God commands. We are, in other words, first defining, or partly defining, God in terms of *goodness,* and then subsequently defining goodness in terms of what is commanded by *God.* . . .

It is possible to combine a variant of the second view with the first if one says that one thing, but not the *only* thing, which makes right actions right is that God has commanded them. Some actions, say Sabbath observance, are right simply because God has commanded them, but other actions, say actions of promise-keeping, are not right simply because God has commanded them, but for some other reason. On this view, being commanded by God is just one of a number of things which make it right for us to do something, but not the only thing which makes right actions right. It is then possible to argue that, since things like promise-keeping and honesty are right, and can be known to be right without its first being known whether or not God commands them, and since God is perfectly good, and will command us to perform actions which are right, he will command us to perform actions like keeping our promises and telling the truth. Since, on this view, being commanded by God is one thing which makes an action right, actions which are right for some reason other than that they are commanded by

God now become right for *two* reasons; since they are right for whatever reason, God will command them, and since they are commanded by God, they will also become right because it is also right for us to obey his commands. Since God may also command some actions which are not antecedently right, there are some actions which are right only because God has commanded them; it will be impossible to infer that God has commanded *these* actions from a prior knowledge of the fact that they are right because, where these actions are concerned, they are not right until God has commanded them.

It might even be possible, on this view, to have a conflict of duties, a conflict between our duty to obey God's commands and our duty to perform an action which is right for some reason other than that God has commanded it. One might say that, when God commanded Abraham to sacrifice Isaac, Abraham was faced with a conflict of duties, a duty to preserve human life and to take care of his offspring, and a duty to obey God's commands. It might seem suitably pious to say that, in the event of such a conflict, one's duty to obey God's commands would take precedence over any other duty.

If there were no God, all the actions which were right for some reason other than that they were commanded by God, might still be right, though in this case they would be right for one reason only, instead of two. They would be right for whatever reason made them right in the first place—say that not to have performed them would have caused other people unnecessary suffering—but they would no longer be right because God, who commands us to perform every action that is right, has commanded us to perform them, for God does not exist. Hence, on this view, or combination of views, there will still be some right actions, if God does not exist, though not so many as there would be if God does exist. One will also have motives, if God exists, for doing what is right, which one will not have, if God does not exist. If God exists, one may wish to do what is right not simply because it is right, but to please the God who has commanded it, and possibly also because one believes that ill will befall one in this world or the next as a result of a persistent adherence to wrong-doing. . . .

If there is a God, and he is omnipotent and omniscient, as by definition he is, then everything that happens in the universe, with the possible exception, already mentioned, of the free actions of human beings, must be something which he has intended or has allowed to happen, and has intended or allowed to happen for some reason. Hence, if something that happens is beneficial to mankind, God must have intended it to be so, and if something that happens is harmful to mankind, God must have intended this to be so also. Now, of course, a great deal of what happens in the world is of benefit to mankind; men are usually born with the tendency to develop abilities, in particular their intelligence, which are useful to them; they have been made sociable to quite a high degree, which enables them to augment their power and their productivity by co-operating with one another; in nature there is a not wholly inadequate supply of the raw materials which they need; and man is quite well adapted to the environment in which he lives. All this, on the assumption that there is a God who is responsible for every contingent matter of fact about the world being as it is, points to the fact that God is well-disposed to mankind. On the other hand, much of what happens in the world does not point to a God who is well-disposed to man. Man would be happier and more successful if he were even more intelligent than God has made him, if he were less prone to quarrel with his fellow men, less prone to physical and mental illness and deformity, had a more adequate supply of the commodities he needs, and was better adapted to his environment. Hence, on the assumption that there is a God, an investigation of the natural world would point to the fact that he is reasonably benevolently disposed to mankind, but by no means wholly so, and, moreover, to the fact that he is much more well-disposed to some men than he is to others. To some men, indeed, he would appear to behave in a manner worse than any human malevolence could possibly imagine or contrive.

Many attempts have been made to reconcile the apparent evil and imperfection in the world with God's benevolence, but they have not been very successful. It has been suggested that some evil in the world enhances the goodness of the whole, much as a discord in music may enhance the beauty of the music or an ugly colour in a painting may enhance the beauty of the painting; it may be argued, however, that the dreadful suffering endured by many is too high a price to pay for this aesthetic beauty. It has also been suggested that the appearance of evil in the world may be due to the fact that man, being finite, sees only a small part of the whole, and that, were he to see the whole, he would realize that the evil in the part he does see is a necessary means to some overriding good. But though this *may* be so, that it is so is simply a possibility—and a remote one, at that—which we have no means of testing unless we do view the whole that we cannot see. It has been suggested, too, that the causal laws which govern the universe make evil a necessary concomitant, and sometimes a necessary means, to a greater good. For example, the function of pain is to warn the person who feels it of something that will do him damage, and, though pain could be dispensed with, it would be at the price of endangering the organism which it is the function of pain to preserve. It is argued that even useless pain is still part of that price which mankind, or rather, sentient creatures in general, have to pay for their preservation, for it would be impossible to have the physiological mechanism which causes us to feel pain unless we also felt pain sometimes when it was too late or impossible for us to take the necessary avoiding action. The difficulty with this defence is that one cannot argue that the causal laws which govern the universe make it inevitable that we should experience pain if we are to be warned of danger, when God is himself supposed to have created the universe and made these causal laws what they are, and so must have the power to alter them at will. It has been suggested that man himself brings evil into the world by his own free will, and that the only way God could have prevented this was by creating men without free will; but a man without free will would be a less admirable being than a man with free will; hence evil is the necessary price we have to pay for freedom. The reply to this is obvious. Not all the evil in the world *is* the result of the operation of man's free will. Earthquake, famine and pestilence are not. It might even be argued that God could, if he had wished to do so, have created man both free and good. What we freely choose to do is to an enormous extent dependent upon the physical state of our brain and nervous system. A woman taking therapeutic drugs for mental illness may freely choose to do many things which the same woman not taking drugs will not freely choose to do. Hence if an ordinary doctor, by giving someone drugs or some other form of treatment, can change the pattern of a person's free and voluntary activity for the better, it is difficult to see how God could find it difficult to have made people better than they are, and at the same time free. Hence, even if we concede that there is a God who for some reason or other brings about or permits everything that happens in the universe, it is difficult to see how one can arrive by the unaided use of reason, at the conclusion that he is perfectly benevolent. (If you say, as I have suggested you should, that God is by definition perfectly benevolent, you must then say that it is difficult to see how you can arrive at the conclusion that the being who governs the universe is God.) For all these reasons one cannot, even granted that there is a God, or at least that the universe is ruled by an omnipotent and omniscient being, come to the conclusion that necessarily he commands us to perform those actions which it would be to our good to perform, for a God who will allow suffering might very well command actions which are *not* conducive to the happiness of his creatures.

If one does *not* allow oneself to assume that there *is* a God, it is still more difficult to produce any reason for thinking that God commands men to perform those actions which further their own happiness. In this case, we are not allowed to assume that there is a God, and simply show that he is benevolent; we must show that there is a God, and that he is benevolent. All the difficulties with the first argument, for the benevolence of God on the assumption that he exists, are also difficulties with the second argument, which purports to show that there is a God who is benevolent; and

there are more as well. The hypothesis that the world is governed by an unobserved but benevolent God is very unlike the hypothesis that there is an unobserved magnet in my pocket, which is causing a compass needle to behave in an unusual way, or that there is an unobserved planet, the existence of which is modifying the behaviour of other planets, even leaving aside the difficulty that it is in principle possible to observe the magnet and the planet, though they are at the moment unobserved, while it may be argued that God is in principle something which it is impossible to observe. Where the hypotheses that there is an unobserved magnet in my pocket or an unobserved planet in the solar system are concerned, one argues to their existence from an apparent irregularity in the normal course of nature, an irregularity in the behaviour of the compass needle or in the behaviour of other planets, which irregularity can be shown to be only apparent if the magnet or the extra planet are postulated. The argument in fact goes as follows: something which happens appears to go against what we expect from what we know of the laws which govern nature; if however, there were an unobserved magnet or an unobserved planet situated in a certain position in space, we could explain what is happening without abandoning any of the laws which we already accept; hence there is very likely an unobserved magnet or an unobserved planet. In the case of the argument to the existence of a benevolent God, however, there *is* no interruption to the normal laws of nature. The fact that man is intelligent and is adapted to his environment can be perfectly well explained without the hypothesis that there is a God. If we discount, for the sake of simplicity, miracles, which are in any case sporadic, unpredictable and imperfectly attested, the argument to the existence of God takes as its premise not apparent irregularities in the course of nature, but the fact that nature is uniform. There is no need, however, to postulate anything at all to explain the fact that nature is uniform. Indeed, it would be impossible to have any explanation of this. For normally the question 'Why' means 'Why in this case but not in that?' and it is impossible to ask the question 'Why is nature uniform in this case but not in that?'—which question *might* be answered by saying there is a God responsible for the uniformity in this case, though there is not in that—for, where the universe is concerned, the universe is the sum total of everything that there is, and hence there are no other cases. Hence, if we are not allowed to assume that there is a God, it is still more difficult to argue to the existence of a benevolent God who makes laws which it is in man's interest to obey.

Perhaps, however, we are wrong to try to make our argument to the nature of God's laws rest upon his benevolence. Perhaps we should argue, instead, that what God intends is the normal or the 'natural', and that deviations from the normal or 'natural' are contrary to his intentions, and so wrong. Hence suicide is wrong because God must have intended man to live out his normal life-span, unless this is shortened by illness which man has no power to control, and contraception is wrong because this is contrary to the normal or natural manner of having sexual intercourse, and sexual perversion is wrong for the same reason.

There are a number of difficulties with this manner of arguing. For one thing, it is very difficult to find any standard of normality other than what is usual or what happens most, and what happens most is obviously quite often wrong. For another thing, if God is omnipotent and omniscient, then he must have intended everything that happens, and be as much responsible for deviations from the norm as he is for the norm itself; hence we cannot argue that the norm is what he intends, but the deviations are not what he intends. And it is very difficult to argue that it is wrong to interfere with the normal course of nature by committing suicide or using contraceptives while stopping short of arguing that it must also be wrong to interfere with the normal course of nature by curing disease or using artificial fertilizers. In any case, the argument would at most allow us to argue to God's intentions given the assumption that there is a God, not at all to the *existence* of a God.

If we cannot argue to the nature of God's commands for man from a consideration of the nature of the world, perhaps we are able to know about him from what we are told about him in the Bible or in some other holy book. Certainly in the Bible we are told things about God, and what he intends, and what he expects of his creatures. The most serious difficulty is that part of the appeal of the Bible is a moral appeal. Christ, for example, is presented not simply as a man who worked miracles and who claimed to be, or to be in a special relationship to, God. He behaved in certain ways which most people regard with at least qualified approval and enunciated certain moral precepts which commend themselves to many people at least in some degree. But for the appeal of Christ to be a moral appeal, it must be presupposed that we have some standards of right and wrong already, by which Christ's behaviour can be morally assessed. For his precepts to commend themselves to us, we must have some insight into what is right and wrong which is independent of his testimony. I personally have no doubt that, if Christ behaved in ways which we would consider quite reprehensible, and enunciated precepts which most people would regard as being outrageous, the claims which he made on his own behalf and on behalf of the religion which he founded would command no serious attention.

It is true that, given that Christ's behaviour appeals to the standards of morality we already have, and given that many of his moral precepts commend themselves to the degree of moral enlightenment we possess at the moment, we may well be prepared to accept some *other* of his precepts simply on his authority, that is, on the authority of someone who has already shown himself to possess moral insight and to be in practice good. But such precepts would supplement the knowledge of right and wrong we already possess, rather than be the sole means of our having any knowledge of right and wrong. Hence the view that we acquire all our knowledge of right and wrong—that is, on the view that 'right' simply means 'commanded by God', all our knowledge of God's commands—upon the authority of some divine being, revealed in some divine book, must be rejected.

In any case, ... all knowledge based upon

testimony presupposes knowledge not based upon testimony. We may know that there are black swans in Australia or that Pythagoras's theorem is true because we have been told, and the person who told us may himself have been told by yet another person, but the chain of testimony must end at some point by someone's having observed the black swans in Australia, or worked out Pythagoras's theorem, for himself. Hence, though we may believe things about God's commands or man's duties on the authority of some holy person or book, there still remains the question how this holy person or the men who wrote the holy book themselves came to know what they claim to know.

Many people believe that our consciences provide a way of knowing what it is that God commands us to perform, and what kind of thing he wishes us to do. I believe that, for many people, conscience presents itself as of divine authority. These people, when they have a guilty conscience, feel as if God is actively displeased with their conduct, and, when they have a clear conscience, feel as if he is not displeased or is positively approving of them. Hence they imagine, if this is not too question-begging a word, their conduct to be under the perpetual review of a being who demands that they do what he enjoins, and that they refrain from doing what he prohibits. I doubt, however, whether conscience does provide us with any means of knowing what God's wishes for us are. For one thing, I do not think it is a universal phenomenon that conscience presents itself as the voice of God. Many who do not even believe in God have a conscience which demands that they behave in some ways and refrain from behaving in others.

For another thing, it is unclear whether conscience is supposed to provide us with a means of inferring what God's commands are, or whether it provides us with some form of direct acquaintance with the wishes of the divinity. If it were to provide us with a means of inferring the commands of the divinity, the argument would, again, have either to be one which rested *upon the assumption* that there is a God who causes us to feel guilty or self-approving in the way we do, and to have the conscientious scruples we do have, or it must itself provide us with a reason for thinking that there *is* a God who causes our consciences to operate as it does. The latter argument would only be plausible if the operations of conscience could not be explained in any other way, but these operations can already be partially explained as being a reaction to the pressures of our environment and the demands made upon us by our community, and it seems quite possible that psychologists will be able to produce a full explanation of the working of conscience in the course of time. And the argument that, *if* there is a God, he must intend us to refrain from performing those actions which are such that they would cause us to have an uneasy conscience if we did perform them is highly precarious. Conscience is moulded by social influences which often seem to have little to do with divine action, and is highly fallible, both because the person who possesses the conscience is mistaken about or ignorant of relevant matters of fact, and also because it appears to enjoin at one time things which we subsequently reject as being wrong. God, if he is omnipotent and omniscient, must be responsible for the deliverances of our conscience when these err just as much as when they do not err.

Perhaps, however, it is not so much a case of arguing to the existence of God, using facts about our consciences as premises, as that, through our consciences, we are brought into some form of direct contact with the divine will, and hence know what he commands not by inference but by something more like direct acquaintance with his commands. It is certainly true that, in many people, though not in all, conscience does present itself as if it were a form of immediate awareness, as if we did not need to infer, from the deliverances of conscience, what God's commands are, but knew them in some more intimate, less discursive way. If this were so, it is important to realize how very different would be our awareness of God's commands from our knowledge of the commands of our human superiors. Where these latter are concerned, we hear words, the meaning of which we understand, and which we believe to emanate from the bodies of the people who are commanding us, which bodies we suppose to be animated by minds, whatever being animated by a mind consists of. Hence we are not directly aware of some entity called a command; what we are directly aware of is a noise, or possibly ink marks on paper, and we infer from the occurrence of the noise or the ink marks that there is some being with a mind like ours who is doing what we are doing when we ourselves command others. In the case of our alleged *acquaintance* with God's commands, however, there can be no question of written marks being made on paper by some divine being, or of sound waves emanating from his vocal chords. We must, if we are aware of his commands at all, and especially if this awareness is supposed not to involve our making any inference, be directly aware of the commands without the intermediary of ink marks on paper producing light waves which modify the retina of our eyes or of noises produced by sound waves affecting our ears.

Personally I find it very difficult to conceive of what such an awareness, the awareness of a command of some being, which does not consist in the first instance of an awareness of symbols the meaning of which we understand, could possibly be. It is true that I am familiar with the experience of imagining myself disapproved of by some superhuman being, as I am with the experience of imagining myself disapproved of by other human beings, but *imagining* oneself disapproved of, even if it is accompanied by a tendency to believe that one actually is disapproved of, is a very different matter from being aware, in some unusual way, of the disapproval which these other beings are supposed to feel.

It is often the case that people who believe that there is some intimate connection between God's commands and man's duties hold their moral opinions with much greater firmness, a firmness which in some cases amounts to an intolerant dogmatism, than people who believe that moral beliefs are not beliefs about God's commands, whether or not these latter people also believe that

there is a God who commands them to perform actions which they think are right. I cannot personally see any reason why the belief that actions are right because they are commanded by God, or the belief that 'right' simply means 'commanded by God' should by itself produce dogmatism or intolerance, but there is a reason why the belief that one arrives at least at some of one's moral tenets upon God's *authority* should produce such dogmatism. The reason, I think, is this. An omniscient being can scarcely be supposed to be mistaken about what is right and wrong; hence, if we are told that something is right upon the authority of an omniscient being, it is natural to suppose that we ourselves cannot be mistaken about this thing's being right. Though this is natural, however, it is mistaken. Though God's 'beliefs' may be superhuman and infallible, our beliefs, even when they are beliefs which we think that God has revealed to us, are all human and fallible. Hence, though God may know that adultery is wrong, and may have told us that adultery is wrong, it does not follow that we ourselves know that adultery is wrong, and it does not follow, therefore, that we are justified in maintaining that adultery is wrong with supreme confidence. For our belief that adultery is wrong, if we believe this because we believe God has revealed it to us, can be no better warranted than our belief that God *has* revealed it to us, and this belief is simply a human fallible belief of ours. We may feel that God has not only revealed to us that adultery is wrong, but has also revealed to us the fact that he has revealed to us that adultery is wrong, and hence that our belief that God has revealed to us that adultery is wrong has a divine backing which justifies us in holding it with a confidence which we would not have in it if we thought it was merely a human belief of our own; but this, again, is a mistake. To argue that we know that God has revealed some fact to us because God has revealed to us the fact that he has revealed this fact would be rather like the notorious argument that God exists because this is revealed in the Bible, which must be infallible, because it is the word of God. Any doubt about whether God has revealed something must imply a like doubt about whether he has revealed to us that he has revealed this: If God does not exist, for example, not only can he not have revealed to us that adultery is wrong; he also cannot have re-vealed to us that he has revealed that adultery is wrong. In any case, it is a peculiar kind of revela-tion which requires another and prior revelation of the fact that it is revelation. . . .

VIII.5   A Modified Divine Command Theory of Ethical Wrongness

ROBERT MERRIHEW ADAMS

Robert Merrihew Adams is professor of philoso-phy at the University of Southern California at Los Angeles. In this reading he attempts to meet the standard criticisms against the divine command theory by modifying it so as to take into account the loving nature of God. Although it is not logi-cally impossible for God to command us to do what is gratuitously cruel, he would not do so be-cause of his love. Adams's essay contains a valu-able section detailing the ways in which secular and religious morality are different and the ways in which they are similar.

I

It is widely held that all those theories are indefen-sible which attempt to explain in terms of the will or commands of God what it is for an act to be ethically right or wrong. In this paper I shall state such a theory, which I believe to be defensible; and I shall try to defend it against what seem to me to be the most important and interesting objec-tions to it. I call my theory a modified divine com-mand theory because in it I renounce certain claims that are commonly made in divine com-mand analyses of ethical terms. (I should add that it is *my* theory only in that I shall state it, and that I

This is a major part of the essay "A Modified Divine Command Theory of Ethical Wrongness" by Robert Merrihew Adams. From *Religion and Morality: A Collection of Essays* (New York: Doubleday, 1973), edited by Gene Outka and John P. Reeder, Jr. Copyright © 1973 by Gene Outka and John P. Reeder, Jr. Reprinted by permission of the author, the editors, and the pub-lisher. Footnotes edited.

believe it is defensible—not that I am sure it is correct.) I present it as a theory of ethical *wrong-ness* partly for convenience. It could also be pre-sented as a theory of the nature of ethical obligato-riness or of ethical permittedness. Indeed, I will have occasion to make some remarks about the concept of ethical permittedness. But as we shall see (in Section IV) I am not prepared to claim that the theory can be extended to all ethical terms; and it is therefore important that it not be pre-sented as a theory about ethical terms in general.

It will be helpful to begin with the statement of a simple, *un-*modified divine command theory of ethical wrongness. This is the theory that ethical wrongness *consists in* being contrary to God's commands, or that the word "wrong" in ethical contexts *means* "contrary to God's commands." It implies that the following two statement forms are logically equivalent.

(1) It is wrong (for A) to do X.
(2) It is contrary to God's commands (for A) to do X.

Of course that is not all that the theory implies. It also implies that (2) is conceptually prior to (1), so that the meaning of (1) is to be explained in terms of (2), and not the other way round. It might prove fairly difficult to state or explain in what that con-ceptual priority consists, but I shall not go into that here. I do not wish ultimately to defend the theory in its unmodified form, and I think I have stated it fully enough for my present purposes.

I have stated it as a theory about the meaning of the word "wrong" in ethical contexts. The most obvious objection to the theory is that the word "wrong" is used in ethical contexts by many people who cannot mean by it what the theory says they must mean, since they do not believe that there exists a God. This objection seems to me sufficient to refute the theory if it is presented as an analysis of what *everybody* means by "wrong" in ethical contexts. The theory cannot reasonably be offered except as a theory about what the word "wrong" means as used by *some but not all* people in ethical contexts. Let us say that the theory offers an analysis of the meaning of "wrong" in Judeo-Christian religious ethical discourse. This restriction of scope will apply to my modified divine command theory too. This restriction obviously gives rise to a possible objection. Isn't it more plausible to suppose that Judeo-Christian believers use "wrong" with the same meaning as other people do? This problem will be discussed in Section VI. . . .

II

The following seems to me to be the gravest objection to the divine command theory of ethical wrongness, in the form in which I have stated it. Suppose God should command me to make it my chief end in life to inflict suffering on other human beings, for no other reason than that He commanded it. (For convenience I shall abbreviate this hypothesis to "Suppose God should command cruelty for its own sake.") Will it seriously be claimed that in that case it would be wrong for me not to practice cruelty for its own sake? I see three possible answers to this question.

(1) It might be claimed that it is logically impossible for God to command cruelty for its own sake. In that case, of course, we need not worry about whether it would be wrong to disobey if He did command it. It is senseless to agonize about what one should do in a logically impossible situation. This solution to the problem seems unlikely to be available to the divine command theorist, however. For why would he hold that it is logically impossible for God to command cruelty for

its own sake? Some theologians (for instance, Thomas Aquinas) have believed (a) that what is right and wrong is independent of God's will, *and* (b) that God always does right by the necessity of His nature. Such theologians, if they believe that it would be wrong for God to command cruelty for its own sake, have reason to believe that it is logically impossible for Him to do so. But the divine command theorist, who does not agree that what is right and wrong is independent of God's will, does not seem to have such a reason to deny that it is logically possible for God to command cruelty for its own sake.

(2) Let us assume that it is logically possible for God to command cruelty for its own sake. In that case the divine command theory seems to imply that it would be wrong not to practice cruelty for its own sake. There have been at least a few adherents of divine command ethics who have been prepared to accept this consequence. William Ockham held that those acts which we call "theft," "adultery," and "hatred of God" would be meritorious if God had commanded them. He would surely have said the same about what I have been calling the practice of "cruelty for its own sake."

This position is one which I suspect most of us are likely to find somewhat shocking, even repulsive. We should therefore be particularly careful not to misunderstand it. We need not imagine that Ockham disciplined himself to be ready to practice cruelty for its own sake if God should command it. It was doubtless an article of faith for him that God is unalterably opposed to any such practice. The mere logical possibility that theft, adultery, and cruelty might have been commanded by God (and therefore meritorious) doubtless did not represent in Ockham's view any real possibility.

(3) Nonetheless, the view that if God commanded cruelty for its own sake it would be wrong not to practice it seems unacceptable to me; and I think many, perhaps most, other Jewish and Christian believers would find it unacceptable too. I must make clear the sense in which I find it unsatisfactory. It is not that I find an internal inconsistency in it. And I would not deny that it may reflect, accurately enough, the way in which some

believers use the word "wrong." I might as well frankly avow that I am looking for a divine command theory which at least might possibly be a correct account of how *I* use the word "wrong." I do not use the word "wrong" in such a way that I would say that it would be wrong not to practice cruelty if God commanded it, and I am sure that many other believers agree with me on this point.

But now have I not rejected the divine command theory? I have assumed that it would be logically possible for God to command cruelty for its own sake. And I have rejected the view that if God commanded cruelty for its own sake, it would be wrong not to obey. It seems to follow that I am committed to the view that in certain logically possible circumstances it would not be wrong to disobey God. This position seems to be inconsistent with the theory that "wrong" means "contrary to God's commands."

I want to argue, however, that it is still open to me to accept a modified form of the divine command theory of ethical wrongness. According to the modified divine command theory, when I say, "It is wrong to do *X*," (at least part of) what I *mean* is that it is contrary to God's commands to do *X*. "It is wrong to do *X*" *implies* "It is contrary to God's commands to do *X*." But "It is contrary to God's commands to do *X*" implies "It is wrong to do *X*" only if certain conditions are assumed— namely, only if it is assumed that God has the character which I believe Him to have, of loving His human creatures. If God were really to command us to make cruelty our goal, then He would not have that character of loving us, and I would not say it would be wrong to disobey Him.

But do I say that it would be wrong to obey Him in such a case? This is the point at which I am in danger of abandoning the divine command theory completely. I do abandon it completely if I say both of the following things.

(A) It would be wrong to obey God if He commanded cruelty for its own sake.

(B) In (A), "wrong" is used in what is for me its normal ethical sense.

If I assert both (A) and (B), it is clear that I cannot consistently maintain that "wrong" in its normal

ethical sense for me means or implies "contrary to God's commands."

But from the fact that I deny that it would be wrong to disobey God if He commanded cruelty for its own sake, it does not follow that I must accept (A) and (B). Of course someone might claim that obedience and disobedience would both be ethically permitted in such a case; but that is not the view that I am suggesting. If I adopt the modified divine command theory as an analysis of my present concept of ethical wrongness (and if I adopt a similar analysis of my concept of ethical permittedness), I will not hold either that it would be wrong to disobey, or that it would be ethically permitted to disobey, or that it would be wrong to obey, or that it would be ethically permitted to obey, if God commanded cruelty for its own sake. For I will say that my concept of ethical wrongness (and my concept of ethical permittedness) would "break down" if I really believed that God commanded cruelty for its own sake. Or to put the matter somewhat more prosaically, I will say that my concepts of ethical wrongness and permittedness could not serve the functions they now serve, because using those concepts I could not call any action ethically wrong or ethically permitted, if I believed that God's will was so unloving. This position can be explained or developed in either of two ways, each of which has its advantages.

I could say that by "*X* is ethically wrong" I mean "*X* is contrary to the commands of a *loving* God" (i.e., "There is a *loving* God and *X* is contrary to His commands") and by "*X* is ethically permitted" I mean "*X* is in accord with the commands of a *loving* God" (i.e., "There is a *loving* God and *X* is not contrary to His commands"). On this analysis we can reason as follows. If there is only one God and He commands cruelty for its own sake, then presumably there is not a *loving* God. If there is not a loving God then neither "*X* is ethically wrong" nor "*X* is ethically permitted" is true of any *X*. Using my present concepts of ethical wrongness and permittedness, therefore, I could not (consistently) call any action ethically wrong or permitted if I believed that God commanded cruelty for its own sake. This way of developing the modified divine command theory is the simpler and neater of the two, and that might reasonably lead one to choose it for the construction of a theological ethical theory. On the other hand, I think it is also simpler and neater than ordinary religious ethical discourse, in which (for example) it may be felt that the statement that a certain act is wrong is *about* the will or commands of God in a way in which it is not about His love.

In this essay I shall prefer a second, rather similar, but somewhat untidier, understanding of the modified divine command theory, because I think it may lead us into some insights about the complexities of actual religious ethical discourse. According to this second version of the theory, the statement that something is ethically wrong (or permitted) says something about the will or commands of God, but not about His love. Every such statement, however, *presupposes* that certain conditions for the applicability of the believer's concepts of ethical right and wrong are satisfied. Among these conditions is that God does not command cruelty for its own sake—or, more generally, that God loves His human creatures. It need not be assumed that God's love is the only such condition.

The modified divine command theorist can say that the possibility of God commanding cruelty for its own sake is not provided for in the Judeo-Christian religious ethical system as he understands it. The possibility is not provided for, in the sense that the concepts of right and wrong have not been developed in such a way that actions could be correctly said to be right or wrong if God were believed to command cruelty for its own sake. The modified divine command theorist agrees that it is logically possible that God should command cruelty for its own sake; but he holds that it is unthinkable that God should do so. To have *faith* in God is not just to believe that He exists, but also to trust in His love for mankind. The believer's concepts of ethical wrongness and permittedness are developed within the framework of his (or the religious community's) religious life, and therefore within the framework of the assumption that God loves us. The concept of the will or commands of God has a certain function in the believer's life, and the use of the words "right"

(in the sense of "ethically permitted") and "wrong" is tied to that function of that concept. But one of the reasons why the concept of the will of God can function as it does is that the love which God is believed to have toward men arouses in the believer certain attitudes of love toward God and devotion to His will. If the believer thinks about the unthinkable but logically possible situation in which God commands cruelty for its own sake, he finds that in relation to that kind of command of God he cannot take up the same attitude, and that the concept of the will or commands of God could not then have the same function in his life. For this reason he will not say that it would be wrong to disobey God, or right to obey Him, in that situation. At the same time he will not say that it would be wrong to obey God in that situation, because he is accustomed to use the word "wrong" to say that something is contrary to the will of God, and it does not seem to him to be the right word to use to express his own personal revulsion toward an act against which there would be no divine authority. Similarly, he will not say that it would be "right," in the sense of "ethically permitted," to disobey God's command of cruelty; for that does not seem to him to be the right way to express his own personal attitude toward an act which would not be in accord with a divine authority. In this way the believer's concepts of ethical rightness and wrongness would break down in the situation in which he believed that God commanded cruelty for its own sake—that is, they would not function as they now do, because he would not be prepared to use them to say that any action was right or wrong.

III

It is clear that according to this modified divine command theory, the meaning of the word "wrong" in Judeo-Christian ethical discourse must be understood in terms of a complex of relations which believers' use of the word has, not only to their beliefs about God's commands, but also to their attitudes toward certain types of action. I think it will help us to understand the theory better if we can give a brief but fairly comprehensive description of the most important features of the Judeo-Christian ethical use of "wrong," from the point of view of the modified divine command theory. That is what I shall try to do in this section.

(1) "Wrong" and "contrary to God's commands" at least contextually imply each other in Judeo-Christian ethical discourse. "It is wrong to do X" will be assented to by the sincere Jewish or Christian believer if and only if he assents to "It is contrary to God's commands to do X." This is a fact sufficiently well known that the known believer who says the one commits himself publicly to the other.

Indeed "wrong" and such expressions as "against the will of God" seem to be used interchangeably in religious ethical discourse. If a believer asks his pastor, "Do you think it's always against the will of God to use contraceptives?" and the pastor replies, "I don't see anything wrong with the use of contraceptives in many cases," the pastor has answered the same question the inquirer asked.

(2) In ethical contexts, the statement that a certain action is wrong normally expresses certain volitional and emotional attitudes toward that action. In particular it normally expresses an intention, or at least an inclination, not to perform the action, and/or dispositions to feel guilty if one has performed it, to discourage others from performing it, and to react with anger, sorrow, or diminished respect toward others if they have performed it. I think this is true of Judeo-Christian ethical discourse as well as of other ethical discourse.

The interchangeability of "wrong" and "against the will of God" applies in full force here. It seems to make no difference to the expressive function of an ethical statement in a Judeo-Christian context which of these expressions is used. So far as I can see, the feelings and dispositions normally expressed by "It is wrong to commit suicide" in a Judeo-Christian context are exactly the same as those normally expressed by "It is against God's will to commit suicide," or by "Suicide is a violation of the commandments of God." . . .

(3) In a Judeo-Christian context, moreover, the attitudes expressed by a statement that something is wrong are normally quite strongly affected and colored by specifically religious feelings and interests. They are apt to be motivated in various degrees by, and mixed in various proportions with, love, devotion, and loyalty toward God, and/or fear of God. Ethical wrongdoing is seen and experienced as *sin*, as rupture of personal or communal relationship with God. The normal feelings and experience of guilt for Judeo-Christian believers surely cannot be separated from beliefs, and ritual and devotional practices, having to do with God's judgment and forgiveness.

In all sin there is offense against a person (God), even when there is no offense against any other human person—for instance, if I have a vice which harms me but does not importantly harm any other human being. Therefore in the Judeo-Christian tradition reactions which are appropriate when one has offended another person are felt to be appropriate reactions to any ethical fault, regardless of whether another human being has been offended. I think this affects rather importantly the emotional connections of the word "wrong" in Judeo-Christian discourse.

(4) When a Judeo-Christian believer is trying to decide, in an ethical way, whether it would be wrong for him to do a certain thing, he typically thinks of himself as trying to determine whether it would be against God's will for him to do it. His deliberations may turn on the interpretation of certain religiously authoritative texts. They may be partly carried out in the form of prayer. It is quite possible, however, that his deliberations will take forms more familiar to the nonbeliever. Possibly his theology will encourage him to give some weight to his own intuitions and feelings about the matter, and those of other people. Such encouragement might be provided, for instance, by a doctrine of the leading of the Holy Spirit. Probably the believer will accept certain very general ethical principles as expressing commandments of God, and most of these may be principles which many nonbelievers would also accept (for instance, that it is always, or with very few exceptions, wrong to kill another human being). The

believer's deliberation might consist entirely of reasoning from such general principles. But he would still regard it as an attempt to discover God's will on the matter.

(5) Typically, the Judeo-Christian believer is a nonnaturalist objectivist about ethical wrongness. When he says that something is (ethically) wrong, he means to be stating what he believes to be a fact of a certain sort—what I shall call a "nonnatural objective fact." Such a fact is objective in the sense that whether it obtains or not does not depend on whether any human being thinks it does. It is harder to give a satisfactory explanation of what I mean by "nonnatural" here. Let us say that a nonnatural fact is one which does not consist simply in any fact or complex of facts which can be stated entirely in the languages of physics, chemistry, biology, and human psychology. That way of putting it obviously raises questions which it leaves unanswered, but I hope it may be clear enough for present purposes.

That ethical facts are objective and nonnatural has been believed by many people, including some famous philosophers—for instance, Plato and G. E. Moore. The term "nonnaturalism" is sometimes used rather narrowly, to refer to a position held by Moore, and positions closely resembling it. Clearly, I am using "nonnaturalist" in a broader sense here.

Given that the facts of wrongness asserted in Judeo-Christian ethics are nonnatural in the sense explained above, and that they accordingly do not consist entirely in facts of physics, chemistry, biology, and human psychology, the question arises, in what they do consist. According to the divine command theory (even the modified divine command theory), in so far as they are nonnatural and objective, they consist in facts about the will or commands of God. I think this is really the central point in a divine command theory of ethical wrongness. This is the point at which the divine command theory is distinguished from alternative theological theories of ethical wrongness, such as the theory that facts of ethical rightness and wrongness are objective, nonnatural facts about ideas or essences subsisting eternally in God's understanding, not subject to His will but guiding it.

The divine command account of the nonnatural fact-stating function of Judeo-Christian ethical discourse has at least one advantage over its competitors. It is clear, I think, that in stating that X is wrong a believer normally commits himself to the view that X is contrary to the will or commands of God. And the fact (if it is a fact) that X is contrary to the will or commands of God is surely a nonnatural objective fact. But it is not nearly so clear that in saying that X is wrong, the believer normally commits himself to belief in any *other* nonnatural objective fact. . . .

(6) The modified divine command theorist cannot consistently claim that "wrong" and "contrary to God's commands" have exactly the same meaning for him. For he admits that there is a logically possible situation which he would describe by saying, "God commands cruelty for its own sake," but not by saying, "It would be wrong not to practice cruelty for its own sake." If there were not at least some little difference between the meanings with which he actually, normally uses the expressions "wrong" and "contrary to God's commands," there would be no reason for them to differ in their applicability or inapplicability to the far-out unthinkable case. We may now be in a position to improve somewhat our understanding of what the modified divine command theorist can suppose that difference in meaning to be, and of why he supposes that the believer is unwilling to say that disobedience to a divine command of cruelty for its own sake would be wrong.

We have seen that the expressions "It is wrong" and "It is contrary to God's commands" or "It is against the will of God" have virtually the same uses in religious ethical discourse, and the same functions in the religious ethical life. No doubt they differ slightly in the situations in which they are most likely to be used and the emotional overtones they are most apt to carry. But in all situations experienced or expected by the believer as a believer they at least contextually imply each other, and normally express the same or extremely similar emotional and volitional attitudes.

There is also a difference in meaning, however, a difference which is normally of no practical importance. All three of the following are aspects of the normal use of "it is wrong" in the life and conversation of believers. (a) It is used to state what are believed to be facts about the will or commands of God. (b) It is used in formulating decisions and arguments about what to do (i.e., not just in deciding what one *ought* to do, but in deciding *what to do*). (c) It expresses certain emotional and volitional attitudes toward the action under discussion. "It is wrong" is commonly used to do all three of those things at once.

The same is true of "It is contrary to God's commands" and "It is against the will of God." They are commonly used by believers to do the same three things, and to do them at once. But because of their grammatical form and their formal relationships with other straightforwardly descriptive expressions about God, they are taken to be, first and last, descriptive expressions about God and His relation to whatever actions are under discussion. They can therefore be used to state what are supposed to be facts about God, even when one's emotional and decision-making attitude toward those supposed facts is quite contrary to the attitudes normally expressed by the words "against the will of God."

In the case of "It is wrong," however, it is not clear that one of its functions, or one of the aspects of its normal use, is to be preferred in case of conflict with the others. I am not willing to say, "It would be wrong not to do X," when both my own attitude and the attitude of most other people toward the doing of X under the indicated circumstances is one of unqualified revulsion. On the other hand, neither am I willing to say, "It would be wrong to do X," when I would merely be expressing my own personal revulsion (and perhaps that of other people as well) but nothing that I could regard as clothed in the majesty of a divine authority. The believer's concept of ethical wrongness therefore breaks down if one tries to apply it to the unthinkable case in which God commands cruelty for its own sake.

None of this seems to me inconsistent with the claim that part of what the believer normally means in saying "X is wrong" is that X is contrary to God's will or commands.

IV

The modified divine command theory clearly conceives of believers as valuing some things independently of their relation to God's commands. If the believer will not say that it would be wrong not to practice cruelty for its own sake if God commanded it, that is because he values kindness, and has a revulsion for cruelty, in a way that is at least so some extent independent of his belief that God commands kindness and forbids cruelty. This point may be made the basis of both philosophical and theological objections to the modified divine command theory, but I think the objections can be answered.

The philosophical objection is, roughly, that if there are some things I value independently of their relation to God's commands, then my value concepts cannot rightly be analyzed in terms of God's commands. According to the modified divine command theory, the acceptability of divine command ethics depends in part on the believer's independent positive valuation of the sorts of things that God is believed to command. But then, the philosophical critic objects, the believer must have a prior, nontheological conception of ethical right and wrong, in terms of which he judges God's commandments to be acceptable—and to admit that the believer has a prior, nontheological conception of ethical right and wrong is to abandon the divine command theory.

The weakness of this philosophical objection is that it fails to note the distinctions that can be drawn among various value concepts. From the fact that the believer values some things independently of his beliefs about God's commands, the objector concludes, illegitimately, that the believer must have a conception of ethical right and wrong that is independent of his beliefs about God's commands. This inference is illegitimate because there can be valuations which do not imply or presuppose a judgment of ethical right or wrong. For instance, I may simply like something, or want something, or feel a revulsion at something.

What the modified divine command theorist will hold, then, is that the believer values some things independently of their relation to God's commands, but that these valuations are not judgments of ethical right and wrong and do not of themselves imply judgments of ethical right and wrong. He will maintain, on the other hand, that such independent valuations are involved in, or even necessary for, judgments of ethical right and wrong which also involve beliefs about God's will or commands. The adherent of a divine command ethics will normally be able to give reasons for his adherence. Such reasons might include: "Because I am grateful to God for His love"; "Because I find it the most satisfying form of ethical life"; "Because there's got to be an objective moral law if life isn't to fall to pieces, and I can't understand what it would be if not the will of God." As we have already noted, the modified divine command theorist also has reasons why he would not accept a divine command ethics in certain logically possible situations which he believes not to be actual. All of these reasons seem to me to involve valuations that are independent of divine command ethics. The person who has such reasons wants certain things—happiness, certain satisfactions—for himself and others; he hates cruelty and loves kindness; he has perhaps a certain unique and "numinous" awe of God. And these are not attitudes which he has simply because of his beliefs about God's commands. They are not attitudes, however, which presuppose judgments of moral right and wrong. . . .

This version of the divine command theory may seem *theologically* objectionable to some believers. One of the reasons, surely, why divine command theories of ethics have appealed to some theologians is that such theories seem especially congruous with the religious demand that God be the object of our highest allegiance. If our supreme commitment in life is to doing what is right just because it is right, and if what is right is right just because God wills or commands it, then surely our highest allegiance is to God. But the modified divine command theory seems not to have this advantage. For the modified divine command theorist is forced to admit, as we have seen, that he has reasons for his adherence to a divine command ethics, and that his having these reasons implies that there are some things which he values independently of his beliefs about God's commands. It is therefore not correct to say of him that he is committed to doing the will of God *just* because it is the will of God; he is committed to doing it partly because of other things which he values independently. Indeed it appears that there are certain logically possible situations in which his present attitudes would not commit him to obey God's commands (for instance, if God commanded cruelty for its own sake). This may even suggest that he values some things, not just independently of God's commands, but more than God's commands.

We have here a real problem in religious ethical motivation. The Judeo-Christian believer is supposed to make God the supreme focus of his loyalties; that is clear. One possible interpretation of this fact is the following. Obedience to whatever God may command is (or at least ought to be) the one thing that the believer values for its own sake and more than anything and everything else. Anything else that he values, he values (or ought to) only to a lesser degree and as a means to obedience to God. This conception of religious ethical motivation is obviously favorable to an *unmodified* divine command theory of ethical wrongness.

But I think it is not a realistic conception. Loyalty to God, for instance, is very often explained, by believers themselves, as motivated by gratitude for benefits conferred. And I think it is clear in most cases that the gratitude presupposes that the benefits are valued, at least to some extent, independently of loyalty to God. Similarly, I do not think that most devout Judeo-Christian believers would say that it would be wrong to disobey God if He commanded cruelty for its own sake. And if I am right about that I think it shows that their positive valuation of (emotional/volitional pro-attitude toward) doing *whatever* God may command is not clearly greater than their independent negative valuation of cruelty.

In analyzing ethical motivation in general, as well as Judeo-Christian ethical motivation in particular, it is probably a mistake to suppose that there is (or can be expected to be) only one thing that is valued supremely and for its own sake, with nothing else being valued independently of it. The motivation for a person's ethical orientation in life is normally much more complex than that, and involves a plurality of emotional and volitional attitudes of different sorts which are at least partly independent of each other. At any rate, I think the modified divine command theorist is bound to say that that is true of his ethical motivation.

In what sense, then, can the modified divine command theorist maintain that God is the supreme focus of his loyalties? I suggest the following interpretation of the single-hearted loyalty to God which is demanded in Judeo-Christian religion. In this interpretation the crucial idea is *not* that some one thing is valued for its own sake and more than anything else, and nothing else valued independently of it. It is freely admitted that the religious person will have a plurality of motives for his ethical position, and that these will be at least partly independent of each other. It is admitted further that a desire to obey the commands of God (*whatever* they may be) may not be the strongest of these motives. What will be claimed is that certain beliefs about God enable the believer to integrate or focus his motives in a loyalty to God and His commands. Some of these beliefs are about what God commands or wills (contingently—that is, although He could logically have commanded or willed something else instead).

Some of the motives in question might be called egoistic; they include desires for satisfactions for oneself—which God is believed to have given or to be going to give. Other motives may be desires for satisfaction for other people; these may be called altruistic. Still other motives might not be desires for anyone's satisfaction, but might be valuations of certain kinds of action for their own sakes; these might be called idealistic. I do not think my argument depends heavily on this particular classification, but it seems plausible that all of these types, and perhaps others as well, might be distinguished among the motives for a religious person's ethical position. Obviously such motives might pull one in different directions, conflicting with one another. But in Judeo-Christian ethics

beliefs about what God does in fact will (although He could have willed otherwise) are supposed to enable one to *fuse* these motives, so to speak, into one's devotion to God and His will, so that they all pull together. Doubtless the believer will still have some motives which conflict with his loyalty to God. But the religious ideal is that these should all be merely momentary desires and impulses, and kept under control. They ought not to be allowed to influence voluntary action. The deeper, more stable, and controlling desires, intentions, and psychic energies are supposed to be fused in devotion to God. As I interpret it, however, it need not be inconsistent with the Judeo-Christian ethical and religious ideal that this fusion of motives, this integration of moral energies, depends on belief in certain propositions which are taken to be contingent truths about God.

Lest it be thought that I am proposing unprecedented theological positions, or simply altering Judeo-Christian religious beliefs to suit my theories, I will call to my aid on this point a theologian known for his insistence on the sovereignty of God. Karl Barth seems to me to hold a divine command theory of ethics. But when he raises the question of why we should obey God, he rejects with scorn the suggestion that God's *power* provides the basis for His claim on us. "By deciding for God [man] has definitely decided not to be obedient to power as power." God's claim on us is based rather on His grace. "God calls us and orders us and claims us by being gracious to us in Jesus Christ." I do not mean to suggest that Barth would agree with everything I have said about motivation, or that he offers a lucid account of a divine command theory. But he does agree with the position I have proposed on this point, that the believer's loyalty is not to be construed as a loyalty to God *as* all-powerful, nor to God *whatever* He might conceivably have willed. It is a loyalty to God *as* having a certain attitude toward us, a certain will for us, which God was free not to have, but to which, in Barth's view, He has committed Himself irrevocably in Jesus Christ. The believer's devotion is not to merely possible commands of God as such, but to God's actual (and gracious) will.

V

The ascription of moral qualities to God is commonly thought to cause problems for divine command theories of ethics. It is doubted that God, as an agent, can properly be called "good" in the moral sense if He is not subject to a moral law that is not of His own making. For if He is morally good, mustn't He do what is right *because* it is right? And how can He do that, if what's right is right because He wills it? Or it may be charged that divine command theories trivialize the claim that God is good. If "X is (morally) good" means roughly "X does what God wills," then "God is (morally) good" means only that God does what He wills—which is surely much less than people are normally taken to mean when they say that God is (morally) good. In this section I will suggest an answer to these objections.

Surely no analysis of Judeo-Christian ethical discourse can be regarded as adequate which does not provide for a sense in which the believer can seriously assert that God is good. Indeed an adequate analysis should provide a plausible account of what believers do in fact mean when they say, "God is good." I believe that a divine command theory of ethical (rightness and) wrongness can include such an account. I will try to indicate its chief features.

(1) In saying "God is good" one is normally expressing a favorable emotional attitude toward God. I shall not try to determine whether or not this is part of the meaning of "God is good"; but it is normally, perhaps almost always, at least one of the things one is doing if one says that God is good. If we were to try to be more precise about the type of favorable emotional attitude normally expressed by "God is good," I suspect we would find that the attitude expressed is most commonly one of *gratitude*.

(2) This leads to a second point, which is that when God is called "good" it is very often meant that He is *good to us*, or *good to* the speaker. "Good" is sometimes virtually a synonym for "kind." And for the modified divine command theorist it is not a trivial truth that God is kind. In

saying that God is good in the sense of "kind," one presupposes, of course, that there are some things which the beneficiaries of God's goodness value. We need not discuss here whether the beneficiaries must value them independently of their beliefs about God's will. For the modified divine command theorist does admit that there are some things which believers value independently of their beliefs about God's commands. Nothing that the modified divine command theorist says about the meaning of ("right" and) "wrong" implies that it is a trivial truth that God bestows on His creatures things that they value.

(3) I would not suggest that the descriptive force of "good" as applied to God is exhausted by the notion of kindness. "God is good" must be taken in many contexts as ascribing to God, rather generally, qualities of character which the believing speaker regards as virtues in human beings. Among such qualities might be faithfulness, ethical consistency, a forgiving disposition, and, in general, various aspects of love, as well as kindness. Not that there is some definite list of qualities, the ascription of which to God is clearly implied by the claim that God is good. But saying that God is good normally commits one to the position that God has some important set of qualities which one regards as virtues in human beings.

(4) It will not be thought that God has *all* the qualities which are virtues in human beings. Some such qualities are logically inapplicable to a being such as God is supposed to be. For example, aside from certain complications arising from the doctrine of the incarnation, it would be logically inappropriate to speak of God as controlling His sexual desires. (He doesn't have any.) And given some widely held conceptions of God and his relation to the world, it would hardly make sense to speak of Him as *courageous*. For if He is impassible and has predetermined absolutely everything that happens, He has no risks to face and cannot endure (because He cannot suffer) pain or displeasure. . . .

(5) If we accept a divine command theory of ethical rightness and wrongness, I think we shall have to say that *dutifulness* is a human virtue which, like sexual chastity, is logically inapplica-

ble to God. God cannot either do or fail to do His duty, since He does not have a duty—at least not in the most important sense in which human beings have a duty. For He is not subject to a moral law not of His own making. Dutifulness is one virtuous disposition which men can have that God cannot have. But there are other virtuous dispositions which God can have as well as men. Love, for instance. It hardly makes sense to say that God does what He does *because* it is right. But it does not follow that God cannot have any reason for doing what He does. It does not even follow that He cannot have reasons of a type on which it would be morally virtuous for a man to act. For example, He might do something because He knew it would make His creatures happier.

(6) The modified divine command theorist must deny that in calling God "good" one presupposes a standard of moral rightness and wrongness superior to the will of God, by reference to which it is determined whether God's character is virtuous or not. And I think he can consistently deny that. He can say that morally virtuous and vicious qualities of character are those which agree and conflict, respectively, with God's commands, and that it is their agreement or disagreement with God's commands that makes them virtuous or vicious. But the believer normally thinks he has at least a general idea of what qualities of character are in fact virtuous and vicious (approved and disapproved by God). Having such an idea, he can apply the word "good" descriptively to God, meaning that (with some exceptions, as I have noted) God has the qualities which the believer regards as virtues, such as faithfulness and kindness. . . .

VI

As I noted at the outset, the divine command theory of ethical wrongness, even in its modified form, has the consequence that believers and nonbelievers use the word "wrong" with different meanings in ethical contexts, since it will hardly be thought that nonbelievers mean by "wrong" what the theory says believers mean by it. This

consequence gives rise to an objection. For the phenomena of common moral discourse between believers and nonbelievers suggest that they mean the same thing by "wrong" in ethical contexts. In the present section I shall try to explain how the modified divine command theorist can account for the facts of common ethical discourse.

I will first indicate what I think the troublesome facts are. Judeo-Christian believers enter into ethical discussions with people whose religious or anti-religious beliefs they do not know. It seems to be possible to conduct quite a lot of ethical discourse, with apparent understanding, without knowing one's partner's views on religious issues. Believers also discuss ethical questions with persons who are known to them to be nonbelievers. They agree with such persons, disagree with them, and try to persuade them, about what acts are morally wrong. (Or at least it is normally *said*, by the participants and others, that they agree and disagree about such issues.) Believers ascribe, to people who are known not to believe in God, beliefs that certain acts are morally wrong. Yet surely believers do not suppose that nonbelievers, in calling acts wrong, mean that they are contrary to the will or commandments of God. Under these circumstances how can the believer really mean "contrary to the will or commandments of God" when he says "wrong"? If he agrees and disagrees with nonbelievers about what is wrong, if he ascribes to them beliefs that certain acts are wrong, must he not be using "wrong" in a nontheological sense?

What I shall argue is that in some ordinary (and I fear imprecise) sense of "mean," what believers and nonbelievers mean by "wrong" in ethical contexts may well be partly the same and partly different. There are agreements between believers and nonbelievers which make common moral discourse between them possible. But these agreements do not show that the two groups mean exactly the same thing by "wrong." They do not show that "contrary to God's will or commands" is not part of what believers mean by "wrong."

Let us consider first the agreements which make possible common moral discourse between believers and nonbelievers. (1) One important agreement, which is so obvious as to be easily overlooked, is that they use many of the same ethical terms—"wrong," "right," "ought," "duty," and others. And they may utter many of the same ethical sentences, such as "Racial discrimination is morally wrong." In determining what people believe we rely very heavily on what they say (when they seem to be speaking sincerely)—and that means in large part, on the words that they use and the sentences they utter. If I know that somebody says, with apparent sincerity, "Racial discrimination is morally wrong," I will normally ascribe to him the belief that racial discrimination is morally wrong, even if I also know that he does not mean *exactly* the same thing as I do by "racial discrimination" or "morally wrong." Of course if I know he means something *completely* different, I would not ascribe the belief to him without explicit qualification.

I would not claim that believers and nonbelievers use *all* the same ethical terms. "Sin," "law of God," and "Christian," for instance, occur as ethical terms in the discourse of many believers, but would be much less likely to occur in the same way in nonbelievers' discourse.

(2) The shared ethical terms have the same basic grammatical status for believers as for nonbelievers, and at least many of the same logical connections with other expressions. Everyone agrees, for instance, in treating "wrong" as an adjective and "Racial discrimination is morally wrong" as a declarative sentence. "(All) racial discrimination is morally wrong" would be treated by all parties as expressing an A-type (universal affirmative) proposition, from which consequences can be drawn by syllogistic reasoning or the predicate calculus. All agree that if *X* is morally wrong, then it isn't morally right and refraining from *X* is morally obligatory. Such grammatical and formal agreements are important to common moral discourse.

(3) There is a great deal of agreement, among believers and nonbelievers, as to what types of action they call "wrong" in an ethical sense and I think that that agreement is one of the things that make common moral discourse possible. It is certainly not complete agreement. Obviously there is a lot of ethical disagreement in the world. Much of it cuts right across religious lines, but not all of it does. There are things which are typically called "wrong" by members of some religious groups, and not by others. Nonetheless there are types of action which everyone or almost everyone would call morally wrong—such as torturing someone to death because he accidentally broke a small window in your house. Moreover any two people (including any one believer and one nonbeliever) are likely to find some actions they both call wrong that not everyone does. I imagine that most ethical discussion takes place among people whose area of agreement in what they call wrong is relatively large.

There is probably much less agreement about the most basic issues in moral theory than there is about many ethical issues of less generality. There is much more unanimity in what people (sincerely) say in answer to such questions as "Was what Hitler did to the Jews wrong?" or "Is it normally wrong to disobey the laws of one's country?" than in what they (sincerely) say in answer to such questions as "Is it always right to do the act which will have the best results?" or "Is pleasure the only thing that is good for its own sake?" The issue between adherents and nonadherents of divine command ethics is typical of basic issues in ethical and metaethical theory in this respect.

(4) The emotional and volitional attitudes normally expressed by the statement that something is "wrong" are similar in believers and nonbelievers. They are not exactly the same; the attitudes typically expressed by the believer's statement that something is "wrong" are importantly related to his religious practice and beliefs about God, and this doubtless makes them different in some ways from the attitudes expressed by nonbelievers uttering the same sentence. But the attitudes are certainly similar, and that is important for the possibility of common moral discourse.

(5) Perhaps even more important is the related fact that the social functions of a statement that something is (morally) "wrong" are similar for believers and nonbelievers. To say that something someone else is known to have done is "wrong" is

commonly to attack him. If you say that something you are known to have done is "wrong," you abandon certain types of defense. To say that a public policy is "wrong" is normally to register oneself as opposed to it, and is sometimes a signal that one is willing to be supportive of common action to change it. These social functions of moral discourse are extremely important. It is perhaps not surprising that we are inclined to say that two people agree with each other when they both utter the same sentence and thereby indicate their readiness to take the same side in a conflict.

Let us sum up these observations about the conditions which make common moral discourse between believers and nonbelievers possible. (1) They use many of the same ethical terms, such as "wrong." (2) They treat those terms as having the same basic grammatical and logical status, and many of the same logical connections with other expressions. (3) They agree to a large extent about what types of action are to be called "wrong." To call an action "wrong" is, among other things, to classify it with certain other actions, and there is considerable agreement between believers and nonbelievers as to what actions those are. (4) The emotional and volitional attitudes which believers and nonbelievers normally express in saying that

something is "wrong" are similar, and (5) saying that something is "wrong" has much the same social functions for believers and nonbelievers.

So far as I can see, none of this is inconsistent with the modified divine command theory of ethical wrongness. According to that theory there are several things which are true of the believer's use of "wrong" which cannot plausibly be supposed to be true of the nonbeliever's. In saying, "X is wrong," the believer commits himself (subjectively, at least, and publicly if he is known to be a believer) to the claim that X is contrary to God's will or commandments. The believer will not say that anything would be wrong, under any possible circumstances, if it were not contrary to God's will or commandments. In many contexts he uses the term "wrong" interchangeably with "against the will of God" or "against the commandments of God." The heart of the modified divine command theory, I have suggested, is the claim that when the believer says, "X is wrong," one thing he means to be doing is stating a nonnatural objective fact about X, and the nonnatural objective fact he means to be stating is that X is contrary to the will or commandments of God. This claim may be true even though the uses of "wrong" by believers and nonbelievers are similar in all five of the ways pointed out above. . . .

Bibliography for Part VIII

Helm, Paul, ed. *The Divine Command Theory of Ethics.* Oxford: Oxford Univ. Press, 1979. This work contains a good selection of the latest material on the subject.

Kierkegaard, Søren. *Fear and Trembling,* translated by Howard V. Hong and Edna H. Hong. Princeton: Princeton Univ. Press, 1983. A classic work on the relation of religion to morality.

Nielsen, Kai. *Ethics without God.* London: Pemberton Books, 1973. A clearly written description of humanistic ethics.

Outka, Gene, and J. P. Reeder, eds. *Religion and Morality: A Collection of Essays.* New York: Anchor Books, 1973. A good collection of essays.

Quinn, Philip. *Divine Commands and Moral Requirements.* Oxford: Clarendon Press, 1978. An incisive treatise on the subject.